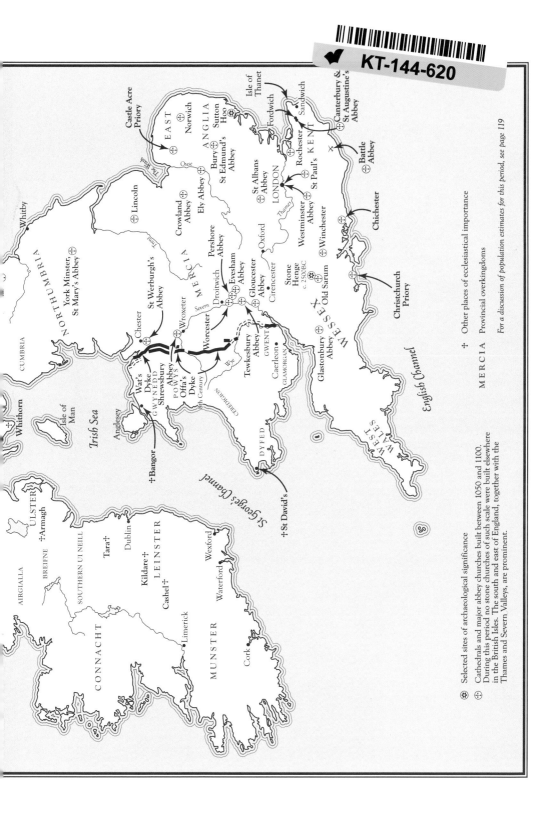

KT-144-620

Castle Acre Priory

Isle of Thanet

Sandwich

Canterbury & St Augustine's Abbey

Fordwich

Rochester

Battle Abbey

EAST

Norwich

ANGLIA

Sutton Hoo

Bury St Edmund's Abbey

St Albans Abbey

LONDON

St Paul's

Westminster Abbey

Winchester

Chichester

Whitby

Lincoln

The Wash

Ouse

Crowland Abbey

Ely Abbey

NORTHUMBRIA

York Minster, St Mary's Abbey

St Werburgh's Abbey

Chester

MERCIA

Pershore Abbey

Droitwich

Evesham Abbey

Oxford

Trent

Wroxeter

Worcester

Severn

Gloucester Abbey

Cirencester

Stone Henge c. 2500BC

Old Sarum

Christchurch Priory

CUMBRIA

Wat's Dyke

GWYNEDD

Shrewsbury Abbey

POWYS

Offa's Dyke 8th Century

Tewkesbury Abbey

GWENT

Caerleon

Wye

GLAMORGAN

WESSEX

Glastonbury Abbey

Isle of Man

Anglesey

Whithorn

Irish Sea

Bangor

CEREDIGION

DYFED

St David's

St George's Channel

WEST WALES

English Channel

ULSTER

Armagh

AIRGIALLA

BREIFNE

SOUTHERN UI NEILL

Tara

Dublin

Kildare

LEINSTER

Cashel

Wexford

Waterford

Limerick

CONNACHT

MUNSTER

Cork

For a discussion of population estimates for this period, see page 119

For a discussion of population estimates for this period, see page 119

Other places of ecclesiastical importance

✠ Provincial overkingdoms

MERCIA Provincial overkingdoms

⊛ Selected sites of archaeological significance

⊕ Cathedrals and major abbey churches built between 1050 and 1100. During this period no stone churches built elsewhere in the British Isles. The south and east of England, together with the Thames and Severn Valleys, are prominent.

A World by Itself

A World by Itself

A History of the British Isles

Edited by Jonathan Clark

Contributors:
James Campbell
John Gillingham
Jenny Wormald
Jonathan Clark
William D. Rubinstein
Robert Skidelsky

WILLIAM HEINEMANN: LONDON

Published by William Heinemann 2010

2 4 6 8 10 9 7 5 3 1

First published in Great Britain in 2010 by
William Heinemann
Random House, 20 Vauxhall Bridge Road,
London SW1V 2SA

www.rbooks.co.uk

Addresses for companies within The Random House Group Limited can be found at:
www.randomhouse.co.uk/offices.htm

The Random House Group Limited Reg. No. 954009

A CIP catalogue record for this book
is available from the British Library

ISBN 9780434009015

The Random House Group Limited supports The Forest Stewardship
Council (FSC), the leading international forest certification organisation. All our
titles that are printed on Greenpeace approved FSC certified paper carry the FSC logo.
Our paper procurement policy can be found at: www.rbooks.co.uk/environment

Mixed Sources
Product group from well-managed
forests and other controlled sources
www.fsc.org Cert no. TT-COC-2139
© 1996 Forest Stewardship Council
FSC

Typeset by SX Composing DTP, Rayleigh, Essex
Printed and bound in Great Britain by
CPI Mackays, Chatham, ME5 8TD

'There be many Caesars,
Ere such another Julius. Britain is
A world by itself; and we will nothing pay
For wearing our own noses.'

Cloten, *Cymbeline*, Act 3, scene 1

Contents

Acknowledgements

The six authors of this volume have accumulated many debts. In particular, they are indebted to each other for discussion, criticism and suggestion as drafts circulated among themselves during the process of composition. Scholarship is cumulative and collaborative: we all profit from the insights of the wider community of historians in innumerable ways. Space prevents full acknowledgement here, but our six authors will supply detailed references and bibliographies when their chapters are published in expanded form as six separate volumes.

Meanwhile, each author also has particular debts of gratitude to repay. James Campbell thanks Dr Bärbel Brodt and Dr John Maddicott, who helped with Part I. Jonathan Clark thanks Patrick O'Brien for reading Part IV. William Rubinstein thanks Dr Hilary Rubinstein for her advice on Part V. Robert Skidelsky thanks the following who have read Part VI in whole or in part: David Ashton, Meghnad Desai, Mrs Jean Floud, Nigel Lawson, Kenneth Morgan, David Owen, Larry Siedentop, Edward Skidelsky, William Skidelsky, Norman Stone. His special thanks go to Pavel Erochkine and Louis Mosley who helped him with the research and ideas for this essay. Collectively, too, the contributors are indebted to Mike Shaw and Jonny Pegg, who steered this project from its conception, and to our editor at William Heinemann, Drummond Moir, who brought it to completion. Our thanks also to Laurie Ip Fung Chun for her assistance with picture research, and to Martin Lubikowski for producing the endpaper maps.

Despite this generous assistance, the authors each wish to emphasise that the views expressed in their chapters are their individual interpretations, and do not represent a group position. Scholarship evolves by disagreement and debate; that is as true of this group of historians as of any other.

Notes on Contributors

JAMES CAMPBELL was a Tutorial Fellow of Worcester College, Oxford, from 1957, and retired as Professor of Medieval History in 2002. A Fellow of the British Academy and an Hon D.Litt. of the University of East Anglia, he is the author of numerous articles on Anglo-Saxon history, many of which are published in *Essays in Anglo-Saxon History* (1986) and *The Anglo-Saxon State* (2000).

JOHN GILLINGHAM is Emeritus Professor of History at the London School of Economics and Political Science and a Fellow of the British Academy. His books include *Richard I* (1999), *The English in the Twelfth Century: Imperialism, National Identity and Political Values* (2000) and *The Angevin Empire* (2001).

JENNY WORMALD is an Honorary Fellow of the University of Edinburgh, and formerly a Tutorial Fellow in St Hilda's College, Oxford. Her publications include *Lords and Men in Scotland: Bonds of Manrent 1442–1603* (1985), *Mary Queen of Scots: A Study in Failure* (revised edn, 2001), and numerous articles on early-modern Scottish and 'British' history.

JONATHAN CLARK is currently Hall Distinguished Professor of British History at the University of Kansas; he was previously a Fellow of Peterhouse, Cambridge, and of All Souls College, Oxford, and was a Visiting Professor at the Committee on Social Thought of the University of Chicago. His best-known book is *English Society 1660–1832* (2000).

WILLIAM D. RUBINSTEIN is Professor of History at the University of Wales, Aberystwyth. He was formerly Professor of Social and

Economic History at Deakin University in Australia. He has written *Men of Property: The Very Wealthy in Britain since the Industrial Revolution* (1981; revised edn, 2006); *Britain's Century: Political and Social History, 1815–1905* (1999), and many other works.

ROBERT SKIDELSKY is Emeritus Professor of Political Economy at Warwick University. His three-volume biography of the economist John Maynard Keynes (1983, 1992, 2000) received numerous prizes, including the Lionel Gelber Prize for International Relations and the Council on Foreign Relations Prize for International Relations. He is the author of *The World after Communism* (1995) and *Keynes: The Return of the Master* (2009). He was made a life peer in 1991, is a member of the House of Lords Select Committee on Economic Affairs, and was elected Fellow of the British Academy in 1994.

Illustrations

photo) by English School, (17th century) Private Collection/ The
Bridgeman Art Library Nationality / copyright status: English /
out of copyright.

p. 324, 'The Horrible Tail-man' © Rijksmuseum, Amsterdam.

p. 347, 'The Coffeehous Mob' © The British Library Board. 1490. d.83.

p. 360, The art of stocking framework knitting, engraved for 'The
Universal Magazine, 1750 (engraving) (b&w photo) by English
School, (18th century) Private Collection/ The Bridgeman Art
Library Nationality / copyright status: English / out of copyright.

p. 383, Hackney Church, London © George Skipper.

p. 399, The Revolution © The Trustees of the British Museum.

p. 425, The Mitred Minuet © The Trustees of the British Museum.

p. 440, 'Death or Liberty' © The Trustees of the British Museum.

p. 450, The Great Exhibition of 1851.

p. 464, The Forth Bridge © Royal Scottish Geographical Society.

p. 475, Eaton Hall © Getty Images.

p. 482, Suffragette campaigner, 1913.

p. 509, Lloyd Family Butchers, Aberystwyth, 1911.

p. 530, the Great Chartist Meeting, Kennington Common, 1848.

p. 577, (l) British Movement rally © Getty Images .

p. 577, (r) boy watching cricket © Getty Images.

p. 588, The Tube Train, c.1934 (linocut) by Power, Cyril Edward
(1874-1951) Private Collection/ © Redfern Gallery, London/ The
Bridgeman Art Library Nationality / copyright status: English / in
copyright until 2022.

p. 614, World War One © Popperfoto/Getty Images.

p. 648, Mercators Projection Map © Time & Life Pictures/Getty
Images.

p. 658, NHS © Time & Life Pictures/Getty Images.

p. 665, Roman Catholic Mass © Getty Images.

Every effort has been made to contact all copyright holders. If notified,
the publisher will be pleased to rectify any errors or omissions at the
earliest opportunity.

Editor's Introduction

These small islands, once regarded as remote by those who under-standably saw themselves as central, have nevertheless played a role in the world's affairs far beyond their size. During Rome's ascendancy they formed a borderland, part within the Roman empire, part beyond it, a division with lasting consequences. After the fall of Rome, they saw the survival in present-day Ireland of Christianity; the re-establishment in present-day England of the first widely monetised economy and the first bureaucratically centralised monarchy north of the Alps; the first society in which a common-law code and a representative assembly were fully developed and lastingly affected governance. England, then Britain, became the linchpin in the survival and spread of international Protestantism; Ireland became a symbol of the role of Catholicism as the matrix of populist resistance.

The islands played a key role in the emergence of the United States and its survival against acquisitive European powers in North America. From Newtonian physics through the splitting of the atom and the invention of the computer, these islands' contributions to science and technology have been without parallel. Britain's empire grew to be comparable with Rome's, with the Mongol empire and with the Islamic empire, but it alone initiated the process we now call globalisation. Without Britain, either world war of the twentieth century would have taken a wholly different course, with incalculable consequences. The cultures of the British Isles looked both inwards to create powerful identities, and outwards to sustain a series of 'special relationships', first with Rome, then Scandinavia, then France, then the United States, now with a global village. Emigration from these islands has populated societies from Alaska to Australia; immigration to them has raised every question of assimilation and conflict. Their law, language and culture have been formative; the history of the USA, especially, would be unintelligible except against this background.

It is not necessary to be triumphalist about these things to acknowledge their reality; and, appropriately, the historiography of these islands – the serious academic analysis of their history – has achieved an equal status as a field of intellectual contest and achievement. Few of the great issues that preoccupy historians are not debated within the history of these islands, and few such debates for other societies reach higher standards of sophistication than here. If the past is now at peace, its English, Welsh, Irish and Scots historians are not.

History, like economics or physics, is a serious subject; it has the widest consequences. Some historians, admittedly, seek to disguise the dangerous element in their craft, presenting their work as popular entertainment or moral uplift. Yet even they know that this is a smokescreen, for on technical debates within academic history depend real outcomes in the world of action – the Reformation, rebellion in 1642 and 1776, industrialisation and world empire, world war, resistance to National Socialism and Marxian Socialism alike.

Historical debates with practical implications have therefore been conducted over many centuries. What were the origins of the Britons? Whence came Christianity? What are the preconditions of political and social cohesion? How are states formed, and how do they survive? How do societies deal with natural or medical catastrophe? Why are wars fought, and what determines their outcomes? What causes civil conflict? What is national identity, and is it easily malleable to fit modern agendas? What causes economic prosperity? What are liberties, and how can they be secured? Do states have moral dimensions, and how is the religious component of life expressed or erased? At its most general, can we give coherent and reasoned accounts of the greatest changes in human affairs, or does the chaos and complexity of events finally overwhelm us? On such issues there has been, and remains, profound disagreement. Yet there is much to be gained by standing back from the historical record of these islands over two millennia and asking these larger and more fraught questions.

History is argument. This is so since professional historians do their work not by unstructured description but by posing exact questions to which (they think) verifiable answers can, at least potentially, be given. Yet (as in the natural sciences) what counts as a question or as an answer is continually challenged: historical writing that conceals its working and so presents a bland, uncontestable story implicitly claims an authority that it does not have. If history is argument it is interpretation, and so also reinterpretation. The authors of this volume are aware that recent decades have seen great changes in our understanding of the history of the British Isles. In their writing on their own areas of expertise they have tried to be open to those challenges rather than resistant to them, and to be willing to call in question what even recently appeared to be knowledge securely gained. So they are here.

Historical advances have escalated in recent decades; but, as was observed even at the outset of the professionalisation of twentieth-century scholarship, 'we are slow in re-valuing the whole and reorganizing the broad outlines of the theme in the light of these discoveries'. This volume is an attempt to redraw some broad outlines. Its subversive moral might be the apparently innocent truth that 'the understanding of the past is not so easy as it is sometimes made to appear'. History is an ongoing enquiry, currently dynamic and inno-vative. This *History* is intended not as a memorial to what has been agreed, but as a signpost to future discovery.

Because history is argument about what is potentially verifiable, it is able to rescue the past from polemical misuse, and several such misuses are implicitly confronted here. It may have become recently fashionable to be too fastidious to confront questions of power, too queasy to mention war, too idealistic to grapple with law, too secularly self-righteous to mention religion. This volume respects none of these inhibitions.

The early centuries covered in this study have been neglected in the popular imagination as the presumed arena of superstition and tyranny, patriarchalism and feudalism. This work emphasises how central and how important were the transitions from late Iron Age societies to the law-bound and monetised economies of the Middle Ages, transitions that long preceded similar trends normally located in later centuries.

Twentieth-century writers were often eager to locate in the history of these islands a great watershed between pre-modern and modern, and merely offered competing locations for such an episode: the Reformation? The Glorious Revolution? The Industrial Revolution? Yet in recent decades the realisation has dawned that there was no sudden discontinuity of social-structural forms, but rather a series of incremental adjustments in which 'the new' and 'the old' survived indefinitely; that political and religious changes were played out against a background of larger continuities; and that even the classic political and religious episodes need reconsideration in consequence.

Historians once often sought to prioritise only one of the causes of conflict, whether ethnicity, religion, class, poverty or constitutional libertarianism. Yet each of these has risen to prominence, declined and risen again: no single logic of historical development emerges from these pages. Especially, 'secularisation' (conventionally the other side of the coin of 'modernisation') can now be understood as a recent project, not a timeless process, and despite that project religion here assumes a major salience as a framework of social life.

Nationalists go to an extreme: they privilege their own polity and imply the existence within it of an unchanging essence. Yet 'nationalism' is the proper name of a nineteenth-century political ideology, not an eternal truth, and an ideology that was received differently in England, Scotland, Ireland and Wales. Political units in these islands have been repeatedly built up, combined and broken down: the record of twenty centuries discourages us from taking any one polity as an exemplar or an inevitable outcome. Postmodernists and their lesser derivatives go to the other extreme, for equally political reasons, claiming the recent origin of states and the transience of their identities. These ideas have become clichés, often asserted, seldom demonstrated. Yet such views seem most plausible to those whose knowledge extends only over short time spans. This book's return to an older attempt to make sense of large themes over centuries or even millennia helps us to undertake more balanced appreciations of continuity and change. It shows that, alongside the extinctions, many things in the life of these islands are very old indeed, tenacious and deeply rooted.

A broad survey illuminates the deep continuities that evolutionary change preserved. Change has been resisted as well as promoted: stability and continuity, even in the face of catastrophe, have characterised life here to a greater degree than in many neighbouring areas of continental Europe. Assertions of the impermanence and shallowness of identities are problematic against the picture of continuity and evolution that emerges in England across many centuries from the Anglo-Saxon era (and, in Scotland, Wales and Ireland, from earlier still). Episodes of armed conflict in these pages are many, and in the seventeenth century these islands acquired a Europe-wide reputation for political instability. Yet by the twenty-first century, the United Kingdom was the only major society in Europe not to have experienced revolution or conquest between 1789 and 1815, not to have suffered defeat in the First or Second World Wars, and not to have gone though social revolution in their wake. How this could have happened is part of the story. So are the dynamic changes that have been built into present-day society, and that challenge confidence in such survivals in future. No achievement is secure, or ever has been.

One explanation for this track record is the remarkable antiquity and durability of the state, especially in England. Yet the political structures seen in these islands have steadily changed, and this succession of state forms, including now some areas and now others in ever-changing frameworks, has been one reason why there has been no single name for a polity embracing all of them (we use 'the British Isles' as the closest functional substitute, not as a normative response to separatist nationalism). Although 'Great Britain' was used to denote the union of 1707 that combined England, Wales and Scotland, the terms 'Britain' and 'England' were also widely used as shorthand for the three kingdoms and a principality assembled by the union of 1801 under the cumbersome formal title 'the United Kingdom of Great Britain and Ireland'. But the authors do not assume a necessary union, or a homogeneous experience, between or even within these components. Ireland, Scotland, Wales and England have their internal divisions as well as their commonalities.

On the contrary, the present authors give priority to the idea that state formation in these islands involved the assembly of diverse groups, developments that were never predetermined and were at times reversed. Unexpectedly, given its legal culture, England was reluctant to seek to define the relations between the polities of the British Isles, just as Britain's reluctance to define the nature of its relationship with its colonies contributed to the American Revolution. Historians are now alive to the dynamic of relations between England, Wales, Ireland and Scotland, and the contributors to this volume often seek to explore familiar themes, like the Reformation or population growth, on a comparative basis.

Because of the way in which it was formed, the 'United Kingdom' was a 'composite monarchy', surviving into the twentieth century from a much older world. It may be asked how well it fared after 1914 compared with Austria-Hungary, Germany and Russia. The independence of the mainly Catholic south of Ireland in 1922 produced political schism in the islands, but as a consequence of the First World War this was arguably modest compared with the price paid by many other European states. Neither unity nor disunity was predetermined. A longer perspective reveals the ethnically mixed nature of most polities and the general prevalence of states that embody, in different formulae, more than one group identifying themselves as 'nations': 'nationalism' as an idea is to be explained historically, not merely used. Nor have the contributors presumed that any particular state form can be labelled 'anachronistic' or 'modern', or that such labels tell us anything of value; in European culture, republics are as old as monarchies.

This book, then, tries to deal with the histories of Wales, Ireland and Scotland as well as England. But it is only an early step in that direction, which must point forward to future endeavours rather than sum up present achievement. Writing a history that includes Scotland, Ireland and Wales rather than treating England as standing proxy for the others has been widely accepted by historians as a goal, yet the increasing volume and sophistication of historical writing on those societies has paradoxically made that challenge easier to issue but harder to meet. The authors of this volume have addressed this challenge, but they recognise how much remains to be done.

These islands have contained many polities, and their interaction has occupied historians from the time of the Anglo-Saxon kingdoms. The personal union with much of present-day France was for some centuries a viable one; whether its breakdown was unavoidable is a matter for debate. From the sixteenth century into the seventeenth, historians have emphasised a 'three kingdoms' dynamic between England (including a relatively integrated Wales), Scotland and Ireland, each with its own parliament; yet, however prominent in that era, this diversity was to some degree overridden by the power of a centralised state after the unions of 1707 and 1801. If the British Isles' internal dynamics, especially ones of denominational conflict, were resolved by exporting them to the American colonies, where they recurred so uncontrollably in 1776, it may equally be asked how far a new set of internal dynamics were projected around the world in the nineteenth and twentieth centuries (anti-slavery and anti-imperialism were successful British exports). Whether we are today witnessing the breakup of the Union is a matter that historians as well as politicians debate, often based as much on their understandings of much earlier centuries as on their understandings of recent decades.

Although the relations between the polities of the British Isles have often featured in this volume, the theme of empire has less often stood out as a dominant one, despite the vogue that it has recently enjoyed. 'Empire' has assumed prominence as a shorthand term that allows a normative denigration of the domination of the weak by the strong. Yet power is an inescapable theme within these islands over many millennia; it does not need to be written on a larger overseas canvas to be assessed. It is also a question whether the experience of overseas rule had a lasting or determinative impact on domestic governance, whatever the claims of Edmund Burke, in his pursuit of Warren Hastings in the 1790s, that tyranny in India would produce tyranny at home. The British Isles contained within themselves the full range of resources to express both rule and resistance; they did not need to call on the experience of empire for these resources to achieve armed expression, for they did so at home.

The possession of colonies was translated by twentieth-century writers into 'imperialism', and imperialism expressed as a process. But are there such things as historical processes, clearly identifiable impersonal dynamics with inner logics? Two developments of method call this in question. Swift change in historical interpretation re-emphasises, say some, the possibilities that did not come to fruition; the many other things, in any situation, that might plausibly have happened instead: in technical terms, the counter-factuals. Pressing this insight further and on a smaller scale reveals, claim other historians, the importance of contingency, the play of infinitely complex causes in an unstable system. Although they pull in different directions, the recent rise of these two preoccupations has helped to change the landscape over which historians look.

By contrast, what we look back on in the late nineteenth and twentieth centuries as 'modernism' shared certain key characteristics: in modernism's vision, all outcomes were overdetermined; counter-factual alternatives were indignantly repudiated; and the categories of enquiry were sacrosanct. Some debate was permitted, for example, on the causes of 'the Industrial Revolution', but it was not permitted to doubt whether such an episode necessarily had to happen or had occurred. No other pathways of economic development were explored or analysed; and similarly with all other major historical

categories. Yet this exclusion rested on an elementary error. The claim
that 'a caused b' is also the counter-factual claim that 'without a, b
would not have occurred'. Whether that was the case cannot be
known in advance of historical enquiry. Much postmodern scholarship
ironically shares this modernist assurance, presenting its postmodern
claims about the instability of identities in equally determinist terms as
developments reflecting objectively identified causes like the decline of
empire and the retreat of Protestantism. Yet scholarship in recent
decades has steadily undermined this complacency, which was indeed
as recent as the 'modernist' project of the late nineteenth century.

At present, the overdetermined certainties of modernism are
everywhere dissolving: uncertainty, instability and the unexpected
now loom larger in the English-speaking world, and research is now
recovering similar preoccupations in past centuries also. Our continuing attempts to reduce chaos to order and to see patterns in the flux
of human affairs therefore take new forms. The authors in this volume
do not fall back on a counsel of despair, and conclude that chance rules
all; but they have all been challenged to set out their understandings of
the alternative paths of development systematically, to analyse
sceptically and without wishful thinking what might otherwise have
happened at key points. The section on counter-factuals with which
each chapter closes is therefore integral to this collaborative project.

This book, then, tries to identify some of the alternative pathways of
development that the British Isles might have pursued. It avoids 'naïve
counter-factualism', the misleading idea that, but for some one error,
all would have been well; but it takes seriously the idea that many
paths of development were feasible, and that the one actually followed
in any situation was not necessarily the most obvious or the most
sought. This approach is one of the distinguishing characteristics of this
book, and it is offered here as an aid to the understanding of wider
patterns of historical development.

Method affects substance. The recent re-awakening to the
importance of contingency and the counter-factual has re-prob-
lematised aspects of the history of these islands, formerly often taken
for granted: the creation and defence of the state, the development of
the rule of law, the achievement of steadily growing population and
prosperity, the assertion, entrenchment and erosion of the Christian
religion: all these and others now emerge as remarkable achievements
or developments, not as the secure outcomes of 'processes', as the

characteristics of 'stages of development' or as the natural reflections of 'underlying causes'.

With the disintegration of the complacencies of modernism has gone a renewed attention to how people in the past understood things rather than to how present-day analysts schematise them. Collective self-images have a large role to play in human affairs, and from the historical writing of the Venerable Bede to the Battle of Britain and beyond, one recurring theme has been providential survival against the odds. This was, moreover, a game that four could play: the Welsh, Scots and Irish often sustained similar senses of survival defined against incursions by the English. All countries have myths of origin; they seldom lack a foundation in the historical record, but are seldom immune to challenge and redefinition.

This volume was written at a time of growing insecurity as terrorism, global climate change and epidemic disease seemed to threaten the social-democratic certainties entrenched in the West by the victory of 1945 (indeed the very idea of 'the West' has come under critical scrutiny). It is written for a generation that has drifted away from modernism without necessarily embracing postmodernism, but it tries to take nothing for granted. The British were long confident about their survival and prosperity, so that it became almost impolite to point out that war might be analysed, for every state, not as an aberration, a suspension of normal security, but as a normal feature of life, even the principal purpose of the state. In these pages war is not glamorised or treated in a triumphalist perspective, but its results are not taken for granted either.

A vision of history over many centuries suggests that war, famine and disease have been the major challenges to human life. Mankind has tried to set up barriers against these disasters, notably through politics, religion and law, more recently through the social and natural sciences; these systems of ideas give structure to the practical activities contained within collective life. This book is an account of how the inhabitants of these islands, over two millennia, encountered successive challenges and, at the price of much suffering and with many setbacks, constructed cultures that have been both widely envied and widely contested.

This is not the story of a single development; call it 'progress' or anything else. It is the story of changing goals, changing values, changing peoples. Ends are no sooner attained than they are abandoned;

secular values are no sooner affirmed than they are negated. It may be
that the unities of collective life lie not in race (a mistake of nineteenth-
century science) nor in wealth (for peoples' ideas of what constitutes
wealth are always evolving) but in shared historical experience. It is
this experience that has created identity, and it is this experience that is
expressed within those two dominant systems of ideas, law and
religion. The historical sense explains why a community often thinks
of itself as immemorially the same, when its component parts are
changing; it may even explain its collective survival of catastrophic
change.

The British Isles were the home to a wide diversity of peoples,
sometimes cooperating, sometimes in conflict. At different times, they
pictured their commonalities in different ways: history, culture,
religion, class, ethnicity and political symbols have each had their
moments when people have held them up as symbols of identity. It is
not necessary to subscribe to mistaken Victorian ideas of race in order
to appreciate long continuities. They can already be demonstrated, for
example, from the remarkable consistency of patterns of surname
distribution within Britain between the census of 1881 and the electoral
register of 1998: major geographical mobility in that period, usually
hailed as the most mobile of all, has been the experience of minorities
only. In future years, DNA mapping of the population may shed even
more light on such phenomena via the new discipline of
archaeogenetics. Such a science refutes the idea of 'race' by showing
the many lineages that go to make up the genetic code of each
individual; but it also emphasises the inescapability of descent, and the
traceability of descent via the special case of mitochondrial DNA. In
several senses, we are the creation of our ancestors.

Shared history is not a share of an unchanging asset, and change
(whether contingent or deterministic) may accelerate. In the present
day, it is not yet clear whether the pace of change will override the
historical enterprise and submerge it in a consumerist presentism. A
society's understanding of its history is continually debated, always
able to be refined, always liable to be diluted or debased. The challenge
to explain a society historically, and to compare it with others, is an
intellectual and, to some, a moral one; how it is met here is a matter for
the reader to judge.

This volume cannot be a universal compendium: it cannot present
all that deserves to be recorded, or all that the reader will wish to

explore. It can, however, give some sense of why historians find history important: the processes of enquiry, the different methods, the rival hypotheses that are debated within the historical arena. This enterprise is not, at the same time, intended to set up a gallery of those historians who were right against a rival gallery of those who were wrong. In the wider picture, such parochial rivalries matter little. Our aim has been to give priority to the arguments, and to help the reader to see how much of our understanding of the past has changed and continues to change.

Counter-factuality also subverts moral self-assurance. It reveals that, despite the demands of present-day interest groups, it cannot be the task of history either to celebrate or to denigrate past causes or groups but to understand them; we might add that this task is more difficult, more important, and more interesting than normative judgements. Consequently, the contributors to this volume have not thought themselves entitled to produce 'a story which is the ratification if not the glorification of the present'.

Such a sense that this might indeed be a legitimate role of historians often encourages within their ranks a subtle divergence, which might be identified as one of demeanour. For some historians, people in the past were politically incorrect, or socially absurd, or both: the ancestors of groups stigmatised in the present are presented by such authors as self-parodies. The present which such writers celebrate is often today a self-denigratory one, but the teleology which is assumed to reinforce the outcome of decline is the same. Other historians approach the past with what might be described as a sense of awe in the face of a vast canvas of human achievement and failure: to them, all the actors in the drama need respect if the technical riddles of cause and effect are to be solved. They are neither triumphalists nor declinists, but it may be that to them the activity of reading, and writing, history is an intellectual discipline and something more: it is also an act of *pietas*. When a country's past is to be addressed across two millennia, these alternative approaches pose ever more urgent choices.

PART I

THE ROMANS TO THE NORMAN CONQUEST, 500 BC–AD 1066

James Campbell

Introduction

The long sweep of the story of the British Isles from prehistory to the Norman Conquest is full of enigmas. But at least one thing is certain. It was determinative for much of what happened in these islands in the centuries which followed; and so, indirectly but importantly, for the history of much of the world and not least of the United States. By the year 100 much of Britain was on the way to becoming an integrated part of a Roman empire which stretched from the Irish Sea to the Tigris. A kind of chaos followed the dissolution of that empire. But by the year 1000 the divisions which still mark the archipelago were already engrained: England, Ireland, Scotland and Wales were distinct political areas. Most striking, England had become the first European nation-state; and this was partly due to economic changes no less significant than those of the eighteenth century.

1. Material Cultures

Geography and Prehistory

Britain and Ireland are not so very large: together they are smaller than are a number of US states. It is their location rather than their size which is crucial. To the Greeks and Romans they seemed remote, the utmost edge of the earth; an early Irish author could refer to his island as a pimple on the chin of the world. But viewed from the north the British Isles are far from remote: the Straits of Dover are the gateway to the Atlantic and Mediterranean for most of the peoples living round the North and Baltic seas; the southern funnelling of the North Sea brings the rich lands of south-east England and those of the Netherlands into easy proximity. The importance of sea communication was captured by the Roman historian Tacitus, writing in about AD 100: 'Nowhere', says he, 'does the sea hold wider sway.' Tacitus knew what he was writing about, for his father-in-law, Agricola, was the governor of Roman Britain from AD 77 (or 78) to 84. Indeed, no single point on either of the main isles is more than eighty miles from the coast, and both have many rivers. Water transport was essential to societies which could not normally manage much more than a daily average of fifteen miles on foot or forty mounted. Compare this with estimates of the speed and range of such a ship as that of about AD 600 excavated at Sutton Hoo – with a fair wind from its Suffolk base it could have reached Canterbury in half a day, Gaul in a day, York in a day and a half, and Jutland in just three days. Journey times by water during the so-called Dark Ages were not very different from those of the eighteenth century.

The major geographical division of the main island of Britain is that between the largely mountainous or hilly 'highland zone' of the north and west and the 'lowland zone' of the south and east, much of which was very fertile. This fertility mattered politically, for a key to power was command over land which was sufficient to produce a surplus above what was needed to feed the men and beasts cultivating it. Crucial in the future political development of England was thus its wide fertile areas, which could provide such a surplus. Similarly, but on a reduced scale, in the largely highland area now called Wales each of the main units of authority had a base in an area of fertile lowland. There were similar determinative geographical factors in Irish history. Although the island has extensive areas of mountain and of bog, it has others which are fertile and productive. The mild Irish climate makes for fine cattle country, one where values were expressed in bovine terms and cattle raids loomed large in poetry and in war. Its areas of fertility and its mild climate together ensured that for much of its history Ireland supported a far larger proportion of the population of the British Isles than it has since the mid-nineteenth century.

Strong geographical forces can, however, sometimes be less historically determinative than one might guess. A paradigm instance is Scotland. The medieval kingdom of Scotland makes little geographical sense: it consisted largely of poor country, with its most-inhabited coastal plains and river valleys separated by mountains and estuaries. The geography of the western Highlands and islands is such as to create stronger links to north-eastern Ireland than to other parts of Scotland: indeed the shortest sea crossing from mainland Scotland to mainland Ireland is just thirteen miles. This helps to explain why Scotland came to be called 'Scotland'. To anyone writing Latin in the seventh century or the eighth *Scotia* meant Ireland, and *Scoti* were Irishmen. During (probably) the fifth century, northern Irish rulers established power in the western islands and Highlands of Scotland creating the extended realm known as Dál Ríata. From the ninth century onwards their descendants gained ascendancy in the much wider area which came to take its name from their Irishness, Scotland. This no more than superficially strange evolution is a reminder that the Irish Sea united rather than divided; so too did the English Channel, at its narrowest twenty-one miles wide. In the fifth and sixth centuries there were Germanic invaders and settlers of related origins on its facing shores. At the western end of the Channel there was a comparable Celtic link. One of the most important facts in the history of the Britons in the post-Roman period is their conquest and settlement of Brittany. Thus Brittany, like Scotland, owes its modern name to Dark Age invasions across the narrow seas.

The attractions of the archipelago made for a rich and interesting prehistory. Human beings first appear in these islands perhaps three quarters of a million years ago, but it was not until approximately the fourth millennium BC that people there began to contribute to the accelerating developments which took a portion of the human race from stone axes to rockets in less than 10,000 years. A rough chronology for the prehistory of the British Isles is as follows: from about the fourth millennium BC settled farming was practised; the use of bronze came in the second millennium; iron was in use from about the later seventh century BC. What had the revolutionary prehistoric millennia accomplished by the time Caesar brought the first Roman army to Britain in 55 BC? Not least, much of the forests of the islands had been cleared; less maybe in Ireland and in what were to become Wales and Scotland than elsewhere, but still extensively. The extent to which early man had taken command of the landscape around him is demonstrated by remarkable discoveries in County Mayo in north-west Ireland. Stone walls, some of them over a kilometre long, defining extensive field systems have been discovered deep in peat bogs. Carbon dating of the peat indicates that the walls belong to the fourth millennium BC, suggesting that closely organised authority goes back so far. Such early political power can be demonstrated elsewhere – the origins of the tremendous, presumably religious, monument of Stonehenge go back to at the latest the fourth millennium BC; the first major stone works there belong to about the middle of the third millennium BC, and were extended and remodelled some thousand years later. The sheer magnitude of Stonehenge is testimony to collective, organised action on a grand scale. Other medieval and Dark Age evidence indicates the presence of extensive systems of assessment and control for such public objectives as roads, defensive works and drainage. There remain unsolved questions about the antiquity and origins of such systems which, if ever answered, would reveal a great deal about the development of social organisation and state power.

Roman Britain

The Romans transformed the material culture of Britain. No sooner had they completed the conquest begun by the emperor Claudius in AD 43 than they set about consolidating their authority in their usual way: by road-building. By the end of the first century Britain boasted a network of roads stretching thousands of miles, well-constructed, properly surveyed, and forming the basis of much of the modern system. The great bridge the Romans built at London, repeatedly repaired and rebuilt, was for many centuries a key to power in south-eastern Britain. One of the main functions of the Roman infrastructure was military: to get a legion to the point of danger as fast as a legion could march. The possibilities for fast transport helped to foster a complex economy in much of Britain. One feature of this was the extensive use of coin. Coin had already been struck by rulers of little Iron Age kingdoms in southern Britain in the generations before the Roman conquest, but in many areas of Roman Britain coin was used in greater abundance. The considerable use of coin was associated with the availability, in wide areas – not all – of manufactured goods for common use, above all of pottery. Roman Britain thus developed an economy which in some ways was much more 'modern' than what had been there before, or was to be there for centuries afterwards.

Tacitus claimed that 'Britain provides gold, silver and other metals such as to make it worth conquering', and Britain was indeed rich in minerals. The Romans worked at least one gold mine there, at Dolau Cothi in South Wales. It was immense: one of the two constructed watercourses which served it was seven miles long and capable of delivering three million gallons daily. Further south, Cornwall was one of the most important European sources of tin. Bronze is composed of copper and tin and so many Roman bronze objects must have had a little bit of Cornwall in them. The Romans lost no time in exploiting British lead; they were mining it in the Mendips within six years of the Claudian conquest (and the lead ore was mixed with a proportion of recoverable silver). Tacitus also stresses the fertility of Britain, insisting that anything could be grown there except such Mediterranean crops as olives.

Two features of the Romano-British countryside and agrarian economy are particularly striking, not least for the (teasingly unanswerable) questions which they pose. The first of these is the layout of the landscape, the second the presence and nature of villas. It is quite possible that in wide areas of England the pattern of fields, paths and little roads is pre-Roman. That it does not conform to the Roman roads suggests that it was older than they were. This kind of arguably very ancient landscape can be found, for example, in parts of Essex, East Anglia and Devonshire; the same could have been true over even wider areas before the reorganisation of much of the countryside from about the tenth century on. Continuities of agrarian landscape could imply continuities of systems of agricultural exploitation and of social organisation. We are reminded that beneath wars, invasions and changes of regime there could have been long rural continuities, no less important for being harder to determine.

'Villas' were a dominant feature of much of the Romano-British countryside, principally in the lowland zone. 'Villa' is a loose term used by modern scholars for a country house: large or not so large, but with some stylistic pretensions. More than six hundred villas or possible villas have been identified in Roman Britain, the grandest of which could rival eighteenth-century ducal mansions. Most were the equivalents of manor houses, large or small. Excavation of a villa commonly takes one into a civilised world, that of a spacious, well-situated house, quite often adorned by fine mosaic floors with religious or cultural references, and equipped with a central heating system. Many villas were flourishing well into the fourth century. It shows how little is really known of Roman Britain that almost nothing is known about who owned the villas. Members of a native British upper class? Expatriate officials? Retired army officers? No doubt patterns of ownership varied from one period to another. It must be significant that villas are not found in all parts even of lowland Britain. Maybe fertile areas in which they are not found, such as the Fenland, were imperial estates.

In recent decades a number of scholars have suggested a fourth-century population of Roman Britain in the neighbourhood of four million, and estimates reaching towards seven million have even been risked. The population of England in 1086 (on the basis of Domesday Book, our first approach to a comprehensive record) is often deduced to have been something under three million. Comparison between these figures gives serious food for thought.

Roman Britain was part of an empire whose life and economy were largely determined by imperial policy and by the presence and demands of the army and bureaucracy. The emperors never found the resources to complete the conquest of the archipelago. Tacitus says that Agricola often maintained that Ireland could have been taken and held by a single legion with auxiliaries, and that this conquest would have made Britain more secure. That no such expedition was launched had effects which endure to this day. Rome's failure to complete the conquest even of the whole of Britain ensured that frontier defence in the north was a heavy burden. Coastal defence also became increasingly important and internal security was not without its costs. Thus war and the vulnerability of lowland Britain would have profound and lasting importance for the material culture of the whole archipelago. This has always been obvious to students of that part of Roman Britain which became England, but less so to those of Ireland, Scotland and Wales. This is largely because the historiographical traditions of these latter areas have tended to rejoice in a culture of victimhood.

Ironically, however, their history from the Roman period into the Dark Ages is one of predation. That the Romans placed two legionary fortresses, at Chester and Caerleon, near the later Anglo-Welsh frontier is indicative of just how vulnerable to western British aggression they felt during the early imperial period; at some stage some 12,000 troops would have been sardined into these bases. How long the Welsh threat remained may be seen by setting beside the Roman garrisons the enormous Anglo-Saxon earthworks on the Welsh frontier (the most extensive in western Europe) and the heavy fortification there later. Our oldest informed description of the Welsh comes from the late twelfth century, and is by an aristocratic Welsh churchman, Gerald of Wales (known variously, and in this volume, as Gerald de Barri). The Welsh, says Gerald, are entirely bred up to the use of arms. Their minds are 'always bent upon the defence of the country', and 'on the means of plunder'. They 'think it right to commit acts of plunder, theft, and robbery, not only against foreigners and hostile nations, but even against their own countrymen'. (This could easily be a nineteenth-century British judgement on the people of the North West Frontier of India.) Consideration should be given to the lively possibility that what Gerald describes for the twelfth century had been true for a very long time. Similarly in the area which came to be called Scotland predation was characteristic in the long career of the people living north of the Forth whom outsiders called Picts (though we do not know the name they gave to themselves). First mentioned about AD 300 as dangerous predators, nearly four centuries later they could bring a Northumbrian king to defeat and death. As for the Irish, a striking description comes from the sixth-century British cleric Gildas. He saw them as 'exceedingly savage', 'like greedy wolves', or as creeping to attack like worms wriggling into the warm sun. The most compelling evidence of Irish aggression is the extent of their conquests and settlements along the western side of Britain. Roman Britain thus presented the not unparalleled picture of a rich, fertile, economically developed area preyed upon by poorer neighbours. The costs of defence and the profits of predation were economic determinants throughout the archipelago. In the end the predators won. Early in the fifth century imperial authority collapsed and the economic, political and social structures of former Roman Britain were transformed.

The fate of towns gives us a thread to follow in tracing material culture through the centuries of Roman rule and Roman collapse, for Roman civilisation was urban and Roman rule town-based. Some of the pre-Roman peoples of Iron Age Britain had had large settlements with some characteristics of towns. But Roman towns had much more to them. Naturally their economic functions varied, ranging from the wide compass of the activities of the mile-square metropolis of London down to simpler roles of the quasi-urban settlements which gathered outside forts. Administrative and social purposes were commonly present and sometimes dominant. Roman Britain was largely subdivided into *civitates* which reflected 'tribal' areas. A *civitas* capital had as its main purpose to be a centre of authority and of civilisation. The importance of civic and governmental functions was proclaimed in magnificent public buildings – the basilica beside the forum of Roman London, for example, occupied a larger floor area than did Christopher Wren's St Paul's Cathedral. To see just the one surviving capital of a column from the colonnade of a temple or basilica at Cirencester, measuring over a yard in diameter, is to catch a thrill of lost magnificence.

The Decline of Roman Britain

Imperial authority in Britain collapsed early in the fifth century. It has been argued that towns were in economic decline from the early fourth century onward. If so, their fate – and maybe that of Roman Britain as a whole – can be seen as reflecting not a sharp and sudden end, but, rather, a long-drawn-out tailing-off. By contrast, the development and nature of villas indicates substantial, maybe unprecedented, prosperity in at least part of the fourth century. Such problems as are presented by what seems to have been happening in towns do not have obvious solutions. Thus the archaeological evidence apparently showing urban decline during the fourth century may have had as much or more to do with political as with economic changes. In general terms *civitas* capitals, which had been the centres of what may have been something like small very subordinated republics, became centres above all for the exertion of imperial power. Yes, public buildings (other than fortifications) did decay. A leading example is that of the great public baths complex at Wroxeter (*Viroconium Cornoviorum*). But it was methodically demolished, and its loss may reflect not so much general economic decline as a change in the imperial system such as to deprive local authorities of the capacity to maintain such establishments. Furthermore, and remarkably, after Wroxeter's baths basilica was demolished the site was neatly levelled and timber buildings were constructed there, one of them was over a hundred feet long. They must belong to the late Roman or early post-Roman period. An important consideration here is that Wroxeter is a 'greenfield' site; all other *civitas* capitals but two were on the sites of modern towns, so the possibility of making discoveries such as those at Wroxeter must be remote. Although the economic role of towns inevitably declined as the Roman empire fell, their role as centres of authority sometimes continued. Thus the historian Bede (*c.* 673–735) is explicit that Canterbury was the capital, *metropolis*, of the dominions of Ethelbert of Kent, *c.* 600. Ethelbert presumably had a palace there. How significant this could prove to be if and when it is uncovered is illustrated by the discovery that at least part of the great headquarters building of the legionary fortress of York could have been still in use until the late Anglo-Saxon period. As nearly always, material culture and political culture interact and overlap. Centres of authority could have economic status by their very nature, attracting men and goods, followers and tribute.

Post-Roman Britain c. 400 – c. 800

The collapse of Roman authority involved the collapse of an economic system. Two simple demonstrations are these: the import of coin from the Continent dried up in the early fifth century (coin, though much used in late Roman Britain, was not struck there); and the mass production of pottery seems to have stopped at about the same time. For some, these changes must have implied economic catastrophe. There are, however, questions about them which are not always asked. How many Roman coins and how many mass-produced pots were there in Britain in, say, 425? Probably hundreds of thousands of each, maybe millions. What happened to them? Surely they would have continued to be used for quite some time; so it could well be that an archaeological site dated, as often, by coins and pottery could have been significantly later than first appears.

The story of what happened in the countryside as Rome fell is as difficult to follow as that of the towns. Landscape survival would be compatible with other elements of agrarian continuity. Pollen analysis suggests that there was no general agricultural abandonment, though there was considerable change from arable to pastoral farming. From the fourth century the climate became colder and wetter; this could have had significant effects on settlement and migration patterns. An enduring mystery is that of the fate of the villas. No British villa site has produced evidence of post-Roman continuity of occupation and life at the level of social or economic sophistication found in late Roman days, continuity such as is sometimes found on the Continent.

Particularly interesting, not to say puzzling, are some of the material remains of the post-Roman period from western Britain, from areas which were long to remain under British rule. There are about 140 memorial inscriptions, for example, from between the fifth century and the eighth from Wales, about forty from the south-west of Britain, and a handful from the southern part of modern Scotland. All are in Latin, though some of those from Wales are also in Irish, reflecting the establishment there of elements of Irish power. The distribution of the stones is remarkable – thus the Welsh ones are largely concentrated in the north-west and south-west, not, as one might have guessed, in the more Romanised south-east. Some of the inscriptions show influences from memorial or lettering styles used in Gaul or Africa and have considerable elements of aesthetic sophistication. A similar tale is told by finds of imported pottery on high-status sites in western Britain and around the Irish Sea dating from between the fifth century and the seventh. Some of this was tableware from south-western France, some was amphorae from as far as the eastern Mediterranean. The general impression from the inscriptions and the imported pottery is one of sophistication and wide contacts. Should such discoveries about Dark

Age society surprise us? Not altogether. This is a period in which Gildas wrote in sophisticated Latin. It is one in which sixth- and seventh-century landowners in south-east Wales could transfer land by Latin documents. (If, as is powerfully argued, though not universally accepted, some of their wording is preserved in much later deeds.) Long-distance trading contacts and the persistence of Latin culture need not have been related, but they could have been.

From the fifth century on there were invasions and settlements in southern and eastern Britain by Angles, Saxons and other German peoples. Their effect on the material life of Britain was considerable but debatable. How numerous were they? Are we looking at a folk migration or rather a takeover by elites? If some combination of the two, what combination? None of the evidence is adequate to answer the main questions. That the English language is overwhelmingly Germanic proves little – French is overwhelmingly derived from Latin, but Romans were never more than a minority of the inhabitants of Gaul. It follows that the dominant extent to which English place names are Germanic need reveal no more than that nearly all the population came to speak English. DNA analysis may in the end answer some of the main problems, but at present doubts and uncertainties prevent its doing so.

In exploring the nature of Germanic invasions we are largely dependent on the evidence of archaeology. More than 30,000 apparently Anglo-Saxon burials have been found in southern and eastern England and grave goods discovered in them demonstrate that the invaders came from lands on the other side of the North Sea. There are, however, major difficulties in using cemetery evidence for weighing the scale and full significance of the invasions and settle-ments. One is that of differential survival of evidence; one can hardly tell how far the distribution of discovered burials accurately reflects past activity. Second, there is the possibility of 'acculturation'. A purely British inhabitant of a sixth-century grave might have entirely Anglo-Saxon personal equipment, but so might a purely Anglo-Saxon inhabitant have adopted British ways and left no grave goods. For, third, and not least, Britons did not bury grave goods. This is a principal reason for their having left but few archaeological traces in Wales even though they were the only inhabitants. Millions of Britons from the post-Roman generations have left no archaeological remains, in burials or otherwise. None of these difficulties prove that the Anglo-Saxon invasions and settlements did not have at least some of the character of a folk migration. All the same it does look as if in wide lands under Anglo-Saxon rule most of the population could very well have been of British origin, and the ultimate effect of Germanic invasion and rule may often have been the creation of groups with new, Germanic, identities which absorbed existing British inhabitants.

The collapse of Roman order could have undermined economic life not least because of the threat to infrastructure: bridges, roads and canals. What would have been the consequences of the collapse of the authority which saw to the maintenance of London Bridge, for example, or to that of the Carr Dyke in Cambridgeshire and Lincolnshire, a major canal nearly a hundred miles long? Did systems for such maintenance remain at least partly in place? If so, who ran them? A related question is that of mineral resources. What did post-Roman Britain do for lead, tin and iron? What did it do for salt? Such a society depended greatly on salt, not least for winter food, and preserving food requires a lot of it. Preserving a single herring takes an ounce of salt at the very least. Under the Romans a major source of salt was the great deposits of rock salt at Droitwich, Worcestershire, as was indicated in its Latin name, *Salinae*. As soon as there are documents which can give relevant information, by about 700, we find salt in production there. We do not know what happened between Roman times and then. Similarly, we know that lead was in production by the end of the late seventh century but on whether there was continuity in lead mining from Roman to later times there is no information (though it is a reasonable guess that it did continue). These are questions not just about economics but also about power – it is worth remembering that when first we have figures (1086) Droitwich was worth more to the king than almost any other provincial town.

Let us approach material life from an altogether different angle. Consider the wonderful artefacts discovered in a ship-burial mound at Sutton Hoo in Suffolk in 1939. It was the burial deposit of a great man, possibly a king. It dates from about 630, maybe somewhat later. The weapons, personal ornaments and tableware found there shed light on, and raise questions about, the position and possessions of the very great.

The first impression is that of wealth: the grave held many gold ornaments and lavish silverware. The second is of the amazing sophistication of the techniques displayed. For example, the gold foil which backs the garnets in the brilliant jewellery is patterned. The patterns are exceedingly regular, involving numerous exactly parallel lines, with several lines to the millimetre. It is not easy to see how such patterns could have been created without the use of a jigged machine such as is otherwise unknown until the sixteenth century, though the possibility of the creation of stamps repeating the patterns of fine silk cloth has been raised.

Whence did such wealth come? Not all the gold and silver of Roman Britain had been taken away by a departing elite. Germanic invaders had much to plunder; whoever was buried at Sutton Hoo was probably the beneficiary of such predation, directly or indirectly. The endemic warfare of sixth-century Britain involved the extortion and concession of treasures. Successful warfare produced another source of profit: slaves to sell abroad. An episode preliminary to the conversion of England was Pope Gregory I's encounter with a consignment of Anglian slaves in the market at Rome. It is no surprise that rich men had sophisticated goods; but such goods raise questions about the range of techniques available to society as a whole. Early Anglo-Saxon society depended for decency and warmth on a wide range of metal goods. Brooches of various kinds were essential (buttons were introduced later). Their varieties were fairly various and their supply must have involved commercial, or quasi-commercial, mechanisms. On another level we see that these peoples had great powers of construction in wood. The Sutton Hoo ship, ninety feet long and beautifully built, shows this. So too does the amazing structure of the towering 'grandstand', rather like a wooden segment of an amphitheatre, traced at Yeavering (Northumberland) and dating from the late sixth or early seventh centuries.

Two other, related, aspects of the Sutton Hoo discovery stand out. One is Romanness – *Romanitas*; the other is the extent of overseas contacts. These two go together: the immediate influences behind the production of the magnificent helmet are Swedish, but its ultimate model was parade gear imitated by the Romans from their Sassanian enemies in Iran. An enormous, and old, silver dish came from Byzantium, and was just such as would have graced a rich late-Roman table. The silver bowls beside it had been made recently, probably in Egypt. In short, the material style of great men of this period was significantly Roman. (One may relate this to their willingness to accept a Roman religion.) Their contacts, whether direct or indirect, whether commercial or political, were wide. Surviving rich church treasures from Ireland and silver from Pictland suggest at least the possibility of wealth comparable to that of Sutton Hoo and the same could have been true of Wales.

Insufficient attention has been given by modern historians to what was possibly the most important event in the material history of the archipelago in the seventh century, and one likely to have had long-enduring effects. Sometime in or around 664 there was an epidemic of what may well have been bubonic plague, and the pestilence returned c. 684–7 and later. The evidence from England includes the death of many kings and bishops, an account of the near extinction of the monastic community at Jarrow, and reference to widespread depopulation. Somewhat more extensive evidence from Ireland at the same time suggests that there was similar devastation and it has been suggested that there this plague, and another in the mid-sixth century, may have considerably affected church organisation, favouring the growth in the power of great monasteries. In the fourteenth century a great plague, the Black Death, killed a third or more of Europe's people. Demonstrably, it transformed social and economic balances. Such certainty is not possible in our period; we depend instead on inferences, anecdotes and speculation. However, these are enough to establish the serious possibility that plague in the seventh century may have had a revolutionary impact comparable to that which it had seven hundred years later.

A major reduction in population could have had significant economic effects. Some Dark Age lands may have had frontier economies depending partly on the availability of manpower. A law of Ine, king of Wessex, c. 700 laid down that a nobleman who left his land could take with him only his reeve, his smith and his children's nurse. By contrast elsewhere overpopulation could be seen as a problem. Thus two Irish sources see plague as, literally, an answer to prayer, because overpopulation was leading to famine. Even if this evidence is not contemporary it still shows an interesting attitude. In some circumstances there could indeed be too many people. A famine in Sussex (678) was so severe that starving people committed suicide, joining hands and jumping over the cliffs to their death. Reduction in population could, of course, benefit the survivors. Thus the fourteenth-century survivors of the Black Death were on average better off than their parents; and plague expanded demand for better goods. The question of whether plague could have produced such a transformation in a much earlier period can be discussed only as Dark Age economic history: that is to say as hopeful guesswork.

It is, however, certain that the later seventh and early eighth centuries saw economic transformations. The key words are *sceattas* and *emporia*. Coins first: no coin was struck in post-Roman Britain until about 600, when small gold coins, insular versions of Merovingian *tremises*, began to be struck in the south-east. During the last quarter of the seventh century the gold coinage was replaced by silver. Numerous small silver coins, called *sceattas* by historians, were produced in the south and east. There were millions of them, and before the mid-eighth century there may well have been as much coin in circulation as there was to be centuries later, perhaps even more than at any other period before 1066. So the first major economic phenomenon of the later seventh and early eighth centuries is, in a considerable part of Britain, an abundant silver coinage. The second great economic phenomenon is that of *emporia*. The Latin term simply means 'trading places', but it is used by scholars to denote extensive trading places which look like towns but which they do not care, or do not dare, to call towns. Three, probably four, such sites are known in England and there were probably others. Bede, writing *c.* 731, says that London was an *emporium* for many people coming by land and by sea, and archaeologists have found widespread traces of such a settlement, not within the Roman walls, but immediately to their west. *Hamwic* (beside medieval Southampton) has been rather more comprehensively excavated. Its origins lie in the seventh century, its decline in the ninth. At its maximum it occupied up to something like a hundred acres (forty hectares), with streets and house plots laid out in an orderly way. Such an area, even if not fully built up, would have been compatible with a population of several thousands. Ipswich was significantly comparable but did not decline in the same way in the ninth century, and from the early eighth it was the centre of an important pottery industry with widely distributed wares. At *Hamwic* there was considerable craftwork in bone: maybe it too was a manufacturing town. There is a likely *emporium* site at York also and names and locations suggest others, e.g. Fordwich and Sandwich. Generalisations about the *emporia* can be made with some confidence. First, these places are near to the sea and are part of a pattern of such places round the narrow seas (compare, for example, Quentovic in

Picardy, and Dorestad in Frisia). Second, their size indicates that their economic functions cannot have been confined to luxury goods. Third, their locations suggest a connection with royal authority. So, the story the *emporia* sites could tell is one of international trade in quite bulky goods, quite possibly involving royal power.

Which goods? The commodity exported from Britain of which we are best informed is slaves, but the scale of the *emporia* suggests that other things must have been involved as exports or imports. Wool? Hides? Timber? Wine? Royal, and other, lordship may have been such as to accumulate exportable commodities. There is a little evidence for the import of wine. Thus we learn from a life of St Cuthbert that on a visit to a distinguished abbess she offered him a drink: 'Wine or beer?' The saint, most properly, chose water, but the incident shows that wine was imported for non-sacramental purposes.

What are we to make of this economy, two of whose distinguishing features are an abundant silver coinage and extensive trading sites? One piece in the puzzle must be that south-eastern Britain and Frisia had what was, effectively, a common currency and that the Frisians were the great trading people of the age. (And we may notice that the Frisian and Old English languages were very close relatives.) Another new and important clue is the discovery of 'productive sites'. These are sites in southern and eastern England where metal detecting has found numbers of coins and/or small pieces of metalwork. Some, at least, of them were probably trading places. This is important in relation to our present enquiry. For if *emporia* handled bulky commodities these were likely to have been agricultural. Some 'productive sites' could have been collecting centres for such commodities and/or distribution centres for manufactured goods.

How was the countryside organised? Again, all that can be offered is a set of related problems and possibilities. How far does archaeology come to the rescue? Alas, not very far. Most Anglo-Saxon archaeology has been of cemeteries. An increasing number of settlements have been excavated, but by no means enough to encourage much safe generalisation. A specially important case is that of a village at West Heslerton in North Yorkshire excavated over many years by Dr Powlesland. What he has found there are the remains of a substantial settlement over a period from the fifth century (or maybe earlier) to the ninth. It seems to have been well-organised and maintained and involved in fairly complicated networks of trade and exchange. The furthest range of its contacts is indicated by such finds as a cowrie shell and elephant ivory rings. The village presents features not yet fully paralleled elsewhere, but, viewed in a wide historical context, the most interesting thing about it is what might loosely be called its normality. It does not seem to have been so very different from many medieval or early modern villages. Our written sources deal largely with violence and change. It is well to be reminded of how much normality and continuity there can have been, even in bad times.

Who owned such a village? Such a crucial question is one which archaeology can seldom answer. Its context can be summed up in three themes or theories: those of the 'extended estate', of the 'mark', and of 'inland and warland'. Once we have fairly detailed knowledge of English estates, i.e. from 1086 on, we find that major ones fairly often form (or, apparently, had once formed), as it were, archipelagos: there was a main estate centre with a number of 'extended' outliers, sometimes distant. Thirteenth-century Welsh law codes describe similarly extended estates which suggests that some of the estate organisation of at least parts of early medieval England may have derived from a Celtic past. There is occasional evidence to support this possibility; for example, the Celtic origins of words sometimes used for certain dues in northern England. The second theme is that of the 'mark' theory developed in Germany and, in the nineteenth century, much canvassed in relation to England. It has recently been revived, though not by the same name. The basic idea is that independently organised groups of free peasants were settled in territorially independent groups in such a way that there was considerable common tenure, above all of grazing land. Quite numerous examples of fairly wide areas with common grazing can be detected in England from Domesday Book and other evidence, and these can be seen as remnants of such earlier 'tribal' settlement. The third approach is that most recently and powerfully put forward by Dr Faith. She detects in medieval sources over much of Anglo-Saxon England the legacy, and continuity, of a pattern such that nuclei of authority, with nearby land, *inland*, cultivated by fairly closely subordinated peasants, were surrounded by, or associated with, wider areas of *warland* occupied by free peasants owing services partly to the lord of the inland but also to rulers. These services were commonly assessed in terms of 'hides'. (The 'hide' was a unit of land measurement and assessment.) This approach can be linked to an interpretation of social history which sees a free peasantry in the early Anglo-Saxon period later being 'manorialised' and sinking to a semi-free system involving economic and personal subjection to manorial lords. All three of these approaches can be reconcilable in various ways and in varying degrees, and each raises questions of continuity or discontinuity. Could it be that estate structures and systems of obligation survived from Roman times or before? How revolutionary were the changes in the country-side in the tenth century and later: the breaking up of large units, the creation of nucleated villages with two- or three-field systems? What difference did the Scandinavian invasions make? (By the eleventh century there was much more peasant freedom in northern, eastern and east midland England than elsewhere, but the connection between this and Scandinavian rule and settlement in these areas is debatable.)

In all these questions political, social and economic considerations meet. Consider, for example, a possible connection between the wide south-western conquests of the kings of Wessex in the later seventh century and the economic developments associated with the *emporia*. Suppose, as is likely, that most of a lord's or a king's rural revenues came from renders in kind. One of King Ine's laws has an air of this: 'ten vats of honey, three hundred loaves, thirty barrels of clear ale, two full grown cows or ten wethers (and so on down to a hundred eels) shall be paid as food rent from every ten hides'. That twelve different commodities are specified could suggest that what we are given may be the specification of the materials for a regular feast for an itinerant king. But such a law indicates that a king or other great man might have large supplies of commodities at his disposal, supplies which could well have been increased by such conquests as those of the kings of Wessex. Could some of these have been exported, for example leather, a key commodity without which life would have been impossible?

There is archaeological evidence for widespread cloth production. Cloth may have been used as currency, as it was at other times in other places. One of Ine's laws (*c.* 700) says that 'the blanket paid as rent from each household shall be worth sixpence'. Wool could thus be seen in cash terms. The same law says that a sheep was to retain its fleece until midsummer and if it was sheared earlier then two pence should be paid for the fleece. Two things should be noticed in these laws: first, that what was specified in apparent cash might well have been paid in goods; second, that the cash value indicated seems to indicate a relatively low value for coin. 'Two pence' was probably two silver *sceattas*. Low value for coinage could go with what the numismatic evidence suggests: considerable use of coin.

This example reflects the fact that early Anglo-Saxon society was, in some important senses, very commercial. It was one in which any illegal or injurious act could be redeemed by payment. Every man had his price, every one of his fingers had its price. According to the *Penitential* attributed to Archbishop Theodore (early eighth century) a man could even sell his son, provided the child was under the age of eight. The nature of the goods found in sixth- and seventh-century graves indicates that there had long been commercial activity of some kind. Brooches, even simple ones, could hardly be made in the ordinary family home. Pots stamped with the same bone stamps but found in cemeteries miles apart tell of professional potters. It is important that the archaeology of metal ornament, especially female ornament, shows that from about the end of the sixth century there was increased resemblance in style over wide areas of future England. This may relate to changes in economic activity such that traders 'going into the interior of the country', mentioned in Ine's laws, played their part, as, in the course of time, 'productive sites' may have done. There seems to have been an increasingly complex economic system, revealing and presumably creating wealth. Production in which lordship could have once played an important role now may have become more market-oriented.

Monasteries demonstrated important wealth. The progress of the Christian Church from 597 was accompanied from the mid-seventh century by monastic foundation on a large, even extravagant, scale. An institution such as the twinned abbey of Monkwearmouth-Jarrow was immensely expensive, not least because of the cost of ornaments and manuscripts. Two examples of monastic wealth are these. The most famous manuscript produced at Monkwearmouth-Jarrow was the *Codex Amiatinus*, a stunning copy of the Bible. It was one of three produced there at the same time. The number of calf skins needed for these masterpieces was approximately 1,550 – a great herd of cattle had been needed, as well as considerable time and immense skill to process the vellum. Another example of monastic wealth is this: as Bede lay dying, he sent for his box so that he might give his personal possessions to his friends. They included *pipera*, pepper, which cannot have come from anywhere much nearer than southern India. Another as yet

imperfectly understood possible link between monasteries and a
burgeoning economy is altogether remarkable: the designs of a
number of *sceatta* types echo illuminated manuscripts of the period.
Does this significantly Christian iconography indicate that such coins
were produced at, and for, monasteries?

The connections between economic activity and royal power
mattered. A crucial question is: even if monasteries were involved in
coining, how far were kings also? When a *sceatta* bore a name it was
almost always that of a moneyer, though there are coins with royal
names from Northumbria and East Anglia. This position changed in
the later eighth century. From about 760 in much of England coins
were struck differently and regularly bore the names of kings. The
coins of Offa (king of Mercia, 757–96, and overlord of other kingdoms)
were of this kind. Statistical analysis shows that Offa's coins must have
numbered many millions. Control over such a coinage must have been
important for the power of a great king. Another major element in
royal authority was treasure, its receipt and not least its gift. *Beowulf*,
the only complete Anglo-Saxon secular epic to survive, may well have
its origin in the eighth century and its frequent use of the epithets 'ring-
giver' and 'gold-friend' is symptomatic of a political economy in which
treasure was important. Treasure included fine weaponry and rich
clothes as well as bullion. How were such things to be obtained? Often
by wresting them violently from those who had them or by levying
them as tribute. How else could war and predation produce treasure?
It might well have been by selling the fruits of conquest, the most
remunerative of which may have been slaves. Perhaps the most
illuminating text on the economics of war in the seventh century is
Bede's account of the adventures of a Northumbrian nobleman
captured at a battle with the Mercians in 679. This man, called Imma,
managed to talk his way out of being killed. Instead, he was bought by
a Frisian merchant who took him towards London in chains. Bede was
interested in this episode because Imma had a priestly brother whose
prayers repeatedly made his chains drop off. By contrast, our interest
lies in the Frisian merchant apparently lurking in the rear of the battle,
and his bearing his purchase off to London. For once one sees an
emporium in action (and it is interesting to see how wide the economic
hinterland of London could be).

A more complicated element in the economics of power is this. In a
society in which currency, especially coin, does not circulate, the larger

part of what the powerful can get from most of subordinated society is food renders and labour services. For bullion they have to look elsewhere, especially to war. But if coin circulates some way down society then bullion can be obtained through rent or tax and the systems of power are modified. By the late eighth century this may have come about in some areas of Britain. This is not to say that royal conquest and predation were not to be determinative for centuries to come, but it does suggest that the internal exploitation of lands and land took on heightened significance.

Early Ireland

The economic circumstances just described were those of the area which came to be called England. What happened in the rest of the archipelago? The economic history of future Wales and Scotland is, at present, obscure. One can attempt rather more for Ireland, and it is important to do so, for we are looking at the bread-and-butter side of intellectual triumphs. Here the following generalisations are possible. Whatever currency was in use, it was not coin – as in other pre-coin economies, there was a system of conventional valuations in which female slaves, for example, were important units. Law tracts are helpfully informative on tenures, even if distorted to an unknowable extent by schematisation. According to these a lord or an abbey could have two kinds of dependant (family and slaves apart): 'free clients' and 'base (which here is used to mean 'lower' not 'unfree') clients'. Both classes were provided with cattle by the lord. A 'free client' would be provided with a number of cattle for which he would pay an annual render in cattle (or an equivalent) for six years. In the seventh year he would return the original grant but keep any surplus. A 'base client' would owe services and renders heavier than those of a 'free client': food rents, labour services and hospitality.

There were no towns in any ordinary sense in Ireland before 800, but there were what historians term 'monastic towns'. A big monastery, with numerous monks, servants and clients would attract other people, too, to meet the needs of a rich community or to seek its protection. There may well have been significant foreign trade, especially along the Atlantic sea routes. When St Columbanus made a return visit to Ireland from Nantes in 610 he found a merchant ship there on which he could take passage. A striking thing about certain Irish works is that they demonstrate very early knowledge of the writings of Isidore of Seville (*c.* 560–636). This speaks for close contact with Spain. From the later Middle Ages a major element in Irish trade with Spain was leather. Could the export of hides from a cattle-dominated society have been intrinsic to the early connection between Ireland and Spain?

Scandinavian Invasions

A striking and surprising thing about the *emporia* and monasteries of England was that they were unfortified. A heavy price was soon paid for this combination of vulnerability and prosperity. The *Anglo-Saxon Chronicle* records, for 793, one early such payment: 'the ravages of heathen men miserably destroyed God's church on Lindisfarne, with plunder and slaughter'. This was one of the first of many Viking raids, both on Britain and on Ireland. From about the mid-ninth century these increased in scale and changed in nature. From at least 841 Scandinavian forces wintered in Ireland, and from 851 in England. From 865 a Danish 'great army' was active in England, and by the 870s some Danes were taking landed power there. Well before 900 the economic life of the archipelago had been transformed by Norse, coming chiefly to the north and west, and by Danes, coming chiefly to the south and the east. Most obviously by physical attacks: monks writing annals may have understandably tended to a degree of hysteria, but cannot have been very wrong in emphasising destruction. Such devastation is hinted at by, for example, the excavation of an otherwise unknown but rich monastery at Brandon, in Suffolk. Aside from a great predominance of men's graves, some writing implements and one fragment of a finely embossed gold book cover, Brandon monastery has left not a wrack or a record behind. Secular institutions suffered no less. It was not for nothing that the *emporium* at *Hamwic* petered out in the ninth century.

The Vikings did not invent pillage and destruction. Irish monasteries had suffered from the attentions of Irish potentates and, not least, from those of rival monasteries well before the Vikings struck. Yet it is likely the Scandinavian invasions increased the role and scale of pillage. The economic effects of pillage were not all negative. The release into circulation of bullion held as treasures, for example by monasteries ('dethesaurisation'), could have been an economic stimulus. Raiders almost inevitably become traders as they need to dispose of their booty, not least of their captives. We are told, for example, that when Vikings returned in 871 from a successful assault on Dumbarton it was with two hundred ships laden with Anglian, British and Pictish slaves. One further effect of Scandinavian conquests and settlements was to create, and stimulate, commerce across the Irish Sea. If a boom in the slave trade was among the economic developments introduced by the Scandinavians, it was not the only one. Between the eighth century and the tenth they learned a great deal about commerce. Their own places of trade and manufacture developed: Hedeby, at the neck of the Jutland peninsula, is just one example.

Before the invasions Ireland had only the 'monastic towns'. The Vikings ('Ostmen') created something more like real towns, in particular Cork, Waterford, Wexford and, above all, Dublin. The first Viking settlement there was destroyed by the Irish in 902. A new one, near the core of modern Dublin, was begun in 917. Part of this tenth- and eleventh-century settlement has been excavated, and the regular division of tenements there, the houses and the general organisation, are those of a significant town. Significant, too, was the incoming Scandinavians' economic sophistication as displayed in northern and eastern England. Excavation at York shows it to have been a counterpart to Dublin as a developed trading town, and coin was struck at York, at Lincoln and in East Anglia. It is revealing of Anglo-Scandinavian assimilation that many of these coins were struck in the name of saints: St Peter, St Michael and, most notably, St Edmund, the king of East Anglia, killed by the Danes in 869. The English towns which were under Danish control came to manufacture quantities of ordinary goods for ordinary people. For example, the production at Stamford of commonly used pottery began before c. 900 and comparable large-scale pottery manufacture grew up in other eastern towns by the tenth century at the latest.

The English Economy in the Tenth and Early Eleventh Centuries

In his contemporary biography of William the Conqueror, William of Poitiers gloats on the wealth of England. The land is extremely fertile, he says, and its wealth is increased by its merchants. The study of

Domesday Book (1086) and of coins enables us to put some figures to such wealth. From *c.* 973 the currency was run on a system whereby at fairly frequent intervals a new type was issued and significant efforts made to withdraw the old type. Analysis of this coinage could indicate that the amount of coin struck in each of the issues *c.* 973 to *c.* 1059, current for periods averaging about six years, varied between forty-seven million pennies and two and a half million, the amount in circulation at a given time from twelve million to 1.3 million. (The scale of these variations has not been fully explained.) The *Anglo-Saxon Chronicle* maintains that 272,147 pounds of silver were paid to buy off Danish invaders between 991 and 1018. Some of these geld figures are questioned, but their message is the same as that of the abundant coinage: England had great wealth and a developed and developing economy.

An important element in England's wealth was its towns. Domesday Book omits the most important town, London, and also Winchester, but its data on other towns indicate that 8 per cent or more of the population lived in settlements of over 450 people. The major provincial towns probably had about the same populations as in 1400 (though they were not necessarily the same towns). Some towns were major centres of trade and industry; witness the importance of urban pottery manufacture.

Sherds are indestructible, and so pottery shouts loudly in the archaeological record. Other urban manufactures were perhaps even more significant. Thus important excavations in Coppergate ('Coopergate'), York, have revealed large traces of extensive wood turning; for example, the manufacture of cups and saucers (shaped just like modern ones except that the cups are handleless). At York, and in other towns, there are extensive indications of metal and bone working. Large-scale production of relatively cheap consumer goods seems to have become a major phenomenon in England at this time. Scrupulous recording of every manufactured scrap turning up in Professor Martin Biddle's important excavations at Winchester in the 1960s further suggests that the availability of manufactured goods increased greatly during the tenth century.

Relationships between town and country are crucial in the developments of the English economy in this period. The countryside supplied towns with food; almost all towns had agricultural land attached to them, but by no means all could have supplied themselves from their own land. An entertaining example of a town being supplied from the country comes in a late tenth-century life of Swithin, the sainted ninth-century bishop of Winchester. An old woman was bringing a basket of eggs into Winchester to sell. By ill chance she dropped them. Naturally, she invoked the saint, and, supernaturally, the eggs were restored to their original integrity. This fortunate lady must stand for many others bringing goods from the countryside to towns. Similarly the early twelfth-century 'Laws of Edward the Confessor' see waterways as primarily a means of conveying supplies, foodstuffs and wood from the countryside to the towns. The reference to wood is important: probably the most bulky item supplied by the countryside was fuel, not least to fuel-hungry pottery towns. Agriculture depends upon tools. An early eleventh-century tract lists more than a hundred kinds of tool, implement and vessel. Some of the iron ones may have been made by rural smiths, but iron-working towns such as Gloucester or Thetford must have been a major source of supply.

Changes which took place in the Anglo-Saxon countryside were no less radical than those in Anglo-Saxon towns. Unsurprisingly there was extensive local variation and there were complicated relationships between economic, social and political developments. Two important and probably related changes were the reorganisation of settlements and settlement patterns, and the restructuring of major estates. Neither can be dated closely; both may have begun before 900, but were certainly important afterwards. Major tracts of south-eastern and of western England still have much the same dispersed pattern of settlement as before the Anglo-Saxons came; even the field patterns can be very old and 'nucleated' villages (that is to say villages in which most habitations are clustered together) are the exception. By contrast, in other areas in the south, the north and much of the midlands, nucleated villages are the norm. It looks as if in wide areas nucleation did not become common until the late Anglo-Saxon period. Sometimes such villages were laid out on an organised plan. This can be seen by considering the layout of, for example, many midland villages as they were until 'enclosure' in the eighteenth and nineteenth centuries. What we commonly find is a nucleated village surrounded by two or three open fields each divided into a neat pattern of strips, often the result of a large-scale reordering of the landscape which could have taken place before 1066. Another change, maybe an associated change, approximately in the same period, was this. In the early Anglo-Saxon period it looks as if much land was held, and organised, in large complexes, sometimes territorially contiguous and sometimes with different parts having different functions. Traces of such systems are widely visible in Domesday and later. But by the time of Domesday many such estates had already been extensively divided up so that there were many land holdings consisting of one village or part of a village. An interesting consequence of this is that by 1066 the estates of many great men, including the king, consisted partly of such villages or parts of villages sometimes scattered over very wide areas. Although our evidence is not good enough to deal in more than instances and hopeful inferences, we can glimpse patterns of change in the organisation of villages and the countryside, and can apprehend their importance.

Five factors, beyond geographical good fortune, lie principally behind English prosperity: royal power, investment, foreign trade (maybe largely in wool), the beneficent interaction of factors for growth and, maybe, fish. The most important royal contribution to the economy was peace, wars against Scandinavian invaders set to one side. There was indeed dynastic violence, in particular c. 900 and c. 978, and the politics of Ethelred II's reign (978–1016) were neither calm nor clean. It is true that the *Anglo-Saxon Chronicle*'s annalists could be misleadingly discreet in concealing disorders. When all that is said, it still matters that so little civil strife was recorded compared to what we find across most of Europe. In the long reign of Edward the Confessor the nearest the English came to civil war was in a standoff in 1051–2 between the king and Earl Godwin with his sons. One factor in the relative absence of civil strife could, however, be the harshness of the ruling order; it is therefore worth mentioning some of the violence which *was* used. For example, note the late chronicler Wendover's account of king Edgar's punishment of the men of Thanet for robbing merchants from York. He 'deprived all of them of their possessions and even deprived some of them of life'. Late Anglo-Saxon government appears to have institutionalised a brutal sense of order.

Not the least contribution power made to prosperity was a coinage which was of good quality and abundant. Coinage had long been a royal monopoly, and in the tenth and eleventh centuries the coin issued for lands under the king's control was uniformly good. Another benefit of royal authority was the upkeep of the communications system. The maintenance of bridges appears in land grants from the eighth century onwards as a public obligation from which no exemption was available, and in the eleventh century damage to major roads and waterways was prohibited under heavy penalty. In such ways the foundations and frameworks for economic advance were provided through the institutions of a well-organised state.

A second key to English prosperity was investment, above all investment in agriculture, one aspect of which is watermills. Domesday records more than six thousand of these, the most complicated machinery the age knew. Even more important were plough beasts. Domesday shows the presence of over 650,000 plough oxen, many owned by peasants. The significance of this large supply of edible traction appears sharply if a contrast is drawn with what is written in 1977 about the modern developing countries of Syria and Dahomey. In Syria, as W.B. Morgan shows, 'Mixed farming techniques have been introduced . . . aimed . . . at the introduction of ox-drawn ploughs in order to eliminate the village bottleneck and make possible larger farms'. In Dahomey animal draught was almost unknown until 1964 and ten years later there were only some 3,600 plough oxen there. Another kind of rural investment was in salvation. The great number of parish churches built at this time reflects both the apparently increasing number of 'one village' estates and mounting agricultural wealth.

William of Poitiers stressed the importance of the third factor, foreign trade. But the same question arises as in the earlier age of *emporia*: trade in what? Later in the Middle Ages the economy rested largely on the export of wool. Peter Sawyer argued brilliantly in 1965 that the same might have been true in the eleventh century, since large amounts of silver went out of England in Danegeld in the early eleventh century while coin issues of very many millions continued. There must, therefore, have been a favourable balance of trade with an inflow of silver, and wool export was the best hypothesis in explaining this. Importantly, this is almost exactly what Henry of Huntingdon, a chronicler writing c. 1140, says. He observes that much silver is brought from Germany in exchange for exports including 'costly wool', so that there was, he said, a larger supply of silver in England than in Germany itself.

Huntingdon also mentions the export of fish. Fish (both freshwater and sea fish) was more important in human diet in the Middle Ages than it is now. There is evidence to suggest that sea-fishing increased in importance in the late Anglo-Saxon period. For much of English history a major source of food has been the East Anglian herring fishery. Until recently, every autumn countless millions of herring shoaled off East Anglia. The fishermen here could win food with an ease unknown to the farmer who had to toil for months to get a crop of three or four times the seed he had sown. The herring fishery was a kind of protein mine. Medieval salt herrings were one of the commonest of cheap food; one might say that the herring was the potato of the Middle Ages. Domesday shows that the East Anglian herring fishery was already important. How important we cannot really tell, but the herrings may have had more than a swimming-on part on the economic scene. To consider the wool possibility and the herring possibility is to be convinced of something crucial: that in seeking understanding of the early economic history of the British Isles hypothesising is not a luxury, but a necessity.

A familiar cliché of economic history comes from the eminent American economist Walt Rostow: the idea of the 'take-off', the situation in which a number of interacting beneficent circles ensure not only quantitative but also qualitative change. In considering economic development one might look back from Rostow to the father of development economics: Adam Smith. Smith emphasised that without density of settlement you are unlikely to have much specialisation of function, and without specialisation of function you cannot have economic advance. Domesday proves that much of England did have dense settlement of various types. Specialisation of function implies a complex relationship within a hierarchy of settlements. In this connection the distinction between 'town' and 'country' is partly misleading. Rather, one should consider a gradation from the most basic hamlet, with, say, three poor peasant families, to more complex villages, then up to important royal or monastic estate centres, like Domesday Glastonbury with its eight smiths, and so further up through small and larger towns to such metropolises as London or York with multiple specialisms, some of them expensive and luxurious. The development and economic effect of such a hierarchy depends on the operation of a complex system of specialisms and exchanges. Important here is a good currency; and here we may note how deeply and widely the good English currency of the period circulated. The numismatic evidence suggests an almost nationally interactive currency. It matters that, of the coins of 1018–87 found singly, slightly more than a third were at more than sixty miles from their minting place. One can imagine how such a degree of economic unity and widespread contact helped in the creation of a number of beneficent circles. Thus the availability of millwrights in major settlements provides for the construction and servicing of the machines which free from grinding labour man or woman power, which is then available for such seasonally demanding tasks as the operation of water meadows, hay-making, shearing and weeding. If urban metalworking makes good, cheap tools more widely available, then food production can rise and the likely relationship between urban wages and food prices can ensure that the cost of production goes down and the availability of tools increases.

On reasonable suppositions, based above all on Domesday Book, much of England's economy was developed and on the move, though there were marked regional variations. The extreme contrast between the fertile fields of Kent and the stark hills of Cumbria was as determinative then as it would be centuries later. More puzzling is the question of similarity or dissimilarity between England and its neighbours. How far are apparent dissimilarities due to England's being illuminated by Domesday Book while other areas are not? Or is it, rather, that the English administration's capacity to produce a Domesday Book shows how different England was? The answer, like most answers, has to be mixed. Quite probably areas across the Narrow Seas such as Flanders had an economy not so very different from that of southern England.

Wales, Ireland and Scotland,
c. 900–c. 1066

The economies of Wales, Scotland and Ireland are much harder to understand than that of England. All that can be done is to hazard generalisations, or at least to pose questions. First, disunited Wales. What economic effects did the Vikings have on Wales? The attacks were serious and prolonged; the Welsh seem to have put up a good fight, but Viking authority appears to have been established for periods in parts of Wales from the ninth century. Wales, perhaps particularly the north-western principality of Gwynedd, became integral to an

'Irish Sea province' which represented an elaborate political/economic nexus, in which Norse Dublin was integral. Some indication of Welsh material circumstances in about 1100, and probably earlier, comes from the twelfth-century biography of Gruffydd ap Cynan, ruler of Gwynedd, 1095–1137. His ancestry and life were rooted in the Welsh–Irish connection. He was born in Dublin. His mother was of high Norse and Irish descent. He repeatedly fled to or visited Ireland and used Irish–Scandinavian troops. His biographer gives harsh indications of elements in the material life of Wales. Here is a vignette of warfare: 'Trahaern was stabbed in his bowels until he was on the ground breathing his last, chewing with his teeth the fresh herbs and groping on top of his arms: and Gwcharki the Irishman made bacon of him as of a pig'(translation by Evans). So much for the cut and thrust of Welsh battle. Here is a more general view of a campaign (twelfth-century, but earlier times would hardly have differed): 'Gruffydd marched towards Arwystli and destroyed and killed its people; he burned its houses, and took its women and maidens captive.' (The 'women and maidens' would either have passed into domestic use or have been put on to the slave market.) Wales, like many areas in this period, had a material culture in which a leading element was society's cruel self-destruction. One passage in the story of Gruffydd illuminates another aspect of Welsh life. It tells how he was saved from imprisonment when he was chained up in the marketplace at Chester. He was freed by a young man who came from Wales to Chester, with a few companions, 'to buy necessities'. Then, as later, urban functions for parts of Wales were performed by towns in England.

Direct evidence for the economy of Scotland is as little, or even less, available than for Wales. Again we can perhaps most helpfully approach the problems with the aid of twelfth-century evidence, in this case the grants made by Scottish kings. Scotland until the twelfth century was, by comparison with England or Flanders, behind the times: no coin was struck there; there were no towns; there were no up-to-date monasteries of the kinds found elsewhere. The first Scottish king to strike coin was David I (1124–53). In twelfth-century Scotland the process of town foundation was organised, involving the introduction of Flemish and French burgesses. The land grants of Malcolm IV (1153–65) reveal something about the connection between towns and coins. His grants involving coin (as contrasted with grants of renders in kind) always have something to do with new towns, and/or with monasteries. The significance of such twelfth-century evidence is that it shows development of the kind of thing which had been present in England in the tenth and eleventh centuries, but not in Scotland.

It is unclear how far the establishment of a Scottish ascendancy over the Pictish lands in the ninth century had economic consequences. It is fairly usual to imagine that what happened came about by a kind of semi-beneficent osmosis, but nothing about ninth-century Scotland is clear. The authors of the great clarion call of Scottish liberty, the Declaration of Arbroath (1320), boasted of the complete extermination of the Picts (*Pictis omnino deletis*). These gloating patriots may well have been ill informed, but perhaps the establishment of a united Alba (the contemporary name for the united realms of the Scots and the Picts) did involve more material glee for some and more material misery for others than the bald, thin annals can show.

Ireland, and its economy, were much involved with other parts of the archipelago: Repeatedly in the early tenth century men of the same families ruled simultaneously, if intermittently, in Dublin and in York. The Irish Sea was not just a theatre of raiding and of war. The extent to which trade with Ireland mattered can be seen in the growing wealth of Chester in the tenth century, and of Bristol in the eleventh. So far as we can tell, a principal export to Ireland was slaves. But what came *from* Ireland? Irish merchants could travel far. We have a reference to some at Cambridge in the late tenth century. But we do not know what they were selling. There is a reference in the Domesday account of Chester to marten skins from Ireland, but the economies of major towns are not founded on marten skins. A principal export, even possibly *the* principal export, from Dublin and the other Scandinavian towns in Ireland was mercenary service. It was not for nothing that dissident English noblemen in 1051–2 and in 1066 fled to Dublin to find support.

Indeed, mercenary service should not be separated too far from commerce; war and trade met and mingled, and their connections are intimate to the whole material history of the archipelago. Consider the great events of 1066. When Harold Hardrada tried for the English throne it was as king of Norway, a position he had gained with the aid of resources built up through outstandingly successful mercenary service in Byzantium. William became a successful Conqueror partly by employing mercenary troops. It is an interesting question as to how he managed to keep his army together for the long weeks before the wind blew the right way for his crossing. One possible answer, that he may have had credit from the Jews of Rouen, is not deprived of all interest by a disagreeable absence of evidence.

The story of the material cultures of the archipelago is full of gaps and contrasts, long continuities and great changes. It must always be borne in mind just how much is not known, and that there is no possibility of constructing anything like a complete picture. Something of which we can, however, be sure is that material culture was partly determined *by* ideas, and partly determinative *of* them. It is to the immense force and effect of Christian ideas that we now turn.

2. Religious Cultures

Religion in Roman Britain

Roman Britain was a country of many religions. The Celtic population must have long continued in the beliefs they held before the Roman conquest. These were joined and modified by the importation of many cults. The assimilation of old belief systems to new, native to imported, was a common feature. Characteristic of great empires and superstates is that they are multicultural, containing all kinds of people from all over the world. Two British examples: a tombstone at South Shields marks the burial of the British wife of a man from Palmyra; a regiment from Syria was stationed at the high, wet, misty head of Eskdale, Cumbria. (They must have needed their hot bathhouse.) Such people brought a variety of religions with them, for example such mystery cults as that of Mithras. Among the imports was a sub-cult of Judaism, named after its founder, a remarkable artisan from Palestine.

How well established did Christianity become in Roman Britain? There was certainly quite a lot of it about, as can be seen, for example, from Christian inscriptions, some quite casual. It was certainly established among the prosperous – witness the mosaic head of Jesus at the centre of the dining-room floor of a very smart fourth-century villa at Hinton St Mary (Dorset), a far cry from Nazareth in more senses than one. Suggestive of the strength of Christianity in Britain by the end of the fourth century was the success of a well-educated Briton, Pelagius, in establishing a powerful heresy at Rome. Pelagius held the attractive view that salvation need not depend entirely on grace.

A likely demonstration of the strength of Christianity is that we hear so little of paganism among the Britons in the post-Roman generations. References are not entirely absent; thus the (later) life of a sixth-century saint, Samson, mentions his coming across pagan ceremonies in, it may be, Cornwall. There could easily have been more paganism than we hear of. Our sources are scanty indeed, and records of paganism would

not be kept or treasured. At a minimum there were bound to have
been some elements of continuity with the pagan past – it would be
odd if some of the holy springs of western Britain had not been holy
long before anyone had heard the name of Jesus. But it must be
significant that the sixth-century writer Gildas says nothing of
paganism in his own day. If the sinful rulers he denounced had
tolerated paganism he would have let us know about it – vehemently.

The nature of Gildas's work tells us much about religious culture.
His complicated Latin and his range of reference speak of a
sophisticated education and an educated audience. His intellectual and
religious context is in accord with the general impression given by
Latin inscriptions and charters from western Britain. What happened
in the east of the island is more obscure. In wide areas there were
several generations between the replacement of Roman authority by
Anglo-Saxon and during these years many, maybe most, of the
inhabitants were Christian. However, the traces of their faith and
church are indeed few. Thus we know that there was until the early
seventh century a British, and presumably Christian, kingdom, Elmet,
in Yorkshire east of the Pennines; yet knowledge of it rests on three
references only, and nothing is known of its church. An arresting,
though enigmatic, indication of the life of the British Church in the east
is the story of the cult of St Alban, a Briton believed to have been
martyred in a Roman persecution. We first hear of him in a life of St
Germanus who first came to Britain in 429 to deal with Pelagian
heretics. Germanus is said to have visited the shrine of St Alban at
Verulamium (modern St Albans). Bede (writing *c.* 730) says that miracles
had continued to be performed there 'from that day to this'. Possibly
he was deploying a conventional phrase: but he could have been telling
of a major Christian cult and shrine continuing in an area which, on
other evidence, may have remained under British control until the late
sixth century.

Religion in Ireland

A powerful demonstration of the strength and learning of the British
Church is the conversion of Ireland. The first certain date in Irish
history is 431. A continental chronicle tells us that in this year someone
called Palladius was sent 'as first bishop to the Irish believing in Christ'.

What is more, he was sent by the pope. The Christian authority of Rome was thus beginning to extend beyond the borders of the lost empire. No one knows who these Irish believers were. A better known missionary is St Patrick, very probably active in the fifth century; it is uncertain quite when. Our only firm knowledge of him comes from a kind of autobiography and a letter. A British Christian, he was captured as a slave and taken to Ireland, spent time in Gaul and ultimately returned to work on the evangelisation of Ireland. Much of what has been supposed about him comes from writings from and after the late seventh century and went with the promotion of his cult which was associated with the power of the Uí Néill dynasties. Two aspects of his life may be mentioned here. First, he had been a slave. Slavery would long be an important force in the diffusion of knowledge and experience. Second, in his *Confession* he gives an impression of defending himself against a charge of making financial gain from his ministry. His defence is accepted as valid; for it is the inevitable posthumous good fortune of saints to be taken at their own valuation. But it is worth remembering that mission could also mean gain.

Knowledge of the Christian Church in Ireland before the seventh century is thin. Christians may have been in a minority well into the sixth century and pagan customs and attitudes appear to have lingered after that. A major characteristic of the organisation of the Church in Ireland is that by the eighth century the dominant forces were monastic. Great abbeys and their abbots, often men of the highest connections, had other abbeys subordinated to them and the units so created were principal ones. By contrast, a bishop could be more a liturgical necessity than an administrative leader. It is not hard to see why abbeys with strong dynastic links might accord more easily with Irish geo-political reality, which was based on 'tribal' and dynastic loyalties, than with an episcopal organisation whose origins lay in an urban-centred empire. Two difficult questions arise here. How far back does the monastery-based organisation go, and how complete did it become? The Irish Church developed largely under the influence of the British Church, in which monks and monasteries were important by the sixth century. Bede thought that by *c.* 616 the community of the Welsh monastery of Bangor was more than two thousand strong. Some major Irish monasteries were founded in the earlier sixth century. More came in the later part of the century; prominent among them was Iona in Dál Ríata, founded in 563 by Columba. Iona became a very important centre of Church authority, intimately connected with the Uí Néills. It was probably largely responsible for the conversion of the Highlands and islands of Scotland, and would play a crucial part in the conversion of England. Some scholars suggest that until the period of rapid monastic growth the Irish Church had been organised on an episcopal and quasi-parochial basis; others that monasteries were important in the organisation of ecclesiastical power from an early date. While there is no telling which theory is correct, we can be reasonably certain that, great though monastic power had become in the Irish Church before the eighth century, some bishops retained authority then and later.

The first page of St Luke's gospel in the Lichfield Gospels ('St Chad Gospels'), thought to be from around the second quarter of the eighth century. Its presentation, resembling that of the better-known Lindisfarne Gospels, shows highly developed sophistication: note the ordered stylisation of the letters and the wonderfully intricate decoration borders whose style owes something to the Celtic world. The great skill of the artist or artists proves that he or they did not come new to their task. This leads one to wonder how many such illuminated manuscripts there may once have been.

An astonishing and irrefutable fact about the early Irish Church is its great learning. The first evidence of this comes from the writings of St Columbanus (*c.* 543–615), whose range of reference and command of Latin speak eloquently for the education he had received partly at the monastery of Bangor (the Irish Bangor, not the Welsh one). Bede emphasises how far Ireland was a centre of education and learning, and describes Anglo-Saxons going there to study. The production of learned works in seventh-century Ireland was extraordinary; just how extraordinary was revealed in 1954 by the German scholar Bernhard Bischoff. He argued powerfully that a major range of works on biblical exegesis was of previously unrecognised Irish origin. A great intellectual feat in about 750 was the production of the 'Irish reference bible', an extensive compendium of biblical exegesis, and the early eighth century saw the compilation of a remarkable canonical collection, the *Collectio Canonum Hiberniensis.* Besides these works there appeared in and after the seventh century a variety of others, commandingly vigorous and exceptionally learned.

How could an island on the edge of the known world have become the brightest centre of learning in the West? There is no clear answer, but relevant factors are these. First, in pagan Ireland there was an important class of learned men, expert in law and poetry, with high status. So, Christian learning was probably grafted on to a tradition in which learning and learned men were valued. A second explanation touches on a mysterious matter: the possibility of intellectual inheritance from the British Church. The traditions of early saints emphasise British–Irish relationships: Gildas, for example, appears as influential in Ireland as well as in Britain. A problem in assessing such connections is our knowing so little of the intellectual life of the British Church beyond what can be deduced from Gildas's work. No manuscript survives which can safely be attributed to the early British Church, though the possibility of a fine manuscript of Virgil having originated in fifth- or sixth-century Britain has been canvassed. There were special features in the organisation and presentation of Irish manuscripts which distinguish them from those of continental origin, and these could have derived from Britain. There were other intellectual influences on Ireland, not least from Spain. The works of Isidore of Seville (*c.* 560–636) were known in Ireland soon after their composition. Another possible factor in Ireland's pre-eminent culture of learning is influence from the Mediterranean world via England.

Irish students were present at the school at Canterbury of Theodore, archbishop 668–90, and this may have influenced the composition of the great Irish canonical collection. The missionary activity of Columbanus after 590 in Gaul and Italy would also have resulted in intellectual connection and impact. Yet it would be wrong to think of Irish learning as above all derivative. One of the simplest, most basic, of original Irish contributions faces us in every page of every book. Strange though it may seem, in manuscripts earlier than the seventh century no spaces were left between words and sentences were not indicated by capitalisation of the first word. The spaces and the capitals were introduced by the Irish.

Anglo-Saxon Paganism

By 600 much of Britain was under Anglo-Saxon dominance. Anglo-Saxon paganism has not had the attention it deserves. Much of what is known of Germanic paganism is only questionably relevant for our period, for evidence is either very early, notably the *c.* 100 *Germania* of Tacitus, or that of Norse sources chiefly from the thirteenth century or later, and thus very late. Such sources are not negligible, but have to be treated with necessary diffidence. There was certainly a Germanic pantheon – we are reminded of it four times weekly by the names of Tuesday, Wednesday, Thursday and Friday, all named after Germanic gods (Tiw, Woden, Thunor and Freya respectively). Tacitus gives a remarkable account of the Germanic cult of the goddess Nerthus ('Mother Earth'). Her home, he says, is in a grove on an island. At intervals she goes on tour in a wagon drawn by oxen and attended by her priest. Wherever she goes there is peace, and objects of iron are put away. After her tour the goddess and her car are washed in a lake, by slaves, who are drowned once their task is completed. We are thus given the impression of elaborate organisation and professional priesthood; and should note that among the peoples participating in this cult were the Angles, some of whom settled, much later, in Britain.

Our best evidence for Anglo-Saxon paganism comes from Bede, who suggests that religion in early seventh-century England had elaborated elements, partly comparable to those which Tacitus describes. This appears specifically in his account of the first conversion of Northumbria, *c.* 625, in which he gives a dramatic description of a

Northumbrian council's deliberation. The words he quotes are doubtless no more than those he believes ought to have been used, but he could hardly have been seeking to mislead his informed audience on the general circumstances. Bede has as principal speaker at this session Coifi, *primus pontificium*, high priest. Coifi speaks first, an indication of his importance. He says, in Bede's terms, the right thing: that loyal service to pagan gods has done him no good, and he will therefore change faiths. Coifi's advice is given poignancy by the philosophical broodings of a second, unnamed, councillor, who likens the life of pagan man to the flight of a sparrow through a banquet hall on a dark winter's night: 'While it is inside, it is safe from the winter storms; but after a few moments of comfort, it vanishes from sight into the wintry world from which it came.' Coifi implements his decision in a most interesting way. First he mounts a stallion (Bede tells us that pagan priests were not supposed to ride stallions), then he rides to a temple, which he desecrates by hurling a spear into it. So, we are shown a pagan religion with a hierarchically organised priesthood, with temples, and with rules governing both priests and temples. This impression of formalised religion is reinforced in another of Bede's works, *De Temporum Ratione*, 'On the Measurement of Time'. He describes a pagan calendar which, unlike its Christian successor, regulated the relation between solar and lunar cycles by the deployment of leap months. Such an elaborate calendar would presumably have required some formal body to regulate and announce its working: a plausible role for the priesthood. There is but one other reference in our written sources to a pagan priest. It comes in the life of bishop Wilfrid by Stephanus. Wilfrid's ship was stranded on the Sussex coast in 666. The natives naturally set to work to loot it, and were encouraged by a pagan chief priest who stood on a high mound overlooking the shore. His intervention was inefficaceous, for one of Wilfrid's escort killed him by a slingshot. We may note two things: one, again the presence of a high priest; two, the *tumulus* overlooking the sea shore must remind one of such prominent burial mounds as those at Sutton Hoo, and of the extent to which such mounds could have been integrated into a pagan religious scheme.

Although what little we are allowed to know suggests, strongly, that paganism was organised and institutionalised rather than trivial or superficial, little else can be gleaned about the pagan religion of the Anglo-Saxons in Britain. Attempts have been made to identify pagan temples archaeologically, but so far without success. Place names suggest two kinds of temple: large important ones and minor local shrines. A fairly general transition from cremation to inhumation burial in the early Anglo-Saxon period suggests the possibility of religious changes in advance of conversion to Christianity. This raises profound questions about the nature of paganism – did it, for example, resemble Hinduism in being receptive to and absorptive of other cults? An important possibility, little discussed, is that pagan temples were endowed and richly furnished so that conversion saw a 'dissolution of the temples' and a significant transfer of assets. A second question relates to the nature of pagan idols, which we know existed – how far did the Christian sculpture of the Anglo-Saxons have pagan antecedents? Finally, and most importantly, could there have been some almost institutionalised continuity between paganism and Christianity, something of the kind which can be glimpsed in Ireland?

The Christian Conversion of England

The official story of the conversion of England begins in 597 and is brilliantly outlined by Bede. In 596 Pope Gregory I, a Roman aristocrat as capable as he was devout, sent a mission to the English, in particular to Ethelbert, king of Kent, who already had a Frankish Christian wife. Gregory's letters make this the best known episode in early English history. They enable us to follow major elements in the mission: Gregory's concern that his emissaries should have the right support in Gaul; his stiffening their resolution when they thought of throwing in the sponge and going home; his plan to establish two Church provinces, one based in London, one in York, each with an archbishop and twelve bishops; his advice to come to terms with paganism on non-essentials. What we cannot be sure of are the pope's motives in their entirety. It was not at all ordinary for a pope to seek to save the souls of distant barbarians, let alone with a mission of most extraordinary size: forty-strong. Gregory's great effort may reflect realpolitik as well as zeal for souls; it could have formed part of diplomatic schemes extending from Byzantium to Picardy.

Gregory's Italian missionaries did not gain lasting success outside Kent. Their last known survivor was Honorius; when he died as archbishop of Canterbury in 653, he must have been old indeed. Indeed by this time Christianity was making good headway in England; but its gains were due largely not to Italian, but to Irish missionaries (and their English disciples). Oswald, king of Northumbria (634–42), had been converted to Christianity while in exile among the Irish, and brought a monk of Iona, Aidan, to Northumbria as a missionary bishop. Aidan, and some of his disciples, won considerable success.

By 690 all the Anglo-Saxon kingdoms (or at least their kings) were converted. The missionary influences had not come from Rome and Iona alone. A Frank, Felix, had played a large part in the conversion of East Anglia. A man of unknown origin (but coming immediately from Italy), Birinus, was similarly instrumental in Wessex. Remarkably, our main authority, Bede, gives no direct account of when the mass of the population became Christians. Probably many of the subjects of some Anglo-Saxon kings were Britons and already Christian or somewhat Christian. That all Northumbrians were formally Christian by 734 is suggested by Bede's letter to Bishop Egbert of York, for he does not include toleration of paganism in his vehement catalogue of episcopal failings.

Burial archaeology can provide an important clue on the development of popular religion. To oversimplify, in all parts of the country in which grave goods were deposited this custom was modified in the later seventh century and entirely disappeared in the eighth. This looks like evidence for widespread Christianisation (though an apparently different relationship in Gaul between Christianisation and changes in burial customs reminds one to be reserved in using such evidence). Other changes which had come about by the 730s are striking indeed, not least a fertile proliferation of monasteries. In the later seventh century in England, as in later sixth-century Ireland, they were founded at a great pace. The most famous is the twin monastery of Monkwearmouth-Jarrow, founded in 674 by Benedict Biscop and the monastic home of Bede. There were many other monasteries, large and small. It is remarkable that there were certainly scores of them and there may have been hundreds. This suggests many thousands of monks and, so, an extensively Christianised society. Many of the most important monasteries were 'double': communities of both monks and nuns, with the abbess, commonly a royal princess, in command. Undoubtedly, and astonishingly, some of these ladies and their establishments were remarkably learned. The leading case is that of Whitby, under Hild, a Northumbrian princess. Bede says that five future bishops were educated there.

Bede himself was the greatest scholar in the western Church of his day. Most of his work was a series of major commentaries on books of the Bible; but he was a great authority on chronology and language, and is chiefly remembered for his *Ecclesiastical History of the English People*, completed not long before his death in 735. In this period there was probably more learning in monasteries than we can trace: the only intellectual in the English Church whose writings deserve to be set beside those of Bede is Aldhelm. Aldhelm was of high rank, connected to the royal family of Wessex; he became (*c.* 675) abbot of Malmesbury (Wiltshire), a monastery of Irish foundation, in 705 was made bishop of Sherborne (Dorset), and died in 709. He was truly learned and armed with a notably ornate prose style. His range of work was in some ways wider than Bede's – including, for example, a collection of one hundred riddles – but there is nothing from Aldhelm to correspond to Bede's great series of works of exegesis, to say nothing of his *History*. We have a handful of works from other monasteries: the first life of Gregory the Great was written at Whitby (perhaps by a nun). Lindisfarne produced a life of its great saint, Cuthbert. One of the followers of Bishop Wilfrid (*c.* 634–709) wrote his life. There is not very much else, mainly because there were far more readers than writers in English monasteries. Here a caveat must be entered, in that the loss and destruction of manuscripts in and after the ninth century was such that some works may have disappeared.

The laws of late seventh-century England, those of Ine of Wessex (688–726) and Wihtred of Kent (690–725), indicate a fierce desire to maintain religious discipline in something of the way in which sixteenth-century reformers sought to do. 'If a servant rides on his own business on that day (sc. Sunday) he is to pay six (shillings) to his lord, or be flogged'; 'If a child has not been baptised within thirty days of birth and dies unbaptised, the father is to compensate for it with all he possesses'. Conversion in England may have depended very much on coercion by royal power. Bede says that Earconberht, king of Kent (640–64), laid down that idols were to be abandoned and destroyed throughout his kingdom. And note what Bede adds: Earconberht ordered the forty days' fast of Lent to be enforced. Destroying idols is one thing; regulating what people have for dinner is another. There was at least an aspiration to drive Christianity home to the domestic hearth.

In discussion of the conversion of England it is tempting, even conventional, to emphasise likely elements of superficiality, mere formality and convergence with the ideals and mores of paganism. All these elements were present. There may have been more to it, though. Christianity or related beliefs can have drastic effects on whole populations. Maybe we should put the conversion of England into a category which includes cargo cults, and the great revivals of nineteenth-century America. By the earlier eighth century the Anglo-Saxons could have been revolutionised by religion.

There are powerful indications that this was broadly true of at least an elite. One such indication is not only the large number of monasteries founded, but also the lavish endowment of some of them. Such a monastery as Monkwearmouth-Jarrow must have cost its founder very dear. Its buildings were at least as grand as those of a good Roman villa (no mosaics though). Its monks were most adequately provided for. The provision of what was required for their manuscript production cannot have been cheap, let alone the treasures required to serve God in their churches (recall the great Bible of Monkwearmouth-Jarrow). Similar conditions applied in other monasteries to which we have no more than casual reference to a nunnery whose church was lit by silver lamps, for example, and to another which could be asked to provide a manuscript written in letters of gold. The endowment of the monastic movement was indicative of an economy which was prospering, even booming.

Another sign of the sharp impact of Christianity is that even kings were moved to withdraw from the world. The first of these of whom we hear was Sigeberht, king of East Anglia for a period after 630 or 631, who gave up his throne to enter a monastery. But, most remarkably, he was forced out of retirement because the East Angles felt they needed his leadership in war. He dutifully did battle against the Mercians, but on principle he came unarmed, carrying just a stick, and so he perished. An alternative to entering a monastery was a terminal journey to Rome. Thus Caedwalla, king of Wessex 685–8, abdicated and retreated to Rome where the next year he died wearing his white baptismal clothes. Though a Christian, he had (like others) postponed baptism. Baptism washed away all sins and so a prudent sinner might postpone it. Caedwalla's timing was excellent (his grave in St Peter's was marked by a finely grandiloquent Latin epitaph). It is true that some royal retreats from the world had more to do with forced abdication or expediency than with piety. This was probably the case with Ceolwulf, king of Northumbria, who entered the monastery of

Lindisfarne twice. In 731 his stay was brief, but he returned to
Lindisfarne in 737 and remained until his death in 764.

Not the least impressive people in the early Anglo-Saxon Church
were the missionaries. Their activities affected the whole history of
Europe. The origins of the missionary movement lay in Ireland (like so
much else which was remarkable). The first great Irish missionary was
Columbanus who began his mission to Gaul in 590. His successes were
impressive: the foundation of great monasteries at Luxeuil (in
Burgundy) and Bobbio (in Italy), and not least the pursuit of a moral
crusade among the Frankish nobility, who needed one. It was in
Ireland that the English missionary campaign on the Continent had its
origins. The first successful English mission overseas was that of
Willibrord to Frisia in 690. He had been inspired by Egberht, an English
monk long resident in Ireland. Willibrord's great successor was
Boniface. In 716, after a monastic career in Wessex, he set forth as a
missionary, first working in Frisia, then in Hesse and Thuringia, later
more widely in west, central and southern Germany. In 722 he was
made a bishop, later becoming archbishop of Mainz. In 753 he resigned
his see and returned to his first mission field in Frisia, where he was
killed by brigands in 754.

If the English missionary impulse owed much to Irish models and
guidance there were nevertheless other major forces involved. Crucial
were the relations between the missionaries and the men of power
among the Franks. Boniface was closely associated with Charles
Martel, the grandfather of Charlemagne. The establishment and
organisation of Christianity in much of Germany went hand in hand
with the consolidation of the power of this dynasty. Both Willibrord
and Boniface acted with repeated reference to another power also, that
of the papacy. In earlier generations popes had had little influence on
the Frankish Church, but the English missionaries brought about
much closer involvement. So it was largely thanks to Boniface that the
pope played a key role in enabling Charles Martel's son, Pippin, to
become king of the Franks, displacing the last Merovingian. The
English missionaries not only converted, they organised. At Boniface's
instigation a series of councils were held in Gaul between 742 and 747.
These were instruments for the reform of the Church, not least in the
establishment of an orderly hierarchy. With the wisdom of the dove
Boniface seems to have combined the cunning of the serpent. Maybe
this is why Bede, somewhat strangely, says nothing about him in his

Ecclesiastical History. Nevertheless, there was much in the activities of Boniface, as in those of other missionaries and reformers, which echoed the values stressed by Bede. There was also something particularly English about the close involvement of Willibrord and Boniface with the papacy, their conjuring up papal power. Bede demonstrates that the English had special veneration for Rome and for Gregory I, seen as their apostle. It was not for nothing that his earliest biography was composed in England. The English Church, though the youngest child of the papacy, was yet the most loyal, its Cordelia.

A determinative contribution made by Rome to the Anglo-Saxons was Archbishop Theodore. Theodore was a Greek refugee at Rome who was sent in 669 to be archbishop, no one else being willing to take this post on. Never can a *faute de mieux* choice have proved more successful. He was electric both in the exercise of ecclesiastical power and as a teacher. Crucial in his establishment of the authority of the see of Canterbury throughout the English Church was the inauguration of regular councils. The first known of these was held at Hertford in 673: it was concerned with the date of Easter, relations between bishops and between bishops and abbots, the need to increase the number of bishops, and the law of marriage. At the same time Theodore established a school at Canterbury with a magnetism which extended far beyond Kent. Bede says instruction was given above all in scripture, but also in astronomy, computation and metrics, and that Greek was known there. The *Penitential* associated with Theodore's name shows his expertise in law. Fairly recent manuscript discoveries have transformed knowledge of his eminence as a theologian, one in the style of the eastern Church, which laid more stress on the literal interpretation of scripture than western scholars did. Granted all that Theodore accomplished in more fields than one, it is hard to believe that he was eighty-eight when he died in 690, but Bede says that this was so; and so the archbishop must have started his great work when well over sixty.

The English Church at the time of the death of Bede in 735 enjoyed a European importance in scholarship and mission which it was never again to reach. English, and Irish, missionaries and scholars laid the foundations for the great developments in learning in the Carolingian empire in the eighth and ninth centuries: the 'Carolingian Renaissance'. Leading among them was the Englishman Alcuin, in Charlemagne's service from 782 until his death in 804. His relationship to the ruler is illuminated by a story of Charlemagne's posing a theological question to him while both were swimming in the baths at Aachen.

A major connection between England and Ireland emerged, stressfully, in the conflict over the calculation of the date of Easter. In the earlier seventh century it was realised that the Irish and Britons were calculating Easter on a different system from those used at Rome. Churchmen lived in a mental world which integrated fact and symbol in such a way as to give such a consideration as that of the date of Easter almost sacramental force. The churches of southern Ireland after due enquiry changed their Easter calculation to those in use at Rome, probably in the 630s. The churches of northern Ireland did not follow them, and a protracted and bitter conflict ensued. Most of the Irish missionaries in England came from the north, and so they and their English disciples celebrated Easter at a date different from that used by those who looked to Canterbury and Rome. The issue came to a head in 664 in a meeting held at Whitby. Oswiu, king of Northumbria, presided, and he decided in favour of the 'Roman' party. Many of the supporters of the 'Celtic' Easter took themselves off to Ireland, though the conflict smouldered among the Anglo-Saxons for some time. The culmination of the conflict came in 716 (or soon after) when Iona itself adopted the Roman Easter. Bede's account of the controversy is characteristically tempered. He acknowledges, indeed emphasises, the English debt to Irish learning. While absolutely opposed to the non-Roman calculation of Easter, he attributed it to the Irish having been isolated from the advice of orthodox calculators. In this he is disingenuous and evades the long conflict in Ireland over Easter, about which he must have known.

Another set of Anglo-Irish interactions emerges from consideration of the work of Theodore. He had Irish pupils at Canterbury (Aldhelm describes them as surrounding him like hounds baying round a boar) and may, via them, have influenced Irish interest in canon law. Conversely, the *Penitential* associated with him probably shows Irish influence. Its first book is indeed a penitential, that is to say a tariff of penances for sins. It is the first such work known to have been produced in England, but earlier penitentials derive from Ireland where this kind of treatise seems to have originally developed. So the *Penitential* of Theodore, indebted to Ireland as to Mediterranean lands, influential on the Continent, stands for rather a lot in the vital intellectual life and influence of the insular churches.

An important feature of Theodore's regular councils was that no king was present, nor any other layman. Decisions of importance to kings could be taken by clerics acting alone. A strongly illuminating instance of independent conciliar power comes from a letter (of 704 or 705) from Wealdhere, bishop of London, to Berhtwald, archbishop of Canterbury. Wealdhere refers to a war between Wessex and Essex and says that bishops from the two kingdoms were arranging a peace. However, 'at the last synod' it had been decided that no churchman should have anything to do with Wessex. Wealdhere asks the archbishop what to do. This letter implies that the conciliar system was in regular operation. No less importantly it shows the bishop of London deferring to the synod and the archbishop, rather than first consulting the interests of his own king and kingdom. Thus for a period synods of the whole English Church and the archbishop enjoyed a degree of authority independent of kings and geographically wider than that of any king.

The eighth century saw important changes in the balance of power between king and synods. On the one hand the power of synods can be seen in their exercising jurisdiction in disputes over Church lands. The extent of such lands would have fostered ecclesiastical power. Thus it has been calculated that by the later ninth century between a third and a half of Kentish lands was in Church hands. On the other hand, such a ruler as Æthelbald, king of Mercia (716–57) and overlord of southern England, strengthened his power over the Church. He was present at Church councils and so were members of his high nobility. It seems likely that he took steps to make sure that monasteries rendered services to the king which they had hardly rendered before. But even great kings could not have it all their own way in conflicts with the Church. Thus Offa, the greatest king of the Mercians (757–96), had a long dispute with Jænberht, archbishop of Canterbury, but he could not simply get rid of him. All he could win was a compromise, a division of the archdiocese, and that was achieved only with papal help.

The Church in Early Ireland

In Ireland some elements in the relations between ecclesiastical and secular authorities differed from those in England, not least because in Ireland the power of abbots and their monasteries was greater, and the power of bishops less than was the case in England. But the similarities, or possible similarities, are thought-provoking. The organisation of the Irish churches was inseparable from a political scene of devolved and fluctuating power, with a hierarchy of rulers headed by great families, holding considerable authority directly or indirectly in wide areas, below them lesser rulers, and further down those with power over very small areas. The organisation of the Church had conformed, by a kind of organic growth, to these systems of power, chiefly by monastic creation and development. Everywhere the Church adopted, reflected and maintained the realities of lay society and rule. Granted such intimate relations, the questions of relationships between ecclesiastical and lay authority become arresting and difficult. Were there Irish Church councils held independently of kings? The evidence, in particular, of the *Collectio Canonum Hiberniensis*, is that there were indeed such councils, sometimes representing the whole – or much – of the island. How far did secular and ecclesiastical authorities integrate in the exercise of power? Crucial here are legislative acts called *cana* or *leges*. There is evidence for at least thirty-three of these between 697 and 842. They were promulgated by ecclesiastical councils or by abbeys and were aimed towards the protection of particular groups. The *Lex Innocentium* (Law of the Innocents) of 697 was the most striking of them. Associated with the great abbot of Iona, Adomnan (679–704), its main aim was the protection of women, children and clerics. It was promulgated by a mighty council, including clerics and rulers from much of Ireland and Dál Ríata and, interestingly, a Pictish prince. The promulgation of such acts was often accompanied by an abbey's sending its relics on a judicial tour. *Cana* enforcement was largely entrusted to secular authorities, who shared the resulting fines. So the purposes of such judicial procedures could have significant financial implications.

The influence of the Irish Church was very important in seventh-century England, above all in Northumbria. The first firm establishment of Christianity there came about because two exiled Northumbrian princes were converted among the Irish and later became successive kings of Northumbria. Three Irishmen were successively bishops of Northumbria from 633 to 664. That Irish connection by no means ended with the 'synod' of Whitby in 664 is well illustrated by the career and work of Adomnan, abbot of Iona. When he became abbot in 679 Iona was probably under the authority of Ecgfrith, king of Northumbria, for Bede, in describing Ecgfrith's defeat and death in 685, which brought about the end of his empire, says that he had had the 'Irish who were in Britain' under his authority. Indeed, Ecgfrith was quite likely buried at Iona. In 684 he had tried to extend his authority by sending an expedition into Ireland. (Bede much disapproved of this; the Irish, he said, had always been very friendly to the English.) In 685–6 Adomnan came to Northumbria, attempting to recover captives whom Ecgfrith had taken (he was on favourable ground since Ecgfrith's half-brother and successor Aldfrith who was now king was half Irish and had lived long in Irish exile). Adomnan's writings illustrate the Anglo-Irish connection in other ways – in his life of Columba, for example, he names two 'Saxon' monks at Iona before Columba's death in 597. So there were evidently Anglo-Saxon Christians at Iona before Augustine came to Kent.

The Church in England in the Ninth Century

The ninth century is a crucial period in the history of the religious culture of England, and a very mysterious one. The Vikings certainly took their toll, as the *Anglo-Saxon Chronicle*'s account of the early assault on Lindisfarne demonstrates. However, the *Chronicle* tells us surprisingly little about the later fate of other monasteries. Striking, if circumstantial, evidence exists for their destruction over wide areas in northern, eastern and central England. By the end of the eighth century it was frequent, indeed maybe normal, for land grants to monasteries to be recorded in written documents, 'charters'. A fair number of these survive from southern and western England, but from the areas conquered and held by the Scandinavians there are almost none. The Scandinavian invasions must thus have hit many English monasteries destructively. However, while King Alfred, in his introduction to the translation of the *Pastoral Care* of Gregory the Great, lamented the state of English monasticism and learning, he did not see the Viking onslaught as the only cause for the decline of learning. He does say that 'everything' had been ransacked and burned. *But* he interprets this as divine punishment for failure to foster learning. There had been, he says, churches all over England, full of books and treasures. But the servants of God, numerous though they were, had no benefit from their books because they could read no language but their own. Alfred was perhaps a little carried away when he said that he could not recall one man south of the Thames who could translate a line of Latin, and hardly one to the north. Nevertheless, our knowledge of learning in ninth-century England (or, rather, our lack of it) bears out Alfred's general claim. Neither Bede nor Theodore left, as theologians, any English heirs. There survives only one *vita* of an English saint written between the death of Bede and the tenth century.

What had happened to learning in that long period? One puzzle is that of the significance of vernacular poetry. Considerable quantities of such poetry, for the most part religious, survive in four manuscripts from about the turn of the tenth century. The works preserved belong to a complex tradition, and sometimes a learned one. Most of this poetry is impossible to date securely – some certainly goes back to the eighth century, but how much of the whole corpus belongs to the eighth or the ninth is unknowable. Even if such poetry fills something of the gap in the history of English learning and monasticism, that gap is still yawning. For example, we know very little of what happened to the royal double monasteries, so impressive in Bede's day. Although some long survived it was without their female element, originally dominant; it is unclear when and how the nuns slipped out of the picture.

Why should Latin learning have evaporated in southern England? One factor was undoubtedly the considerable elements in monastic life that were hardly conducive to study. Bede, in his *Letter to Egbert*, denounced 'false' monasteries, set up by nobles to gain tenurial and fiscal advantages. Some of these, he says, did have monks, but they were bad lots, recruited from anywhere. He emphasises that some monastic founders lived in their monasteries with their wives and families. When the council of Clovesho (747) condemns showy clothes for monks and nuns and urges monks to avoid drunkenness like 'mortal poison', this suggests that even the more orthodox monasteries had their failings, something which other evidence supports. Thus Alcuin writes to the bishop of Lindisfarne in 797 protesting against men of religion listening to secular songs to the strains of the lyre rather than to devotional readings: 'what has Ingeld [the legendary Germanic warrior] to do with Christ?'. Indeed, Lindisfarne seems to have had a long tradition of conviviality. Alcuin's disquiet finds an echo in Cuthbert's earlier unease when he spent Christmas Day with his brethren feasting, rejoicing and storytelling.

The monastic attitude to drink was ambiguous. Drunkenness was regarded as a sin; but not always. A provision, to the modern eye surprising, of Theodore's *Penitential* says of a monk's drinking that if 'drunkenness is for gladness at Christmas or Easter or for any festival of a saint, and he then has imbibed no more than is commanded by his seniors, no offence is committed. If a bishop commands it no offence is committed.' This is the milieu in which monastic obedience met with native conviviality, and one questioned by Bede, who comments with distaste on episcopal entertainment. It is rumoured, he says, that certain bishops have men about them who are given to laughter, jests, tales, feasting and drunkenness. In short, the mores and indeed the values of a rich and largely aristocratic Church may not have been such as to encourage intellectual endeavour. It must, however, be borne in mind that criticism of monastic standards of learning and life comes from the learned themselves. Historians may sometimes adopt, half unconsciously, and rather uncritically, the values of contemporaries who disapproved of monasteries in traditions and with aims other than their own.

Thus in Ireland there was a process of adaptation and absorption which may sometimes too easily be categorised as one of decay and decline. It is clear that even before 800 it had become common for some abbots to be married. Abbeys came to descend by hereditary succession. Boys of high birth could be fostered in monasteries. An abbot could help to choose a king. Thus Aédan Mac Gabrain owed his accession as king of Dál Ríata to Columba. In Munster an abbot might actually *be* a king. Such conduct hardly accorded with the teaching of the gospels, the Fathers or the councils of the Church; but, all the same, it was not so very different from what happened in the Church in other areas of the British Isles.

How is it that we know so much about the state of affairs in Ireland? Largely because there is a considerable annalistic record. It is annals, chiefly, which provide information about, for example, abbatial successions. In England the annalistic record is exceedingly thin, and for many areas non-existent. Suppose we did have fairly detailed annals for ninth-century England such as we have for Ireland – might they not show a monastic scene resembling the Irish one; a scene which would help to explain the disappearance of English learning? This could indeed be so: though one has to bear in mind that Irish monastic accommodation to the ways of the secular world did not extinguish learning. On the contrary, some of the most remarkable Irish scholars

belonged to the ninth century, leading among them Sedulius Scotus –
poet, theologian and grammarian – and John Eriugena – poet,
contentious theologian, and maybe the very first post-classical scholar
who may be called a philosopher.

That intellectual activity could be compatible with accommodation
to the ways of the world is demonstrated by a remarkable account,
from the early ninth century, of an unidentified English monastery.
This history is a long, instructive and evasive Latin poem on the abbots
of a Northumbrian house. The founder of this house was, we are told,
a *dux*, Eanmund. The foundation is put into the context of the
tyrannical rule of Osred, king of Northumbria (705/6–16) who
'destroyed many by a pitiable death, but forced others to serve their
parent above, and to live in monastic enclosures after receiving
tonsure'. We may note here the force (and obscure conventions) of the
idea of the monastery as a retreat from the world. A passage shows that
one of the monks had been twice married (indeed, it may just be
plausible that he was still married). The competence and art of the
poem are evidence of living intellectual activity, and we learn that the
monastery employed an Irish illuminator, Ultan. Matrimony and
learning need not have been incompatible. Nor indeed need artistic or
craft skill have been incompatible with self-indulgence. Bede tells us of
a famous smith in 'a noble monastery' who was always drunk.

Something may be imagined about the condition of English
monasteries in the ninth century by considering what happened to
many of them afterwards. In the history of the English Church the
religious houses which shine most brightly are the great monasteries in
the Benedictine tradition, founded or refounded in the tenth century.
But there were many others, not necessarily negligible because they
were much less wealthy and conspicuous than the Elys and the
Glastonburys. Characteristic is St Frideswide's monastery at Oxford. It
came to claim quasi-legendary, but not entirely implausible,
foundation by an eighth-century Mercian princess, presumably as a
double monastery. It does not appear in any written record until a
charter of Ethelred II's reign (978–1016). By 1066, and probably long
before, it had become an all-male institution and Domesday records
something of its property. It comes nearer to the surface of historical
recognition in Henry I's reign (1100–35) when it was tidied up into a
house of Augustinian canons. Its later consequence can be judged from
its great church, now Oxford cathedral. Such institutions, communities

of priests, probably all married, outnumbered the reformed Benedictine houses of late Anglo-Saxon England and had a much wider distribution. A number survived as communities of secular priests into the Middle Ages, or even beyond. A characteristic of nearly all such communities in the Anglo-Saxon period was their failure to leave a written record: most English religious communities, whether in the ninth century or the tenth, did not put pen to parchment. There was a striking contrast between England and the Continent on the one hand during the decades on either side of 700 and on the other in the ninth century. The extraordinary thing is that the nature of this contrast was completely reversed between one era and the other. In the early eighth century English scholars and clergy were in the lead; through the ninth century if there was significant learning in England very little of it survives. In contrast, the intellectual life of the Carolingian empire was astonishing. The total number of manuscripts written in Carolingian scriptoria in the eighth and ninth centuries is estimated at thirty thousand. English production may hardly have reached a hundredth of that. Of course the Carolingian empire was far wider than England. Still, the contrast is formidable.

King Alfred, the Church and Learning

These contrasts between English and Carolingian intellectual activity are the essential background to the singular learned campaign of King Alfred (871–99). This campaign had four related elements. First, the translation from Latin into English of key works, some claiming to have been translated by the king himself (though some recent scholarship has raised doubts about this). Second, an attempt to extend literacy. Third, the employment of foreign scholars. Fourth, the deployment of a palace school in which teaching was in both English and Latin. All four initiatives converged on one aim: the furthering of God's purpose as it was embodied in Alfred, his person, policy and regime. The translated works were: the *Pastoral Care* and *Dialogues* of Gregory the Great, the histories of Orosius and of Bede, Boethius's *The Consolation of Philosophy*, the *Soliloquies* of Augustine, and the first fifty psalms. In association with the same programme a 'national' chronicle was composed and circulated. The form of Alfred's law code fitted with this. It was introduced by a long preface, heavily biblical and

homilectic in tone; it was 'national' in claiming to call on previous laws
from Kent and Mercia as well as from Wessex; and it had a dimension
of West Saxon historic continuity in containing the laws of Alfred's
distant predecessor Ine as well as his own. The literacy campaign is
described by his Welsh biographer, Asser, as one for adults, Alfred
insisting that officials, men of power, should learn to read if they were
at all capable of doing so. Alfred even bought the services of foreign
scholars to aid him in his mission, salient among them Asser himself.
As, or more, important was Grimbald, a Frank, whom Alfred seems to
have thought of as a possible archbishop of Canterbury. Another
foreigner, John the Old Saxon, was made abbot of the only monastery
for men which Alfred founded, Athelney.

Alfred was not a great benefactor of monasteries; besides Athelney he
founded only one other such institution, Shaftesbury, for women. This
demonstrates that the emphases of his piety differed from those of his
seventh- or early eighth-century predecessors. For him, as for some
continental contemporaries, monasteries, or at least some of them, could
be seen as essentially property. It was on such a basis that Alfred gave two
monasteries to Asser. Possibly he even took land from monasteries;
certainly, nearly three hundred years later, the monks of Abingdon
believed that Alfred had robbed them. Another contrast between Alfred's
regime and that of his eighth-century predecessors is this. Church
councils, so important in the eighth century, are not heard of after the
mid-ninth century. Thus Alfred may have deployed more ecclesiastical
authority than, for example, his great Mercian predecessors.

One must have a care here, however, because our evidence is so
limited. An example of our ignorance is our insecure knowledge on the
introduction of trial by ordeal and of royal enforcement for tithe.
These were two fundamental elements in the religious culture of late
Anglo-Saxon England. Before the tenth century ended, royal enforcement of tithe (the payment of a tenth of produce to the Church) was
established. Similarly normal by the same time was ordeal, the use of
various devices to obtain God's judgement in criminal cases. The
scriptural ideal of tithe was known in pre-tenth-century England, and
sometimes applied, but there is no evidence for a universal system.
There are two (somewhat uncertain) references to ordeal in the laws
of Ine (c. 700), which Alfred put together with his own laws and so may
in some sense have been included in his own legislation; otherwise
there is no English evidence until the tenth century. By contrast, both

tithe and ordeal are widely evidenced in the Carolingian empire. Both institutions would have been much in accord with the general direction of Alfred's apparent policies, yet somewhat puzzlingly; so far as our limited evidence goes, royal enforcement of tithe, and possibly the use of ordeal, were not introduced until the time of his successors.

The emphasis on literacy and learning in the Alfredian programme is fiercely interesting. A modern reader may be more surprised by it than he ought to be. There were important laymen in the Carolingian empire who could write perfectly good Latin. All the same, it is doubtful whether there was much lay literacy in ninth-century England before Alfred. Asser gives an arresting (if confused) account of the difficulty with which the king himself learned to read; he may never have learned to write. (Charlemagne also found this difficult.) It is not possible to be sure how far Alfred's campaign for literacy succeeded, but there is evidence for fairly widespread literacy in tenth-century England. The most remarkable, one might say extraordinary, instance is from the 980s, when a great noble, Æthelweard, produced, or was contemporaneously claimed to have produced, a Latin version of the *Anglo-Saxon Chronicle*. His is a suggestive case, though a unique and, maybe, a deceptive one, since the main direction of the Alfredian programme was towards the vernacular, and the vast majority of written culture of tenth-century England was in accordance with this. Though the origins of much of the surviving Anglo-Saxon poetry, including *Beowulf*, may well lie before the tenth century, it still matters that the earliest manuscripts for nearly all of it date from around about 1000, demonstrating a strong interest in such literature. Alfred's patronage of vernacular literature was part of a history (a considerably lost history) extending from the eighth century or earlier to the tenth. Granted that Alfred had vernacular foundations on which to build, he nevertheless built high: his translations represent an energetic attempt to bridge the gap between vernacular and Latin culture. There is a contrast with Charlemagne here. For, although Charlemagne took an interest in the vernacular, he did not see it as a vehicle for high learning, as a substitute for Latin. The only area where the vernacular had a status comparably high to that which it gained in England was Ireland.

Asser's account of the palace school is particularly interesting. The school was partly intended for the royal children, some of whom were taught in Latin and in English, some just in English. Asser also states that those educated there included not only nobles but boys who were not noble. The mention of nobles reminds one of how far the 'palace school' may have been an extension of fosterage, the practice whereby boys from one noble family were brought up in another. The presence of the less noble also suggests a wish to create a new elite, a career open to talent.

How did it come about that a Welshman, Asser, was so prominent among Alfred's scholar courtiers? What learning was there in Wales? Asser would not have been (expensively) employed had he not been importantly and usefully learned. Possibly he had been educated to an impressive standard in Gaul, but some learning must also have been available in Wales. What little surviving evidence there is for ninth-century Welsh intellectual life comes largely from North Wales, and includes a letter from a group of Irish scholars in Gaul to their teacher at home. In it, they warn him to prepare others for a test of learning which had been set for them by Merfynn, king of Gwynedd (d. 844). The test was a riddling poem by another Irish scholar. They had solved the riddle, but felt that others should be prepared for it. In another instance, the Irish poet Sedulius wrote a panegyric on 'Roricus', who seems to have been Rhodri Mawr, another ruler of Gwynedd, who would therefore seem to have had links to Irish intellectuals. Such, almost chance, instances put Welsh learning on a footing otherwise hard to apprehend.

Religion was crucial in creating and sustaining Alfred's widening power. It looks as if it might also have played a considerable role in the remarkable creation of the kingdom of Alba in the ninth century. This process, traditionally associated with Kenneth MacAlpine (Cinaed Mac Alpin), king of Dál Ríata, involved the absorption of the Pictish lands (and sooner or later the extinction of the Pictish language) by a Gaelic dynasty. The sources are wretchedly thin and no doubt skewed, but among the theories sensibly canvassed is one which argues that religion played its part. It emphasises that from the later eighth century there was a reform movement in the Irish Church. Its adherents were called *Celi Dei*, 'servants of God', anglicised as 'Culdees'. They laid stress on clerical celibacy, close observance of the Sabbath and other strictnesses. There are some reasons for guessing that this movement may have played a part in the Irish penetration and ultimate gain of control over Pictland. The transfer of relics of Columba from Iona to Brechin could have been a straw in the wind here. In short, feeble though our knowledge of ninth-century Scotland is, by setting Scotland beside England one can imagine a quasi-Alfredian element in the creation of the kingdom of Alba, one with some element of religious drive.

The (probably later eighth-century) 'Coppergate Helmet', found in York, is one of only three complete Anglo-Saxon helmets. Finely made, it has Latin inscriptions set out across its top (most demonstrably made by an illiterate craftsman). The more complete one rather incoherently reads in translation: 'In the name of our lord Jesus the Holy Spirit, God and with all we pray. Amen. Oshere [the owner?]. Christ'. The inscriptions show how God and war could be brought together in an artefact, as in other ways, and before King Alfred sought to turn his wars into proto-crusades. Note that the helmets shown on the Aberlemno stone (p. 99) resembles this one, which is now held in the Castle museum, York.

The Church in Tenth- and Early Eleventh-Century England

Alfred's immediate successors were Edward (899–924) and Athelstan (924–39). One conquered much of the area under Scandinavian control (the 'Danelaw'), the other established himself as the most powerful ruler in Britain. Their achievements stand out but the details of their deeds are often misted. Thus, for the religious climate and policies of their reigns, one can see no more than salient features. Under Edward there was some reorganisation tending towards a system of one bishop per shire. Athelstan's widespread power was mirrored by his collecting famous relics, radiantly holy treasures, from far and wide. We know little about most bishops of the earlier tenth century other than their names. We do know, however, of Oda, archbishop of Canterbury 941–58, that he was of Danish origin. This reminds us of how little is known of the conversion of Scandinavian immigrants or settlers. There is little evidence for long continued paganism among them. Nevertheless, earlier Danish invasions had not only ravaged monastic life but had also damaged the administrative structure of the Church: the episcopal succession was interrupted in much of the Danelaw. The reaction of Edward (or his immediate successors) was instructive: a new see was established for a wide area running from the Thames to the Humber with its seat at Dorchester-on-Thames (Oxfordshire). It seems strange that it should have been placed on the far southern edge of so vast a diocese. Presumably it was thought best to have it near the centres of royal authority. The same apparently centralising concern can be seen in leaving East Anglia under the authority of the bishop of London until the mid-tenth century.

The laws of Edward and of Athelstan suggest extension of Alfredian schemes for the institutionalisation of a royal quasi-theocracy. Ordeal appears in a law of Edward's as a recourse for dealing with perjury, and Athelstan prescribed its wider use. General tithe is not mentioned until Athelstan's reign when he lays down that it is to be paid from his lands and those of his ealdormen, bishops and reeves. The obligation was certainly extended before the end of the century. The scale of the tenth-century rulers' piety can be seen at Winchester, the nearest thing they had to a capital. There had been a cathedral there since the seventh century. Edward, in accord with his father's wishes, built another major church right beside it, just yards away. This was the New Minster in which Alfred was buried. A royal nunnery, the Nunnaminster, was built just across the road. Winchester became a holy city as well as a focus of power.

The greatest, or most conspicuous, innovations in the English Church came later in the century. They are summed up in the term 'tenth-century Reformation', somewhat paradoxically since they largely had to do with the foundation of monasteries not with their dissolution. The heroes of the epic are three bishops, Dunstan of Canterbury (959–88), Æthelwold of Winchester (963–84) and Oswald, bishop of Worcester from 961 and simultaneously archbishop of York from 971 until his death in 992. All three were highly connected and involved in major struggles for power, but we can do no more than apprehend tensions and guess at alignments. The movement was one for the foundation or refoundation of abbeys largely following continental models. Dunstan may be differentiated from the other two: his zeal for Benedictinism was perhaps less absolute, his secular role more important. The devotion of these men, their connections and the attractions of the movement for which they stood took major effect in the reign of their great patron, King Edgar (959–75). This saw the foundation or refoundation of monasteries on the grandest scale.

Just how expensive such a grand project could be was exemplified by Ely, one of the greatest of these monasteries, refounded and endowed by Æthelwold in c. 970. Its wealth was vast. Ely, which owned very little in the early tenth century, by 1066 owned land in 116 villages and its free dependants were numbered in thousands. Monastic reform could produce seismic changes in ownership – an extreme example is that of Huntingdonshire where eighty-three vills recorded by Domesday Book had passed into monastic hands as a result of the 'Reformation'. No less remarkable than great gifts of land were great gifts of treasure, such as the silver-gilt and bejewelled shrine given by Edgar to house the body of St Swithun at Winchester, and which weighed three hundred pounds. For many the most important endowments of the great monasteries would have been not land, but massive, sumptuous, treasures.

Why was there monastic foundation on so magnificent a scale? Explanations in terms of ulterior political motive, the wish to establish new focuses of royal power, must weigh. But in the past, as well as in the present, people often did things for the reasons stated by themselves, at least in part. It is rather more than a good guess that Edgar and his bishops believed in God. They lived near to death, in a world which they probably believed to be no more than two hundred generations old, one from which heaven and hell were not so many miles away. Their God was a royal God; in this period even Jesus on the cross sometimes appeared crowned. This God needed to be served royally if he was to extend His powerful protection. He required magnificent service by men of the right sort: chaste monks of high birth.

Reformed monasticism could provide this. In monastic reform, as in much else, England was heir to the Carolingian empire, and not least to the great Benedictine reformer of the early ninth century, Benedict of Aniane. Major influences in England came from continental abbeys reformed in the earlier tenth century such as Gorze in Lorraine, St Bavon in Flanders and Fleury in France. One distinguishing feature of such abbeys was concentration on the liturgy. The monks spent longer in church than their predecessors in earlier centuries, and the services had great dramatic power, music being specially important. Our account of the service for the dedication of the abbey church at Ramsey in 991, for example, describes antiphonal singing so sophisticated that the service would not have been out of place in a great fifteenth-century church. At the Old Minster at Winchester the organ was so grand that it took seventy men to pump it. Great churches had a monopoly of serious music; they were the nearest thing to opera houses the age knew.

By 1066 monastic domination of the Church was less marked. In the early eleventh century secular clerks, i.e. men who were in holy orders at some level, but were not monks, were becoming bishops. Some of these had served in the royal household or were otherwise royally connected. The most successful of them was Stigand, archbishop of Canterbury from 1052 until his deposition in 1070. He held the rich see of Canterbury in combination with the comparably rich see of Winchester, and used his position to batten on several rich abbeys. One of the earliest of the long line of English clerical pluralists, he was also the most successful. He must have been richer than any nobleman other than the earls, yet does not seem to have had grand origins. How had he risen so far? One possibility is that his success was related to the power and complexity of the English royal administration. Maybe he was the king's chief agent, comparable to Roger of Salisbury or

Cardinal Wolsey, later prelates whose rise to ecclesiastical pinnacles depended on indispensable administrative serviceability. Stigand's position had its difficulties, such, indeed, that they played some part in the initiation of the Norman Conquest. Archbishops of Canterbury were expected to have their appointment confirmed by the pope, but Stigand could obtain such confirmation only from a pope whose own legitimacy was contested. This was at a time when papal power was on the way up, one which saw the beginnings of 'Gregorian reform', which was to transform both papal ambitions and attitudes towards the papacy. Thus English monasteries now sought papal privileges as a hundred years before they would not have done. Very great English magnates went on pilgrimage to Rome as their grandfathers had not done. It was a sign of papal influence in England that, because Stigand lacked adequate papal recognition, English bishops were wary of being consecrated by him. Pope Alexander II's support for William the Conqueror was probably connected to hostility to Stigand's questionable position.

Stigand's uncanonical position was not the only aspect of the English Church which was to offend Normans in their pious triumph, though their exclamations should not to be taken at unquestioned face value. It is as well to bear in mind that the Norman Conquest brought the takeover of most of the high positions and wealth (great wealth) of the English Church by the clerical followers and courtiers of the new king. Denunciations of the expropriated by the expropriators can produce no more than a cracked ring of conviction. But Norman criticisms, if not always fair, were meaningful, and Norman judgements on the English Church provide a starting point for ours.

The godly colonisers of the English Church found particular fault with both some of its bishops and some of its saints. Stigand was undoubtedly open to criticism, as was his brother Æthelmaer, bishop of East Anglia. Nevertheless, Edward the Confessor's episcopal appointments in general show something more than the operation of a spoils system. Significant was the choice of some bishops from Lorraine, where there were important centres of learning and reform. The plainest case of a reforming Edwardian bishop is that of Leofric, bishop of Devon and Cornwall (1046–72). English (or maybe Cornish) by birth, he had been educated in Lotharingia, became a cleric in Edward's household and, like other such, was made a bishop. With papal approval Leofric moved the seat of his see from Crediton to

Exeter, thus meeting the canonical requirement that a *sedes* should be at a significant population centre. He had his new cathedral manned by regular canons living according to the rule of Chrodegang, a rule favoured in Germany and Lotharingia. Leofric was a sound moderniser. His policy shows that major elements in the pre-1066 Church were on the move.

The Normans found some very special, even peculiar, saints in England. The early twelfth-century historian William of Malmesbury said that there were cults of saints who were nothing but bare names, *nuda nomina*. New Norman abbots found doubts about old Saxon saints, though they could overcome such censorious flurries when fundraising was in hand. The cults of ancient, more than half-forgotten, saints indicate something important about the Anglo-Saxon Church: the memory and influence of the distant past. Much of the English Church had not been transformed by the movements of the tenth and eleventh centuries. Most religious houses in England were not those which had been reformed into neo-Carolingian Benedictinism, but were communities of secular clerks, some with a long monastic history. Many such communities were small, others less so, and one was very important indeed: the community of St Cuthbert. After the Viking assault on Lindisfarne the community took the body of their saint with some other valued possessions and fled. At one stage they thought of retreat to Ireland. But they settled down, first at Chester-le-Street, and from 995, on a height overlooking the River Wear, at Durham. Their extensive judicial privileges, which continued to be exercised by the bishops of Durham until 1836, may have been granted by Viking rulers at York. Their saint (whose body remained largely undisturbed until 1827) was venerated and feared as no other in the north. No known attempt was made to 'reform' Durham until after the Conquest. All over England there were comparable, if lesser, communities. If ancient communities survived, so too did a number of ancient Church buildings, for example the church built by king Ine at Glastonbury, which was still there in 1066. At St Augustine's abbey Canterbury there was a striking example of reverence for a venerable building. Abbot Wilfrid (1045–61) had a building scheme which involved the partial demolition of a church or chapel dedicated to St Mary, but died before it could be completed. His death was attributed to Mary's displeasure; his successor, prudently, did not pursue the scheme. The first Norman abbot characteristically went much further

Tower of the parish church at Earls Barton, Northamptonshire. This tower is one of the few significant late Anglo-Saxon buildings still standing. It dates from the early eleventh century, and the decoration is characteristic of the period (the battlemented top is much later). This tower is a reminder of how slight is the visual evidence for the architecture of the late Anglo-Saxon church – although Anglo-Saxon stonework remains in well over two hundred parish churches, no major churches as those of such great monasteries as Winchester survive. Often what is left is a mere fragment, which might easily have perished: a reminder that there must have been far more stone Anglo-Saxon churches than can now be identified, which in turn indicates the wealth of England and the extent to which its investment could be spiritual as well as material.

in innovation: he knocked the Anglo-Saxon buildings down and built a
very grand modern abbey church, with the tombs of St Augustine, the
early archbishops and early kings of Kent impressively deployed.
Norman bishops and abbots could be more energetic than historically
sensitive.

A remarkable legacy from the past was a peculiarly English
institution, the monastic cathedral; that is to say one in which the usual
chapter (a group of secular priests serving the cathedral) was replaced
by a Benedictine monastery with the bishop as abbot. By 1066 four
English sees were in this position: Canterbury, Winchester, Worcester
and Sherborne. Others were added after the Conquest. The 'cathedral
monastery' is abnormal in the western Church. How had this English
divergence come about? A likely element is that there had been similar
arrangements in the early English Church; indeed, Bede had recommended something of the kind in his *Letter to Egbert*. Here, as in other
respects, the English Church was probably affected not only by
innovatory schemes with foreign origins, but also by conscious regard
to its own past.

One of the most notable things in England is the parochial system,
as it stood until fairly recently, and, to quite an extent, still stands. The
English are so familiar with the physical expression of the system that
they take it for granted that in nearly all villages there is an old stone
church of commanding presence. Approaching three hundred of these
contain at least a little Anglo-Saxon stonework. Before the eleventh
century ended there must have been even more stone churches than
these, though stone churches were probably well outnumbered by
wooden ones. The parochial system for many centuries provided a
church and a priest for thousands of villages; often enough a priest for
every twenty families or even fewer. This was for century after century
a most important strand of England's social fabric. Historians disagree
about the nature of pastoral provision in the period before the Viking
assault. This dispute centres round the 'minster hypothesis'. The
hypothesis is that in early days pastoral care was largely, or almost
exclusively, the responsibility of religious communities of varying
kinds: 'minster communities'. The 'minsters' are seen as providing
most of the framework from which the later parochial system grew. It
is suggested that some were founded to provide pastoral care for
particular areas of authority: thus there could have been a minster for
each of the sub-units ('lathes') of Kent. Even communities whose *raison*

d'être was not pastoral might, all the same, undertake such work on their estates and round about. But it seems that starting from about the tenth century the large 'minster parishes' were commonly divided up into the parishes of a type normal in the Middle Ages and later, this division being related to that of large estates into smaller units.

The 'minster hypothesis' is largely incontrovertible, but its possible limitations must be borne in mind. The thesis does not, and cannot, deprive bishops of a central responsibility for pastoral care, nor can it deny the existence of some diocesan organisation. Undeniably there were from an early date focuses of religious activity which were not 'minsters': these were oratories, cemeteries, crosses, churches directly associated with noblemen. Some contemporary accounts, especially of missionary activity, distinguish between monasteries and 'churches'. Perhaps more emphasis should be given to the possibility that English pastoral provision should be seen partly in terms of a network (maybe an increasingly close network) of oratories, chapels, estate churches, cemeteries, crosses and holy wells, set aside for religious use and served by clergy whose activities were largely itinerant or occasional. A large role in early pastoral care was played by bishops themselves, travelling round their dioceses. What the car is to pastoral care now so the horse was then. Theodore rebuked Bishop Chad (Ceadda) for refusing to ride. When the missionary Bishop Willibrord went to do God's work, he and his companions were mounted. We know this because on one occasion they pastured their horses 'in the meadows of a certain wealthy man'. When the 'wealthy man' jibbed he was punished by a most unpleasant miracle.

By 1066 in much of England the parochial organisation of country and town had become what it was long to remain and to a significant extent still remains. Thus, although the Domesday survey does not set out methodically to record parish churches, it mentions many, for example some three hundred in Norfolk. Our most detailed eleventh-century records come from Kent. They show that before 1100 the complement of rural parishes there was nearly as full as it was to be in 1800, though this cannot have been the case in all parts of the country. What paid for all this, for all these churches (increasingly stone churches) and all those priests? They must largely have been funded by tithe, which at least from Edgar's time was royally enforced, and harshly so. If due tithes were not paid, then the king's reeve, the bishop's reeve, the lord of the land's reeve and 'the priest of the minster' (presumably the priest of the antecedent 'minster parish') were to take the produce of the land: the priest of the minster would get a tenth, the bishop and the lord would get two-fifths each. The unhappy delinquent was to be left with only a tenth of his crop. A major issue (and subject of legislation) was the division of tithe between the 'old minsters' and the new 'parish churches' created within their areas of authority.

Three factors stand out in the long, strange story of religion in the archipelago in the first millennium. First is, of course, the complete success of Christianity. Its earliest beginnings here go back probably to the second century. The last century in which there were ostensible pagans before the Vikings came was probably the seventh century or possibly the eighth. Christian progress illustrates all the means by which a religion can spread, from royal force to missionary sacrifice. The second major phenomenon, and not the least remarkable, is the development of Christian learning, above all in Ireland but also in English monasteries in the years between the conversion and the Scandinavian invasions. The origins of this development present problems still no more than half solved. Third, that there is so little evidence for enduring Scandinavian paganism in England suggests that, notwithstanding the damage the Vikings did to the organisation and culture of the English Church, that Church had the capacity to absorb its rivals. By 1066 the most striking phenomenon of all is the divergence of the religious culture of England from that of the rest of the archipelago. England had become a normal part of the western Church: its sees and parishes and its relationship to Rome fitted into a general pattern. Until the tenth century the religious culture in much of Britain bore important resemblances to that of Ireland. By the eleventh century there were strong contrasts. They paralleled and reflected comparable changes in political culture. Both in Church and in State England by 1066 had – as one might put it – rejoined what had been the Roman empire: Ireland, Scotland and Wales had not.

3. Political Cultures

Roman Britain

The story of Roman Britain begins with probing expeditions in great force, launched by Julius Caesar in 55 and 54 BC. He came, he saw but he did not conquer, though he may have hoped to do so. Lasting conquest in the island was begun by the emperor Claudius in AD 43 and had reached its full extent by about AD 90. Britain slipped out of the Roman empire in stressed and obscure circumstances, the final sequence beginning in 406. Yet what the Romans conquered, they transformed.

In Britain the Romans met an old and a sophisticated society. Much of immediately pre-Roman Britain was divided among kings, a number of whom were already striking coin, something that their Anglo-Saxon successors could not manage until over five centuries later. By early in the first century AD Roman material culture had already attracted and affected ruling groups in Britain. Britain was in the penumbra of Roman power and Rome had, for example, provided refuge for an important British exile. Likely enough by AD 43 some favoured Britons were subsidised clients of Rome.

The nature of the new Roman regime in Britain was such as to allow for friendly relations with British elites. Of course such friendship was anything but universal. The conquest of (future) Wales and much of northern Britain required repeated and hard campaigns. Roman brutality and British hatred were also plain in the origins and devastating repression of the revolt of Boudicca in AD 61. A contrasting account of early Roman policy in Britain comes from Tacitus in his memoir of Agricola. Tacitus shows how far Roman–British relations were assimilative. He is mordant on how Agricola worked to make leading Britons pleasantly inured to peace and ease, speaks of introduction to such amenities as baths and banquets as making vice agreeable and sums up by saying that what was spoken of as civilisation (*humanitas*) was really part of enslavement (*pars servitutis*).

Cultural transformation was integral to an imperial policy of creating devolved local administration. This depended on the division of a province into *civitates*, areas of authority often approximating to earlier tribal spheres. Much, but not necessarily all, of Roman Britain was divided up in this way. The administration of *civitates* was entrusted to local notables, 'decurions'. Outstanding importance was attached to the provision of public buildings in *civitas* capitals. Well within a century of Claudius's invasion, baths and basilicas stood out nobly in such British places as *Durovernum Cantiacorum* (later, and still, Canterbury). Dominant power remained safely in non-British hands. All high political officials were men of appropriately grand status from elsewhere in the empire, serving in Britain as part of a career, civil and military, which took them from province to province.

As we have seen, by the fourth century the fine public buildings of British *civitas* capitals were often neglected, ruined or even demolished. This probably reflected drastic changes in the political structure of the empire. Much of the second century and the earliest part of the third had been a time of peace and prosperity. But the middle decades of the third century brought near collapse: defeats on more frontiers than one and political chaos at home, with sixteen emperors or would-be emperors in under twenty years. Diocletian (286–305) and Constantine (306–37) held the boundaries and restored the empire. But theirs was a different empire, more of an oriental despotism, with a reorganised army largely independent of civil powers, and with harsher, more oppressive tax systems. Ruinous civic buildings in Britain tell of decurions who had lost local means; new military buildings proclaim the other side of the late imperial system. Nowhere was there a tougher demonstration of the confident power of the new regime than at York. The great façade of the legionary fortress (rebuilt *c.* 300) loured across the Ouse with eight tremendous towers.

That much, but nevertheless not enough, of Britain had been conquered in the first century soon presented Rome with serious problems of defence. The emperor Hadrian faced these, and in about AD 122 began the construction of a wall (Hadrian's Wall) stretching eighty miles across a northern neck of Britain from the Tyne to the Solway Firth. It required thirty million facing stones. Equally, but differently, remarkable is an excavated site over a hundred miles further north. Agricola made a powerful effort to carry Roman power to the far north of Britain, and in AD 83 began the construction of a legionary fortress at Inchtuthil (near modern Perth), a tremendous base extending over fifty acres (twenty hectares). Within a very few years the work was methodically abandoned, apparently because a legion had to be withdrawn from Britain for service on the Danube. This abandonment of Inchtuthil in *c.* AD 87 (leaving over a million unused nails behind) can be set beside the defeat in AD 9 of the last Roman effort to conquer Germany. An empire which had financed expansion by conquest was being pressed back to the defensive, and defence was dear. The Romans kept larger forces in Britain than any later ruler could possibly have afforded to pay, until, maybe, Oliver Cromwell. Roman armies were professional, always needing pay and often demanding bribes.

The importance of expensive Britain to Rome can be seen from the number of emperors and future emperors who came and even died there. Admittedly, the initial conqueror, Claudius, was across the

Hadrian's Wall, built following the emperor's visit to Britain in AD 122. The might and complexity of the Roman systems of defence and control in the north are tributes not only to the power of the empire but also to that of its opponents and potentially rebellious subjects. They also invite reflections such as those of R. A. Fletcher: '. . . the building history of the Wall is intensely complicated and displays many of the characteristics which we associate with large-scale government works: capricious changes of plan, oscillation between extravagance and parsimony, and a strong dose of muddle.'

Channel for only sixteen days, but one of his legions was commanded by a future emperor, Vespasian. The emperor Septimius Severus died in Britain in 211 while on an expedition against the Picts. So did Constantius in 306, which is why his son Constantine was proclaimed emperor at York. It is likely that Constantine made two or three more visits. Constans made a hasty winter visit in 342 or 343. The future emperor Theodosius came with his father to restore the military position in 368–9.

Thus Britain was by no means seen as being marginal or expendable. Why did the empire hang on there with such expensive tenacity? A quick answer is that hanging on is what great empires do. A more sophisticated answer would seek statistics relating to balance of advantage; but since all the relevant (and doubtless vast) archives have gone we are reduced to estimations and impressions. British mineral resources must have been worth a lot. Impressions of prosperity in Britain and of high population in parts at least of the late imperial period could justify a most interesting allegation by a panegyrist of c. 300: that Britain was fruitful in taxes. A remarkable account of how the emperor Julian used a fleet of transports to shift supplies of grain from Britain to the army of the Rhine in 358–9 suggests that Britain might have been an imperial breadbasket comparable to parts of North Africa. Britain could have been valued also because it provided remunerative commands and offices for high elites.

One commodity of which Britain was certainly productive was mutiny. The strength of the forces stationed there tempted commanders to set up as usurpers. The first such attempt was made by the governor Claudius Albinus in 193–7. In 286 or 287 a naval commander, Carausius, seized power in Britain and Gaul. His authority and that of his successor, Allectus, lasted until 296. Not the least remarkable usurper was Magnus Maximus. A Spaniard, he took advantage of high command in Britain to rebel in 383, to cross the Channel and to establish himself at Trier, with authority over Britain, Gaul and Spain. He made a power-sharing agreement with the emperor Theodosius, but it collapsed; and so he was killed in 388.

That two emperors, Septimius Severus and Constantius, died in Britain while on campaign against Rome's northern enemies shows how deeply Roman rulers could feel the burden of inability to fulfil the Agricolan ambition for conquest of the far north. The northern threats these emperors faced could have been partly an unintended creation of Roman policy. In an earlier period of Roman Britain there seem to have been a number of tribes north of the Forth. The Picts' establishment of some united authority there may derive from Roman pressure, maybe even from Roman subsidy. For in Britain, as elsewhere on the imperial frontiers, the Roman adoption of an essentially defensive position could transform and strengthen the enemies outside, not least because their restraint or cooperation could be well paid for. Danger did not threaten only from the north. The construction from the later third century of powerful forts on the east and south coasts shows how threatening were German sea raiders. A general concern for security is demonstrated by the fortification of towns large and small from the late second and early third century on.

That Roman Britain was on the defensive on every coast and frontier must have affected the inhabitants' view of imperial authority. They needed defence by imperial forces, but those who valued imperial protection may well have resented the severe taxes needed to pay for it. Some troops, above all the mobile forces of the field army, could have welcomed the opportunity to adventure with a would-be emperor; other units would have become much more part of the countryside or town in which they had long been settled. If a number of people lived well from the governmental system, there must have been many more who were stressed and oppressed by state levies, by enemy raids, and maybe by breakdowns of order.

Echoes of these stresses can be heard in our meagre information on the end of imperial power in Britain. The import of coin to Britain seems largely to have ceased in c. 402. Thus lack of pay may partly explain the army's having brought three usurpers successively to power, 406–7. The last of these, 'Constantine III', is the only Romano-Britain whose secular career has won him a place in the history books. In 407 he led the army, or much of it, across the Channel. There he was successful in coping with barbarian invaders and gained authority in Spain as well as in Gaul. In 409 the emperor Honorius even accepted him as a colleague. Thus his career echoed that of Magnus Maximus. So too did his fate: Honorius had him killed in 411.

While 'Constantine III' sought to establish himself across the Channel major events were taking place in Britain. A Saxon invasion in 408 was defeated by the Britons who at that time also, a chronicler says, expelled 'the Romans' (presumably the high-ranking expatriates?). Historians with certain political attitudes hope that this rebellion was a 'popular' one, but in truth there is no telling. Confusion is increased by a statement by the fifth-century historian Zosimus that the emperor Honorius told the Britons that they should look to their own defence. Not only is it unclear what is meant, but it is possible that the reference is not to Britain but to a part of Italy with a similar name.

Clouded and scanty though our information is, we can at least be fairly certain that institutional connection with Roman emperors and the presence of organised Roman troops in Britain ceased at about this time.

From Roman Departure to Viking Assault

What happened in Britain in the fifth and sixth centuries will never be fully known and understood. It can be argued that the life and authority continued in a 'late Antique' mode in some areas and for a long time. By contrast, a case can be made for early 'systems collapse', such that lack of evidence can be equated with the disappearance of *Romanitas*. That there certainly was major collapse at some stage is demonstrable by contrasting Britain with Gaul. For example, in both areas episcopal sees had been established in Roman towns. In Gaulish towns a succession of bishops continued; in Britain it did not. The best source we have in writing is Gildas's diatribe on the fall of Britain, written in the mid-sixth century (or, some suggest, earlier). Some of what he says about the last period and failure of Roman power shows him as the first (though not the last) intellectual to misrepresent challenging sources here. In particular he gives utterly misleading explanations for the great northern fortifications of Roman Britain.

He can hardly, however, have been mistaken in his emphasis on there having been long periods of successful British resistance to invaders. This resistance distinguishes Britain. In Gaul and in other parts of the former empire 'barbarian' invaders took over the Roman system of government which partly continued to function, if in a rundown way. Of course there was warfare, but there was not a long continued struggle between inhabitants of the former Roman empire and invaders, with long fluctuations of success and failure such as Gildas describes in Britain. The Britons fought the invaders as others did not. Maybe this capacity for resistance was due to forces from the highland zone, such as may not have become fully absorbed into the imperial system and demilitarised. A striking indication of the power of British resistance is that Wales was the only part of the western empire which remained in the control of the people who had held it before the Romans came. Gildas suggests some united authority among the Britons in the fifth century, but he shows division of power in his own times. It is plain that, at least in the areas which concerned him, minor kingdoms, resembling those later found in Wales, were normal. We should, however, not be too eager to assume that significant elements of more widely organised authority did not survive in Britain. The reader may ask: 'How does Arthur come into this scene?' The answer has to be that, though some such person may have existed, and may even have been very important, the sources are insufficient to tell us who he was or what he did. He is first mentioned in a source which may or may not be as early as 600, which says merely that someone else was 'not Arthur'. The great merit of Arthurian studies, perhaps the sole one, is that they show how tremendous are the gaps in knowledge of this period; so stimulating has speculation been that it blurs captivatingly into fiction.

Ireland remained untouched by direct Roman rule. A distinguished scholar (D. A. Binchy) has characterised early Ireland as 'tribal, rural, hierarchical and familiar' ('familiar' in the sense of being such that family relationships were crucial there). He could with justice have added a sharper adjective, such as 'predatory'. Certainly the Irish were major invaders of Britain, establishing power in (future) Scotland and Wales. An Irish leader could come in warfare across the Irish Sea, as when we find an Uí Néill prince in battle against Æthelfrith, king of Northumbria, in 603. Yet relationships across the Irish Sea could not have been entirely hostile. Æthelfrith's sons later fled as exiles to the Irish (and the Picts), and this ultimately led to the Christian conversion of much of England.

Of the invaders whom Gildas stigmatised (and also welcomed as instruments of God's wrath) those with the most successful career to come were the 'Saxons'. He describes some of them as entering British service in the fifth century as mercenaries, then as mutineers bringing compatriots in, and conquering much of the island (though with fluctuating fortunes). His story is plausible as an outline of what happened or of some of it; but he may err in putting a crucial initial stage in the mid- rather than the earlier fifth century. We know that 'Saxons' were not the only continental peoples involved: there were

others also from northern Germany and from the Danish peninsula:
Angles, Jutes, Frisians, Franks and others. By the early seventh century
Germanic invaders had control of a great deal of what was to become
'England', though important gains, not least in the south-west, were
made later.

The scale and nature of such settlement and occupation is
problematical. Particularly uncertain is its impact on institutions of
rule. Were some Anglo-Saxon kingdoms the successors of Romano-
British *civitates* in serious ways? Kent, for example: its name follows
that of the *Cantiaci*. Was there a deeper continuity? The early kingdom
of Kent had a system of subdivisions into 'lathes', and of assessments in
'sulungs'. Were they created by the post-Roman regime or were they
inherited from Roman times? This leads to a broader question: how far
were there Roman origins of assessment for services and taxes which
were determinative in the centralised organisation of the late Anglo-
Saxon state?

A people whose ferocity Gildas does not bring out were the Britons.
Seen from the east they were victims; seen from the south-west they
were conquerors. It is uncertain when the Britons conquered Brittany,
but conquer it they did, and it retained substantial independence for
centuries. A relevant date is 461 when a British bishop, possibly from
Brittany, attended a Gaulish synod. Even more remarkably, some
Britons established themselves in north-west Spain, where we also find
a British bishop. Add to the Britons' establishment in Gaul and Spain
their major role in the conversion of Ireland and some part in the
conversion of the Picts, and it is hardly too much to speak of a First
British Empire.

Predation was fundamental to the political economy of the
archipelago in this period. Not for nothing is the earliest Irish epic titled
'The Cattle Raid of Cooley'; not for nothing could certain Irish kings
be required to undertake a ritual cattle raid upon accession. Cattle
counted for a lot, in Britain as in Ireland, but the politics of war
included more than stolen cattle. Bede shows that there could also be
royal treasures to win, and – perhaps most important of all – captives
to be enslaved and sold. It was significant that the kingdoms which
developed as the most powerful – Wessex, Mercia and Northumbria –
were those which had frontiers on which they could expand at the
expense of Celtic peoples. Raids and conquests could be cruel. When
Bede describes invasions of Anglian lands by the British king

Cadwallon in the early seventh century, he says that he was bestial in cruelty, sparing neither women nor innocent children. At the same time Bede almost glories in the conquests of the Angle Æthelfrith, king of the Northumbrians (d. 616), who may well not have differed particularly from Cadwallon in his modus operandi: Bede says that Æthelfrith occupied more British land than had any other ruler, 'exterminating or subjugating' the inhabitants. 'Ethnic cleansing' was no more foreign to the seventh century than it is to the twenty-first.

Most of the polities of the archipelago were fairly small kingdoms. The Anglo-Saxon lands as they were by c. 800 had recently contained a dozen or more of these. In this, post-Roman Britain differed from post-Roman Gaul, Spain and Italy, areas which did not divide to the same extent or in the same way; indeed, such division was more character-istic of areas which had not been part of the Roman empire, in particular Scandinavia and Ireland. It is unclear how far the kingdoms of early Anglo-Saxon England were consistently independent of one another; and their number was falling. Thus eighth-century Northumbria represented the two former kingdoms of Bernicia and Deira. Mercia absorbed such lesser kingdoms as that of the Hwicce in the west midlands. Sometimes greater kings had overlordship over lesser. Bede refers to seven kings who held *imperium*, the first four over all kingdoms south of the Humber, the last three over those to the north as well. The earliest overlord was, he says, Ælle, king of the South Saxons in the late fifth century; his successors, in a chronologically discontinuous series, were kings of Wessex, Kent and East Anglia. After an interval followed three kings of the Northumbrians with wide authority for considerable parts of the period from 616 to 670. Bede also says that Æthelbald, king of the Mercians (716–57) had authority over all the kings and kingdoms south of the Humber. Æthelbald's successor, Offa (757–96), certainly extended authority over kingdoms south of the Humber, claiming, for example, the right to control the disposal of land in Kent, and having a king of East Anglia executed. Offa had relations on something like equal terms with Charlemagne, and his fame extended to Ireland. In considering the nature of the organisation of power in early Anglo-Saxon England one should bear in mind that Germanic polities on the Continent, thought apt to shift in their composition and organisation, had nevertheless long been organised in various, and sometimes in apparently sophisticated, ways. Bede describes such a system when he says of the continental Saxons that in his own day they were divided into sub-divisions each under a leader whom he calls a 'satrap'. When war threatened, these 'satraps' cast lots and he upon whom the lot fell was followed and obeyed, but only for as long as the war lasted.

There does seem to have developed a degree of unified power in the Anglo-Saxon lands but one cannot be confident in assuming a steady or uniform progression. It is impossible to tell what Bede meant when he says that Ælle, king of the later unimportant kingdom of Sussex, c. 490, held *imperium*. Historians are apt to describe such authority as he may have had as 'vague': all they mean is that they have to be vague about it. It could well be that the political system of early England not only involved fluctuations of authority but also the expression of authority in organised systems of tribute taking. Even if there was a development in 'overlordship' (as quite likely there was) it was not a linear progress. Thus by Bede's account Æthelbald and Offa had less geographically extensive authority than did their Northumbrian predecessors. Although the number of kingdoms certainly, in the long term, diminished, one should bear in mind that some of the small ones may have started life as fragments of others previously larger.

We should take seriously Bede's observations on Northumbrian power. He must have moved in Northumbrian circles high enough to give him accurate information about the circumstances of a generation or so before. He indicates that Edwin (616–33) had some authority in Wales and that he gained Anglesey and Man (in this showing the importance of sea power). Of Oswiu (655–70) he says that he overwhelmed and made tributary the peoples of the north of the island, the Picts and the Irish. He seems to indicate that such kings enjoyed wide authority, in Oswiu's case and that of his successor Ecgfrith (670–85) wider than that enjoyed by any ruler until James I and VI.

The post-Roman centuries are sometimes seen as a period of what is termed 'state formation'. A simplified view of this theory runs like this. It may be that in some parts of Britain, units of Roman or Roman–British authority were taken over by Germanic rulers, e.g. Kent. In wide areas there was probably no such extensive authority; rather were there small units under chieftains of some kind. These then merged, the stronger ones assimilating the weaker, so that, over generations, larger units with more powerful dynasties were built up; the later stages of such development appear in the seventh- and eighth-century moves towards 'overlordship'. There are plausible elements in such hypotheses on circumstances about which little is known for certain. But it could be that areas of authority, even from the fifth century, were often much larger than this theory suggests.

A key document in arguments about the organisation of power is the 'Tribal Hidage', believed to belong to the seventh or the eighth century. It is a list of areas, denominated in hides, and identified by names in the genitive plural. Thus it begins with the land of the Mercians and goes on to list the lands of others. Some of the areas concerned are vast (the largest is Wessex, assessed at a hundred thousand hides), while others are very small (five are assessed at no more than three hundred hides). This list could be one of tribute obligations to an overlord, likely enough a Mercian or Northumbrian one. If so, it suggests organised tribute taking, which raises the question of just how far one should interpret the 'Hidage' in terms of 'tribes' in accordance with the title given to it in the nineteenth century. The assumption is that many of the names in the *Hidage* are those of little 'peoples' who settled in limited areas and were subsequently incorporated into, in particular, Mercia. There could well be something in this, but one cannot be sure how much, not least because of a Germanic usage whereby apparently 'tribal' names could perform a function later fulfilled by 'area' names (for example, the early term for Somerset is *Sumærsæte*, a 'people' name, but in denoting those people ruled from Somerton it indicates not a 'tribe' but an area of authority). The 'Tribal Hidage' may tell us more about administration than about settlement. Assessment in hides appears in other contexts. Land grants ('charters') from the late seventh century on describe estates in terms of Latin equivalents of 'hides'; some demonstrate that separate places or estates had individual assessments. What appears from references to assessments both in the charters and in the *Hidage* is that we are dealing with organised rule via possibly elaborate systems.

This impression is reinforced by the early laws. Four 'codes' survive from the seventh century: from Kent those of Ethelbert (*c.* 597–616), of Hlothere and Eadric (673–?676), and of Wihtred (690–725); and from Wessex of Ine (688–*c.* 726). Royal authority seems fairly strong in the first two, but even stronger in the second two. Thus the laws of Ine seek to control movement between *scirs* (quite possibly the historic shires of Wessex) and lay down strict requirements in regard to infant baptism and Sabbath observance. It can be argued that the impression given of detailed control lacked substance and that such laws were largely for show. Evidence to the contrary, supporting the impression they give of strong royal authority, is that of many tens of thousands of tons of earth: that is to say the great dykes built in this period. The greatest of all is Offa's Dyke, separating the English from the Welsh by a barrier over a hundred miles long, well over twenty feet high from the bottom of the ditch to the top of the bank: still the most imposing earthwork in western Europe and the most compelling evidence for the scope and scale of royal administrative power in early England. There is little reason to doubt that it was – as a near contemporary, Asser, maintains – built (at least in part) by Offa, king of the Mercians (757–96). Offa's Dyke has lesser, but still massive, counterparts in other kingdoms. All tell of organised power and suggest that we should take the early laws seriously when they too imply this.

How far did the political culture and developments of the other parts of the archipelago resemble those of the Anglo-Saxon lands? Taking Ireland first, there was an obvious major difference: Ireland had not been subject to conquests as England had been. It was a land of many small kingdoms and complicated hierarchies of supremacy. Historians of Ireland agree in suggesting political development (which can be no more than vaguely delineated) from a 'tribal' political system of numerous such *tuaths* to one which was increasingly 'dynastically' orientated, 'territorialised'. There certainly was an 'all-Irish' conscious-ness hardly paralleled at an early date in the Anglo-Saxon lands. The laws or conventions expressed in the legal tracts were seen as valid for the whole of Ireland. The hereditary class of learned men responsible for their preservation and implementation had an 'inter-kingdom' status, and the Irish language as written was uniform throughout the island. The prestige of the 'king of Tara' was all-Irish, if varyingly so.

This 'kingship of Tara' played an important part in political develop-ments from the seventh century onwards. In large parts of northern and midland Ireland two branches of the Uí Néill family, the 'northern' and 'southern', became dominant, and had reached a peak of authority by the end of the eighth century. The importantly honorific 'kingship of Tara' was sometimes held by one branch, sometimes by the other. Another family, the Éogonacht, became dominant in the south-west, in Munster. Such overlordships were complicated, not least in regard to the relationships between different branches of the dominant families and the obligations and status of subordinated families or 'tribes'.

It is not easy to ascertain exactly what the powers of kings in seventh- and eighth-century Ireland were: the search for administrative structure is frustratingly inconclusive. A key document may be *Senchus Fir nAlban* (History of the Men of Scotland), which sets out the military and naval service owed from components of Dál Ríata in relation to the number of 'houses' in component settlements. The leading modern expert argues it to be 'overwhelmingly likely' that the surviving text derives from one of the seventh century. Maybe the organisation of Dál Ríata was entirely exceptional, but it is equally possibly that the *Senchus* gives insight into elements of administrative organisation in Irish polities that eludes other sources. In regard to legislation the law tracts from the seventh and eighth centuries suggest that the legislative capacity of kings was largely limited to emergencies; but the *cana* provide a different impression, one of the early importance of the profits of justice.

If there is much that is obscure about the distribution of power and the nature of government in early Ireland, almost everything is obscure about them in Wales. Wales was always an area of divided and fluctuating power in which the most important kingdoms were Gwynedd, Powys, Deheubarth and Dyfed. A critical question in understanding the seventh and eighth centuries is that of how far laws first revealed in the late twelfth century may relate to much earlier circumstances. It is hard to do much more than to state a possibility, an important one. There are indications that systems of estate organisation and elements of royal authority which appear in the earliest Welsh laws may have existed in areas outside what became Wales and thus may indicate the survival, or partial survival, not only in Wales but elsewhere in Britain, of systems and institutions possibly predating even the Roman conquest. Arguments for this are incon- clusive, but the possibility, however shadowy, is important, and not least for considering how early Wales may have been organised.

While we know almost nothing of law and administration in the very large part of north Britain ruled by the Picts, we can, however, quote one most extraordinary statement by Bede about the response of Nectan, king of the Picts, when he became converted to the Roman system for calculating Easter (*c.* 717): 'The nineteen-year cycles for Easter were forthwith sent out by public order throughout all the Pictish kingdoms to be copied, learned and acted upon.' This might just be an unrealistic commonplace, a standardised account of what a king was supposed to do, but Bede knew men who must have known the Pictish set-up well. He may be giving a glimpse of how well the Pictish realm was organised. There are indications in later sources (from the twelfth century on) of an orderly system of authority in areas which had been ruled by the Picts.

How far did conversion to Christianity affect the exercise of royal power in England? Interesting possibilities arise from a comparison between two earlier seventh-century codes and the two later. The earlier laws are notable for the absence of physical penalties: no hanging, no flogging. By contrast, the later codes abound in such punishments; thus, similar offences attract penalties in the later codes very different from those which appear in the earlier. This puts one in mind of Tacitus stating in his *Germania* that the imposition of physical penalties was the province of priests. There are more than five hundred years between Tacitus and the early English codes. Still, it is an interesting possibility that conversion, by removing the power of a pagan priesthood, enhanced that of kings. Certainly one can see how royal power and the imposition of Christianity and Christian ways went hand in hand. Conversion to Christianity had an element of re-Romanisation: it was not for nothing that Christianity and coinage came in at about the same time.

In Ireland, too, secular and ecclesiastical power assimilated to one another: it could be that the new class of the ecclesiastically important was derived from that of pagan intellectuals who, *inter alia*, declared the law; maybe the two classes more or less merged. The early law tracts were affected by canon law, and ecclesiastics had views on secular law. A distinguished Irish historian (Professor Dáibhí Ó Cróinín) writes of 'clerical enthusiasm for capital punishment' in eighth-century Ireland (though not all clerics need have shared it). Monasteries, increasingly secularised, became major players in the game of power.

Response to the Scandinavian Invasions

'The pagans desecrated the sanctuaries of God, and poured out the blood of saints around the altar . . . trampled on the bodies of saints in the house of God, like dung in the streets . . . Truly this has not happened by chance, rather is it a sign that it was well merited by someone . . . if anything ought to be corrected in your grace's habits, correct it quickly.' Thus the Northumbrian Alcuin, leading theologian at the court of Charlemagne, wrote to the bishop/abbot of Lindisfarne in the aftermath of the Viking assault on his abbey in 793. This disaster was early in a series of moves by which, over two centuries, Scandinavians made themselves felt by raid, trade or settlement from Newfoundland to the Volga River.

Four important generalisations about the Vikings are these. First, the time span involved is long indeed. The Scandinavian assault on England begins towards the end of the eighth century; the threat of a major invasion loomed recurrently until 1085. There would have been vast differences between a man who enjoyed the loot of Lindisfarne in 793 and a distant descendant in the service of Danish Cnut when he made himself king of England in 1016. Second, although there was passionate anti-Viking feeling, often religiously inspired, the story is by no means simply one of hostility between Scandinavians and their victims. The invaders were soon involved on one side or another in civil wars and local quarrels: thus they assisted Carolingian rebels, made themselves serviceable in Irish feuds and ran a puppet ruler in Mercia. (Indeed, Alfred himself may for a time have been subject to Danish authority.) Third, they were by no means always united: in particular hostility between Danes and Norse was serious in Ireland from the ninth century, in England from the tenth. Fourth, the consequences of the 'Viking' movements could be, in economic terms, positive. Traders as well as raiders, Scandinavians were involved in the foundation of towns, from Cork to Kiev. Not for nothing was a considerable part of Scandinavian-occupied Britain known as 'the land of the five boroughs'.

A series of assaults on and from the coasts of Britain and Ireland were made in the early decades of the ninth century. Their aims were plunder, capture of slaves and the exaction of tribute. The proximity to the coast of rich but undefended monasteries and trading places made the invaders' task all the easier. Towards the middle of the century things changed for the worse. Both in Ireland and in Britain Viking forces began to overwinter and their assaults increased in force. By the 870s the invaders had transformed the political geography of England. In 800 there had been four remaining kingdoms: Northumbria, East Anglia, Mercia and Wessex (now holding everything south of the Thames, bar Cornwall). The invaders destroyed, took over and partly settled the first two of these and Mercia was carved up by a treaty (of 886 or maybe a little earlier) between the Danish king Guthrum and Alfred, king of Wessex, the only English kingdom left. In no other part of the archipelago did Scandinavians achieve such extensive control.

The survival of Wessex is an oft-told tale, the hero of which is King Alfred, though contemporary sources, such as the *Chronicle* and Asser's biography, both the work of clerical courtiers, are likely to be biased and certainly cannot tell us all we would like to know. When Alfred acceded in 871 his country's predicament was looking increasingly bleak, and for some years complete defeat loomed. A major victory over the Danes in 878, at Edington, marked the turn of the tide. By the time of his death in 899 Alfred was secure; indeed, thanks to his Mercian gains, his dominions were far wider than those of his forbears.

The Alfred Jewel, found in 1693 near Athelney. Its inscription saying 'Alfred had me made' and its high craftsmanship suggest connection with King Alfred's court. It appears to be the head of a shaft, possibly the head of an *aestel*, a pointer to assist in reading. At least six comparable (but somewhat lesser) objects have been found, all but one recently, and all (like the Alfred Jewel) as casual finds. The chance discovery of so many objects suggests that once they were numerous. Were there hundreds? Thousands? Should we imagine many Anglo-Saxons, no less numerous than prosperous, poring over manuscripts *aestel* in hand? Or were these items heads of shafts with another purpose – wands of office, perhaps?

Alfred's success was largely due to his naval and military organisation. Specially important was the West Saxon fortress system. This is set out in a document from Alfred's time (or that of his son, Edward). It lists thirty-three fortresses (*burhs*), nearly all of which lay on the borders of Wessex. Virtually all have been identified, solidly on the ground. This was no mere parchment scheme, but one which reflects the deployment of organised power, reminding us of what must have lain behind the great dykes of rather earlier days.

Alfred's fame rests significantly on his patronage of learning. His biographer's account of this is borne out by the survival of the translations of works from Latin into English with which the king was associated. Alcuin's observations on the sack of Lindisfarne are a reminder that the origins of Viking assault could be seen as moral, provocation of God's justified wrath. Alfred was similarly concerned to harness royal intentions to God's will (and conversely). The translations are part of such a programme. The histories of Bede and Orosius show history determined by divine judgement; the *Pastoral Care* of Gregory the Great showed how godly rule should be exercised; Boethius's book on the consolation of philosophy taught the vanity of earthly things, the need for fortitude and (especially with Alfred's own additions) how social function should fit with divine plan. Alfred was concerned that his aristocrats should become literate, with their hearts, minds and loyalties in the right place. The *Anglo-Saxon Chronicle*, produced at his court, set the history of Wessex into a wider frame such that West Saxon history appeared almost that of the Anglo-Saxon peoples as a whole. Alfred's law code claimed descent from Mercia and Kent as well as Wessex. In short, the writings associated with Alfred and his court reflect the concerns of a threatened kingdom and an ambitious king.

What happened in Ireland was notably different from what happened in England. Two opinions have been held about the impact of Scandinavian invaders there. One suggests that it transformed Irish political culture. On this view, before the Vikings came warfare had been controlled, almost ritualised. The other view is that Ireland was already so violent that the addition of foreign violence would not have made much difference to a world where Christian potentates raided monasteries much as Vikings were to do, and indeed where annals record monasteries in armed conflict. The likely truth is, almost needless to say, intermediate. There had been a good deal of violence in

pre-Viking Ireland; on the other hand Viking assaults on monasteries
were more indiscriminate, less inhibited than those by Christian
warriors. Episodes such as that of 821 when Vikings 'made a great prey
of women' at Howth may have been hard to parallel in pre-Viking days.

The most lasting Scandinavian contribution to Ireland was urban,
and above all lay in the creation of Dublin as a centre of trade and of
(fluctuating) power. Dublin and its surroundings came to comprise a
kind of city-state under the influence of surrounding Irish rulers,
sometimes more, sometimes less. Dublin stands as the product of an
era of high activity, predatory and commercial, all around the Irish Sea.
The impact of such activity on the eastern shores of that sea has to be
estimated from inadequate annals. Thus there were several assaults on
Iona, and a major Norse incursion into central Scotland in 839. An
attack launched on Dumbarton in 870–71 produced a mighty haul of
Angle, British and Pictish slaves carried off to Dublin. But we have no
details for the Norse acquisition and settlement of the Hebrides
and Man.

Wales suffered a similar fate. West Wales looks, naturally, towards
Ireland (witness the location of its principal see at St David's); Welsh
Latin learning and culture owed much to Ireland; and in the ninth
century Vikings were heavily involved in Wales via Ireland. Thus
Rhodri Mawr ('the Great'), ruler of Gwynedd, 844–78, for a time
successfully fought against Viking invaders, but in 877 was driven into
exile, to be killed in the following year not by the Norse, but by the
English. Scandinavians from Dublin continued to have major parts to
play in Wales, and some Welsh princes came to be much involved in
the power politics of the Irish Sea. Coastal place names of Wales are
often of Scandinavian origin, for example Anglesey or Swansea: such
names are much more numerous in Wales than in Ireland. Yet if one
asks how far the obvious Norse influence in Wales may have extended
to actual rule for periods, how far the coastal place names may have
stood for coastal settlement, secure answers come there none.

England, c. 900–c. 1066

Success was a dominant theme in English monarchy between the
death of Alfred in 899, when the area of England under Scandinavian
control included much of the north, the midlands and the east, and that

of his great-grandson, Edgar, in 975, by which time it had become possible to speak of a unified England. Alfred's son Edward 'the Elder' (899–924) conquered East Anglia and most of the midlands in a series of smashing campaigns. Norse and Danes remained seemingly powerful in northern England until Alfred's grandson, Eadred, made a final conquest of the Scandinavian kingdom of York in 954. The triumphant success was achieved on a political stage that encompassed the entire archipelago. Athelstan (924–39) in 937 won a victory at Brunanburh over Olaf, king of Dublin (and claimant to York), and his allies, the kings of the Scots and of Strathclyde. Athelstan's power was felt in west Britain also, where he made Welsh princes tributary. According to William of Malmesbury the Welsh promised an enormous annual tribute of twenty pounds of gold, three hundred pounds of silver, and twenty-five thousand cattle. Alfred had already claimed some authority in Wales and Athelstan was not the last Anglo-Saxon king to claim 'imperial' authority in Britain. Witness the optimistic view taken by an obituarist of Edward the Confessor: 'he governed the Welsh, ruled Britons and Scots, Angles, and Saxons'. Perhaps the most impressive demonstration of the grand prestige of the West Saxon royal house and of Athelstan was the marriage of his half-sisters to some of the greatest men of the Continent, most eminent among them the future emperor Otto I. During the reign of Edgar (957–75) the kingdom reached an apogee of power and even of peace. An expression of this was a remarkable performance which took place at Chester in 973, when six kings from around the Irish Sea came and promised service to him (it was later said that there were eight kings and that they rowed him ceremonially on the Dee). An early twelfth-century author gives an extraordinary account of Edgar's naval power, saying that he circumnavigated Britain every year, employing three great fleets, each of 1,200 ships. This may be too much to believe. But certainly by the eleventh century Anglo-Saxon kings had an organised system for the provision of ships and crews for the royal fleet, a system applied to inland as well as to coastal areas. This could have given them important naval capacity to act beyond England, one which their twelfth-century successors may well have lacked.

After the death of Edgar events took an exciting, but less gratifying, turn. There was a succession dispute: Edgar's son Edward ('the Martyr', king 975–8) was assassinated in the interest of his half-brother Ethelred (II, 'the Unready', 978–1016). During Ethelred's reign the

Danes resumed their invasions with increasing force and frequency. In 1016 Cnut, a Danish prince, won the kingship of England, to which he soon added Denmark and, later, Norway. After Cnut's death in 1035 the short reigns of two of his sons were followed, remarkably enough, by the succession in 1042 of Ethelred II's son Edward ('the Confessor'). Edward was a fairly successful king, one might even say very successful if one considers how peaceful his reign was compared to those of continental contemporaries. But he was childless and the consequence of this was the struggles for the succession which culminated in the Norman Conquest.

More, much more, is known about late Anglo-Saxon England than about any other part of contemporary Europe. This is thanks to Domesday Book. Although the survey it records was made in 1086 on the orders of William the Conqueror, the astonishing administrative system it reveals was created before the Conquest. The survey covers the whole country, the far north apart, and mentions and deals with more than four-fifths of the places of modern England. It is plain that most places in Domesday had clear boundaries, many of which still exist today. The area surveyed was divided into thirty-three shires (later also termed counties) which formed the framework of local government for many centuries to come, and to an extent still do. Some of these already had long histories – Hampshire, for example, is a territorial unit of human organisation older than any European state. Most of the midland shires were created at some stage in the tenth century. These were usually laid out neatly with a river as a spine, and took their names from shire towns at nodal points on the river system. Some other shires were based on former kingdoms: Kent, Sussex, Essex. Some were much bigger and/or more populous than others. There were differences between the organisation of shires in different areas. Thus the sub-divisions ('hundreds', or 'wapentakes') had more uniform neatness in the midlands than in Wessex. Still, all told, the shire system was one of important uniformity, more closely resembling the *départements* of post-Revolutionary France than pre-Revolutionary France's unwieldy systems of feudally derived subdivision. The durability of the system is best demonstrated by its transfer to and persistence in the United States. 'County' was the term used there, but the word shire survives in 'sheriff', meaning 'shire reeve' – 'officer in charge of a shire'.

Dominant in Domesday is the detailed assessment of landholdings for tax or service in terms of 'hides' (in some shires 'carucates'): the survey records an assessment for every significant holding in every village. The level of detail is amazing. Such assessment relates largely, of course, to royal dues and renders. At least from the early eleventh century the main tax was that termed 'Danegeld' (tax for the Danes), or alternatively 'heregeld' (army tax). Crucial knowledge of this tax in this century comes from a passage in the *Anglo-Saxon Chronicle* (D version) for 1051. 'In this year King Edward abolished that tax which King Ethelred had instituted to buy off the Danes: and this was in the thirty-ninth year since he had introduced it . . . it always had priority over other taxes which were paid in various ways, and was the most generally oppressive.' This puts the introduction of the Danegeld/heregeld to about 1012. What happened before 1012, then? According to the *Chronicle*, sums totalling £137,000 were paid to the Danes between 991 and 1012. The plausibility of these alleged payments has been challenged, but effectively defended as indicative of, at a minimum, orders of magnitude. We do not know in any detail before *c.* 1012 how so very much money was raised, though hidage assessments probably played a major part. The geld raised from *c.* 1012 to 1051 was used to maintain a standing force of warships and their crews. Standing armies are sometimes said characteristically to appear in the sixteenth century, but England had such a force in the early eleventh.

Characteristic of the late Anglo-Saxon regime were two tendencies apparently almost contradictory but in fact largely complementary: on the one hand tight social control and on the other considerably wider participation in government. Knowledge of control comes largely from contemporary legislation. Late Anglo-Saxon 'codes' are a mixed bag. We have surviving laws from every king between Alfred and Cnut who reigned for any length of time, but none of these comprise what could now be called a code; and large subjects, above all land law, are hardly touched upon. Laws of wide importance and apparently intended durability accompany others of more limited significance. Some laws were essentially practical and pragmatic; others, such as some of those of Ethelred II, are written in a powerfully homilectic vein. Some 'codes' are not essentially royal: one is the regulations of a local association of thief pursuers. Undoubtedly some, maybe many, laws which were laid down do not survive.

Some of the laws demand, or display, terrible brutality. An example, from Cnut's second code, is that of a much-suspected man who, having failed twice at the ordeal, must have his hands or feet cut off, 'or both'.

If he is guilty of 'still further crimes' 'he shall have his eyes put out and his nose and ears and upper lip cut off or his scalp removed'. One might hope that such horrors existed on parchment only. But a late tenth-century account of the miracles of St Swithin refers to the miraculous healing of a man who had suffered just such punishment which the (contemporary) author says had been introduced by King Edgar, thus not only showing that such dreadful penalties were imposed, but also indicating otherwise unknown legislation by Edgar.

The authorities were concerned to maintain tight social control, in particular to ensure that everyone was in a system to ensure that he should be brought before the law as required. It is likely that already in force over much of England before the Conquest was the organised system ('frankpledge') of which we have detailed knowledge by the thirteenth century. Its essence was the division of the population into groups, the members of each being mutually responsible for the production before the law of any one of their numbers. These groups were of ten or twelve, or comprised the inhabitants of a minor settlement. Tight social control involved a significant and close relationship between central authority and the individual. A general requirement for an oath of obedience to the king first appears in a law of Edmund, 939–46. It probably applied to all freemen and may well not have been new.

The system of legal organisation had a more positive side. It is likely that a fairly high proportion of the population was involved in courts. It has been estimated that in the eleventh century at least one adult male in twenty might have attended these monthly 'hundred' courts held for ordinary business. There are other indications of the possibility of there having been rather a wide 'political nation' in late Anglo-Saxon England. One sign of this is Cnut's distribution of two letters, or proclamations, presumably designed for shire and hundred courts: one, c. 1020, deals with the king's recent doings and with the estab-lishment of peace and justice; the other describes his visit to Rome in 1027. One has to wonder how far kings might find it expedient to appeal to a constituency much wider than that of the nobility. May the Confessor's abolition of Danegeld/heregeld in 1051 have been a political move aimed at an audience both wide and significant?

There is, of course, an important area in which political history meets social and economic history. How far was the social balance such as to give significant power to classes of men who would later have been termed 'gentry' or 'yeomen'? Domesday shows that there were indeed such classes. The tendency, at least from the tenth century, for the division of big estates in such a way as to foster a class of lesser landowners, many of whom were based in a single village, could have created or increased a class of 'gentry'. English society was at least in some extensive areas one in which free peasants, or partly free peasants, were important. The English polity was one in which classes well below the aristocracy had to be taken seriously.

Relations between Anglo-Saxon kings and nobles were of a kind no more than imperfectly matched abroad; though the position of the ealdormen (otherwise earls) with their wide provincial authority to an extent paralleled that of dukes and margraves in post-Carolingian France and Germany. (The title 'ealdorman' had been replaced by 'earl' by about the early eleventh century.) In the ninth century each of the ancient shires of Wessex had had at its head a noble termed *ealdorman*: not so long before he might have been seen as, and termed, a sub-king. By the ninth century he had apparently come to resemble a Carolingian count. Probably early in the tenth century a different system, maybe connected with the conquests of Edward the Elder, came into play. The ealdorman was now at the head of a former kingdom or a large part of one: e.g. East or West Wessex, East Anglia, Essex, West Mercia. This system continued until the Norman Conquest, though there was hardly a completely continuous succession of earls, in any earldom. It is important that the territorial composition of an earldom could be varied from time to time, presumably by royal decree. There is Domesday evidence that important lands were associated with the office of ealdorman / earl and moved from one holder to another, and it is unclear how far this system was in decline before 1066 – though it may have been.

All, or almost all, tenth-century ealdormen probably came from an extended cousinhood with rather a lot of West Saxon royal blood. This cousinhood was naturally prone to factious crises, but had powerful inclinations towards unity. Son often followed father in high office, but ealdormanries should be seen as confined to a small class of very high aristocracy, rather than as strictly hereditary, and royal control in the disposition of ealdordoms / earldoms and their accompanying landed endowments was not insignificant. The previous division of England into independent kingdoms left notably little of a tradition of provincial consciousness, except in Northumbria and Kent. Mercia last appears as a quasi-independent entity in 957–9 when Edgar was briefly recognised as king of the Mercians and Northumbrians. A powerful counterbalance against the possibility of provincialisms leading to civil war is indicated by Domesday Book. The estates of important noblemen were sometimes widely scattered, and in more earldoms and ancient kingdoms than one: such scattering must have been a disincentive to civil war.

Among the ancient southern kingdoms Kent did retain a strong sense of identity; indeed, it retained some land laws of its own until the twentieth century. Yet Kent's integration into a national system was expressed in the convention that Kentish levies should lead the army. Indeed, one of the great successes of the English state was the integration of local loyalties towards national goals. A powerful, and early, demonstration of this appears in the *Anglo-Saxon Chronicle*'s account of a losing battle against the Danes in 1010: 'the men of Cambridgeshire stood firm against them'. Cambridgeshire can hardly have been a political unit for even so much as a hundred years; yet here we have its forces praised in a national context.

Royal relations with the high nobility changed from the eleventh century. A palace revolution in 1005–1007 marked the waning of the power of the royally related cousinhood. Of the cousinhood's members, the ealdorman Ordgar and Æthelmaer retired from active life in 1005 (one permanently, the other temporarily). In the next year Æthelmaer, earldorman of Northumbria, and two of his sons were murdered. It seems that the moving spirit here was Eadric Streona ('the Gainer'), who became ealdorman in 1007. The inner workings of the politics behind the changes are beyond our knowledge. It is no surprise that the accession of the Dane Cnut to authority over all of England in 1018 brought new and drastic changes to the tenure of earldoms. He had Eadric Streona decapitated at Christmas 1017 and appointed Scandinavian followers to English earldoms. More lastingly important, however, were his promotions of Englishmen. In 1018 he raised to the earldom of Wessex Godwin, a member of a not very important English family. Leofric, whom he made earl of Mercia, came of more important – but probably not royally connected – stock. These two men, and later their children, came virtually to dominate English politics. Edward the Confessor married Godwin's daughter, Edith, in 1043. After 1053 all the great earldoms, those of East Anglia, Mercia, Northumbria and Wessex, were held by sons of either Godwin or

Leofric. Godwin's son, Harold, succeeded him as earl of Wessex, and, best of all, but as it proved to be, fatally, succeeded Edward the Confessor as king of England in January 1066.

The position of the two great earlish families for so many years presents many problems. What, in particular, were the power and powers of an earl? Domesday Book shows that these families had become very rich. There is some dispute about the calculation of the figures concerned, but it is clear that the annual landed income (not the whole income) of the crown at the death of Edward the Confessor was of the order of £9,500, that of the Godwin family of the order of £5,500, of the Leofrics of about half as much. It is reasonably certain that many of the properties attributed to earls in Domesday were associated with their office, though such lands may have been increasingly regarded as family property. It is important to consider powers which earls did not have. Their authority cannot have been entirely vice-regal. Under Cnut and Edward the Confessor all England was divided up into earldoms; if earls had all the royal powers, kings would have had hardly any. There is no clear evidence for earls having any share of Danegeld/heregeld, except possibly in Northumbria, where one source says that the rebellion of 1065 against Tostig was partly caused by his having levied an enormous tax. This issue of the earls' relationship to tax is very important: thus if, until 1051, Edward the Confessor had exclusive access to the heregeld and was using it to maintain a strong standing force of ships and men, then the balance of power was very much in his favour. Another important question, easier to pose than to solve, is that of how far sheriffs were under the control of kings rather than of earls.

Three things stand out about the non-earlish nobility in the late Anglo-Saxon period. One is that Domesday indicates that the wealth even of the richest of them was low compared to that at the disposal of the Godwin and Leofric families. Of noblemen who did not belong to these families only one had more than £400 worth of land, only another fifteen more than £150 worth. Second, and this is in marked contrast with what happened in the former Carolingian empire, although a few great ecclesiastics such as the bishop of Durham and the abbot of Ely held important quasi-independent jurisdiction, otherwise there was very little important seigneurial jurisdiction, secular or ecclesiastical, except, as may be, at a low level. Third, relations between kings and noblemen must have been considerably affected by the frequency of forfeiture. At least one of Alfred's noblemen forfeited his lands for desertion. Forfeiture, generally decreed at a major council meeting, could follow outlawry, harbouring an internal exile, committing a major crime, being a non-celibate clergyman. Extensive forfeiture may well have been a key element in the dynamics of the Anglo-Saxon polity, not least in the *bouleversements* of the reigns of Ethelred II and Cnut.

One of the most eminent historians of Anglo-Saxon England, the great F. M. Stenton, has made an observation about late Anglo-Saxon England which is surprising, even superficially anachronistic. He says of it that the nature of the royal council gave 'in however narrow a form' 'the characters of a constitutional monarchy to the Old English state'. What supports this contention? Indications can be found in accounts of the tribulations, and in particular trials, of the dissension between Edward the Confessor and the Godwin family in 1051–2. There were something like state trials, and they appear to have been conducted with formality. For example, the D version of the *Chronicle* describes how in 1051 summonses were issued throughout England, including Northumbria, to hear Godwin defend himself. The king seems to have formal powers of a remarkable kind. Thus, in the crisis just mentioned, all the thegns of Harold were 'transferred to the king's allegiance'. Not only can a king circulate letters to his subjects, he can make them promises. After the rebellion of 1065 the Northumbrians were promised the laws they had enjoyed in the days of Cnut. Part of one of Ethelred's 'codes' looks as if it may be a proclamation of promises made by the king after his return from exile in 1013. This may indeed have been a violent society. But it was also one very conscious of laws and rights, what should happen, and how things should be done, how state business should be conducted.

Ireland, c. 900–c. 1066

The political culture of other parts of the archipelago contrasts strikingly with that of England in this period. The distinction may be one not so much between the actual circumstances as in the nature of the surviving sources. Constant awareness of the incompleteness of our sources for all countries in such periods is essential. One should bear in mind, for example, how little one would know of the astounding detail and power of the English taxation system were it not for the survival of Domesday Book and for just the one annal in the D version of the *Chronicle*. In Irish lands it is only *Senchus Fir nAlban* which raises the possibility of systems for military service methodically assessed and recorded. One may wonder how far taxation systems in Ireland were more elaborate than the bulk of our sources allow us to see. At least it is plain that the Irish polity was very different from the English: England was united as Ireland was not.

Historians do, however, see Ireland as progressing towards something like greater unity in the eleventh century, by which time circumstances had changed greatly from those in which the Uí Néill families and the Éogonacht had extensive and long-lasting power. The consensus between the Ui Néill branches had collapsed and their power had diminished. Similarly with the Éogonacht, they were largely displaced in the tenth century by a previously minor dynasty. Its most famous member, Brián Bóruma (Brian Boru), succeeded in 976, made himself the most powerful ruler in Ireland and was claimed to be 'emperor' of the Irish. He was killed in a final, and famous, battle, Clontarf, in 1014. His opponents included Sihtric Silkbeard, the Norse ruler of Dublin. So the battle came in the twelfth century to be presented as an epic conflict between Irish and Norse. This was a fairly early effort in the long task of fictionalising the history of Ireland. In reality the conflict was between, on the one side, Brian aided by the Limerick Vikings and, on the other, Sihtric, allied to Irish Leinster forces. Brian was killed at Clontarf, but Sihtric wisely confined himself to observation from the walls of Dublin. It is worthwhile noting that he was a Christian and later a pilgrim to Jerusalem. The pattern of warfare in Ireland in the eleventh century is thought to have been changing; in particular the campaigns became more extensive and more cavalry was used. Some historians have seen in this a movement towards unity and order, one which tended towards a more 'modern' Ireland. Others find such argument forced or anachronistic.

Wales, c. 900 – c. 1066

Wales, like Ireland, was an area in which there was a small number of relatively important rulers. These had fluctuating relations with one another and with lesser authorities. The evidence for what went on is poor. Important here is the extent to which English rulers claimed (and to an extent enjoyed) power in Wales. From time to time a Welsh prince would establish widespread authority in Wales; but his gains would normally be dispersed on his death. Conspicuous among such princes was Gruffudd ap Llywelyn, who from 1039 until his death in 1063 was prince of Gwynedd and Powys, to which he added Deheubarth in 1055. Some of his relations with England were indeed friendly: notably he married the daughter of Ælfgar, earl of Mercia, but such cordiality was anything but continuous. Gruffudd had not only imposed unity on Wales by force but had led successful raids into England especially in the years 1052 and 1053. He was ultimately defeated by Harold and in 1063 was killed – by his own men. His power is demonstrated by the force needed to defeat him: the final campaigns against him required the forces both of Harold, earl of Wessex, and of Tostig, the earl of Northumbria. After his death two trophies were sent to Edward the Confessor: one was Llywelyn's head, the other the prow of his ship, a reminder of how far he was involved in the violent web of Irish Sea politics.

From the late twelfth century we have written laws from Wales. They are attributed to Hywel Dda ('the Good') who gained extensive authority in Wales between his accession to Dyfed, c. 904, and his death in 949 or 950, and they may indeed owe something to him. They show a sophisticated system of law, partly the responsibility of a professional (and probably hereditary) legal class, and with some Anglo-Saxon influence. The fairly orderly subdivision of Welsh principalities into cantreds and commotes is by this time apparent though the age of this system is unknown. However divided Wales was, there is no doubt of the unity of Welsh consciousness: Welsh people had not only a single language, but a common culture and a sense of a common history.

Granted the plain power of the Anglo-Saxon kings, why did the conquest of Wales from England not get seriously under way until *after* the Conquest, apart from fluctuating English gains along the north coast and one significant gain on the central border? Geography makes it fairly easy to understand why Scotland and Ireland were exceedingly hard to swallow. But mountainous though much of Wales is, it is not so easy to see why its final conquest took until the time of Edward I. Part of the explanation must lie in the long history and experience of the Welsh as an armed and, not least, a divided people. By contrast it was the *unity* of England which helped William of Normandy to conquer so much, so quickly, in 1066. It could be that the very success of Gruffudd ap Llywelyn in establishing a degree of unified power in Wales helped to pave the way for Norman success. But in the last resort the Norman expansion of conquest in Wales must tell one at least as much about the Normans as about the Welsh.

The Creation of a Scottish Kingdom

As Patrick Wormald put it, 'We do not know how the kingdom of the Scots came into being and we never shall.' Until the ninth century the geographical and political structures of Scotland more or less coincided. In the south-east what became Lothian was part of Anglian Northumbria; Strathclyde in the south-west was British; the larger part of the lands north of the Forth was Pictish; the Western Isles and part of the adjacent mainland formed the Irish ('Scottish') domain of Dál Ríata. Well before 1100 one royal house had authority over all these lands, except the western and northern isles and parts of the far northern mainland, which were under Scandinavian control. The crucial episode in the construction of a unified kingdom of Scotland ('Alba') came in the years c. 843–c. 850 when a ruler of Dál Ríata, Kenneth MacAlpine, acquired the realm of the Picts also. Most of what is known about this depends on scrappy annals. It seems that the ruling families of the Picts and of the Dalriadic Scots were much involved together, their relationships being complicated by matrilineal succession among the Picts. A consequence of such relationships was the rule or overlordship of Pictish rulers in Dál Ríata in the early ninth century. How this came to be succeeded by the events of the 840s is unclear. How could it be otherwise? No historians, no matter how learned, thoughtful or contentious can conjure certain knowledge from a few hundred words about what happened in several decades to many thousands of people living in very wide areas. Maybe the rulers of Dál Ríata were driven to move their power eastwards and bring rulers of Irish origin to wide power, because they were under Scandinavian pressure in the west; or maybe they made use of Scandinavian forces. Some Scottish historians have seen a merger of 'Scots' and Picts as almost natural and inevitable, a natural reaction to external pressures. However, violence and a serious transfer of power may well have been involved. A likely indication of this is the disappearance of the Pictish language. That language seems to have been P-Celtic, i.e. of the same family as Welsh, long distant from Irish (Gaelic) which is Q-Celtic. Traces of Pictish remain only in place names and in a handful of inscriptions.

In ways of long-lasting importance the most significant component in the Scottish state was English: the south-eastern area known as Lothian. It is impossible to be certain when Lothian was acquired. A fair guess is that it was in the earlier tenth century at some time when the Scandinavian regime based on York limited the northern reach of English kings. But there were relevant dealings between Scottish and English rulers in the later tenth and earlier eleventh centuries; a main transfer of authority may have taken place then and the whole story must have been more complicated than we can tell. The picture in regard to the British lands in the south-west, Strathclyde, is similar: Strathclyde seems to have had rulers which came under the authority of the kings of Scotland and who ceased to be kings in their own right in the earlier eleventh century.

Much about the Scottish regime is obscure, not least in regard to law and government. An arresting element is that of Scottish 'shires' and 'thanes'. It is strongly arguable, principally from charters of the twelfth century or later, that in central eastern Scotland there were at least some seventy units of authority sometimes called 'shires'. Each of these was in the charge of a 'thane'. Shires related to royal rights and dues which it was the duty of a thane to collect and guard. Thanages became hereditary but they do not appear always to have been so. What was the origin of this plainly important institution? The terms 'shire' and 'thane' are of English origin, but this could have been a matter of nomenclature rather than of substance. The 'shires' seem to be of Celtic origin, resemble the 'small shires' (sub-units, to be distinguished from the major shires otherwise called counties) of areas of northern England, and can plausibly be argued to fall into a pattern extending over much of Britain and to be of Celtic origin. It is important that 'shires' and 'thanes' do not appear in former Dál Ríata, and that they cluster in the eastern areas likely to have been at the heart of Pictish power. Perhaps they reflect English influence in the eighth century and should be associated with the one sentence in Bede which suggested organised Pictish power.

The Aberlemno Stone, one of the finest and most interesting Dark Age sculptures, is Pictish. This great slab (7 ft 6 in high) is probably eighth century and may depict a battle scene. It has been suggested that it concludes by showing the death of Ecgfrith, king of Northumbria, in battle with the Picts in 685 (bottom right). In any case, to see those caparisoned horsemen riding by gives a likely and rare glimpse of past reality. The device in the top right-hand corner is one of the 'symbols' which appear on many Pictish stones and are plausibly argued to have genealogical significance. The protagonists wear helmets resembling the Coppergate helmet (p.59).

The Political Culture of the Archipelago,
c. 600–c. 1066: an Overview

In the seventh century one can seem to see elements of uniformity in the political culture of the whole archipelago: rather small units of authority, overlordships of varying authority, a political economy in which predatory raids played a large part, administrative systems, which, though they may sometimes have been effective, are exceedingly hard to explore. By the eleventh century the position was very different: above all in the strong contrast presented by England as opposed to Ireland, Scotland and Wales. Domesday Book shows us an English state remarkably well, indeed tightly, organised and centralised to an extent which helped a conqueror in 1066 to establish full power once he had killed his royal rival. What theories may help to explain English divergence in organisation and power?

Something may have been owed to Carolingian influence. Much in the organisation of tenth-century England considerably resembles that of the Carolingian empire in the ninth – English shires recall Carolingian counties; hundreds as sub-divisions had the same name (one new to England) as the corresponding sub-divisions across the Channel; and the peace oath taken by all freemen in England had its close Carolingian counterpart. The mechanisms which possibly expressed or determined such connection are, however, exceedingly hard to trace.

A major, even dominant, factor in the exceptional position of England was economic, for it was the accumulated wealth of England which gave it the capacity to sustain large-scale authority. To put the matter crudely, there was enough surplus product to sustain powerful kings, a heavyweight high aristocracy and a fabulously wealthy Church. England was the only part of the archipelago in which coin was struck (other than to a certain extent and from c. 1000 in Dublin). The abundant and controlled coinage of late Anglo-Saxon England was part of, and instrumental in, a developed economy. Kings of England had a taxation system fit to exploit such an economy, and royal power and economic prosperity helped one another. When Cnut circulated his letter in 1027 describing his Roman visit to attend the coronation of Conrad II he emphasised what he had done to prevent his subjects' being harassed by unjust tolls. Royal organisation of England thus integrated the economic and the political. The creation of most of the midland shires involved division on a basis of relationship to the crucial inland waterways such as to grant major economic privileges to the shire towns at key nodes of the major river systems. Generally important was the maintenance of peace, shown by the relative absence of civil war, and of order, signalled by the harsh and detailed provisions of the laws. In other parts of Europe, not least in much of France, a higher level of predation probably went with a lower level of prosperity. The enormous number of plough oxen revealed in Domesday is an index of peace and order, for such beasts are especially vulnerable to predation.

In societies ruled by dynasties successions are of dominating importance. If one asks 'Why was there a Norman Conquest of England?' the first answer has to be 'Because Edward the Confessor died childless and without leaving an heir of full age'. Those who believe that the determinants of history are economic and social tides such that particular events are no more than products or symptoms, may find such an answer crude. But it must be the first answer to the question. In worlds ruled by dynastic chance not only the chances of individual successions, but the nature of succession systems are important indeed. A major, and it may be a determinative, difference between England and the other polities in the archipelago was the system of succession which came to prevail in the royal house of Wessex. Until the accession of Æthelwulf in 839 the West Saxon succession was very open. Kings such as Æthelwulf's father Ecgberht succeeded predecessors to whom they were at best very distantly related. From 839 until 1066, except in circumstances of foreign conquest, succession always went to a son, a brother or a half-brother of a previous king. The situation was different in Wales and Ireland, where there was a tendency to make separate provision for cadet lines, sometimes using conquered lands. The systems were 'segmental', that is to say with a number of branches of major families in union or competition and such that, while a particular man or line could become temporarily dominant, this dominance was not durable.

Another key to England's great success may well have been conquest, above all conquest of the Danelaw. Successful regimes depended substantially on the fruits of plunder. If one asks why the Carolingian regime could afford so expensive a religious/cultural establishment, part of the answer must be the enjoyment of the fruits of conquest in several directions. Why were the rulers of tenth-century Germany more powerful than those of France? Because they had remuneratively exploitable frontiers to their east and south. Such explanations must be incomplete, but it must be roughly true that England's remarkable development was partly fuelled by the conquests made by the kings of the house of Wessex. In an earlier period a great nobleman might take to ravaging for his own hand. Witness what his biographer says about the (future) St Guthlac (d. 714). As he reached manhood he 'took up arms . . . devastated the towns and residences of his foes . . . with fire and sword and gathering together companions . . . amassed immense booty'. Rulers such as Edward the Elder and Athelstan harnessed such noble instincts and ambitions in the royal, one might even say in the national, interest.

Something which distinguishes England in a most definite way from the rest of the archipelago was the nature and position of the Church there. Well before the Conquest it fitted naturally into the normal pattern of the western Church as a whole, while the ecclesiastical establishments of Scotland, Ireland and Wales were very different. Three prominent features of the English Church were its great wealth, its extensive organisation and its close links with the crown. By the time of Domesday Book roughly a quarter of the landed wealth recorded and valued there belonged to the Church. The holders of such wealth were more often than not appointed by the king and close to royal power. Naturally bishops and abbots could become involved in the factious tensions which followed such succession disputes as those that arose on the death of Edgar. But the close relationship of kings to bishops and abbots is plain. There could be limits to royal power to appoint: Edward the Confessor caused a near revolt when he sought to make a Norman archbishop of Canterbury, but he had previously managed to make him bishop of London and was able to appoint men of Lotharingian origin or upbringing to important sees. Ecclesiastical and secular government was integrated in more ways than one. Kings were solemnly anointed, probably at latest from the time of Edward the Elder. Shire court and bishop's court met jointly. At the latest from the early tenth century ordeal played a major part in judicial procedure. Royal laws could have a strongly homiletic nature, emphasising unity between divine and royal purpose. The organisation of the Domesday enquiry tells something of the administrative role of the increasing number of parish priests. We are told that witnesses from each village were to be four villagers, the reeve and the parish priest. To the extent that Church government and royal government were integrated parish priests could be part of a web of control.

When all is said and done one is still left to wonder how much of the underlying basis of state power in England was very old, even immemorial. Offa's Dyke stands boldly to warn one how much early Anglo-Saxon government could achieve. Hidage assessment was probably involved here, and it remains a crucial and unanswered question as to where the origins of the hidage system lay. In pre-Roman Britain? In Roman Britain? In non-Roman Germany? In some widely diffused Indo-European grammar of administration which could have had much the same rules in many areas? Such questions remind us of how far there may have been underlying, residual, and/or hidden systems of government or exploitation in parts of the archipelago other than England. Be that as it may, the development of England was altogether extraordinary. In an obituary poem for Edward the Confessor an annalist wrote: 'Danes had rule over *this noble realm of England* for twenty-eight years' (my italics). Not for nothing was this the rhetoric of the nation-state. In 1066 William of Normandy conquered a nation-state: maybe the first one.

4. Some Counter-Factuals

Agricola nearly conquered all Britain, and Ireland seemed almost within his grasp. Yet what if he had conquered the whole British Isles? If he had secured the whole archipelago, maybe the western empire centuries later would not have fallen. Along the threatened imperial frontiers, though attack may have been the best form of defence, it still often had a serious defect: successful attack could widen the area needing defence. But the British Isles were at the very edge of the inhabited world. Had they been fully conquered, most of the enormous burden of defending Britain, which rested on the empire for over three hundred years, would have disappeared, freeing resources not only to stave off North Sea raiders, but to make major contributions to imperial defence elsewhere.

Complete Roman conquest of Britain and Ireland would have ensured that the dominant language or languages of the archipelago would have become Romance ones. The consequences for the cultural history of the British Isles would have been tremendous. We have enough evidence for active intellectual life in immediately post-Roman Britain to suggest how much more there might have been had Britain remained Roman. But there would have been great losses, above all in Ireland. No Dark Age writings are of such unique importance as those in Old Irish. Though none (in their existing form) antedate the seventh century, some, especially the laws, take one into the sophistications and regularities of a prehistoric world so old that it has links to very early India. By contrast, virtually nothing remains in writing from Gaul before the Romans conquered it but one (very large) metal plate, with calendrical details.

Something else which survived in the British Isles, thanks both to Celtic survival and to Germanic invasion, was a system, a set of traditions and assumptions for the allocation of power, which contrasted with those of Rome. Roman governance depended on clearly (and quasi-permanently) defined areas and levels of authority. By contrast in the Germanic or Celtic worlds there prevailed systems which can too easily be dismissed as expressive of competitive chaos, but which had their capacity for creating and defining peace and order. Thus particular peoples or associations could have complicated constitutions. Systems had been developed for expressing and institutionalising political subordination of varying and complex kinds combining elements of lordship, confederacy or family arrangement. One can imagine such 'prehistoric' systematisations and systems of 'Roman' type in interaction or even conflict when one considers, for example, the debate over the implications of the 'Tribal Hidage'. Or similarly one can interpret the reintroduction of coin and of permanent and plain geographically defined divisions of authority as 're-Romanisation'.

Thus, if the Romans had conquered the whole archipelago their authority might never have vanished in the way that it did when they had faced the problems intrinsic to holding only the southern two-thirds of Britain. It might even have been that they would have retained power in the western empire as they did in the eastern. More probably the development of Britain and Ireland would have resembled that of Gaul and Spain. Beyond doubt their language, literature and social fabric would have been very different from what they actually became in the long centuries of the disunited archipelago, in which no later ruler had effective authority over the whole until the later seventeenth century – and even this unity did not last far into the twentieth century.

More than nine hundred years after the death of Agricola a series of events in England provokes questions and doubts about the chances and organisation of power; and about the possible delusions of historians. The key question is 'What would have happened if King Alfred had been succeeded not by his son Edward, as he was, but by his nephew Æthelwald, the son of his elder brother Æthelberht?'

Æthelwald certainly made a bid for the crown in 899. A surprising story can be pieced together from limited annals. He seized an important royal centre, Wimborne, and, when Edward moved against him, slipped to Northumbria where (and this is a big surprise) the Danes made him king. We are then told that he came by sea to Essex (though not whence he came) and that he was recognised as king there. He moved into Mercia, later raiding into Wessex. Edward led an army against him and in a brutally hard-fought battle Æthelwald was defeated and killed. It is an odd tale, and a revealing one.

Historians term Æthelwald's move 'rebellion', though he may have had as good a claim, or a better one, than did his cousin Edward. However, Alfred's courtier historians emphasise (plausibly) that there had been efforts as early as Æthelwulf's reign to attach special significance to Alfred's royal claim (and even to that of his line) as against those of his three brothers who had reigned before him. We can imagine (though hardly discern) the chances and manoeuvres which led to the prevalence of a linear rather than a partible or segmental succession system in Wessex.

That Æthelwald had Danish support should surprise only those who are all too happy to see Alfred, as he probably wished himself to be seen, as the leader of something like a Christian crusade. There are, however, several indications of friendly relations between Danes and English. Alfred himself was not only an enemy of the Danes but something like an ally when Guthrum (newly baptised) and he carved up Mercia between them. Alfred had Scandinavians at his court, not least Othere, whose remarkable account of Scandinavia was added to the Alfredian translation of Orosius. Alfred even had Scandinavians among the monks of his royal monastery of Athelney: Asser says that these included *pagani*. He cannot mean pagans and so he must mean Scandinavians. Had Æthelwald become king historians would probably not have written about the unification of England in terms of 'reconquest' by West Saxon kings and in particular by Edward the Elder. 'Reconquest' is indeed an odd term, for none of the lands in question, except Essex, had previously been ruled by any member of the West Saxon dynasty.

One account of Æthelwald's lost battle says that among those who perished with him was Brihtsige, son of Beornoth 'the Atheling' (i.e. prince): it is likely that this man came of a line with a claim to the Mercian throne, if so one which had been squeezed out of its claims or rights by Alfred and his deal with Guthrum. One can readily imagine how, had Æthelwald won the great battle, as he might have done, there might have been a different allocation of power in England, in which Danish and Mercian claims were recognised under a West Saxon regime which had more of suzerainty than sovereignty about it.

Finally, perhaps the most compelling counter-factual of all: what if King Harold II of England had won the Battle of Hastings in 1066? Indeed, he might well have won the battle, the long duration of which suggests how near he must have come to victory. In this period battles normally lasted for only a few hours, but Hastings lasted from just after dawn until dusk. Harold would have been very powerful, and the foundations of his power would have been partly the same as those which, in the real event, underlay the power of William. First, a strong and largely uniform administration framework. Second, a fiscal system apt to exploit a wealthy country. Third, a hierarchy of courts and assemblies combining effective social control with significant participation of the not very rich. Fourth, a powerful landed basis which had been strengthened by the addition of the royal demesne of the wide lands of the house of Godwin. Had Harold defeated William at Hastings historians would have made much of this last factor.

Harold's aristocracy would have been very different from William's. Domesday witnesses that the Norman Conquest displaced a whole dominant class to an extent unparalleled elsewhere in British history. True, till 1075, Edward the Confessor's widow Edith and Earl Waltheof survived in wealth and honour. Otherwise, however, the high Anglo-Saxon aristocracy was displaced and so too were many landed families lower down the scale. William not only created a new aristocracy, he created a pattern of landed power. Though his friends and relations were made very rich, he did not have families so overwhelmingly rich as those of Godwin and Leofric had been. The pyramid of power descended rather more gently than it had in late Saxon times.

In one way William's high nobility resembled Edward's: the lands of most of them were very scattered. But in another way hypothetically long-reigning Harold could have been much better off than real William. His nobility might well have been less rebellious. The late Anglo-Saxon kings had, compared to their continental contemporaries, few noble revolts to face. William and his successor faced a number of such, only to a limited extent due to Anglo-Saxon resentment and dissidence. (Though one must remember that Harold's being the first non-Scandinavian king without a drop of royal blood would not have been an asset.) Harold's English aristocracy would have been un-Norman in two other ways. One is obvious: some of them would have been interested in English, as opposed to French literature. The Conquest led interest in such literature to dwindle and it remained limited for nearly three hundred years. Second, the Norman aristocracy were not only more rebellious than the Anglo-Saxons they had displaced. They were also more expansively greedy, especially in Wales. It is a reasonable supposition that had Harold survived Hastings far more of Wales would, by 1100, have remained under Welsh rule than proved the case. In actual fact Norman lords went far in the advances which ended in the total subjugation of Wales by Edward I. Several powerful drives towards the unity of the archipelago followed 1066: mounting conquest in Wales; peaceful penetration in Scotland; and, from 1169, penetration and conquest in Ireland.

The secular architecture of late Anglo-Saxon England was that of a land ruled largely by consent. William I's England was dominated by force. So, if Harold had survived, his realm would have differed from William's in this crucial respect. Eleventh-century Anglo-Saxon aristocrats did not live in strongly fortified dwellings, but Normans did, in castles of earth and timber and, increasingly, of stone. Very significantly, Anglo-Saxon towns were surrounded by earthworks or walls, designed to protect the whole place. By contrast, important towns after the Conquest were commanded by a royal castle, built at least as much to subjugate as to protect. The visitor to England during Harold II's hypothetical long reign would have seen far fewer massive signs of domination expressed in hundreds of thousands of tons of earth and stone than actually came to be there.

Nor would he have seen so many astounding and vast expressions of ecclesiastical triumphalism. A majority of the biggest churches built in Europe between 1050 and 1150 were those of Anglo-Norman England. Edward the Confessor had indeed built one big new church, Westminster Abbey, in a fashionable 'Romanesque' style, but Westminster was the only major Anglo-Saxon example of this. The Anglo-Saxons were much more attached to old buildings than were the Normans. Had Harold survived not only the buildings but also the organisation of his Church would not have been by any means so searchingly reformed. William I had strong religious principles, partly exemplified in his being an almost uniquely faithful royal husband, but expressed, via his Italian archbishop Lanfranc, in extensive reform of the administration and law of the Church. Harold would have reformed less and exploited more.

PART II

CONQUESTS, CATASTROPHE AND RECOVERY, 1066–*c.* 1485

John Gillingham

Introduction

During these centuries Britain and Ireland were transformed. Perhaps most striking is the issue of individual liberty: in the eleventh century slavery was still an important source of labour; by the end of the period slavery no longer existed, and nor did its lesser cousin, serfdom. Men and women – especially the latter, the chief victims of the slave trade – were freer than they had ever been before.

Economically, there were similarly radical changes. Although looking back from the twenty-first century it may seem to us that Britain and Ireland remained overwhelmingly rural economies, this is not how it seemed to those who participated in a process of urbanisation and commercialisation which saw the foundation of more than *six hundred* new towns.

A series of invasions shaped the languages and political geography of present-day Britain and Ireland: the Norman invasion of England in 1066, the English invasions of Ireland, Wales and Scotland; the Scottish invasions of the Highlands and islands – violent events which remain more firmly in the memories of those whose lands were invaded than in the memories of the invaders' descendants. In English history 1066 – from the point of view of the English ruling elite its worst crisis so far – is the one universally remembered date, so well-known that banks advise customers not to choose it as their PIN number.

More catastrophic than 1066 was the Black Death of 1348–9, the greatest disaster to strike the people of Europe in recorded history. But despite that massive mortality, the institutional, technological and cultural infrastructure built up in the previous centuries did not wither, as such things had after the withdrawal of the Roman government from Britain. The achievements of the pre-Black Death centuries were retained by those who survived. Indeed, many of the houses, castles and churches which they built can still been seen in the landscape today.

1. Material Cultures

When Duke William of Normandy invaded England in 1066, he intended to conquer a kingdom whose wealth was the envy of its neighbours. According to the duke's chaplain, William of Poitiers, England was much richer than Gaul: 'Wonderfully rich in grain, it should be called the granary of Ceres; fabulously rich in gold, a veritable treasury of Arabia.' If the wealth of eleventh-century England fascinated ambitious contemporaries, so too a record of that wealth, in the shape of Domesday Book, has mesmerised modern historians. No other part of early medieval Europe lies as seductively open as that part of the kingdom covered by Domesday Book, the extraordinary document compiled in 1086 on William the Conqueror's orders. It stands as a monumental signpost at the beginning of a series of documents that tell us much about English society, economy and government. But for Ireland, Scotland and Wales there is neither a Domesday Book nor anything to match the subsequent richness of English administrative records. The skewed survival of evidence makes it hard to know whether historians are exaggerating or minimising when we discuss the differences between England and the other three.

Crucially important differences there were. South and east Britain has always enjoyed the advantage of being nearer the Continent, facilitating easier trade with the varied economies across the Channel and North Sea. When the Italian Aeneas Sylvius Piccolomini reached Newcastle on his way south from Scotland in 1435, he felt he was once again in a civilised country. Geology and climate meant that England contained a much higher proportion of good fertile soil, as opposed to mountain, bog and moor, than Ireland, Wales and Scotland. Almost everywhere in Britain a mixed farming regime prevailed, but in the south and east there was always a higher proportion of the land surface under the plough. A wider variety of crops, including wheat and legumes, could be grown successfully, and summer temperatures allowed vineyards to be planted as far north as Ely. In the north and west there was greater dependence on oats, barley and animal husbandry. Thus the genuine contrasts exaggerated by Gerald de Barri, the earliest author (c. 1190) to describe the economy and society of Ireland and Wales. Ireland, he wrote, was 'more grass than grain' and 'its pastures more productive than its ploughed fields'. As for the Welsh, they 'are used to plenty of meat but not so much to bread . . . They live off their herds, oats, milk, cheese and butter.' In the north and west, cattle, providing milk, meat, traction and leather, 'the plastic of the middle ages', were far more important than sheep. Where there was plenty of pasture, herdsmen practised transhumance, moving to and fro with their livestock and their families between winter and summer pastures. The Irish word for farmer, *bóaire*, means 'lord of cows'. Taken together with archaeological evidence of anything between two-thirds and 90 per cent of animal bones from settlement sites being of cattle (and sheep rarely more than 20 per cent), this implies an economy of dairying, and the regular slaughter of male calves. In south and east Britain sheep were of vital economic importance, and known to be so. 'The wool of England,' asserted a petition sent to Edward I in 1297, 'is worth half the value of all the land.'

But the developments of this period suggest a division not into two economic zones (Highland and Lowland) but into three. The first zone lay in the rich kingdom that William conquered. Domesday Book records the existence of 112 towns and another thirty-nine places where markets were held. In about forty of those towns coins were minted. All the towns and markets lay south and east of a line drawn from York to Exeter via Chester and Gloucester. In Britain north and west of this line only Durham could be considered a town – defined here as a permanent concentration of at least a few hundred people, some following a variety of non-agricultural occupations. There were also a very few Viking ('Ostman') port towns on river estuaries in Ireland: Waterford, Wexford, Cork, Limerick and, above all, Dublin, where indeed coins had been minted c. 1000. But when William conquered England, it looks as though there were no towns in Scotland and Wales, and no coins minted there either.

In the twelfth and thirteenth centuries, however, a tide of economic and commercial expansion swept into northern England, Wales,

Ireland and Scotland. The kings of Scots began to mint their own coin in 1136. As a result of the English conquest of Wales and invasion of Ireland, coin issued by the kings of England circulated in both those countries. By 1300 there were about sixty burghs in southern and eastern Scotland, more than fifty towns in southern and eastern Ireland, and perhaps as many in Wales. This was zone two. But in zone three it looks as though material conditions remained much as in the Iron Age. There were no towns and markets in parts of the far west of Ireland or in late medieval Scotland north and west of a line from Cromarty to Kintyre.

Since most of Part One is about developments in zones one and two, it is worth staying for a moment in the third zone. The *Orkneyinga Saga* (c. 1200) describes the hands-on economy of one of the lords of Orkney, Svein Asleifarson of Gairsay:

> In the spring he was busy, with a great deal of seed to sow which he saw to carefully himself. That done, he would go off plundering in the Hebrides and Ireland on what he called the 'spring trip'. He returned home just after midsummer, staying until the fields had been reaped and the grain safely in. Then he was away raiding again until after the end of the first month of winter. This he called the 'autumn trip'.

The fourteenth-century Scottish historian John Fordun contrasted the inhabitants of the second and third zones:

> The people of the lowlands speak English; those who live in the high-lands and outer isles speak Gaelic. The lowlanders are docile, civilized, trustworthy, tolerant and polite, dress decently and are affable and pious. The islanders and highlanders are a wild untamed people, uncouth and turbulent, given to plunder and the easy life, clever and quick to learn, handsome in appearance but slovenly in dress.

Similar things were written about Gaelic societies in Ireland. When Raymond of Perelhos (in the Pyrenees) went on a pilgrimage to St Patrick's Purgatory (in Donegal) in 1397, he saw a warrior society of impoverished herders, living in close contact with their cattle and horses. They didn't eat bread or drink wine; instead they ate beef and, while the lords drank milk or beef tea, the common people made do with water. All wore a tunic down to the knee, but no shoes, no hose, no breeches. In consequence both men and women showed 'all they had and with as little shame as showing their faces'. But, Raymond discovered, their king considered that Irish customs were the best in the world. In their society cattle raiding was as honourable a pursuit as duelling would be in eighteenth-century England.

Domesday England

Early in 1086 William launched an enquiry. In the words of the *Anglo-Saxon Chronicle*:

> he sent his men over all England into every shire and had them find out how many hundred hides there were in the shire and what land and cattle the king himself had in the country, and what dues he ought to have annually from the shire. Also he had a record made of how much every landholder in England had in land and cattle and how much money it was worth.

The main outcome of that enquiry was Domesday Book. It names and gives details about over 13,400 places in England. By the twelfth century the book was already part of the mythical history of England, called by a name – 'Domesday' – that linked it with the Last Judgement.

Historians have often been tempted to use Domesday Book as though it were an economic survey of England. But this it was not. The king wanted to know how rich the lords of manors were. He was interested in the rents, whether in money or services, that tenants paid to lords of manors, but not in the other resources of those tenants. Hence we know that four thousand herrings were owed to William de Warenne from the Sussex fishing village of Brighton, but we do not know the size of the catch. The only livestock belonging to the tenants that interested him were those draught animals that performed ploughing services on the lords' demesnes (their home farms). Domesday records altogether 81,184 plough teams (at eight oxen per team), but takes no account of the plough animals that belonged to tenants who owed only a money rent. Domesday tells us how many hides there were in each manor, but this represents the size of its tax liability, not its size on the ground (though the two were often in some way related). Statistics derived from Domesday Book and its satellites have to be used with extreme caution. Adding up all Domesday's valuations of manors, we reach a total of about £73,000, but this represents the annual income of lords, not an estimate of GNP. An entirely unquantifiable part of economic output went unrecorded. Nonetheless, these records provide us with remarkable glimpses of the economy and administration of eleventh-century England, both 'now' (i.e. 1086) and on the eve of the Conquest. In Oakley (Buckinghamshire), for example, 'Ælfgyth the maid had half a hide which Godric the sheriff granted her as long as he was sheriff, on condition of her teaching his daughter gold embroidery work. This land Robert FitzWalter holds now.'

Ælfgyth's special skill made her an unusual tenant. Domesday Book shows that over 70 per cent of rural tenants were either farmers (*villani* in Domesday Latin), typically holding 15–40 acres each, or cottagers, often with five acres or less. Although the former should have been able to support themselves and their families from the produce of their farms, the latter would certainly have depended upon wages to supplement what they grew themselves. Several early twelfth-century estate surveys indicate that *villani* owed heavy labour services, sometimes as much as three days' work a week on their lord's farm. To meet this obligation they almost certainly employed slaves or waged servants, some doubtless being cottagers.

Slaves and Serfs, 1066–c. 1350

In the eleventh century slavery was still basic to British and Irish society. About 10 per cent of the recorded Domesday population were slaves. Thousands of entries contain items like this one for Cuxham (Oxfordshire): 'In demesne there are 2 ploughs and 4 slaves.' At times of famine, the threat of starvation led to parents selling children into slavery. Slaves were exported to Ireland from Bristol and Chester. Domesday records the toll to be paid for each slave sold at Lewes (Sussex) market. A major source of slaves was war – 'Five times', wrote Symeon of Durham, 'King Malcolm (III) of Scotland raided Northumbria, devastating the land and carrying the wretched inhabitants off into slavery.' Decades later it was still being alleged that every Scottish household had its English slave.

But in northern France slavery was a thing of the past by 1066. In consequence the Norman Conquest was the first conquest in the history of Britain and Ireland that did not result in more slaves being taken to market. King and archbishop forbade the export of slaves. Although many French lords retained the slave workforces they took over from their English predecessors, it is clear from Domesday Book that slave numbers at this time were declining. The council of Westminster in 1102 was the last Church council in England to prohibit the slave trade. Slave replacement costs meant that in a time of rising population and increasing labour supply, lords found other forms of labour more attractive. Some owners freed slaves and even provided them with a few acres of land. Writing in the 1130s Lawrence of Durham observed:

> After England was ruled by Norman lords then the English no longer suffered from outsiders that which they had suffered at their own hands. In this respect they found that foreigners treated them better than they had themselves. Meanwhile in Scotland and Ireland, where the natives are still the lords, the old custom of slavery continues, though on a lesser scale now.

Twenty years later John of Salisbury criticised the Welsh for carrying on 'a regular slave trade'; Lawrence could have added Wales to the list of lands where 'the old custom' still prevailed.

For the first time in their history the English, now that they no longer kept slaves themselves, were struck by the barbarity of the raid for human cattle. Consider this contemporary description of a Scottish raid in 1138:

> They slaughtered the sick on their beds, women who were pregnant or in labour, babies in their cradles or at their mothers' breasts. They slaughtered the disabled, worn-out old men and feeble old women. They killed husbands in front of their wives. Then they carried off their plunder and their captives, women and girls, stripped, roped together, using their spears as goads to drive them on. Their fate was either to be kept as slaves or sold to other barbarians in exchange for cattle.

But in Scotland also modernising rulers came under pressure to limit slavery. In 1138 a papal legate at the court of King David I of Scotland made the Scots promise to release the slaves taken during their recent raids into northern England. By c. 1200 slavery was a thing of the past throughout Britain and Ireland.

The great variety of terms of tenure meant there were everywhere and always many degrees of economic freedom and unfreedom. Tenant farmers who owed heavy labour services had only limited free time to work in their own fields. Tenants who could give, sell or leave their lands without their lord's licence were privileged; most were tied to their holdings, entitled to leave only with permission – and payment of a fee (chevage). The English cottagers and farmers of Domesday Book were presumably less free than that 14 per cent of the recorded population who were called precisely 'free men'.

In England c. 1200 judges stepped in to create a new legal distinction between free and unfree. It had long been part of the morality of kingship that kings should protect freemen from oppression, but the massive expansion of royal justice resulting from the development of the common law opened the door to the possibility that the 'lord king' would constantly be called upon to intervene on the side of rustics against lords. To prevent this happening, the judges formulated rules whose effect was to disbar the more disadvantaged tenants from access to the public courts. From now on those who had the right to have their property disputes heard in the royal courts were regarded as being free; those who did not were 'servile' and were called serfs or *villani* (now better translated as 'villeins' rather than farmers). Their disputes, whether with each other or with their landlords, could only be heard in their landlord's court, the court of the manor. Technically not only the villein's land but also his house and chattels belonged to his lord; in practice the lord's need for services meant that manorial custom allowed, at a price, both family succession to a tenancy and inheritance of the chattels. But the children of serfs were born into serfdom and all serfs, even the wealthier, knew that they enjoyed less freedom than many of their neighbours. The stigma was highlighted by having to pay manorial fines such as 'merchet' when a daughter married, and 'leyrwite' if she had sex before marriage. Similarly harsh terms applied in Scotland to tenants known as 'bondsmen', as well as to those known in Welsh as *taeog* and in Irish as *betaghs*. Yet however servile the conditions of their lives, at least they were not slaves. Families could no longer be broken up, individuals taken to market and sold. Nor was it lawful for their landlord to kill or wound them – in contrast to the view of the author of the early twelfth-century *Leges Henrici Primi*, who had held that a master who killed his slave was guilty of a sin, but not a crime.

Population Growth

We can only guess at the population of Britain and Ireland in this period. Historians have often turned to Domesday Book in the hope of estimating the population of England in 1086. It records the existence of 283,240 people, and it is generally assumed that almost all of them, with the exception of many of the slaves, were heads of household. Depending on whether we opt for an average household size of three and a half or – as most demographers prefer – of five, we might be tempted to think of a population in the order of one to one and a half million. Unfortunately the fact that in 1086 the king and his advisers were not interested in people whose labours did not directly contribute to the incomes of manorial lords (manorial sub-tenants, for example) means that there may have been more households than 283,240, but we have no way of estimating how many more. Thus Domesday Book can yield a population minimum of a million or so, but the actual number could have been two or three times that.

It is possible to make an estimate of the size of the English population three centuries later on the basis of the poll tax of 1377. It was levied on all lay people over fourteen, except for the very poor and the exempt counties of Cheshire and Durham. The returns reveal a total recorded taxed population of 1,355,201. Depending on assumptions about the age structure of the population and allowances for those exempted, we can estimate a population of between two and three million. What is certain is that the population of the whole of Britain and Ireland had been much bigger in 1300 than it was in 1377. The cumulative effect of the plagues of 1348–9, 1361–2 and 1368–9 may well have reduced their populations by over a half. Estimates for England in 1300 thus range from four to 6.5 million; what the populations of Ireland, Scotland and Wales were at this date is anybody's guess. If the relative sizes were of the same order as in 1660 – a big if – then these combined might have been three to four million *c.* 1300.

These estimates, plus evidence for particular English manors, do at least make it clear that population grew during the twelfth and thirteenth centuries. There were, of course, setbacks – in 1258, as Matthew Paris wrote, 'Such great famine and mortality prevailed in the country that . . . the dead lay swollen and rotting in the streets and on dunghills, and there was scarcely anyone to bury them.' Yet despite such episodes, population continued to grow, probably as a consequence of a continuing tradition of early marriage. If mortality rates were as high as forty per thousand per year, as has been suggested for tenants of the bishop of Winchester in the 1240s, then birth rates could have reached fifty per thousand.

For all its limitations, Domesday Book can be made to reveal important things about population. In 1086 East Anglia and the south-eastern coastal regions were the most densely populated parts of England; north and west of the Trent the least populated. Where opening up hitherto uncultivated land created opportunities for younger sons, most farmers practised impartible inheritance, usually primogeniture (inheritance by the eldest son), sometimes ulti-mogeniture (inheritance by the youngest). A characteristic feature of East Anglia and Kent, where there was less room to clear land and make new holdings, was that all male children inherited equally. The 1377 tax returns show that three centuries after Domesday, the north and west were still the most thinly populated parts, but that the area of relatively dense population now took in a wider area of south and east Britain, including the midlands and Holland (south-east Lincolnshire) – this last the result of draining in the fens. Throughout the twelfth and thirteenth centuries one option taken by people who saw few prospects in England was migration to Wales, Scotland and, after 1169, to Ireland. This westward and northward movement has been termed a 'second tidal wave of Anglo-Saxon colonization'.

Towns and Markets

Many English towns suffered badly during the Norman Conquest, with streets and houses demolished to make way for castles. But by 1100 Norman lords had already founded about twenty new towns and during the course of the next hundred years the trend towards urbanisation, visible in England since the tenth century, clearly accelerated. With the population rising, most new towns developed 'naturally' as villages grew in size. By 1200 there were six to seven hundred places where weekly markets were held by ancient right or royal charter; in the next hundred years another 1,100 market charters were granted. By 1300 everyone in England lived close enough to a market to be able to walk there and back during the hours of daylight. Most market settlements remained villages. But in places where booths and shops were busy not just on market day, some people were able to specialise as craftsmen or shopkeepers, making and selling goods in exchange for the agricultural production of the countryside or raw materials from forest, quarries and mines. Most such new towns remained small, with a population of only a few hundred, and many residents combined a craft or trade with farming. Yet however small they were, by 1300 there were more than five hundred towns in England, at least four times as many as in 1086.

Analysis of three well-established towns, Norwich, Winchester and York, indicates that by 1300 nearly half of those whose occupations are known were involved in manufacturing, working in textiles (woollen cloth, linen), leather and metal; about 40 per cent were in retail trade, and about 10 per cent in service occupations such as transport, clerical work, law and medicine. Almost everywhere, in village and town, women were prominent in brewing and selling ale, and in selling poultry, fish and dairy produce; in larger towns prostitution was an option, though the authorities tried to restrict it to a suburb, in London's case to Southwark. The larger self-governing towns generated a mass of regulations intended to prevent profiteering in basic foodstuffs and to control the activities of artisans by bringing them within 'craft guilds' such as those of weavers, bakers, fish-mongers and saddlers. Reality was presumably more flexible than the regulations suggest.

By 1300 there had been major developments in municipal self-government. Towns had long been administratively distinct from the countryside around them, but they had belonged to lords, from the lord king downwards, and the men who presided over town courts and collected revenues were the lords' agents; they remained so unless and until he granted his townsmen 'liberties and free customs'. From the twelfth century onwards records of such grants survive in increasing numbers, mostly in the form of borough charters. Typically these granted the burgesses the right to sell, sub-let, mortgage or bequeath their tenements (burgages); and freed them from performing labour services and paying servile dues or toll at the borough's weekly market, and at other markets owned by the same lord. Where the lord was the king this was an extremely valuable privilege, since he was lord of most of the oldest and biggest towns in England. The law came to recognise the custom that a man able to live in a borough as a burgess for a year and a day would thenceforth be regarded as a freeman (hence the proverb: 'Town air makes you free'). By granting these freedoms to his tenants the lord gave up some profitable rights, but he did so in the expectation that the town would flourish, bringing in a higher overall income. He could guarantee himself a useful annual sum with virtually no effort on his part by leasing to the burgesses the right to administer the town and collect the revenues. By 1130 both London and Lincoln had bought these rights from the king. In this way municipal self-government was born. From 1191 London was administered by a mayor and aldermen who headed the wards; Winchester had a mayor by 1200, Exeter by 1205. By 1300 some fifty English towns enjoyed a significant degree of self-government. The growing importance of such towns is indicated by their being, from 1265, required to send representatives to parliament.

The most dramatic sign of urban growth was the number of towns set up on new sites. In England between 1066 and 1330 more than 150 planned towns were established, among them Arundel, Boston, Chelmsford, Devizes, Egremont, Hull, Liverpool, Maidenhead, Newcastle upon Tyne, Okehampton, Portsmouth, Reigate, Salisbury, Truro, Uxbridge, Watford, Yarmouth (Isle of Wight) and South Zeal (Devon). Kings continued to found towns; Portsmouth, for example, by Richard I, Liverpool by John. In the twelfth and thirteenth centuries, however, most foundations were by wealthy landowners. Founding new towns involved considerable capital expenditure, the laying out of houses, streets and market, and often a church. The grant of borough status, offering burgages at low rent, usually 12d. a year, was intended to attract settlers. Kings and aristocrats, far from being contemptuous of commerce, actively encouraged such developments. In the mid-twelfth century the Templars founded a town in Hertfordshire, diverting the road leading north from London to bring it into their new marketplace. Ambitiously they named it Baghdad (now Baldock). Much effort went into improving communications, in particular by bridge building – most of the bridges of England *c.* 1750 were already there by 1300. Not all new towns prospered. The prospects for those founded later in the thirteenth century, such as South Zeal, when the country was already well provided with markets, were poor. But these 'failed towns' reflect a climate of commercial vibrancy and optimism.

In Wales, Scotland and Ireland, the role of town founders was even more prominent. The Normans who invaded South Wales founded towns to provide for the needs of their castle garrisons at such places as Brecon, Chepstow, Kidwelly, Monmouth and Pembroke. English burgesses worked and traded in relative safety behind town walls. Edward I's conquest of North Wales led to the foundation of a dozen fortified boroughs such as Aberystwyth, Beaumaris and Caernarvon. Most of the seventy-five or so towns in Wales c. 1300 were very small; probably only Cardiff, Carmarthen and Haverford contained much more than a thousand inhabitants. Yet they had a major economic impact on a previously townless country. The lion's share of the profits

The great majority of English medieval stone bridges were demolished in the nineteenth century. By the thirteenth century, when Monnow Bridge at Monmouth (shown here) replaced an earlier timber structure, the bridge network which would last until the eighteenth century was in place. Might this imply that there was little economic development between the thirteenth century and the Industrial Revolution?

went to 'the English burgesses of the English boroughs of Wales', as
they called themselves. According to Gerald de Barri, the Welsh 'do
not engage in trade or industry nor live in towns, villages or castles'.
Since the invaders grabbed the most promising regions, it is hardly
surprising that it was not until the thirteenth century that native Welsh
princes began to promote towns of their own such as Welshpool
(Powys) and Llanfaes (Anglesey).

In Ireland, too, although the Ostman towns of Dublin, Waterford,
Wexford, Cork and Limerick were almost certainly growing in size
before 1169, and some Gaelic centres such as Kells and Kildare showed
signs of urban development, undoubtedly the great surge after that
date was the work of invaders and settlers. By 1275 New Ross, founded
by William Marshal, had become the principal wool and grain
exporting port of Ireland, outstripping Waterford and Wexford. Civic
pride is revealed in the poem on the building of New Ross's town wall
in the 1260s, welcoming all foreigners wishing to buy and sell there. By
1300 English colonists had founded at least fifty towns as focal points in
a new landscape of villages, mills and bridges in southern and eastern
Ireland. By contrast there were very few towns west and north of a line
from Cork to Galway and Carlingford. The towns were inhabited by
the Gaelic-Irish as well as by the English, though the number of
'Irishtowns' in the larger towns, even, as at Limerick and Kilkenny,
enclosed within walls of their own, implies a degree of segregation.

But in Scotland it was the native rulers, in particular the anglicised
David I (1124–53), who made the running in the urbanisation of the
country. He promoted old centres such as Berwick, Roxburgh,
Edinburgh, Stirling, Dunfermline, Perth and Aberdeen, granting
burghal status and monopolies of local trade. His extension of royal
authority into Moray was reinforced by the creation of burghs at
Forres and Elgin. Burghal customs were based on those of Newcastle
upon Tyne, and many of the settlers were English. David's example
was followed by his successors, by the bishops at St Andrews and
Glasgow and then by other lords. By 1300 there were about sixty
Scottish burghs, more than thirty of them royal foundations.

Throughout Britain and Ireland it was generally the older towns that
were the richest, whether they went back to the tenth century such as
Dublin, Norwich and (probably) Bristol, or to Roman times, for
example York, Winchester, Lincoln, Canterbury, Colchester and
London. According to a tax assessment in 1334, London was five times

richer than the next most affluent town, Bristol. (Significantly for the geographical distribution of wealth the next six were all eastern towns: York, Newcastle on Tyne, Boston, Yarmouth, Lincoln and Norwich). With a population, *c.* 1300, of about 80,000, London was by contemporary European standards the only genuinely big town in Britain. Its strategic position within the road network was reinforced by the building of a stone bridge across the Thames – one of the great engineering achievements of the twelfth century. To allow large ships upstream, it incorporated a drawbridge which remained operational until 1476. In the 1170s William FitzStephen composed a panegyric in praise of his fellow Londoners, 'known everywhere', as he put it, 'for the elegance of their manners, dress and cuisine'. He counted 139 churches within the city and its suburbs. He was proud of the cookshops, fast-food places where 'halfpenny pies' could be bought. Yet twenty years later a Winchester author saw London very differently:

> Whatever evil or malicious thing can be found anywhere can also be found there: actors, jesters, smooth-skinned lads, Moors, flatterers, pretty boys, effeminates, pederasts, singing and dancing girls, quacks, belly-dancers, sorcerers, extortioners, night-wanderers, magicians, mimes, beggars, buffoons.

Two miles to the west, and already joined to London by a continuous line of development, lay the palace and abbey of Westminster. Many nobles possessed town houses in London, Westminster or Southwark, and the archbishop of Canterbury built a palace in Lambeth. London and Westminster were seen in combination, one the commercial, the other the political capital of the nation. Inevitably there were tensions between the two, most dramatically expressed in 1215 when London opened its gates to the rebels, forcing King John to accept Magna Carta. In consequence the charter reinforced London's pre-eminence by making its weights and measures standard throughout the kingdom.

Coins I: 1066–1344

For more than two hundred years after 1066 the silver penny remained the only coin minted in England, mostly by moneyers at London and Canterbury, though other mints were opened when the king ordered a recoinage. For some high-value transactions the penny was supplemented by gold coins (bezants) minted abroad. Throughout this period the proportion of silver in the penny was generally at least 92.5 per cent. When Henry I's soldiers complained in 1124 that they were being paid in debased coin, the king had the moneyers castrated. All this resulted in a highly valued and stable currency (the term 'sterling' probably derives from the Old English word *ster*, meaning strong). In 1130 Henry of Huntingdon associated sterling with a flourishing export trade. German silver, he wrote, 'is brought down the Rhine in exchange for huge quantities of fish, meat and wool so that there seems to be more silver in Britain than in Germany. Hence its coinage is made from pure silver.'

The most recent estimates of the volume of coin in circulation in England and Wales suggest that until the mid-twelfth century it fluctuated at late Anglo-Saxon levels, i.e. between £30,000 and £80,000 (between eight and twenty million pennies), then expanded greatly during the next 150 years. Thanks to England's favourable balance of trade, silver flowed in from newly opened mines in Germany, Italy and Bohemia. By 1310 the English currency, with over twenty times more coin in circulation than in 1066, approached £2 million. The weight of silver passing through the mints was not to be regularly exceeded until after the Napoleonic Wars. For most transactions the penny, a day's pay for many labourers, was an impossibly large unit of currency. People took the matter into their own hands, cutting pennies into halves and even quarters. But small transactions were often based on barter and credit, and wages paid in produce, especially grain. The government finally addressed the matter in the recoinage of 1279–80; the Tower mint at London issued 20 million halfpennies and 13 million farthings, as well as 72 million pennies. Thus day rates for men labouring on Edward I's castle building in Wales were set at 1¼d. or 1½d.

The first Scottish king to issue his own coin was David I. For more than two hundred years the Scottish currency shadowed the English one; many of the coins circulating in Scotland were English. Twelfth-century Irish kings minted a few silver coins, known as bracteates, at Ferns and Clonmacnoise, but it was only after the English invasion that the monetisation of Ireland took off. The new government began to mint coin principally at Dublin, including remarkably early issues of halfpennies and farthings. All this represented a massive commercialisation of the economy of Britain and Ireland.

Foreign Trade

As early as the eleventh century England's favourable balance of trade may well have been based on demand for wool from the booming Flemish cloth industry. For bulk goods such as wool, counted in sacks, each weighing 364 pounds, or wine, stored in tuns each containing 252 gallons, water transport was much more efficient than land, especially over longer distances. It cost as much to move a tun of wine fifty miles overland as to bring it from Bordeaux to Southampton. In the twelfth century a newly developed ship type, the round-bellied cog carrying larger cargoes, at a lower cost per ton, further increased the economic advantages of sea transport. The cog's deeper draft required deep water harbours. Hence many of the new towns were ports equipped with quays and cranes.

Trade routes ran in all directions, including to Iceland and Greenland, but the most important ones went south, to France, the Low Countries, the Rhineland, and increasingly also to Spain and the Mediterranean, bringing silk, sugar, rice, almonds and oriental spices. A series of 'southern' queens – Eleanor of Aquitaine, Isabella of Angoulême, Eleanor of Provence, Eleanor of Castile – gave royal and aristocratic society a taste for spicier food. From the later twelfth century the fairs of Champagne functioned as key points of exchange between north-western Europe and Italy, linking north and south into a single European trading zone. The same period saw the development of 'great fairs' at Boston, Winchester, Bishop's (later King's) Lynn, Stamford and St Ives (Cambridgeshire). Most English towns enjoyed the right to hold an annual fair, serving a local or regional market and lasting for two or three days. The 'great fairs' lasted several weeks, during which trade was free of the restrictions which towns normally imposed; they attracted rich Londoners and buyers from aristocratic households, as well as merchants from Scandinavia, Germany and Spain. Late in the thirteenth century Italian ships sailed to Southampton and London, returning with cargoes of English wool. All this ensured a volume and regularity of business sufficient to generate the changes in business techniques, credit and banking which have been dubbed the thirteenth-century commercial revolution. By 1300 Londoners were using negotiable credit instruments and bills of exchange. Contacts with the Continent and the Mediterranean were now on a scale not seen since the days when Britain had been a province of the Roman empire.

These developments did not suit everyone, however. English winegrowers could not compete with better wines imported from La Rochelle and Bordeaux. Towns celebrated for cloth-making in the twelfth and early thirteenth centuries such as Stamford and Lincoln suffered as a result of competition from Flanders and Italy. The superiority of Italian banks and credit systems allowed firms such as the Riccardi of Lucca to buy up wool clips for years ahead. By lending to the crown they gained royal patronage and protection; in 1275 Edward I appointed the Riccardi as collectors of customs in England and Ireland. By then even Flemish businessmen were being elbowed out of England's commerce by Italians, though they retained their leading position in Scotland's, as reflected by the presence of a Scottish business community at Bruges. Significant though economic growth in Britain was, the economies of Flanders and northern Italy were developing even faster. By 1300 England and Ireland were provinces producing raw materials for an Italian commercial empire. The Business Charter (*carta mercatoria*) issued by Edward I in 1303 laid down that in disputes between native and foreign businessmen half the jury was to be composed of the foreigner's nation. Native businessmen had a smaller share of the trade of Britain and Ireland than for many centuries, though the total volume was now so much greater that arguably both groups gained. Certainly both gained from the developing network of courts, including specialist courts to settle commercial disputes, register debts and pursue debtors.

In the Countryside, 1086–1315

Even in relatively urbanised England at least 80 per cent of the population lived in the countryside. The most obvious way to feed the growing numbers was to farm more land, since most of Britain and Ireland had room for expansion. The introduction of rabbits and rabbit warrens into twelfth-century England (and then into Ireland) exploited infertile land such as the Breckland (East Anglia) and Dartmoor in a new way. Even so, varying soil quality meant there was a limit. In some parts of England this point may have been reached by 1086, but elsewhere large areas of forest, fen, marsh and upland were cleared, drained and farmed. By 1300 there was probably 30 per cent more land in agricultural use than in 1086. One consequence was that numbers of wild pigs and wolves dwindled; by 1300 they had been hunted to extinction in England and Wales (though not yet in Ireland and Scotland). So much woodland was cleared that some parts of England became virtually treeless; what remained had to be carefully managed through coppicing. Growing timber shortage meant that coal-mining became an increasingly attractive proposition. By 1300 Newcastle was supplying coal to east-coast towns, above all London, and to the Continent.

Some of the newly made land was good soil, as in the silt belt around the Wash. More ploughing required more draught animals, so much reclamation was for pasture – Glastonbury Abbey, for example, reclaimed thousands of acres in the Somerset Levels, creating high-quality hay meadow. From the south of England to the Cheviot Hills in Scotland sheep farming became increasingly big business. English customs records (extant from 1279) show annual English wool exports rising to the equivalent of twelve million fleeces by 1304–5. The earliest Scottish records (for 1327–33) indicate an annual export of 1.5 million fleeces and 35,000 hides. Irish customs records do not distinguish between fleeces and hides, but point to a late thirteenth-century export peak of one million fleeces, or 450,000 hides. More wool must have come from the thousands of small flocks kept by tenant farmers than from the large flocks of the great landlords, though the latter commonly acted as the middlemen between farmers and the international market.

In continuation of trends visible long before 1066, a midland zone of nucleated settlements (villages rather than hamlets or scattered farmsteads) extended into northern England and southern Scotland. In villages farming was a communal enterprise, for by cooperating with his neighbours the farmer who owned two oxen could take advantage of the most up-to-date farm machinery: the heavy plough drawn by eight oxen. Because heavy ploughs were much harder to turn than the old-fashioned scratch plough, it made sense for the land they worked to be divided into long strips. Each householder held strips scattered throughout the two (or three) large fields attached to each village. Good and bad soil was shared out fairly, and all lived more or less equidistant from their work. After 1170 English emigration took this pattern into south-eastern Ireland.

One consequence of the proliferation of markets and the increasing volume of coin in circulation was that on many manors lords took rents in money rather than in produce or in labour services. First seen in England, this trend can be traced in southern Scotland by the 1140s, and in thirteenth-century Wales and Ireland. Those who owed money rents were, by and large, free to raise the cash by whatever means they chose. In eastern England, where landlords had early given up labour services and regulation of the tenantry, the result had been both partible inheritance and an active land market. Free tenants were better placed to take advantage of market forces – but were also more vulnerable to them. To some extent manorial custom protected servile tenancies; by 1300 free tenants were more likely than serfs to have holdings of less than five acres. Smallholders with families could not have survived unless they supplemented their income by part-time employment as craftsmen or as labourers on neighbouring farms. But rising population meant a greater pool of labour and low wages. The real wages of English farm workers were at their lowest in the decades either side of 1300.

Rising demand for basic foodstuffs made growing crops for the market an increasingly profitable activity, especially in the more urbanised south and east of England. Hitherto most manors belonging to the greatest lords had been leased to tenants, either in return for knight service or for a money rent. This system gave lords a predictable income at minimal administrative cost. But it also meant that tenants, especially those with long leases, profited most from rising prices. From the late twelfth century, lords began to take back control of their manors, appointing bailiffs and reeves as managers. On each manor detailed accounts were kept and then checked by auditors; since expenses and profits were bound to vary from year to year, it would otherwise have been easy for manorial managers to cheat. The auditors had a policy-making as well as a fraud-detecting role, fixing targets and taking investment decisions. A new literature emerged, treatises on agriculture and estate management such as the *Husbandry* attributed to Walter of Henley. To look after livestock kept in the yard – pigs, chickens, geese – Walter recommended employing a woman 'at much less cost than a man'. These changes presuppose a society capable of producing numerate and literate men in numbers, and must be associated with an increasing number of schools.

The survival of thousands of accounts from *c.* 1270 to *c.* 1380, especially from southern and midland England, all using the same measures (4 pecks = 1 bushel, 8 bushels = 1 quarter) has enabled historians to study the manorial economy in detail. On many great estates managers achieved returns of no more than three- or fourfold. If the wealthiest employed the most advanced agricultural techniques, and yet yields remained stubbornly low while the population continued to rise, it is not surprising that historians generally painted a gloomy picture of a countryside choked with people, a land threatened by soil exhaustion as each year farmers were forced to plough an increasingly high proportion of their fields. It seemed that by 1300 England was on the brink of a Malthusian catastrophe.

But more recent research has shown that much higher yields were achieved in some areas. In part this was done by growing legumes such as peas and beans. Legumes were used as fodder for animals kept in stalls, whose manure was collected and then spread on the soil at the optimum moment – just before ploughing, more efficient than relying on the droppings of grazing animals, much of which would be washed away by rain. Human excrement (known as 'nightsoil' because collected at night) was similarly recycled. Moreover, whereas human and animal dung merely recycled nitrogen, legumes added new nitrogen to the soil. The science of this would not be understood until the late nineteenth century, but experienced farmers were well aware of the importance of legumes in keeping the land 'in good heart'. By ploughing and weeding more often and speeding up the ploughing by using horses instead of oxen, better results could be obtained. Yields of over twenty bushels an acre could be achieved, standing comparison with yields obtained by Norfolk farmers in the eighteenth century.

The key was evidently the intensive use of labour: ploughing, weeding, spreading manure. For most wealthy landlords, however, as their auditors would have told them, there was no point in achieving high yields if it meant higher labour costs. On their estates low yields could make better financial sense. But ordinary tenant farmers, with their wives and children, were their own labour force. Many were prepared to put in the time and effort involved in intensive cultivation. Since approximately three-quarters of the land of England was occupied by farmers of this kind, productivity per acre over most of the country was probably higher than it was on the well-recorded great estates. Productivity per capita was another thing altogether – despite all their hard work, the standard of living of the poor fell during the later thirteenth century. For smallholders and low wage-earners c. 1300 staying alive was a struggle. Bad harvests such as those of 1294 and 1295 meant that smallholders suffered badly, while those with larger farms made bigger profits than in years of good harvest. For many English families, emigration had long offered a way out. But at the end of the thirteenth century political changes turned both Ireland and Scotland into war zones into which it was increasingly dangerous to venture. The frontiers were being shut down.

The Great European Famine

In the winter of 1309–10 the Thames froze over; Europe's climate was entering a colder phase. A poor harvest in 1314 meant that less grain than usual could be put aside for seed, then from spring 1315 until summer 1316 torrential rain affected all Europe north of the Alps. Two successive years of harvest failure meant record prices for foodstuffs, not just cereals but also meat and animal products, because wet weather and hay shortage combined to spread disease among cattle and sheep. Price fixing, as by the London magistrates' order that a gallon of the best ale should cost no more than 1½d., proved useless. Allegedly, starving people ate grass, cats, dogs and dung, or turned to murder and cannibalism, even eating their own children. Record evidence – principally from England and Flanders – demonstrates significant increases in rates of mortality and accusations of theft. Not until 1318 did prices drop back to normal levels. Even then another round of livestock diseases in 1319–21 added to the miseries. In both north Britain and Ireland the famine was made more terrible by the devastation caused by the wars with the Bruces. Those who grew enough grain even in years of poor harvest to be able to take some to market made a huge profit. Others were so desperate that they sold their few acres in order to survive for one more year.

From England a new literary genre emerged in this period, the song of social protest; if any had been written before, none survive. Even if not composed by the poor themselves – though some may have been – they reflect a recognition that the lot of the poor was worsening as a consequence of a crisis in the manorial economy, with bad weather and heavy royal taxation the last straws. In the *Song of the Husbandman*, composed *c*. 1340, the husbandman laments that, after being 'picked full clean' by manorial officials, 'I sold my seed to seek silver for the king, wherefore my land lies fallow and learns to sleep'. In the *Song*

Against the King's Taxes, the ills of the time were such that 'common folk must sell their cows, their utensils and even their clothes'. At least they did not sell their children into slavery as they had in the famines of the eleventh century and earlier. Instead they put increasing numbers of them into service with better-off farmers.

Coins II: 1344–c. 1470

In the fourteenth century the currency of Britain was transformed. A rapid growth in supply allowed gold to be increasingly used in international transactions, both commercial and political, such as the subsidies paid to allies in the Hundred Years War. In 1344 the English crown issued its first effective gold coin (the noble) valued at half a mark (6s. 8d.); in 1357 the Scots followed suit. In 1351 the English government increased the flexibility of silver by issuing groats and half-groats (4d. and 2d.) – useful in light of the wage rise that followed the Black Death of 1348–9. But over the next hundred years the supply of silver dwindled. In Edward I's recoinage (1279) about one hundred tonnes of silver had been reminted; in Henry IV's (1411–14) only two tonnes were – although at the same time gold equivalent to seventy tonnes of silver was reminted. Current estimates suggest that whereas the stock of silver was at least 4s. per head in 1300, by 1422 it had fallen to at most 2s. A mid-fifteenth-century European 'bullion famine' had a damaging effect on international trade that was not alleviated until new silver-bearing ores were discovered in the Tirol and Saxony in the 1460s and improved pumps allowed old mines to be reopened.

European governments explained the difficulties which their subjects faced in monetary terms, talking about 'scarcity of bullion', and devising policies intended to keep bullion within the country. Weight reductions encouraged merchants to take coin to mints because at face value they received more money back than they brought in. By 1464 the penny sterling had been reduced in weight from 1.44 grams to 0.78 grams. Even so, England's favourable balance of trade enabled the crown to avoid the instability and inflationary effect of debasement more successfully than all other contemporary governments. Throughout the long period of silver shortage the English crown, unlike governments elsewhere, never minted 'black money', a billon or copper coinage, and by 1470 the silver stock per capita may well have climbed back to the *c.* 1300 level. By contrast, the Scottish government, wishing to attract more silver into the country to pay David II's ransom, ended the policy of shadowing England's currency in 1367 and began one of debasement that over the next century whittled away at the penny until, by 1470, it was mostly copper, and worth only a third of an English one. In Ireland in the 1460s the mints of Dublin, Waterford and Drogheda began to strike not only pennies, halfpence and farthings at three-quarters of the weight of English counterparts, but even half-farthings in copper. Beyond the Pale – but not in the far west – Gaelic imitations, known as 'O'Reilly's money', were minted. Despite the bullion famine, there were still very few self-respecting regimes which did not issue their own money.

The Black Death

The received view that the Black Death, a name invented in the nineteenth century, was a form of plague (bubonic, pneumonic or septicaemic) has recently been seriously questioned. Many scholars now think it may have been a viral haemorrhagic disease in which people were infectious for three to four weeks before plague-like symptoms such as boils or abscesses in groin and armpit appeared. Whatever the disease, it affected virtually the whole known world and spread death on a scale unparalleled since.

The pestilence arrived in south-west England in June 1348; a few weeks later it reached Ireland. In 1349 the mortality attained staggering proportions. William Dene of Rochester wrote that 'men and women threw the bodies of their children into mass graves, from which there came such a stink that it was barely possible to walk by a churchyard'. At Cuxham, Oxfordshire, every one of the twelve tenant farmers died in 1349, and four of the eight cottagers. According to Henry Knighton, 'sheep and cattle wandered through the fields and among the crops. There was no one to round them up, and for want of a keeper they perished amongst the furrows and under hedges in numbers beyond reckoning.' The Scots, he wrote, mockingly called it 'God's judgement on the English', and were preparing an army of invasion when they too were struck down in their thousands. In Ireland Friar John Clyn of Kilkenny described himself in March 1349 as 'waiting among the dead for the coming of death. I have committed to writing those things that

I have truly heard and seen; I leave behind parchment just in case any survivor should remain who might wish to continue my work.' He died soon afterwards, as did millions of others. Current estimates, based on many local studies, have revised the traditional estimate of mortality throughout Britain and Ireland upwards from about one-third to nearer one-half of the population. Yet in the face of this barely imaginable catastrophe, society did not collapse. Parliament was postponed, but at Westminster, exchequer, chancery and the law courts continued to operate, and taxes were still collected. In 1349 more than any other year the two certainties were death and taxes.

After the Black Death: the Countryside

The alarmingly sudden labour shortage experienced after 1348 led to the rich and powerful fearing conspiracies of the many against the few. The English government issued the Ordinance of Labourers (1349), aimed at pegging wages at pre-1348 levels. When parliament finally reconvened in 1351 after a two-year prorogation, the Statute of Labourers reiterated the provisions of the Ordinance in language that spoke of a world turned suddenly upside down by 'the malice of servants' who 'for the sake of their own comfort and greed completely disregard the said Ordinance'. Justices were appointed to enforce the statute in Wales and Ireland as well as in England. The fact that their king was a prisoner in England probably explains the apparent lack of equivalent Scottish action.

Despite their fears, wealthy landowners in fact did quite well in the 1350s. Initially there was no difficulty in finding tenants to replace those who died; heriots (death duties) and entry fines boosted landlords' incomes, enabling them to pay higher wages – economic reality proving stronger than the Justices of Labourers. Post-pestilence dislocation and poor harvests combined to keep grain prices relatively high. But developments in the 1360s and 1370s – first the second epidemic, the so-called Grey Plague, in 1361–2, then a series of good harvests in the later 1370s – ensured that the generation born around the time of the Black Death lived through one of the greatest reversals in British economic history. Grain prices tumbled and stayed low. Labour was in such short supply that even the most powerful lords had to pay high wages. The poet William Langland looked askance at the demands of those who had, as he put it, 'no land to live on but their shovels':

> Draught-ale was not good enough for them, nor bacon, but they must
> have fresh meat or fish, fried or baked and *chaud* or *plus chaud* at that,
> lest they catch a chill on their stomachs. So it is nowadays. The labourer
> is angry unless he gets high wages.

A craftsman's real wages were now three times higher than they had been *c.* 1300. Some workers even had paid holidays. Throughout the fifteenth century the real wages of agricultural workers were higher than in all subsequent centuries before the twentieth. The labour shortage also created opportunities for paid employment for women and the young, and although both continued to be paid lower wages than grown men it may be that some women were able to become more independent. Whether the period 1350–1450 deserves the label 'a golden age for women', however, remains controversial.

The removal of population pressure dramatically changed the appearance of the countryside. In many places land reverted to its former uncultivated state. Drainage systems and dykes were neglected; reclaimed marshland was abandoned. Settlements contracted and in time many, such as those high on the Lammermuir hills in southern Scotland, came to be abandoned altogether. In England perhaps as many as three thousand former settlements became 'ghost villages', their traces visible in aerial photographs. Since demand for meat, leather and wool was more much more elastic than demand for grain, it made sense for landowners to switch to grazing sheep and cattle. Where heavy clay land was returned to pasture, the evidence of former generations of ploughing can be seen in ridge and furrow undulations in the grass. Zooarchaeological evidence shows that farm animals, presumably better fed, increased in size. In some regions, such as the English midlands, the shift from arable to livestock husbandry may have been on a scale sufficient to curtail female employment.

Those manorial lords who had resisted the temptation to turn the labour services of their villeins into money rents were now in a relatively strong position – if, that is, they could keep their serfs on their manors. Consequently they put legal obstacles and high costs in the way of any servile tenant who wanted to leave. But competition for labour led to other employers welcoming runaway serfs and treating them as free men. Now that the terms of a free market in labour were all on the side of the employee, serfdom – the condition in which hundreds of thousands still lived – became an explosive issue. In purely economic terms labour shortage might have led to the reintroduction of forced labour, but after two centuries without slavery its reimposition was evidently inconceivable. Indeed, the abolition of serfdom became one of the central demands of rebels who led the Peasants' Revolt in 1381. It was in the prosperous south-east where opportunities and hence frustrations were at their greatest that men rebelled. According to one account, the rebellion in Kent was triggered by the recapture of an escaped serf.

In the event serfdom was never formally abolished, but the fundamentals of the economic situation meant that it slowly withered away. After the rebellion of 1381 few attempts were made to enforce the oppressive new labour laws. Within many manors servile tenure was replaced by copyhold; the tenant was given a copy of the entry in the manor court roll that recorded his title and terms of tenure. In parts of England copyhold (which survived until 1926) became the most common form of landholding. Many lords gave up the direct management of their estates and reverted to leasing their manors, even though land plenty meant that they were in no position to dictate terms. One consequence was that detailed manorial records were no longer needed. Hence estate management throughout Britain and Ireland in the century after c. 1380 is much less well documented than before – although this means only that it becomes less visible to the historian, not that it became less sophisticated. The emergence of a new word, 'yeoman', reflected the rise of a class of substantial tenant farmers, many of them able to take on extra acres, particularly if they switched to less labour-intensive pastoral farming. Sir John Fortescue, writing in the mid-fifteenth century, liked to imagine an England in which 'there is no hamlet, however small, in which not only a rich knight, esquire or franklin could be found, but also many other free tenants and yeomen'.

It is likely that crop yields per acre declined as less effort was put into back-breaking tasks such as weeding; on the other hand productivity per capita improved. After the Black Death the poor no longer died of starvation. Wet weather in successive years in 1437 and 1438 caused the worst harvests of the century, yet there is no evidence of greater mortality. The fact that chroniclers report how people were reduced to the extremity of eating barley, peas and beans instead of wheat demonstrates just how much had changed since the Great Famine of the early fourteenth century. In imitation of aristocratic manners, people ate more roast meat and fried fresh fish (rather than dried or salted) and no longer depended quite so much on a diet of vegetables and fruit. Beer made with hops could be stored for longer than ale and distributed over longer distances; this encouraged brewing and buying in larger quantities. In the fifteenth century breweries brewing a thousand gallons of beer at a time helped preserve the venerable English tradition of boozing and added the pub to the amenities of the village. More people than ever before could afford to travel or go on pilgrimage, and more could be fashionable. Instead of wearing loose woollen tunics, men began to wear stockings (hose) and a close-fitting tunic, often lined and therefore using double the amount of cloth; 'doublet and hose' became the standard male costume. So offended were the nation's elites by such trends that in 1363 parliament passed laws against people dressing, eating and drinking above their station on pain of forfeiting to the king all 'the outrageous and excessive apparel' they had worn – inevitably to no effect whatever.

Comparatively little is known about the economic impact of the Black Death in the rest of Britain and Ireland. Even if in the north and west mortality was on an English scale, this would not have had so drastic an economic effect on regions which previously had suffered less from land hunger. In Scotland the government's policy of debasing the coinage may have meant that demands for higher wages seemed less 'outrageous' than in England. There was no equivalent of the 1381 rebellion. Aeneas Sylvius Piccolomini was struck by just how much meat and fish was consumed by 'the poor, rough common people' of Scotland. In Wales families were keen to leave bond land in the search for greater freedom and/or better soil. Since all the owners of great estates were English, there was an ethnic edge to the tensions between landlords, tenants and labourers. Owain Glyn Dwr's revolt (1400– c. 1410) precipitated a collapse of landlord control and the end of serfdom, allowing tenants to obtain more favourable terms. In Ireland the reversion to pastoral farming was hastened by the Gaelic recovery. Many English returned to the greater security of England, reversing the earlier direction of migration. The abandonment of many English settlements under the twin pressures of war and disease doubtless contributed to the belief of Richard FitzRalph, archbishop of Armagh during the years of the Black Death, that plague destroyed two-thirds of the English nation in Ireland.

After the Black Death: Towns and Markets

Many village markets disappeared, but the network of towns remained; the infrastructure of roads, bridges and waterways was maintained. Despite high rates of mortality in towns, they continued to draw immigrants from the countryside. Even so there is no doubt that almost everywhere towns were declining in size, including ones as important as London, York, Bristol and Coventry. Some over-ambitious foundations reverted to the status of villages. The overriding impression given by town records is one of gloom. But the number of town inhabitants is one thing, their per capita income another. High wages and increased spending power, by women as well as men, boosted the demand for all manner of goods – as suggested by the increasing number of household utensils, kitchenware and personal items such as finger-rings found in the excavation of late medieval sites.

The English cloth industry revived. Just over 4,400 broadcloths (each twenty-four yards long and one and a half to two yards wide) were exported in 1347–8 (the year of the earliest cloth custom records); this soared to 40,000 by the 1390s and 60,000 by the 1440s. The 'bullion famine' meant that cloth exports dipped between 1450 and 1470, but they then rose again, reaching almost 80,000 by the end of the century. Burgeoning exports created employment for a wide range of skills, some of them traditionally women's work such as carding and spinning – with the spinning wheel increasingly replacing the distaff or spindle. Much of the cloth dying, weaving, fulling and finishing was done in newly prospering rural areas such as Stroudwater in Gloucestershire or the Stour valley on the Essex–Suffolk border, where water power was used to drive fulling mills. Here places such as Lavenham and Hadleigh grew in size and specialism sufficient to rank as towns – though without borough status. The fashion for close-fitting clothes required more cutting and sewing from an increasing number of tailors. In London the most common occupation of those who had their wills registered between 1374 and 1488 was that of tailor, and the next brewer.

A Venetian visiting London *c.* 1500 was impressed by its wealth. He counted fifty-two goldsmiths' shops in Cheapside 'so full of silver vessels, great and small, that in all the shops in Milan, Rome, Venice and Florence put together, I do not think there would be so many of the magnificence to be seen in London'. In his view English pewter dishes were hardly inferior to silver. Pewter goods, using the tin of Devon and Cornwall, were – after cloth – England's second most valuable manufactured export. London metalworkers supplied the finest memorial brasses and church bells all over England; many still survive, including no fewer than seven bells made in the well-recorded Aldgate foundry during the year it was run by a woman, Johanna Hill (d. 1441). Fifteenth-century towns, with less unemployment, less destitution and less squalor, had become pleasanter places to live in than their thirteenth-century counterparts.

Population: Delaying Marriage?

While population levels seem to have recovered fairly quickly after the 'great European famine' of 1315 and 1316, there was no such recovery from the Black Death and its aftershocks (including further visitations in 1361–2, 1375, 1390 and then a dozen fifteenth-century local outbreaks). Most estimates of the late fifteenth-century population of England put it at not much over two million, perhaps no bigger than it had been in 1086. Why should population levels have remained low when economic circumstances (land plenty, high wages, low food prices and rents) appear to have been ideal for early marriage and a rising birth rate? Was it simply a consequence of higher mortality rates, perhaps as a consequence of people being more susceptible to influenza and other diseases (tuberculosis, dysentery) in a damper and colder climate, as some historians have suggested? As yet the study of human skeletal remains gives little support to this hypothesis.

One possible explanation might lie in the convention that led to children leaving home in their early teens to enter service with other families until they were in the twenties, while their parents took other children into their home. To the Venetian visitor the presence of so many 'life-cycle servants' seemed strange and cruel.

When I asked the reason for this severity, they answered that they did it
so that their children might learn better manners. But I believe that they
do it because they like their comforts and are better served by others
than by their own children. Anyway it saves them money because they
do not have to feed them so well.

Such customs probably inhibited sons and daughters from marrying in
their teens. Apprentices in late medieval England, for example, were
typically bound to their masters for seven years, and during that time
were not permitted to marry. More numerous than apprentices were
young servants taken on at hiring fairs and employed on contracts
renewable annually or half-annually. Evidence of the hopes of 'life-
cycle servants' is naturally hard to come by. One thirteenth-century
preacher described a servant girl walking to market with milk and
poultry to sell, and day-dreaming about advancing to dealing first in
pigs and sheep and then in oxen, until she was rich enough to ride on
horseback and marry a nobleman. Such servants might have deferred
marriage until they felt they had reached the point beyond which they
were unlikely to climb. If in England a late medieval pattern of later
marriage marks a shift from an earlier pattern of earlier marriage, it is
not easy to explain so fundamental a change except as a response to a
perceived crisis such as that of the early fourteenth century. In the
world of opportunity that subsequently opened up for those who
survived the Black Death did delayed marriage remain an attractive
option? Such questions are probably unanswerable. Whatever the
causes, so few children were born that provision for old age began to
shift from family to charity, both private charity, as in the foundation
of almshouses, and communal, as in the parish 'common box'.

Houses and Homes

Houses represent one of the best indicators of the gradual development of material culture over these centuries. Despite the increasing
wealth of the elites in the tenth and eleventh centuries, nothing of their
houses survives above ground, except in timberless places such as the
Orkneys and Shetland. Everywhere else the residences of the powerful
consisted of an enclosure containing a number of timber buildings: a
hall, chambers for the lord and his family, accommodation for visitors

and senior servants, a kitchen, brewhouse, workshops, stables and at least one privy, generally all of them single-storey buildings, visible today only as excavated post-holes, since they were constructed using earth-fast timbers which rotted away.

But the Normans, unlike the Danish conquerors, celebrated their triumph in stone. Stone, much more expensive than timber, brought huge advantages. Fireplaces and chimneys could safely be set in walls, so that it was no longer necessary to rely for warmth upon open fires or braziers in the centre of the floor space. Thick walls could house corridors and private rooms, above all privies. The increasing use of

Alston Court, a fine late- fifteenth-century house in the village of Nayland, Suffolk. The jetty, by which the front of the upper floor jutted out a few feet beyond the ground floor, was a design feature of town houses from the twelfth century onwards. In towns where streets were narrow and crowded, it had an obvious function; in the late medieval countryside it was a fashion statement.

glass allowed rooms to be better lit; window seats set into the walls gave people better views of their gardens, fishponds, orchards and parks. Except in the borderlands with Wales and Scotland, most castles built in England from the twelfth century onwards were 'power houses' in which comfort and display counted for more than defence. Unsurprisingly the kings of England set the fashion. Edward I and his wife had separate bathrooms at Westminster; by the fifteenth century the provision of bathrooms at Caister Castle indicates they were widely fashionable among the aristocracy. Country gentry continued to build in timber, often using timber from their own estate, but increasingly on stone foundations. By the thirteenth century once separate buildings were increasingly being brought together to make a single whole, with hall, chambers and service rooms (buttery and pantry) all under one roof: the standard 'English medieval house'.

A few twelfth-century town houses still survive, in Lincoln and Waterford, for example. Two storeys high and built in stone, such houses seemed to be urban palaces. By 1300 London's houses, timber-built on stone cellars, roof-tiled, three- or four-storeys high, towered over the one- or two-storey houses typical of English market towns. The urban poor lived in rented accommodation. Lady Row in Goodramgate in York is a surviving range of two-storey jettied houses built in 1316, with just one room on each floor, ten feet by fifteen. Those who crowded into them, with little or no space for cooking, must sometimes have relied on fast-food shops for hot meals. Thanks to the gradual adoption of improved methods of construction – setting timber houses on pad stones or low stone walls – a few small thirteenth-century village houses still stand in southern England. The redistribution of wealth after the Black Death meant that in the century after 1375 many thousands of substantial two-storey houses were erected in the countryside as well as in town. With slate or tile roofs, stone hearths and chimneys, they were built to a standard that has allowed several thousand to stand to the present day, mostly in the south-east of England – perhaps over two thousand in Kent alone. The insertion of a second storey, with a number of smaller rooms taking up the space once occupied by a 'public' hall, implies the continuing development of ideas of private domestic space. Since the richer lords had reverted to leasing their manors, they travelled around their estates a great deal less than before. Like more recent landed aristocrats they divided their time between a London house and just two or three country houses. With fewer homes to call their own, when they and their households needed somewhere to stay the night, they called in at the large inns now being opened in towns on well-travelled roads.

Elsewhere building materials and techniques were not such as would either leave much archaeological record or survive for centuries above ground. Not until the later Middle Ages can stone houses, often in the form of 'tower houses', be found in both town and country in Ireland, Scotland and Wales. In Ireland the earliest were built in English areas, but by the fifteenth century the form had been adopted, as at Bunratty, by the most powerful Irish. Gerald de Barri's description of Welsh houses in the 1190s as 'wattled huts, sturdy enough to last a year or two' may be unduly condescending, but visitors to Ireland and to the north and west of Britain continued to comment on the primitiveness of houses made of wattle and clay with turf roofs and oxhide doors. The greater settlement mobility characteristic of a more pastoral economy meant that in these regions comparatively little was invested in house building.

In some fundamental ways Britain and Ireland changed little during these centuries. The overwhelming bulk of the population still lived and worked on small farms, kept animals and grew crops. Although the climate may have entered a colder phase in the fourteenth century, it is hard to demonstrate consequential changes in farming practices. The family and the household remained the basic unit of economic as well as of social life. From the age of seven or eight children were expected to help with the unremitting round of gender-divided work described in the fifteenth-century *Ballad of the Tyrannical Husband*. Here, a ploughman, returning home after work, complains that his dinner is not ready because his wife has been gossiping with the neighbours; her furious answer is a long list of the tasks that keep her busy night and day.

But in other ways Britain and Ireland had been transformed. Without either slavery or serfdom being formally abolished, both withered away. By the end of the period both men and women were freer than ever before. These were not the achievements of a more enlightened governing class, but the outcomes of changing economic conditions, reinforced by rebellion, in England in 1381, and in Wales under Owain Glyn Dwr after 1400. By the end of the period more than six hundred new towns had been founded, and hundreds of new markets had appeared. There was more money per capita in circulation. Inflation combined with the widening range of denominations (from 10s. down to farthings) meant that coins were more useful than they had been when only pennies were minted. The average real income of the English is thought to have been twice as high in 1470 as in 1050 and people everywhere lived in better houses. In terms of loss of life the Black Death of 1348–9 was the greatest catastrophe in recorded European history. But although it undoubtedly resulted in some economic setbacks, the institutional, technological and cultural innovations of the pre-Black Death period survived, to the great benefit of the peoples of Britain and Ireland.

2. Religious and Secular Cultures

By the eleventh century the people of Britain and Ireland had been Christian for centuries. Christianity had taken over the ancient religious rituals of the farming year. Most people went to church on Sundays and on the great feast days; nearly all were buried in churchyards. The only important exceptions were the Jews who came to England after 1066. After their expulsion in 1290, England became once again as uniformly Christian as Wales, Scotland and Ireland. Virtually everyone recognised, at least nominally, the authority of the bishop of Rome in matters of religion. More than ever before the churches in Britain and Ireland became parts of a single whole, everywhere moved by the same commands and obeying – more or less – the same rules.

Within Britain and Ireland the English Church set the pace. The life of Margaret, the English wife of King Malcolm of Scotland, represents her as insisting, against opposition, that all Scots should take Easter communion. In 1170 the synod of Cashel, as part of a drive to 'anglicise' the Irish Church, ordered that children should be baptised in the font – as had long been obligatory in England. In England Sunday church attendance was enforceable in a court of law. No doubt most did their duty. A few did not, such as two women from Hungerford who failed to attend church or take communion for five years, and were excommunicated and imprisoned in 1409. Whether or not people followed Christianity's rules of moral conduct, most accepted its code of ritual obligations. Few heretics were found and persecuted: nearly all of them in England, mostly between 1380 and 1450, a tiny handful in Scotland and none in Ireland and Wales. By comparison with much of continental Europe, in Britain and Ireland there was little open religious dissent.

An Age of Faith?

Whether this meant that virtually all the inhabitants of these islands believed in the God of the Christians is another question, and one with no certain answer. Pope Alexander IV was probably misinformed when in 1261 he instructed the bishop of Raphoe (Donegal) to stop the idol worship in his diocese. But, according to Peter of Cornwall, Prior of Holy Trinity, Aldgate (London), writing in about 1200, 'There are many people who do not believe that God exists, nor do they think that a human soul lives on after the death of the body. They consider that the universe has always been as it is now and is ruled by chance rather than by providence.' We do not know whether Peter was right, nor what he meant by 'many people'. None of these 'many' unbelievers wrote anything that has survived. Nor indeed was anyone prosecuted for atheism, although fifteenth-century worries about heresy led to the uncovering of opinions such as John Brewer of Albourne's view that there was more good in a cask of ale than in the four gospels.

Inevitably many of the Church's rules such as the requirement that every year all farmers should hand over a tithe (in Scotland, a teind) – one-tenth of their produce – caused resentment, especially in Ireland and Scotland. According to the Melrose chronicle, Bishop Adam of Caithness was murdered in 1225 because he had insisted on people saving their souls by paying tithes. Many were undoubtedly also angered by the rule against working on Sundays and holy days. When a man working on the feast day of St Erkenwald (London's saint) was rebuked for doing so, he 'belched out', in the words of a twelfth-century canon of St Paul's, 'his poisonous brew of insults':

> You clerics have so much time on your hands that you meddle with what's none of your business. You lot grow fat and soft with idleness. With your everlasting useless dirges you despise us, though we are the ones who do all the real work. And you go and bring in some Erkenwald or other to justify your idleness and try to stop me doing the job that I need to stay alive. Why should I pray alongside drones like you? When we've made a bit of money, enough so we can eat – and a bit more too, so we can drink – then we have a holiday, and a good time dancing and singing. You keep your festivals, your mouldy old tunes and your Erkenwald to yourselves. Leave us alone.

That for our sense of what a hard-pressed working man might have said, we have to rely, as here, on words written by an ecclesiastic, illustrates the historian's problem. It is not just that clerics did most of the writing. Not all clerics were particularly pious. The main problem is that those writings which have survived the centuries best are those which were kept in the libraries or archives of bodies which came to enjoy a long institutional life: the English and Scottish monarchies, some towns and many churches. Inevitably we know much more about the thoughts of ecclesiastics than we do about the thoughts of laymen and women. Likewise Church buildings survive better than any other sort of building, as do the artefacts kept within them. For those who love medieval cathedrals and parish churches it cannot but seem that this was, as it is often called, an 'Age of Faith'. Why else would people have spent such huge sums in erecting and furnishing churches? Yet the rich and the powerful spent far more money on building and decorating houses to live in than on churches to pray in. It is just that thousands of non-monastic medieval churches survive while virtually all the great houses have been demolished and rebuilt in line with ever-changing ideas of domestic comfort. The surviving evidence exaggerates the role played by religion in the life and culture of the people – but by how much? How many believed in a steady-state Godless universe? We cannot tell.

Gregorian 'Reform'

What is certain is that the beginning of this period witnessed a papally-led Europe-wide campaign aiming at radical changes in Church and society. Conventionally known as Gregorians (from Gregory VII, pope 1073–85), these ambitious radicals set out to abolish both secular control of the Church and the family life of the clergy. They believed that for the clergy to be pure, the Church must be free. It ought not to be subject to the jurisdiction of the laity, nor should it be required to pay taxes to them. By exploiting more systematically an income stream from the wider population, i.e. tithes, it was hoped to free the Church from dependence on secular lords. But throughout Christian Europe churches owed their existence to the generosity of those wealthy landowners who had endowed them, so it is hardly surprising that kings and secular lords should choose the bishops, abbots and priests who headed their churches. Despite the fact that western canon law had long held that priests could not marry, only monks chose celibacy; other churchmen everywhere had partners and families. For the Gregorians, however, most of them monks, sexual and familial ties threatened the spiritual life of the clergy, undermining their claim to moral superiority over the laity.

William I was sympathetic to those parts of their programme that posed no threat to his own authority. To implement and control this programme he chose the learned abbot of St Stephen's, Caen, the Italian-born Lanfranc, as his archbishop of Canterbury. Lanfranc summoned general councils of the English Church with unprecedented frequency; priests and deacons were ordered not to hunt, carry arms, marry or have sex. Although priests tended to share the lifestyle of their social equals – village priests often inherited their church from their father, since learning at home was a practical way of training priests – over subsequent centuries the pro-celibacy campaign and the growing number of schools gradually led to the disappearance of the married priest in England. Elsewhere in Britain and Ireland, however, the campaign was less successful. Church court records show Welsh priests making wills providing for their children. Within Gaelic Ireland the priesthood remained hereditary. Familial succession to bishoprics remained as common in the later Middle Ages as earlier. Eoin O'Grady, archbishop of Tuam (1364–71), Oxford graduate in canon law, was the son of an archbishop of Cashel. Such men bought the papal dispensations which allowed them to be bishops despite their canonical illegitimacy.

In Gregorian eyes the ceremonies (investiture and homage) by which a new bishop or abbot received his office from a secular ruler were hated symbols of dependence. They demanded free election: of bishops by the canons of the cathedral, of abbots by the monks. Anselm, Lanfranc's successor as archbishop of Canterbury, refused to do homage to King Henry I or to consecrate those bishops whom Henry invested. In 1106 a compromise was reached whereby Henry renounced investiture, but prelates continued to do homage. Both parties saw this as a temporary concession, but it endured. Domesday Book demonstrates that churches held one-seventh of the total assessed wealth of the kingdom. Since churchmen could not bring themselves to renounce those rich estates which, they claimed, were held by the saints to whom each church was dedicated, rulers could make life uncomfortable for those canons or monks who refused to elect the king's candidate. Only when the king held no strong view was free election more than a façade. Kings of England regularly promised that the Church should be free – as in clause one of Magna Carta – but the occasions when they did not get the bishops they wanted, no matter how unsuitable, remained very few. Like Thomas Becket, Henry II's chancellor, most bishops earned their promotion by working in the king's administrative or diplomatic service, and many continued to do so after their 'election'.

Unfortunately for the ecclesiastical theory that even the humblest priest counted for more than a king, on the grounds that priests cared for souls while kings ruled only bodies, most people did not see it that way. When Pope Innocent III, intending to bring pressure to bear on King John, imposed an interdict on England in 1208, banning church services and burials in consecrated ground, the clergy obeyed his instructions. But John profited, confiscating the clergy's assets, then allowing them to buy back the privilege of managing their own lands. In 1209 Innocent III excommunicated John in the hope of increasing the pressure on him. Not until King Philip of France threatened to invade England in 1213 did John submit to the pope. On their own excommunication and interdict, the strongest weapons in the Church's armoury, were effective only against extremely pious laymen, and most were not.

The theory of papal plenitude of power justified the pope's right to make appointments – to 'provide' – to benefices throughout Christendom. But only rarely did the pope provide a bishop against the king's wishes. Edward I reluctantly acquiesced in the provision of the Franciscan John Pecham to Canterbury in 1278, then informed the bishops of the consequences of obeying their archbishop contrary to his wishes: 'know for certain that if you so act, we shall seize your baronies by force'. By the fourteenth century all bishops were appointed by papal provision, but popes had learned to provide men keen to continue working with kings. Indeed, in 1326, 1381 and 1450 bishops Walter Stapledon of Exeter, Simon Sudbury of Canterbury, William Ayscough of Salisbury and Adam Moleyns of Chichester were lynched for the offence of being too closely involved with unpopular governments. Not just in England, but throughout Britain and Ireland, rulers continued to dominate appointments to major ecclesiastical office.

Dioceses

Christian doctrine gave overall responsibility for pastoral care to bishops, and bishops could be found throughout eleventh-century Britain and Ireland. In England there were two archbishoprics – Canterbury and York – and thirteen bishoprics with defined borders; but in Ireland, Scotland and Wales there were as yet no cathedral cities, no dioceses with fixed boundaries, and no archbishops, a situation which allowed York to claim authority over Scotland, and Canterbury over the whole of Britain and Ireland. There was some movement in England after 1066 – a few bishops moved their seats to more populous cities, notably to Norwich, Lincoln and Chester, and two new bishoprics were established, at Ely (1108) and Carlisle (1133), bringing the total to seventeen. After that no more dioceses were created until after the Reformation.

In the rest of Britain and Ireland, the changes made were much greater. By 1200 the diocesan structures that were to frame church life through all subsequent centuries had been put in place. In Wales four dioceses, more or less corresponding to the kingdoms of Deheubarth, Morgannwg (Glamorgan), Gwynedd and Powys, had emerged by 1150: St David's, Llandaff, Bangor and St Asaph. Canterbury, supported by English political and military power, succeeded in defeating attempts to make St David's an independent archbishopric for Wales. On mainland Scotland nine dioceses were established within the dominion of the kings of Scots. The rulers of Galloway managed, with English support, to keep their independence until 1235; in consequence Galloway's bishopric, Whithorn, accepted the authority of York. From David I on, several kings urged the pope to make Scotland an ecclesiastical province with its own archbishop, but in vain. What saved their nine sees from ecclesiastical subjection to York was a papal declaration, made by 1192, that the Scottish Church was the pope's 'special daughter'. In the absence of a metropolitan, the nine bishops took it in turns to summon provincial Church councils. Beyond the mainland, two dioceses (the Isles and Orkney) owed formal ecclesiastical obedience to the Norwegian archbishop of Nidaros (Trondheim), although after the thirteenth century their bishops were usually Scotsmen. When in 1472 St Andrews was at last made an archbishopric, both Galloway and the 'Norwegian' dioceses were formally added to its province.

In Ireland where there were lots of kings, there were also plenty of bishops. The territorial extent of their responsibilities fluctuated according to the rise and fall of kingships until two twelfth-century councils, both chaired by papal legates, systematically restructured the Irish Church – and ended Canterbury's claim to authority there. At Raith Bresail in 1111 two provinces were established under the archbishops of Cashel and Armagh; at Kells in 1152 the creation of two more provinces, Dublin and Tuam, ensured that better account was taken of Irish political divisions. After a few minor adjustments early thirteenth-century Ireland was left with four archbishoprics and no fewer than thirty-three dioceses. But the theoretical stability of this structure was complicated by ethnic divisions. After the death of Laurence O'Toole in 1180, one of Henry II's English clerks, John Cumin, was made archbishop of Dublin. The gradual extension of English control over the island was reflected in the increasing numbers of English or Anglo-Irish bishops, until the Gaelic revival of the fourteenth century reversed the process.

Parishes

At the beginning of this period nearly all the major churches in Britain and Ireland were 'minsters' (Latin *monasteria*), collegiate churches staffed by groups of priests who provided services and burial in consecrated ground, and in return received renders and/or tithes from the people living within the large area, the parish, which they served. In the more populous south and east of England many of these large parishes had already fragmented by 1066 as lesser churches acquired burial rights and a portion (usually a third) of the tithes. Over the next two hundred years the process of small parish formation continued, and spread north and west. When the English invaded Ireland, they took the pattern of small parishes with them. In 1300 there were about 9,500 parishes in England and 1,000 in Scotland and the Isles. By this date, with innumerable vested interests protected by the growing influence of lawyers, the church's territorial organisation had frozen. The thirteenth-century parochial grid survived until the nineteenth century. Many of these small parish churches were built in stone rather than timber. Hence they achieved an enduring presence in the landscape, creating the archetypal English village scene: manor house and nearby church, squire and parson. The pattern of small parishes never reached the less densely populated parts – upland Wales, the far south-west and north of England, the west of Scotland, Gaelic Ireland. Here other centres of pastoral care and preaching remained more important: oratories, standing crosses and holy wells.

A conscientious parish priest, even when helped by two or three assistant clergy, was a busy man. He recited the daily office, or at least matins and vespers. Although his parishioners were required to attend only on Sundays, he celebrated mass daily. He baptised babies, received confessions and administered the last rites. Official doctrine was that although no fee could be charged *for* the services of baptism, marriage and burial, it was acceptable for priests to receive gifts *at* such ceremonies. By 1300 the laity could bring complaints against the clergy to local Church courts. The most common single charge was of sexual misconduct. English priests had been brought to renounce marriage, but many found chastity impossible.

Complaints about their inadequate education led to more systematic attempts to school priests in their duties. In 1281 Archbishop Pecham of Canterbury published a Latin manual of instruction (later translated into English), requiring each parish priest four times a year to explain the rudiments of the Christian religion in his mother tongue and without any 'fancifully woven subtleties'. According to John Mirk, fourteenth-century author of *Festial*, a collection of English sermons for priests' use, 'it is much more useful and of greater merit for you to say your Pater noster in English than in such Latin as you do. For when you speak in English, then you know and understand well what you say.' Yet the words of the Eucharistic sacrament itself, the miracle by which the bread and wine, while still appearing unchanged, were turned into Christ's body and blood, were not translated. The priest performed this miracle at the altar, partly hidden by a rood screen, inaudible to the Sunday congregation and, in Latin, incomprehensible. Alexander Ashby complained that it was commonly at this most solemn moment that gossiping and joking broke out among the congregation. When during the interdict parish priests stopped celebrating Sunday mass, no layman is known to have complained.

Because most parish churches owed their existence to the generosity of the local lord, the founder's descendants tended to take it for granted that they should have the right to choose (in technical language 'present') the priest, even if they accepted that he could not enter into his duties until approved and ordained by the bishop. In societies such as Wales, where property rights were partible among males, the right to present was also partitioned. Tithes often generated far more revenue than was necessary to support a village priest living among his parishioners like one of them. In many cases this led to a division of the revenue, the greater part going to an absentee rector, and the remainder to a vicar who did the work. Thirteenth-century synodal and diocesan legislation made explicit the responsibilities of the laity for the fabric and furnishings of their parish church. Hence the provision of pulpits (more than two hundred pre-Reformation examples survive in English parish churches) and, from the fifteenth century, fixed seating in the form of pews. Previously people sat on benches or stood – so that they could leave quickly if they did not like what they heard, some said. Organising these responsibilities led to the development of the office of churchwarden and a proliferation of parish guilds and fraternities, voluntary associations of pious laymen (and sometimes women) for mutual benefit.

Church Courts

During the two centuries after 1066 a system of ecclesiastical law was developed which, in addition to dealing with the Church's internal business, touched the lives of laymen at many critical points: the legitimacy of their birth, their sexual conduct, their marriages and divorces, the distribution of their property after death. This law – canon law – came to be defined with increasing precision and subtlety as a result of its systematic study, initially at Bologna and then at law faculties in universities throughout Europe. It was administered separately from the law of the land by a network of ecclesiastical courts, with the papal court having the last word. In Britain, as a result of the Reformation, the papacy was shut out, but in other respects the system continued – indeed, the jurisdiction of Church courts over probate, testaments and matrimonial causes survived well into the nineteenth century.

Its beginnings in England go back to the 1070s when William I issued a writ setting out the principle of separate spiritual and temporal jurisdictions in conscious departure from the previous practice of churchmen and laymen acting in joint sessions. 'Before my time,' ran the words of William's writ, 'episcopal laws were not properly administered in England according to the precepts of the holy canons.' William's Archbishop Lanfranc ordered bishops to appoint arch-deacons in order to implement the Church's law locally and soon all English dioceses were divided into archdeaconries and their sub-divisions, rural deaneries. Archdeacons, operating an inquisitorial system developed from Roman law and empowered to impose fines as well as penances, were able to make a good living out of the failures of both clergy and laity to live up to the standards, especially in sexual matters, set by canon law. Episcopal courts were then established, partly owing to the volume of complaints against the venality of archdeacons, although in practice the expense of going to appeal meant that the greater part of the population remained at the mercy of 'rural chapters', i.e. archidiaconal and diaconal courts. In the hope of creating safeguards for the accused, increasingly complex procedural rules were devised. Things had to be done by the book. All this helped to transform the Church into a structure in which officials and lawyers counted for as much as – and many said more than – priests.

Although rulers throughout Europe accepted the principle of separate courts, there were inevitably disputes about where the boundary between ecclesiastical and secular jurisdiction should be drawn. Henry II set out his view in the sixteen chapters of the Constitutions of Clarendon (1164); Pope Alexander III (1159–81) rejected most of them, including chapter three, which dealt with 'benefit of clergy'. Since Church courts could not impose the death penalty, many reckoned that allowing the clergy the benefit of freedom from secular judicial process was tantamount to encouraging crime. But Thomas Becket fiercely defended the right of the Church to have exclusive jurisdiction over 'criminous clerks'. The quarrel over this and other issues led to Becket fleeing the country to escape the king's wrath. It simmered for six years and then exploded when Becket was murdered soon after his negotiated return to Canterbury in 1170. The damage this did to Henry's reputation forced the king to give way on several of the points at stake – on appeals to Rome, for instance, and on benefit of the clergy, which was to last in England, though in modified form, until 1827. Nonetheless, Henry calculated that by doing public penance for his involvement in Becket's death, and by coming to terms with Pope Alexander, he was able to preserve the essentials of royal power over the Church, including jurisdiction over disputes concerning

ecclesiastical patronage, which he and his successors regarded as part
of their jurisdiction over land. Despite Edward I's writ *circumspecte
agatis* (issued in 1286) ordering his judges to 'act circumspectly' and
recognising tithes, parochial dues, defamation and attacks on clergy as
matters for the Church courts, the clergy continued to complain to
king and parliament about what they regarded as infringements of
their jurisdiction.

Astonishingly little resistance came from the king of England's
judges as thirteenth-century Church courts extended their jurisdiction
to cover not just pious and charitable bequests but all testamentary
bequests of movable property. By this time they routinely passed
questions of the validity of a marriage to the Church courts, where
rules such as the ban on marriages within seven degrees of kinship (i.e.
between couples who had great-great-great-great grandparents in
common) were followed. One consequence was that marriage now
became a contract for life – previously secular custom had permitted
divorce. Judicial separation was possible, but in this case neither party
could remarry. If a couple had made an invalid marriage, then it was
annulled. This was relatively common on grounds of consanguinity
before 1215, but much harder after the Lateran Council reduced
the 'forbidden degrees' from seven to four. Until their conquest by the
English, Ireland and Wales were different. The Irish *Cain Lanama*
(the law of couples) took polygyny and divorce for granted, including
'no-fault' divorce and the corresponding property arrangements.
Welsh law as reflected in thirteenth-century lawbooks was similarly
open to divorce.

By this time Alexander III had decided that if two people who were
free to marry and old enough (fourteen for boys, twelve for girls),
freely exchanged words of consent spoken in the present tense (*verba de
presenti*) – 'I, John, take thee, Agnes', for example – then they were
married. In earlier legal traditions – Roman, Germanic, Jewish,
Christian – the consent of parents or guardians and a public ceremony
had been the two basic criteria for testing the validity of a marriage.
Not any longer. Clandestine marriages were now relatively easy. In
practice, no doubt, most marriages were made with the consent of
family and friends. Sensible people realised that marriage, with all its
consequences for the descent of property, was too serious a business to
be left to lovers. But in the earliest extant substantial collection of
private letters, the fifteenth-century Paston letters, the case of Margery

Paston and Richard Calle shows that there were a few who used the Church's law to marry in defiance of the pressure of both family and Church. The Church taught that marriage was one of the seven sacraments, yet allowed it to become the one significant rite of passage beyond its control – indeed, since a collusive claim of prior contract by *verba de presenti* was easy to make, it opened a back door to divorce. This extraordinary law of marriage survived in England until the eighteenth century, and in Scotland for longer.

Jews

Throughout most of the twelfth and thirteenth centuries there was one small non-Christian religious community in England: the Jews. So far as is known none lived in England before 1066, but by c. 1090 French-speaking Jews from Rouen had settled in London. A hundred years later there were small Jewish communities in more than twenty other English towns, as far west as Exeter and as far north as Newcastle upon Tyne. In practice the Jews were restricted to one economic activity, moneylending. With interest rates set at one, two or occasionally three pence per pound per week (i.e. 22 per cent, 44 per cent or 66 per cent per annum) this was an occupation which brought them great profits and at times even greater unpopularity. A twelfth-century monk, Thomas of Monmouth, alleged that the Jews of Norwich had ritually murdered a young boy called William. His book on the subject helped to launch the anti-Jewish 'blood libel' which was to scar subsequent European history.

Crusades, with their reminders of Christ's crucifixion, tended to stimulate anti-Jewish sentiment; plundering Jews sometimes seemed an all too appropriate way of raising the cash to make good a crusading vow. Anti-Jewish riots and killings reached a climax at York in 1190. A mob led by some of the local gentry, crusaders among them, attacked the royal castle where Jews were sheltering. Seeing no hope, most of the Jewish men killed their wives and children, then committed suicide. The rest surrendered when promised that their lives would be spared if they accepted Christian baptism; on leaving the castle they were killed. In York Minster the mob made a bonfire of the records of debts owed to Jews. But the government tried to punish those responsible for the massacre of York, and over the next few decades

Jews returned to the city until it, once again, contained one of the richest communities in England.

As a small, wealthy, exclusive and culturally distinctive minority faced by anti-Semitism and religious discrimination, Jews looked to the king for protection. In return kings exacted a heavy price, regulating their business dealings closely and at times taxing them very harshly. In 1210 John demanded the staggering sum of £44,000 from the Jews, employing mass arrests and brutal measures to enforce payment. 'Jews are the sponges of kings', wrote one theologian. When Jewish money-lenders died, the crown collected the outstanding debts, and in clauses 10 and 11 of Magna Carta John was forced to promise that he would deal sympathetically with the widows and children of any landowner who died in debt to Jews. In 1215 Pope Innocent III decreed that Jews and Muslims were 'to be publicly distinguished from other people by their dress'. In England, however, the king was happy to exempt individuals or communities from the obligation to wear the Jewish badge – at a price. From the 1240s onwards Henry III's shortage of money led him to tax them even more aggressively. Over the next forty years the Jewish sponges were pressed so hard that little more could be squeezed out of them. They had always been a tiny minority, at most little more than five thousand, counting men, women and children; by the late thirteenth century there were as few as two thousand. In 1275 Edward I banned moneylending by Jews; in 1290 he expelled them. On both occasions he was rewarded by general applause and generous grants of taxation.

Monasteries

There was little that was 'monastic' about most of the *monasteria* of eleventh-century Britain and Ireland, even if many were headed by a man bearing the title 'abbot'. They were collegiate churches staffed by clergy, often members of the founding family, who shared the revenues, but did not generally eat together in a refectory or – since many of them were married – sleep in a dormitory as required in those communities which followed the Benedictine rule (*regula*). Only in the southern half of England were 'regular' monasteries to be found, in all fewer than fifty, including ten for women. Reform-minded twelfth-century commentators were shocked by the traditional lifestyle of the members of such family churches (*clasau* in Wales). A decree of the 1101 council of Cashel, the first Irish council to be presided over by a papal legate, ordered that in future no head (*erenagh*) of a *monasterium* could be a layman.

The monastic impulse so prominent among eleventh-century ecclesiastical activists contributed to a massive increase in the number of monks and nuns in the 150 years after 1066. By the 1220s there were about 550 regular abbeys and priories for men in England, about 200 in Ireland, 46 in Scotland and 33 in Wales. In England there were also about 150 religious houses for women. Proportionally women were less well provided for in Ireland and Wales – probably reflecting secular inheritance customs there. The violence of the Norman Conquest meant that there were many from the king downwards who felt in dire need of prayer, and who suddenly had the wealth to be generous. During the reigns of William I and William II thirty Benedictine abbeys and priories were founded in England. When the Normans invaded Wales, they 'reformed' *clasau* by turning out the natives and bringing in monks from outside. By 1100 the Benedictine model had also been adopted in Dublin and at Queen Margaret of Scotland's priory at Dunfermline. The role of monks and nuns was to chant each day the full cycle of prayer, in the belief that this was a way to save not just themselves, but also, and especially, those who had founded or endowed their community. Although they took a vow of personal poverty, they lived in property-owning communities, some – such as Glastonbury, Ely and Winchester – very rich indeed. The sheer scale of the abbey churches built after 1066, whether in ruins or still standing, astonishes even today. The scale on which food was provided also astonished. Gerald de Barri claimed that lunch at Christ Church, Canterbury, consisted of no less than sixteen dishes. Not surprisingly, Benedictines acquired a reputation for gluttony.

In the twelfth century shortcomings such as these – used in the sixteenth century to justify the dissolution of monasteries – provoked instead the creation of new orders, each with its own distinctive style and ethos: Cistercians, Augustinians, Templars, Hospitallers, Premonstratensians, Carthusians and Gilbertines. Of the new orders the Gilbertine, founded by Gilbert of Sempringham (Lincolnshire), was confined to England. Almost all the others had their origins in France, a reflection of the extent to which religious life in Britain was bound into a single, largely Francophone, Latin Christendom. It was also a

militant Christendom, with two of the new orders, the Templars and
Hospitallers, keyed into the crusading movement. All their houses
were parts of two networks of assistance for the crusader states in
Palestine and Syria. The most high profile of the new orders, the
Cistercian, was also the most consciously international. Representatives from each house were obliged to travel to an annual general
chapter at Cîteaux. Their austerity led to them giving up the linen
underwear and black woollen top garment of the Benedictines (the
Black Monks), and wearing nothing but an undyed woollen habit,
hence coming to be known as White Monks. Whereas Benedictine
houses recruited largely children (oblates), given by their aristocratic
parents to be brought up in the cloister, the Cistercians prohibited
entry for anyone under sixteen, and required a year's novitiate. By the
end of the twelfth century even the Benedictines felt compelled to
follow the Cistercian example. From now on the new model army of
monks and nuns consisted only of adult volunteers. And since the army
was increasing in size – at a much faster rate than overall population
growth – it recruited people from a wider social range than before. For
a while the Cistercians even offered a half share in the religious life to
the poor, allowing them to take the vow and wear the habit in return
for doing manual labour.

Lanfranc's foundation of a leper hospital outside Canterbury was
the first of nearly 350 hospitals founded in medieval England. As
religious establishments endowed with one or more priests, hospitals
offered the sick, who were themselves expected to follow a quasi-
monastic life, a full range of pastoral care – sometimes to the irritation
of parish priests. Hospital founders often brought in Augustinian (or
Austin) regular canons, members of an order which valued pastoral
work unusually highly, to run them (as, for example, London's St
Bartholomew's). Their pastoral work led to Augustinians being invited
to take over the properties and functions of many minsters throughout
Britain and Ireland, expelling those 'secular' canons who refused to
give up their families. This made founding Augustinian houses
relatively cheap. They never matched the spirituality of Cistercian
authors such as Ailred of Rievaulx, nor indeed the grandeur of
Cistercian building (as at Fountains Abbey), but at their height there
were 274 houses of Austin canons in England, more than the combined
total of 219 Benedictines and Cistercians.

Yet the very success of the new orders in obtaining endowments as well as recruits meant that they too tended to slip into comfortable ways. Fresh inspiration came in the shape of two radically different new orders, both originating in southern Europe in the early thirteenth century: the Franciscans and Dominicans. Determined to own nothing, their mission was to preach penance and sustain themselves by begging. They concentrated on towns, where their preaching was badly needed and where begging was easier. Such idealism and dedication was impressive, and they attracted thousands of recruits, often to the dismay of well-off parents who were shocked to see their children begging. Dominicans and Franciscans came to England in the 1220s. Two more mendicant orders, the Carmelites and the Austin friars, arrived in the 1240s. By the 1340s there were about five thousand friars in England (housed in 190 friaries); in Ireland eighty-five friaries, more than twenty in Scotland and eight in Wales. Although friars never became great property owners, they attracted many small gifts in money, often in the form of bequests (as is clear from the evidence of wills, which survive in increasing numbers from the late thirteenth century on). They too began to attract criticism as hypocrites (as has been said, in the field of religious enthusiasm nothing fails like success). Nonetheless, the success of the mendicant orders marked the culmination of two centuries of astonishing creativity in the development of religious institutions, catering for almost every conceivable variety of religious life, contemplative, ascetic, active, rural, urban.

In 1215 the Fourth Lateran Council decreed that no more new orders should be founded, and hardly any were. The flow of land into ecclesiastical hands slowed down. Great landowners had long been unhappy at the loss of future reliefs and profits of wardship suffered when their tenants gave estates to institutions which did not die. In 1279 Edward I issued the Statute of Mortmain, forbidding grants of land into the 'dead hand' of the Church. In fact, grants continued, but only with the king's licence, which had to be paid for. In the fourteenth and fifteenth centuries only ten monasteries with an income of more than £100 a year were founded in England, in sharp contrast to the 220 founded in the previous two hundred years.

The Black Death struck religious communities hard. Some smaller houses never recovered. In England anti-French sentiments, stirred up by the Hundred Years War, led to the suppression of alien priories (daughter houses of foreign abbeys). By the beginning of Henry VIII's reign there were fewer than six hundred religious houses as opposed to about a thousand before the Black Death. The monasteries that had the greatest staying power were the richest ones, almost always the oldest – of the twenty-four houses assessed at the time of the dissolution as having a net annual income of over £1,000, twenty-three had been founded by the mid-twelfth century, and seventeen before 1066. These were the houses in which standards had always tended to be relaxed, and often still were. Fifteenth-century Westminster Abbey kitchen accounts indicate that each monk had a daily ration of two pounds of meat or fish, two pounds of bread and a gallon of ale. The generally less well-resourced Irish monasteries suffered particularly badly. Within Anglo-Irish areas the number of Benedictine houses plummeted from eighteen to three at the Dissolution.

Only one order saw an increase in number. The Carthusian brand of austerity, in which the monks lived as solitaries in cells grouped around a cloister, observing a strict rule of silence, found admirers at the highest level when kings such as Henry V at Sheen in 1415 and James I at Perth in 1429 followed the example set by Sir Walter Manny, who founded the London Charterhouse in 1371. But Carthusian houses were always few; the late foundations brought the total in Britain up to only nine. In terms of number, the one major exception is the success of the Observant branches of the mendicant orders in Ireland, where no fewer than ninety Observant friaries were established in the fifteenth century. They did particularly well among the Gaels, where their strict observance of the rule stood out sharply in a traditional religious culture in which family values still sometimes led to son succeeding father as abbot. The presence of so many Observant friars would stiffen Irish resistance to Protestant Reformation.

Religious Decline?

Protestants have often read the declining number of religious houses in Britain as an indicator of a general decline in religion. Others have disagreed, pointing out that instead chantries (chaplainries in Scotland) and almshouses became the principal beneficiaries of lay endowment. Because the inmates of almshouses (the poor and old rather than the sick) were expected to attend the parish church, almshouses caused less parochial tension than hospitals did. Chantries, which first appear in the historical record in the twelfth century, could be separate chapels,

but were often 'private' altars in an existing church, with an endowment so that priests said daily masses on behalf of the dead. Their
proliferation meant that in many churches the office was virtually
continuously celebrated. By the time they were suppressed by Henry
VIII there were at least two thousand chantries in England. The
survival of wills from the late thirteenth century onwards shows that
testators from an increasingly wide social range were able to secure
this kind of spiritual comfort for themselves, their families and often
also for the souls of 'all the faithful departed'.

The growing number of religious works written in English for clerks
to read to a lay audience suggests that religious enthusiasm was far
from declining. Some of the most popular, judged by the number of

The Resurrection. The artist of this *c*. 1400 alabaster depiction persuades us that for him the
resurrection of Christ was as real and as present as the contemporary armour and gear
illustrated in his representation of the soldiers at the tomb.

surviving manuscripts, reinforced traditional confessional and penitential discipline. *The Prick of Conscience*, composed *c.* 1360, for example,
encouraged self-examination in terms of the four last things: death,
judgement, hell and heaven. Other works, such as those written by
Richard Rolle (d. 1349), and Walter Hilton (1396), developed the idea of
a 'mixed life', combining life in secular society with periods of intense
contemplation, even direct and mystical communion with God. This
offered a way as open to women as to men, as the lives and books of
Julian of Norwich (d. *c.* 1416), whose *Revelations of Divine Love* may well
have been the first book in English composed by a woman, and
Margery Kempe (d. *c.* 1440), author of the first autobiography in the
language, demonstrate.

Nonetheless, developments in the practice of indulgence (the
remission of part or all of the penance imposed on a contrite sinner)
and in the doctrine of purgatory have also been regarded as evidence
of decline. Indulgences had been issued since the twelfth century. They
were intended to encourage pious acts such as alms giving and church
attendance on saints' days, or contributing to causes such as the
crusades and church, hospital and bridge building. Since to obtain an
indulgence it was necessary to have confessed, one effect was to
encourage lay people not to wait, as previously nearly everyone had,
until they were dying before confessing their sins. In this religious
climate Pope Innocent III decreed that everyone should confess once a
year. Indulgences were sometimes offered to the dying; evidently they
were already expected to have an effect in the afterlife. Although not
formally defined until 1274, the concept of purgatory as a place where
the dead were chastised for their sins and purified by fire in preparation
for heaven was much older. The length of time spent in purgatory –
potentially tens of thousands of years – could be reduced by the
intercession of saints, by the prayers of the living, and by priests' saying
mass. As always the pious and wealthy made the most of their
purchasing power – William Courtenay, archbishop of Canterbury
(1381–96), for example, bought 10,000 masses for his soul. The
development of indulgences to the point at which they could be
bought by the living on behalf of the souls of the dead facilitated
further reductions in the length of time spent in purgatory. Initially
indulgences remitted no more than a few days, but the law of
competitive generosity gradually took its toll. Arguably this demand
led Christianity to become a less demanding religion to live by, and the

great majority were content with that. They accepted a set of values that bound together not only communities of the living but also, through the doctrine of purgatory and the value placed on intercession, those of the living with the dead. In the next century a demand-led religion would face greater problems.

Heresy

In the fifteenth century the mystic's claim to direct communion with God worried the authorities more than it had in earlier times. The Oxford theologian John Wyclif was largely responsible for this heightened nervousness. Employed in the 1370s by Edward III's government when it wanted to justify taxing the Church to pay for war with France, Wyclif argued that in the present state of ecclesiastical corruption, kings, as stewards of the nation's wealth, were entitled to seize Church property. Pope Gregory XI condemned the argument. At this point, instead of turning to safer academic questions, Wyclif launched fundamental attacks on the structure and doctrine of the Catholic Church. In 1378 he argued that because all people were predestined to either salvation or damnation, priests were superfluous as channels of grace. All they could usefully do was preach God's word as it appeared in the Bible – where, as he pointed out, there was no mention of popes, bishops or property-owning prelates. In 1379 in his treatise *On the Eucharist* he denied transubstantiation – the ritual which, above all others, was held to express priestly authority. Condemned as a heretic in 1380, in May 1381 he defiantly reaffirmed his beliefs. The outbreak of the great rebellion of 1381 a month later made him an easy target for those who looked for someone to blame. He was driven out of Oxford, but continued to write until his death in 1384. Meanwhile, some of his Oxford followers took his ideas to a wider audience, going on preaching tours and composing, in English, Wycliffite sermons, treatises and broadsheets such as the satirical *Letter from Satan*, praising the clergy of the day. Above all they embarked on the unprecedented act of translating the Bible into English. They rapidly won adherents in towns such as Leicester, Coventry and Bristol. A few of the gentry were persuaded, prominent among them the soldier and courtier Sir John Oldcastle. In pointed contrast to the worldliness of many of the higher clergy, the simple lifestyle adopted by the Lollards, as

Wycliffites came to be called, was attractive. They concealed – as their enemies put it – 'the perversity of their doctrines under a veil of sanctity'.

In fact their numbers were always few, but the orthodox could not be sure; energetically led by Archbishop Thomas Arundel of Canterbury, they exaggerated the danger. In 1401 the continental use of the death penalty for relapsed heretics was introduced into English law. In 1407 Arundel ordered that all preaching had to be licensed, and all translations of the scriptures approved by the diocesan. Oldcastle was sent to the Tower in 1413, but soon escaped. He was captured and executed in 1417. His alleged leadership of a small rising at St Giles' Fields, just outside London, in January 1414, was exploited by the government in order to tar Lollardy with the brush of sedition. This put an end to support for Lollardy among the elite. After the middle of the century, since it no longer won recruits among the politically influential, the authorities gradually lost interest in it. But it survived, and to some extent thrived, as an underground movement with its own literature (in English). In the view of some scholars it was 'the premature reformation'.

Schools and Universities

In the eleventh century and earlier very few children received any schooling in the sense of entering the world of letters. Those with a parent who could read, often their mother, were expected to follow suit through parental instruction. A few children were taught the Latin alphabet and prayers such as the Pater Noster and Ave Maria by their parish priest. Christianity being a religion of a book, a bookish education was available in major churches throughout Britain and Ireland. According to a poem written by Ieuean ap Sulien, his father spent five years learning in Scotland, then ten years in Ireland, before returning to Wales to teach at Llanbadarn Fawr. Such is the absence of evidence from Scotland that we don't know where he might have found scholars there, whereas in Ireland churches such as Armagh, Glendalough and Lismore still enjoyed a reputation as centres of learning.

Hitherto educational provision, no matter how good, had always been ancillary to the main business of the institutions which offered it, whether cathedrals, religious houses or the households of prelates, nobles and kings. But in twelfth-century England the growth of towns made it possible for a man to make a living by charging fees for teaching reading and writing. 'Are not teachers,' one mid-twelfth-century commentator complained, 'now as common as royal tax-collectors?' There was evidently a growing demand for education, not fully met by the 1179 papal decree requiring all cathedrals to maintain a schoolmaster to teach poor scholars for nothing. By the late twelfth century one learned clerk, Walter Map, asserted that rustics sent their sons to school so that they could become clerics and get rich. Few clerks wanted to become priests; most became administrators and secretaries. The increasing output of documents implies a growing number of clerical staff; William FitzStephen asserted that, as chancellor, Becket employed fifty-two clerks.

As, through the centuries, the volume of surviving documents increases, so also the number of known schools, rising from about forty in twelfth-century England to about three hundred in the fifteenth. The establishment of public elementary schools – 'public' in the sense of being open to anyone whose parents or patrons could afford the fees – was the educational environment out of which the universities of Oxford and Cambridge evolved c. 1200. By this date the pattern of the modern school year was set: three terms starting in September and ending in June. In the fourteenth century benefactors founded grammar schools where boys could be taught free of charge. Although endowed schools were for boys only, by this date in towns such as London and Oxford there were also schoolmistresses teaching girls how to read. The widespread use of bureaucratic Latin in government and manorial administration implies that the gentry could read it well enough. Writing was another matter – usually that could be left to clerks, as to typists and secretaries in the twentieth century. Once pupils had mastered Latin, many switched to reading and writing in their vernaculars: English and French. The ideal from the later twelfth century onwards was to be able to read in all three languages.

In Ireland and the less urbanised parts of Britain few such grammar schools were founded. Education remained in the hands of either the Church, in particular Dominican and Franciscan friaries in the later centuries, or was left to those learned familial groups such as the O'Dalys of Ireland or the Mhuirichs of the Western Isles which flourished in Welsh Wales, Gaelic Ireland and Scotland and kept alive a vibrant vernacular culture.

In 1188 the innovative and ambitious Anglo-Welsh scholar Gerald de
Barri put on a one-man literary festival at Oxford. Over three days he
staged readings of his new work, *The Topography of Ireland*, and paid for
three book launch parties. He chose Oxford, he explained, because that
was 'the place in England where the clergy were the most numerous and
most learned'. At this stage there were just informal gatherings of teachers
and learners, living in lodgings or rented houses, no universities in the
sense of bodies (corporations) recognised as such in law. At Oxford a
quarrel between the scholars and the town authorities over the hanging
of three allegedly innocent clerks led, in 1214, to the establishment of a
formal union of masters and students, a university. The quarrel also led to
the beginnings of Cambridge University since many clerks migrated
there, withdrawing their purchasing power to put pressure on Oxford. By
the mid-fifteenth century both English universities were venerable
institutions, their colleges and halls containing about three thousand
teachers and students. The arts degree took seven years (four for the BA,
and three more for the MA). The baccalaureate consisted mainly of
Grammar, Logic and Rhetoric, the three arts of the Trivium – in practice
an intensive training in linguistic analysis, logic and the techniques of
presenting an argument. For the master's degree they employed these
techniques to debate philosophical questions. This was a formidable
training in transferable skills which made its products desirable
commodities in the upper reaches of the labour market, since both secular
and ecclesiastical princes wanted men who could present a good case, or
demolish a competitor's, as well as act as administrators, managers and
consultants. Not many students stayed on to work for doctorates in the
three higher faculties: law, medicine, theology. Theology was recognised,
principally by theologians, as the 'queen of sciences', but law and
medicine were the 'lucrative sciences'. At Oxford and Cambridge more
than two-thirds of the few who stayed on chose law. These remained the
only two universities in Britain and Ireland until 1412, when St Andrews
was founded, soon followed by Glasgow (1451) and Aberdeen (1495).

Secular Culture

The limitations of the surviving evidence mean that for what little we
know about the leisure pursuits and cultural interests of those men,
women and children who did not belong to the elite, we depend chiefly

upon comments made by people who wanted to curb them: church-men who disapproved of the pleasure taken in 'lascivious' music and dance, or complained that too many people preferred watching wrestling matches to listening to sermons; secular authorities who wanted to see free time used for archery practice rather than on football or golf. Such spoilsport voices are at least sufficiently numerous to indicate that early versions of most modern games in which players use bats, clubs or their feet in order to knock a ball about were widespread. Archaeological evidence – items such as musical instruments, toys, dice or pieces for board games – allows us to 'see' the objects and make replicas, but otherwise adds little to what written sources tell us about the social milieux in which they were used.

What appear to be the oldest stories to represent secular values from the 'inside' are the vernacular tales of the violent deeds of long dead heroes such as Beowulf, Cú Chulainn and Roland. A few such works, *Beowulf*, for example, survive in early eleventh-century form, but most are known only from manuscripts written in the twelfth century, such as the Irish Book of Leinster and the Chanson de Roland, or from even later, such as the fourteenth-century Welsh books containing the earliest known vernacular Arthurian tale, *Culhwch and Olwen*. After the Norman Conquest, the Old English *Beowulf* was largely forgotten until the nineteenth century. The Irish heroes lived on in the literature of Gaeldom, but made little impact outside Scotland and Ireland until the invention of an imaginary Celtic world in the nineteenth century. By contrast, thanks to Geoffrey of Monmouth's *History of the Kings of Britain*, probably composed at Oxford in the 1130s, the court of King Arthur rapidly became the setting for some of the finest works of European secular literature. Being written in Latin, the *History of the Kings of Britain* entered the wider world of learning; in number of extant manuscripts it far outstrips any other history written anywhere in Europe during the twelfth century.

Whether its readers believed it to be true or not, they were bowled over by a history that celebrated kings, both pagan and Christian, and measured their success by non-religious criteria: victory in war, law-making, road building, town founding, and the holding of magnificent courts. It was immediately turned into French verse by Geoffrey Gaimar and Wace; then into English verse by Layamon. The imagined world of rulers such as King Arthur or Mark of Cornwall was the setting for a new kind of literature: the prose romance. Authors such as

Chrétien of Troyes and Thomas, author of the *Romance of Horn* (both more or less speculatively linked with the court of Henry II) set out a code of noble conduct for women and men, models of behaviour in peace as well as war. Descriptions of evening entertainment reveal that the well-brought-up aristocrat was expected to be able to play a musical instrument. Chess, a game which came to Europe via the Arab world, reached England soon after 1066. As a fashionable game of skill played by women as well as men, it offered opportunities, in the words of the *Romance of Alexander*, 'to speak courteously of love to ladies'. In exploring the effects of passion on men and women the romances took a relaxed attitude to sex. Nonetheless, sexual relationships as presented in them were models of restraint when compared with the exuberant bawdiness in the *fabliaux*. These give us, as few other surviving sources do, some idea of what less earnest people liked to laugh about. Chaucer's *Miller's Tale* looks very tame when compared with the abandon with which the 'crude' French equivalents for words such as 'fuck', 'prick' and 'balls' were thrown about in stories such as *Le Chevalier qui fist parler les cons*.

The deathbed scene in the early thirteenth-century biography *L'Histoire de Guillaume le Maréchal* throws a revealing light on the piety of a man regarded as a model knight. During his final illness William confessed his sins every week and obtained a plenary indulgence from the papal legate. Even when preparing for death, however, he knew his own mind. When told that he could go to heaven only if he returned all his tournament winnings, William's answer was that 'churchmen shave us too closely. If the kingdom of heaven is closed to me because I captured 500 knights and kept their arms, horses and equipment, then so be it. Either their argument is false or no man can be saved.' Later a clerk advised him to sell eighty fine robes and spend the money for the salvation of his soul. William rounded on him: 'Be quiet you wretch. Whitsun, when I hand out new robes to my knights, is coming and this will be my last chance to do so.' His determination to leave behind a reputation as a good knight and an honourable lord outweighed everything else.

However many clerks there were, they were never more than a tiny minority of the total population. Moreover many, perhaps most, were more interested in secular culture than in religion. One of the priests in William Langland's *Piers Plowman* (late fourteenth century) confesses: 'I don't even know the Paternoster perfectly, not as a priest should really sing it. I know plenty of ballads about Robin Hood and Randolph Earl of Chester, but not a verse about our Lord or our Lady.' But no ballads of Randolph of Chester survive, and none of Robin Hood pre-date the fifteenth century. Indeed, although works written in English survive from every century in this period, more survive from the fifteenth than from all the previous centuries combined. In part this was due to the achievement of late fourteenth-century poets such as Langland, John Gower, the unknown author of *Sir Gawain and the Green Knight* and, above all, Geoffrey Chaucer in demonstrating to what sophisticated uses the English language could now be put. The immediate popularity of Chaucer's masterpiece, *The Canterbury Tales*, unsurpassed in fluency and wit, helped to establish English as the main language of the nation's literature.

One consequence of this is that the pleasures and values of the secular world are more in evidence in the fifteenth century than earlier – which would appear to fit neatly into a scheme of 'decline' in religious vitality before the Reformation. It is, however, likely that even in periods of active religious reform such as the early twelfth century, elite secular culture was both dominant and self-confident. Eadmer, Anselm of Canterbury's biographer, remarked that the long-haired and courtly aristocrats of his day mocked those who cut their hair short, calling them peasants (*rustici*) or priests, both evidently terms of abuse.

Words such as *rustici* and *rusticitas* (boorishness) are key terms in the earliest extant courtesy books. 'Do not grab the tastiest morsels,' wrote one author, 'or you will be reproached for your *rusticitas*.' Table manners were particularly important in an age when food was served in units, known as messes, shared between two, three or four people, and when in the absence of forks – which only gradually came into use from the late fourteenth century onward – diners used their fingers to help themselves. Bodily functions were to be kept under control. Daniel of Beccles, author of the longest of all courtesy poems, the twelfth-century *Liber Urbani*, The Book of the Civilised Man, advised on when, where and how to belch, defecate, fart, spit and urinate politely; only the head of a household, for example, was entitled to urinate in the hall. But courtesy books, extant in Latin from the twelfth century, Anglo-Norman from the thirteenth, and English from the fourteenth, were much more than books of etiquette. Often in the guise of advice from father to son, or in one case from mother to daughter, they instructed their readers in deportment, dress and on a wide range of social relationships (between men and women, master and servant, host and guest), on how, in Daniel's phrase, to lead a civilised life. The much shorter twelfth-century Latin poem *Facetus* ('The man of refinement'), which became a standard text in English schools, contains the dictum: 'he who speaks badly of women is a boor (*rusticus*), for truly we are all born of women'. Such language reflects courtesy literature's claim to teach a code of conduct appropriate to people of rank. The image of a gentleman as someone who looks after his estates, lives on friendly terms with neighbours with whom he exchanges visits, and who acts as local magistrate can be found as far back as the *Liber Urbani* – and may well be older than that.

The emphasis on elegant manners and polished speech, leading to the coining of words such as *courtoisie*, meant that men who took a monk's view of Christianity were disturbed by the values of the courtesy books. These, however, were the values which were taught in the schools and great houses of England and Lowland Scotland. Throughout this period households remained the principal schools of the elite. In them future heads of households served as pages, experiencing what lordship and service meant.

Languages

In every part of north-western Europe in the eleventh century at least two languages were in use: the regional vernacular for everyday speech, and Latin, the language written and spoken by clerks. In some regions the absence of records means that hypotheses about the spoken languages have to be based on the fragile evidence of later place names, though the survival of Norn in Orkney and Shetland until the eighteenth century leaves little room for doubt about the vernacular of the far north. In some regions there may well have been two vernaculars – Gaelic and Norse in the Western Isles and in some Irish ports, for example, or Cornish and English in the far south-west. The Scottish Highlands and islands were part of Gaeldom, sharing the same legends and mythical heroes such as Finn McCool; in the fourteenth century the Bruces, looking for alliances with Irish chiefs, appealed to their common language and way of life.

Only a handful of words attest to the existence of written Gaelic in early Scotland and written Cornish in Cornwall, but Ireland and Wales were, in European terms, unusual in having a developed vernacular literature. Pre-Norman England was even more unusual since English was used not only for verse and religious writing but had become the predominant language of law, historical writing and government. The Norman Conquest brought over thousands of French settlers who called their own language 'roman' and who looked upon English as a barbarous language, not to be used in polite society. Religious works and poetry continued to be composed in English, but as the written language of law and government it was rapidly ousted by Latin. By the mid-twelfth century the descendants of the conquerors, or at any rate those who did not also possess great estates in Normandy, thought of themselves as English, and could speak English, but they continued to identify themselves as a cosmopolitan elite by using Anglo-Norman French as their preferred language. Indeed the oldest extant works of French literature in several genres were composed in twelfth-century multi-lingual England. When francophone settlers were invited into Scotland and invaded Ireland, they took their culture with them. Hence the composition of the thirteenth-century *Roman de Fergus de Galloway* whose hero swears by St Mungo, and narratives of the English conquest of Ireland written in both Latin and French.

The ability to speak French offered so many advantages that it did not remain exclusive to the ruling class. Some knowledge of it was indispensable for those involved in the workings of the king's courts. The syntax and vocabulary of English was dramatically altered by French influence in a way that is explicable only in terms of widespread bilingualism. At the same time and partly as a result of English immigration into Scottish towns, English (first called 'Scots' in 1494) came to be more widely spoken north of the Forth. Not until the later fourteenth century, the age of Chaucer, did English become a high-status language in England, and not until the fifteenth was it routinely used in the business of government, in Scotland as well as in England, while the use of French declined rapidly – although Law French survived until 1731. Latin remained everywhere the language of the Church and of the learned, in science until the seventeenth century. One consequence of the Chaucerian revolution was to return authors writing in English to the relative isolation of the time before the Norman Conquest when readers on the Continent knew nothing of their works. Not until the eighteenth century did people outside England want to read Shakespeare. Within England, however, the proliferation of schools and wider distribution of wealth created the demand which William Caxton met when, in 1475, he began printing books in English, in the process contributing, for good or ill, to the standardisation of the language.

3. Political and National Cultures

In 1066 England, its borders already very similar to those of modern England, was much the largest and richest of the political units in Britain and Ireland. To its north and west stretched an arc containing a fluctuating number of smaller kingdoms, expanding and contracting as the military fortunes of individual kings waxed and waned. In the eleventh century the kings of the Scots were the most successful of these, but they were far from ruling anything like modern Scotland. Driving southwards from their core territory (the rich farmlands of Fife), they had imposed their rule on Cumbrians and the English of Lothian. To the south-west, however, the Galwegians still resisted, as did the kings of Moray to the north. Further north still, Caithness was ruled by the earls of Orkney; they, like the kings of Man and the Isles in the west, acknowledged Norwegian overlordship. In Wales there were usually at least four or five kingships at any one time: Gwynedd, Powys, Deheubarth, Morgannwg and Gwent. Ireland was even more fragmented. The learned thought of it as divided into two halves, northern and southern, into five provinces – Leinster, Munster, Ulster, Connacht and Meath – and into more than a hundred peoples (*tuatha*), each one ruled over by a chief (*toisech*) or king (*rí*). Each *rí túaithe* owed tribute and military service to more powerful neighbours. As scores of kings fought to be the strongest king in a province, or even to be the greatest king in all Ireland, sometimes known as *rí Erenn*, king of Ireland, or 'high-king', Ireland remained in a state of constant flux.

A major theme of the next five hundred years of political history is the English attempt to rule the rest. By 1300 the kings of England had conquered Wales, taken over the Isle of Man, seemed to be on the point of completing a conquest of Ireland, and had just launched an invasion of Scotland. Peter Langtoft, writing late in Edward I's reign

(1272–1307), believed he was witnessing the triumphant recreation of
King Arthur's legendary empire under the English crown:

> Now are all the islanders joined together
> And Albany [Scotland] reunited to the regalities
> Of which King Edward is proclaimed lord.
> Cornwall and Wales are in his power
> And Ireland the Great is at his will.
> Arthur never held the lands so fully.

But in Ireland a Gaelic resurgence turned the tide, and the Scottish
kingdom was too big to swallow easily. A series of expansionist kings
had pushed northwards and westwards until, by 1300, their realm
included the far north of mainland Scotland and the Western Isles. This
sequence of invasions, conquests and failed conquests has left an
indelible mark on the political geography of Britain and Ireland.
Ironically, of course, the richest and most powerful of the kingdoms of
Britain and Ireland was the one most comprehensively conquered.

The Norman Conquest

Throughout these five centuries the flow of political power was
generally from south-east to north and west. The single most abrupt
moment in this flow occurred during the night of 27–28 September
1066 when the fleet of William, duke of Normandy, sailed from
St Valéry-sur-Somme to Pevensey on the south coast of England. Two
weeks later, on 14 October, on a ridge a few miles north of Hastings,
William won a close-run battle against King Harold, who was killed
alongside his two brothers. Exploiting the consequent lack of
leadership, William forced London's surrender. He was crowned king
in Westminster Abbey on Christmas Day 1066. In order to persuade so
many to risk life and limb in one of the most hazardous military
operations of the century, he had promised to reward them with the
lands of the followers of 'the usurper' Harold. Keeping this promise
entailed the confiscations and resentments that led to English risings in
every year from 1067 to 1070. Each rebellion triggered further confiscations. Initially the Normans had to live as an army of occupation,
building castles in an effort to control the towns and main roads while

the countryside belonged to the resistance. Memories of the struggle survived in the tales of Hereward the Wake, one of this guerrilla movement's last leaders. Inevitably William had the greatest trouble in controlling England north of the Humber, difficult to access from the south and wide open to armed intervention from both Danes and Scots. When King Swein of Denmark sent a fleet to assist Northumbrian rebels in 1069, William's response was the 'harrying of the North', the systematic destruction of an entire society and its stock of food and seed: massacre by famine.

In the end the War of English Independence was lost, the English political nation destroyed. By 1086, as Domesday Book makes plain, the Norman Conquest had resulted in the old English upper class suffering the virtually total loss of property or status, or both, an event unparalleled in European history, and the greatest crisis – so far – in English political history. By 1100 not a single bishopric or major abbey was ruled by an Englishman. The new regime imposed itself on a gargantuan scale. William I's Colchester Castle, Bishop Walkelin's Winchester Cathedral and William II's Westminster Hall were the largest buildings of their kind erected north of the Alps since the fall of Rome. The new castles were characterised by distinctively French design features such as great towers and mottes. The old cathedrals and monastic churches were demolished and replaced by new ones built in a new style, influenced by models from France and the Rhineland.

England: the French Connection

The Normans were the first French dynasty to come to power in England. Two more followed: the house of Blois in 1135, the house of Anjou in 1154. In 1216 the French royal dynasty, the Capetians, almost became kings of England too. The two royal families had been closely related since 1140 when King Stephen's son and heir Eustace married Constance, sister of Louis VII. From 1338 onwards the king of England claimed to be king of France. From 1066 to 1453 the kings of England also held substantial territories in France, and most of them had French wives. In consequence most of them spent some time in France, and some of them spent most of the time in France. English and French politics were inextricably entangled.

William I had not intended to integrate England and Normandy into a single kingdom. When he died in 1087 he split them between his two older sons, Normandy for Robert 'Curthose', and England for William, known as Rufus. But, driven by short-term military and political expediency, he had also created a new class, a cross-Channel aristocracy holding lands in both England and France. It suited this powerful interest group when first Rufus and then the youngest of the Conqueror's sons, Henry I, used English wealth to make themselves rulers of Normandy too. In the event England and Normandy shared the same ruler from 1106 until 1204, except for ten years, 1145–54, during the war of succession between Stephen of Blois and the Angevins. Even then both contestants claimed to be rightful ruler on both sides of the Channel.

The accession of Henry II in 1154 brought to the throne a ruler who was, as contemporaries put it, 'in extent of his dominions greater than any previous king of England'. His seal lists his titles: king of England, duke of the Normans and Aquitanians, count of the Angevins. The extent of his dominions, in part due to his marriage in 1152 to Eleanor of Aquitaine, meant that he ruled more of France than did King Louis VII (Eleanor's ex-husband). His empire was passed on virtually intact to his sons, Richard I and John. John's ineptitude, however, culminating in his responsibility for the murder of his nephew, Arthur of Brittany, meant that almost no one would fight for him when Philip II of France (Louis VII's son) invaded Anjou and Normandy in 1203–4. When Eleanor died in March 1204, the Poitevins did homage to the king of France. In Gascony, the towns' commercial ties with England, above all through the Bordeaux wine trade, were so central to their interests that they stayed loyal to John. But the combined loss of Normandy, Anjou and inland Poitou was one of the most comprehensive defeats ever suffered by a king of England. A new fact of European political geography was established, and one that turned out to be near permanent: two rival nation-states separated by the Channel, France the larger and richer of them. John's belated attempt to recover his lands ended disastrously at the Battle of Bouvines in 1214 – a defeat that led directly to the Magna Carta rebellion and the invasion of England by Philip's son Louis. Eventually Henry III accepted the loss of Normandy and Anjou (the Treaty of Paris, 1259), in return for the king of France's recognition of him as duke of a truncated Aquitaine.

The costs of defending Aquitaine against the lawyers and armies of the king of France remained high. To meet them Edward I pushed through the changes which amounted to the creation of a state financed by parliamentary taxation. Further French threats to Gascony in the 1320s and 1330s provoked Edward III into claiming the crown of France for himself in opposition to his Valois cousins. During the War of French Succession, usually known as the Hundred Years War, fortunes fluctuated dramatically. Edward III's and the Black Prince's victories in the 1340s and 1350s were followed by a period of French recovery. The war of conquest relaunched by Henry V after Agincourt (1415) saw his son Henry VI crowned king of France in Paris, but was brought to a standstill by Joan of Arc, the most extraordinary war leader in European history. Even so the rapid collapse of their empire in France between 1449 and 1453 shocked all Englishmen and precipitated the violent quarrels between the houses of York and

A rare illustration of a house being ransacked. More commonly medieval representations of war focus on the heroic moments of battle and siege. Why might that be? And is it possible to decide whether one kind of image is more realistic or informative about soldiers' motives in going to war than the other?

Lancaster known as the Wars of the Roses. Although the Hundred Years War is conventionally said to have ended in 1453, when Gascony was finally lost, so long as kings of England claimed to be kings of France – as they did until 1801 – there was always the possibility that, given the opportunity, they might reactivate the claim. The French fear that Richard III might do just that led them to provide an obscure exile named Henry Tudor with ships, money and troops. There is a case for seeing Bosworth (1485) not merely as the decisive battle of the Wars of the Roses but also as the last battle of the Hundred Years War.

Scotland: the English Connection

Malcolm III (1058–93) was one of the most successful of all Scottish kings, yet everything we know about his reign is due to the fact that, by marrying Margaret, sister of Edgar the Atheling and great-niece of Edward the Confessor, he became of interest to the compilers of the *Anglo-Saxon Chronicle* and the monks of Durham. If any documents were issued in his name they do not survive; nor does any historical narrative composed in Scotland until a hundred years later. The names given to their children are revealing: Edward, Edgar, Edmund, Æthelred, Alexander, David, Edith and Mary – five of them names used by the English royal house, and none of them names of her husband's ancestors. According to Symeon of Durham, Margaret was a civilising influence.

Malcolm's role as protector of English refugees, including the displaced royal family, lent a new tincture of righteousness to his leadership of predatory raids on Northumbria. But he was killed in 1093 during one of those raids, and in the violent succession dispute which followed, Duncan II, Malcolm's son by an earlier wife, promised that 'he would never bring Englishmen or Frenchmen into the country'. Not until 1097, when Edgar the Atheling was given command of an army that put his nephew Edgar on the Scottish throne as William II's client, was the struggle for the throne settled. A generation of peace on the Anglo-Scottish border then followed as a result of Henry I's marriage to Malcolm's and Margaret's daughter Edith and the succession to the Scottish throne of two of Edith's brothers: Alexander I (1107–24), and David I (1124–53).

A familiar figure at the English court since 1093, David welcomed Anglo-Norman nobles to Scotland and endowed them generously in Lothian. His monastic foundations at Kelso, Holyrood and Melrose not only brought in English and continental religious fashions, they also involved the production of the earliest undoubtedly genuine Scottish royal charters. Conceivably some of 'his' innovations – the foundation of the earliest Scottish towns and of a parish system – had been anticipated by his predecessors, but, if so, the evidence does not survive. He was certainly, however, the first Scottish king to issue his own coin, modelled on Henry I's. In William of Malmesbury's opinion, 'the rust of his native barbarism had been polished away by his upbringing amongst us'. The opposition he faced from Alexander I's illegitimate son Malcolm mac Heth in 1124, and from Angus of Moray in 1130, may reflect the hostility of traditionalists to new-fangled foreign ways. Over three decades of peace came to an end when David launched several invasions of England after 1135, both to support his niece, the Empress Matilda, and to press his wife's claim to Northumbria. Although defeated at the Battle of the Standard in 1138, he overran Cumbria and secured the recognition of his son, Henry, as earl of Northumbria. This meant that for once in British history, a Scottish king, in possession of Newcastle and Carlisle, could hope to match his southern neighbour.

Henry died in 1152, however, and David's decision to designate his eleven-year-old grandson, Malcolm IV, as his heir put this achievement at risk. In 1157 the young king was compelled to return Cumbria and Northumbria to Henry II of England, perhaps the better to face a rival king to the west, Somerled, the Gaelic-Norse king of Argyll and the Western Isles. Malcolm IV died unmarried and childless in 1165, and was succeeded by his younger brother William, whom David had proclaimed earl of Northumbria. Naturally William I took advantage of rebellion against Henry II to invade and reclaim his earldom, but he was captured in 1174. To obtain his release he was forced to do homage to Henry II for Scotland, and accept English garrisons in the castles of Edinburgh, Berwick and Roxburgh. This gave the mac Williams, descendants of Duncan II, an opportunity to challenge the throne right of Margaret's line. But William, later known as 'the Lion', overcame the mac Williams, purchased Scottish independence from Richard I for 10,000 marks in 1189, and was subsequently able to extend royal authority northwards across the Moray Firth.

William's son Alexander II (1214–49) was drawn into supporting the Magna Carta rebellion by the promise of the northern counties, but withdrew once Henry III appeared to be secure. This ushered in an eighty-year period of peace between the two countries, formalised by Alexander's marriage to Henry's sister Joan in 1221, and then by the treaty of York (1237), finally establishing the Tweed–Solway line as the border. He and his son, Alexander III (1249–86), continued the policy of expansion west and north, provoking a vigorous reaction from their rival King Haakon of Norway. But Haakon's successor, King Magnus, sold off all Norwegian rights over Man and the Western Isles (the treaty of Perth, 1266). Apart from the Orkneys and Shetland, which remained Norwegian, the political geography of modern Scotland was now in place. The early deaths of his children led Alexander III to make his granddaughter Margaret, 'the Maid of Norway', his heir presumptive. When he died in a horse-riding accident, she was recognised as queen and betrothed to Edward, Edward I's eldest son. Her death, aged seven, in 1290, precipitated the great crisis in Anglo-Scottish relations.

Thirteen 'competitors' claimed the Scottish throne, recognised Edward I's overlordship and agreed to accept his verdict. In 1292 he awarded the throne to John Balliol. But by then treating him as though he were an English baron, not king of another country, he drove him into opposition and interpreted it as rebellion. The Scots turned to Philip IV of France, making the treaty which traditionally marks the beginning of the Auld Alliance. Edward invaded, captured Berwick (Scotland's largest burgh) in 1296, took Balliol prisoner and carried off the Stone of Scone on which Scottish kings had been enthroned. The Scottish aristocracy recognised defeat, but two esquires, Andrew Moray and William Wallace, did not. They inflicted a humiliating defeat upon the overconfident English at Stirling Bridge (September 1297), though in the battle Moray was mortally wounded. For the next ten months Wallace was the unrivalled leader of the Scots. In July 1298, however, he unwisely engaged Edward himself in battle at Falkirk. The Scottish spearmen were overwhelmed by the massive English superiority in archers and cavalry. Wallace returned to relative obscurity, but fought on until betrayed and executed in 1305. The War of Scottish Independence went on far longer than Edward had imagined possible, for the Highlands, too extensive to be ringed round with castles like North Wales, provided a safe refuge for determined patriots. Even so, by the end of 1306 it seemed that Edward had won. A desperate bid for the throne by Robert Bruce had fizzled out. So tarnished a figure – he had committed murder and sacrilege, killing John Comyn of Badenoch in the Greyfriars' church in Dumfries – was easily disposed of, hounded by the English and the Comyns until he disappeared beyond the horizon of historians into a legendary world of caves and spiders.

The story of Bruce's re-emergence in 1307, of how he overcame each setback until at last, at Bannockburn in 1314, he routed an army led by the king of England in person, is one of the great more or less true romances of history, and told as such in the earliest known life of Robert, John Barbour's epic poem *The Bruce*. A letter drafted in Bruce's chancery, known as the Declaration of Arbroath (1320), summed up the cause: 'we fight not for glory, nor for riches, nor honours, but for freedom alone, which no good man gives up except for his life'. Initially the fightback was made possible by Edward I's counter-productive policy of treating Robert's friends and kinsmen not as honourable enemies but as traitors. Political disarray in England during Edward II's reign then gave Bruce the breathing space that allowed him to overcome his Scottish enemies, partisans of Comyn and Balliol, giving their estates to his own followers, before launching the raids into England that turned the fight for survival into a war of profit. After Bannockburn he opened up another front, sending his brother Edward Bruce with an army to Ireland, appealing to pan-Gaelic patriotism. In 1328 an enfeebled English government formally recognised Robert's kingship and the existence of an independent Scotland.

But yet again the priority given to the claims of family put the kingdom at risk. In 1326 Robert had settled the succession on David, his recently born and only legitimate son. David's accession in 1329 presented Edward III with a golden opportunity to avenge recent humiliations. In return for the promise of much of southern Scotland, he encouraged John Balliol's son Edward to claim the Scottish throne. From 1332 to 1338 a triple alliance of Balliol, the 'Disinherited' – those whose lands had been confiscated by Robert Bruce – and the king of England campaigned in Scotland, but met fierce resistance from those, notably the Douglas family, who had acquired what the 'Disinherited' had lost. When Edward III's ambitions turned south, David II, as a good ally of France, invaded England and was captured in battle (1346).

While he remained a prisoner, Robert 'the Steward', son of Robert Bruce's daughter Marjory, governed as lieutenant of Scotland. In 1357 David was released in return for the promise of a ransom of 100,000 marks. He died, still childless, in 1371, enabling Robert II to come to the throne some fifty-three years after he had first been made heir presumptive. Since Robert had five legitimate sons (as well as seventeen other children), there was little danger of the Stewart dynasty dying out in the male line. Providing his children with great estates did, however, add to the amount of power in the hands of regional magnates. For over thirty years Scottish political life was dominated by the duke of Albany, acting in turn as lieutenant for his father (Robert II), brother (Robert III) and nephew, James I (1406–37). Captured by the English in 1406, James remained their prisoner for eighteen years. When finally released he arrested and executed those whom he accused of leaving him to rot. By confiscating their estates he reclaimed control of the crown's material resources. He used parliament to introduce a flood of statutes, including the prohibition of football. So interventionist a king made many enemies and in 1437 he was assassinated, leaving a six-year-old boy as his heir.

Revulsion at his father's murder helped to keep James II safe while various factions, including the Douglases, struggled for control of him during the twelve years of his minority. When he came of age he resumed his father's policy of attacking some of the most powerful families. In 1452 he murdered William, earl of Douglas, and in the next few years used gunpowder artillery to bring down the castles of the earl's kin, adding their estates to the crown lands. In compliant parliaments he proclaimed his concern for law and order, economic stability and royal authority. The Wars of the Roses in England gave him the opportunity to recover territory. He was killed (3 August 1460) when one of the guns with which he was bombarding Roxburgh exploded. Five days later the battered town submitted. On 10 August the ten-year-old James III was crowned and anointed at nearby Kelso Abbey. The following year Margaret of Anjou, desperate for help, gave back Berwick. In 1469 James III began to rule in person. His marriage in that year to Margaret of Denmark led to the acquisition of Orkney and Shetland in 1472. In the same decade substantial inroads were made into the power of the last of the great regional magnates, the Macdonald lords of the Isles, who had been semi-independent rulers of the Hebrides ever since they had ousted their rivals by backing the winning side in the civil wars of Robert Bruce's reign. The growing authority of the crown meant that its reach extended further into Gaelic and Scandinavian regions, but the social and cultural contrast between Highland and Lowland, east/southern and west/northern, Gaelic-speaking and English-speaking Scotland still remained strong. So did Scottish Anglophobia, the legacy of the previous 170 years.

Wales: the English Conquest

Norman invasions of Wales followed hard on the heels of the Norman conquest of England. By the 1090s the Welsh scholar Rhigyfarch ap Sulien lamented:

> The people and the priest are despised
> By the words, hearts and deeds of the Frenchmen.
> They burden us with tribute and consume our possessions.

With the Frenchmen came English settlers to populate the new towns of the southern coastal region. Further inland the Welsh were better able to resist. The terrain meant that the conquest of Wales remained difficult and piecemeal, undertaken on the initiative of individual baronial families (Marcher lords) such as the Braoses, Clares and Mortimers, with only occasional intervention by kings of England more interested in the richer land of France. The leaders of Welsh resistance, men such as Owain ap Gruffydd (d. 1170) of Gwynedd and Rhys ap Gruffydd (known as the Lord Rhys) who ruled Deheubarth until 1197, won great reputations. But even they recognised English overlordship to the extent of no longer calling themselves kings. After their deaths, traditional succession customs led to the fragmentation of their principalities.

The first Welsh ruler to establish a longer-lasting principality was Llywelyn ap Iorwerth of Gwynedd, known as 'the Great'. Gwynedd, thanks to its mountains and tidal estuaries, was the most defensible of the ancient Welsh kingdoms. Even so, when King John concentrated his forces against it in 1211 and 1212, Llywelyn was forced to surrender Perfeddwlad (the four cantrefs east of Conwy). But John's high-handed exploitation of this triumph united the Welsh people against him, and catapulted Llywelyn into leadership of a national revolt. So effectively did Llwelyn take advantage of John's troubles in 1214–16 that he was able to persuade other Welsh rulers to swear allegiance to his son Dafydd. As a modernising ruler he built stone castles, preferred to collect revenues in coin rather than in produce, and in administration increasingly used written documents authenticated by his seal.

But after Dafydd's death in 1247, the English government imposed the Treaty of Woodstock, annexing Perfeddwlad and, posing as the guardian of Welsh tradition, dividing the lands west of Conwy between Dafydd's two nephews, Owain and Llwelyn ap Gruffydd. 'Now Wales,' wrote Matthew Paris, 'has been brought to nothing.' The threat of further partitions of Gwynedd provoked Llywelyn to fight. In 1256 he recovered Perfeddwlad where the Welsh, according to the *Brut Y Tywysogion*, 'preferred to be killed fighting for their liberty rather than suffer themselves to be unjustly trampled over by foreigners'. He was joined by the Welsh rulers in Ceredigion, Powys and Deheubarth, in part thanks to his policy of restoring territories recovered from Marcher lords to their former Welsh owners, 'keeping naught for himself', in the words of the *Brut*, 'save fame and honour'. Henry III's political difficulties after 1258 played into his hands to such an extent that the English king felt obliged, in the treaty of Montgomery (1267), to accept the reality of Llywelyn ap Gruffydd's conquests and title: Prince of Wales.

But since 'Welsh' Wales produced insufficient salt, wheat, iron and cloth to be economically independent of England, the new principality would survive only if the king of England accepted it. For this reason Llywelyn had agreed to pay a huge price, £16,667 – about three times his annual revenue – in return for English recognition. But after Edward I's accession in 1272 Llywelyn miscalculated badly, paying the new king neither homage nor the instalments due. In autumn 1277 an English army landed on Anglesey, the 'breadbasket' of Wales, and harvested the grain. Llywelyn surrendered, yielding Perfeddwlad and accepting that Welsh barons owed homage to the king. It was agreed that all disputes within Wales should be settled 'according to the laws and customs of those parts', but it was Edward who picked the judges. This, and the building of castles at Flint, Rhuddlan, Aberystwyth and Builth, made the Welsh feel that once again they were being bullied. Revolt broke out in March 1282; on 11 December the first and last native Prince of Wales was killed and his head sent to London. In January 1283 in an unprecedented winter campaign Edward's troops overran

Snowdonia. The principality of Wales was annexed to the English crown, and divided into shires (Anglesey, Caernarfonshire and Merionethshire) on the English model. The Statute of Wales (1284), while tolerating Welsh law in some spheres, introduced the forms and substance of English common law.

In spite of rebellions in 1287 and 1294–5, further castles at Harlech, Caernarfon, Conwy and Beaumaris ensured the permanence of the Edwardian conquest. In 1301 Edward of Caernarfon became the first heir to the English throne to bear the title Prince of Wales, but Wales remained a fragmented country. Outside the principality the numerous lordships known collectively as the March of Wales continued to be held by English baronial families, largely independent of each other and of the crown. The division between the native Welsh and English settler population, especially the commercial privileges of the burgesses of the English towns in Wales (the Welsh were not allowed to live in them or trade outside them), caused significant tension, and a glass ceiling made it difficult for natives to obtain high office. In September 1400 Owain Glyn Dwr, a descendant of the princes of Powys and Deheubarth, exploited the turmoil caused by the dethronement of Richard II to have himself proclaimed Prince of Wales. His rising was rapidly put down, but when the English parliament of 1401 reacted by sharpening anti-Welsh legislation, the revolt flared up again. Henry IV faced too many threats to be able to give Wales a high priority. In 1403 and 1405 the French sent military aid; in 1404 and 1405 Owain held Welsh parliaments at Machynlleth and Harlech. Also in 1405 the Percys, Edmund Mortimer and Owain drew up the Tripartite Indenture, agreeing to divide England and Wales between them, Owain's share being essentially an extended Wales. But once Henry IV had survived his early difficulties, the much greater English resources ground out an English victory. Owain himself never submitted and his capacity to inspire loyalty meant that he was still at large when he died, place and date unknown. In the words of the Welsh annalist: 'Very many say he died; the prophets insist he has not.' But although poetry and prophecy continued to fuel Welsh resentment, there was no further revolt.

Ireland: the Land of War

The most northerly of the Ostman towns, Dublin, lay within range of kings from all parts of Ireland; its central position in the Irish Sea economy made it the most desirable of prizes. One after the other dominant kings fought or negotiated their way into Dublin. While their control of Dublin lasted, all of these kings had a prima facie case to be regarded as *rí Erenn*, even if not all the other kings of Ireland accepted this – a state of affairs indicated by the phrase, almost a title, 'king of Ireland with opposition'. Several appointed sons of theirs as kings of Dublin, hoping that its resources would enable that son to build up a power base of his own. But in the succession struggles that followed every king's death very few sons managed to hold on to the supremacy their father had won. Not that any king's position, whether local, provincial or national, was ever secure. Some rulers dealt ferociously with threats from kinsmen and other dynasties. In 1141, for example, Diarmait Mac Murchada killed or blinded seventeen members of the royal families of Leinster. When Muirchertach Mac Loughlin of Ailech (Tyrone), 'king of Ireland without opposition', was killed in battle in 1166, Diarmait Mac Murchada, one of the kings who had enjoyed Muirchertach's protection, was overwhelmed by old enemies and fled.

He went to Henry II and received permission to recruit soldiers. A contemporary poem summarised Diarmait's offer:

> If anyone wishes to have land or money,
> Horses, equipment or chargers,
> Gold or silver, I will give him generous payment.

From 1167 onwards, attracted by these prospects, small bands of English adventurers sailed to Ireland. The most prominent was Richard de Clare, known as Strongbow, to whom Diarmait offered the hand of a daughter and succession to Leinster. Before Diarmait died, he and Richard captured Waterford and Dublin. The prospect of Strongbow as king so alarmed Henry II that in 1171 he took a massive English army across the Irish Sea. Most Irish kings submitted, though not the last 'high king', Rory O'Connor of Connacht. Henry assumed the title 'lord of Ireland'. 'Modernisers' among the Irish churchmen welcomed Henry's presence as a means of pushing ahead with reform.

Letters from them led Pope Alexander III to express his joy at the news that 'a barbarous and uncivilized people has been made subject to the noble king of the English'. Writing twenty-five years later, the historian William of Newburgh, in a chapter he entitled 'The Conquest of the Irish by the English', observed that 'a people who had been free since time immemorial, unconquered even by the Romans, a people for whom liberty seemed an inborn right, were now fallen into the power of the king of England'.

But Henry II did not stay long. As early as the spring of 1172 he was called away by urgent business in Normandy. He kept Dublin, Wexford and Waterford to be administered by royal officials, confirmed Strongbow in his possession of Leinster and granted Meath to Hugh de Lacy. Subsequent kings followed Henry II's lead, granting

'The Strangeness of Ireland'. According to Gerald de Barri, the inauguration ceremony of a king in Tir Connail (a part of Ireland which Gerald never visited) involved the king copulating with a white mare. The mare was then killed and turned into a stew in which the new king sat while, as shown here, distributing the meat to his followers. If this did not actually happen, then why might Gerald have thought it did, and why should he repeat the story?

other – as yet unconquered – Irish kingdoms to English lords to see what they could make of them. Until 1541 all kings of England retained the title 'lord of Ireland', but in their eyes other things would always matter more. Only two of them ever visited Ireland: John and Richard II. Ireland became a land of opportunity for farmers, craftsmen, merchants, labourers and clerks who came over from England and Wales, settling in their thousands along the south and east coasts and the river valleys from Cork to Carrickfergus. Anglicisation became official policy. The Irish who submitted had to swear to learn English and wear English clothes. Legislation made in England was routinely dispatched to Dublin. The apparatus of English government was transferred to Ireland: central courts (exchequer and bench) presided over by the justiciar (in place of the absentee king), chancellor, counties (twelve by 1300), sheriffs, councils and parliaments, the system of taxation. The modern Irish legal system, pattern of local government and parliamentary tradition all derive from the innovations made in this period.

Early attempts by the Irish to coordinate resistance, such as the 1258 alliance between Aedh O'Connor and Brian O'Neill, were crushed. Irish kingdoms continued to be bestowed on English lords as when the Ui Briain kingdom of Thomond was granted to Thomas de Clare in 1276, but the pace of English migration gradually slowed down. In some parts of Ireland English lords seized power, but could not introduce settlers in numbers sufficient to replace the native inhabitants. That two hundred or so places were accorded borough status yet never developed into towns – some never even became villages – is a measure both of the strenuous efforts that were made to attract immigrants, and of the fact that not as many came as had been hoped. Other parts such as the O'Donnell and O'Neill territories in the north escaped the colonising process altogether. There were always internal military frontiers, war zones in which Irish and English fought not only each other but also between themselves. A society already under pressure from Edward I's government, determined to make Ireland contribute to the cost of his many wars, suffered more severely still after the arrival of Edward Bruce's Scottish army in 1315. Many Irish recognised Bruce as king, but he was unable to win over the Anglo-Irish or capture Dublin, and was killed in battle at Fochart in October 1318. The Scottish challenge proved, none the less, to be a turning point. The turmoil of invasion, coinciding with a disastrous famine, caused a marked contraction in the area controlled by the Dublin government. Another battle fought in 1318, at Dysart O' Dea, saw the death of Thomas de Clare's son Richard and the restoration of Ui Briain power in Thomond. From now on Ireland cost the kings of England more than it brought in.

Only during the interludes of peace in the war with France were the English prepared to divert substantial resources to Ireland. From 1361 to 1367 Edward III's son, Lionel of Clarence, governed Ireland as Lieutenant. He was funded from English resources to the tune of £43,000, but since there was no united organised Irish enemy for him to find, let alone defeat, his troops made little military impact. Richard II took an even larger army to Ireland in 1394–5. He recognised, as he wrote, that 'Irish rebels are rebels only because of wrongs done to them and lack of remedy', but neither on this occasion nor in 1399 did he stay long enough to provide remedy. The Dublin government was trapped in a downward spiral of diminishing authority and declining revenue. Receipts at the Irish exchequer, over £6,000 a year during Edward I's reign, averaged only £1,000 a year in the fifteenth century. By the 1470s taxes could be collected only in Waterford, Wexford and the Pale (the four counties of Dublin, Meath, Louth and Kildare).

Beyond the Pale traditional political life continued. More exposed colonists had to pay 'black rent' – protection money – to neighbouring Gaelic chiefs. The lifestyles, fashions and houses of the two peoples became hard to distinguish. The English who adopted 'degenerate' Irish customs in dress and hairstyle were condemned in the Dublin parliament of 1297 and again in the Statutes of Kilkenny (1366) which prohibited marriages and alliances between English and Irish. Anglo-Irish lords such as the earls of Desmond and Ormond ruled their territories much as Gaelic lords did, launching summer cattle raids as one of the means by which they jockeyed for position within their regions. Gerald 'the Rhymer', third earl of Desmond, wrote Irish verse. Close ties to Gaelic society could make an office holder vulnerable to accusations of treason; this led to the summary execution of the seventh earl of Desmond in 1468. But since the English government would not provide Lieutenants with adequate salaries and resources, only men with great estates in Ireland could afford to take the office. In the 1470s and 1480s under successive earls of Kildare, the Dublin government became noticeably independent of Westminster. Yet the kings of England upheld their claim to be lords of Ireland, and this, taken together with the presence of Anglo-Irish chieftains beyond the Pale, meant that very few outsiders thought of the Gaelic chiefs as kings, whatever their own bards continued to call them.

Kings and Queens

The expectations placed in kings were high and everywhere broadly similar: to keep the peace, ensure that justice was done and protect their people in times of war. In 1485 just as much as in 1066, it was taken for granted that kingdoms, like landed estates and businesses, were family firms. When family quarrels erupted the result was often political crises that shook whole kingdoms. When peace was made it took the form of a family arrangement, as when Stephen adopted Henry of Anjou as his son in 1153, or when Henry Tudor married Elizabeth of York in 1486. Throughout these centuries the single most important political factor was the personality of the head of the family, his capacity to get on well with those to whom he was closest. *His* capacity, not hers, because it was also taken for granted that the head of the family would be a man. Nowhere in Britain and Ireland did a woman come to the throne in this period (though two came close. Henry I of England, lacking a legitimate son, bullied assemblies into swearing that his daughter, 'Empress' Matilda, would inherit his throne, but once he was dead (1135), oaths counted for little compared with the preference for a man, Henry's nephew Stephen. In 1286 Alexander III's granddaughter, Margaret, was recognised as queen of Scots, but died soon afterwards). Rulers were expected to be warriors. Not even peace-loving kings such as Henry III and Henry VI of England were able to avoid wars. Unlike today, it was assumed that competent adult rulers would accompany their armies and share the risks themselves when they sent their people to war. Extraordinary circumstances led to a few women such as 'Empress' Matilda and Margaret of Anjou becoming in effect commanders-in-chief. Even fewer took part in battle, though one exception was Gwenllian, wife of Gruffydd ap Rhys, king of Deheubarth, who rode at the head of her army 'like a second Queen of the Amazons', and was killed in battle against the Anglo-Norman invaders of Wales in 1136. Leadership in war was for men.

Since kingdoms were family firms, kings' wives were hard to dispense with. Of the twenty-nine kings of England (not counting Edward V) and Scotland who came to the throne after 1100, only Malcolm IV, a victim of Paget's disease, never married. Queens and their ladies were expected to add glamour and a frisson of sexual tension to the other excitements of court life. King's wives enjoyed fewer opportunities than aristocratic wives, who were often entrusted with important managerial work, running the estates while their husbands were away, usually at court or with the king's army. But, by definition, adult kings could never be 'away' from the centre of patronage and power – except on extraordinary occasions such as during Stephen's captivity or Henry VI's mental breakdown, when their wives, Matilda of Boulogne and Margaret of Anjou, stepped into the breach, the former proving an effective campaign manager. William I, Henry I, until 1118, and Henry II, until 1173, i.e. married kings of England who had large dominions in France, routinely asked their wives to act as their representatives on the other side of the Channel from the one they themselves were on. Kings of smaller kingdoms were never tempted to do this, and after 1173 kings of England almost never let their wives off the leash until Edward II allowed Isabella to go to France in 1325, with catastrophic consequences for him. It did not happen again. As wives, queens were well placed to give confidential advice; no doubt many did and many husbands were happy to follow it. A few queens, such as Margaret of Scotland and Margaret of Anjou, were reputed to wield great influence. But it was always taken for granted that they should submit to their husbands' authority. Eleanor of Aquitaine's involvement in the 1173 rebellion against Henry II came as a great shock, whereas contemporaries disapproved of, but were not surprised by, the rebellions of his sons.

A queen who was a first wife was expected to bear her husband's children; her sexuality was closely guarded. Hence in 1352 an English parliamentary statute declared rape of the king's wife – as well as of his eldest daughter and the wife of his eldest son and heir – to be high treason. Queens were expected to oversee the education of their children, both daughters and, in the boys' early years, sons. The care that some queens took over their children's education may well have encouraged clerks to look to them for patronage and to see in them, as in aristocratic women more generally, suitable dedicatees of works of literature, particularly in the vernacular. As widowed mothers, queens could wield significant political influence over their sons, as Eleanor of Aquitaine did in Richard I's reign, and several queens of Scotland during the minorities of the fifteenth century.

In the public mind the queen was often seen as an intercessor, much as the Virgin Mary was perceived. This allowed a king to appear gracious rather than weak when changing – or appearing to change – his mind, as when Edward III pardoned the burghers of Calais in 1347 (Calais was surrendered to Edward III in August 1347 after an eleven-month siege on terms which required six of the port's richest citizens to volunteer to appear before him with ropes around their necks. In return for their sacrifice, he would spare the lives of their fellow 'rebels'. When the six knelt before him, he ordered their immediate execution, relenting only when Queen Philippa publicly begged him to show mercy. This piece of political theatre became a famous theme of art and literature). The fact that after 1100 nearly all queens of England and Scotland came from outside their husband's kingdom helped them to appear to be non-partisan mediators in internal quarrels. The Black Prince broke with more than 250 years of convention when he fell in love with and married Joan of Kent in 1361. Three years later David II also married an insider, Margaret Logie; when she bore no children, he divorced her. When Edward IV married Elizabeth Woodville in 1464, he created a tense political situation that had not been seen since the reign of Edward the Confessor: a queen of England with many English relatives looking to her for advancement. 'Take heed,' wrote a contemporary, 'what love may do.'

Royal Households

Wherever a king went, his household went with him; part domestic, part administrative, part political, it was indispensable. Irish bardic poetry, Welsh legal texts, English and Scottish administrative documents all reflect this same basic reality. The most elaborate household ordinance of the period, Edward IV's *Black Book of the Household*, imagined England as a hierarchy of households, the king with a household of 500, then dukes with households of 240, earls 140, barons 40, knights 16, and esquires with 10. 'Duke' was a new title, created in the fourteenth century, but there was nothing new or particularly English about a hierarchy of households. Between households in the various kingdoms the differences were above all ones of scale. The nature of the surviving evidence means that we know little about early households except when they went to war, creating the impression of development from war band to court as a centre of display and conspicuous consumption. Later English records distinguish between the 'house of magnificence' and the 'house of supply', in effect between 'upstairs' and 'downstairs'; but in one form or other these two parts had always existed, both integral to the political process.

Common to royal households everywhere were three senior officers: steward, chamberlain and constable (or their equivalents). The steward, normally a lord, was responsible for overall management of the household, but the chamberlain, controlling access to the chambers where the king slept and where a store of money and treasure was kept, was often more influential. The responsibilities of the constable were primarily military. When a king went to war, the core of his army, sometimes the whole of it, comprised an expanded household, drawing in not just the king's domestic household (*domus*), but also the wider household (*familia*), composed of men (*familiares*) retained to perform political and military services when called upon.

Only in England was the use of the written word for government already so common by the eleventh century that the royal household included an official responsible for the seal and writing office, a chancellor. Not until the twelfth century did the rulers of smaller kingdoms, led by the Scottish kings, feel the need for a secretariat. The oldest extant documents are charters recording grants of estates or privileges, copies of which were made and kept by the beneficiaries. For historians of English government 1199 marks a crucial turning point: the chancery began to keep registers (in the form of rolls) of copies of outgoing letters. Once again the Scottish kings followed suit. Although historians, English ones especially, have been impressed by the increasing use of documents, contemporaries took more notice of those men close enough to the king to hear his orders out of his own mouth than of those who received his commands in writing. They were even more impressed when they themselves heard the king's words. Hence kings constantly travelled from one part of their territories to another.

Initially they moved from one centre to another, consuming the customary renders in cows, pigs, sheep, cheese, loaves of bread and vats of ale brought in by local agents. The system could get conspicuously out of hand. According to the *Anglo-Saxon Chronicle* for 1104, 'wherever the king went, there were burnings and killings as his wretched people suffered from the ravages of his household'. As the use of money increased and markets proliferated, households were less constrained to visit the places of production. Richard FitzNigel, Henry II's treasurer, said he knew people who had seen supplies brought to the court at fixed times, but that this practice had been discontinued as being convenient to neither king nor farmers – as they had demonstrated by marching on the court brandishing their ploughshares. Renders were replaced by money rents. The cash was used to buy goods, either in towns or in what Walter Map called 'the fair that travelled with the king'. In England this process was largely complete by 1130. In Scotland it was still ongoing in the thirteenth century. But political imperatives – and the pleasure of hunting – meant that even the kings of England continued to travel, in order to see and be seen. Hence throughout this period and beyond kings insisted on retaining 'purveyance' (the right to commandeer provisions notionally in return for fair payment).

Thanks to the survival of the chancery rolls, the itineraries of the kings of England from 1199 onwards can be established with much greater precision than those of other rulers. John averaged no less than three moves a week, winter and summer, throughout his reign (1199–1216). Since he and his predecessors were as much French princes as kings of England, they spent a great deal of time in France, particularly between 1154 and 1203. After 1203 English royal itineraries were increasingly confined to England. The rest of Britain and Ireland they rarely visited except at the head of an army. Even after Edward III claimed the throne of France, the only king of England to spend much time in his other kingdom was Henry V. By the fifteenth century English kings travelled less than John had, averaging two moves a week in the summer, and tending to spend the winter in and around London/Westminster. The rise of a money economy probably enabled other rulers to travel less too, though in the absence of records it is hard to be sure. In Ireland Gaelic chiefs continued to demand 'coign and livery' (billeting rights and produce rents), a traditional practice that to English observers now seemed wicked.

Choosing Rulers

The extent to which kings succeeded or failed in living up to their responsibilities depended more on themselves as individuals than on any machinery of government. As the violent ends to the reigns of James I, James III, Henry VI and Richard III all testify, this applied almost as much in the fifteenth-century kingdoms of Scotland and England as it had done in the much less bureaucratic kingships of eleventh-century Britain and Ireland. Choosing a king was a matter of the greatest importance. It was taken for granted that he would be a member of the reigning family. Father-to-son succession was the norm in England by 1100, and in Scotland fifty years later – though here the norm faced a number of challenges from the mac William dynasty. But in Ireland and Wales the way to the throne remained open to any member of the dynasty who had followers and resources, the twin levers of power. Since candidates for kingship could come from fairly distant segments of the ruling dynasty, anthropologically minded historians have called the succession disputes that resulted 'segmentary strife'. A son who had been favoured by his father, perhaps chosen as 'tanist' (deputy), certainly possessed an advantage over his rivals, but what counted above all were the skills to win men to his side – political intelligence, military prowess, ruthlessness when necessary. In Ireland and Wales there were no boy kings. Where economic conditions combined with fierce competition for resources made cattle raiding a *sine qua non* of kingship, it was crucial to have a king who could do this. In Ireland tradition required a king to inaugurate his reign with an armed raid, his *crech ríg*. The 'open' system of succession in Wales and Ireland created a permanent stock of eligible kings and, inevitably, more bids for kingship. It resulted quite often in shared kingships and in partitions of kingdoms. Kingdoms fluctuated in size depending upon the outcome of each round of 'segmentary strife'. To English commentators, politics in contemporary Wales and Ireland always seemed chronically unstable.

Where kings did not have to go to war every year, then boy kings could be tolerated in the – not always fulfilled – expectation that they would grow up to be warriors. Boys aged ten or younger came to the throne in England in 1216 (Henry III), 1377 (Richard II), 1422 (Henry VI) and 1483 (Edward V); in Scotland in 1249 (Alexander III), 1329 (David II), 1437 (James II) and 1460 (James III). Evidently in both countries by the

thirteenth century there were systems of government in place capable
of functioning for some years without the king himself having to play
an active managerial role. Richard I's three-year absence on crusade
and in captivity suggests that England had reached that point earlier;
that his father, Henry II, spent most of his reign out of England may
have contributed here. In crisis the Scots showed that they were loyal
to more than a person. In 1296 when Edward I forced John Balliol to
renounce the throne and royal regalia, leaving him only his bare sur-
coat, 'toom tabard', the Scots continued to resist English aggression. At
the siege of Stirling in 1304 they proclaimed their allegiance not to a
person but to the Lion of Scotland. Nonetheless, in this period none of
the peoples of Britain and Ireland deliberately chose to do without
a king.

If a king had more than one son, then the question arose: which son?
Where the sons of many different women could bid for the throne,
then kingship was an office open, if not to all, then at least to many
talents. Henry I's son, Robert of Gloucester, admired as a politician and
patron, would surely have become king of England when his father
died in 1135 had he not been regarded as illegitimate. The same may
also have applied in Scotland in 1124 when Alexander I's son Malcolm
mac Heth was defeated by Alexander's brother, David. (It had been
different in Normandy in 1035 when William the Bastard became
duke.) The ecclesiastical theory of illegitimacy added to the number of
boy kings in England and Scotland, though in 1483 it suggested to
Richard of Gloucester a way of eliminating one of them (Edward V).
By the thirteenth century such notions had came to count for something in Welsh politics; in Ireland they still had not by the fifteenth.

In eleventh- and twelfth-century England it was not a foregone
conclusion that legitimate sons would succeed to the throne in order
of seniority. There was no prescribed order of succession. It is clear that
the wishes of the previous king, in particular his testamentary
dispositions, were widely regarded as creating an acceptable title. In
1087 William I designated his younger son, William Rufus, as his heir
in England. In the absence of legitimate sons, as in 1066, 1135 and 1199,
the old king's right to designate a successor was all the more evident.
But this rarely settled the matter, certainly not between 1066 and 1135
when each king's death was followed by a war of succession. In that
sense the successful claimant was always the one chosen by the people.
In the more legalistic thirteenth century people in England and

Scotland were increasingly inclined to apply the laws governing descent of property even at the highly politicised level of a kingdom. In the 1280s Alexander III had tailzies (entails) drawn up combining the principle of primogeniture in the male line with, in the absence of male heirs, female succession to the throne. In 1290 Edward I followed suit in England. In 1292 he adjudicated the 'Great Cause' by awarding Scotland to John Balliol as the nearest heir. For as long as it seemed natural that a war of succession would follow the death of the previous king, new reigns were not formally held to begin until the day of coronation or inauguration. But Edward I's reign began on the day of his father's funeral, and from Edward II onwards it was conventional to date a new king's reign from the day after his predecessor's death. In 1329 the Scots went one better, starting the new reign on the day the old king died. The emergence of rules of succession eased the king's task of managing his own family. Edward III's relationships with his sons were always likely to have been less awkward than Henry II's. Although a tendency towards primogeniture has been discerned in Irish succession practice, to a commentator writing c. 1500 it still seemed that 'he that hath the strongest army and hardest sword among them, hath best right and title'.

The right of women to inherit or transmit title to thrones was never recognised in Welsh or Irish law; Strongbow's claim to inherit Leinster on the death of his father-in-law, King Diarmait, used foreign law to justify foreign conquest. In England Henry II's accession in 1154 could be seen in retrospect to have strengthened the claim (his mother's) that had failed in 1135; at the time he succeeded only by forcing Stephen to adopt him as a son. In Scotland the challenge to Alexander II via the female line of the mac Williams was sufficient to cause the murder of a child, her brains dashed out against the market cross at Forfar in 1235. Edward III's claim to France ran through the female line. Despite this, in 1376 he entailed the throne of England in the male line. This did not settle the matter. Richard of York's claim to the throne, pressed in 1460, went through the female line. When Henry VI regained the throne in 1470, the entail in the male line was reasserted in parliament. Richard of York's son, Edward IV, not only fought his way back to the throne in 1471, he also had the records of Henry VI's parliament destroyed. What one king did, a later king could undo.

Although it became conventional to see the Wars of the Roses (1455–87) as phases in a single war of succession between Lancaster and

York, the risings against Henry VI and Edward IV were in fact
something different. Like the revolts against Henry II, John, Henry III,
Edward II, Richard II and Henry IV, they occurred some years after
their accession and were caused by dissatisfaction with the way they
ruled. The one exception to what had become the normal pattern of
political crisis occurred in 1483 when Richard of Gloucester seized the
throne before Edward V could even be crowned. In that sense Richard
III put the clock back several centuries. Henry Tudor's response led in
1485 to a king of England being killed in battle for the throne for the first
time since 1066, and the accession of a king whose dynastic title was as
weak as William I's had been.

Magna Carta and Reform

By 1215 it was plain that John was a poor war leader and an untrust-
worthy and oppressive ruler. But in one crucial respect the rebellion
against him was unprecedented. There was no obvious alternative
ruler; John's own sons were too young to lead a rebellion. In this
situation the opposition barons took the revolutionary step of
inventing a new kind of focus for revolt: a document. They drew up a
long charter containing something for nearly everyone and forced
John to grant it 'to all the freemen of the realm and their heirs for ever'.
Its sixty-three chapters were primarily a commentary on John's rule,
but some applied to English royal government in general. Above all,
chapter thirty-nine became and remains an iconic statement of the
rights of the subject: 'No free man shall be taken or imprisoned or
deprived or outlawed or exiled or in any way ruined except by the
lawful judgement of his peers or by the law of the land'. Two more
controversial chapters undermined the sovereignty of the crown by
making John's decisions subject to a review committee composed of
his enemies. Hence John sealed the charter at Runnymede on 15 June
1215 only to gain time to hire an army of mercenaries. War broke out
in September 1215. In desperation the rebels turned to Louis, heir to the
throne of France. In consequence when John died in October 1216, the
war became a succession dispute between Louis and John's oldest son,
Henry. A boy of nine thus proved a more acceptable ruler than John
had been, particularly when his advisers cut the ground from under the
feet of the opposition by reissuing a modified Magna Carta. In 1217

Louis withdrew and Henry III's government reissued the charter again, with further modifications, including a supplementary document dealing exclusively with forest law. It was in contrast with this shorter Forest Charter that the Big Charter (*magna carta*) acquired its familiar name. The reissues of 1216, 1217 and 1225 ensured that Magna Carta became in effect a written constitution – the earliest in the history of European states – limiting the powers of English kings.

Henry III proved to be a feeble king with an overambitious and expensive foreign policy. In 1258 he was forced, under threat of rebellion, to acquiesce in the Provisions of Oxford, which imposed on him a council of fifteen chosen by four electors, only two of whom were the king's men. This council was authorised to appoint the king's principal officials, chancellor, treasurer and justiciar, and was answerable to the barons in parliament. As a constitutional experiment 1258 was more radical even than 1215. But once Henry changed his foreign policy, the united opposition of 1258 fragmented; only a few hardliners such as Simon de Montfort continued to insist on depriving the king of his right to choose his own counsellors. On this issue civil war broke out in 1264. The Montfortian victory at Lewes led to the establishment, in the name of the captured king, of a conciliar government. Next year Earl Simon and thirty of his friends were killed in the battle that became known as the 'murder of Evesham'. Although later attempts to impose constitutional limits on royal authority did not go as far as 1258, the events of Edward II's, Richard II's and Henry VI's reigns in England – as also of Robert II's and Robert III's in Scotland – all suggest that opposition magnates now preferred to think not of alternative kings, but of institutional constraints on royal freedom of action.

Shedding Royal and Noble Blood

In the last resort, however, no formal arrangement could stop an adult king taking over the reins of government if he were free and wished to do so. In England this awkward fact provoked five dethronements of four kings: Edward II's (1327), Richard II's (1399), Henry VI's (1461 and 1471), and Edward V's in 1483. All four were subsequently murdered. Indeed, in 1484 the chancellor of France publicly commented on the English habit of murdering their kings. Richard III's conduct shocked the political community, and his reign was correspondingly brief, but both Henry IV and Edward IV were able to rule successfully despite their responsibility for killing their predecessors. This acquiescence in political murder reflected a change in English political values following Edward II's execution of his cousin Thomas of Lancaster and two dozen other aristocratic rebels after the Battle of Boroughbridge (1322). In the twelfth and thirteenth centuries the worst treatment meted out to high-status English rebels had been exile and confiscation of property. Edward II caused such outrage that it became possible to depose and murder him – a fate that in England had not befallen kings and would-be kings captured by their enemies for over four hundred years. After Edward III took power himself in 1330, he ruled without such bloodshed, but the execution of leading opponents became a feature of the reigns of Richard II and of all the rulers of England for the next three hundred years – although it was not until Henry VIII's reign that monarchs began to execute women for political reasons.

Even during the more 'chivalrous' twelfth and thirteenth centuries, however, English kings treated the Welsh and Irish brutally, regarding them as inferiors who understood only savage medicine. Indeed, Gaelic Irish politics remained a bloody business throughout the medieval centuries. Welsh politics became less bloody after 1200, with Llywelyn ap Iorwerth setting an example of more merciful treatment of his rivals. This did not prevent Edward I, the victor of Evesham, from executing Welsh resistance leaders in 1283, 1292 and 1295. Scottish politics also became less bloody in the later thirteenth century, but the murder of Comyn provoked Edward I into hanging six members of Robert Bruce's family and the earl of Atholl in 1306. Atholl was the first earl executed by a king of England since the beheading of Earl Waltheof of Northumbria in 1076. Although the fierce conduct of Gaelic clansmen, 'wyld wykkyd Heland-men' as Andrew of Wyntoun called them, alarmed English-speaking lowlanders, politics in later medieval Scotland remained less bloody than in England until 1425, after which a spate of killings included the murder of James II.

Rebellions of the People

English rule in Scotland and Wales triggered popular risings in which William Wallace and Owain Glyn Dwr acted as the champions of national resistance. The English rising of June 1381, however, was different. Although commonly known as the Peasants' Revolt, towns-people and artisans were also prominent when well-coordinated rebel armies from Essex and Kent rode and marched on London, taking up arms against a government which took the side of lords and employers against labour at a time when, for once, the economic tide was in the latter's favour. The last straw came with the imposition of a flat-rate poll tax in 1380 and the stringent measures taken, particularly in the wealthy counties of south-east England, to enforce its collection. Catching the government completely unawares – hardly surprising since nothing like this had happened before – the rebels captured London, executed several government advisers and ministers (including the treasurer and the chancellor, who was also archbishop of Canterbury), and seemed to have the fourteen-year-old king, Richard II, at their mercy. But they did not hold him responsible for 'his' government's failings; many went home on 14 June when he agreed that serfdom should be abolished. Those who remained in London, hoping for further reforms and still trusting Richard, allowed

The Peasants' Revolt. Here we see two of the dramatic events of 15 June 1381 at Smithfield: first the attack on Wat Tyler, and then King Richard II addressing the rebels, who appear to be anything but a disorganised and poorly armed rabble. Artistic licence or a reflection of the reality of the revolt?

themselves to be dispersed when their leader, Wat Tyler, was killed during a conference with the king's party at Smithfield (15 June). Richard revoked his concessions and the remaining rebel leaders were rounded up. At least 150 were hanged, including John Ball, preacher of sermons reminding his audience of the theoretical egalitarianism of Christianity. Risings elsewhere, notably in East Anglia, though provoked by local grievances, were inspired by the news of the march on London, and did not long survive its collapse.

1381 signalled the violent entry of the underprivileged into politics. Nothing quite like it happened again. But their more active participation in 'high' politics, whether in the form of lynching nobles in 1400 and 1450 or in the support given to the gentry-led Cade's revolt in 1450, shows that the fear that it might was not entirely groundless. It would be a long time before another English government introduced a poll tax or interfered so blatantly with the laws of supply and demand.

Lordship

The most influential people, of course, were those who had great households of their own, but who spent a part of the year as servants in the royal household, enjoying a courtier's access to favour and the levers of power, before returning to their own town houses and country mansions. In kingdoms with relatively stable borders such as England and Scotland, political cohesion depended primarily upon the ruler's ability to manage the relationship of mutual interdependence between him and the lords who comprised his wealthiest tenants. Even in societies, notably Ireland, where frontiers between kingdoms were chronically unstable, skilful leadership in war was not enough. Rulers everywhere were expected to distribute resources in ways that contented their most powerful subjects, including members of their own family.

The number and wealth of such subjects, as well as the formal and informal terms of their tenancies, naturally varied considerably over time and space. As always, the evidence allows us to see English developments more clearly than those elsewhere. The fact that William I created a new aristocracy led to an exceptional strengthening of royal lordship. Wealthy landholders could no longer make wills bequeathing some of their estates, their 'bookland', to whomever they wished. But the notion that the conqueror introduced an entirely new and 'feudal' form of tenure, based on the tenants' obligation to provide 'knight service', is a myth created in the seventeenth century. Long before 1066 many of a lord's dependants had also been his tenants, paying rent in many forms, including an obligation to provide military service. Elsewhere in Britain and Ireland the absence of relevant evidence makes it difficult to speculate about changes which may – or may not – have occurred within the structures of lordship. Although Lowland Scotland, for example, is commonly said to have been 'feudalised' in the twelfth century as the result of an influx of Anglo-Norman settlers, this is because it is from then that the earliest royal charters survive.

If estates held by tenants fragmented then extracting rent or services became more complicated. In England the right of the eldest legitimate son to succeed to the whole (male primogeniture) became the common-law rule. Division occurred only when there was no legitimate son and more than one daughter. By contrast, Celtic custom excluded daughters and tended to give all sons a share. In England heirs of those who held estates from the king – tenants-in-chief in the jargon of the time – had to pay a charge, known as a relief, before they could possess their inheritance; if under age, they and their estates were taken into royal custody, allowing the king either to pocket the income or to grant the custody and marriage of the ward to whomever he chose. If there were no direct heirs then, after provision had been made for the widow, whose own remarriage was also under royal control, the king could make a new grant of the estate. A document from 1185 listed 'the ladies, boys and girls in the king's gift', and assessed their market value. These were desirable assets and ambitious men were tempted to bid highly for them. This could yield a tidy revenue, but was more useful as an instrument of political control. By making little or no effort to collect the sums bid and agreed, kings could keep men in their debt and serving faithfully in the hope of never having to pay what they had offered. By the thirteenth century English inheritance customs had been adopted in Scotland where the kings enjoyed similar powers.

These rights over his tenants gave the lord king a strong hand. It was one which, in principle, his tenants accepted because they depended on the same rights for the effective exploitation of their own estates. But it was a hand which the king had to play skilfully if he were not to

alienate too many of those families on whose cooperation he
ultimately depended. Henry I's Coronation Charter (1100) shows that
relief, wardship and marriage were already points of tension in the
relationship between king and nobility. It was largely by overplaying
this strong hand that King John brought about his downfall. In Magna
Carta reliefs, previously negotiable, were fixed at £100 for an earl's or
baron's estate, and £5 for a knight's. The crown's rights over wardship
and marriage were less easy to limit. A father's premature death could
still deliver the wardship and marriage of his heir to the crown – in 1380,
for example, this allowed John of Gaunt to buy the marriage of an
heiress for his son Henry. But the development of legal devices such as
jointures (which strengthened the position of widows) and 'uses' went
some way to circumscribe the lord king's power over his tenants. In
particular the 'use', the grant of estates to trustees to be held for
specified uses, meant that privileged landholders could once again, as
before 1066, bequeath land by will. In these respects late medieval
English kings were weaker than their Norman and Angevin predecessors. On the other hand, the fewer the structural causes of tension
between crown and nobility the easier the cooperation between them,
to the advantage of both.

Taxes and Customary Revenues

The capacity to levy general taxes on the population at large has long
been regarded as a defining mark of the modern state. Traditional
rulers, by contrast, relied on revenues which, whether paid in produce
or money, came from their own estates – in England this included
nearly all the major towns – or were derived from their relationship
with their tenants-in-chief. Living on rents and the profits of jurisdiction and lordship including some tax-like levies such as 'scutages'
(payments in lieu of military service) and 'tallages' (imposed on Jews
and townspeople), traditional kings were essentially just higher status
lords. Seen in this light, England, Ireland and Scotland (but not Wales)
all underwent significant modernisation during these centuries,
though with striking differences in chronology and intensity. English
kings already levied a land tax, known as the *geld* (later Danegeld)
before 1066. In Scotland the 'common aid', a land tax equivalent to the
geld, was occasionally levied from the later twelfth century on.

General taxation was first levied in English Ireland during John's reign, and might well have been developed by the native princes of Wales had they not been eliminated by Edward I. By contrast, taxation remained as absent from Gaelic Ireland in the fifteenth century as it had been in the eleventh. A significant difference between traditional revenues and taxes was that the latter – originally at least – were thought of as extraordinary, justified only in special circumstances. Rulers had to obtain the consent of their subjects before they taxed them. In 1204, for example, King John wrote to 'all his faithful subjects of Ireland' asking them for financial aid 'not as a matter of custom but out of friendship'. By contrast, in conquered Wales the English did not levy direct taxes, but exploited customary ways of extracting revenue, leading a modern Welsh historian (Rees Davies) to write of 'the systematic financial rape of the country'.

Although eleventh-century Danish kings of England apparently employed the geld to raise very large sums, by the time of the earliest document enabling historians to compare the yields from various sources, the 1130 exchequer roll, taxation was relatively unimportant. This records a total of about £23,000 paid into the treasury that year, of which less than £2,500 came from taxation. Nearly £10,000 came from the county 'farms', fixed sums paid into the treasury by the sheriffs responsible for managing the crown estate in their shires. Their predictable yield made them the backbone of crown finances. Including estates that were temporarily in Henry I's hands (as a result of confiscation, for example), revenue from land came to almost £13,000, more than half the total. Other sources of customary income, fines imposed in the king's courts and the profits of his rights of lordship over tenants-in-chief, varied considerably from year to year. In 1130 they totalled about £7,000, of which about half came from wardship and marriage. The earliest Scottish account, a fragment of a chamberlain's roll, indicates that in 1264 the king was entirely dependent on traditional revenues; out of a total receipt of over £5,400, two-thirds came from the fermes of sheriffs and burghs and one-third from reliefs and payments for grants of wardship and marriage.

Royal estates were, however, a declining asset. Kings had to be generous; in political crises they rewarded their key supporters with land, the most desirable of commodities. The county farms still produced no more than £10,000 a year in 1300 – much less in real terms than in 1130. The underlying trend was for there to be an outflow of

royal estates into private hands. It was wiser not to attempt to reverse
the flow. Kings who adopted a policy of wholesale confiscation of
estates paid for it with their lives: in England, Edward II, Richard II and
Richard III; in Scotland, James I and James III. Yet other sources of
customary revenue could be made to yield substantially more only at
high political cost. It was one thing to derive an income from judicial
fines, another to give the impression that the king saw justice primarily
as a money-raising operation. It was one thing to have powerful men in
the king's debt, another to shape their indebtedness into a stick to beat
them with, as John too often did. Between 1208 and 1213 he exploited his
traditional revenues to the full, imposing both frequent scutages and
heavy tallages. In 1211 income audited at the exchequer came to over
£83,000. But as Magna Carta demonstrates, this offended contemporary
notions of good lordship. Later kings of England learned the lesson.
After 1215 the profits of justice and lordship rarely yielded more than
£5,000 a year, in real terms massively less than the £7,000 of 1130.

   So little did the geld contribute to Henry II's revenues that he chose
to do without it. But then appeals for help from the crusader states, and
the need to find a ransom for Richard I, meant that the kings of
England had unassailably good causes when they asked their 'faithful
subjects' to grant them a tax. This enabled them to experiment with a
new kind of tax, assessed on a valuation of movable property. In the
long run this tax, later known as the subsidy, was to revolutionise the
government's financial base. The first subsidy for which an official
record of yield survives, the thirteenth of 1207, brought in no less than
£57,000. Not surprisingly such tax grants long remained rare. After 1237,
for example, Henry III was granted no more until 1269, when he
obtained a subsidy for his son Edward's crusade.

   The turning point came after 1294 when Edward I found himself
faced by war on three fronts, in Gascony, Scotland and Wales, and
managed to win consent to five tax grants in the next eight years. From
1294 to the end of his reign he averaged £20,000 a year from this source
alone. From then on the near permanent state of war against the Scots
and/or the French meant that direct taxation, generally in the form of
tenths from towns and fifteenths from shires, became a major part of
English royal finances. In 1334, to save the expense of a reassessment
each time a tax was levied, the yield of a tenth and fifteenth was fixed
at £37,800, with a known sum laid upon each borough and village.
Convocations of the English Church were also persuaded to make

grants of direct taxation (clerical tenths, each one bringing in about £15,000).

The Scottish kings were more successful in retaining the stock of royal lands until Robert Bruce had to give much away during the long war he fought against both Scottish and English enemies. The parliament of Cambuskenneth (1326) responded by granting him an annual subsidy of a tenth, assessed on lands and rents. This precedent was occasionally followed, notably in the 1350s and 1360s in order to raise the ransom for David II, but in Scotland direct taxation, known as the 'contribution', never became as frequent as in England. By 1469 it had been levied just twenty-two times, and rarely raised as much as £2,000.

Britain's coastline had long enabled its kings to profit from charges on seaborne trade, but it was, once again, in Edward I's reign that indirect taxation first began to play a major role in state finance. By the late thirteenth century the rise of the international banking system combined with growing demand for wool from the Flemish and Italian cloth industries had created new opportunities. In 1275 Edward obtained consent to a duty on the export of wool and hides from an assembly in which towns and merchants were strongly represented. The assumption that the cost would be borne by overseas customers paying higher prices disarmed opposition. At the rate of 6/8d. on each sack of wool and every one hundred hides, collected at Irish and Welsh ports as well as English, it regularly produced about £10,000 a year, enabling Edward I to repay loans made him by Italian bankers. In Scotland Alexander III followed suit, adding some £2,000 a year to his income. In 1294 Edward I increased the rate sixfold to £2 a sack, and Edward III would do the same thing again in 1337; both pleaded military necessity. Edward I backed down in 1297, but Edward III's military successes against France and Scotland in the 1340s and 1350s allowed him to turn the wool subsidy into a fixture. By 1370 revenue from overseas trade was averaging £70,000 a year (over 80 per cent of it from the export tax on wool). This was *two-thirds* of his total income, collected by less than a hundred crown agents, three-quarters of them unpaid. Once again the Scots followed suit, quadrupling the rate of duty in order to ransom David II. Granted for the lifetimes of kings the wool tax became part of their customary revenue – which is why such charges are still called 'customs'.

Under Henry IV and Henry V, 85–90 per cent of the king of England's annual income came from taxes, direct and indirect; the

ratio between taxation and traditional revenue was now almost exactly
the reverse of what it had been in 1130. The trend was not, however,
irreversible. Wool exports gradually declined, in part a consequence of
the high export duty inducing customers to look elsewhere. The
export duty on cloth was low and not easily increased without
damaging the ability of English cloth producers to compete in
continental markets. Hence the changing pattern of international trade
caused a long-term decline in the proceeds of indirect taxation; in
England down to about £40,000 a year in the 1470s, in Scotland to about
£3,000. In England the turbulence of the Wars of the Roses meant that
rulers were reluctant to risk the unpopularity associated with direct
taxation. In both kingdoms old-fashioned sources of revenue made
something of a comeback in the later fifteenth century.

Law

Throughout eleventh-century Britain and Ireland law and order was
maintained in broadly similar and very local ways. If anyone were
insulted, injured or killed, it was the duty of their kin to exact
vengeance or to take the matter to court and demand compensation in
the form of an honour price. The accused looked to their kin,
neighbours and friends to be oath-helpers, to swear in court to their
good standing. Courts were local assemblies in which the role of any
royal official present was limited to chairing the meeting; judgements
were made by 'law-worthy' men of local eminence. This often
amounted to arbitration of the dispute in the light of local custom by a
panel acceptable to both sides, occasionally guided by the opinions of
learned men who read or produced written codes of law. Whenever
possible trials were decided on the basis of evidence and character
witness; if that wasn't possible, questions of guilt or innocence might
be decided by ordeal, either of water or iron. In this sphere William I's
one innovation was to introduce the French practice of trial by battle.

Much more significant was the emergence in England of a public
prosecution service. In 1166 the sheriffs were ordered to empanel in
every hundred a jury of twelve men whose job it was to present (i.e.
name) those whom they believed guilty of serious offences; sheriffs
then had to arrest and hold them until they could be tried before the
king's judges in the county courts. A country-wide jail-building

campaign demonstrates the seriousness with which Henry II launched this drive against crime. Those found guilty were punished by mutilation or death, but did not have to pay compensation to the victim. Only if victims themselves or their relatives were prepared to bring private prosecutions (appeals) and risk trial by battle did they have a hope of compensation. By Edward I's reign such appeals were rare. Major crimes were treated as breaches of the king's peace which could no longer be privately settled by the offer of compensation ('blood money'). Those legal systems which were still based on the old ways now seemed inferior, even morally wrong.

A second important development occurred when Henry II's chancery encouraged litigation in disputes about possession of land by making available to plaintiffs, for a fee, standardised written orders (writs) addressed to the appropriate sheriff ordering him to arrange for a jury to decide the case on the basis of their local knowledge before the king's judges. Such writs were more easily obtained after the 1170s when a branch of the chancery settled permanently at Westminster, no matter where the king or his itinerant representative in England, the justiciar, happened to be. From now on royal judges, mostly laymen, made frequent tours – eyres (derived from the Latin *errantes* meaning 'travelling') – of the counties. They had so much business that they continued to work on their return to Westminster, establishing for the first time a central court of justice at a fixed point. Rich landowners had long retained legal advisers to look after their interests, but by 1200 the increasing volume of litigation, especially in and around Westminster, led to the emergence of professional lawyers – attorneys who, for a fee, were willing to represent any client. These developments meant that from now on there was a single framework of serious crime and property law common to the whole country: the Common Law.

In 1210 King John had the main rules of English law put into writing; the resulting document, the first official definition of the Common Law, was sent to Dublin. Although it may then have been assumed that in time English law would apply to all Ireland's inhabitants, subsequent events ensured that outside the areas of English settlement, traditional Irish law continued to prevail. The differences in the ways the two laws dealt with crime, marriage and inheritance persuaded the English that Irish ('brehon') law was both primitive and immoral. In a similar spirit Edward I insisted on a wholesale 'reform' of Welsh law, imposing both English criminal law and rules of inheritance, giving women greater rights than they had enjoyed under native custom. Had he conquered Scotland, he would not have felt the need for such drastic action since by then a century of close relations between the two kingdoms had led to the Scots adopting and adapting a good deal of English law; much of *Regiam Maiestatem*, a summary of Scottish law *c.* 1300, was based on 'Glanvill's' *Treatise*. In Scotland, moreover, unlike Ireland, there was one law for both Gaelic- and English-speakers.

By this time trial by jury had become a standard feature of both English and Scottish criminal law. Trial by ordeal, requiring God to decide cases too difficult for men, depended upon priests blessing the red-hot iron or the pits of water. But in 1215 Innocent III prohibited priests from taking part. Scottish kings responded by allowing defendants to choose between trial by jury and trial by combat; English judges kept them in prison in increasingly intolerable circumstances (*peine forte et dure*) until they did opt for jury trial. As late as 1722 stubborn defendants could choose to be pressed to death, allowing them to die deemed innocent. Throughout Latin Christendom people faced the same problem after 1215 and only in Denmark and Britain did men replace God with a jury. Elsewhere they went down the path of Roman law, increasingly using torture as a way of getting at 'the truth'.

Scottish law, though anglicised, remained relatively uncomplicated. But English law grew increasingly complex and incomprehensible. Specialists became indispensable: to advise litigants, to represent them in court or to act as judges. These experts were trained by attending courts and studying a technical literature written in Law French. By the mid-fourteenth century the Inns of Court both served as London hostels for law students and provided them with teaching. By this date all those appointed as justices in the two central courts, Common Bench and King's Bench, were salaried professionals who had served their time as apprentices and as serjeants (advocates) in Common Bench. In the later fourteenth century chancery developed as a court intended to provide justice where the common law failed. Although the eyre system broke down *c.* 1300, central court judges continued to be dispatched to act as justices of assize or of gaol delivery in the county courts. Here and in English Ireland, the outline of a legal profession split into two branches – attorneys and serjeants, today's solicitors and barristers – had emerged.

Capital Cities

Capital cities – central places for routine government business, no matter where the king was – emerged, first in England, then in English Ireland and finally in Scotland. In 1066 the kings of England already possessed a permanently staffed royal treasury and depository for fiscal records at the old West Saxon centre of Winchester. By the 1180s, however, thanks to the pulling power of a great port and its international commerce, London and the nearby palace of Westminster had replaced Winchester. A decisive stage in the emergence of a settled centre of English government occurred during the reigns of Henry II and Richard I, i.e. in that half-century when the royal household was frequently abroad, often for years at a time. Although it was from the household offices of chamber and wardrobe that kings spent money to meet the daily needs of pleasure and politics, it was in their interest to have a fixed place where the accounts of the sheriffs were regularly examined. By the 1180s the exchequer routinely did this at Westminster. Similarly a judicial committee, the embryonic Court of Common Pleas or Common Bench, met in Westminster Hall (where it and the other central courts remained until 1884). There was in effect a government machine operated by two panels of specialists, according to the rules of their profession as set out in the two earliest administrative handbooks in British history, *The Dialogue of the Exchequer* written in the late 1170s by Richard Fitz Nigel, treasurer of the exchequer, and *The treatise on the laws and customs of England*, written in the 1180s by an unidentified author, though often attributed to Ranulf Glanvill, Henry II's justiciar. A secretariat permanently based at Westminster provided the routine documentation which the law courts and the exchequer required. During John's reign the Westminster model was transferred to Dublin. In Scotland by contrast, as in Wales before the loss of independence in the late thirteenth century, the ruler's itinerant household remained the only hub of government. Not until the later fifteenth century did Edinburgh begin to function as Scotland's capital.

In England the elaboration of central offices continued. The formerly itinerant King's Bench of judges (specialising in cases in which the king had an interest) increasingly sat at Westminster. A Westminster council, presided over by the chancellor, began to meet daily during the law terms, usually in the Star Chamber, functioning as a supplement to the more informal counsel that the king had by him as and when he chose. Except for brief periods during Edward I's and Edward III's wars against the Scots, when the administration moved to York, it remained at Westminster and was serviced by the city of London. The Inns of Court were here. The main royal mint was in the Tower of London, as was its principal arms factory and arsenal, by the mid-fourteenth century employing more than three hundred engineers, armourers, gunners and carpenters. When the rebels of 1381 seized the Tower, they knew what they were doing. By 1400 at least two hundred officials (many of whom had clerical staffs of their own) were employed in the central departments of state: the law courts, chancery, exchequer and privy seal. That they served 'the state' rather than the king is shown by the fact that when Richard II was deposed in 1399, none of those who held office in these departments lost their jobs.

Government in England

The Norman Conquest, following upon conquests by West Saxon and Danish kings in the tenth and early eleventh centuries, meant that by 1086 England was already, in Maitland's phrase, 'a well conquered, much governed kingdom'. Given that it lacked a bureaucracy, a standing army and a police force, a phrase such as 'much governed' can seem odd. But if we compare it with other eleventh-century European polities, then the force of the remark is clear. In England, centres of wealth and local power such as towns and castles were enclosed within a remarkably uniform network of shires, hundreds and vills which, with some exceptions such as the palatinates of Durham and Cheshire, covered the entire kingdom. Shire reeves (sheriffs) and hundred reeves held courts, the latter every three or four weeks; together with village reeves they were responsible for policing their districts. Most of them received no pay. What they got was something better: prestige and local influence, commodities which, in turn, brought material rewards, often in the shape of gifts. Indeed, so profitable was the office of sheriff that men habitually bid for it.

By the fifteenth century, England was even more intensively administered. The increasing use of writing in government meant more paid employment for increasing numbers of clerical staff. Supplementary tasks were imposed on the sheriffs, and new kinds of local officials were introduced to help the overworked sheriff: coroners, escheators, keepers of the peace and, after 1361, JPs. The numbers of JPs grew. In Wiltshire there were six JPs in 1368, seventeen by 1478. In addition special commissions were appointed *ad hoc*, for example to recruit soldiers. By 1400 there were as many as fifty individuals active in the government of a single large shire such as Norfolk. But England was still far from being a bureaucratic state. The court in the itinerant royal household remained at the heart of politics and fashion, and outside London there were almost no full-time paid officials. Local government was the preserve of part-time amateurs, the landed aristocracy and gentry. They were the king's servants, but their active cooperation, without which the king's commands were unenforceable, could not be taken for granted. It had to be won by the exercise of patronage, and by drawing some of them into parliament.

Parliaments

It has long been conventional to reserve the term 'parliament' for a national assembly summoned by a king and attended by the 'Commons', members of the 'Third Estate'. This usage is followed here. In this sense parliaments first appear in England and Ireland in the later thirteenth century, in Scotland in the fourteenth century, but in Wales only in 1404–5 during the brief period of Owain Glyn Dwr's rule. When compared with the representative institutions which developed in continental Europe during the later Middle Ages, the parliament of England was odd in the sense that here the three estates did not sit separately; instead the nobles and upper clergy sat together with the king's council in one place, while the commons met in another. The commons, it appeared, represented the nation, while the lords were part of the government.

All government rested, in practice and in theory, on the help of its leading subjects, who were assumed to represent the rest. Kings everywhere held assemblies of their greater subjects, their barons, both ecclesiastical and lay, to advise them and to act as judges in their courts. Up to a point this expectation was met by the 'great courts' which all rulers held at the major festivals of the Christian year. But 'great councils' were also summoned whenever rulers sensed a political need or opportunity, such as the Council of Clarendon in 1164 when Henry II intended to deal with Becket, or when William the Lion asked for the grant of a 'common aid' in 1190 so that he could buy Scotland's release from servitude to England. No doubt the voices which counted in such assemblies were those of the lords, both secular and ecclesiastical, though equally it seems likely that sensible lords took note of the opinions of other members of the 'community of the realm', particularly in a crisis such as 1264–5 when Simon de Montfort challenged the king or when questions of taxation were discussed.

It was on the matter of taxation that it was for the first time spelled out, in Magna Carta, precisely how 'the common counsel of the realm' was to be obtained. It was on this issue in 1254 that barons, who previously had both agreed and refused taxation, for the first time announced that they were unwilling to represent others. From the later 1290s, when Edward I's wars led him to make massive financial demands, the presence of the Commons in parliaments, hitherto occasional, became increasingly frequent. Edward I's advisers drafted a formula for the writs of summons emphasising that those who represented the communities of shires and towns in parliament had the power to commit their constituents. The fiscal revolution that took place in the fifty years between the 1290s and the 1340s meant that the Commons became a fixture. At the same time other representatives, the proctors of the clergy, now dropped out of parliament, since they would only assent to taxation of the clergy subject to its subsequent ratification in convocation.

In 1278 Edward I encouraged people to bring petitions to him in parliament. From then on, petitions flooded in. In Edward II's reign, the Commons as a body supplemented petitions from individuals by drawing up requests which they claimed to be in the 'common' interest. By the 1340s the common petitions and the replies given them by king and council were recorded in the official record of parliament. Not surprisingly, special interest groups lobbied the Commons in the hope, often justified, that their own requests would be presented as common petitions. By the fifteenth century procedures for considering petitions, by then known as 'bills', were well developed. The Commons role as petitioners reinforced the bicameral character of the English parliament. They petitioned; the king took counsel with the lords and answered. As petitioners, pressing matters of local concern, MPs were valued by the communities that sent them to parliament, but it was as answerers to royal requests for money that MPs came to wield some real political clout, in, for instance, campaigning successfully that men of their sort, the gentry of shire and town, should be given real local authority as JPs. By the late fourteenth century it had become usual for the Commons to delay their answer to any request for a tax until the last day of parliament when the king's answers to petitions were read out.

Between 1376 (when Edward III was in his dotage and the French war going badly) and 1406 (while Henry IV was still facing rebellions in England and Wales) the Commons enjoyed greater influence over central government than at any time before the seventeenth century. Taxes were refused or negotiated downwards and new procedures were devised, such as the election of Commons Speakers and the impeachment of unpopular ministers. But the Commons' businesslike cooperation with Henry V, to the crown's great profit, was more typical of fourteenth- and fifteenth-century practice than the dramatic confrontations of the previous generation. It was by frequently consenting to taxation that they won the right to consent. It was in the justified expectation that they would continue to negotiate and consent that kings in England, unlike kings elsewhere, went on summoning them to parliament.

4. Some Counter-Factuals

It is hard to imagine Britain and Ireland not sharing in the great economic, social and religious transformations common to the whole of medieval Europe: the end of slavery, population growth, the proliferation of towns and schools, markets and monasteries, the Black Death and its consequences. Historians of religion have often observed that, compared with the Continent, Britain was relatively free of heresy. But it might have been different. After all, the Hussite revolution in Bohemia was inspired by the heretical ideas of an Oxford academic, John Wyclif. If his attacks on ecclesiastical authority had not happened to coincide with the Peasants' Revolt of 1381, the rulers of England might have seen their attractive side. In 1410 a petition to parliament calculated that the estates of English prelates, if confiscated, would fund the creation of 15 earls, 1,500 knights, 6,200 esquires, 100 almshouses, 15 universities and 1,500 Wycliffite priests, and still leave the crown with a tidy income from the proceeds.

Alternative political histories are easy to imagine. Whereas the long, if intermittent, history of English pressure, both invasion and migration, suggests that Wales was ultimately bound to succumb to the wealth and military power of its eastern neighbour, the process might well have lasted much longer. It was far from inevitable that the first Prince of Wales, Llywelyn ap Gruffydd, would also be 'Llywelyn the Last'. Although the policy choices which Llywelyn made after 1272 proved to be disastrous both for him and for Welsh independence, they were at least understandable in light of previous centuries of Anglo-Welsh relations. Other rulers made much more surprising choices. If in 1171 Henry II had not decided to invade Ireland – an island to which he had no hereditary claim and over which none of his predecessors had ever ruled – it might well have been many centuries before any subsequent English government, given the low priority they generally gave to Ireland, took a similarly fateful decision.

At a more structural level, because the kingdoms in Britain and Ireland were family firms, hereditary monarchies of one sort or another, they were always subject to biological accident. Two of the most famous examples suggest that the political map of Britain in 1485 was far from inevitable. If, for example, David I's adult son Henry, earl of Northumbria, had not predeceased his father in 1152, then the Anglo-Scottish border might have become established at the Humber. Alternatively, a union of the royal houses of England and Scotland might have occurred three hundred years before it eventually did, had Margaret, the 'Maid of Norway', survived and married, as planned, Edward (later Edward II of England). The rulers of a united Anglo-Scottish realm might then have been able to complete the conquest of Ireland. Not that hereditary monarchy was itself a foregone conclusion. The English crisis of 1215–16 that generated a document as unprecedented as Magna Carta, might also have shifted the balance between inheritance and election as the theoretical basis of monarchy. Louis of France's supporters argued that he was rightfully king because he had been chosen by the people. Had he successfully dethroned John – as he might well have done if John hadn't died first (allegedly as a result of gorging himself on peaches and new cider) – then kingship in thirteenth-century England might have become as elective as it was in contemporary Germany. Among the probable consequences of such a shift is the avoidance of minorities such as those of Richard II, Henry VI and Edward V. Nor would it have been necessary for Edward IV's sons to be eliminated in order for Edward IV's brother, Richard of Gloucester, to ascend the throne.

Finally, the most well-known of counter-factuals should not be omitted. If it had been Duke William who died at Hastings – and, according to his chaplain, he had three horses killed under him – there would have been no Norman Conquest. Although many of the changes often attributed to the Conquest would probably have happened anyway, there can be little doubt that an entirely different, and much less rich, English language would have developed. For the acquisition of over 10,000 French words in the centuries after the Conquest not only doubled the size of the English lexicon, it also created a language more receptive to further borrowings from French and Latin in subsequent centuries.

PART III

REFORMATIONS, UNIONS AND CIVIL WARS, 1485–1660

Jenny Wormald

Introduction

It is a truism that no society is ever static; change, for good or ill, is an eternal fact of life. It is not a truism that attitudes to change have altered profoundly. To modern British eyes, it is highly desirable, even essential; it must be for the better; and when it does not happen quickly or successfully enough frustration sets in and politicians are pilloried. It cannot be stated too strongly that this – except in the field of learning – is the antithesis of expectations in the early-modern British Isles: change was unwelcome, frightening, traumatic. Yet the sixteenth century witnessed the wrenching away of the inhabitants of the three kingdoms from their long-accepted religious norms, on a scale not seen since the earliest centuries of missionary Christian activity. In the mid-seventeenth, the Wars of the Three Kingdoms, themselves in part religiously inspired and therefore a consequence of the dislocation of Reformation, smashed for good what had been vaguely understood as political and constitutional reality in a way which made dreaded memories of the Wars of the Roses look paltry by comparison. Add to this the shocking fact that in 1603 a Scottish king took over the English kingdom – the profoundly ironic answer to the imperialist ambitions of the medieval English monarchy – so that for the first time the idea of Britain might have some justification, jolting the English out of ingrained and automatic assumptions of superiority. The age of Renaissance, of expansion, of Shakespeare begins to look less joyous; and if this was, as has been argued, the time when the medieval world gave way to the modern – a highly dubious concept anyway – it can only be said that it was a very protracted, painful and unwelcome birth, presided over by midwives who were, in terms of their commitment, conviction, even fanaticism, very much in the minority.

1. Material Cultures

Time and the Calendar

That this was a period of unprecedented conflict within the British Isles is reflected in the fact that even the most basic of concepts – time, date and the calendar itself – became sources of protracted dispute. Light and dark marked out the division of the working day, the calendar of the church and the months the divisions of the year. In 1500 the British Isles shared that calendar in common with the rest of western Christendom, the only variations being the feasts of local saints and the continued observance of pagan feasts such as Beltane (1 May) and Lammas (1 August). By 1600 they did not – or not officially. Unity broke down in the face of the ideas of the Protestant reformers in each kingdom; no longer was there a common pattern with regional variations, but fundamental differences between the kingdoms.

Godly Scotland witnessed the most determined onslaught on the medieval calendar. Not only were all saints days abolished after the Protestant success in 1560, but so were Christmas and Easter, as too redolent of papist rather than Christian celebration. Moreover, a strongly sabbatarian Kirk made Sunday a day of sermon and prayer, and certainly not of relaxation and enjoyment. The Scots especially, therefore, suffered from godliness, which bore down harshly on a working population (though in 1598 the Scottish parliament, reacting against the Kirk's austerity, made Monday the day for necessary recreation). At the other end of the spectrum, in Ireland, the saints not only survived, their number actually increased. Indeed, seventeenth-century Irishmen did not necessarily wait for Rome to canonise, but did it themselves in the case of local martyrs such as Cornelius, bishop of Down, and Connor, executed in 1611. Saints days and pilgrimages to holy places therefore meant that the Irish calendar was the least disrupted by religious change, and, to an extent, this might also be said for Protestant Ireland as a whole. In the middle – or, one might say, in a muddle – were England and Wales. Henry VIII was the most ruthless destroyer of saints days, abolishing some and merging others into one feast day, the first Sunday in October. In 1552, the Edwardian regime, despite generally pushing reform further, mitigated this harshness, introducing a calendar which restored some of the major feasts, though carefully emphasising that these holidays were to honour God, that the choice came from the government, and that work was permitted. It was this calendar which would survive for the future. But the whole issue was complicated by the lawyers; for neither the civil nor, paradoxically, the ecclesiastical courts changed the traditional calendar, and saints days abounded. In any event, nowhere – not even in Scotland – were the purges universally observed. This worried some, comforted others. It is a measure of the confusion of the age.

Part of the confusion is reflected in the English government's attempt to compensate further for what had been lost by introducing new annual celebrations, a mixture of bell ringing and festivity, prayer and sermons: Elizabeth's Accession day (19 November), the Gunpowder Plot (5 November) and, later, Charles I's execution (30 January) and Charles II's escape after the Battle of Worcester, Royal Oak Day (29 May); Scotland got the Gowrie Conspiracy (5 August). There was one way in which the Scots clarified the calendar, though only for themselves; it took the rest of the British Isles some considerable time to catch up. When was New Year's Day? 1 January was certainly used. But so also – and more typically – was Annunciation Day (Lady Day), 25 March. Thus, for example, Charles I was executed, according to contemporary English records, not on 30 January 1649, but on 30 January 1648. In 1599, however, the king of Scotland and future king of England declared (as king of Scotland) that New Year's Day would be fixed on 1 January, bringing Scotland into line with 'all utheris weill governit commoun welthis'. England was therefore, by implication, not well governed; and on this matter, having no doubt enjoyed his sideswipe in 1599, he apparently never felt it necessary to make it so.

Hierarchy and Status

Not until the nineteenth century is it possible to speak of class, with its connotation of conflict. But throughout recorded history there was a strong consciousness of degrees of men within a strictly hierarchical

society and, at least in theory, of the responsibilities as well as the rights
of those in its upper echelons: the obligations of protection and service
fundamental to personal lordship and kinship. To a varying extent
within the British Isles, personal lordship, however much overlain by
the complexities introduced by what historians refer to (sweepingly
and often without adequate definition) as feudalism – when the
holding of land became integral to lordship and service – still mattered
much. Whether for military purposes, or counsel in their affairs, or the
visible demonstration of their status, the great needed their affinities
and retinues, the lesser the advice and protection of their lords: good
lordship in England, maintenance and manrent in Scotland. This was
the case even in early-modern England, where throughout the
medieval period the precocious development of central justice had had
its inevitable effect on the exercise of what was primarily local lordship;
by the sixteenth century that was also to an extent true of Wales. But
in Scotland and Ireland the local justice of kin and lord, in the shape of
the justice of the feud – sometimes bloody, often highly effective – was
still flourishing. It continued throughout the sixteenth century in
Lowland Scotland and beyond that in Ireland and the Scottish
Highlands.

In another way there was a distinct contrast between England and
Scotland. By 1400 the great men of the English realm were divided into
two groups, nobility and gentry, signified by the right of the first to an
individual summons to the House of Lords, and of the second to seek
election to the House of Commons. The unusual bicameral nature of
the English Parliament, indeed, was integral to the social division. (The
less clearly structured Irish parliament was also loosely bicameral, but
as it was hardly representative of Irish as opposed to Anglo-Irish society
it cannot readily be included in the argument here.) By contrast, as
elsewhere in Europe, Scotland's parliament was unicameral, a meeting
of the three estates. As in Europe, its landowners were higher and
lesser nobility, the Scottish word laird meaning lord, not gentleman;
and the same lack of division held good in Gaelic Ireland. How far this
mattered is a subject for debate. Yet for those who cared about such
things, the fundamental social division between gentle and non-gentle
was complicated in England when those above the great dividing line
were no longer all possessed of nobility as well as gentility, especially
in an age when humanist scholars were at pains to define nobility and
gentility as a single concept, not in terms of birth but of innate virtue.

Uniquely, English gentry had to fight to defend their gentle status, especially at the lower end where economically they might merge into the ranks of the upper yeomen.

This may help to explain the self-conscious use of the word 'gentleman' which the English gentry attached to their names, and the groping efforts of early-modern gentlemen to define their gentility through somewhat vague ideas about its being established after three generations and not working with ones hands. It may also explain the tracts on hierarchical divisions written by William Harrison and Thomas Wilson in the late sixteenth century and Edward Chamberlayne in the late seventeenth. Chamberlayne demonstrates how much these divisions still mattered, writing at a time when a changed world was showing a new concern with economic divisions, exemplified most famously in 1696 in the work of one of the new group of 'Politick Arithmeticians', Gregory King. A century earlier, Wilson had been at pains to complain about the habit of wealthy yeomen of dressing in the silks of the gentry, a message reinforced by the sumptuary legislation of the late-medieval and early-modern period, which attempted to regulate the dress and food of the various social orders. Scotland also had its sumptuary legislation in this period, which meant that not only in England were the upper orders feeling under the pressure from below, which produced such legislation. Scotland might have a higher and a lesser nobility, but the lesser nobility were not allowed the same number of dishes as the higher, and if a higher noble went to dine with a lesser one, he had to provide his own extra dishes.

No hierarchical society is, of course, ever rigid. But it does seem that this was an age when those at the top of society were feeling particularly challenged. In 1649 the proto-sociologist Patrick Gordon of Ruthven, writing of the disorders of the time in *Britanes Distemper* (by which he actually meant his own locality, north-east Scotland) poured contempt on what he called the English devil, the keeping of state, the particularly deferential form of behaviour demanded by the great. This he ascribed to England having been a conquered nation, unlike Scotland. But now, as a consequence of the union of 1603 his own local lord, the marquis of Huntly, was adopting English practice and distancing himself from his men and servants; even that great hero the marquis of Montrose was guilty of similar arrogance. Gordon might lament the changed relationship; but English style appeared to have had something to offer the hitherto more relaxed but now worried Scottish higher nobility.

Learning and the Professions

With the partial exception of England, the medieval British Isles depended on their clerics for the literate arts and skills. England was unusual, in that by the beginning of the fourteenth century laymen were becoming lawyers; even so, the king's government was still very heavily clerical. The clergy were, therefore, an elite, but also a service elite, useful in government and in royal and aristocratic households where reading and writing were necessary for business and for entertainment. Great laymen were not philistines; they had the literature of the day read to them. But it was not part of their *raison d'être* to read it for themselves. Why this changed is one of the great imponderables of the period. They did not *need* to become literate; we can only observe that, from *c.* 1300, they did. It was a massive social change when kings and nobles began to read and write, and gradually, though very slowly, that spread down the social scale. And it had a considerable impact on hierarchical relationships.

Education certainly offered a wonderful new opportunity for the English gentry to recapture the prestige which they may have felt they had lost. Under the influence of humanist scholars, though themselves divided on the issue (as Sir Thomas More found when he discovered that Erasmus, whose approbation he so much sought, disapproved of men of learning directly serving their prince), education did provide them with a new role in royal service as councillors, administrators and diplomats on a much more extensive scale than formerly. Well before the Reformation, laymen were replacing clerics, in government and in the law. Thomas More himself, son of a London lawyer, who began in his father's profession and rose in royal government to become Lord Chancellor, is a spectacular example of this new development. There had been a few lay Chancellors in England, the first in the thirteenth century, six in the fourteenth century and two in the fifteenth, but they were knights or earls; and even Scotland had its occasional high-born medieval lay Chancellor. But in both countries the overwhelming number had been clerics, most of them bishops. More was the first of a virtually unbroken line of lay Chancellors in England. And there were others making their mark, such as Thomas Wyatt, court poet and diplomat in Henry VIII's later years, to the perplexity of his contemporary court poet Henry Howard, earl of Surrey, who loathed this breed of men whom he regarded as upstarts but deeply admired Wyatt's poetry. What such men were doing was finding a new role for themselves, that of service to the crown.

By the late sixteenth century lay gentlemen were thoroughly entrenched in government, holding the great offices of state and dominant in the royal council, no longer intermittent visitors at court but permanent members of it. Whereas in the past the rewards for such men had been benefices in the Church, now, from the reign of Henry VIII, the laymen could look for peerage titles, and a few even got them from the parsimonious Elizabeth, though not until James's reign were they given out with a more lavish hand. By that time, the pressure for place and office was such that demand far outran supply, clogging up the patronage networks and creating huge tensions and rivalries in court and government. It was an unforeseen and unwelcome development of the fact that education was now as necessary for gentility as military prowess had been, and Castiglione's *Il Cortegiano* – The Book of the Courtier – became the essential manual for all aspiring gentlemen.

The same phenomenon was observable in Wales and Ireland, although inevitably the results were different, for neither Welsh nor Irish gentry could flock to the centre. The shiring of Wales and the extension of law courts after the Act of Union of 1536 did, however, offer more jobs for Welshmen; and Sir John Price and William Salusbury, humanists and lawyers, whose influential writings combined admiration for both Welsh language and literature and the new dispensation created by the Act of Union, were a powerful voice for the acceptability of that union. In Ireland, the literate government gentleman tended to be English; the great poet and brutal despiser of Ireland Edmund Spenser is the outstanding example. Inevitably, however, religious divisions produced a different pattern, with Protestant and Catholic Irish, lay and clerical, pressed into the service of the rival Churches.

Scotland, however, more closely resembled England in the sixteenth century, perhaps more remarkably because coming from further behind. James IV's Education Act of 1496 enjoined on the eldest sons of landowners the possibly unwelcome burden of going to school until they had learned 'perfyte Latyne'. By James V's reign (1513–42), educated laymen were coming into the king's government, men such as Sir Thomas Erskine, first lay royal secretary, who had studied law at Pavia, and that dazzling courtier, diplomat and poet, Sir David Lindsay of the Mount. As in England, laymen were the dominant force in government by the later sixteenth century, helped on by the insistence of the Kirk in pulling the ministry out of royal service, as enacted in 1584. The Maitlands, east Lothian lairds, were the Scottish equivalent of the English Cecils; a father and two sons were respectively Keeper of the Privy Seal, Secretary and Chancellor to Mary and to James VI – examples of minor local landowners becoming major political figures. The number of these men in Scotland was never so great as to create the severe strains visible in England. But it was from this group that James VI, after 1603, could create his absentee government in Scotland, and, by raising them to the peerage, establish what was effectively a *noblesse de robe*.

Religious considerations came to play a part in all this, as well as the earlier influence of the humanists, with their enthusiastic encourage-ment of lay literacy. The drive for an educated laity is associated with the reformed churches, but it also motivated Counter Reformation Catholicism. What is striking in the British Isles, however, is the very different impact of reforming thought on education in England and Scotland. Scottish Calvinists, following the lead of the great reformers of Strasbourg and Geneva, had a vision of universal education, movingly set out in the First Book of Discipline of 1560, which was very much local education; home, school and Kirk would together create the godly individual. It was not immediately realised; the money was not there. But it was not lost sight of, and by the later seventeenth century the main burghs and most Lowland and north-eastern parishes had a grammar or parish school. The same thinking lay behind the extension of university education; again, it was to be local. To the three medieval universities of St Andrews, Glasgow and King's College, Aberdeen, were added three more, the 'tounis college' of Edinburgh founded in 1582, Marischal College, Aberdeen, founded by the earl Marischal in 1593, and in the same decade Fraserburgh, founded by a laird, Fraser of Phillorth, although three in the north-east proved one too many and it did not survive (sadly, its buildings were taken over by members of the universities of Aberdeen, in time of plague). But the others flourished, with all the excitement of the challenge to Aristotle, the extension of the curriculum and the introduction of specialist teachers. They produced an educated ministry; they also educated the laity, the greatest of whom combined education at home with a taste for foreign travel, to Paris, Orleans, Pavia, Montpellier.

In England, the idea of local and universal education had much less appeal. The much-vaunted Tudor grammar schools, founded on the proceeds of the dissolution of the monasteries and the chantries, are now seen as less impressive than used to be thought; indeed the money was there to found more of them, had there been the will. The great medieval charitable foundations for poor scholars, like Eton and Winchester, now began their lives as bastions of the elite. Oxford and Cambridge retained their exclusive grip; it is an irony that Oliver Cromwell could cut off a king of England's head, but fail in his attempt to found a university at Durham. For this was an age of the founding of Oxbridge colleges, by laymen. And if Wales did not get its own university, Welsh students flocked into Oxford and, to a lesser extent, Cambridge, getting their own Oxford college, Jesus, founded by Hugh Price in 1571. Ireland did get its first university, Trinity College Dublin, founded with some imput from the University of Glasgow; again, to an even greater degree than elsewhere, the motivation here was to support and strengthen the Protestant Church of Ireland. In contrast to Scotland, in all three countries education was more elitist; and more people had to travel away from home to get it.

Yet even in England this was not the whole story. If lay literacy was still, in the sixteenth century, mainly associated with the upper orders, by the seventeenth it had visibly spread beyond such elite confines. It is very difficult to estimate its extent, partly because reading and writing were taught as separate skills, and partly because it is impossible to deduce a general ability to write from the evidence only of a signature. And it is important to forget modern assumptions that literacy is an essential part of life and remember that then it was not; it may very often have been fashion, the desire to emulate one's neighbours, which provided the spur to learning, rather than any actual need which drove literacy down the social scale. Indeed, need could militate against learning, for children were required not for the luxury of schooling, but to work. Yet while much of the population, and especially the female population, remained illiterate, the change is obvious enough, as seen in the chapbooks – romantic, historical, godly – which were now included in the packs of the pedlars on the roads of

England. The greatest of them all is *The Pilgrim's Progress*, with its combination of medieval romance and intense godliness, written by John Bunyan, son of a tinker, given basic education by his mother until forced to work, but going on to educate himself and produce one of the most remarkable writings of early-modern England. Not every child was a Bunyan; even Shakespeare went 'unwillingly to school'. But knowledge of the written word was opening up new possibilities; by the mid-seventeenth century these were beginning to include heightened political debate, with the introduction of the news-sheets, first in London and then spreading throughout the kingdoms.

Moreover, reading was not the only source of entertainment, learning and growing political awareness. In 1576, a public theatre – called, graphically, 'The Theatre' – opened in London. It was only the second in Europe since the days of classical Rome, and the first of many in the British Isles, originally in England and then, in the mid-1630s, Dublin. Another belatedly followed in godly Scotland in 1660, although plays were performed there in the late sixteenth century, initially with the concurrence of the Kirk and then under royal protection. Indeed, a troupe of English players, who just possibly included Shakespeare, and who went on to become the King's Men after 1603, were invited by James VI in 1601 to give a Scottish tour, to the impotent fury of a now hostile Kirk. Not only did this call into existence the professional play-wright and actor. Erratic censorship – heavier under both Elizabeth and Charles I than it was under James VI and I – meant that British audiences were treated to a feast of history, both classical and medieval, comedy, black and blood-stained drama and political satire. The explosion of material available on the public stage is breathtaking. It certainly argues for informed and interested audiences, the poorer members willing to stand for hours in often packed theatres. Even more than the gradual spread of literacy, the public stage surely transformed political and social awareness.

A new professionalism was not only associated with the theatre. If professionalism in this period can be defined as a means for the upper ranks of society to carve out new careers for themselves, it extended, as has been seen, to the government, and also to the law. In part this was a product of economic pressures as well as educational aspirations. Except in Ireland, where outside the Pale gavelkind (partible inheritance) still survived, succession by primogeniture and the practice of entailing land ensured that estates, or the lion's share of them, passed to the eldest son. For younger sons, the pre-Reformation Church had offered a haven, in the extensive priesthood and the monasteries. So also, in late medieval England at least, had war. Neither, except briefly and intermittently in the second case, was now available. There was, therefore, a need for new opportunities. By the second half of the sixteenth century, the Inns of Court in England were operating alongside the universities as the training ground for gentlemen, combining professional legal training with a wider curriculum including history, geography, languages, astronomy, mathematics; that self-consciously perfect English gentleman and extensive traveller Fynes Morryson boasted that he had been educated at Cambridge and Oxford and the Inns of Court, which perhaps makes it unsurprising that when he visited Scotland in 1598 he wrote of it with contempt. It was Elizabeth's misfortune that the 1601 parliament, the most contentious of her reign, which launched a determined attack on monopolies, should contain 253 barristers and gentry trained at the Inns of Court. The process did not begin there; lawyers had been a problem in the parliament of 1372. But there was a difference, when Thomas Cromwell, son of a Putney clothworker, rose to pre-eminence as a lawyer and also a merchant. He was one of the two dramatic cases of men rising to the top from the lower orders, the other being Cardinal Wolsey, son of an Ipswich butcher. But Wolsey took the traditional route, the Church. Cromwell was unusual in his origins, and hated for it; no medieval lay lawyer of lowly origin achieved what Cromwell did. Yet, as a layman, he was the man of the future.

The same process was happening in Scotland as younger sons and heads of cadet branches of the great aristocratic families went into the law; in the course of the sixteenth century, Edinburgh became the home of legal dynasties, the Hays, the Colvilles and others. Perhaps the most famous was Thomas Hamilton, heir of four generations of a legal family, descendant of the Hamiltons of Innerwick; his father and two brothers were Lords of Council and Session, and he himself became Lord Advocate and President of the Court of Session before going on to become, in 1612, the King's Secretary, and entering the ranks of the peerage. And it was laymen who were prominent in the plan, beginning in the 1570s, to digest and codify the jungle of the 'auld laws', men like Sir James Balfour of Pittendreich who produced his *Practicks* in 1579, and in the early seventeenth century Sir John Skene of Curriehill and Sir Thomas Craig of Riccarton. These were lawyers who began the academic and philosophical study of Scots law more normally associated with the *Institutes* of James Dalrymple, first viscount Stair, published in 1681; Dalrymple's is the famous work, but he was building on a century of legal thinking. More generally, it was the professional lawyers who by 1600 were well on the way to undermining the amateur justice of kin and lord, not because it was ineffective but because it was amateur; the aura of legal professionalism – not to say the insinuous aura of legal obscurity – would have an ever-increasing appeal, and this meant that in Scotland the rise of the professional lawyer had a much more profound social impact than in England.

Law was clearly the most dramatic and visible area in which the lives of the gentry took on a new dimension. But it was not the only one. In the long run even more important and exciting were science and medicine. The great politician, lawyer and polymath Francis Bacon may have died of an experiment in the freezing of food, but before that lamentable end his approach to scientific discovery – his *Instauratio Magna*, inductive and experimental rather than contemplative, as derived from Aristotle – was an influential part of the new approach to the study of science. In medicine, there was even a certain pleasing 'British' aspect; William Harvey, discoverer of the circulation of the blood, was given the freedom of Edinburgh and Aberdeen, even if Scottish physicians did not necessarily agree with his findings. English contempt for the Irish may have extended to their poets and historians, but not to their doctors, because of a distinguished tradition, both clerical and lay, stretching back into medieval times; one, James Neylon, even managed to graduate in medicine at Oxford. The enthusiasm for new investigation reached out beyond natural philosophy and medicine. John Napier of Merchiston invented logarithms and followed Leonardo da Vinci in designing submarines. Map-making was beginning to be more than an art form. Sir George Bruce's underwater coal mine in the Firth of Forth at Culross became a major tourist attraction. This was not only an age of cultural transformation, as gentlemen redefined themselves. It was a time of thrilling intellectual achievement.

Marriage and the Family

A great deal more has been written on this subject for England than for Scotland, Ireland and Wales. This section, therefore, is inevitably Anglocentric. Yet when looking at the way in which reforming thought affected attitudes to marriage, as it did in three of the four parts of the British Isles, though only partially in Ireland, we can begin with one surprise. Scotland experienced the most thoroughgoing Calvinist reformation. But from the beginning, Scotland was much more willing to countenance divorce than England. The 'double standard' did exist in Scotland; a woman's adultery, with the possibility of doubtful paternity should there be a child, was as much a matter of concern for property owners as anywhere else. But divorce for adultery was allowed, for both men and women. It was also allowed, albeit by a pretty tortuous process, for desertion. And it was granted initially, in the years of legal confusion after 1560, by Kirk sessions, and then by the new central and local commissary courts. In England, by contrast, divorce was allowed only by Act of Parliament, which meant that if divorces in Scotland were few, in England they were virtually non-existent, the first case being brought as late as 1698.

Actually it is less surprising than may at first sight appear. It was not because the Scots were instinctively more tolerant of those trapped in unhappy marriages; in England as in Scotland it was possible to arrange separations. It was because the Scots were more logical than the English about the implications of marriage no longer being a sacrament, but only a contract. Milton pointedly asked why the marriage contract could not be broken, as other contracts could be, but his was a lone English voice. As with education, so with marriage law: the Scots were more in line with European Calvinism. As Calvin himself asserted, 'a man may hold the primacy in other things, but in bed he and his wife are equal'. This is not to say that Scotland did not have its own muddles. 'Habit and repute' remained grounds for a valid marriage; so did marriage according to medieval canon law, which, rather confusingly, had acknowledged that although it was then a sacrament, a man over the age of fourteen and a woman over the age of twelve could create a legal marriage by agreeing to marry and sleeping together, without parental consent, witnesses or priest. No wonder the eighteenth century saw English couples fleeing north to Gretna, just over the border in godly Scotland. Moreover, what ensured that the Kirk's initial attitude to divorce was maintained was the fact that, fortunately for divorcing couples, the commissary courts were secularised; the Kirk, after all, while in 1560 accepting the logic of the new sacramental theology, would have preferred adulterers to be executed.

What does not distinguish Scotland from England or, for that matter, other parts of the British Isles, is the highly problematic question of patriarchalism and familial affection. This has certainly been a subject of considerable debate among historians, and probably always will be, because a lot of the evidence for early-modern marriage is anecdotal, or comes from the conduct books written by men, and is therefore conflicting. It is almost tempting to say that then, as now, and no doubt at any time, some marriages were made in heaven, some in hell; indeed in 1617, for example, William Whateley's *Bride's Bush* described marriage as a 'little hell'. The real difficulty is to try to understand the social mores of the period, without going to extremes. On the one hand, they cannot be underestimated, and treated as a veneer overlaying modern attitudes to marriage. What western modern woman would say, as Mary, countess of Warwick, did, that 'my lord fell, without any occasion given by me, into a great passion with me, which troubled me so much that I fell into a dispute with him . . . and spake unadvisedly'? But Mary was undoubtedly sincere; she asked God's forgiveness for 'shedding so many teares for anything but my sinnes and for not being content with what his providence was pleased to order for me'. On the other hand, the argument for lack of affection, especially focused on the idea that high infant mortality meant that parents avoided investing in love for their children, is equally doubtful; Ben Jonson's heartbreaking poems on the deaths of his children, and the agonising sense of loss recorded in women's diaries, are testimony to the very reverse.

The conduct books themselves offer us a fascinating insight into practice as opposed to theory; they tell us what the authors thought should not happen. One of the best known, *Of Domesticall Duties* (1622) by William Gouge, minister of Blackfriars in London, for example, adjures wives not to address their husbands by pet names such as 'sweetheart . . . duck . . . chick' or even by their first names; the correct form was 'Husband'. Gouge was clearly not popular with the female members of his congregation, who showed their disapproval when the second edition of his work was published in 1634. Like Hannah

Woolley, in her *Gentlewomen's Companion* (1675), Gouge stressed patriarchal discipline, and the inferiority and subjection of wives, children and servants. Yet this is not the whole story. He was firmly against wife beating, on the grounds that it humiliated the wife and reduced her authority over her children and servants. And if the wife was inferior, that was nevertheless tempered by the fact that she was her husband's companion, there to offer spiritual support and comfort. The idea of the companionate marriage was now very much emphasised, and the same was true of writings on the family in late seventeenth-century Scotland. Predictably, the godly marriage was given even more weight in Scotland. And the Scottish enthusiasm for threatening children with hell, and for children dying godly deaths, can be, to the modern reader, spine-chilling. Yet even contemporaries seem to have sympathised with the wife and children of the impassioned covenanter Archibald Johnson of Wariston, whose 'inexhaustible copiousness' in family prayers was undoubtedly excessive.

Reforming thought undoubtedly did enhance the married state; for it was no longer seen as inferior to celibacy and, to Elizabeth's intense fury, the clergy now had wives and children. More specifically, they enhanced the status of married women, and especially godly married women, whether Protestant or Catholic, like Lady Margaret Hoby and Magdalen, viscountess Montague, both of whom strenuously upheld their faiths in their households, the first observing the official faith, the second preserving the forbidden one. Woolley might comment bitterly that 'vain man is apt to think we were merely intended for the world's propagation . . . Most in this depraved age think a woman learned enough if she can distinguish her husband's bed from another's', which echoes James VI and I's brutal comment that to educate women was as difficult as taming foxes. Neither was wholly accurate. The educated woman, from the aristocratic lady to John Bunyan's mother, who taught her son to read, was a powerful force in marriage, the family and the household. If she was too powerful that might be a cause for criticism. The cuckolded or bullied husband was the object of contempt in local communities, expressed in the skimmington rides, public spectacles designed to make him the object of ridicule. Taming the shrew was a familiar literary theme, normally straightforward enough. But in the early 1590s, Shakespeare wrote *The Taming of the Shrew*; and while we can only guess how in his day Kate delivered her final speech, in which she appears to accept patriarchy unreservedly, it is sufficiently ambiguous to have given later actresses plenty of scope for interpretation.

That women were not the depressed creatures of patriarchal theory was not, of course, a new phenomenon. What was, perhaps, new was that this was more fully acknowledged, with approval. The word 'couple' appears in 1611, to denote the married couple. But if this looks like an advance, it has to be set alongside a quite different trend, reflected in another word which took on a new meaning. From the 1590s, 'spinster' no longer only referred to a way of earning a living; it referred to the way of life of an unmarried woman. 'Couple' was a concept, 'spinster' a fact. The age of marriage among the upper orders rose from the early twenties of the sixteenth century to the mid-twenties in the seventeenth, and this in itself reflects the changing patterns of male lifestyle, with the appeal of the Inns of Court and the beginnings of the Grand Tour. But also rising were the number who did not marry, reaching one in four by the late seventeenth century. That is a significant proportion of the population. Women's writings of the period, while admitting the inferiority of the female to the male author, were beginning to comment on the loss of liberty which marriage entailed. In the often vitriolic satire *The Ten Pleasures of Marriage*, attributed to Aphra Behn, the author roundly proclaims that 'for my part, I believe that of all the disasters we are subject to in our life-time, that of marriage takes preference from the rest'. Certainly a group of late seventeenth-century women writers, Woolley, Behn – the first woman in England to make her living from writing – and Mary Astell, called for more education for women and more freedom from the chains of marriage. It may be going too far to label them, as some writers have done, as 'feminists', but they were undoubtedly challenging accepted norms. More prosaically, and very practically, the doughty widows of Abingdon in Berkshire in the seventeenth century were less inclined to remarry than their sixteenth-century predecessors; the proportion fell from 50 per cent in the mid-sixteenth century to 37.5 per cent in the first half of the seventeenth century and 23.5 per cent in the second. In part this was for economic reasons; increasingly husbands included penalty clauses in their wills, depriving the widow of her inheritance, or reducing it if she remarried. But a new husband would provide economic support. Surely, therefore, it was the chance of independence which was a powerful motivation. The Homily on Matrimony, read in church since Elizabeth's reign, did after all remind widows that to remarry was 'to relinquish the liberty of their own rule'.

Evidence about attitudes to marriage and the family is therefore very far from straightforward. One could say that that is the human condition.

The Economics of an Expanding World

It must have seemed an exciting age. In the late fifteenth and early sixteenth centuries, helped on by innovative developments in the design of ships and a new interest in geography, based on Ptolemy's second-century *Geographia*, men began to explore their world. Columbus's discovery of the West Indies in 1492 is the most famous; twenty-eight years later, Magellan's expedition circumnavigated the globe for the first time. Curiously, it took some time for this to rouse interest; travel accounts were not much read until the mid-sixteenth century. But in 1496–8 Henry VII provided money and ships for John Cabot's voyages of discovery and, in 1508, for his son Sebastian. It is not entirely clear what they found, though John Cabot did land in America. There was further exploration in the mid-sixteenth century, with voyages to Muscovy and the Gold Coast in 1553. Englishmen were going out not only to discover but to colonise, beginning with Raleigh's unsuccessful and mysterious colony at Roanoke in 1585–7, and followed after 1603 by expeditions to Virginia, New England, Maryland and Pennsylvania; emigration in the seventeenth century was higher than it would be again before the twentieth century. New trading companies were established, among them the Muscovy (1555), Levant (1581) East India (1600) and Virginia (1606). Meanwhile, in the later sixteenth century, the privateering of Francis Drake (who also circumnavigated the globe in 1577–80), Richard Hawkins and Thomas Cavendish was proving profitable to the crown and to themselves. The Scottish bid to join in this development was short-lived and unsuccessful; the attempt to seize the French Canadian colony of Port Royal in 1629 and establish Nova Scotia lasted only three years before Charles I restored it to the French. But England's world was dramatically expanding.

It was also an age of projects. In the scholar and diplomat Thomas Smith's *Discourse of the Commonweal* (1549) plans were set out for creating new industries and planting new crops. Woad was grown, and from the 1580s spread extensively, first in southern England and then further north. Iron founding flourished from 1543, significantly expanding that begun by the French in Sussex fifty years earlier. Stocking knitting became popular, as did the making of caps, hats, pins, gloves and much else. In 1549 the duke of Somerset settled Flemings in Glastonbury, to improve the making and dying of worsteds. More and more avenues were explored by the projectors: tobacco growing, soap making, starch making. In the 1580s, woad and a superior form of madder growing, and the production of rape oil were introduced in Ireland. Stockings were being knitted in Wales by the seventeenth century. At its best, this was intended to provide work at home and help the export trade while reducing imports. At its worst, it was a field day for monopolists; this had become a major political issue by the late sixteenth century which would drag on into the seventeenth. Exactly the same trends were evident in Scotland, particularly in the reign of James VI. Already the Edinburgh gold- and silversmiths of the second half of the sixteenth century were producing work of remarkable quality. In James's reign, 'projectis' became the rage, and Venetians were brought in for the new industry of glass making, English for leather and sugar refining, and Flemish and English for weaving and spinning; and efforts were made to develop the fisheries in the interests of the Scots and not the Dutch, whose ships operated round the Scottish coasts. And Scottish monopolists were as unpopular as English ones.

Discovery, colonisation and projects – despite the monopolists – and the expansion of trade all sound very positive. Both English trade and English shipping were significant growth areas and even Scottish trade was growing in the later sixteenth century; to its traditional partners, notably France and the Baltic countries, it added Catholic Spain – to the indignation of the Kirk. But there were severe economic problems. Europe as a whole was hit by inflation in the sixteenth century, and this included all parts of the British Isles. Prices in Spain doubled in the first half of the sixteenth century, and inexorably the price rise spread. It took some time for men to realise that this was caused by the influx of the New World silver; Thomas Smith was one of the first to make this argument. He was also the only commentator who was aware of the effect of the vicious debasement of the English coinage in the 1540s; for others, it was easier to blame the highly unpopular enclosures. The debasement of the 1540s was embarked on because of the need to finance the French and Scottish wars of Somerset and Henry VIII. It was dramatic in its speed and extent. But from 1552 it was reversed, although the heavily debased coinage was not fully withdrawn from circulation until the early years of Elizabeth's reign. Much more severe and long lasting was the debasement of the Scottish coinage, beginning in the 1520s. This was not a peculiarly Scottish problem; it was happening also to the coinages of France and the Italian cities. But in Scotland it was happening on a bigger scale. By 1601 the silver content of the pound Scots was one-fifth of what it had been in 1500; and the exchange rate with the pound sterling fell from 3:1 in the mid-fifteenth century to 12:1 in 1603.

A further problem was population increase. After the ravages of the Black Death in the fourteenth century, the population in the sixteenth century was beginning to recover, though probably only reaching pre-plague levels at the beginning of the seventeenth. Between the mid-sixteenth and mid-seventeenth centuries, the English population virtually doubled; and although there was no overall pattern, the urban population rose more rapidly than the rural, although whereas York, for example, sustained its growth, Norwich did not. What skewed the urban rise was the extraordinary phenomenon of the exceptional growth of London, from 50,000 in the 1520s to 200,000 by the end of the sixteenth century and 400,000 by the mid-seventeenth. After 1650, when the population ceased to increase and even slightly declined, London continued to grow. Economically, socially, administratively, professionally and culturally, London had an increasingly irresistible pull which brought men and women flocking to it. In Wales, the population likewise increased, apparently more in the north, which experienced a rise of about 66 per cent, than the south. Although Cardiff's population increased, it was the northern towns which grew more notably, Caernarfon's population rising by 120 per cent, Wrexham's by 112 per cent. But numbers were still small; Caernarfon in 1670 reached 1,755, Wrexham 3,225. Ireland appears to have had a slower rising population, in both rural and urban areas; war and famine took their toll. In Scotland, Edinburgh by the later seventeenth century had more than 30,000 inhabitants, while Glasgow, Dundee and Aberdeen had reached 10,000 by the mid-seventeenth century, Glasgow continuing to grow to c. 14,000 by the end of the century.

The population increase was, inevitably, a source of worry, and
even of some lurid efforts to explain it; in 1605 Sir Thomas Craig of
Riccarton ascribed it to the fact that in Scotland 'our women do not
indulge themselves with wine, exotic foodstuffs and spices from distant
lands, so harmful to the womb, hence the more readily do they
conceive'. It certainly created new levels of social tensions and concern
about how to cope with the increase in numbers of the poor. It was
part of man's Christian duty to help the sick and the poor, and efforts
were made to fill the vacuum created by the destruction of the
monasteries, hospitals and almshouses of the pre-Reformation
Church. Doubt has been cast on the accuracy of describing that group
who in Edward VI's reign (1547–53) did show awareness of the problem
as 'the common-wealth men', but there were certainly people like
Hugh Latimer, bishop of Worcester, and the evangelical clergyman
Robert Crowley who were highly critical of the greed of the rich
and their indifference to the poor. The London hospitals, St
Bartholomew's, St Thomas', Christ's, Bridewell and Bedlam, were re-
established or founded between 1544 and 1557. Robert Dudley, earl of
Leicester, founded his own hospital in Warwick. Towns began to
make censuses of their poor; in 1577, Norwich recorded 2,359, 18 per
cent of the population, and Huddersfield in 1622 had over 20 per cent.
As well as individuals and local communities, central government now
stepped in, in both England and Scotland, with the Poor Laws. In
England, efforts to put the able-bodied poor to work and support the
impotent poor go back to Cardinal Wolsey, and there were various
attempts to legislate, including the notorious Vagrancy Act of 1547,
which allowed vagrants to be bound as slaves for two years. But
legislation really got going in 1572, to be followed up by further Acts
in 1576, 1593, 1598 and 1601. The government was terrified of rising
vagrancy – the roads of England were, in its fevered imagination,
overrun with criminal vagrants – and so punishment of vagrants was a
major concern. The other strand in its legislation was provision for the
deserving poor; responsibility for them was to be held by church-
wardens and overseers of the poor in each parish, poor relief being
provided by taxing every inhabitant. Begging was banned. The
problem about this, well-intentioned though it was, lay in the fact that
it sought to change, virtually overnight, traditional habits based on
kinship and neighbourliness and impose a 'state'-run system. There
were objections to compulsory poor relief and the ban on begging,

which removed the opportunity to assist the poor by giving in kind – so it was argued by parishioners in the West Riding and in Ormskirk. The new legislation did not work in England and Wales, especially in times of dearth; only over time would the new system become familiar and acceptable. In 1574 and 1579, however, the policy seemed attractive enough to be borrowed by the Scots, who passed their own Poor Laws. To the list of those described as vagrants the Scots added 'vagabond scholars' of the three universities. Begging was allowed by 'cruikit folk seik impotent folk and waik folk'. Those who did not belong to the parish would be sent from parish to parish until they came to their parish of birth – thus adding to the numbers of beggars on the roads. Its real weakness, however, was that unlike the English legislation it made no attempt to provide work for the able-bodied poor; there was in Scotland no dawning awareness that being idle was not necessarily the poor man's fault.

In the period of this legislation death was still a grim reality throughout the British Isles. The 1590s was a particularly bad decade; in the early seventeenth century matters improved, until the horrors of the year 1623, especially in Scotland and northern England, perhaps the worst famine year of the period. Thereafter experience diverged. In England, Wales and Ireland, where war was a more devastating force than famine, there were still years of shortage, but no longer on the level of the past. In Scotland, by contrast, the mid-1690s saw a recurrence of the famines in which people starved to death. And although plague was no longer the national killer it had been, there were still local outbreaks, continuing until 1666 when the villagers of Eyham in Derbyshire made their heroic sacrifice, barricading themselves in during their effort to contain it. Meanwhile, there was a new scourge, syphilis, which arrived in Italy in 1494 and spread rapidly throughout Europe; it is first mentioned in England and Scotland in 1497. Less of a killer than plague, it was still a loathsome, painful and frightening disease.

There was undoubtedly innovation and expansion in this period, and much to create a sense of achievement. There was also all too much which was beyond the power of men to cope with adequately or effectively. Early-modern governments simply did not have the resources to implement their policies; such things as the movement of food in time of dearth were beyond their capacities. But there is a certain anachronism in that comment. What the inhabitants of the

British Isles saw was central and local authorities trying to meet new pressures. They may have been encouraged to assume that governments could solve economic problems, as we are today. They may have been no more or less mistaken.

2. Politics and Religion in the Sixteenth Century

The Polities of the British Isles in 1485

1485, which saw the accession of the victorious Henry Tudor to the throne, used to be seen as a critical date in English history; sloppy assumptions about the end of the Middle Ages and the beginning of the modern world were once appealed to, as intolerably powerful medieval magnates supposedly woke up to become the more civilised Tudor aristocracy. As the reign of James III of Scotland conveniently came to an end in 1488 it was possible to see the same thing happening at the same time to the Scottish magnates, whose spots equally changed in the reign of James IV. This is so old-fashioned an idea that it may seem curious to mention it here; English historians have long been identifying Tudor innovations in government, especially in the area of finance, as being anticipated by the Yorkist kings, in particular Edward IV, and Scottish historians no longer regard the fifteenth-century crown as endlessly in conflict with overmighty magnates.

Nevertheless, the late fifteenth century was a low point in English and, to some extent, Scottish political life. The balance of power in Europe had shifted decisively away from England; not until the beginning of the eighteenth century would England once again become a major player in European politics. The immediate beneficiary was France, whose rise to become one of the two super-powers after its final defeat of England in the Hundred Years War was dramatic; its economic recovery in the second half of the century was such that in the 1490s Charles VIII, not himself a personally impressive king, could lead an army accompanied by a vast and glittering artillery train down through Italy to assert his right to the kingdom of Naples, thanks to a full treasury. The Spanish kingdoms, brought together into personal union with the marriage of Ferdinand and Isabella, and with the huge bonus of the silver of the New World after Columbus's discoveries in 1492, emerged out of relative isolation beyond the

Pyrenees to become the other superpower. For the next two centuries it was France and Spain which dominated European affairs. England would sink into the position which Scotland was already in, that of a minor offshore kingdom. Its monarchs would have to learn – and did learn – the lesson which Scottish kings had already successfully grasped, that shouting about their importance was the only way to sustain the notion that they were in fact important. That was no doubt good for consumption at home. But it worked better in Scotland, which had never attempted to act the part of a major European power. The very fact that England had done so throughout the high and late Middle Ages meant that it could never really throw off the consciousness of defeat and decline. That uneasy awareness would do much to determine its dealings with its other territories within the British Isles, Ireland and Wales, and, crucially, because of the impact of religious reform and the dynastic failure of the Tudors, its relationship with Scotland.

Moreover, whatever the relevance of governmental developments in the Yorkist period to the undermining of the idea of 1485 as a turning point, it is still possible to see it as a date which does mark a decisive shift, even if 1487 – the date of Stoke, the last battle of the Wars of the Roses – might be more precisely accurate. For the dismal end of the Hundred Years War in 1453 was accompanied by the equally dismal beginning of dynastic civil war between the houses of York and Lancaster, which would last for three decades. It is possible to play down its importance on the grounds that war was intermittent and, despite the extreme bloodletting of the Battle of Towton in 1461 (in which perhaps some nine thousand men were slain), not one of much fighting and loss of life. But the accession of Henry Tudor in 1485, a man without any claim to the throne, dramatically exemplifies the low state to which the English monarchy had sunk; and the sustained development of the sixteenth-century myth that the Tudors had rescued England from the chaos of the Wars of the Roses and given it dynastic stability would, as it turned out, be no more than myth. But both testify to the extent of English dislocation in the second half of the fifteenth century.

The accession of James IV to the Scottish throne in 1488, after the *coup d'état* in which his unpopular father was killed and in which he was involved with those who opposed James III, suggests that Scotland also had its share of political violence; but this was on a much smaller scale than its English counterpart. Sauchieburn, where James III died, was a one-off affair; compared to the six usurpations and three murders of English kings since 1399, this was only the second challenge to a Scottish one (the other being the murder of James I in 1437). There were fewer aristocratic rebellions and no drawn-out civil war; furthermore, the new Scottish king was not some relatively unknown chancer from abroad who had to include right of conquest in his justification of his title, but the undoubted heir to the throne. Before 1488, Scotland had been a politically more stable kingdom than England. After 1488, there was less need for political adjustment, and none of the war weariness which assailed the English aristocracy.

In October 1488, the Scots parliament laconically recorded the field of Stirling (Sauchieburn) where the late king 'happinit to have bene slane', and tapped into traditional hostility to England by exaggerating James's appeal to Henry VII for aid in the last months of his life, cheerfully turning it into the charge that he had been plotting 'the inbringing of Inglissmen to the perpetuale subieccione of the realme'. Yet in 1489 the new regime faced a major rebellion. Unlike the efforts to displace Henry VII with the Yorkist pretenders Lambert Simnel and Perkin Warbeck, however, this was not directly against the king; James III was undoubtedly dead and there were no Scottish Princes of the Tower whose deaths were mysterious enough to allow men to resurrect pretenders. Rather, although it used the pretext of bringing the late king's murderers to justice, it was against the narrowness of the new regime; too many had been crowded out by the families of Hepburn and Hume, who exercised too much control over the fifteen-year-old James IV. Militarily, the rebellion was a stalemate. Politically, it was a success; the political nation was widened. Although the dead James III would go on to become in the sixteenth century the most myth-laden king of late medieval Scotland, with his low-born favourites and his increasingly elaborated death at Sauchieburn, the crisis itself was over.

The overthrow of any king is, of course, a major political event. Yet 1488 compared to 1485 was a comparatively superficial and certainly short-lived affair. The myths surrounding James III had none of the essential propaganda value so necessary to the Tudors; they grew up not to underpin the legitimacy of a usurping monarchy but to explain the specific failure of an individual king, with the bonus of pointing the moral about what successful kings should avoid, in James's case

primarily too much dependence on low-born favourites. More immediately, it is a comment on the contrast between the unchallenged
survival of the Stewart monarchy and the final overthrow of the
Plantagenet one that the first Tudor king's panicky reaction to the
Battle of Sauchieburn was to issue orders for the strengthening of
the border garrisons; while the Scots were moving to establish James
IV's succession with as little trouble as possible – something which left
them no time or inclination to threaten England – a nervous Henry
VII, still not yet secure on his throne, and with problems enough, was
inventing another one.

   1488, though in the short term dramatic enough, was not of major
significance in Scottish terms. The importance of 1485 has been
exaggerated, though it undoubtedly represented a greater political
shift than 1488. Both are worth spending a little time on, however,
because taken together the events of the 1480s tell us much about the
nature and strength of the monarchies of England and Scotland and
about the political elites of both. Nor was this relevant only to the late
fifteenth century. Henry VII's desire for friendship with his northern
neighbour led him to press for the marriage of his elder daughter
Margaret to James IV, a marriage which took place in 1503, a year after
the Treaty of Perpetual Peace of 1502, and it was that marriage which
would lead to the union of the crowns of 1603. It was the event which
made union possible. Even more to the point, it was the state of
Scotland and England in the late fifteenth century which would
determine Anglo-Scottish relations in the sixteenth, and the form
which union took in the seventeenth; far from being the lesser mortals
the English would have liked to regard them as, the Scots had no
reason to feel any sense of inferiority to their southern neighbours.

The Early Tudor Composite Monarchy:
Henry VII and Henry VIII

Tudor England witnessed two of the great monarchs of English
history, Henry VIII and Elizabeth. Arguably, however, the monarchy
had to do a lot more shouting to keep its courage up than its great
medieval predecessors; witness, for example, Henry VIII's deliberate
identification of himself with one of them, Henry V. Such success as

the monarchy had may owe more to the unpopular and uncharismatic Henry VII than to his son and granddaughter. For it was Henry VII who came to terms with England's decline in European status and set about restoring the morale of the monarchy with intelligence and style. In part this was done at home; Henry attracted to his court major European humanist scholars, Polydore Vergil and Bernard André, setting them to work at, among other things, the beginnings of the creation of the Tudor myth. He married Elizabeth of York, daughter of Edward IV, thus giving himself contact with the last ruling house, however careful he was to deny that Elizabeth in any way gave him a claim to the throne.

Establishing the monarchy's morale also meant re-establishing England's presence abroad. It is not wholly true that Henry VII would not spend money on warfare. In 1492 he did some sword-rattling with France, successful enough for him to get from Charles VIII money and a promise not to support Yorkist pretenders. But on the whole it was the diplomatic rather than the military which appealed. He went for alliance with the rising power of Spain, marrying his son and heir Arthur to Katherine of Aragon, daughter of Ferdinand and Isabella. A lesser target, but in its way an equally important one, was Scotland. James III had departed from traditional Scottish foreign policy, alliance with France, turning instead, with a series of proposed marriage alliances, to England; 1474 had seen the first treaty, as opposed to truce, between the two countries. His son had reversed that, going back to France and renewing hostility to England to the extent of supporting the pretender Perkin Warbeck. But, as we have seen, he was persuaded into alliance with England in 1502 and marriage to Henry's daughter the following year. England might no longer be a major European power; but it had a major European ally, and, for the moment, a peaceful kingdom to the north.

These relatively good relations did not last. His son Henry VIII (Henry V *redivivus* or, in other moments, David or Arthur) was one of those larger-than-life characters, and not only in his physical appearance. He came to the throne in 1509 as king of England; he died in 1547 as king of England and Ireland, Defender of the (Roman Catholic) Faith and Supreme Head of the (non-Roman) Church. Despite his French wars at the beginning and end of his reign he did not actually revive Henry V's ambitions to become king of France, and it is unlikely that he intended to. Like his ambitious predecessors, he failed

to establish his overlordship of Scotland, although he did try. Nevertheless, as far as England was concerned, his was quite an achievement.
It gave him a false sense of his own importance, as he saw himself as
the equal of those genuinely first-rank monarchs Francis I and Charles
V; in fact, they picked him up and dropped him entirely in their own
interests, which was one reason why his potential for being a player in
international dynastic politics, based on the existence of two daughters
and a son, was never realised. But their interests did enable him to act
the part of the warrior king, going to war on behalf of one or the other,
which fed his self-fantasy. It was not too financially ruinous, especially
in the 1540s when he invaded France in support of Charles V, because
of the windfall from the recent dissolution of the monasteries.

He had another way of enhancing his power, of course, because he
ruled over Wales and Ireland. In 1536 he united the first to England, a
union enshrined in the Act of 1543, and in 1541 he made himself king of
the second. Wales was the easier of the two. Henry VII's emphasis on
his Welsh ancestry had done something to undercut the idea of a
foreign king ruling from London, and his strengthening of the Council
of the Marches, presided over by Arthur, Prince of Wales, did add to
his modicum of control. Moreover, though linguistically and culturally
Welshness was strong, Wales was not in any way a united community,
likely to or capable of offering serious resistance. Union offered new
opportunity to Welsh gentry who had been denied English office. The
insistence, in the Act of Union, on replacing the Welsh language with
English might look like a hint of the belief in Ireland that the
eradication of Irishness was the only way forward, and did stir up a
certain opposition. But it was not greatly resisted, partly because of the
advantages offered by a knowledge of English, mainly because it was
not rigidly enforced. Welsh did not cease to be a spoken or literary
language; indeed, in 1567, to advance the Reformation in Wales,
Elizabeth authorised a translation of the Prayer Book and New
Testament into Welsh, followed by a Welsh Bible in 1588. Welsh –
British – history was allowed to flourish. The Marches were shired,
English law ran throughout Wales, and the Welsh were represented in
the English Parliament. The ferocious overreaction of Bishop Rowland
Lee, President of the Council of Wales, fearful that this would not
work and overenthusiastic about executions, was entirely misplaced. It
did work, the only successful union of the period.

Ireland was a wholly different matter. There was no sense of a shared ancestry with the English crown. The foreign English imposed the rules, such as Poynings Law, which made the Irish parliament subservient to the English king and Privy Council. Henry VIII appeared to think that the way to control Ireland was to encourage feuding between powerful families, the Fitzgerald earls of Kildare who were dominant and the Butler earls of Ormond, set up to rival them. Kildare's rebellion in 1534, which led to his defeat in 1536 and execution in 1537, suggested that there was room for a different approach. Ireland got it: Henry made himself king of Ireland and settled down to rule through a series of more or less successful viceroys. But there was no attempt to assimilate Ireland into England. It was now, and would remain, a kingdom, but never treated as one; at best it was a dependent kingdom, ruled not by the king of Ireland but by the king of England; at worst, as was normally the case, it was regarded as a particularly uncivilised and barbaric province. Moreover, if Wales – however grudgingly – went along with the religious reforms of Henry and his successors, Ireland emphatically did not. It was the worst of all political and religious worlds. From 1541, Henry was king of England and Ireland, as well as Defender of the Faith and Supreme Head of the Church; he was also self-styled king of France. No doubt it gave him the same pleasure that adding strings of letters after their names gives to scholars. But the title of king of France, though claimed by every English monarch from Edward III to George III, was entirely bogus; and Henry's kingship of Ireland was highly problematic and highly tenuous.

Stewart Scotland: James IV and James V

It is in comparing Henry's England with Scotland, however, that the real limitations of his monarchy and his status as a European king become clear. It is not normally recognised, at any time in the history of the British Isles, that Scotland might be at least as flourishing and successful a kingdom, and possibly even more successful; but there is a strong case for the claim in the early-modern period. Two European leaders gave it a place which Henry VIII certainly would not have done. Not only Henry VII but Pope Julius II had already shown awareness that Scotland was not to be despised; in Julius's ranking of European rulers in 1504, it was in the middle group, two places below

England, but above Hungary, Bohemia, Poland, Denmark and others. The Holy Roman Emperor Maximilian I went even further; in Dürer's triumphal arch commissioned by him in 1515, the twelve Caesars were paralleled by twelve contemporary kings, and there James IV was portrayed along with Francis I and Henry VIII as one of the great kings of Europe.

There was some justification for this. Both James IV and, even more so, James V exploited their limited resources to the full, and with considerable intelligence, in maintaining their European presence. Both could draw on imagery established in the reign of James III. In 1469, sixty-four years before Henry VIII's Act of Appeals (1533) famously stated that 'this realm of England is an empire', the Scottish parliament chose the more minor matter of the appointment of notaries to declare that 'oure soverane lord has full jursidictione and fre impire within his realme'; and in what has been called the first Renaissance coin portrait north of the Alps, James III's silver groat of *c.* 1485 displayed him three-quarters face, wearing the closed crown of the emperor, three or four years before Henry VII saw the advantages of the device.

James IV fulfilled these two basic requirements of kingship, to do justice and to defend his kingdom – to be loosely interpreted in practice as to govern well and win military renown – successfully and on the cheap. Effective Scottish kingship was still peripatetic kingship; the centralising tendencies of James III, in whose reign Edinburgh can perhaps for the first time be regarded as the capital city, on the lines of Paris or London, were part of the problems of his kingship. James IV did not wholly reverse this; the Court of Session, the supreme civil court, began for the first time to sit regularly in Edinburgh. He was also a king on the move, travelling throughout his kingdom in a combination of pilgrimages, driving the justice ayres and mistress-visiting, which did much for the popularity which, tragically, would bring out his subjects in droves to fight with him at Flodden in 1513.

Flodden was an interruption of a pattern which saw him con-centrating on the trappings of warfare rather than its reality; he was, for example, a passionate ship builder, his mightiest ship, the *Great Michael*, reducing Henry VIII to paroxysms of envy until he built his own, the *Henri Grâce à Dieu*, to the same specifications. His other approach was warfare through diplomacy. Julius II – the 'warrior pope' – was hell bent on stirring up warfare within western Europe with his

The glorious heraldic ceiling of St Machar's Cathedral, Aberdeen (1519–22), has forty-eight coats of arms, in three lines of sixteen. The centre has those of the pope, Leo X, the archbishops and bishops of Scotland and the university of Aberdeen; on the right are those of James V, St Margaret, the leading nobles and the royal burgh of Aberdeen; on the left, the Holy Roman Emperor Charles V, the principal European kings and dukes, and the burgh of Old Aberdeen. This is a powerful depiction of Scotland's status as a European kingdom. The arms shown here, of Henry VIII and James V, make a more specific Anglo-Scottish point: the English king has an open crown, the Scottish king the closed imperial one. It is surely notable that at a time of considerable vulnerability to England the Scots chose to make this defiant gesture.

wholly misnamed Holy League aimed against France. James, to counter this, pursued a policy of appealing to western rulers to unite in a campaign against the Turks. To modern eyes, the spectacle of a king from small and far-off Scotland trying to dictate policy to the great powers of Europe might look faintly ludicrous. In fact, the Ottoman threat was all too real, and would be a Habsburg nightmare for most of the sixteenth century. What he was doing, therefore, was thinking on a European scale in the only way in which a Scottish king without the resources for full-scale warfare might hope to have some influence. What brought him to actual warfare and to grief was precisely his European engagement; insisting on maintaining the long-standing

Auld Alliance with France, against papal policy, made friendship with both England and France impossible. In 1513 he attacked England in defence of the French against Henry VIII's invasion, but was out-manoeuvred and killed.

This should have been disaster. For a king and a considerable number of the governing elite to die in battle, with only a baby, the sole surviving child of James and Margaret, to succeed, left the Scots surely very vulnerable. So why was it not? Fortunately Henry was sufficiently engaged in France not to pursue his advantage, and the Scots had the sense to ignore French blandishments to try again. But the real explanation for the Scots' survival lies beyond the immediate political circumstances: the underlying strength and the unusual nature of the political nation. For this was not just that very threatening thing, a minority; 'woe unto thee, oh land, when thy king is a child' as the scriptures had it. For the Scots, it was *yet another* minority, of which they had already had more than their fair share in the fifteenth century. They could deal with minorities; and they could do so without serious disturbance to political and social stability because, in contrast to the more centralising kingdoms of England, France and the Spanish realms, Scotland remained a decentralised nation. The Stewart kings, from James I onwards, were all remarkably tough, as any dissident noble, and indeed English kings, had found. But an almost total lack of warfare, as opposed to sporadic battles against the English, had a significant effect on the relationship between the crown and its subjects, including, as a group, its greatest subjects; it had not pressed down on them with repeated demands for men and money.

No early-modern kingdom could fully centralise; justice from the centre was always paralleled by justice in the localities. In Scotland, the balance simply remained more tilted towards local justice, not only through local courts but through the personal and amateur justice meted out by heads of kin and local lords. This is not to say, of course, that kings were not immensely important. But this was a kingdom which demonstrated that it was possible to cope if kings were incompetent or children. Scotland is therefore something of an object lesson in the fact that the increasingly lofty claims which early-modern kings were beginning to make for the power of monarchy – those highly problematic concepts of autocracy and absolutism – were not necessarily required to run a successful kingdom.

Thus the minority of James V, who came to the throne in 1513, was complicated by both the machinations of his erratic mother Margaret Tudor (Henry VIII's sister) and the marital antics which seemed to run in that generation of the family. These inevitably led to faction, and the habitual need to turn to a regent who carried some legitimacy, in this case James's uncle John, duke of Albany, brought up in France and acting in French interests. So there were occasional factional troubles in Edinburgh; and the regent in 1523, in one of his two brief periods in Scotland, led French troops south against the English accompanied by Scots who sat on the sidelines while the French and English fought the Battle of Wark, which the English won. Yet none of this seriously undermined the stability of the kingdom at large.

Five years later, at the age of fifteen, James V began his personal rule, tidying up minority factions by ousting the powerful house of Angus; the earl would spend James's reign in England. Margaret Tudor, like Henry VII's mothers Margaret Beaufort, lived on for most of his reign, but, unlike Margaret Beaufort, without influence on her son. Indeed, no one influenced James V, though many, including most furiously his uncle in England, and also Francis I of France, tried. Tension between James and Henry lay not, as it had with James IV, in the bigger ships and infinitely more distinguished court culture of the Scottish king; James V also presided over a distinguished court, but Henry, thanks to the existence of Wyatt and Surrey, had caught up.

Where James really scored was in foreign relations. A brilliant opportunist with a nice taste for blackmailing the pope for money, and the French king for his marital ambitions, he made full use of the religious divisions now assailing Europe to get his way. Rarely, indeed, had a Scottish king been such a prize; both Clement VII and Charles V considered him as a potential bridegroom, though his different intentions spared him Catherine de' Medici. What he wanted, and got, by the expedient of threatening to break the Auld Alliance, was Francis's daughter Madeleine; then, after her early death, he married a lady from one of the great aristocratic families of Europe, Mary of Guise. It did nothing to help relations with his uncle that Henry too was casting his eyes on Mary. All of this meant that he could ignore Henry's efforts to persuade him to join with him in breaking from Rome, and, at a more personal level, offer the English king the crowning insult of failing to turn up to Henry's proposed meeting at York. The outcome was an English invasion, the defeat of the Scots at Solway Moss in 1542, and the death of James V shortly afterwards. He was thirty, and he left as his heir a baby daughter one week old. It was a sad end to an impressive reign.

Already religious issues had made themselves felt in political matters, and from now on they would become inextricably intertwined, although it was not until the late sixteenth century that one can really begin to speak of confessional politics. France and Spain were, after all, still engaged on their long struggle in the Italian peninsula; in the 1530s the Most Christian King of France actually allied with the Turk against the Very Catholic King of Spain. It was not until 1559 that they finally realised that heresy was becoming rampant in Europe while they distracted themselves elsewhere, and made peace. But religious division was a complicating factor which would certainly have a profound effect on domestic politics. Meanwhile, the balance of power within the British Isles showed the viability of Scotland. The English king struggled to preside over a kingdom which demanded an interventionist level of kingship, and over a composite monarchy in which one of his territories seemed beyond resolution.

In Scotland the crises of Flodden and Solway Moss were actually small interruptions to a more confident and stylish kingship; Henry VIII's historical researches into English overlordship of Scotland in 1542 tell us more about his frustration and fury than any realistic possibility of imposing it. Dynastically, both lived on a knife edge. James IV and James V each had dead sons, leaving infants as their heirs, and in the second case a female infant. Under Henry VII, the Tudors had seemed more secure, despite the death of his elder son Arthur. Henry VIII destroyed that; for only twenty years after 1509 was there an undisputed heir to the throne – the ten years from Mary's birth until Henry's challenge to the legitimacy of his marriage to Katherine of Aragon, and the last ten years of his life, with his son Edward. Otherwise, doubts hung over Mary and Elizabeth, and the dynastic record of all three children was disastrous. Three living Tudor siblings were, paradoxically, more of a problem than two Stewart babies. No amount of Henrician bombast can really obscure the fact that the more stable kingdom was Scotland. It remained to be seen what would happen when Scotland, like England, was pitchforked from what might be called normality, for all its problems, into that uniquely dislocating force – reform of the churches.

Reformations

In 1500, none of the intense dislocation which would characterise the sixteenth and seventeenth centuries could have been foreseen. In England and Scotland, at least, the present looked good, the future presumably assured; the decades of civil war in England, and the brief year of civil war in Scotland, 1488, were over. Martin Luther was an unknown and insignificant monk. Lollardy in England, its intellectual impetus substantially diminished, had retreated into being a sort of puritanical wing of the Church. In Scotland it is difficult to find much evidence of heresy at all; a brief and disapproving mention of it in the verse chronicle of the early fifteenth-century Andrew of Wyntoun, John Knox's approving but cryptic reference to the Lollards of Kyle (south-west Scotland), and the failure of that terrifying pillar of orthodoxy, Laurence of Lindores, first principal of the University of St Andrews, to find more than two heretics to burn, add up to virtual insignificance. Ireland, from the point of view of English ecclesiastical authorities, might cause deep offence because of its married clergy, but it too seemed happy enough, and, indeed, would be the one part of the British Isles which strenuously fought for Catholic happiness rather than reformed rigour.

Yet twenty years later, it was all too evident that Luther's ideas had travelled fast, and that from then on his teaching on the Eucharist, justification by faith alone, penitence, predestinarianism and the papacy would plunge the theologians of Europe into fundamental and bitter division, and split Christendom. First publicly urged by him in 1517 primarily on the issue of the sale of indulgences, and developed over the next four years when he defended them at the Diet of Worms in 1521 and beyond, they had reached north-east Scotland by that year, when an Aberdeen schoolmaster was forced to recant his Lutheran heresy, and from 1525 there was legislation in Scotland against the bringing in of heretical books. Also in 1521, in England, Cardinal Wolsey held a meeting of Oxford and Cambridge theologians in an attempt to mount an attack on Luther, whose books were burned at Paul's Cross in London. Yet at the White Horse tavern in Cambridge men aware of Luther's works came together to discuss them, and from 1525 began to preach against what they saw as distracting and even idolatrous: images and pilgrimages. In the later 1520s, Bible reading, hitherto associated with the Lollards and therefore unacceptable, now had a new and considerable appeal; despite efforts to ban it, Tyndale's 1526 translation of the New Testament was widely sold and read in Cambridge, Oxford, London and Suffolk. A desire for reform was certainly in the air. But what kind of reform?

The answer given by historians used to be simple, based on the idea of a Church so corrupt, so worldly, so lacking in spirituality, that Luther had only to begin his attack and it would collapse. It is a good Reforming myth, mercifully now exploded. Whatever the course of reformations within the British Isles, or elsewhere, their starting point did not lie in an enthusiastic rush away from the Catholic Church. The call for reform began *within* the Catholic Church in the fifteenth and early sixteenth centuries. Pope Leo X's claim to fame would become the sale of indulgences for the rebuilding of St Peter's (an ambition which was not necessarily wholly at odds with those who sought to serve God by contributing their mite, as could be seen throughout Europe in the way in which local churches were made glorious by those living on the breadline) and the excommunication of Luther in 1520. But it was he who summoned a reforming council, the Fifth Lateran, between 1512 and 1517; though motivated by broadly similar ideals, its efforts at reform were far less dramatic than Luther's, and therefore vulnerable to being drowned out. Luther himself seems initially to have thought that his thunderous attacks would be listened to by the pope he was criticising, which indicates that he was still in the world of those who recognised the need for reform from within. What was common ground between those who remained within and those who left was the desire for greater purity within the Church, a renewed emphasis on the centrality of Christ, with a corresponding playing down of traditional ceremonies which might blur that centrality in men's minds. But it has to be borne in mind that reform was primarily the desire of the educated, rather than of the illiterate majority of the population, whether of Europe or the British Isles.

In England in the 1520s, Scotland in the 1550s – on the eve of Reformation – and throughout the sixteenth century in Ireland, there were always those who sought reform from within. Those who met in the White Horse tavern, or who read Tyndale, cannot simply be forced into the Lutheran mould. Cardinal Wolsey himself, hated – as Cardinal David Beaton was hated in Scotland in the 1530s – for his power, ostentation and wealth, was, despite his fear of Luther and of Tyndale, a reformer, fully in tune with the educational aspirations of those who saw the need to improve standards in the Church. Hence, for example, his foundation of Cardinal's College, Oxford, in 1526 (to be taken over by Henry VIII, and refounded as Christ Church). And to his new college he brought leading Cambridge theologians from the White Horse group, as well as, unsuccessfully, trying to tempt the conciliarist theologian and leading academic John Mair from Scotland. This is a powerful indication of that common ground which existed, even if individuals might find the heady ideas in circulation taking them in ultimately very different directions. There was far more to Wolsey than a single-minded greed for power, even – as his pursuit of Mair demonstrates – papal power. Fluidity as well as fear marked the decade of the 1520s until, after 1529 – largely inspired by the passionate fear and hatred of heresy which marked out that man with an almost certainly exaggerated reputation for saintliness, Sir Thomas More – heretics began to be burned. Wolsey, who had burned heretical literature, was by then gone; More's target was the heretics themselves. It was a hardening of attitude, which was shortly to be undermined by the antics of Henry VIII.

How far the ideas of the elite appealed to ordinary Catholics is a very different matter. We know all too little about the religious enthusiasms, or lack of them, of the ordinary inhabitants of the British Isles. But we can find out more in this period, precisely because of reactions to the demands for reform. What should not be given too much slavish attention is what Protestant reformers who loathed pre-Reformation religion, condemning it in the misleading and pernicious terms of superstition and idolatry, said about this; they tell us about what they insisted people should want, rather than about what they did want. We can be certain enough about the socio-religious centrality of the parish church in local communities. And there was safety to be found in the observances of the Christian year and in the mediation of local saints in times of disease and bad harvests, or in individual cases of distress and hardship. Thus it is wholly unsurprising to find examples of strong reaction against the attack on pilgrimages, relics and images, already evident in the 1520s and growing more pervasive in the 1530s, such as the defence of the crucifix in the church at Ashford as late as 1539, in opposition to the sermons attacking it by the reforming Henry Goderick. It may be unpleasant to modern eyes to read about enthusiasm for heretic burning, but it undoubtedly existed; even children were hurling wood on to the fire which consumed the heretical Thomas Harding at Chesham in 1532.

Yet by 1550, in England and Wales certainly, to an extent in Scotland and even in Ireland, traditional certainties had been substantially undermined. The reasons why are, of course, extraordinarily complex. But in the fractured world of the Reformation, one thing emerged: the crucial importance of the ruler, as Calvin and his successor in Geneva, Theodore Beza, fully recognised, and as the Peace of Augsburg of 1555 proclaimed. The well-known assertion *cuius regio eius religio* (roughly translated to mean that the religion of the ruler would be the religion of his country) may never actually have been enunciated, but the principle was clear enough. For the rulers of sixteenth-century Europe, whether Catholic, Lutheran or Calvinist, this new level of responsibility for the souls as well as the bodies of their subjects, under the pope (at least nominally) if Catholic, absolute if Protestant, gave in theory a new meaning to the old idea of monarchy by divine right, and in practice permanent and sometimes crippling headaches; for with the exception of Philip II of Spain, none of them succeeded in eradicating significant numbers of religious and therefore dangerous dissidents within their territories. Charles V, as Holy Roman Emperor, spent much of his life in battle with the Lutheran princes of his empire; late sixteenth-century France was bedevilled and weakened by the Wars of Religion. Conversely, the Huguenot Henri IV of France did the opposite; famously declaring that Paris was worth a mass, he converted to the majority religion in his kingdom. He then upheld it, although departing from usual practice by finding a haven, through the Edict of Nantes, for his Huguenot subjects which worked while he lived but would be under threat when he was dead.

The Beginnings of Reform in England: Henry VIII

Against this European background, the monarchies of the British Isles had a dismal record. Confusion reigned in England, Wales and Ireland; and in Scotland monarchical direction for the first twenty-five years of the Reformation was entirely absent. This may sound odd in view of the traditional assumption that the Reformation in England began in the reign of Henry VIII, that monstrous and dominating figure who terrified (and killed) those who disagreed with him. It used to be thought that the Reformation 'happened' during Henry's reign; it is only comparatively recently that historians of the English Reformation have convincingly pointed out that it was a long process, going on well into the reign of Elizabeth. Indeed, England appears to have been all too subject to the monarchical principle, for its religious state changed with every ruler from Henry VIII to James II to a greater or lesser degree. In the early 1640s, as England slid towards civil war, a few godly souls positively rejoiced in impending chaos. They looked back to a sort of mathematical progression whereby Henry VIII began Protestant reform, Edward VI extended it and Mary reversed it; Elizabeth got it going again, James I consolidated it, Charles I reversed it. Charles' present troubles therefore heralded the advent of the third Reformation. They were to be disappointed, but they were right about the shifts in religion under each monarch. And the shifts went on; godliness during the Interregnum (1649–60) gave way to the episcopal Anglicanism of Charles II, and that in turn was threatened by the Catholicising tendencies of James II. It settled down to become a Protestant kingdom, after a lurch from 1685 to 1688 towards some measure of Catholic restoration, only in the reign of William III. That, when compared with the track record of the kings of the Spanish *monarchia* or France or the Scandinavian kingdoms, is hardly inspiring.

Nor is the king who began it. One sorry aspect of Reformation studies – or some of them – is a reluctance to allow religion a central role. There is a tendency to scurry after apparently more acceptable factors, political, social, economic. Of course, in a movement as huge as the Reformation all these played an often important part. Politics could undoubtedly inform the timing of Reformation; and it was certainly the case that no king, whether *dévot* or *politique*, had the luxury of being as single-minded and committed as the great religious reformers. But Henry VIII, more than his European counterparts, has been the particular target for the charge of political motivation – or even sexual motivation.

The search for greater power and Henry's desire for a male heir raises a possible political dimension. Would there have been a Reformation in the 1530s had Pope Clement VII agreed to annul Henry's marriage – as popes had obligingly done in the past, most

recently in the case of Louis XII of France in 1498 – instead of being
constantly frightened off by the political fact that Queen Katherine was
the aunt of Charles V, always a threatening figure to Rome and never
more so than when his imperial armies sacked the city in 1527? The
logical conclusion of this is that it was Katherine's stubborn refusal to
get herself to a nunnery and release Henry which caused the English
Reformation; and as that would be a massive oversimplification, it can
safely be assumed that Henry's dynastic and political problems are only
part of the story.

Indeed, we know that Henry was a devout man, even if he used his
time at mass for getting business done. In 1521, desperate to rival the
kings of France and Spain with their prestigious papal titles, Most
Christian King and Very Catholic King, he wrote (or had ghost-written
for him) an attack on Luther, the *Assertio Septem Sacramentorum*, as a
prize essay for the pope. He got his prize, the title of Defender of the
Faith, a title which, from the papal point of view, would soon turn out
to be disastrously misplaced. Only thirteen years later, this loyal son of
the Church abolished papal authority and gave himself a new title,
Supreme Head of the Church; and in 1543 the Defender of the Faith was
writing (or having ghost-written) his own account of the faith, *A
Necessary Doctrine and Erudition for Any Christian Man*, known as *The
King's Book* (1543). Doctrinally it was highly conservative; the only
problem was that it was written in a kingdom without pope or
monasteries, a kingdom which had, in the 1530s, witnessed a lurch
towards evangelical reform and then swung back again. For this was
Henry's difficulty as Supreme Head of the Church; much as he adored
his new status, he was simply not up to the role. This was a king of first-
rate ambition and third-rate intelligence who could be remarkably
easily led, and who was singularly short of ideas of his own. Even in his
most dramatic action (other than the rejection of papal authority), the
Dissolution of the Monasteries in 1536 and 1539, he was not being
original; he was copying Gustavus I of Sweden, who had done the
same thing in 1527. Moreover, he was inconsistent; the great Dissolver
actually founded a monastery, at Bisham, in 1536.

Yet the Dissolution, perhaps even more than the break from Rome,
ensured that even though modern historians are right to emphasise the
long timescale of the Reformation, Henry's subjects in the later 1530s
were aware of change on a stunning level. Not every loyal subject
followed royal orders and erased the pope from liturgical books, or the

name of Henry's most hated saint, Thomas Becket; at Barking in Suffolk and Newbury and Henley in Berkshire, for example, they survived. But no one living in the vicinity of any abbey or priory could ignore the visual impact of great stone buildings – probably the only stone buildings in the area, with their appearance of massive and unchallengeable permanence – being emptied of their monks and nuns, having their roofs stripped off, their fabric plundered. It was as unthinkable as if, say, students at Oxford and Cambridge came back from vacation to find their medieval and early-modern college buildings and libraries emptied and gutted. Moreover, the monasteries were utterly integral to the lives of their local communities, as centres for hospitality, poor relief, care for the sick, even as custodians of the holy girdles used to ease the pains of childbirth, such as St Aelred's girdle at Rievaulx.

Financially, the beneficiaries were those of the gentry who secured monastic lands and buildings, and of course the crown, which sold them off; in 1544, for example, the sale of monastic lead alone swelled the royal coffers by £30,000, and in the eight years after the first dissolution of 1536 the crown got some £900,000 overall, providing an annual income equal to Henry VII's ordinary income in 1509. Greed, therefore, looks a very obvious motive for Henry VIII and his great servant Thomas Cromwell, especially in the case of a king whose grandiose ideas of warmongering made him frantic for money. The wanton grabbing of the treasures and libraries of the monasteries, their dispersal and destruction, reinforces the impression of unscrupulous and ruthless pursuit of wealth. Nevertheless, there may well have been more to it. The history of monasticism, from its beginning, is the history of the rise and fall of the monastic ideal. The great monastic reforms of the eleventh and twelfth centuries which preceded the next, inevitable, stage of decline were not repeated in the fifteenth and sixteenth centuries. In England, Henry V had attempted to reimpose austerity with his foundations of the Charterhouse at Sheen and the Brigittine house at Syon. By the 1520s, internal reform seems to have lost its impetus. Those very unlikely soulmates Thomas Wolsey and the more spiritual bishop of Rochester, John Fisher, were both dissolving monasteries, with the intention of endowing Oxford and Cambridge colleges, and as late as April 1536, a month before her downfall and execution, Anne Boleyn was urging educational reform rather than total dissolution.

Moreover, Luther and Erasmus might fall out spectacularly over the issue of free will, but they were at one in attacking not only monastic decline, but the very essence of monasticism itself; the Christian should be out in the world, not shut behind stone walls offering his prayers. And, indeed, the new orders founded in the course of the Counter Reformation, from Jesuits to Theatines and Ursulines, were not enclosed, but emphatically out in the world, in their revival of educational and charitable activities. Nor was monasticism enthusiastically re-embraced under Mary Tudor's Catholic restoration; it was not high on her order of priorities, and even the restored abbey of Westminster, despite the distinction of its abbot, John Feckenham, was a community of middle-aged men, failing to attract younger recruits. It is, therefore, possible that Henry VIII, self-believer in his theological skills, and his distinctly more intelligent sidekick, Cromwell, were motivated by principle as well as profit. Nevertheless, profit certainly mattered. The evangelical and humanist push to turn the monasteries into secular educational institutions had little appeal for those cultured and humanist creatures, Henry VIII and Cromwell; indeed, it has been tantalisingly suggested that to the usual reasons adduced for Anne's remarkably sudden downfall (incest and adultery) can be added Cromwell's determination not to let an evangelical queen get in the way of gain.

In any case, the idea that there might be a case for reform hardly counted with the defenders of the monasteries, the monks themselves, like those at Hexham in 1536, who, with the support of the townspeople, successfully if temporarily resisted the first arrival of the king's commissioners, and the vast numbers of men in the seven northern counties who flocked to join the greatest rebellion England had experienced since the Peasants' Revolt of 1381, the Pilgrimage of Grace of 1536–7. It was the first of five major rebellions which would threaten Henry and his three successors between 1536 and 1571. All of them have been particular targets in the debate about political, economic and religious motivation. As against those who give what might be regarded as undue weight to political and economic factors, it can be argued that five massive expressions of dissent within thirty-five years do suggest that there was more to them than, for example, economic distress, in a population long accustomed to the vagaries of weather and the harvest, but encountering for the first time not only religious change but rapid religious change in mid-sixteenth-century England.

It is true that the harvest of 1535 had been bad, that of 1536 not good; but do men march under the banner of the five wounds of Christ, or call their rebellion, as their leader Robert Aske did, the Pilgrimage of Grace, if their main concern was poor harvests and high taxation? The widespread rebellions of 1549 throughout southern England, from Cornwall to East Anglia, offer the same conclusion. Much has been made of the fact that the detailed, highly conservative and peremptory articles of the western rising ('we will have . . .') were drawn up by priests, as though this somehow undermines the idea that their congregations may have been in agreement; by contrast, those of East Anglia ('we pray that . . .') were much more socio-economic. The religious articles from East Anglia suggest that, in stark contrast to the west, the rebels thought that the reforming regime of Edward VI, which clarified many of the ambiguities inherent in Henry's reforms of the 1530s, had not gone far enough. Taken together, they surely tell us of a society not only angry and frustrated because of socio-economic problems but riven and confused by the upheavals in the Church. The same arguments can be adduced for the Wyatt rebellion of 1554, despite Wyatt's apparent attempt to play down religion and emphasise hostility to Mary's marriage to Philip of Spain; the Northern Rising of 1569 and the smaller Ridolfi plot of 1571 both combined wishful thinking about getting the (dubiously) Catholic Mary Queen of Scots on to the English throne with pipedreams of support from Spain. England took a very long time to become Protestant England; indeed, it never was wholly Protestant England. But from the 1530s, English men and women were aware that they no longer had the spiritual assurances enjoyed by their ancestors, and their reactions in these decades could be violent.

It can have done nothing to help them come to terms with the changes that they were never given enough time to discover what the changes actually were. Parishioners in the mid-1530s were made very aware of alterations in their parish churches, when Henry was at his most reforming, his ears attuned to the genuine push for reform coming from Cromwell, Archbishop Cranmer and, initially, Anne Boleyn. Of these three, two were executed by Henry, Anne for treason and adultery in 1536, Cromwell for treason and heresy in 1540, and the third, Cranmer, was lucky to escape with his life – his fate reserved for the reign of the vengeful Mary Tudor – when at the end of the 1530s and in the 1540s Henry ran scared, started listening to the conservatives, and tried to stop the reforming clock in almost every way other than the break with Rome. But before 1538 there was little evidence that he would do so.

The Ten Articles and Injunctions to the clergy in the summer of 1536 gave force to ideas already causing dissension within the parishes. It has been argued that the Ten Articles were relatively moderate; but they can hardly have seemed so, in the circumstances in which they were issued by Convocation. The opening sermon of Hugh Latimer, bishop of Worcester, a typically vitriolic piece of rhetoric, was a call for demolition on a wide front. The response by the lower house, the *mala dogmata*, rejected Latimer's call for wholesale condemnation of established practices, attacking those who 'woll nedes have the thing itself taken away and not enough the abuses to be reformed'. The Ten Articles did take away. Purgatory was out, four of the seven sacraments were passed over in silence, and the cult of saints, though not yet condemned, was to lose its 'superstitious' element through the medium of reforming preaching. What was certainly noticeable was the ban on pilgrimages, and the Act of 1536 which swept away all but the most major feasts of the Church in time of harvest, from 1 July until 29 August, while individual celebrations of patronal festivals were no longer to take place at their accustomed times but to be observed uniformly on 1 October. It can only have added to the confusion that this Act was introduced during time of harvest. And it was particularly unfortunate, for Archbishop Cranmer, that in 1537 his inconsistent Supreme Head was celebrating the feast of St Laurence, a banned saint, at court.

There was already dislocation, therefore – and reaction to the changes, seen in the determination with which some parishes insisted on maintaining the traditional holy days – before the next set of Injunctions, in 1538. Images were already being despoiled, especially at pilgrimage centres; most horribly, though to the visible delight of Latimer, the friar John Forest was slowly burned to death over a fire provided by the image of the Welsh saint Darvell Gadern four months before the Injunctions. These ensured that, at least where they could be enforced, churchgoers found the appearance of their churches changed, with the ban on candles and tapers before the images of saints. And there was another direct attack on the cult of saints: no longer were congregations to respond to the litanies of saints with 'ora pro nobis' at the mention of each name. Emphasis was shifted further away from traditional religion to preaching and scripture; the Injunctions instructed that English bibles were to be made available in all churches, and, in 1539, Coverdale's new and authorised translation, the Great Bible, was to be chained to reading desks.

All this might look as though, however slowly and falteringly, the Church in England was being reformed. In late 1538, however, reform stopped; the Supreme Head had had enough. The Injunctions were issued in September. In November, Henry, dressed in white, and supported by ten bishops, presided over the heresy trial of the anabaptist John Lambert; Lambert was duly and agonisingly burned. In the same month, Henry issued a proclamation giving his strenuous backing to ceremonies much assailed by the reformers; ashes on Ash Wednesday, 'creeping to the Cross', the Easter sepulchre and others were now given the king's approval. And this return to a more conservative position was reinforced in June 1539 by the Act of the Six Articles. Even purgatory and prayers for the dead came back. At his death in 1547, Henry left money – admittedly not on a generous scale – for masses to be said for his soul. This, after the debates and upheavals of the mid-1530s, all suggests that the Church was coming back into a Catholic line: 'English Catholicism'. It is easy to see why. One strong argument against the playing down of religion as the central factor in the Reformation movement is that the stakes were so high: eternal salvation, not just earthly considerations. Those forced to accept religious change might have an excuse at the Day of Judgement. It was not so simple for the leaders of reform, religious and secular; they had to be certain. Henry himself had a nice way of identifying himself with God. But unlike those pressing him for reform – Cranmer, Cromwell and Latimer – he himself had instinctively been a natural conservative, a cleaner-up of what could be urged as abuses in the Church rather than in any way a religious radical. Playing safe – fire insurance – is therefore entirely understandable.

The trouble, as far as his subjects were concerned, was that stopping the clock, let alone turning it back, was impossible. A genuinely 'English Catholic' Church, under the Supreme Head rather than the pope, could have quietened fear and dissension. Since the mid-fourteenth century the English had had a tradition of resisting papal claims to authority, mainly in the area of appointments to benefices and clerical appeals to Rome, as laid down in repeated Acts of Provisors and Praemunire from 1351 onwards. Moreover, papal prestige was low

in the fifteenth and early sixteenth centuries. The Great Schism
(1378–1415) had dramatically undermined papal authority; the papacy's
attempt at recovery, by re-establishing itself as the judicial, fiscal and
legislative head of Christendom, which it had built up so successfully
since the eleventh century, was not in itself notably successful. This left
it highly vulnerable to the charge that what was lacking was its spiritual
role, which would not be effectively reasserted until the Council of
Trent, between 1545 and 1563, that council which, in response to the
challenge of the reformers, comprehensively defined Roman Catholic
doctrine. To calls for reform, initially internal and then external, the
papacy not only did not give a lead; it dragged its feet. The nadir was
the 'warrior pope', Julius II, who was far more concerned in the first
decade of the sixteenth century to fight off his enemies; his 'Holy
League' against France was one of the great misnomers of history.

Henry VIII had made capital out of this in the early 1530s,
threatening the clergy with praemunire in 1530 (which brought him a
large fine in 1531) and between 1532 and 1534 with the Acts on annates,
first fruits and tenths, depriving the pope of any revenue from the
Church. In 1533 came the Act on Appeals, with its famous clarion call
that 'this realm of England is an empire . . . governed by one supreme
head and king'. 'Empire' did not mean centre and provinces, core and
colonies; it meant that England was an authority unto itself, recognising no other. The king could do all this, with relative ease, to an
institution remote from England and seen to be interested in politics
and money rather than the cure of souls. There were defenders of the
papacy, like Thomas More, Bishop John Fisher and friar Forest. But in
the Pilgrimage of Grace, the destruction of Cromwell appeared to
weigh more than the restoration of the pope, who in the Pontefract
articles was mentioned only once, though given a little more attention
by the clergy; any desire for the renewal of the link with Rome was
only obliquely hinted at by the western rebels of 1549. Although men
might come out on the streets in defence of their religious practices, it
was unlikely that they would do so for the papacy.

Yet even after Henry's lurch back to his more conservative position,
there were still reasons for them to come out. The king still insisted on
the vernacular Bible in the churches, even though here again he showed
signs of panic; in 1543, his Statute of Artificers forbade the reading of the
Bible by the lower orders – and women – 'for the advancement of true
religion'. 'True religion' was, of course, a great slogan in this age of

shifts, turns and uncertainties, but it is difficult to see much consistency about what was 'religious truth'. And Henry's 'English Catholic' phase was to show cracks at the end of his life. Despite the apparent dominance of Stephen Gardiner, bishop of Winchester, and his adherents, litanies and primers in English were appearing. Cranmer felt confident enough to produce a litany in 1544 which reduced the number of saints, and in 1546 to mount a new attack on 'creeping to the Cross' and other Easter ceremonies. It is perhaps fitting that it was Cranmer who was at Henry's side when he died, the last meeting of the king who had never been quite sure what he wanted with the archbishop who was, had been frustrated, and could now go ahead.

In the fifteenth and early sixteenth centuries there was a general awareness among Catholic and then Protestant reformers alike that reform of the Church was becoming ever more essential as educational, charitable and moral aspirations changed. This used to be associated, in England, with rampant early sixteenth-century anti-clericalism, an idea which has been fortunately laid to rest. There were critics of clerics, particularly and naturally Cardinal Wolsey, though it is notable that his main clerical attacker, the bad-tempered and old-fashioned poet John Skelton, himself an absentee parish priest, and useful in the main for writing vitriolic anti-Scottish and French poems, dropped his criticism instantly when Wolsey renewed his patronage.

The other great plank for the anti-clerical school was the mysterious death of the London merchant tailor Richard Hunne in prison in 1515. Hunne's initial offence had been the refusal to pay a mortuary due; but such an offence was not necessarily pursued, and it was Hunne's opposition to ecclesiastical authority and his heretical views which made him a thorn in the ecclesiastical flesh from 1511 until 1515. His death was originally claimed as suicide, but the coroner's jury established it as murder. It was a huge London *cause célèbre*; and it undoubtedly stirred up considerable anti-clerical feeling in London. But a single case, however sensational, is hardly evidence of wide-spread anti-clericalism, any more than are attacks on the uniquely powerful figure of Wolsey, dominant in state as well as Church. Blaming corrupt priests and running individual cases into an over-arching whole were far too simple as an explanation of the problems of the Church. In England, as elsewhere, contemporaries seem to have been more aware that individual clerics were human and therefore, to a greater or lesser degree, sinful; they did not expect saints on earth.

'Anti-clericalism', therefore, has been a hindrance rather than a help in seeking to explain what was happening in and to the Church.

In no society in fractured Christendom was reformation ever straightforward; that was the inevitable outcome of the fracturing. In Henrician England, the 'Reformation' was a uniquely spectacular mess because no one was really in control. The king flapped about, adopting positions urged on him by those in favour. When they fell out of favour, he tended to murder them, which gave them no chance to continue to exert or renew influence. If the presence of Cranmer at his deathbed is symbolic, so too is the fact that Cromwell, Henry's vice-gerent in ecclesiastical matters, was executed for heresy. And one can add to that the survival of his last wife, the evangelical Katherine Parr, despite coming within an inch of being brought down by the conservative faction, and the survival of the leading layman of that faction, the duke of Norfolk, in the Tower awaiting execution and saved only because the king died a few hours before the axe was due to fall.

The initial years of the English Reformation, from one point of view, were a bloodbath, presided over by an increasingly megalo-maniac king who did not really know his own mind. For those poor souls who saw no compelling reason for religious upheaval, let alone upheavals, security was gone. For those genuinely committed to reform, the upheavals posed equally grievous problems. In both cases, given the king's uncertain and shifting moods, and if they came to the king's attention, they were likely to die, for clinging to their security and for their commitment.

Resistance to Reform in Scotland: James V

In 1541 James V held a reformation parliament. It was profoundly different from Henry VIII's Reformation parliament of 1529–36, not only in being – as was typical of Scottish parliaments – much shorter. For it was a determined defender of the Catholic Church; the seven sacraments, the Virgin and the saints, statues and images, the authority of the pope were all resolutely asserted. 'To the confusioun of all heresy that all the sacramentis be haldin and honourit as thai have bene in all tymes bygane as thai have bene within this realme conforme to the lawis and doctryne of halykirk' ran the first Act. But the warning note was there. These Acts were necessary, as that on 'the reforming of kirkis and kirkmen' made clear. There was lack of observance of the eucharist and lack of honour to the Virgin and saints; and churchmen were lacking in 'witt knawledge and maneris'. A further Act forbade private meetings held to dispute about the scriptures. Scotland was, in other words, experiencing exactly the same pressures and conflicts which were assailing England and the European kingdoms in general. Unlike Henry VIII, however, James V was quite clear about what he wanted. His early death at the age of thirty in the following year would remove that certainty, destroy the lead from the throne which would not return for some forty years and plunge Scottish religion into the same confusion as existed in Henrician England.

The reasons why James V insisted on upholding the Catholic Church are, however, a good deal less clear. As with any secular ruler, whether advancing or holding back reform, religion and politics were entirely intertwined; and in James's case the tendency has been to assume political opportunism rather than religious commitment. It is certainly the case that this brilliant opportunist used Henry VIII's break with Rome to considerable effect. The Stewart kings of this small, remote and potentially insignificant kingdom had an impressive track record of making themselves heard in Europe, but none had had such an opportunity as now offered itself to James V. Mentioning the pressure put on him by his uncle Henry to follow him in challenging the papacy and ultimately breaking with Rome was enough to bring him a series of enormous payments from the pope; as the Scottish parliament said, as early as 1532, the present pope, Clement VII, 'has bene mair gracius and benevolent till his grace than to all his forbearis', so that James, to show himself a 'thankfulle and obedient sone', would 'manteine and defend the auctorite liberte and fredome of the sete of Rome and halikirk'.

Moreover, the increasing religio-political tensions of the late 1520s and early 1530s meant that proposed marriage alliances for the King of Scots were particularly prestigious. This is a reminder that modern historians play down too much Scotland's position in Europe in the early sixteenth century. Contemporary Scots thought very differently, and rightly so. Those who worshipped in St Machar's Cathedral, Aberdeen, could look up at the dramatic heraldic ceiling which showed in the centre the arms of Pope Leo X and the thirteen archbishops and bishops of Scotland, with the prior of St Andrews and the University of Aberdeen, on the right James V, St Margaret and the leading nobles, with the royal burgh of Aberdeen, and on the left the Holy Roman Emperor, Charles V, the major European kings and dukes, and the burgh of Old Aberdeen. But this was not just the Scottish perspective, as Julius II and Maximilian I had shown.

We need to see James V, therefore, as a European monarch embroiled not only in traditional international politics, but in the troubled international politics of the Reformation era, and in his case doing well out of it, rather than in the more narrow-minded terms of a particularly cynical and self-seeking king; and, indeed, this is how he is now beginning to be seen. He, like his fellow monarchs, saw the papacy in its early sixteenth-century state, not yet endowed with the spiritual authority given to it by the Council of Trent. He had reason to view the imbalance of a Church whose income was ten times that of the crown; his transference of that income to the crown was by no means wholly unscrupulous in intention, as opposed, perhaps, to means, in that some of it at least was given to his College of Justice. We cannot, of course, be certain about his religious commitment. But there is no reason to assume that he was unusually indifferent to his immortal soul.

He had his relics, as other monarchs did. He went on pilgrimage. It was in his reign that the new cult of the Virgin's house, created by Julius II when the 'house' arrived in Loretto in Italy, came to Scotland, and a Scottish Loretto was established. Now, Loretto is one of Scotland's few notable public schools; then, it was the pilgrimage centre to which the king journeyed. He was a less determined hunter of heretics than Cardinal Beaton, although even Beaton's record was comparatively modest; he burned fourteen. But according to John Knox, he kept a scroll of heretics, urged on him by the prelates in 1540 – probably the better-born heretics – in 'his own pocket' until the day of his death. On the other hand, on 6 January 1540 there was performed at the court at Linlithgow an interlude, possibly written by Sir David Lindsay of the Mount, and perhaps an early version of his spectacular *Ane Satire of the Thrie Estaittis*, which portrayed to a silent king watching the portrayal of the evils of his realm, and in the end approving reform. Among the evils were those of the clergy. It is said that at the end James V turned on the bishops and threatened to pack them off to Henry VIII if they did not reform their lives and excessive exactions on the poor. Even the hostile Knox recounts a similar threat: when the bishops offered him wealth if he listened to them, his response was to tell them to reform, and if they did not, he would reform them, though 'neither yet as the King of England does, by hanging and heading'.

But what was meant by reform? There is no doubt that in the 1520s and 1530s fears of Lutheran heresy were rising in Scotland as in England. Yet whereas in the upper echelons of English society it was in the 1520s that the intellectual excitement of reforming ideas – which did not yet mean 'Reformation' – were prevalent, before giving way to the darker problems of the 1530s, it was in the 1530s in Scotland that such excitement could still flourish. It is unnecessary to see Luther behind every reforming idea, for the Council of Trent had not yet imposed its ruthless clarification on Catholic doctrine. Erasmian ideas and criticisms of the Church, and even Lutheran solifidianism, were still heady matters for discussion. They were certainly discussed at the court of James V, as the works of the greatest of the court poets, Lindsay, savage critic of the Church and yet never avowedly 'heretic' or Lutheran, make clear. Within twenty years of the death of James V, Scotland would move into a much more thorough-going reformation than England. Yet in James's reign, unlike Henry VIII's, the survival and revival of the Catholic Church under the authority of Rome would have been the prudent man's bet. A counter, or Catholic, Reformation in Scotland still looked eminently possible, and would do so even as late as the 1550s.

It is easy to say that the Scottish Church was in particular need of reform, being especially corrupt. Scotland's relationship with Rome had been peculiar, for, uniquely, Scotland had lacked an archbishop; in 1192, the solution to demands from York for control of the Scottish Church had been found when Celestine III designated the Scottish church *filia specialis* – special daughter – of the papacy. In the later fifteenth century, as the papacy was struggling out of the nadir of the Great and Little Schisms, that changed; Scotland got its first arch-bishopric, St Andrews, in 1472, and its second, Glasgow, twenty years later. Popes were understandably wary of archiepiscopal power, which might challenge their own in the individual provinces of the Church. These creations represented, therefore, a change in the relationship between Rome and the Church, and crown, of Scotland.

Moreover, under pressure the papacy was driven to concede to kings rights of appointment to major benefices, thus giving up a major source of control, long fought over and jealously preserved. The famous and most important concessions on this issue were to the

Spanish and French monarchies, but the first of them, the Indult of 1487, was made to the Scots. With a new and very free hand, Scottish kings could now make their own appointments; and the result was little short of spectacular. The archbishopric of St Andrews, for example, went to James IV's younger brother, James, duke of Ross, in 1497, and then, in 1504, to his illegitimate son Alexander. Between 1487 and 1569 the bishopric of Dunblane was held by three successive members of the Chisholm family. The number of appropriated parishes soared; in England, a third of parishes were appropriated, in Scotland the figure was 86 per cent.

This was no doubt of considerable advantage to the major ecclesiastical institutions and to the universities, and by no means wholly undesirable, but it often left the vicars in the parishes, educationally and economically the dregs of the Church, in dire straits, and money for repairing parish church buildings was in short supply. Above all was the rise in lay commendatorships, which diverted monastic revenue into lay hands. Thus various bastard sons of James V, children of apparently remarkable piety, as James explained to the pope, became commendators of the monasteries of Coldingham, Holyrood, Kelso, Melrose and St Andrews. More generally, the feuing of Church lands to laymen, especially in the 1530s when the Church was under severe financial pressure from the crown, again transferred wealth from the Church to the laity. And as elsewhere, monasticism was in decline, despite sporadic efforts to improve standards, like those of the Cistercians, with their visitations from Cîteaux after 1500. It all sounds grim.

Yet to condemn the Church on these grounds is, in part, to misunderstand the nature of Scottish society, and in part to listen too closely to the voices of satirists and of Protestant reformers and their heirs, historians and godly ministers of the Kirk in later centuries. In a society such as that of sixteenth-century Scotland, where obligations of kinship were still of fundamental importance, and no self-respecting layman would have dreamt of not helping his kin, it is no surprise to find the same principle alive and well in the Church. It was all too easy for a David Lindsay to pour out his scorn and contempt for the parish clergy, with their outrageous financial exactions from their impoverished parishioners, in the harrowing speech put into the mouth of the Poor Man in the *Thrie Estaittis* who is ruined by clerical demands on the successive deaths of his parents and his wife. There

was undoubtedly something in this; but it underplayed the impoverish-
ment of the parish clergy themselves, some of them resorting to
moonlighting to make a living, and it ignored the widow's mite.
Indeed, reactions of ordinary parishioners when the reformed Kirk
imposed its programme of the (excessively) lengthy preaching and
teaching of the Word suggests that it was the model of Chaucer's Poor
Parson rather than that of the learned Calvinist minister which
appealed, and understandably so.

Education was not confined to the verbal and literary. It could be
provided by the visual, with its greater impact on an illiterate
population, and was. Reformation iconoclasm – the 'cassin doun'
(casting down) of furnishings, decorations and images – means that
very little has survived from pre-Reformation Scotland; reformation
whitewash was all too successful. But there is just enough left, and
evidence of what had been, to indicate what once existed. Doom
paintings – that most powerful of visual messages – existed, for
example, in Elgin Cathedral, and that of Guthrie church in Angus
survives today. The painting in the little church of Foulis Easter in
Perthshire of the crucifixion survives, remarkably, *in situ*, along with
paintings of Christ and the apostles and saints, and Christ as saviour of
the world, and the medieval font, carved with scenes of the crucifixion.
Foulis Easter provides one example of the sacrament house, the
elaborately carved and adorned stone cupboard in which the consecrated host was reserved. Sacrament houses became fashionable in the
north-east in the century before the Reformation, one, at Cullen in
Banffshire, being constructed as late as the 1550s by the local laird,
Alexander Ogilvy of Findlater, as part of the general remodelling of the
choir; the reformers' attack on the eucharistic doctrine of transubstantiation was clearly not finding general acceptance.

Moreover, although we have much less evidence of this for Scotland
as compared to England, there was undoubtedly preservation of relics
and images, as the griping of the later presbyteries and Kirk sessions of
the reformed Kirk demonstrate; relics of St Duthac at Tain were
hidden by Alexander Ross of Balnagown, a kinsman of the provost, and
the presbytery of Dalkeith was exercised by the difficulty of forcing the
Sinclairs of Roslin to destroy imagery in their astonishing mid-
fifteenth-century chapel, fortunately with less than success, for its
glorious mid-fifteenth-century carvings, including saints, angels, the
seven deadly sins and seven virtues, and a dance of death still entrance

visitors today, making their visits utterly rewarding even if they fail to find what they have come for, any trace of Dan Brown's invented Holy Grail. Moreover, as we shall see later, Scottish parishioners after the Reformation showed a dogged and infuriating persistence in preserving traditional customs on saints days.

The tough moral stance of Protestant reformers, and of contemporary Catholic ones, also falls far short of reflecting general aspirations and expectations. Concubinage in Scotland as elsewhere was rife. It had been condemned, unsuccessfully, by the Council of Basle in 1549. But a celibate clergy is not, and never has been, a truly celibate clergy; and illicit relationships and bastard children, anathema to leading reformers on both sides of the religious divide, were not, it seems, the object of widespread obloquy. Cardinal Beaton could be attacked for many things, but his long-standing relationship with his mistress Marion Ogilvy, with whom he had eight children, was not one of the main ones; even Lindsay, in his *Tragedie of the Cardinall*, chose to ignore this. At the other end of the social spectrum is the fourteenth-century stone cross set up by two Argyllshire priests, father and son, and brought to Campbeltown after the Reformation, in 1607; we know about it because no outraged parishioners, nor even the reformers, ever knocked it down, and it still stands today. Possibly the strength of kinship within Scottish society had some bearing on this, but given that concubinage existed throughout Christendom this cannot be given too much weight. More to the point is the possibility that pre-Tridentine churchmen still thought it possible that the Church would end the ban on clerical marriage, which in any case went back not to the days of the early Church but to the eleventh century, only to be disappointed when Trent firmly closed the door on that idea.

This takes us on to the question of monasteries as dens of iniquity and lust. As in England, so in Scotland: it was a *topos*. So when Lindsay's Abbot, in the *Thrie Estaittis*, boasted that

> My paramours is baith als fat and fair
> As ony wench into the toun of Ayr

was the poet actually pointing to particular immorality in south-west Scotland, or using a town name which provided him with a rhyme, in order to invoke a convenient and general theme? Lindsay's satires were undoubtedly devastating. But Lindsay – courtier, diplomat, poet and humanist – moved in the elite of his society, and was using Scotland to illustrate what he and those like him saw as the need for reform of abuses throughout the western Church. Indeed, he could import into Scotland abuses which were not a notable feature of the Scottish Church. This can be very clearly seen in another brilliant character in the *Thrie Estaittis*, the Pardoner, who offers a series of wholly bogus relics, like the rope which hanged the borderer Johnnie Armstrong, for sale. A familiar figure indeed, a Scottish Tetzel – until one remembers that there is only one very slight hint of the existence of any pardoner in Scotland.

Satire, almost by definition, exaggerates; and Lindsay certainly exaggerated, if with a great deal more wit and style than the grumpy John Skelton. His lust-ridden abbeys are far from the whole story. For there were Scottish abbeys which, in this age of turning away from traditional monasticism, were realising the educational ideal which was not achieved in the English monasteries, thanks to the vision of their abbots. Dunfermline and Culross had a distinguished tradition as centres of learning. Two successive abbots of Kinloss in Aberdeenshire channelled their efforts into making their abbey a place of clerical learning, building up a library, forging links with the University of Aberdeen, and bringing a noted European scholar, Giovanni Ferrerio, to teach in the abbey in the 1530s and 1540s; a similar reforming abbot, Alexander Miln, presided over the abbey of Cambuskenneth. More prosaically, numbers of monks did not necessarily reflect declining enthusiasm. It was English destruction in 1545 which was mainly responsible for reducing the community of monks at the border abbey of Melrose from thirty-two in the 1530s to seventeen in the 1550s.

The same point can be made about the friaries, which, unlike the monasteries, had been given renewed impetus in the late fifteenth century and continued to receive endowments right up to the Reformation. Far from rejecting books, as Lindsay's Pardoner did, friars were establishing libraries, under the direction of John Adamson, provincial of the Black Friars, in Aberdeen, Edinburgh, Elgin, Glasgow, Perth and St Andrews; they were noted for the number who had degrees, and were teaching in the three universities.

What all this amounts to is that Scotland was fully in tune with the idea evident throughout Europe that there were aspects of the Church that were faltering or failing, and that reform, whether from within or without, was necessary. Within the British Isles, there is less to say about the Scotland of James V than the England of Henry VIII because the Scottish Church in the 1530s was not yet disturbed and dislocated like its southern neighbour. Heresy was an issue; heretics were burned, more enthusiastically by Cardinal Beaton than by King James, but in fewer numbers than in England; they were still seen as containable, and, remarkably, could still be viewed as containable as late as the 1550s. That is one strand of the history of the Reformation in Scotland after James V's death. But that death ushered in a period of shifts and turns and confusion, parallel, and indeed interacting, with that in England. Domestic and international politics were already a visible factor in influencing, or even dictating, the extent and nature of reform in both kingdoms. After 1542, conflicting religious aspirations and conflicting political ambitions would become crucial.

Reformation or Counter Reformation?
The 1540s and 1550s

In the early months of 1541 it looked as though a miracle was about to happen in Europe: reconciliation. The Catholic Hermann von Wied, archbishop of Cologne, the theologians Johann Gropper and also Johann Eck, who had famously debated with Luther in 1519, came together with the Protestant Philipp Melanchthon, once Luther's foremost disciple but now distancing himself from him, and Martin Bucer of Strasbourg, to join in debate, and reach an astonishing level of unity on original sin and even on the doctrine of justification. Briefly hopes soared; and the last Imperial Diet which might have had a chance of resolving theological divisions opened at Regensburg in March. Even England was represented, in the person of Stephen Gardiner, bishop of Winchester, there on the Catholic side. It failed, just as its forerunner, the Diet of Augsburg, had failed in 1530, and fundamentally for the same reason: the impossibility of finding agreement on the eucharist. But perhaps even more clearly than in 1530, 1541 showed not only the depth of the rift between Catholic and Protestant, but the widening rifts within the Protestant side of the divide, as the doctrine of the real presence became ever more the central point of contention; and to this would be added Lutheran and Calvinist predestinarianism.

Not only was there now no hope of reuniting Christendom, but those who had attacked the Catholic Church were increasingly and with mounting passion fundamentally disagreeing with one another. With this as the context, the superficially simple patterns of religious change in England and Scotland, and their impact on political relations, emerge as anything but straightforward. The terms Protestants, Lutherans and Calvinists, while convenient and regularly used short-hand, and thus used here, were in fact considerably less clear-cut. 'Protestant' came from the *Protestatio* issued by the supporters of Luther and Zwingli at the imperial Diet of Speyer in 1529, and until the later sixteenth century referred exclusively to the Germans; 'Calvinist' began its life as a term of abuse. The keynote to any discussion of reformation, therefore, is conflict and debate, and certainly not clarity, a point over which reformers themselves, seeking to advance God's cause, would agonise. Yet there is no doubt that in the sixteenth century men were keenly aware that they were lining up on different sides, fighting for different beliefs.

One person, however, who did believe that he was advancing God's cause, even if it was difficult for others to follow his twisting path, was Henry VIII; and from his point of view, James V's early death in December 1542 was, on two counts, wonderful news. First, a Scotland whose monarch was a baby girl was now vulnerable to English inter-vention; indeed, the fact that she was a girl offered the opportunity for a marriage alliance with the son he had moved heaven, earth and five wives to get. Second, there was no longer a mighty defender of the Catholic Church. After an initial and brief power struggle, James Hamilton, earl of Arran and heir presumptive to the throne, emerged as regent. It was to Henry's considerable additional advantage that Arran, though apparently Protestant in leaning, was not an utterly committed one. Henry himself cannot be called a Protestant, but Scotland under regent Arran offered him more of an opportunity to detach it from Rome.

In the early months of 1543 events seemed to move as Henry wished, as diplomats and cartloads of Bibles made their way north; ironically, in the very year when, by his Statute of Artificers, Henry was banning the reading of the Bible by labourers, apprentices and women in England, he was encouraging it in Scotland, where a very different Act had been passed, making it lawful to read the Bible in Scots or English. His ambassador Ralph Sadler talked of the Bible and other vernacular

works as 'marvellously desired now of the people of Scotland'. As John
Knox, describing the Act as 'no small victory of Christ Jesus', famously
and triumphantly recorded, 'then might have been seen the Bible lying
upon every gentleman's table. The New Testament was borne about
in many men's hands . . . thereby did the knowledge of God won-
drously increase, and God give his Holy Spirit in simple men to great
abundance.' Knox, it appears, had less fear of simple men than did
Henry VIII.

It was a chimera. By July 1543, Henry's marriage plans were in ruins,
smashed by his own overplaying of his hand, with his insistent demand
that Mary Queen of Scots should be brought up in England. From 1544,
he would press his policy by brutal and savagely destructive warfare,
the so-called 'Rough Wooing', issuing instructions for mass slaughter
to his commander, Edward Seymour, earl of Hertford, in which he
clearly identified himself with God; there should 'remain forever a
perpetual memory of the vengeance of God lightened upon' the Scots.
So there would be no political alliance between Scotland and England.
Ironically, however, it was not only that which weakened his religious
policy towards Scotland. An equal problem was his own dubious
religious position. Knox had over optimistically written that 'all men
esteemed the Governor [Arran] to have been the most fervent
Protestant that was in Europe', which was certainly an exaggeration,
but Arran's Protestantism was in any case undermined by Sadler's
warning to him of the need to go carefully with Henry VIII.

It is in the early 1540s that we hear for the first time, and as yet fairly
faintly, a note which would over the following century swell to a
fortissimo roar. Sadler had naturally pushed on the Scots the *Necessary
Doctrine and Erudition of a Christian Man*, ghost-written by English
bishops, but known as the 'King's Book' because Henry VIII had some
part in it. For Scottish Protestants, it was lacking in doctrinal clarity;
their feet were already set on a far more radical road, away from a
Lutheran or evangelical position, and certainly far beyond Henrician
Catholicism. In 1544 George Wishart was preaching in Ayrshire, Fife,
Angus, Lothian and Perth, with Knox bearing a two-handed sword for
his protection. Wishart was a Zwinglian, and in 1546 he burned for it.
But Wishart undoubtedly inspired Knox, the man who in 1536 had been
ordained Catholic priest; and by 1547, the year in which, as he later said,
he rejected Lutheranism, Knox, in the first of his surviving sermons,
attacked the mass as 'abominable idolatry, blasphemous to the death of

Christ and a profanation of the Lord's Supper', and identified the papacy with Antichrist; 'others', it was said, 'sned [lop] the branches of the Papistry, but he strikes at the root, to destroy the whole'. We are seeing here the first signs of that strain which would enable the Scots in the later sixteenth and seventeenth centuries to claim that they were more pure, more godly in religion than their English counterparts.

It was hardly enough, however, at this early stage, to bring about a reformation movement with any chance of success. After Henry VIII's death, Hertford, now duke of Somerset and protector for Edward VI, presided over a regime which undoubtedly sought to move the Church away from Henry's theological dither towards a more Protestant position – though it remains difficult to pin this down to any of the great Protestant movements, Lutheran, Zwinglian or Calvinist. Somerset continued Henry's military onslaught on Scotland, but this time with a clearly missionary intent. He himself regarded his stunning defeat of the Scots at Pinkie in 1547 as a victory against the Catholic faith; the provision of ministers and bibles in the garrisons he set up in Lowland Scotland, his appeal to the Scots, in his *Epistle or exhortacion to unitie & peace of 1548*, that there should be a Protestant union of two equal kingdoms – no more talk of English overlordship such as Henry VIII had recently indulged in – shows the same commitment. Conciliatory letters, however, were hardly likely to have much effect when sent to a people who were witnessing English garrisons in Lowland Scotland, just as they had witnessed them back in the reign of Edward I; for Somerset had no new military policy to offer. In any case, the coup against him in 1549 by English politicians who had had enough, *inter alia*, of his expensive and unpopular war brought it to an end in 1550.

Peace brought no joy to the Scottish Protestants, for there was no help which the Protestant Edwardian regime could offer them. Already it had been up against a rival power, for in 1547 the French had intervened. A year earlier, Cardinal Beaton had been murdered in his castle at St Andrews by a group of Protestant Fife lairds, with the backing of Henry VIII. These lairds installed themselves in the castle, where they were joined by Knox – St Andrews was the scene for his first sermon – and remained there until a French fleet turned up. The resulting siege of the castle produced the amazing spectacle of an air battle, as cannonballs whistled over the heads of the citizens from cannon hauled on to the castle battlements and the tower of the church of St Rule; and those tunnelling in and those tunnelling out managed to miss one another by a very narrow margin. The outcome was predictable; the Protestants were defeated, and Knox went off to the French galleys, not to die as was the fate of most galley slaves, but to survive and get out after eighteen months. In 1548, the five-year-old Mary was sent off to France for her safety. Again, there was a strong echo of the past; in 1332 that was exactly what had been done to the ten-year-old David II.

For the next decade, therefore, Scottish Protestants of whatever persuasion would languish in impotence, while England continued in religious confusion. The six-year reign of Edward VI was an increasingly heady time for English reformers. Priests could now marry; this at last resolved Cranmer's own marital problems, and in the south two-thirds of the clergy did marry, as compared to one-third in the north. In 1547, chantries went the way of the Henrician monasteries, thus clarifying the uncertainty left by Henry VIII, who had abolished purgatory but played safe by providing money for prayers for his soul; prayers for the dead, that comfort for the living, were now, at least officially, out. From 1547, although initially with a certain caution, and only where the arm of the royal commissioners could reach, injunctions against images came into effect; and while among the elite theological debate might rage, nothing forced the reality of religious change on ordinary parishioners so much as the visual destruction of the traditional and the habitual in their churches, the rood, the statues and the paintings. Removal and whitewash are very potent weapons in the hands of reformers.

Archbishop Cranmer, at last freed from the straitjacketing from which he had suffered under the tyranny of his late master, began to move the Church away from an uncertain Catholicism in the direction of a more clearly defined reformed body. The two great milestones were his Prayer Books of 1549 and 1552. The first was ambivalent on the subject of the Real Presence, producing a formulation which the Catholic bishop Gardiner could just about accept, from his prison in the Tower where he had been sent in 1548. Where it was not ambivalent was in imposing the vernacular for religious services, and removing some of the ceremonial. The result was the massive rising in Devon and Cornwall in reaction against the Prayer Book.

The articles of the rebels set out clearly what had gone, in a detailed list of processions, the ashes on Ash Wednesday, the palms, and much more besides, already banned by Edwardian injunctions before the final blow of the Prayer Book. It has been suggested that, as they were drawn up by priests, they are not necessarily a guide to what the laity thought. But why should they not reflect the profound distress of laymen and women who saw the comforts of their faith dramatically demolished? The articles are in fact one of the best records we have of the practices which had been taken for granted and were therefore all the more devastating when banned. Economic grievances do not explain why it was the reading of the Prayer Book which sparked this rebellion. Religious grievances do. And to that extent, though from the other extreme of the spectrum, 1549 has something in common with 1637 in Scotland, when another Prayer Book would begin the chain of events which would bring down Charles I.

It was not only in the south-west that rebellion flared. There was a string of risings in the south and the midlands in the summer of 1549, and one in East Anglia which rivalled the western rising in scale. In these, economic factors did play an important part, as, in East Anglia, did social ones: the hatred of the gentry, in an area bereft of its great magnate, the duke of Norfolk, languishing in the Tower where he had been since late 1546 awaiting the execution which never came because Henry VIII was shorn of at least one of his victims by dying a few hours before Norfolk was due to do so. But these two rebellions tell us much about the religious confusion of Edward's reign. The extreme conservative stance of the south-west was matched by the much more radical one of the east. In the godly camps set up by Sir Robert Ket and his followers, notably at Mousehold in Norfolk, what was being demanded was not a return to the old but an extension of the new. The peculiar form of enclosure might be a major cause of grievance, but so was the lack of quality of the reformed clergy; and the rebels' articles contained the spectacular clause that 'we pray thatt all bonde men may be made ffre for god made all ffre with his precious blode sheddyng', a demand borrowed straight from the German Peasants' revolt of 1525.

From the reformed point of view, exciting things were happening in the Edwardian Church, things which, had they not been cut short by Edward's death in 1553, might well have led to developments very similar to those which would take place in Scotland, and therefore to reformed religion becoming more of a unifying force than it would actually be. Under Cranmer's leadership, the Church moved steadily away from both English Catholicism and Lutheranism. Calvin's influence was hardly felt until the end of the reign. But that of Zwingli and the moderate Strasbourg reformer Martin Bucer most certainly was, even if this in itself led to clashes within the Church between ecclesiastics such as the Zwinglian John Hooper, bishop of Gloucester, Cranmer himself and Nicholas Ridley, bishop of London, drawn to the more conciliatory Bucer. Among other things, this period saw the beginnings of what would become a major issue in the 1560s, the controversy over vestments, with Hooper's refusal to be consecrated in traditional vestments. The Church became briefly international, as Zwinglian refugees poured into London, to set up a Zwinglian 'Strangers' Church'. More pleasing to Cranmer, three major European reformers with close ties to Strasbourg, Jan Laski, Peter Martyr Vermigli and Bucer himself, accepted his invitation to come to England, in the case of Vermigli and Bucer to be given chairs at Oxford and Cambridge.

What this demonstrates is that in microcosm England was reflecting the struggles throughout Europe to find an acceptable form of reformed theology and liturgy. It was a brief heady moment which would not recur in later decades, as the English Church closed in on itself. And certain things were becoming clearer in the last three years of the reign. In 1550, altars were replaced by communion tables; the sacrifice of the mass was decisively rejected, as was the sacrificial role of the priest, to be replaced by that of preacher and pastor. Then in 1552 came the stunning changes ushered in by the new Prayer Book. So much that was familiar was now to disappear. The funeral rites made it clear that at the moment of death the individual disappeared from human ken; he would be buried, but he would not be prayed for. Before his death, he was no longer granted the comfort of private communion; communion could now take place only in the face of the congregation, which meant either in church or, if in a private household, in the presence of 'a good nombre', all receiving communion. Above all, there was the intense visual demonstration of change at the communion service. The priest officiated wearing an ordinary surplice; there was no longer a prayer over the elements, nor the sign of the cross; any bread and wine left over, clearly unconsecrated, was taken home by the priest for his own consumption, and not – as had been the case with the consecrated bread of the past – taken to be given to the sick. All this represented a huge advance on 1549. And there were no rebellions.

What there was is much more difficult to assess. The Edwardian regime was remarkably gentle in its approach to dissenters. No Catholics were burned, but only two Protestants. Reform inevitably brought extremists in its wake, and one at least, Joan Bocher, made it virtually impossible for the authorities not to burn her. But equally inevitably it was unable to cope with the social deprivation and suffering created by the destruction of the Catholic institutions for poor relief, monasteries, hospitals, almshouses; in February 1548 the fiery Hugh Latimer, bishop of Worcester, chillingly referred to the dead lying unburied in the streets of London. 'Sin' was much in vogue, whether indulged in by the grasping and uncharitable rich, or by the poor, branded, since the 1530s, as lazy and indigent to an extent not thought of before. Even in remote corners of the land, the attack on images was being pressed; a year before the western rising of 1549, the thoroughly unpleasant William Body, archdeacon of Cornwall, turning up in Cornwall to check on their destruction, was murdered by a mob at Helston. Godliness will always both inspire and repel. Dislocation simply repels.

That being so, it is surprising that the idea that the reign of Mary Tudor – Bloody Mary – was a brutal and mercifully brief interruption to the steady advance of Protestantism in England had such a long run among historians. Much less surprising is that Edward's death saw his Catholic half-sister's successful coup against the successor chosen by Edward and Northumberland, the deeply Protestant Lady Jane Grey. There was strong enough reaction against uncertainty and dislocation to ensure that not only Catholics but Protestants, in that very region which had witnessed the 1549 rising and deeply resented Northumberland's brutal suppression of it, Norfolk, turned out in support of the legitimate heir, despite the antics of Henry VIII which had disturbed not only religion but the succession; and from Norfolk, Mary went on to be roared home in triumph to London on 3 August. The fact that within a few days there were Londoners who were demonstrating violently against the mass at St Bartholomew's and at an anti-Protestant sermon at Paul's Cross shows not that Mary's accession was interrupting an inexorable process, but that confusion still reigned.

For many, like the Yorkshire curate Robert Parkyn, it was the later years of Henry VIII and the reign of Edward which had been an aberration, now happily over. For others, Edward's death was a blow which was inexplicable; they who had been so strenuously serving

God's cause now found themselves unable to understand why God did not seem to be equally enthusiastic about it. Blaming God was, of course, not an option. What a number of the leaders of the Edwardian reformation did instead was to rush off abroad and develop a resistance theory much more extreme than anything which had gone before in the medieval and early reformation periods. Caution and ambivalence over the question of how far a tyrant could be resisted were now thrown to the winds. They exonerated God from imposing a tyrant as punishment for His sinning people – hitherto the accepted argument – for God could not be the author of evil. It was the people who erred, in choosing a tyrant; and freeing themselves from error meant removing him or her, from power and from life.

Revolution and tyrannicide were therefore urged by John Ponet in his *A Shorte Treatise of Politike Power* (1556) and the highly misogynistic Christopher Goodman in his *How Superior Powers Oght to be Obeyd* (1558). Even more hysterically misogynistic was John Knox, with his famous, tedious and ultimately disastrous *First Blast of the Trumpet against the Monstrous Regiment of Women* (1558), although this was less resistance theory per se than a focused attack on female rule, directed at Mary Tudor with a sideswipe at the Scottish regent, Mary of Guise, mother of Mary Queen of Scots. These writers may have resolved the problem of making God responsible for evil, but had the unintended result of making Him less than all-powerful, unlike those who had linked tyranny with divine punishment. More prosaically, the problem about this new definition of zeal in God's cause was that these doughty resistance theorists wrote about it from the safety of the Protestant bastions of Strasbourg, Frankfurt and Geneva; none came back to England for a practical demonstration. Instead, it was four Edwardian bishops – Hooper, Latimer, Ridley and Cranmer himself – and some three hundred lesser people who remained at home who burned for their reformed faith; many knew what that was, but there were others who could not understand why the beliefs which had been orthodox in Edward's reign were now a heresy which could lead to a frightful death.

The Marian burnings were, and remain, extremely contentious. They should not obscure the fact that what destroyed the Marian restoration was not Protestant zeal. At the beginning of her reign there had been tension over the former ecclesiastical lands; would restoration of religion mean restoration of these lands? Cardinal Pole thought yes, and was held up on the Continent by more realistic minds, notably that of Charles V. The answer was in fact no, and that eased the path of Catholic reform. There has also been debate about the nature of that reform, the point being urged that England took no part in the Tridentine movement, and these most inspirational and militant reformers, the Jesuits, were not invited in to strengthen the English cause. This is to ignore the very few years granted to Mary. For these few years do not indicate a conservative return to a pre-Henrician past. Pole himself, the man who was devising a financial restructuring of the Church which would have had a profound effect on the standards of the parish clergy, had not spent his years in Rome with his eyes shut and ears blocked; he had been a leader among moderate Catholic reformers. The queen herself, though she did restore the abbey of Westminster, did not have monastic restoration among her priorities; as elsewhere in Counter Reformation Europe, the monastic ideal burned very low. More to the point was a highly reputable bench of bishops, whose resistance to Elizabeth does not suggest lack of commitment. There is little reason to doubt that, had Mary lived, a thoroughly up-to-date Catholic Church in England would have put down ever deeper roots. She did not; the Church which did put down roots would be a curious hybrid, peculiarly English and peculiarly difficult to define. But her death in 1558 did not only affect England. It had a profound impact on the fate of Protestantism in Scotland.

Becoming Protestant Kingdoms? The Later Sixteenth Century

It has been possible to argue – as with the Henrician Reformation – that what drove the Scottish Reformation of 1559–60 was politics; its secular leaders wanted to break the long-standing alliance with France and turn to the 'auld enemie', England. It was certainly changed political considerations which allowed them to push it through. Mary Tudor's death offered a way out of the limbo in which Scottish Protestants had found themselves, when their ally France and both Spain and England were Catholic. In 1559, while the Elizabethan regime struggled to establish its new Church, five leading Scottish Protestants who had tried to struggle out of their limbo with the 'First Band of the Lords of

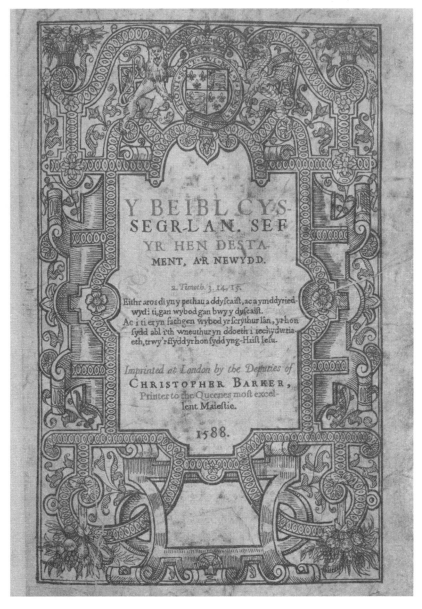

Frontispage of the Welsh Bible, 1588, translated by William Morgan, later bishop of Llandaff and then St Asaph's. This magnificent translation – built on the earlier uncompleted work of William Salusbury and others, and produced with encouragement from John Whitgift, Archbishop of Canterbury – was of both religious and cultural significance, being one of many scholarly publications in Welsh. By contrast, in Scotland only the Book of Common Order was translated into Gaelic, by John Carswell in 1567, but there was no translation of the Bible until 1801. The belated Irish New Testament of 1602–3 had very little impact. It is a reminder that the spreading of the Word was pushed less vigorously than might have been expected.

the Congregation' of December 1557, made to advance the true cause of God, now began to do so decisively.

Knox, kept out of Scotland, to his fury, in the 1550s, was allowed to return, for his inflammatory sermons could now be put to good use; Edinburgh witnessed the rival forces of the queen regent and the Protestant lords chasing one another in and out of the city and the city council. Yet there was still stalemate, until two decisive moments in 1560: after the Tumult of Amboise, the Guises were forced to pull Mary of Guise's French soldiers out of Scotland, and Mary herself died in June. Then came the Protestant explosion: in August 1560 the Reformation parliament met, and in three weeks, and with three Acts and a Confession of Faith, dismantled the Catholic Church; it went for the jugular, as Henry VIII's seven-year Reformation parliament had not done, with a decisiveness and instinct for the essentials which contrasted it sharply with its English counterpart. The mass was abolished, the authority of the pope declared illegal, and all former Acts in favour of the old Church annulled. Scotland was now legally Protestant. That decisiveness is strikingly demonstrated by the fact that the Scots immediately began to use the word 'Reformation'. What is usually referred to today as *The Book of Discipline* was, in 1560, entitled *The Buik of Reformatioun and Discipline of the Kirk*, and in 1563 the Catholic apologist Ninian Winzet was attacking 'the new impietie, callit be sum the Reformatioun of the Protestantis'. In England, by contrast, it was rarely used, and more ambiguous. John Foxe used it in his *Actes and Monuments*, that best-selling martyrology first published in 1563; and it was picked up again in the early seventeenth century by John Donne and the Arminian bishop Lancelot Andrewes. In each case there was more of a sense of long-term process than dramatic event, and not all within the 'Protestant' camp welcomed it. In 1559 the strongly Protestant Antony Gilby attacked the reformation of 'that tyrant and lecherous monster' Henry VIII as 'deformation'; in 1630 the Arminian John Cosin likewise referred to deformation – 'they called it a Reformation, but it was indeed a Deformation' – but the 'they' in this case was applied to the more militant Calvinists.

But was this 'political'? The Protestant lords had not only signed the First Band. In 1558 they had backed the cornerstone of the regent's policy, the marriage of her daughter Mary Queen of Scots to the Dauphin Francis. They did not know that that icon of Scottish romantic history had privately signed away the independence of her kingdom; the most likely explanation for their support is that they were prepared to shore up the Auld Alliance in the interests of keeping Mary out of Scotland, in the hope of somehow moving the Protestant cause forward, even though it smacked of wishful thinking with Mary Tudor not yet dead. They did not respond to veiled hints from Elizabeth's minister William Cecil about the creation of 'Britain' under the Protestant Queen Elizabeth. The most prominent among them, James Stewart, bastard half-brother of Mary, was described by the English ambassador Nicholas Throckmorton as a figure from the Old Testament; he was a skilled politician as well, but this hardly suggests lack of religious commitment.

Knox would, of course, condemn them for lack of zeal, but secular leaders never did have the luxury of the impassioned single-mindedness of the Knoxes of the Reformation movement, and Knox's *History of the Reformation*, written in the late 1550s and first half of the 1560s, however powerful, is not the infallible account of the Scottish Reformation. What should be emphasised instead is that these men were attempting, and achieving, something remarkable; they were reforming the kingdom without a lead from the throne, and indeed in defiance of it, for Mary refused to ratify the Acts of the Reformation parliament. Calvin and Beza both knew the importance of the monarch; the nobility, powerful as they were, were second best, and in France, where some half of them were Huguenot in 1560, the refusal of the crown to turn from Catholicism – indeed Henry IV actually turned from Protestantism to Catholicism – showed why. The religious state of England altered, more or less dramatically, with every monarch from Henry VIII to William III. Scotland did have a 'top-down' Reformation, but it was, uniquely, presided over by the leaders of society under the crown. It was to their great advantage that Mary, in her brief reign, shored up rather than challenged the embryonic reformed Kirk, and that the long minority of her son James enabled it further to establish itself.

Moreover, playing down the religious motivation of those who triumphed in 1560 sits very oddly with the insistence on the especial godliness of the reformed Kirk, that remarkably persistent theme which was already evident among those who strove for it in the pre-Reformation era, and which has survived with prehensile tenacity until the modern day. Following Knox, it would be further fuelled by the great early seventeenth-century Presbyterian writers David

Calderwood and John Row; the prose style of the one who told a rather different tale, John Spottiswoode, archbishop of St Andrews, was less compelling, and in any case did not suit the later belief that a key to the Kirk's godliness had been its anti-episcopal stance from the beginning, that myth which obscures the fact that origins of this position can be traced back convincingly only to the 1630s. Nevertheless, pride in the Kirk as 'one of the purest under heaven this day', as the 1616 Confession claimed, both in its early years, when it outshone England as part of the European Reformed (Calvinist) Church, and in the seventeenth century, when union with England brought a narrowing of Scottish horizons, was undoubtedly a crucial factor in sustaining Scottish identity and explains much of the history of Anglo-Scottish relations in the period before the Restoration of 1660.

More immediately, however, the idea which still lingered on into the later twentieth century, that Scotland became godly in 1560, is surely too extreme. We cannot simply assume, for example, that Scotland became a major witch-persecuting society on a scale much greater than England because of its particular godliness; witch-hunting throughout early-modern Catholic and Protestant Europe, and its regional variations, is a far more complex subject than that. Moreover, Scottish Catholicism was visibly not eradicated. It was flourishing in the south-west, the same area which produced notable reforming zeal; somewhat overcrowded with earls, the Protestant earls of Glencairn and Eglinton were unable to prevent the Kennedies, under the Catholic earl of Cassillis, holding a public mass at Kirkoswald at Easter 1563. In the north-east, under the Catholic earls of Huntly and Erroll, it again survived, to topple over into the treasonable activities of the Catholic earls between 1588 and 1594, seeking the help of Philip II to advance the Counter Reformation. But it existed not only in the remoter parts of the kingdom. In Edinburgh itself, there were still more Catholics than Protestants at the end of Mary's personal rule. It seems, therefore, that there is much to be said for the lament of the Jesuits who came to Scotland in 1562–3 that it was the queen's failure to give a lead to her co-religionists which prevented a thoroughgoing Catholic fightback; Catholicism remained regionalised and therefore politically incoherent. Even before her return to Scotland in August 1561 she had made it clear that her political allies would be Lord James and his party, and she resisted an appeal from Huntly to land in Aberdeen and travel south, re-establishing Catholicism with his support. If religion and politics were fundamentally intertwined, it must be said that here was the exception: political considerations – the succession to the Protestant English throne – mattered more to Mary than religious ones, and this, despite her theatrical and dramatic playing out of the role of the Catholic martyr when she went to execution in 1587, was to be the pattern of her life.

Nor were those who did become members of, or were forced into, the reformed Kirk necessarily enthusiastic about godliness. Calvinist discipline in Scotland was tough from the beginning, exercised by the hierarchy of courts from General Assembly at national level to the parochial Kirk sessions. Their records make it all too clear what the godly were up against; apart from the inevitable quantity of sexual sins, praying for the dead, visiting holy wells, staging civic entertainments and celebrating Christmas – while for those who could not there was the pagan festival of Hogmanay – frustrated and infuriated the godly. Satirical poems and laments for what had gone testify to the same thing. There is nothing surprising about this. All that is surprising is that passive or active resistance to the new dispensation has been so played down, overtaken by the persuasive literature of those who have been interpreted as being more triumphalist than in fact they were.

Equally, of course, the reformed Kirk did have an appeal. It offered the great in the land, nobles and lairds, the opportunity to add the role of godly magistrate to their traditional secular position of the national and local governing elite. Vernacular services and congregational psalm singing brought a new level of involvement in parish worship, even to those who yawned, coughed and slept their way through excessively lengthy sermons. The Protestant God might be a more terrifying and immediately present judge than the Catholic one, but with all intermediaries, priests and saints, cut away, He was also more directly approachable. All of these had a powerful impact.

The main battle within the Kirk was over control. In the 1580s and 1590s, the king's consistent religious and political policy turned on the need to catch up after twenty -five years of royal inadequacy and assert authority over those who claimed the separation of the powers of Church and State; it was the old medieval battle between pope and emperor fought anew, between the Calvinist James and the Calvinist Presbyterians led by Andrew Melville. It was a bitter and prolonged struggle, but one which the king won, perhaps inevitably. He could tap into support from more moderate opinion among the ministry; in theory his authority might be denied, but in practice it could not; and shot through the writings of the Presbyterians is fear of the crown's actions, a fear all too justified. James was not acknowledged as supreme governor until 1612. He had already established a de facto position as such by 1600.

The English Reformed Church and the other Churches of the composite monarchy, Wales and Ireland, were in deeper trouble from the beginning: rent in England and Wales with internal divisions, in Ireland up against successful resistance from Irish and Old English Catholics, and unable to put down roots which would spread widely. There were too many conflicting voices when the Elizabethan Church was established, from the queen (certainly not Catholic but conservative in nature) to the ardent Calvinist Marian exiles who flocked home. We now know that the old idea, put forward by Sir John Neale, that the main difficulty in Elizabeth's first parliament in 1559 came from the 'puritans' – a word not in fact invented until the mid-1560s – cannot be sustained. The main problem was the conservatives. The Act of Uniformity was pushed through with considerable difficulty; and what 'uniformity' meant was anyone's guess. The Act of Supremacy was also passed, but changed Elizabeth's title from Supreme Head to Supreme Governor, possibly, if illogically, because the queen could inherit all the powers of monarchy but could not, as a woman, be Head of the Church.

The attempt to reconcile the Prayer Books of 1549 and 1552, though heavily biased towards the latter, was enough to give rise to the equally erroneous modern idea that it was designed to hold out some hope to the Catholics. The contemporary hope was as vain: that the 1559 settlement, reinforced by the Thirty-Nine Articles issued in 1563, was a starting point for further reform. In one sense, Elizabeth had a triumphant success; the Articles remain the basis for the Anglican Church today. In another, her consistent blocking of any move forward meant that there was always a high level of discontent and disagreement within her Church – which might also be said to have been her legacy to later centuries – and encouraged in the queen a growing neurosis about religious dissent, on the political as well as religious stage.

Catholics were, of course, anathema, especially after the folly of Pius V's excommunication of Elizabeth in 1570; the pope was disastrously encouraged by the rising of the Northern Earls of 1569, which was in

fact a total failure. But so were those who did have ascribed to them the
thorny title of 'puritan' at the time of the vestiarian controversy, the
row over what ecclesiastical vestments were appropriate, which began
in 1565 with their criticism that in structure and outward appearance
the Reformed Church appeared to be no different from the
unreformed one. Unlike in Scotland, those who wanted a more austere
Church in England were always in a minority, and those who objected
to episcopacy in a very small minority, and they never exercised the
same political influence. But they terrified the queen and, increasingly,
her bishops; by the 1590s, John Whitgift, archbishop of Canterbury,
and, even more notably, Richard Bancroft, bishop of London, shared
her fears.

Archbishop Whitgift's position was ambiguous because he was
strenuously Calvinist, and therefore not without appeal to the hard-
line Calvinists. His main battle was, rather, with the anti-Calvinist
group, centred in Cambridge and attracted by the beliefs of the Dutch
theologian Arminius, and with the queen, who refused to ratify his
Calvinist Lambeth Articles of 1595. Bancroft was also theologically a
Calvinist, but hysterically anti-puritan; he caused an international
incident with his notorious Paul's Cross sermon of 1589 and tracts of
1592 in which he associated king James with his own position, which
was no help to a king trying to establish control over the Kirk; Bancroft
appeared to think that Scottish puritans were worse than Catholic
ones. But both naturally upheld episcopacy; it was in this decade that
the theory of *iure divino* (divine right) episcopacy developed, to store
up trouble for the future.

Apart from the Bancroft case, a certain light relief spilled over into
Anglo-Scottish politics because of problems within the English
Church. For all her hatred of puritans, Elizabeth was prepared to allow
their Scottish counterparts, expelled from Scotland by James, to preach
from London pulpits; embarrassing her brother monarch was not
without its attractions. Conversely, when the London printer Robert
Waldegrave got into trouble for printing the highly provocative
puritanical 'Martin Marprelate' tracts, James promptly gave him the
job of royal printer in Scotland. But these cases underlined the
widening differences between the Churches of England and Scotland,
whose Protestantism was supposed to be the source of Anglo-Scottish
friendship. Indeed, however convenient, 'Protestant' is the wrong
word for the English Church. At one end of the spectrum, its future

Anglo-Catholicism was anticipated by Richard Hooker, who asserted that the medieval Church was the true Church, that the English Church was its descendant, and that even now Rome, though riddled with errors, was still part of the visible Church – an idea with which King James, to the horror of Robert Cecil, agreed. At the other end were the puritans, still clinging on to membership of the Church; not until after 1660 would they be driven out. Perhaps it is an extreme version of the problem that Reformation did not bring religious clarity, but it is a unique example of confusion within one Reformed Church. It left plenty of scope for debate; and within half a century of Elizabeth's death that debate would be a crucial factor in bringing England to civil war.

The Elizabethan regime's religious fears spilled over into foreign politics. It was notably Anglocentric, based on the belief that from 1558 the great Catholic powers regarded heretic England as their prime target. Hence, however unsatisfactory Scotland was, it was an attractive ally. Actually the great Catholic powers had far greater problems of their own: France was plunged into internal religious wars as well as wars with Spain for much of Elizabeth's reign, and Spain was far more exercised by the Netherlands and the Ottomans than by the offshore kingdom of England. Philip II simply wanted England left alone, and was therefore horrified by the papal excommunication. Only when Elizabeth was driven into her half-hearted intervention on behalf of his rebellious subjects in the Netherlands in 1585 was he forced to act. The outcome was that iconic moment in English history, the defeat of the Armada in 1588. This did bring England, now at war with the most powerful kingdom in Europe, firmly on to the international stage, but it was a battle which in the long run resolved nothing; war with Spain dragged on for the rest of Elizabeth's reign, expensive, indecisive and leading only to heightened fears about Catholic Ireland as the launching point for renewed Spanish Catholic invasions of England. This indeed happened when a new Spanish armada – the fourth – reached Kinsale in 1601, with no greater success than the other three.

Even foreign relations with Protestant Scotland were far from soothing. For the first of four occasions in her life – the others being the Huguenots, the Dutch and the execution of Mary Queen of Scots – Elizabeth in 1560 was pushed by Cecil into departing from her principle of divine right monarchy and supporting rebels against their divinely ordained monarchs. In 1560 she gave military aid to the Scottish

Protestants against their Catholic Queen Mary. During Mary's personal rule of 1561–7, Elizabeth backed the Protestant party and tried to keep Mary under control through marriage, the insulting proposed marriage to her favourite Robert Dudley, earl of Leicester. Mary's rejection of this is understandable, but her alternative, her cousin Henry Lord Darnley, himself with a claim to the English throne which was Mary's obsession, was a disaster. After two years of political stalemate and scandal, culminating in Darnley's murder in 1567, Mary – having fulfilled that fundamental duty of monarchy and given her kingdom an heir – was too much for a majority of the Scots. She was deposed and stupidly fled to England, where she assumed she would be helped back to her throne by its queen.

Instead, Elizabeth continued to work with the Protestants while paying the supreme penalty for Mary's follies: Elizabeth, not the Scots, had to deal with her for the rest of Mary's life, fighting off pressure from councillors and parliament to execute her. She succeeded until even Mary's plotting could no longer be borne, and condemned her to death in 1587. That should have eased the situation, and to some extent did. But while there was now a Protestant king on the Scottish throne, to Elizabeth's abiding fury he was not one who simply danced to her tune, being less obsessed by, and probably more confident about, the English throne. In any case, as he well knew, Elizabeth would one day be dead; it would be the support of the English political nation and the successful fighting off of any challenge from France or Spain which would matter. He maintained his own foreign policy; and if that included dealings with Spain, so be it. Any suggestion that the English succession put James in Elizabeth's pocket collapses in the face of the virtually annual pension, amounting to £58,000, which this most parsimonious of monarchs paid in an attempt to keep the King of Scots sweet, not only at times of crisis like the Armada, but steadily from 1586 until 1603.

It has been argued that Elizabeth's reign can be divided into two: success until 1588, and then a fifteen-year decline. There is much to be said for this. Certainly the last decade or so was a dismal period. Her refusal to marry and have an heir was a political issue which had agonised her subjects from the beginning of the reign. Now it was clear that there was no acceptable English heir, and time was running out. War with Spain was a dismal slog. In Ireland, the particular severity of the Lord Deputy Sir Henry Sidney led to a major revolt between 1579 and 1583; this was followed in 1594 by the outbreak of open warfare, the Nine Years War, in which the Irish were led by Hugh O'Neill, earl of Tyrone.

Elizabeth had coped no better with Ireland than her predecessors. In the 1560s, she had even rejected assistance from Protestant Scotland, in the person of the earl of Argyll, the prominent magnate of the western Highlands and isles, whose closeness to Ireland made his offer one which it would have been intelligent to accept. Now, war in Ireland split the English body politic, in the rivalry between the Cecils and Essex, and, like the war with Spain, dragged on without obvious resolution. As at the beginning of the century, so at the end: it was Scotland which was the flourishing and successful kingdom, England whose morale had collapsed. As Elizabeth insisted on living on and on, worries and fears increased; the best that could be hoped for was the Scottish succession, and that did nothing to increase morale. However much the English had sought to sustain a self-perception of greatness which had in fact disappeared in the mid-fifteenth century, to the extent that an English divine, John Aylmer, even claimed in 1559 that God Himself was English, there was little left for them to pride themselves on when at long last Elizabeth died.

3. Politics and Religion in the Seventeenth Century

Union

It is temptingly easy to see the union of the crowns of 1603 as something which the Scots wanted, but the English did not. The veneer of unity created by a common cause in religion was just that; the English Church and the Scottish Kirk were very different, and the underlying fact that both were reformed was not enough to counteract long-standing mutual dislike. Moreover, it had hardly been palatable that the English had more to gain from the Amity than the Scots. For the English government, it reduced the old fear of being caught between two hostile allies, France and Scotland. The Scottish government, on the other hand – despite the Kirk's desire to see it reject any dealings with Catholic powers – was naturally less ready to think only in terms of English interests; James VI remained a European king, as Elizabeth had found to her hysterical fury in the 1590s. His accession to the English throne might be deeply satisfying for the Scots, who had the last laugh in the long battle fought by English kings to annex Scotland, last revived by Henry VIII only sixty years earlier. They also, it must be said – from the king downwards – could look forward, over-optimistically, to the greater riches of England. But for the English, the accession of a Scottish king was humiliation: a Scottish, not an English, king would fulfil the English dream of uniting the kingdoms; and beggarly Scots, as plenty of Englishmen said, would get their grasping and greedy hands on English wealth. There is much to be said for this argument, but there are two reservations: for the English, union resolved a massive succession crisis; for the Scots, it meant the loss of the personal presence of their king.

So James's accession removed English fears of a foreign invasion from France or Spain and of a rerun of the dynastic civil strife of the Wars of the Roses; and it added considerably to such security as the Amity had brought. But what would they do with their Scottish king?

What would the Scots do without him? And how would he run the English composite monarchy, with Scotland now added in? These were practical questions, or so it would seem. But in a sense they are historians' questions, because only King James really tried to force the issue of the implications of union; and while he could not be ignored, everyone else preferred to avoid them.

On the surface, of course, much lip service was paid in England to the joy of James's accession. Lord Keeper Egerton, opening his first English parliament in 1604, spoke not without sincerity of the benefits of a king of middle years with a family over a queen of old age and childless; Elizabeth's reputation would take some time to revive, when hindsight became blurred by the contemporary reality of James's rule. But Egerton was thinking of James as king of England. The same parliament utterly rejected the king's desire for the style of King of Great Britain, going into paroxysms of anxiety about the loss of the name of England. The earl of Northumberland had already told him, before his accession, that he – unlike the 'wulgar' among James's future subjects – had no doubt that he would regard his greatest honour as being King of England, allowing his Scottish kingship to slide into obscurity, and that was pretty much what the English assumed. They also took it for granted that long experience of rule in Scotland was irrelevant; in the English parliament of 1610, the MP and common lawyer Nicholas Fuller told the Commons that it was their duty to tell the king of England what by the laws of England he could do, an astonishing and patronising claim which could never have been made to his predecessors. This was not concern about how the new union might work. It was concern about Anglicising the king.

Frieze showing entwined thistles and roses in the Long Gallery at Haddon Hall, Derbyshire. This loyal recognition of the Union of the Crowns by Sir John Manners was paralleled by his relative the earl of Rutland, who in 1608 bought the lowly Scottish oatcake, regarded by the English as food for horses, for human consumption by Lord Burghley. The rarity of such gestures, on both sides of the border, may only serve to emphasise the lack of real enthusiasm for the union.

For the Scots, absentee monarchy might appear to be mitigated by their extensive experience of minority government; they knew better than most how to cope without an adult king. But marking time until the king grew up was a very different thing from seeing an adult king depart for another kingdom which would undoubtedly seek to absorb him. The main problem was not his famous failure to honour his promise to return to Scotland every three years; that has been much exaggerated. His difficulty was getting out of England: in 1617, when he was determined to return to Scotland, he had to run the gauntlet of Buckingham and other courtiers kneeling in his bedchamber, begging him not to go. And earlier, he had terrified the English with periodic threats to move his capital to York, as geographically more suitable for his Anglo-Scottish monarchy.

Moreover, in the first part of his rule, the earl of Dunbar was a genuinely Anglo-Scottish politician, moving endlessly between London and Edinburgh until his death in 1611; although he was not replaced, the postal service, much improved in 1603, ensured regular contact between the king and his Scottish council throughout the reign. What really rattled the Scots was the hostility of the English to any attempt to define the nature of the union. By 1607, they were expressing fears of becoming a province; the example they used was the Spanish *monarchia*, but undoubtedly Ireland was also in their minds. Much earlier, in 1603, they had insisted that they be shown copies of treaties made by England, revealing an instinct for being left out of the formation of foreign policy which would be proved all too justified in the later seventeenth century. In the union tracts of 1603–5 the king was already being urged not to neglect his ancient and native kingdom.

These tracts, poured out in the first two years of union, testify not to enthusiasm but to the lack of it. The Anglo-Scottish union came late among the many unions of the early-modern period, with their varied histories; it was small, geographically coherent and therefore comparatively manageable when set against the vast Spanish multiple monarchy, or the union of Poland and Lithuania (complicated in the later sixteenth century by the Polish enthusiasm for extending it by electing kings from other royal houses of Europe, first France and then Sweden. Neither was successful). The 'British' tracts, therefore, had plenty to draw on when looking for models, and draw they did; they were stuffed with accounts of other unions, along with discussion of divine intention, sovereignty, office holding, economic considerations, the history of England and Scotland, the world of antiquity. They were scholarly, wide-ranging and futile. Perhaps the Scottish reference to neglect, and the exceedingly tactless English one to overlordship, are the best clues to real reactions to the union which no one really wanted. Certainly no one bothered to write about it after 1605. Not until a century later, in a very different international world when Anglo-Scottish union became a serious issue because it offered real protection against the 'universal monarchy' of Louis XIV, would pamphleteers once again take up their pens and address the subject; even then, old habits died hard because English overlordship was once again raised, disturbing and infuriating already touchy and fearful Scots.

The king himself did press for some form of incorporating union, or appeared to do so; certainly his rhetoric about *unus rex, una lex, unus grex* – one king, one law, one people – suggested this. Any hope of creating such a union was dead by 1607, killed by the English parliament. But did James even seriously consider such a creation? Rhetoric is not a self-evident medium; witness his speech to the 1607 parliament with its notorious and infinitely misunderstood claim to govern Scotland with his pen. His bogus portrayal of the Scots as easily governable, and the Scottish parliament as docile and subservient, was not actually a statement about his Scottish kingship; none knew better than he its inaccuracy. It was the very reverse of the feared neglect; it was the first part of a careful and skilful balancing act between his two kingdoms.

In the early part of his reign, he was concentrating on reassuring the Scots by attempting to portray them in a favourable light to his wholly sceptical English audience. Later, he would begin to soothe his English subjects, acknowledging in 1616, for example, that England was the mightier nation, a very different rhetoric from the 'two mighty nations' of his proclamation of 1604 asserting the title of King of Great Britain. This involved a considerable risk given that the English parliament had rejected the idea, and was surely, therefore, itself a refusal to see Scotland reduced to secondary status. The striking fact is that none of this amounted to a serious plan for incorporating union; only Francis Bacon made a brief nod in the direction of the uniting of the institutions of government. What James was doing was something very different: his carefully chosen rhetoric was designed to remind both his Scottish and his English subjects that they could survive under his dual kingship. And if it is easy to see the point as far as the Scots are concerned, it should also be emphasised how necessary it was to reassure the English, whose morale had been infinitely lower on the eve of union than that of the Scots, and who were endlessly worried about James's refusal to learn, and accept, the role of an English king.

So we can forget about the idea that James was motivated by the desire for incorporating union. What he was intent on was the survival of the personal monarchy of Scotland and England, the need to keep both his kingdoms satisfied under one king. In other words, this was about his compelling interest, kingship and sovereignty. The question of sovereignty was recognised as an integral part of the union debate in the early eighteenth century, yet the theme goes right back to its beginning. Nor was James's demand for the name of Great Britain a drive for incorporating union. It reflected his other compelling interest, that of Europe, with himself as a king of European stature – a vision which he pursued, often to the intense annoyance of his English subjects, throughout his life. Great Britain had a cachet which could underpin the importance of this European king, far greater than the England of Elizabeth or the Scotland of James; and the 'Union Jack' which he invented, used exclusively for shipping, was the visual symbol of this, designed for foreign, not domestic consumption. On his death in 1625, therefore, he had not failed in his intentions because there was still no more than personal union. He had succeeded; on both sides of the border men had come to realise that the unthinkable – the coming together of two hostile, mutually suspicious nations – was actually possible.

Ireland and Wales

Attention was, and is, inevitably focused on the union of England and Scotland in the seventeenth century. But James did not only inherit the kingdom of England. He was also king of Ireland, as well as ruler of the principality of Wales. It cannot be said that he showed a great deal of interest in Wales, no doubt because it was by far the least problematic of his dominions. He did refer to the advantages of the union of England with Wales (1536) in his speech to parliament in 1607; but the Welsh showed virtually no enthusiasm for taking up the issue of union when the opportunity presented itself, apart from one Welsh MP, William Maurice of Clenennau, who in the 1609 parliament revived the idea of 'King of Great Britain'. Neither Henry nor Charles, as Princes of Wales, went anywhere near the principality. What did loom large were the jurisdictions of the Council of the Marches, and the Henrician Act of 1543 which allowed the king to legislate for Wales without parliament. The first came about because of the attempt to redefine 'Marches' to exclude the English shires and exempt Englishmen from its jurisdiction. This was raised by English border gentry, resisted by the councillors, and had petered out by 1617. The Welsh themselves were much more concerned with the second, arguing in the parliament of 1610 that it smacked of conquest and the threat of arbitrary government, and trying to associate it only with Henry VIII. The king did not wholly give way until 1624, when an Act of Grace repealed the 1543 Act, but a Bill of Grace was passed in every parliament between 1610 and 1624. As monarchs had not in fact legislated independently for Wales it was a constitutional rather than a practical problem.

If Wales was the low-key part of the British Isles, it was a very different matter with Ireland. James arrived just after the Nine Years War had ended, apparently in victory for the English, but actually leaving their *bête noire* the earl of Tyrone's wings dangerously unclipped. Moreover, royal policy changed. There was a visible clash between James's attitude to Ireland and that of most of his English councillors. Lord Deputy Sir John Davies, in his *Discovery of the True Causes why Ireland was never entirely Subdued . . . until the Beginning of His Majesty's Happy Reign* (1612), showed him to be the heir of Edmund Spenser, Sir Thomas Smith and Henry VIII. If the Scots were barbaric, the Irish were worse; the only way to civilise them was to force them to accept English law, English manners, English dress – and, of course, English religion. Ironically, what Davies wanted was a 'perfect' union – a union of laws – such as existed between England and Wales, while the English were strenuously resisting such an idea with Scotland, where they just as strenuously upheld the 'imperfect' union; it is a measure of the extent to which the English still thought about the English composite monarchy and tried to ignore the additional problem of the 'British' one.

Moreover, while Ireland was indeed a kingdom under Henrician law, in practice it was treated as a colony. It was not in fact subdued at

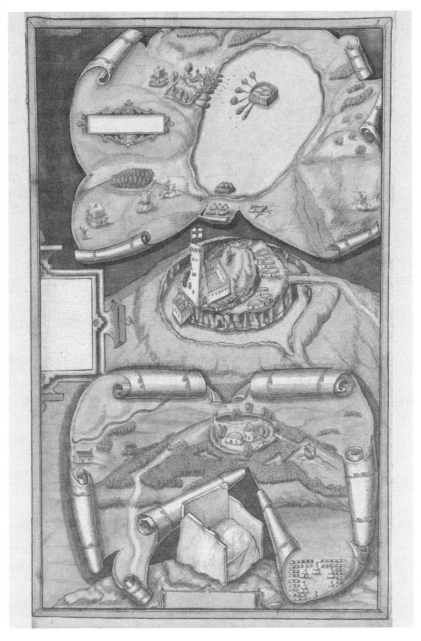

The inauguration stone of the O'Neills at Tullaghoge, Ulster. This drawing was made by Richard Bartlett, a cartographer in the service of the English during the Nine Years War. Hugh O'Neill, earl of Tyrone, apparently went to the stone early in the rebellion, in 1595. It was destroyed by Lord Deputy Mountjoy, to his considerable satisfaction, in 1602. English contempt for this Irish practice was apparently not disturbed by the fact that their monarchs were seated on a stone at their coronations, and still are today, making them the last of all western European rulers, by a long way, to maintain the ceremony.

the beginning of his majesty's happy reign, but James's approach, less fearful and more laid back than Elizabeth's and her councillors', did offer something. He certainly regarded it as a kingdom, not a colony; he, a Scottish king, had a far better understanding of a kin-based and feuding society than English monarchs. He brought to bear a Scottish perspective, to the extent that it is possible that he saw the great Irish magnates, Tyrone and Tyrconnell, as men he could work with, just as he had worked with the great Scottish magnates as his instruments of government in the localities. In the event, however, it was the policy of rule by military power of Davies's predecessor, Sir Arthur Chichester, which prevailed, and which drove the earls into flight in 1607.

The king's great plantation scheme of 1610 certainly had Scottish roots, somewhat oddly in view of the fact that his earlier efforts to plant men from Fife in Lewis had been wholly disastrous. But it rested on the idea of assimilation rather than the imposition of an alien culture. The statutes of Iona in 1609, with their follow-up in 1615, insisted on clan chiefs and their eldest sons learning English and coming to the Lowlands, but they were not a full-blown attack on Gaelic culture; and it is worth noting that the man who worked most closely with him, Andrew Knox, bishop of the Isles, was translated in 1611 to the Irish bishopric of Raphoe. Moreover, those who seek an explanation of modern Irish troubles in James's plantation of Ulster would do well to remember that not only English and Lowland-Scottish Protestants were settled; Scottish Catholics and Scots from partially Gaelic areas also went to Ireland. The Scottish crown was, it seems, more at ease with cultural mix than its English counterpart had been. Ireland was undoubtedly a far more intractable problem than the Scottish Highlands, and James's approach was peculiar to him. Nevertheless, during his reign, and despite the efforts of those who despised the Irish, tensions were temporarily reduced.

The Churches

The major difficulty with Ireland was the failure of the Protestant Reformation. Religious divisions shattered the multiple monarchy of Spain and the Netherlands, and in the case of the Holy Roman Empire and Bohemia, led to the Thirty Years War. Only Huguenot Béarn remained within the French orbit. The difference was that Béarnais Huguenots and Catholics could see common ground with French Huguenots and Catholics, and while Louis XIII offered concessions to the latter, he did not mount a full-scale attack on the former; the division in the French case was less stark than in the Spanish. This might suggest that some sort of a parallel with Ireland and France can be pursued, though only up to a point; for Catholics within the British Isles had none of the limited toleration which the Huguenots enjoyed.

Nevertheless, the ambivalent nature of the Elizabethan Church was such that the drive from the controlling power, in both political and religious terms, lacked clarity. The idea that James failed to take advantage of the defeat of Tyrone to crush the growing Counter Reformation, and thus stored up trouble for the future, while no doubt valid in theory does not allow sufficiently for the fact that the problem for his advisers was that James's genes simply did not include a persecuting one. In the Irish Parliament of 1613–15, with its hilarious – and symbolic – opening, when a Catholic and a Protestant both squeezed on to the Speaker's chair, there was some tough royal talking about penal legislation. In the event, less was done than intended, although efforts were made to enforce anti-recusancy laws; the conciliatory side of James's approach ensured that, at the eleventh hour, he got what was desperately needed, a subsidy Bill. If Catholics were prepared to show their loyalty by supporting it, were they so very bad?

The real difficulty was that no royal policy or efforts by the Church of Ireland, which were in any case not concerted, could effectively counteract the success of the flourishing Counter Reformation, helped on by the quality of priests returning from continental seminaries, the support of the Old English and the backing of Catholic landowners. Apart from anything else, it was difficult to enforce recusancy fines where local Catholics were in control. Catholics could justifiably claim that they were as much concerned to 'civilise' Ireland as the Protestant government, if not on its harsh and Anglicising lines. What has been called a 'shadow hierarchy' was coming into existence after 1610, appointed by the pope; and synods were being held. How objectionable this was to the man who presided over his three kingdoms is questionable. His foreign policy – friendship with Spain – both reduced the threat of Spain's using Ireland for the invasion of England, as had happened in the 1590s, and made him less inclined to be seen as a Catholic persecutor. But above all, James's ecumenism, which was the search not for enforced unification but for harmony, meant that he would never have Elizabethan nightmares about religious dissidents.

What, then, of his other two kingdoms, those which were already reformed? Compared to his experience of the Kirk, that of the English Church was in many ways soothing. Only a small minority challenged its episcopal nature; its puritans, as James found at the Hampton Court Conference in 1604, were a mild lot compared to the Scottish variety. But it is going too far to argue that this led to efforts to Anglicise the Kirk, even in a limited way. James was not a whole-hearted admirer of the English Church. Early in his reign, he showed that he had much in common with his Scottish puritans by objecting to the poorer standards of the parish clergy, though his attempt to do something about it, by ploughing Oxbridge tithes into education of the clergy, came up against vested interests too strong to allow him to succeed. The King James Bible, the one success of Hampton Court, had its origins in the king's desire for a translation of the Bible, as raised at the general assembly at Burntisland in 1601. On a rather different tack, the attempt to blow up him, his heir and his government by a small group of Catholic terrorists, the Gunpowder Plotters of 1605, was hardly soothing. He then upset his English subjects by doing two things: refusing to blame the Catholics of England, and proposing to send his heir, Henry, back to Scotland for his safety. The first is the important point; English Catholics, like all but the most extreme of English puritans, had a much quieter time in Jacobean than Elizabethan England.

The test case for 'Anglicising' is provided by the notorious Five Articles of Perth, introduced by the king in 1617, pushed through a General Assembly at Perth in 1618, after failure at the first attempt, in St Andrews, and then a carefully managed parliament in 1621. They asserted celebrating Christmas and Easter – in the form of sermons – private baptism and communion, confirmation and, most objectionable, kneeling at communion. But this was not the king against the Kirk. This was the king against a powerfully vocal section of the Kirk. He certainly had a constituency which welcomed the amelioration of some of the harsher of its practices. Christmas, despite the Kirk's ban, was certainly celebrated, in Perth and by the judges of the Court of Session, for example, and not only by listening to sermons, as the king's Article enjoined; the celebration of the purely pagan festival of Hogmanay is a telling reminder that not all Scots welcomed godliness.

As late as 1650, at the height of the Kirk's power, the parishioners of St Machar's, Aberdeen, still had to be instructed not to kneel at communion. And the refusal of private baptism and communion for the sick and the dying was certainly not universally acceptable.

What James was doing was fulfilling his role as supreme governor of the Kirk, finally acknowledged by the General Assembly in 1610 and parliament in 1612. How far he was from Anglicising is dramatically demonstrated by the visual appearance of his Scottish bishops; he, who determined their dress, as he did the dress of members of parliament and judges, kept them in plain ministerial black. At the time of the row over the introduction of the Articles, he was pushing forward his scheme for better stipends for the ministry, which was to lead to the complaint by Benjamin Rudyerd in the English Parliament of 1628 that wealthy England paid its clergy less than impoverished Scotland. As in his secular policy, so in his ecclesiastical one. This was James as 'king of all and king of each', not 'king of all Britain', with a discernable preference for its Anglican part.

Foreign Policy

Spain was Catholic and tyrannical, as all good Protestant Englishmen – and Scotsmen – knew. James, after 1603, was the most powerful Protestant prince in Europe, whose mission was to defend the embattled Protestants of Europe, as Elizabeth – it was now claimed, with notable inaccuracy – had done. James arrived in England to make peace with Spain in 1604, the policy Robert Cecil had hoped for, and maintained friendship with Spain for the rest of his life until it became impossible in 1624, when the two nations went to war. The case for the prosecution is obvious enough; and many made it, at home and abroad, especially when he refused to give military aid to his son-in-law, Frederick, Elector Palatine – thus failing on the grounds of both religion and kinship – after Frederick's unsuccessful assumption of the Bohemian crown and his expulsion from the Palatinate by the Holy Roman Emperor, which led to the Thirty Years War of 1618–48.

What about the case for the defence? Neither before nor after 1603 was royal policy determined by confessional politics. What James, father of two surviving sons and a daughter, could do, as Elizabeth could not, was to play dynastic politics. It was this which gave him his clout, as a major European ruler, and it was used in another balancing act; a Spanish match for a son, ultimately Charles, a Protestant one for his daughter Elizabeth, married in 1613 to Elector Frederick. After the outbreak of the Thirty Years War, British and Spanish policy, the latter represented by the Spanish ambassador Gondomar, a man very close to the king and backed by Philip III, made the Spanish match the cornerstone of a policy designed to persuade the imperial Habsburgs to compromise and restore Frederick at least to the Palatinate. In the end it failed, largely because of Philip III's death and the declining influence of Gondomar, edged out by the rising Olivares, principal minister of Philip IV. Charles, after his mad dash to Spain with Buckingham in 1623 to claim his bride, came home empty-handed, to the most popular moment in his life. He and Buckingham now spearheaded the war party in parliament, noisy enough in 1621, unstoppable in 1624. James's pacific policy was in ruins, and he had no alternative to offer. England went to war with Spain; Charles married a French bride, Louis XIII's daughter Henrietta Maria. Huge numbers of Europeans died in the course of the Thirty Years War. If James died a success in domestic politics, he undoubtedly died a failure in foreign ones. Yet the case for the defence can be made; and it is strengthened by what happened next.

Mid-Seventeenth-Century Britain: Chaos and Experiment

We no longer subscribe to the old 'Whig' idea that the road to the English civil war began in 1603, with the advent of those grisly Siamese twins, the 'early Stuarts', whose autocratic tendencies drove to breaking point the liberty-loving members of the English House of Commons. For James VI and I was a very different king from his son Charles I, and it is the 'Wars of the Three Kingdoms', not just the English Civil War, which now rightly engage historians' attention. It remains open for debate when the crisis which swept through the British Isles in the late 1630s and 1640s became 'inevitable', and it is unlikely that that debate will ever be resolved. It is surely putting too much responsibility on the shoulders of two men, James and Charles, to see 1625 as the turning point; that is only to change the chronology but not the over-personalised approach of the Whig historians.

Other questions certainly come into play: the strains imposed by the union of the crowns, in the early years when James's Scottishness, and his sometimes alarming non-English political rhetoric on the subject of kingship and the law, did cause unease to his English subjects, and later when Scottish fears of neglect were enhanced by the death of the king they had known and accession of the king they did not; the increasing fiscal weakness of the crown which forced it to find ways of supplementing revenue by non-parliamentary means; the growing inefficiency of government, especially in England, overburdened with burgeoning business and bureaucracy and unable to satisfy the relentless rise in demands for place and office which put severe strains on the working of patronage. None of these meant that civil war was inevitable, either in 1603 or in 1625. Nevertheless, the accession of Charles I did mean a dramatic change in the style of kingship, from the laid-back to the profoundly interventionist. In theory, perhaps more intervention was needed to do something about the ramshackle nature of the union and the government, and Charles, one of the great tidiers-up of history, undoubtedly thought so. The question was whether he had the ability to do so.

Parliamentary and Personal Rule

If the English had complained that James did not understand England, the Scots could very well complain that Charles did not understand Scotland. As the earl of Kellie wrote from England to his cousin John, earl of Mar, as early as 1623, 'it maye cume that the young folks shall have their world. I know not if that wilbe fitt for your Lordshipe and me'. Both had known King James since their youth in the 1570s; they were lamenting the passing of *their* world, and fearing the world of Charles and his favourite, Buckingham. Certainly Charles's interventions in Scottish affairs, which began in 1625, seemed both unnecessary and inexplicable. There was no obvious point to changing the personnel of Privy Council and Court of Session so that members of one could not sit on the other, thus denying legal expertise to the Council. Even worse was his Act of Revocation. Acts of Revocation had been passed by every Stuart king since the mid-fifteenth century; they were designed to allow the king, when he began his personal rule after minority, to revoke grants made in his name which might have damaged his patrimony – though normally they were regranted. Charles, the first king to come to the Scottish throne as an adult since 1406, decided on a dubious technicality that, being some months short of his twenty-fifth birthday, he was a minor. But his Act did not cover his minority; it went back to 1542 and beyond. He claimed to be cutting through the jungle of land law, in the interests of better financing the Kirk. The legal nightmare which resulted was understood by no one, whether king, lawyers or landowners; it dragged on for at least eight years, achieving nothing but uncertainty about title before fizzling out. And this was rule from afar; Charles finally arrived for his Scottish coronation in 1633, eight years late.

Even more ominous, however, were the early years of his English rule. It is well known that the four sessions of his first three parliaments in 1625–9 were disastrous, leading to the eleven-year 'Personal Rule'. And it is easy enough to put the blame on the king, with his favourite Buckingham, even more hated than he had been as James's favourite. It is worth noting that there was no hint of a homosexual relationship, though, to be fair, James's homosexuality has been much more a subject of interest and scandal for modern scholars than his contemporaries; what was wrong was that Buckingham had a degree of control over the new king which he had not had under the old. But there is another side to the matter. Only a year before Charles's first parliament as king he and Buckingham had appeared to be the darlings of the hour, with their enthusiasm for war with Spain. Why, then, did his first parliament make it so difficult for him to pursue that war, which put huge strain on royal finances? Why did it choose this moment to enquire into what he reasonably assumed would be the traditional grant of tonnage and poundage for life, hark back to the supposedly great days of Elizabeth and the Armada by insisting on a naval war against Spain, leading to the disaster at Cadiz, and force Charles to dissolve parliament prematurely by threatening to impeach Buckingham, the man putting his own wealth into the more useful land war? And then, of course, it objected strenuously when Charles took the much-needed tonnage and poundage anyway.

The 1626 parliament was just as bad; lacking subsidy, Charles, still at war, still desperately needing money, imposed the Forced Loan. The 1628 session saw the Petition of Right, one of whose objections was to the billeting of troops. England was not suffering from the actual horrors of the war fought out on the Continent; the minor matter of troop movement was necessary to support that war which England had apparently wanted so enthusiastically. Yet it became a 'constitutional' issue. Buckingham's assassination in that year did nothing to improve matters. In 1629, when Arminianism became a particular issue, the king's attempt to dissolve parliament was delayed while the Speaker was held down in his chair, unable to pronounce the dissolution until MPs had finished shouting. This was not a blow for liberty. It was an astonishing breakdown of royal authority and respect for the crown, after only four years. The king's reaction was the Personal Rule.

Part of the problem was that England was neither financially nor militarily able to sustain the demands of early-modern warfare, whose scale had increased dramatically in the later sixteenth century; and having hardly been at war since the mid-sixteenth century, the English were without sufficient experience of what it would involve. As the pacifist James had warned Charles and Buckingham in 1624, parliament wanted war, but would not pay for it, a prophecy which turned out to be horribly true. That was reason enough for tension and con-frontation. It became worse when, in 1627, Buckingham achieved the incredible folly of being at war with both Spain and France at the same time, even if the war with Spain had been desired, and the war with France fought for what should have been the acceptable reason of sustaining the Huguenots. By 1630, the lamentable enterprise was all over. Peace was made with France in 1629; negotiations for peace with Spain were begun in the same year and concluded in 1630 (Philip IV had the wit to include Peter Paul Rubens in his embassy, an attractive proposition for an art-loving king, and producing the one lasting memorial to this dismal period, the ceiling of the Banqueting House in Whitehall). This did not undo the harm of the previous five years. It did, however, greatly reduce the strains on royal finance, and made the Personal Rule possible.

But there was surely something more. We tend to think of kings when they come to the throne, and perhaps pay too little attention to what they were like before. But Charles, as Prince of Wales, had sat assiduously in the House of Lords in the parliaments of 1621 and 1624. He happened to be in tune with the mood of parliament in 1624. But MPs knew the king they were going to get: inflexible, ill at ease with his fellow men, reluctant to have his opinions swayed by advice, likely to treat his parliament as the junior partner rather than James's sparring partner. It is difficult to avoid the speculation that, rather than give him a honeymoon period when he became king, they were out to assert themselves, to an unacceptable and even unreasonable degree.

This was not yet, however, a collision course, and certainly not the run-up to civil war. It was a remarkable piece of political bravery by a parliament unaccustomed to direct challenges to its monarchy. Indeed, the level of flattery which Henry VIII, and even more so Elizabeth, had demanded of their subjects was such that James, as James I, found it hard to cope with; for James VI, men 'not of the best temper', as he described his Scottish subjects in a complaint to the English about how flattery could mislead, had at least been direct. Charles, on the other hand, could cocoon himself from the unseemly behaviour of unruly members of parliament in his court. James's court has been unfairly pilloried for its sleazy and disordered behaviour; two drunken episodes, in 1616 and 1618, and one court scandal, do not quite justify that critical view. But Charles certainly found it unacceptable, for his distinction was between the more informal French style, which his father had enjoyed both in Scotland and in England, and the intense formality of Spain, which he experienced in 1623 and which absolutely suited his temperament.

Access to the king now became more restricted, as keys were issued to those allowed into the inner sanctum. Noises off could be disregarded by the king who in 1637, at the time when he was enjoying practising his dance steps for that year's court masque extolling the peace and harmony of his rule, could describe himself as the happiest king in Christendom. Astonishing as hindsight makes that seem, it did have a kind of reality; compared to the monarchs of Europe, he was correct, and the Personal Rule seemed all too successful. Flattery at court and lack of a forum for opposition outside gave a not altogether false sense of security, and there was no reason to think that it could not last. Even the hated Ship Money appeared to be a successful tax. More generally, royal finances seemed to be on a secure footing – provided nothing happened to demand more expenditure than was necessary for peace. A tin-pot war with the Scots would shatter that security.

The issue was religion. The Scots were less interested in constitutional matters than the English; they were instead deeply focused on religious issues. And Charles went much further than his father in attacking that primary source of pride, the purity of the Kirk. Of course he had stirred up trouble in England by wrenching the Church in the direction of his own beliefs, marginalising James's Calvinist archbishop of Canterbury, George Abbott, who had the misfortune to survive under Charles until 1633, and promoting the man whom James had identified as a trouble-maker, William Laud, bishop of London and then Abbott's successor at Canterbury. For those who now found themselves regarded as unorthodox where, until 1625, they had been orthodox – including one John Pym – deep disturbance had flared into open objection in the 1629 parliament. But the attack on the Kirk, more thoroughly Calvinist in both theology and structure, was much more dangerous. Charles was no Scottish historian; expecting obedience, and accustomed to the greater deference with which the English treated their kings, he was wholly unaware of a political tradition in Scotland reaching back to the Middle Ages. Faced with unacceptable monarchs, the Scots had not indulged in the kind of agonised political theorising which had accompanied efforts to remove their English counterparts, and they had not bothered with the fiction of 'evil counsellors'. They removed them. This did not necessarily mean deposition and death; fewer Scottish kings suffered that fate than English ones. They also sidelined them, as in the case of Robert II and Robert III (the latter bluntly told that he had failed), replacing them with hopefully more effective governors. All this Charles ignored.

Ironically, he did attempt to dig into Scottish history when he came north for his coronation in 1633, ordering the antiquary James Balfour of Denmilne to search out its correct form. The result was anything but 'correct'; forcing the bishops into English vestments – which some refused – and installing a large crucifix was not a reformed coronation, Scottish-style. Equally worrying was his insistence in promoting Arminians to the Scottish bench in the mid-1630s and giving the bishops more political power than they had had under James. The unfortunate Spottiswoode, archbishop of St Andrews, who had refused to take part in James's funeral procession rather than wear English dress, found himself unable to resist his monarch, adopted English dress, and became the first (and only) clerical Chancellor since 1546.

Worst of all were Charles's liturgical changes, in particular the imposition in 1637 of a Prayer Book which was extensively English, with few concessions to Scottish practice, and issued all too publicly in the name of the king. The result – riots throughout Scotland, the collapse of Charles's government, and, in 1638, the widespread signing of the National Covenant, which galvanised Scottish resistance to the crown – is well known. Twice Charles, King of Scotland, used his English subjects to make war on his Scottish ones: the 'Bishops' Wars'. Twice he lost. The jubilant Covenanters went ahead and held a parliament in 1640, like the Reformation parliament in defiance of the crown. It passed a Triennial Act and abolished bishops and the prerogative courts. The first 'British' civil war and 'constitutional revolution' were complete in Scotland, with the king as decisive loser. It was a highly dangerous example to set his critics in his other kingdoms; and the emptying of his English treasury to pay for these puny wars ended the Personal Rule.

Charles blundered grotesquely in his dealings with the Scots. Yet there could be something to be said for his point of view. The advent of reform had added an awesome dimension to royal authority, whether Catholic or Protestant; kings were now responsible for the souls as well as the bodies of their subjects. For a man like Charles, it was therefore impossible to conceive of variant Churches in his kingdoms of England and Scotland; religious schizophrenia was not an option, and it was for the king and supreme governor of both to determine what the Church should be. This is fair enough, up to a point. Where Charles undercut his own philosophy was Ireland. Uniformity in three kingdoms might have been a coherent policy. Uniformity in two was not.

It may be that Charles was less interested in Ireland than in what he persisted in regarding, for all his ignorance, as his ancient and native kingdom of Scotland. It may be that even this most determined smoother out of wrinkles thought of Scotland as an easier target than Ireland. This may hardly square with his appointment of that ruthless and clear-sighted man Thomas Wentworth, earl of Strafford, as Lord Deputy of Ireland in 1632. Six years previously, however, desperate for money and men from Ireland for the war effort, Charles had offered 'the graces', which made remarkable concessions to Catholics: the suspension of recusancy fines and the removal of the ban on Catholics from holding office. It was too early in the reign to ascribe it to the baleful influence of Henrietta Maria, for at that stage she had no influence; only in the 1630s would her all too public Catholicism and proselytising become a major political issue, especially in England. It seemed, rather, that problems in England of financing the war took precedence in Charles's mind over the souls of his Irish subjects. In the face of this, efforts by the Church of Ireland to challenge Catholicism were inevitably undercut. Ireland remained the running sore in the English/British Protestant composite monarchy. Worse, the monarch was not treating it as a province, but as somewhere to be wooed, in the interests of its Catholics.

This analysis was incorrect. What Charles wanted from Ireland was money, and that remained the case when Wentworth was Lord Deputy. He also wanted men, whether in the 1620s or at the time of mounting crisis in 1640–41. So he could play fast and loose, without scruple, according to his political circumstances in England. The 'graces' were not delivered, because when war ended in 1629–30 Charles felt neither the need nor the obligation to deliver. That did not mean that the Irish so readily forgot about them, and they became an issue again in 1641 when Charles, now in dire straits with both England and Scotland, once again promised them. Once again he reneged, when he realised that granting them would involve not money coming from Ireland to England, but money going from England to Ireland. That was a major reason why rebellion broke out, during which the Catholics embarked on a Protestant bloodbath. Charles was in Scotland when it happened, naïvely believing that he and his Scots were now in perfect harmony. He rushed south, to find that Pym and his associates were far less interested in suppressing the rebellion than using it to put pressure on the king to make concessions which were wholly and understandably unacceptable: parliament should take over control of the militia, parliament should appoint the king's councillors. As so often, Ireland was not a constituent part of the multiple monarchy; it was the convenient punchbag.

Modern scholarship has concentrated on seeing what was happening as a British problem, and to an extent this has to be right. But arguably what we are seeing is the ultimate breakdown of the English composite monarchy, with Scotland as a complicating factor. After 1603, there was indeed a new problem: instead of a dominant kingdom with its conquered satellites, there were now two sovereign kingdoms, one of which had its satellites. Scotland's initial challenge to King Charles certainly led to what Conrad Russell famously called 'the billiard ball effect'. The Covenanters showed great confidence and acted far more decisively than the English, who in 1640 dithered their way through the paralysed Short Parliament and then the ineffective early months of the Long Parliament; these Covenanters cannot be left out of the reckoning if only because they offered Charles's English opponents a way forward. The contact between the Scots who went to London and these opponents is a unique example of Anglo-Scottish cooperation. Yet Charles was paying for unfinished English business.

Wales had been the 'easy' English takeover: vulnerable because of its long Anglo-Welsh border, and even more vulnerable because of internal feuding between the princes, who were not averse to invoking the English crown's support in their quarrels. This meant that when up against the imperialist ambitions of Edward I they went down in defeat. Only in the Glyn Dwr rising of the 1400s was there serious resistance to English conquest, and even then by no means universal resistance. Ireland was a very different matter. It was singularly unfortunate that Henry II's initial move into Ireland was not followed through, as later English kings set their eyes on greater prizes, notably France and also Scotland. It was equally unfortunate that the determined efforts of the Tudors to assert control over the whole of Ireland coincided with religious division. And it was particularly unfortunate that England both wanted Ireland and despised it. It was not only Charles who in the mid-seventeenth century made a mess of the English composite monarchy. Pym's use of the Irish rebellion to push his wholly English cause was equally damaging.

So Scotland, pursuing its own agenda, began the troubles. Ireland, equally with its own agenda, compounded them. England, demanding that Charles was king by English rules, or, rather, what were now reinterpreted as English rules, lurched painfully and hesitantly into the third of the civil wars. And then there was a British problem.

Civil Wars and the Republican Experiment

In the 1640s every part of the British Isles was at war. In the 1650s, the monarchy had been abolished, a republic created, and Oliver Cromwell and his associates were desperately trying to establish the 'Rule of Saints'. Of course, it is a grotesque oversimplification to say that the responsibility for cataclysm lay squarely with Charles I, but it is also the case that he had to work very hard to bring it about; even in Scotland and certainly in England men did not embark on outright defiance of the monarchy unless pushed beyond endurance, as Charles finally pushed them when he went to war first with his Scottish and then with his English subjects. The only men who reacted to the spiral down to disaster with any sort of confidence were the king himself, assured of the justice of his cause – as he would be until the day of his death – and a handful of godly English preachers who saw the chaos of 1641–2 as the prelude to the coming of the third and perfect Reformation (see above, p.216). Otherwise war – civil war – was viewed with horror; the parliamentarian Sir William Waller summed up what was felt when he wrote to his old friend the royalist Sir Ralph Hopton on 16 June 1642 lamenting 'this war without an enemy'. And none of Charles's opponents, in any of his three kingdoms, in the first years of conflict, sought to get rid of the king, let alone the monarchy; they fought for an accommodation with him, in which the more unacceptable aspects of his arbitrary rule would be curbed.

But the wars changed all the rules of politics. Charles lost two civil wars, in 1645 and 1648. It became possible to ask whether God was on the side of the king. Not many found the answer to that question in the destruction of Charles I. But one who came to do so was a minor country gentleman, Oliver Cromwell, who had made no particular mark as a member of parliament, but had come to dominance by the late 1640s through military brilliance. The godly soldier was a new and often frightening phenomenon; from 1648 Cromwell and his Army determined political events. Parliament, who had gone to war with the king intending to change but sustain his kingship, was reduced to a rump. The king was executed. And 'Britain', under a union imposed from London, became a republic.

More accurately, it tried to become one – and failed. The Rule of Saints lasted four years before giving way to a rather more monarchical experiment in 1653, when Cromwell became Lord Protector of England, Scotland and Ireland. His dealings with parliament were dictatorial and disastrous; Charles I, one feels, must have smiled in his grave. Cromwell's attempts to find a solution to the problems of the republic included establishing direct military rule in 1655. It was deeply unpopular and abandoned in 1657; but the Army as a political force would not go away. His death in 1658 and the failed regime of his son Richard brought the whole unhappy experiment crashing down. In 1660, it seemed, men wanted nothing more than to forget the passions and agonies of the 1640s and 1650s, and have a king again.

It is a riveting period, and one which inevitably had consequences for the future of the British Isles. Yet these consequences fell very far short of what at least some who lived through the period dreamed. War did not only shatter political traditions. Under the pressures of war, fascinating ideas began to crawl out of the woodwork: if the body politic was in chaos, why should not men, and women, begin to think of a new and very different world? Hence Colonel Thomas Rainborowe's astonishing call for universal male suffrage at the Putney Debates in 1647. Hence, in England, the Levellers, the Ranters and the Diggers, three radical and anti-monarchical groups who, in their separate ways, sought to advance the causes of political and economic equality and religious toleration.

Inevitably these movements struck fear into those who tried to preserve some measure of stability in a world so singularly lacking it. As an opponent of Charles I, the Leveller John Lilburne had had a certain popularity. In 1650, Cromwell – with a greater brutality than that normally associated with Charles I's dealings with his critics in the 1630s, when the pillory and the whip had been familiar sights in London – had four leading Levellers shot in the churchyard at Burford in Oxfordshire. They were martyrs, but martyrs to a doomed cause; this was no time for their quasi-democratic ideas, especially for the minor country gentleman who now sought to control England. In the same year the Digger movement collapsed, and the pantheistic Ranters were the target of the Blasphemy Act passed by the Rump Parliament in August 1650. For the rest of the decade Cromwell's regime had to deal with Fifth Monarchists and Quakers, and did so equally repressively. Those who in 1640–42 had had a vision of England as a balanced commonwealth, in which the king had a role shorn of most of what had been the accepted norms of royal authority – in the battle over legality and precedent, Charles I always had a stronger case than his opponents – might put forward new and dangerous ideas themselves, but there was no place in this dislocated age for others to do likewise.

More generally, there was no common cause between the opponents of Charles I throughout his realms. Whatever else they did, civil wars did not strengthen union; as it turned out, the real 'British' problem was the fact that one man was king of three kingdoms. The Scots, temporarily united – with few dissidents – at the height of their belief in their godliness, went ahead with missionary zeal. Their decision in 1643 to throw in their lot with the English Parliament rather than the king was based on their belief that parliament, not the king, would advance their godly cause in England and Ireland; as the Solemn League and Covenant said, it was made for the *preservation* of the Kirk, but the *reformation* of the Churches of England and Ireland. In 1646 they cheerfully changed tack and began to negotiate with Charles I, weakened by his defeat in the first English civil war, in the hope that, if they restored him, it would be he who would force Presbyterianism on England. In December 1647 the Scottish political nation split. All were Presbyterians, but now a gulf opened up between the moderate and the extremist godly. The moderates, a majority of the nobility and lairds, agreed to the Engagement with Charles I, in which they offered him support in return for a three-year trial period of Presbyterianism in England; and in 1648 the Engagers duly marched into England to fight for the king in the second civil war, where he fared no better than in the first. The Engagers were defeated at Preston, and Cromwell came to Scotland to make terms with the extreme Presbyterians, and to presage Pride's Purge of the Long Parliament in 1649 by expelling the Engagers – more than half the political nation – from the Scottish parliament. In Ireland, the intention of the Catholic Confederation of Kilkenny of 1642 appeared to be an independent kingdom or even republic. Meanwhile, as Catholics and Protestants divided over what they actually did want, Protestants fought Protestants, Catholics, Catholics.

In England, the Protestant Church was as always more divided than its Scottish counterpart; anti-episcopacy would be sustained until 1660, but the brief triumph of Presbyterianism would not. Nor was it as clear to Englishmen as it was to Scotsmen what their constitutional position should be, as the lunacy of 'King-in-Parliament' officially fighting 'the King' made clear. As late as 1647, Cromwell and other parliamentary leaders still sought an accommodation with the king, and parliament was desperately negotiating with him at the end of 1648. By then, however, Cromwell and the Army had had enough. In a mockery of what parliamentarians had stood for in 1642, the Long Parliament was purged by Colonel Pride, and the king brought to trial and executed in January 1649. Legally, the trial was a farce, as Charles brilliantly demonstrated; the High Court of Justice, established by an Act of the House of Commons alone, was no court at all. Politically, it was a success, willed by a minority. The Scots, who had begun it all, howled with fury when 'the English' killed their king.

Few knew what would happen next; and no one in the British Isles can be said to have enjoyed what did eventually happen. It is always dangerous to ascribe too much to the dominance and actions of one man, and yet in the 1650s it is hard to play down Oliver Cromwell, 'heaven's angry flame', the 'three-forked lightning' as Andrew Marvell called him. His initial failure was to break the union with Scotland, leaving Charles II as King of Scotland while England became a republic. Neither Charles nor the hideous group of Scottish godly clergy, now in full control after the defeat of the Engagers, and, with the Act of Classes of 1649, further purging the political nation of all dissenters – 80 per cent of the nobility, 60–70 per cent of the lairds – would accept that. Charles was forced to take the covenants and to be crowned at a travesty of a coronation at Scone. Failure became success. In 1651 Cromwell defeated the Scots at Dunbar in a battle which reinforced his belief in the Lord's divine approval of his enterprises; more probably it was because the ungodly among the Scots were not allowed to fight.

The coronation of Charles II at Scone, January 1652. Charles and the Scots insisted on retaining the monarchy, rejecting Cromwell's republican England. But this was surely the nadir of Stuart kingship. The coronation was a humiliating travesty: Charles, having been forced to take the Covenants of 1638 and 1643, was crowned not by a cleric but by the marquis of Argyll, and hectored about the sins of himself and his forbears.

He went on to win again at Worcester in 1651, after which Charles II fled abroad.

If the Scots wanted union, union they would have – and why not Ireland as well? In 1653, a 'British' parliament sat – the Barebones Parliament – which included Scottish and Irish MPs, and in 1654 the first protectorate parliament passed an Act of Union. The Scots would have thirty seats, most held by English officers. More to the point, it was under English military rule, Cromwell's real solution to 'union'. It was suffered in grim and defeated silence, interrupted only by the unsuccessful rising in 1653–5 by the earl of Glencairn, an act of defiance paralleled by the equally unsuccessful Penrudock's rising in England in 1655. The only irony to Cromwellian rule of Scotland was that it was his English army, led south by General Monck in 1659, which began the process which led to the restoration of Charles II in 1660.

What happened in Ireland was infinitely worse. Here, there was no attempt to do anything other than suppress. Best remembered are the hideous massacres at Drogheda and Wexford presided over by Cromwell in 1649; and it is no justification to say that this was to avenge the still-remembered Irish massacres of 1641–2. But these were the prelude to a much more thoroughgoing onslaught on the Irish in what John Morrill has rightly condemned as 'perhaps the greatest exercise in ethnic cleansing in early modern Europe'. By the Act of Settlement of 1652 it became clear that only the New English were acceptable inhabitants of Ireland. Gaelic Irish and Old English – Protestant as well as Catholic – were not. They were dispossessed of their lands, the majority of which went to English and Scottish soldiers, the rest to lawyers, merchants and gentry. Of the *c.* 12,000 Cromwellian soldiers who got lands, almost two-thirds hung on to them after the Restoration.

The government's intention was not wholly matched by its ability to implement it, but, from its point of view, it did remarkably well: the dispossessed landowners saw their share drop from 58 to 15 per cent, and to 10 per cent by the end of the century. But this was not the full extent of the ethnic cleansing. About half of the adult male population – Catholics who had taken part in the rebellion – was rendered liable to the death penalty under the Act; of the 80,000 people involved, it was, in the event, hundreds rather than thousands who suffered, but lack of fulfilment does nothing to mitigate the horror of the proposed slaughter. It was accompanied by a policy of transportation, sustained between 1653 and 1656, as well as a strenuous attempt to eradicate the Catholic faith. Of course, Cromwell is singled out as the villain, but Cromwell could not, and did not, carry through this policy alone. Far too many good and godly Englishmen and Scotsmen hated the Irish, and hated their popery. It is the extreme example of the fact that the Irish problem within the three kingdoms could not be resolved, because the dominant power, England, with some help from the Scots, never conceived of resolving it on any other than the most unequal and repressive terms.

Despite Cromwell's overpowering greatness, the dominant power was itself unable to resolve its own affairs. The various constitutional experiments in England make some of the follies and errors of Charles I look positively moderate. For all its appeal, so firmly grounded in the classical past, republicanism was a heady dream rather than a practical reality. Contemporary republics did not give grounds for optimism. The Venetian republic was, after all, presided over by the Doge, his power restricted by term of office but not much else. The curious hybrid of Poland, a republic under a nominally elective monarchy, worked because no one really tried to tip the balance too far in the republican direction. Even the Dutch republic, carefully maintained by its constitution, was vulnerable, as the house of Orange, steadily and constitutionally established its control in the second half of the seventeenth century over the Seven Provinces.

The English version lasted for precisely four years. When, today, the annual opening of parliament recalls Charles I's arrest of the Five Members in 1642, his final 'tyrannical' act, in the ceremony of the door slammed in Black Rod's face, it is worth asking why Cromwell's far more 'tyrannical' act, lining up troops in the chamber to expel the Rump Parliament in 1653, is not so hallowed in English political consciousness. Instead, Cromwell's nineteenth-century statue stands outside the House of Commons in its misleading guise as the champion of parliamentary democracy. By the end of that year, the republic was over and Cromwell was Lord Protector of England, Scotland and Ireland under the 'Instrument of Government', that rare attempt to have a written 'British' constitution. Ireland and Scotland were already under military rule. Despairing of any other solution, Cromwell pushed England in the same direction, with the rule of the major generals between 1655 and 1657. In 1657 came the final irony, when Cromwell was offered the crown. Perhaps 'King Oliver' sounded too odd in his ears; certainly he rejected it. Yet he had taken on the trappings of kingship, moving into the royal palaces, addressed as 'his highness the lord protector', with his wife 'her highness the lady protectress'; what he did not retain, sadly, was Charles I's glorious art collection, which was sold off. And the principle of monarchical hereditary succession was re-established, with the succession of his son Richard on his death in 1658.

Cromwell was not a man of overweening personal ambition. He genuinely believed in the republic. But he was driven forward by the twin recognition that it could not be made to work, and that he, inspired by God, was the only person who could give England some measure of political and military security. For the unpalatable fact was that none of the breakdown and the drama of the 1640s, the civil war,

Cromwell 'the Horrible Tail-man' (1652). This print from a Dutch pamphlet shows hostility to a different kind of ruler. It draws on the myth that Englishmen had tails, and provides Cromwell with a tail stuffed with gold coins, which he will use to oppress his enemies at home and abroad. A royalist, a Scot, an Irishman and a Dutchman threaten to cut off the tail. Another Dutch print of the same year also showed Cromwell with a tail; this time he is disgorging the royal treasure which he had stolen. This illustration stands as a good indication of the confusion and bitterness of the 1650s which sat alongside the hopes for the new world of the republic.

the public execution of the king, had done anything to create an acceptable way forward. As the experience of the rest of Europe showed, monarchical rather than republican rule was the more effective form of government. When Charles I, at his trial, floored his judges when he reminded them that 'England was never an elective kingdom but a hereditary kingdom for near these thousand years' he was not simply debating the issue of elective monarchy but pointing to the fact that an immediate crisis did nothing to undermine hereditary modes and structures of government.

Moreover, the interregnum witnessed not just the struggle to find a different kind of government, but found an utterly unacceptable form of government: rule by the military. In England, it was not permanent. What was permanent was the presence and power of the Army. Ultimately, Cromwell's inability to distance himself from the Army made it impossible for him to try to establish local control through the civilian country gentry, which would have had some semblance of normality, though he may have been attempting to do this in the last years of his life. After his death, and the succession of his civilian son Richard, there was breakdown. In 1660, General Monck arrived from Scotland. The Rump Parliament, reconvened, expelled and reconvened again by the Army in 1659, now dissolved itself. A Convention Parliament, elected by the free elections called for by Monck, agreed to the restoration of the monarchy. Life returned, it seemed, to normality. In fact, the desire to look back to 1641 and the impossibility of going back to 1641 meant that there was unfinished business which the so-called Glorious Revolution of 1688–9 would try – not wholly successfully – to resolve.

The British Isles were not the only regions to experience disorder in the 1640s. In France, political stability had been seriously threatened by the Fronde in 1647–8. The young Louis XIV went on to distance himself from Paris and develop his 'absolutist' monarchy. Charles I did not have the same option; unlike French kings, English, Scottish and Irish ones were dependent on their representative assemblies for supply. The attack on him, appalling as it seemed, would in the future look small, compared to the French Revolution. It loomed large enough at the time to ensure that when the next crisis for the monarchy came, in 1688–9, it would be James VII and II's good fortune that memories of the 1640s and 1650s produced a determination that this crisis should not be a rerun of those years; his fate was luxurious exile, not death.

The early-modern period in the British Isles, despite its achievements and, in the case of science, exploration and literature, glories,
was a distressed and disturbed age, beset with new problems too great
for it. The trauma of Reformation and religious division was not
resolved, and never would be; it was the cooling of religious passions,
not any real solution, which made it less of an issue in future centuries.
Nor was the other great problem of the era, the British composite
monarchy, settled. That would come in 1707, at least for England and
Scotland, though not Ireland, not because the seventeenth century had
seen efforts to find an answer to the nature of union, which it had not,
but because by the early eighteenth century there were new political,
economic and, crucially, international reasons to make it for the first
time desirable. For too much of the sixteenth and seventeenth
centuries men lived in an uncertain political, constitutional and
religious world. Theirs was not an enviable lot.

4. Some Counter-Factuals

Of the many changes which affected men's lives between the late fifteenth and mid-seventeenth centuries, the three most dramatic were the Reformations, the union of 1603 and the civil wars. Historians know that all three happened; their job is to seek to interpret and make sense of them. Contemporaries had to find out that they were happening, and wonder what to make of them as they did. The value of counter-factual history is that it is a reminder that they did not know that events were set in stone.

The nature of the Reformations within the British Isles was in large measure determined by events and personalities in the three kingdoms. But as they were not a British phenomenon it is worth beginning by asking what might have happened had Luther been listened to, instead of condemned, by Pope Leo X. Luther, after all, fiery though his initial attack in 1517 was, saw himself as attempting to reform from within; he even disingenuously claimed that he had not intended his writings to be published. He could, therefore, have been part of that impressive group of fifteenth- and early sixteenth-century Catholics who did believe in the need for reform. Even Leo X might have classed himself among that group, for it was he who summoned the Fifth Lateran Council of 1512–17, which did make attempts at reform only to have them overtaken by Luther. And not for another thirty years was it acknowledged that the divisions of Christendom might be altered, but were fundamentally irreversible. Yet there is a problem here. By the early sixteenth century, the papacy had lost its pre-eminent spiritual authority. From the eleventh century, with the pontificate of Gregory VII – 'Holy Satan' – it had built up immense legal, fiscal and bureaucratic power, and in so doing significantly changed its image. The scandal of the Great and Little Schisms in the late fourteenth and mid-fifteenth centuries had severely damaged it.

The sixteenth-century papacy was slow to see the need to establish itself at the head of the movement for reform; only after the Council of Trent, whose last session was in 1563, did its spiritual role clearly re-emerge. Thus, for example, the Scottish Catholic reforming councils of 1549–59 had very little to say about the papacy. By contrast, the Louvain exiles of the 1560s – those Catholics who went into exile after Elizabeth's accession – had a lot to say about the spiritual authority of the pope. This is not to say that Protestant or Catholic reformations inevitably took the form they did. But it does seem that with a papacy which had for too long been effectively holding back on reform that frustrations had gone too far to be readily accommodated within the single Church.

We are thus forced back on the experience of individual kingdoms, and indeed forced back on their rulers. Unsatisfactory as it may be to focus on monarchs, the fact is that, for good or ill, in this age when monarchical power was growing to new heights, they led and others, willingly or not, had to follow; they were therefore crucial to all three cataclysmic or, in the case of union, dislocating movements of the early-modern British Isles. What, then, would have happened had Katherine of Aragon had a son? Or, having failed to do so, had she accepted defeat and gone, as she was begged to do by Cardinal Campeggio, Clement VII's representative in England in 1529, into a nunnery? Henry VIII may have been influenced by those more strongly desirous of reform than he was, and may have been attracted, once the idea occurred or was suggested to him, by becoming Supreme Head of the Church. But it is at least possible to argue that, had it not been for the dynastic problem which loomed large in his mind, he would not have cut the English Church off from Rome. That does not mean that there would never have been Reformation in England; but it might have come later, and it might have taken a different form. Conversely, it is possible to ask whether, once he had split the Church, anything could have been done to push more strenuously the early Reformation in Ireland, and the answer is possibly yes; it was in the later sixteenth and the seventeenth centuries that the Counter Reformation Church in Ireland really took on its impressive vibrancy. In which case Ireland, as the impossible member of a Protestant composite monarchy, might have fitted in more comfortably – though other factors perhaps make this a particularly long shot.

Dynastic problems, indeed, continue to give grounds for counter-factual questions. Had Mary Tudor lived longer, and had she had a son, it is impossible not to think that her Catholic restoration might have dug in so deep that a Catholic Tudor dynasty could well have survived to rule a Catholic England. When that did not happen, the next obvious question concerns Elizabeth's refusal to marry, a singular abnegation of the responsibility of monarchs to provide an heir and one which led directly to the union of the crowns of 1603. Nothing else would have brought the flourishing independent kingdom of Scotland into dynastic partnership with England, Ireland and Wales. The fact that Scotland provided the English composite monarchy with a Protestant king was the result of another of history's counter-factuals: what if Mary Queen of Scots, unlike Mary Tudor young and capable of producing an heir, had had the intelligence, desire and strength of character to emulate Mary Tudor in choking off the embryonic Protestant Reformation in her kingdom of Scotland?

Mary Queen of Scots in fact allowed the Scottish Protestants to establish their Kirk, and provoked a short-lived civil war. Her grandson Charles I managed to create civil wars in all his dominions. In many ways he showed lamentable similarities to his grandmother, in his lack of sensitivity to political issues and problems, in his unwillingness to listen to counsel, and in his predilection for duplicity – though both would certainly have defended themselves against that charge, seeing their actions as necessary in defence of their sovereignty. Had he been a different ruler, would the problems of fiscal weakness and overburdened government, which particularly assailed the English government by the seventeenth century, have been resolved more peaceably and without the significant readjustment of political power between crown and parliament?

None of these things happened. But we can wonder what would have been the outcome had they done so. The probable answer is that different sets of people would have been happy and unhappy, satisfied and dissatisfied, in this age of upheaval. That may not appear to amount to much; but it would have mattered much to those who lived through it.

PART IV

Restoration to Reform, 1660–1832

Jonathan Clark

Introduction

All of the chapters in this volume reveal the same central truth: each period (and not just one, formative period) witnessed unanticipated, crucial and determinative events or episodes, the outcomes of which could not have been foreseen but which set momentous new courses for what was to follow. This truth applies equally in the period covered here. Far from being the scene of political stability and social convention in which – as used to be assumed – reassuringly little happened, the decades between the 1660s and the 1830s display astonishing reversals, achievements and new departures.

First was the failure of English republicanism and sectarianism, registered in 1660 in the restoration, against all odds, of the monarchy. This event entrenched a royalist Anglicanism in England and so set guidelines for England's subsequent fraught relations with Scotland, Ireland and Wales. But the exact nature and implications of that royalist, aristocratic order were yet to be worked out. The Revolution of 1688 ensured that the hegemonic formula, under which Britain's geopolitical position was transformed by 1815, would be narrower and more exclusive than that envisaged by Charles II and James II – namely a religiously plural society, accommodating Catholics.

The improbable deposition of James II in 1688 had profound consequences for the governance of each of our four polities: the executive arm of government and representative assemblies in London, Edinburgh (until 1707) and Dublin (until 1801) worked out a pattern of party government far more manipulative, corrupt and centrally directed than the turbulent histories of early Stuart parliaments would have implied. The deposition of a sovereign and the growth of oligarchy to defend his replacements meant that England became a lastingly divided society; Scotland and Ireland were more divided still. The resulting conflicts between centre and periphery in the British Isles were managed in the medium term only by exporting them to the North American colonies, where they recurred in 1776 in a wholly insoluble form.

The American Revolution, generally now seen as an unquestioned starting-point of modern values because of the present-day dominance of the United States, deserves to be taken far more seriously, and must be analysed as an episode in British political and religious history. It was the first in a line of geopolitical dominoes to fall; its fall ushered in an age of world war and social revolution that devastated first the eastern seaboard of the Thirteen Colonies, then the European continent. In the cataclysms of 1776–83 and 1793–1815, Britain's initial achievement was negative: survival. Yet even this could not be predicted, and was far from assured.

How Britain escaped defeat and revolutionary transformation in these years and in their postwar aftermath continues to fascinate historians. Yet out of victory itself came political and social transformations no less dramatic than those threatened by the Jacobins: Britain embarked on an era of reform after 1828 that left it, a century later, with much continuity of political forms but much less continuity of the life lived within them. How far this survival of adversity and the achievement of prosperity is to be traced to an autonomous material realm of demography and economics is another area of passionate historical controversy, and so it is with material considerations that we begin.

1. Material Cultures

In material terms, the British Isles in the mid-seventeenth century were as marginal as they had been for centuries. Thinly populated, with few significant towns compared to the most prosperous areas of continental Europe, they were largely tangential to the wider European economy. The archipelago also counted for less than the sum of its parts. Its population was divided among three polities (England and Wales; Ireland, and Scotland) that had long been in political conflict, and would remain so. Yet by 1832 this weak position had been transformed into one of strength. The British Isles now counted for considerably more than the sum of their parts; they were politically united as never before; their population had grown by a factor of three where the populations of many rival states on the European continent had grown slowly or were sometimes stagnant; Britain's wealth and military power had increased by even more than her population.

To explain this transformation we must reject the assumption that such changes had to happen as they did. They took place because incremental economic developments in agriculture, commerce and manufacture just managed to exceed major population growth; because social change, although continual, was evolutionary rather than revolutionary; and because (with the key exception of the American Revolution) political action succeeded in building up rather than breaking down the state.

Gender: The Role of Marriage and Population

Why did the population grow in such a dynamic way? More than by any other factor, population increase or decrease was determined by gender relations. This is currently a growth area of scholarship, often based on evidence from ecclesiastical or civil courts: evidence, that is, of what happened when relations between the sexes went disastrously wrong. Yet using such material as proof of male domination and female oppression is difficult since we do not know how representative these breakdowns were. The evidence for gender relations that left no record of litigation mainly relates to marriage, birth and death.

Gender roles set marriage patterns, and the family was the main determinant of long-term population change. At the time, there was no reliable information on population trends, so anxiety about any apparent decline could easily spread; even in the early nineteenth century, the journalist William Cobbett (1763–1835) could cite the social problems of his own day as evidence that England's population had fallen since the 1200s. A century earlier Cobbett's theory might have held true. The recent discipline of demography allows us to paint a more accurate picture, however, and, for England at least, the overall pattern is now clear. The story was initially one of failure: England's population boom of c. 1550–1650 slowed down and stopped during the Commonwealth; the population actually declined from the 1650s to c. 1700, and rose little before the 1750s. Demographic historians have recently solved this old problem for England: which was the stronger influence on population trends, fertility or mortality, births or deaths? In sixteenth- and seventeenth-century England the two seem to have been equally balanced, and low compared to other societies of that time, but from the mid-eighteenth century it was more a rise in fertility than a fall in mortality that boosted the total. Responding to the insecurity and disruption of c. 1640–60, marriage strategies changed: the average age at marriage increased, and a larger proportion of people never married at all. Ireland and Scotland, often closer to the margin of subsistence, were perhaps harder hit by mortality crises. Subsequently, however, growth recovered, and from the 1780s it grew faster than at any other time.

A rise in fertility posed considerable risks. England's first major demographer, the Anglican clergyman Thomas Malthus, explained the problem in 1798: population naturally tended to increase in a geometric ratio (1, 2, 4, 8 . . .), but the output of food could rise only in an arithmetic ratio (1, 2, 3, 4 . . .). Population would therefore (he claimed) overshoot subsistence until it was reduced by the 'positive checks' of war, famine (after high food prices) and disease: the crises in mortality which they produced were normally the chief agents restraining population. These savage setbacks could only be avoided, urged Malthus, by a form of social control on personal conduct he called the 'preventive check'. Through such measures as chastity before marriage and marrying at a later age (within wedlock, he assumed, children follow inevitably), population would be restrained within available resources. If this were true, it could seem that England, Wales and Scotland, with effective preventive checks, narrowly remained within these constraints until the 1810s, but that Ireland increasingly did not, with catastrophic results seen in the population boom and collapse at the time of the Irish famine of the 1840s.

Was Malthus's analysis correct? Not if we understand it to mean that all pre-industrial societies were trapped at the same low standard of living; on the contrary, they differed greatly in wealth. We now know that even by 1700 England had moved beyond the ancient demographic regime in which mortality fluctuated closely with food prices: this correlation steadily weakened after the 1640s, largely cured by the market and an increase in real wages. English poor relief based on local taxation was effective by the 1630s; by the end of the seventeenth century, a national market for wheat had developed in England to the point where it ironed out local harvest failures. Even so, there was no sudden and decisive escape from old perils. Crises of mortality meant absolute falls of about 200,000 in England's population between 1678 and 1686, and again between 1727 and 1730. Substantial emigration during c. 1650–1750 helped stabilise England's population, and birth rates began consistently to pull ahead of death rates from the late 1740s. Yet it was not clear at the time that this was occurring, and the interaction of these wider demographic pressures was not fully understood. Anxiety and argument therefore continued: 'preventive checks' were still seen as crucial in keeping population growth sustainable and defending a standard of living much higher than subsistence level.

If population growth in the south of England was triggered by rising real wages before c. 1780, as Malthus's analysis might suggest, that growth continued, once real wages stabilised (or, especially for agricultural labourers, were often eroded), for other reasons including the impact of enclosures, the demise of living-in farm labour, and the decline of apprenticeship and of opportunities for female employment. As urban economic opportunity expanded in the late eighteenth century, the 'preventive check' was not wholly discarded; but what was seen as a prudent response to limited rural economic horizons was increasingly offset by wider, urban, horizons. If elite culture became ever more preoccupied with 'respectability', an ethic of control and postponement, urban life often widened economic opportunities for the non-elite: economic opportunity now depended less and less on having access to land, and so England's population growth accelerated. In the late seventeenth century its rate of increase per annum was zero; by the early nineteenth it was about 1.75 per cent, the highest England ever experienced. But it was a growth rate that still did not revolutionise family structure.

English population history has been brilliantly reconstructed on the basis of evidence from parish registers kept by the established Church, but in Ireland, Scotland and Wales the fragmentary nature of such sources obscures our understanding of those areas before the early nineteenth century. In Ireland, Scotland and to a lesser extent Wales, it seems that war, famine and disease continued to produce the crises of mortality that England increasingly escaped: if so, Malthus's 'positive check' continued to operate in different ways across the British Isles.

Where England is said to have had a 'low pressure' demographic regime of low fertility and mortality rates by European standards, Ireland and Scotland had 'high pressure' regimes with the opposite characteristics. How they coped with the differences determined their demographic outcomes. In Ireland the rate of growth accelerated after c. 1750, reaching three times Scotland's rate of increase in 1755–1801. Scotland's population growth came later than England's, and was less rapid. By contrast, the Catholic Irish hardly emigrated before the famine of the 1840s, and Ireland's growth exceeded England's: between 1781 and 1831, the population of Wales grew by about 48 per cent, of Scotland by 65 per cent, of England by 84 per cent, but of Ireland by 92 per cent.

What caused such divergent demographic outcomes? We still hardly know, although the different operation of 'social control' in different societies must have contributed. The alienation of the Irish elite from the masses for religious reasons may have weakened the force of elite doctrine and the 'preventive check'. The easy availability of farm tenancies in Ireland probably kept the age at marriage low, and a fall in mortality (especially infant mortality) in the late eighteenth century with the disappearance of famine in Ireland also contributed to growth. Ireland followed a pattern that was only narrowly avoided in England and Scotland: in Ireland the strong growth of population from the mid-eighteenth century outstripped the growth of the economy, which prospered in Ulster but stagnated elsewhere.

In demographic terms, it may be that the British Isles only narrowly escaped a general crisis. England's 'low pressure' regime allowed a substantial population increase that ran ahead of agricultural output. Overall economic growth was, on the most optimistic estimates, only just enough to sustain a much larger population without an average reduction in real wages, but in some areas precisely this reduction occurred: by 1820 the countryside in the south and midlands of England too often saw a local world polarised between the mean, grasping farmer and the resentful, welfare-dependent labourer for whom there was too little work. Even in manufacturing areas, threats of revolution produced by economic distress were taken seriously by the government. Outside England, things were worse. Scotland's demographic regime now threatened to revert to its previous state: the second decade of the nineteenth century saw the return of crises of mortality caused by the diseases rampant in the new industrial slums. Although there is evidence of improving conditions of life for the Irish agricultural labourer to 1815, Ireland's 'high pressure' regime was heading for disaster: the stage was being set by population boom and dependency on the potato for the massive mortality of the 1840s.

What did Malthus's 'preventive check' depend on? Older histories treated the forces of capitalism and democracy as the locomotives of history; today, demography seems a more plausible driving force, and demography describes marriage. Female 'virtue' was central to Malthus's 'preventive check': eighteenth-century female authors today labelled feminists generally sought to establish the dignity of their sex, or personal independence, by ostentatious chastity rather than to advance their careers by exploiting their sexuality (the second strategy was open to only a small number of courtesans, and not at every court: William III and Anne looked coldly on sexual licence). For the majority of women, stable marriage was their aim. For them, it is not clear that any fundamental qualitative change in gender relations came about in this period. What changed was the average age at marriage, and the percentage of the population marrying.

Nevertheless, two rival models asserting profound change currently contest this thesis. One, dating from Engels, urges that the decline of production in family units, the growth of the factory and the rise of wage labour increasingly divided the sexes during the working day, diminishing women's power and wealth: patriarchy strengthened. This thesis is contradicted by another which claims that the Industrial Revolution eroded patriarchy and transformed relations between the sexes by expanding opportunities for female employment. Although these explanations cannot simultaneously be true, both might be false, and may fail to do justice to a complex picture in which overall shifts towards or away from 'patriarchy' were absent. Most obviously, a population boom meant that more women spent more of their lives bearing and raising children, a picture not greatly modified until the twentieth century; but this may have added to women's importance. Many enterprises had never relied on family production; those that did had hardly provided for the economic equality or independence of the sexes. For the great majority of women there was no transition from patriarchal subordination to radical-individualist emancipation, or from economic activity to leisured indolence, but merely incremental shifts from certain forms of work discipline and authority to other forms. In some regions women's employment was actually curtailed by economic change: population pressure in the countryside, and male monopolies in many industries, reduced opportunities; elsewhere, factories widened them. In many areas, especially towns, the pattern of female employment remained much the same over long time spans. No single trend is apparent.

These enquiries have not yet been conducted on a comparative basis: currently we do not know how Scotland, Ireland, Wales and England compared in respect of gender relations, or how each compared with continental Europe. The most accurate sorts of evidence are figures for the population; these show the continuing centrality of the institution of marriage and its increasing triumph over mortality. The family remained the basic social unit, and household size (at least in England) was roughly constant between the sixteenth century and the early twentieth: recent demographic history shows that there was no transition from a patriarchal, 'extended' family to a 'nuclear' family under the impact of 'capitalism', as some sociologists used to claim. The nuclear family seems also to have been the norm in Scotland and Wales as well as England. Only in Ireland did ancient assumptions about the primacy of the kin group give family life a more collective character, but this calls for more research.

One marked change was a considerable increase in female literacy in the fifty years after *c.* 1670. Yet this new skill was initially put to old uses, to reinforce ideas of chastity and restraint. The Anglican clergyman Richard Allestree produced his classic work, *The Ladies Calling*, in 1673 (it was very often reprinted); it called on women to develop the religious virtues appropriate to domesticity. Few women writers stepped outside this model: Lady Mary Wortley Montagu (1689–1762) and Catherine Macaulay (1731–91), who seemed openly to challenge men's roles in society, were rare exceptions. The object of 'conduct books' was still to shape women's characters as wives and mothers. What the Church taught as a route to morality, the political economists taught as a route to economic survival. Adam Smith distinguished between 'strict' and 'liberal' schemes of morality: the first meant breaking even, the second would be 'ruinous to the common people'. In the decades in which England's population stagnated and sometimes fell, authors like Mary Astell were urging a retreat from the world; as the doctrine of the moral dignity of family life was re-emphasised, population began to move upward again. How these things were linked we do not yet know.

Contemporary debate on gender relations was limited in scale and small in practical impact. The main changes in 1660–1832 were in numbers of children rather than in gender roles, and changes in family structure were not striking except in one respect. Fewer apprentices and servants 'lived in' with employers, and on this (perhaps minor) fact some historians build a major argument: that this meant a narrowing of 'the household' to create the nuclear family of husband, wife and children. This argument often claims that such a trend was driven primarily by economics (the extension of a monetised, market economy), but it is also linked to an argument about sentiment (the alleged rise of 'affective individualism', which turned the family into a more egalitarian site of warm emotional relationships between kin). Yet demographers have now shown that the 'nuclear family' was by this time very old in Britain, and statistically changed little in the eighteenth century. The argument about a transition from 'patriarchy' to 'affective individualism' also looks less strong if we dispense with the major premise that the seventeenth century was dominated by 'patriarchy': much evidence exists not only for loving marriages in the seventeenth century but also for male domination in the eighteenth and later. It seems likely that opposites were more compatible than we thought: male authority was consistent with loving relationships; the nuclear family was consistent with the wider and affective kin group.

The object of the family was not to fulfil present-day notions regarding gender relations, but to ensure demographic survival. For most people, family formation and success depended on Adam Smith's 'strict code' of morality. Because women had most to lose, conventional gender relations were defended more often by women than by men, and the rise of the female author is therefore revealing: many, like Mary Astell (1666–1731), Aphra Behn (1640?–89) and Delariviere Manley (1663–1724), sympathised with the Tory, and sometimes the Jacobite, cause (explained below) as a route to asserting a larger social role for their sex. Only occasionally did the female voice take a libertine form, as with Behn; sometimes, as with Astell, it generated an opposite ambition of creating separate communities for women.

If 'early feminists' looked to chastity to defend the independence of their sex, this ideal faded in the eighteenth century with significant falls in the percentage never marrying and in the average age at marriage. In this sense 'early feminism' failed: the key women authors of the end of the period were Sarah Trimmer (1741–1810) and Hannah More (1745–1833), Evangelicals, apologists for the family, propagandists for the education of children. Their adult lives, and the years of fastest population growth from the 1790s to the 1840s, were overshadowed by war and the threat of revolution. Women writers who saw the French Revolution as a helpful bandwagon suffered by identifying their cause with an episode whose unfolding horrors polarised opinion against them; of these the most famous was Mary Wollstonecraft (1759–97). But just as the French Revolution diminished the role of women in France, its British supporters did the same in Britain: instead it was Evangelicals, firm friends to the established order, who pioneered a growing role for women as agents of philanthropy, exporting the domestic virtues of the middling ranks to the poor. Women's roles into the nineteenth century were dominated by demography, not democracy.

Open Society or Ancien Regime?

Whether Britain in this period may be termed an ancien regime society was not a question asked before 1789, since no such concept then existed. Indeed, at the outbreak of the French Revolution both the Prime Minister, William Pitt, and his chief opponent, Charles James Fox, were hopeful and optimistic about that episode. It was revolutionary France's declaration of war on Britain in 1793 that defined the question, and Britain's key role as the most tenacious and consistent enemy of international Jacobinism then carved this identity in stone. In daily politics, the postwar ministry of Lord Liverpool often pursued reform, but this did not prevent the profoundly disaffected from reaching for a characterisation of the regime as 'Old Corruption'.

The question, then, was made real by politics, but this key aspect is missed when historians frame a false antithesis, asking whether Britain was an open society *or* an ancien regime. In some ways it was both, since those who supported the existing order (of Church and State, peer and bishop, squire and parson) supported what they saw as the most advanced, most rational option, a social form that had guaranteed security of property and encouraged commercial growth and the progress of knowledge. The French word *ancien* meant 'old' mainly in the sense of 'previous' rather than in the sense of 'outdated'. The real issue is not whether society before 1832 was outdated (which would be a weak claim) but whether the different world that followed 1832 represented a fundamental break with what went before (which is more plausible). This question is keenly debated.

It was also the case that the degree of effective 'openness' in society varied in different social strata. Least open was the world of the great landowners and the peerage. City wealth, not city air, made free; yet across Britain most wealth was still derived from land, which continued to be owned by the few. In 1688, the year of the Revolution, Gregory King estimated that 45–50 per cent of English land was owned by the great landowners, 25–33 per cent by small owner-occupiers. From 1688 to 1790 the second group probably declined slightly, while the tenure of a third group, the tenant farmers, became more insecure. The rise of the great estates and the decline of small proprietors went together, not necessarily in the interests of agricultural productivity but certainly promoting the power of the great landowner.

Scotland's landed society was even more polarised between great landowners and dependent tenants than England's, with a much smaller class of gentry. Scotland's landownership pattern also changed more than its southern neighbour's, as the customary relations of clanship gave way to landlordism in the Highlands. Wales, meanwhile, largely lacked its own nobility. The strange failure of many gentry families in the early eighteenth century to produce a male heir led to a restructuring of its landowning society: perhaps half of Wales's

wealthiest families in the mid-eighteenth century were English new-
comers. Wealth mattered; and in Scotland, Ireland and Wales landed
wealth mattered even more.

At the very top, therefore, society was largely 'closed', the position
of the large landowner even strengthening from the late seventeenth
century to the agricultural depression of the late nineteenth. As
revealed by John Bateman's survey of 1870, the families of more than
nine-tenths of the richest landowners had owned their lands since
before 1700. Few 'new men' bought great estates, although many of
them bought small ones: the gentry was far more 'open' than the
nobility. The peerage even became more closed: of the 117 new peers
created in the eighteenth century only seven came from outside the
gentry. But the lower down the scale of landed wealth, the more
movement there was into the ranks of the landed elite. Land was
business, indeed the biggest business of all, and landowners had to be
open to entrepreneurial opportunity if they were to prosper. Trade,
therefore, did not automatically rule a line between 'open' and 'closed'
sectors of society.

With the domination of landowning by the great estates went the
domination of national politics by the great landlords, usually peers, a
dominance which persisted into the late nineteenth century: the huge
preponderance of peers in successive cabinets is easily established.
Although 'new men' increasingly bought their way into parliament,
the number of MPs who were sons or clients of peers also rose over the
eighteenth century: the old society was strengthening, so that 'the old'
and 'the new' were scarcely yet defined as antithetical: here as
elsewhere, it is not clear that we can speak of a 'new' society rising to
challenge an 'old' one. They merged and cooperated far more than
they divided and fought each other.

In Scotland, the smaller landowners had much less political power
than their English counterparts: the tiny electorate, and the distance
from Westminster, locked them out. In Scottish counties, even among
the landowners only a small fraction possessed the parliamentary
franchise. But their local role was much stronger than the English
gentry's: these 'heritors' held large and growing power within the Kirk
sessions, where civil and ecclesiastical jurisdiction coincided. In
Ireland, the power of the landlords was magnified, and its significance
embittered, by the alternating dominance of Catholic and Protestant
communities. There the major shifts of landholding were the result of

political vicissitude, as the Catholic interest backed the losing dynasty and was penalised by expropriation.

In some ways, British society had long been 'open', and remained so; in others it was not, and would not become so until the social revolution of the 1960s. Yet the 'open' aspects could be very old indeed. In England, representatives from the counties and the boroughs had sat in the same House of Parliament, the Commons, since the reign of Edward I; their children had intermarried; younger sons of landowners had pursued careers in the professions or as merchants. The social distance at any moment between patrician and plebeian was real, but identities over time were not indelible. Nevertheless, not until the agricultural slump of the late nineteenth century did landed wealth weaken its grip on society and the political machinery. It was not clear that merchants made much headway in status or political power, although their well-endowed daughters long found it possible to marry for status. The parliament of 1641 had included fifty-five merchants; that of 1754 included only five more. The group which did increase its representation among MPs was that of the professions, especially lawyers and army and navy officers.

Some historians have celebrated the growth of English towns in the eighteenth century as a proof of increasing 'openness', and there is indeed evidence of urban growth. Towns have sometimes been hailed as a magic marker of modernity; the same statistical evidence, however, calls this into doubt. Against that conclusion are the facts that most 'towns' remained very small by today's standards; that there was only one large English city, London, which accounted for a large share of the urban sector of the population; and that England had little to compare with the network of very substantial towns and cities that characterised long-developed areas of the continental economy, including France, northern Italy, the Low Countries and the Rhineland. Towns were not a prerequisite of political consciousness or political change: the American Revolution broke out in a society even less urbanised. Until after 1800, Scotland, Ireland and Wales were substantially lower in the league tables of urbanisation than England, yet Scotland and Ireland were major destabilisers. Historians' rhetoric about the effects of urbanisation assumes an English model that hardly fits England's nearest neighbours, let alone agricultural North America.

Towns had representative institutions, but they were not essentially democratic in our sense. They varied greatly in their structures of government: Manchester, the archetypal city of Victorian progress, was still administered in the eighteenth century by its court leet, a medieval survival. Yet such structures could be well or badly run: many towns in the eighteenth century pursued schemes of improvement while still being in the hands of oligarchies, while other towns did little. Many corporations were well conducted before the Municipal Corporations Act of 1835 reorganised and opened up their governance; many were badly conducted after it. Corrupt enclaves persisted through subsequent centuries, merely serving new interest groups; it is not clear that an 'open society' argument can be sustained on such evidence.

A preoccupation of the eighteenth century came to be the theme of 'improvement'. Daniel Defoe, in his *A Tour Thro' the Whole Island of Great Britain* (1724–6), celebrated 'the Improvements in the Soil, the Product of the Earth, the Labour of the Poor, the Improvement in Manufactures, in Merchandizes, in Navigation'. Remarkably, this awareness did not generate a generalised idea of 'progress': that term still meant movement, not the amelioration of the human condition. Defoe also described a society that was run by local elites (as was even more true in Scotland, Ireland and Wales) without major intervention from the central government except for the collection of excise (a tax on commodities like beer and tobacco) and the periodic visits of assize judges. Local elites, not subject to the spotlight of publicity, could be more unaccountable than national elites: the idea of the 'open society' is partly an invention of twentieth-century cities.

Some historians have adopted the recent German notion of a 'public sphere' to argue that government became more subject to popular participation and consent, but this thesis must be qualified. The coffee house, the pamphlet and the newspaper, spreading rapidly after 1660, had long been preceded by the tavern, the sermon and the newsletter, and these older forms and forums of communication continued: the culture symbolised by the periodical *The Spectator* (1711–12, 1714) was arguably not as antithetical to this older culture as it now appears. An informed public outside parliament grew with the proliferation of newspapers, and participated even though they lacked the vote. Yet this was not new: the Reformation, and the wars of the 1640s, showed informed participation before the advent of newspapers, and eighteenth-century newspapers were far from populist. The concept of *communitas regni*, the community of the realm, can be traced to the thirteenth century or even the eleventh in England, and the Reformation revealed a similar solidarity in Scotland. In Ireland, sectarian communities were aware of themselves as such for centuries before the franchise became an issue. People had long felt involved (or

Politeness. The rise of coffee-house culture and the periodical, notably *The Spectator*, is sometimes held to symbolise a new polite culture, part of a secular Enlightenment. But this print shows a cup of coffee being thrown in a man's face during a heated argument. Did people continue locked in acrimonious conflict over the old issues? The year is 1710: perhaps the argument was over the trial of Dr Sacheverell and the interpretation of the Revolution of 1688 that it raised.

excluded where they expected involvement); this assumption did not wait for the invention of a concept of 'society' distinct from 'the state'. 'Society' in this sense was unknown to Locke and was an idea only invented, for polemical reasons, by authors like Thomas Paine. Nor did the career or writings of Locke validate the notion of a 'public sphere'. Locke's political theory was underpinned chiefly by natural law, not by contract, and Locke cannot be used to prove the essentially contractual or voluntary character of social relations. Contract was an ancient device, but not necessarily a revolutionary one; it did not automatically supersede status and custom.

Social mobility, too, is not a single and easily measurable thing. Whether 'new men' were acceptable in elite landed society is a question that some historians seek to answer with a simple 'yes', others with a robust 'no'. The situation is likely to have varied greatly by region (London being almost a different world) and occupation (different occupations of equal wealth commanded different statuses). Yet however closed the landed elite and the political class, society in the middle was increasingly 'open'. In a diversified economy, growth meant thousands of new opportunities, seized by men of little or no fortune. This quickly became an easy boast. In 1728 Defoe claimed that

> It is the Trade that has made the common People rich, as Pride has made the Gentry poor . . . however the Gentlemen may value themselves upon their Birth and Blood, the Case begins to turn against them so evidently, as to Fortune and Estate, that tho' they say, the Tradesmen cannot be made Gentlemen; yet the Tradesmen are, at this Time, able to buy the Gentlemen almost in every part of the Kingdom.

Yet Defoe exaggerated. Statistics now available suggest that although *income* did flow into 'new' hands, it flowed into 'old' hands just as much, except in a few areas; meanwhile, the balance of *wealth* at this point was still heavily towards land. Nor did the rise of manufacturing always have an egalitarian outcome. Some enterprises fell into the pattern of the 'artisan republic', the workshop coercively dominated by the customary expectations of groups of skilled artisans; others were organised on a top-down basis by the employer. New manufacturers from the ironmaster Ambrose Crowley through the social reformer Robert Owen and others into the nineteenth century borrowed from the gentry a patriarchal model of labour relations, sometimes idealised, often coercive. Openness depended on one's location and ambitions. The son of a farm labourer who rose to be an innkeeper might consider himself well rewarded; a struggling author who narrowly failed to be accepted as a gentleman might become a Jacobin and an enemy of the aristocratic ideal.

To the rural poor, society could seem much more 'closed', especially when economic change undermined living standards and eroded customary entitlements. Scotland saw a similar transition to England's as customary use-rights slowly gave way to commercially disposable freeholds. In Scotland, even before the suppression of the final Jacobite rebellion, the Forty-five, the Gaelic idea of landowning (*duthchas*, or heritable trusteeship, whereby the clan chiefs were obliged to provide security of possession to their kin), began to give way to an idea of heritable freehold title (*oighreachd*). This 'legalist concept of heritage', as Allan Macinnes has called it, entailed a sub-ordination of traditional ideas of entitlement to market opportunities, growing after 1745, in full flood by the 1820s. This legal shift in ideas of land tenure, it has been argued, was the most important cause of the demise of clanship; and it was a change equally promoted by landowners who inclined to the Houses of Stuart and Hanover. Eighteenth-century Britons competed without our sense of 'the new' transforming 'the old'.

'Class' is normally taken to be a marker of a 'closed society', and class analysis is sometimes postponed by a claim of the survival of paternalism over the unfettered free market, but this antithesis needs careful examination. Such an argument takes paternalism to be in good repair in the early eighteenth century, but undermined by the decline of yearly hirings, the rise of wage labour, the progressive difficulty of obtaining a poor law entitlement (a 'settlement') and a wave of enclosures that eroded economic independence. It has been argued that there was a watershed in the mid-eighteenth century when practices in the labour market moved away from ones that respected paternal relationships towards those that attended only to market forces. This scenario seems most persuasive as a general model, but the local variations were so great as to make it problem-atic as an account of England as a whole, let alone Wales, Ireland and Scotland.

Perhaps what mattered with any system was the degree of humanity with which it was run, and this varied unpredictably.

Overall, it might be argued that compassion and coercion still alternated, the first reasserted as in the Speenhamland poor relief system of 1798 which indexed cash handouts to the price of grain. Yet there was no natural pendulum: the old statutes regulating prices and apprenticeship regulations weakened as the eighteenth century went on; the old assize of bread, allowing local Justices of the Peace to set prices, disappeared after the 1790s. So did traditional rural entertainments, once provided by farmers for labourers: social distances were increasing in the countryside, as in manufacture. Even so, one study of Lincolnshire has postponed the essential shift in labourers' attitudes to the 1840s.

Changes in paternal relationships were not necessarily all in the libertarian direction of individual autonomy. The historian Richard Price has argued for a revival of paternalism in the late eighteenth and early nineteenth centuries, after a period in which many complaints had been made of the self-interest of rural elites. From the middle of the eighteenth century, this argument runs, the rural gentry acquired a new interest in their local roles, a trend that found one expression in the much larger number of country clergy appointed as JPs. This revival of paternalism, it is argued, mitigated the wave of violence, arson and strikes in the 1830s and 1840s caused by the triumph of *laissez-faire* principles, not least in the new poor law of 1834. Whether this 'revival' was sufficient to count as a new paternalism is a subject for debate.

Paternalism and free market forces had co-existed all along. Old assumptions about community and reciprocity, sometimes overstated by historians' use of the term 'paternalism', were perhaps undermined less by the rise of industry (for factories were highly organised and their owners sometimes showed much involvement in workers' lives) than by unemployment in the countryside: total annual expenditure on poor relief in England and Wales rose from just over £2 million in 1783–5 to a peak of £7.87 million in 1818 before being pared away by Whig reforms to about £4 million in the later 1830s. The rural population boom had produced a workforce often too large for the rural economy to sustain in full employment. Wages were eroded; poor relief had to take up the slack. Landowners blamed the labourers; the labourers blamed the landowners, but often also the clergy. Apart from a long-standing drain to London from neighbouring counties, not until after the arrival of the railway did unskilled rural labour become much more mobile, the rural population decline, and the problem of rural poverty shrink. It was not solved.

'Paternalism' partly overlaps with another ill-defined concept, 'patriarchalism', used as a shorthand for hierarchical and male-dominated political ideas. There has been much debate on the ways in which 'patriarchalism' survived from the seventeenth century into the eighteenth. Yet if 'patriarchalism' is a synonym for collectivism rather than for divine right, then, however dominant the assumptions of individualism were in the early nineteenth century, the ideals of collectivism or corporatism survived, too, and found new and powerful expression after 1900 in socialism. Patriarchalism in the political sense of the doctrines peculiar to the political theorist Sir Robert Filmer (1588–1653) was not prominent after 1688, but patriarchalism in the social sense of the doctrines (more numerous and more important in practice) that Filmer and Locke shared was lastingly influential, namely the origins of the state in the family and the rootedness of the social hierarchy in natural law: as Locke expressed it, the ascendancy of gentlemen over plebeians, masters over servants, husbands over wives.

'Patriarchalism' is too fashionable a concept. Much recent writing on gender relations assumes that a social anthropological 'patriarchal model' of the family characterised the seventeenth century but was dismantled by social change in the eighteenth. This draws on an older model of the 'extended' peasant family, holding land in 'impartible inheritance' by collective family ownership, a model once beloved of European sociologists and social anthropologists and held by them to characterise a 'peasant society'. Yet it has now been shown by Alan Macfarlane and others that this pattern was absent in England even in c. 1200. That classic text, Filmer's *Patriarcha* (a defence of the divine right of kings written in c. 1630), had nothing to say about gender relations in his own day. Patriarchalism as a social formation is a construction of recent feminism. As argued in the previous section, gender relations in the long eighteenth century displayed a range of patterns from independence to dominance, centred on a norm taught by the conduct books: companionate marriage, mutual deference, ultimate male legal authority, offset against some legal defences for women. John Locke's *Two Treatises of Government* (1690) was widely regarded as having refuted Filmer, but had no measurable impact on gender relations. Indeed, the bachelor Locke there clearly set out that what a wife owed her husband was 'subjection'.

Reformers seldom protested. From the 1820s, radicalism had much to say about landlords, taxes, debt, governmental corruption and the baneful effect of the established Church; but it had almost nothing to say about gender relations. Radicalism failed to make common cause with the small number of women who followed the path of Mary Wollstonecraft. As a result, the reform movements of the 1820s and 1830s had almost no impact on the position of women. James Mill's *Essay on Government* (1821) ruled out women's franchise on the grounds that their interest was 'included in' that of their parents or husbands. In the eighteenth century, a few women burgage owners could vote in parliamentary elections; this right was terminated by the Whigs' 1832 Reform Act.

Some historians have argued that the period *c.* 1780–1830 saw the emergence of a Victorian 'domestic ideology' that divided women and men into 'separate spheres', confining women to home and family. This trend is variously linked to an Industrial Revolution, the birth of class and evangelicalism. Against this view it has been urged that conduct books and religious teaching had described such a sexual division of labour from at least the Reformation. This teaching hardly changed over time, while other things did change: a growing expectation of women's roles in moral reform, a growing demand that men temper their aggression and pride by good manners and 'politeness'. But it seems likely that these ideals made a practical difference for only a few with leisure and money to act on them: for the majority, the growing necessities of daily life confined them to ancient roles, and ancient responses.

The debate over the 'open society' largely depends on what is being argued against. It has been claimed that the 'ancien regime' model is static, and unable to account for undoubted change in such areas as urban growth and the 'rise of the middle class'. Yet it is not clear that stasis has ever been argued for by the model's proponents. Change was constant, even in earlier centuries, but incremental. What is open to doubt is whether any such changes can be labelled 'forward looking' or 'progressive': the future was to change too much for there to be one set of unmoved goalposts that Locke, Defoe, Hume, Smith, Fox or Shelley all tried to reach. Nor did the English rhetoric of progress fit Scotland, Ireland or Wales nearly as well. They remained much less urbanised; more swayed by great landowners; their hinterlands far less penetrated by urban culture, than England. Scotland was more dominated by Edinburgh, Ireland even more dominated by Dublin, than England was by London. Even the late growth of Glasgow and Belfast did not turn Scotland and Ireland into devolved societies. Wales, meanwhile, was even more lacking in substantial towns until the early nineteenth century. Both the 'open' and the 'closed' models often treat social relations as being of one kind or the other, but basically unproblematic. We should, rather, see social relations as endlessly contested.

The Wealth of Nations: the Economy

The keynote of the pre-industrial, commercial economy, according to Defoe in 1724, was change:

> The Fate of Things . . . plants and supplants Families, raises and sinks Towns, removes Manufactures, and Trade; Great Towns decay, and small Towns rise; new Towns, new Palaces, new Seats are Built every Day; great Rivers and good Harbours dry up, and grow useless; again, new Ports are open'd, Brooks are made Rivers, small Rivers, navigable Ports and Harbours are made where none were before, and the like.

There was always something new: 'new Trades are every Day erected, new Projects enterpriz'd, new Designs laid'; England was 'a trading, improving Nation'. But all this he ascribed to the 'Fate of Things': observers did not yet identify an economic dynamic of progress. Constant change and adaptation did not entail the arrival of any single new model of economy or society. Adam Smith's *An Inquiry into the Nature and Causes of the Wealth of Nations* (1776) did not mention 'capitalism' explicitly or implicitly, and attached no overriding importance to manufactures; Smith's dynamic of growth was the division of labour, the specialisation of function that had already developed within an advanced commercial economy.

More obvious than any economic dynamic were prosperity's pre-conditions: political stability, the avoidance of civil war and revolution, the development of a sophisticated financial system, the absence of inflation, the rule of law and the security of property. Adam Smith could take for granted 'the sacred rights of private property'; he did not elaborate. In 1660 the economy of the British Isles reflected the long-term

consequences of the efficient monetisation of English society under the
Anglo-Saxon monarchs: trade and the monetary expression of
economic relationships had already progressed over many centuries to
produce a sophisticated English economy with the specialisation of
function that Smith was to point to as the key to maximising
productivity. Behind the political disunity of the archipelago lay the
economic introversion of parts of Wales, of Ireland and of Scotland, a
self-sufficiency that left much scope for growth within an economy
that evolved, rather than being transformed in kind, as economic
integration progressed. The Union of 1707 removed tariff barriers and
made England, Wales and Scotland the largest internal free-trade zone
in Europe. Political tension and economic rivalry prevented the
extension of this principle to Ireland, with profound consequences:
where the English and Scottish economies broadly converged in the
long eighteenth century, the British and Irish economies did not.

Yet they might have done so. In 1660, much of the British Isles
already displayed diversity of employment and geographical mobility.
The integration of landed and urban-professional elites dated in
England from the fifteenth century, as a result of their sitting together
in the lower House of the Westminster Parliament. This meant that, as
the trading sector developed after 1660, a sense of antagonism between
land and trade did not become entrenched. Such a sense there was,
strengthened by high taxes to fund the wars of the 1690s; but it tended
to weaken over time, partly thanks to Sir Robert Walpole's anxiety
over the landed interest. Not until the agricultural boom of the
Napoleonic Wars (1803–15), postwar protection and the economic
analysis of the political economist David Ricardo in and after the 1810s
was the idea widely persuasive that society was divided by the
operation of the economy into blocs, each of which had an inherent
interest antithetical to another bloc. Even then, the sense of
antagonism was temporary: the abolition of agricultural protection
with the repeal of the Corn Laws in 1846 tended to restore the deeply
etched symbiosis of land and trade, with important consequences for
politics thereafter.

Everything still depended on the surpluses produced by farmers.
Adam Smith, in 1776, reviewing 'the manufactures of Leeds, Halifax,
Sheffield, Birmingham and Wolverhampton', concluded: 'Such manufactures are the offspring of agriculture.' Even England's relatively
commercial economy was built on farming. In 1688 the workforce was

divided about 60/40 between agriculture and commerce; it took until 1800 to reverse this balance. By the time of the 1851 census, agriculture was still the largest single employer of labour. England's neighbours were even more weighted towards agriculture. Farming in the British Isles was also diverse, ranging from England's 'chalk and cheese', the productive arable and grasslands from the south and midlands, to the Scottish Lowlands, but petering out in the undeveloped Highlands, and confronting the less advanced farming practices of much of Ireland. This diversity did not diminish; indeed, the productivity gap between innovative agricultural regions and backward areas may have widened. What was unusual in Europe was that there was no productivity gap between English agriculture and English manufactures.

The ubiquity of trade is striking: of the 5,034 men who sat in the House of Commons between 1734 and 1832, 897 were associated in some way with business, rising from 1 in 9 in 1734–61 to 1 in 4 in 1818–32. Yet of these most were financiers, merchants or lawyers; only some 29 were manufacturers, 20 of whom entered the House after 1800. Of all 'interests' in the Commons the dominant one was land. Reflecting this cultural dominance, a landed qualification was required of MPs. An Act of 1710 set the requirement for a county seat at a landed estate worth £600 per annum, and £300 for a borough seat (although this hurdle added to a sense of social difference between land and trade, there were occasional attempts to raise it). Swift expressed a lasting ideal of the 'country party' when he wrote in 1721: 'there could not be a truer maxim in our government than this, That the Possessors of the soil are the best judges of what is for the advantage of the kingdom'. Only in 1838 was this qualification expanded to include non-landed forms of wealth. Yet this requirement, initially expressing a rivalry between land and trade, contributed in the longer term to the tendency for successful traders to buy landed estates: symbiosis rather than conflict was the general pattern.

Britain's mixed economy grew steadily, moving away from its medieval focus on a particular sector, the export of woollen cloth. Its pattern was of productivity gains across the board, in agriculture, commerce and extractive industries; these gradually led to the rise of manufactures, although manufacturing was not dominant even by 1832. Commerce rather than manufactures was the key. Centuries of monetary exchange and social mobility had already produced a specialised, trading, financially advanced economy able to support much higher public expenditure than its continental rivals; it used this power in war to build up trade, which grew considerably in this period.

England's commercial prosperity was widely celebrated from the early eighteenth century. But poverty is relative, and Defoe's praise of England's wealth may also be interpreted as Whig propaganda. In the 1790s, the artist James Gillray created images satirising English discontent amid plenty contrasted with French Jacobin self-congratulation in the midst of want; these images too need to be interpreted. Although some historians have emphasised England's growing prosperity in the eighteenth century, this wealth tended to be concentrated in few hands. By present-day (and even by eighteenth-century) standards, 'the poor' were everywhere. There is another, unrelated, debate among historians over whether an 'Industrial Revolution' at the end of the century raised or lowered the standard of living of the workers caught up in it. It is a question too simply framed to yield an answer that will fit the widely varied life experiences of workers in a diverse economy: some gained, some lost; measuring from the top of a boom to the bottom of a slump gives a pessimistic answer, while measuring from a slump to a boom seems to show a strong growth in real wages.

The debate on living standards is fraught because it is still linked with another preoccupation of historians, the alleged triumph of 'capitalism' (by which they normally mean 'factory manufacturing'). Yet even if this concept is valid (all economic systems employ 'capital', not just privately owned, free-market ones), an economy dominated by fixed capital in manufactures was not in place before 1832. 'Industry' then meant the virtue of industriousness, not manufacturing. The earlier economy was preoccupied by 'trade' and working capital (credit), not the fixed capital (factories, machines) implied by 'capitalism'.

What, then, made for success in commerce? The security of private property, restored in 1660 after the lawlessness of rebellion, made possible the further development of a monetised economy, with price stability, sophisticated means of exchange and credit, mobility of labour and increasingly efficient transport. Historians also debate whether an important element was a code of labour law that favoured the employer and facilitated capital formation at the expense of wages. Yet this may be a misconception: the Combination Acts of 1799 and 1800 did not upset the joint regulation of prices in unionised trades like framework knitting, but only penalised 'industrial action' to achieve such ends. Those Acts sought to preserve older practices of mediation and conciliation, the setting of wages and prices by magistrates; for that reason, they were repealed in 1824. Even after that date, it was the 'trades', like bricklayers, carpenters and shoemakers, that pioneered the development of unions, not workers in large factories: hence the term *trades union*, not *working class union*.

Beneath this legal umbrella, industries changed and grew as technological advances were linked to production for a broadening market. This became true of commodity after commodity. Beer was once brewed in the household; increasingly it was produced in industrial breweries. Textiles, glass, salt and soap moved from small-scale to large-scale production. But the site of production, except in naval dockyards, brewing and a few other sectors, was still normally the craft workshop. This meant that, although manufacturing increased, its overall share of the growing English economy was for a long time stable. What grew most was trade.

Overseas trade, in particular, supported a larger and larger fraction of England's non-agricultural population. As Lord Haversham reminded the House of Lords as early as 1707, 'Your Fleet, and your Trade, have so near a relation, and such mutual influence upon each other, they cannot well be separated: your trade is the mother and nurse of your seamen; your seamen are the life of your fleet, and your fleet is the security and protection of your trade, and both together are the wealth, strength, security and glory of Britain.' Over time, this symbiosis strengthened still further, and export trade produced a host of connections with domestic demand and technology. How significant exports were in the overall growth of GNP is, however, still debated. Overseas trade grew, although not as much as eighteenth-century political rhetoric suggests: from 1700 to 1850 exports increased from 8 to 19 per cent of GNP. Yet there was no steady forward march: exports rose and fell, only moving ahead to about 15 per cent in *c.* 1780–1800. The next decisive shift, to about 30 per cent, did not come until 1870–1914. The home market was all-important. There is little room for the argument that 'imperialism', by grabbing overseas markets, was the main engine of growth, or that 'proto-industrialisation', by creating capitalism before the arrival of the word, fulfilled that role. The fashionable demonology of the sources of economic growth is largely mythical. Those sources were mostly domestic and prosaic.

Historians now attend more to the preconditions of economic growth than to what used to be celebrated as its specific triggers; and many of these preconditions were outside of economics: political, legal and financial stability, sustainable demography and, of course, survival in war. Whether war was good or bad for the British economy has been disputed. Some have pointed to the often larger share of military expenditure than of civilian capital formation in GNP; to the periodic disruptions to trade and to domestic demand; to the diversion of resources away from consumption and capital formation; and to the cycles of boom and slump that war caused. Others have argued that war promoted technological innovation and stimulated certain areas of manufacture; that it took up slack in the economy rather than producing a diversion of manpower from productive employment; and that capital diversion took place chiefly away from house building rather than from capital investment in manufacturing or transport. This debate is not yet decided, partly because war had different impacts on different sectors of the economy; partly because different wars had different impacts; and partly because the alternatives (defeats in war and their disastrous economic consequences) are seldom made part of the calculation.

To imagine a long eighteenth century without war is to imagine a utopia that could never have existed. Wars could be expected; but more adverse outcomes to Britain's wars than actually occurred were perfectly feasible. Victory in war, or at least a draw, was a precondition of prosperity less because war per se was an economic stimulus than because the devastation, disruption and death that went with military defeat were definitely adverse to growth. Nevertheless, there is much evidence that Britain's wars, especially from 1776 to 1815, produced a diversion of capital and manpower away from production. The real acceleration in growth rates came in and after the 1820s, as Britain began to recover. And if the wars of 1793–1815 hindered economic growth, was the same true of others of the wars that followed the Revolution of 1688? Work on this question has only begun.

An 'Industrial Revolution'?

The 'Industrial Revolution' is one of those subjects (like 'the Enlightenment', examined below) that have been encased in historians' rhetoric. It is conventionally not just described but celebrated as a 'moment' of mankind's 'emancipation', both from poverty and from the social relations held to stem from poverty. It is depicted as an integrated process that brought transformations in manufactures, transport and agriculture. Technological change now allegedly set mankind on the road to vastly higher Gross National Products, and initiated the 'modern world'. Yet historians need to be more cautious about the idea of a turning point. For good reasons, 'The Industrial Revolution' was a concept unknown in the eighteenth century; it was a term of historical art popularised in English usage only from the 1880s. It evidently originated in France: where France had its political revolution in 1789, Britain was said to have had its economic one, equally sudden. Even then it was not quickly taken into English discourse (one might have expected a quick adoption, had it matched widespread domestic perceptions). Arnold Toynbee (1852–83), a leading agent in its naturalisation, intended the idea of a fundamental divide produced by industrialisation to prove the need for moral and spiritual regeneration. But others from the late nineteenth century took the idea in another direction, launching the movement that we now look back on as 'modernism'; by an 'Industrial Revolution' they meant an assertion of the priority of material considerations in human affairs and of supply-side issues in the economy.

The term was intended to privilege the idea that there was an essential transition between the pre-modern and the modern; it pointed to industrialisation (specifically, to technology-driven manufactures) as the motor of that transition. Yet even if production determines everything (which is questionable) an economy built around manufacturing industry, with coal and steel at its heart, and producing the great industrial conurbations in which most of the population spent their lives, was not mature until about the 1880s – not coincidentally the period when the term '*Industrial* Revolution' was popularised. The rate of growth of England's GNP was also substantially lower in the eighteenth century than it was to be in many continental economies that industrialised in the late nineteenth (when the idea of an 'Industrial *Revolution*' began to look plausible). In the eighteenth century, evolution, not revolution, was the key.

Until about the 1980s, available statistics of economic output seemed to bear out the idea of a sharp discontinuity and a major acceleration in the annual growth of GNP. Since then, economic

Proto-industrialisation. This image records the art of stocking framework knitting. Before the rise of factories, the artisan workshop was often, to some degree, dependent on machinery. Historians debate how much of a difference 'industrialisation' made, and when the major changes occurred.

historians have argued over these figures, intensely difficult as they are to reconstruct for past ages. In general, the recent school of 'econometric' historians (those who apply sophisticated statistical modelling techniques to the data) has steadily scaled down the rate of acceleration of GNP to the point where a clear change of gear is now hard to detect. The English, then the British, economy certainly grew in the eighteenth century, but its growth had been somewhat greater in earlier centuries, and was less in the late eighteenth and early nineteenth, than was recently believed. If economic growth in England as a whole was slower than was once thought, of much older origin, and more protracted, however, this model of gradual evolution hardly applies to Clydeside, Belfast or the valleys of South Wales: there, industrial growth was indeed sudden and fraught, with larger consequences for the host society. Industrial development was highly localised in England also, but England's larger population, and the wide extent of trade and pre-factory manufacture, cushioned and averaged the effects.

No single model of industrialisation fits all four cases. Yet the old historiography advanced just such a single model and a single chronology. It depicted a 'take-off into self-sustained growth' in about the 1780s. Since the 1980s, this model has been largely discarded by economic historians. It tended to single out and celebrate central causes of economic growth (steam engines, transport, technological innovation, capital formation); economic history increasingly records that, when quantified, none of these 'usual suspects' can be shown to have made more than a modest contribution to the twelvefold increase in real income per head of the population in Britain from c. 1780 to the present. Nevertheless, assertions of the transforming and unprecedented effect of industrialisation have proved remarkably durable in the pages of other historians because of the survival of the polemical purposes that the term 'Industrial Revolution' originally promoted. Economic change was, of course, continual. But against the traditional thesis of an essential discontinuity must be set evidence for change being evolutionary rather than revolutionary; for important changes in many areas of economic life, not just manufactures; for more important changes at much earlier periods, notably the introduction of arable farming and the widespread use of coinage; and for economic change preceding the traditional period of c. 1780–1830, notably in the century after 1660. The major quantifiable change was a tripling of population in 1660–1830, but the life experiences of the new millions changed less.

Nor are there just two sorts of society, 'pre-industrial' and 'industrial': many models are found, mixing sectors in different proportions and with different effects. As to an industrial revolution being produced by technological innovation, this has to be measured by productivity growth; and over the eighteenth century, it has been argued that, for England at least, productivity growth was as great in agriculture as in manufactures. Nor was change all one way, for the prosperity of sectors fluctuated: as the iron and steel centre of Sheffield boomed, the iron industry of the Sussex Weald declined; growth in the textile trades of the West Riding of Yorkshire was partly at the cost of decline in the woollen trades of the west of England.

Some have argued that the phenomenal growth in cotton manufacture at the end of the eighteenth century acted to draw other sectors like transport and machine tools into industrialisation, but the links are debatable. Others contend that a series of changes over a long period produced a 'critical mass', so that no single sector was responsible; but this analysis still depends on there being a single thing, an integrated Industrial Revolution, to explain. It seems, rather, that 'industrialisation' as a logic that would link and propel the whole economy was a later concept that does not fully capture the diversity of what happened in the eighteenth century.

The preconditions of late eighteenth-century economic growth now seem more important compared with any later dynamic, and we often find these preconditions in much earlier periods. Yet historians still disagree over more immediate causes of economic change in Britain. Some see the country as the first industrial nation, writing a narrative of the growth of an economy in which technological innovation, or consumption, triggered higher production. Others stress that Britain was already an advanced commercial economy with a highly developed financial system, high labour mobility and specialisation of function; that Britain developed from the seventeenth century an important imperial trading dimension; and that before the nineteenth century this broadly based trading economy still generated much more wealth than the small sectors based on factory production. This debate has often been framed as a choice between two alternatives, since it is phrased as a misleading question: what caused the Industrial Revolution? Once we cease to look for a sudden discontinuity, a *revolution* created by manufacturing *industry*, we can ask how these two economies gradually promoted each other.

If technological change, consumer demand, improvements in transport and the development of domestic and overseas trade were preconditions of faster growth, they were all present before *c.* 1750 without producing a sharp upturn in productivity. It is still a question whether expanding population thereafter provided both a growing market and a growing labour supply, or whether, by outstripping production, it threatened the continuation of the very growth with which the idea of a unitary 'Industrial Revolution' associates it.

Population growth, which was undoubted, has been enlisted by some historians to prove the reality of an Industrial Revolution by taking population growth as the cause of increased domestic demand, fuelling industrialisation by a novel thirst for consumer goods. By this means a 'consumer revolution', held to be evidence of a new *mentalité*, is therefore linked to the old scenario and made to function as a marker of a transition to an 'industrial society' more widely understood. But this argument is undermined if population growth was an extraneous variable (as it clearly was in Ireland and probably elsewhere too), and if rates of growth of productivity were similar across a mobile economy, not concentrated in an industrial leading sector. It is more likely that the 'optimistic' view of the standard of living question has been appropriated by those who wish to rescue the old account of an Industrial Revolution as social and economic *transformation*. But the new school is built on false economics. If all else in a society remains the same (notably per capita savings; and this was probably the case, since most of the population in the eighteenth century was too poor to spend much out of savings) then people cannot improve their standard of living by autonomously consuming more, any more than individuals can lift themselves off the floor by pulling on their shoelaces. All else did not, of course, remain the same (overseas trade and the inputs of factors of production grew); but it is doubtful whether such changes were enough to *transform* the economy as a whole.

An important reason why contemporaries did not see a decisive discontinuity is that there was no overall breakthrough in productivity. This grew at a similar rate across the eighteenth and nineteenth centuries with a partial exception in the mid-nineteenth, although some sectors clearly transformed their positions. Overall productivity growth in England, Wales and Scotland never reached 1.5 per cent per annum in these years, and was probably significantly less in Ireland. Between *c.* 1700 and 1851, a fairly constant 60 per cent of British economic growth was due to greater inputs of land, labour and capital, about 40 per cent to the improved productivity of these factors of production: productivity growth accelerated in the early nineteenth century, but not enough to transform this picture. Much was happening in the British economy as a whole, but none of these things was an essential prerequisite for economic transformation.

Contemporaries, especially from the early nineteenth century, praised the shipping, commercial prosperity, towns and manufactures, but few before 1832 argued that these things had produced a fundamental social change. Their localised impact was one thing; their overall effect on the economy another. No one hailed the arrival of 'modernity': no such concept yet existed, and 'improvement' fell far short of that idea. Even those who might be expected to understand their own day best, the political economists, had no sense that ancient constraints had been escaped, and that an era of exponential growth was beginning that would transform human lives: Adam Smith (1723–90), Thomas Malthus (1766–1834) and David Ricardo (1772–1823) had no such expectation. Most political economists, on the contrary, were preoccupied by the limits to economic growth, and sought to discern when and why a stationary state would be reached. Consequently, they lacked any generalised optimism about the human condition. Even into the 1870s, standard economics textbooks identified the finite nature of land as the final limitation on economic advance.

Some acceleration in the rate of growth of GNP and of real income per capita undoubtedly occurred. Recent quantitative economic history has merely proposed that this acceleration was less than we once thought; that it happened later than we once thought; and that mid-nineteenth-century growth rates look fast chiefly by contrast with a modest eighteenth-century starting point. Other historians have concluded that the term 'revolution' now looks implausible, and that 'evolution' is the more appropriate. Few still insist that the new figures, by delivering substantial growth over a century and a half, disclose a 'fundamental change'; but the key term here is 'fundamental'. The debate therefore goes beyond the questions 'how many is a lot?' and 'how rapid is fast?'. What is ultimately at issue in these debates is whether 'being determines consciousness', and on this philosophical (and ultimately religious) question no ultimate agreement is likely. All that can be said is that everything changes, but normally so slowly that almost everything seems for most people to remain much the same.

Class: the Changing Nature of Social Images

Did 'the Industrial Revolution' create class? We need first to set this question in a longer perspective. The ways in which people pictured the identity of groups in society, and relations between them, changed greatly over time. In 1660 the leading categories were national and religious: the Scots, Irish, Welsh and English were all keenly aware of themselves as such, and aware too of their denominational identities. Other things mattered much less, although Scotland saw a continuing cultural divide between Highland and Lowland society that was only partly denominational. Some craft-based occupations, like stone-masons and shoemakers, had developed a sense of solidarity, but this was specific to each trade and was not generalised to create a 'working class'. The social elite was aware of its group identity but traced this to 'gentility' or 'honour', not to its location within the means of production.

The term 'class' still meant 'group', not 'stratum'. It derived from the Latin 'classis', used also within early seventeenth-century Puritanism to mean a group meeting to worship separately from the established Church. The same usage continued in eighteenth-century Methodism. Since it echoed the Calvinist idea of a 'gathered church' of the 'elect', predestined to salvation, it resisted being generalised to mean a whole social category, universally possessing an identity by virtue of some economic location. Although gradations of wealth from rich to poor were obvious over many centuries, and poverty for the many still a grinding reality, this had not generated a picture of society in terms of strata. Since historians still try to find earlier origins for Marxist social class, it creates confusion that the word 'class' was common in eighteenth-century usage. We must instead work backwards from the idea that 'class' (in the sense of an identity created by the mechanism of production and exchange) was a new ideology in the early nineteenth century, not a natural reflex to changing economic relations.

A key component of an adequate history of class would be a comparison between the different track records of the idea in England, Scotland, Ireland and Wales (and even within those geographically diverse areas); yet such work has not yet been attempted, in part because many aspects of the social history of England's neighbours are still overshadowed by an older and essentially English debate about conditions in industrial England. In Scots historiography, this English Marxist tradition is modified chiefly by crediting a Scots 'working-class movement' with nationalist desires to create a Scottish republic, a movement, visible or 'underground', presumed to last from the 1790s into at least the 1820s. Such theories await scrutiny from less committed researchers. It is at present equally plausible that the ultimate outcome, 'Red Clydeside' or the cultures of the Ulster shipyards and the Welsh valleys, represented specifically Scots, Irish or Welsh phenomena more than local examples of developments more clearly and classically found in England. We do not know.

We can, however, show that before the arrival of this new language the social order had long been diverse: there were large numbers of people in England, especially in the more commercial south, with middling incomes and properties. This was less true in the north of England, and less true again in Scotland, Ireland and Wales, where social divides were starker. Yet it was not in the Welsh valleys or on Clydeside, but in early nineteenth-century England, that the idea of class was coined. In other words, neither poverty, nor inequality, nor the conflict of rich and poor, of themselves created class. Class was an ideology, not an objective response to circumstances.

This argument is not widely accepted, and most historians still write the history of eighteenth-century class relations as prefiguring the forms taken in the nineteenth century. Those inspired by E. P. Thompson's *The Making of the English Working Class* (1963) sometimes tried to spot other classes being formed in other periods. The years *c.* 1660–1730 have been proposed, variously, as the birthplace of the middle class and the site of the 'making of the English ruling class', but both arguments are open to doubt. People in middle conditions of wealth had long existed without giving rise to the ideology of class identity that was novel in the early nineteenth century; the English elite were conscious of their separate status for many centuries earlier still, without generating a class analysis either among themselves or among their opponents. Even Thomas Paine, hostile as he was to the England of his day, did not invent 'class'.

This theme of early class formation continually recurs in the works of some writers, where it performs a variety of present-day tasks. Some wish to hasten the arrival of a well-defined but unattractive middle class in order more easily to argue for the emergence of that more diffuse phenomenon, a working class. Others reverse the values and wish to depict a burgeoning but more appealing middle class as a sensible, pragmatic social constituency whose expansion refutes a stress either on the emergence of a militant working class or on the long survival of the power of the old elite, the nobility and gentry. Scholarship on this question is inconclusive not least since the purposes of too many participants in the debate are still overtly polemical.

Crowd action, riots and conflict in the workplace have sometimes been used as keys to class formation: as E. P. Thompson wrote, 'we can read eighteenth-century social history as a succession of confrontations between an innovative market economy and the customary moral economy of the plebs'. 'The people', in this view, appealed to old ideas of paternalist regulation; but the decline in the power of the gentry and the Church, and the rise of the capitalist cash nexus, steadily eroded the 'moral economy'. These protesters eventually cohered in a plebeian, working-class culture, defined against capitalism. Such a scenario appears to be Marxist, but it is worth considering how far it belongs instead to a romantic or nostalgic idealisation of a 'world we have lost'. Yet if there ever was such a world, it was lost in a much earlier era. Alan Macfarlane's research on the origins of English individualism locates it in the centuries after the Norman Conquest, while historians of Anglo-Saxon England have their own stories of the spread of coinage and monetary relations (see Part I above). Labour relations at all times may express greed and resentment on both sides as well as the defence or violation of paternalist decencies. Once we abandon the idea that the emergence of 'class' in an 'Industrial Revolution' is an unchallengeable end point at which history has to arrive, it becomes possible to see paternalism and altruism, profit and selfishness at work at all points on the social spectrum and in all centuries.

Treating 'class' as a descriptive language has not completely solved the problem, since 'class' was indeed an eighteenth-century term, but, confusingly, with a meaning that was part of the existing terminology of 'ranks', 'orders' and 'degrees'. Some historians, not recognising this older meaning, wish to trace a transition in the middle of the eighteenth century from the old terminology to a wholly new language of 'class', but this claim is problematic. Even when the term 'working classes' is first found in England, in 1789, the plural contradicted the idea of a single identity, objectively generated. The singular terms 'working class' and 'middle class' were in occasional usage from the 1790s: they could have represented a quantum leap in attitudes, but there is no evidence that they actually did so. When this leap occurred, class analysis did not derive from social observation or enquiry: even that acute social commentator Henry Mayhew, famously exploring the culture of the London poor in the 1850s, did not use the categories of class. Scotland had equally lacked any sense of class identities and was slower than England to adopt the new language. Sir John Sinclair's careful social survey, *A Statistical Account of Scotland* (1791–7), compiled in the 1780s, still used the language of 'ranks and orders' and 'people of quality'; it was this that created the plural when it described the 'lower classes' and 'higher classes' in Glasgow. The same was true of Ireland. 'Class' in the nineteenth-century sense was the result of a specifically English debate, and it is to England's conflicts and polemics that we must look for answers.

This image of class as social stratum arrived only very late; the ancient realities of rich, middle income and poor had not created it. Nor was class as stratum evidently a metaphor drawn from new developments in geology, associated for example with James Hutton from the 1780s. It came, initially, from political economy in the 1810s. David Ricardo's *Principles of Political Economy and Taxation* (1817) built on Adam Smith to give a clear tripartite division of society, based on function and source of income: landlords (rent), capitalists (profits) and workers (wages). It was an academic analysis of 'factors of production', those ideal types of the economists; it did not attempt to do justice to the complexities of the old economy, with its overlaps between land, extractive industries, manufacture and urban development; its merchants; its domestic industry and small workshops; and its professionals. But it suited a developing social polemic, the radical campaign against the Anglican, landowning elite, and was therefore taken up and used.

Even Ricardo's polemic was not enough to create 'class'. An additional stream, joined to Ricardian economics, was necessary: the polemic mounted by men such as John Wade, a Unitarian, and James Mill, a religious sceptic, against what they depicted as the aristocratic order and the established Church that underpinned it. Into this alleged clash of interests between the old elite and what the Wades and the Mills hailed as a new 'middle class' intruded the issues raised by nascent trades unions and by the developing ideologies of radicalism and socialism, inheritors but novel developers of Thomas Paine's polemic of the 1790s against kings, aristocrats and priests. These polemics now acted to give new meanings to an old vocabulary.

From the mid-1830s the 'middle classes', until now a diverse collection of groups with different interests and aims, came widely to be called 'the middle class' and to be ascribed its own attributes; later in the 1830s the 'working classes', an even more diverse collection, was increasingly termed 'the working class'. The singular term implied a unity of nature and goal, but was not necessarily evidence that such a unity had emerged on the ground. On the contrary, into the nineteenth century the conflicts within these 'classes' were more important than any solidarities: the conflicts between skilled and unskilled workers, between Irish, Scots and English workers, between 'respectable' and 'unrespectable', between affluent professionals and the 'lower middle class'. Meanwhile, land, industry and labour also showed much cooperation, failing to fulfil predictions of a necessary clash of interests, as well as showing the age-old frictions between employers and employees. Class solidarity, in so far as it ever existed, came later, in the cultural uniformities brought by life in the mass urban conglomerations of the late nineteenth century; even then, solidarity was more solid in some areas (like mining districts) than others; more solid in communitarian Wales and Scotland than in individualist England.

The idea of class was invented in the early nineteenth century in the south-east of England, but took root most strongly elsewhere: it was not that industry created class, but rather that class grew up and became persuasive in areas that had been least diversified by commerce, least opened to social and geographical mobility by employment opportunities in a monetised economy, least susceptible to Anglican ideas of a seamless social hierarchy. Historians imbued with mid-twentieth-century ideas of class tended to read them back into the past and see class conflicts everywhere. Yet it is now by no means clear that even the Chartist disturbances of 1838–48 can be categorised as the first working-class movement, let alone Jacobinism in the 1790s or labour unrest after 1815. If a study of the eighteenth century shows that class was not a thing but a doctrine, then the social history of the nineteenth and twentieth needs to be rethought.

2. Religious Cultures

Religious Pluralism as a Source of Armed Conflict

From the Reformation into the 1640s, Europe was devastated by wars of religion. Even short of war, religion remained into the eighteenth century the most potent cause of domestic political and social conflict. Statesmen and clerics were torn between the ideals of truth and peace, and a succession of solutions was proposed to the horrendous conflicts that principled commitment had sanctioned. How to order the relations of Church and State was therefore the most fraught and urgent of practical problems, and historians still debate whether this practical dimension led to the secularisation of British society.

Over several centuries, three main responses to religious diversity were worked out in England. Before the 1660s the dominant ideal was unity: a single Church, rightly ordered, was seen as the appropriate and attainable solution. From the 1660s to the early nineteenth century a system of 'toleration' was developed: a dominant Church was entrenched as the Establishment, committed to guaranteeing freedom of worship for intolerant minorities by not granting them the political power that they were expected to misuse to persecute others. From the 1830s the state's increasing reluctance to endorse any single Church created a third system of pluralism which sought to distance contests over public morality from denominational rivalries. None of these systems was 'modern'; all evolved by political contingency more than design; none was the certain antidote to conflict over ultimate values. Nor were any of them ever consensual: disagreement on whether uniformity might legitimately be imposed preceded 1660 and continued long after the Revolution of 1688. It may be that British society did not become more tolerant; it only became intolerant of different things.

England, Scotland and Ireland dealt with the issue of religious pluralism in different ways; even so, the ideal of a single, national

Church remained powerful in all three into the early nineteenth century. Each polity had a national Church, as did Hanover, of which British monarchs from 1714 were first Electors, then (from 1815 to 1837) kings. Each national Church had different fortunes, but each was underpinned by a sophisticated body of theory (subtly or substantially different). Despite religious Nonconformity (sometimes growing, sometimes shrinking), despite challenges to orthodox theology, and despite sometimes ambiguous support from monarchs (most dramatically James II), large majorities both of the rank and file and of the intelligentsia wished to see a close relationship between Church and State. Despite what historians much later termed 'secularisation' and 'modernisation', this confessional system was eventually upset not by Enlightenment secularism but by Irish Catholicism in 1828-9 (see below). Meanwhile, the ideal of Christian unity was not abandoned; instead, other denominations than one's own were blamed for violating it.

Everywhere denominational structures continued to colour social life. Although Scotland had an historic parliament before 1707, and forty-five MPs in the Westminster Commons after the union, this did little to make Scots life, in a broad sense, democratic: even in 1830, the Scottish electorate totalled only a minuscule 4,500 out of a population of some 2.3 million. Participation in national life (in the currently fashionable phrase, in the 'public sphere') was exercised via religious denominations, primarily the national Church.

The British Isles shared in the Europe-wide problem of religious pluralism, and it was Scotland's 'Bishops' Wars' of 1639 and 1640 that triggered the 'English' civil war. At issue were attempts to take control of Scotland's national Church and steer it in a particular direction; yet war soon brought to prominence in England a sectarian Protestantism that in its extreme forms rejected the validity of the state Church ideal itself and sought instead to create 'gathered churches' of religious zealots. It was the revolutionary potential of this upsurge of religious feeling that made the re-establishment of an episcopal Anglicanism in 1660 so important, but also so unlikely.

Much depended on the monarch's choice. Read closely, Charles II's Declaration of Breda of 4 April 1660, issued just before his restoration, committed him only to 'the Protestant religion', not to the Church of England as such; he also promised an unspecified 'liberty to tender consciences'. The first could be seized on by Presbyterians, the second by all forms of sectary. It seems that Charles's personal preference was for the policy termed 'comprehension', that is, the inclusion of as many as possible within a more loosely defined national Church. In 1660, he offered bishoprics to three moderate Presbyterians, although on the crown's terms: acknowledgement of both the royal supremacy and episcopal Church order. In 1660, the court managed to prevent the still largely Presbyterian Convention Parliament from defining the religious settlement (that task was left to its successor). Yet this body, nicknamed the Cavalier Parliament, expressed commitments that had evolved since the 1640s, under adversity and persecution, in a High Church direction: a greater stress on sacramental religion, on the divine right of episcopacy, and on a formal liturgy. These things were then enforced by a developing legal code that penalised Non-conformity; as with the Elizabethan laws against Catholic recusants, the official case was that the laws were safeguards against political rebellion and not aimed against religious belief as such. Yet even within the public realm, it was clear that what was at issue was not just an internal matter of Church government; this was recognised to be emblematic of a whole social system. To this uneasy 'settlement' there were to be three main challenges.

Challenges to the National Churches: Catholicism

Resurgent Catholicism was a challenge made plausible by its inter-national dimension rather than by the numbers of English Catholics. The Council of Trent, held in 1545–63, had been the Catholic Church's own Reformation; inspired by a renewed vision and backed by armed force, Counter Reformation Catholicism made steady gains across Europe and continued to press forward even after the Peace of Westphalia of 1648 ended the Thirty Years War.

Within England, Catholicism was a minority movement but, with elite support, it stood a good chance of making significant gains among the powerful, if not of converting a deeply Protestant and still more deeply anti-Catholic majority in Scotland, England and Ulster. Elite patronage was the key at local level; at national level, what mattered most was the monarch. Rumours circulated of Charles II's private inclinations, and while he worshipped in the established Church during his life he was received into the Catholic Church on his deathbed. Meanwhile, his subjects debated whether his instincts were for toleration or 'Popery' (most were sure that these two were inconsistent). In December 1662, Charles issued the first Declaration of Indulgence, an attempt to provide for religious toleration by royal prerogative. Conspiracy theorists had free rein, and seemed vindicated when in 1672 the heir presumptive, Charles's brother James, duke of York, ceased to take communion in the Church of England; the next year, his resignation as Lord High Admiral was interpreted as evidence of his conversion to Catholicism, a fact openly acknowledged from 1676.

The political stance of the Catholic gentry was the key to their denomination's fortunes, and here they were severely handicapped by their past: the Gunpowder Plot of 1605 and the Catholic massacre of Protestants in Ireland in 1641 were public relations disasters that made it easy for the anti-Catholic Whigs to depict James II as determined on imposing 'Popery and arbitrary power'. The Church of England responded during the 1680s with a huge outpouring of anti-Catholic theological writing; together with James II's deposition, it ensured that Catholicism was taboo in England and Scotland until the 1820s. In Ireland the Catholics' position was much more adverse: there the Church of Ireland mounted a sustained campaign, seeking to win what it saw as the benighted populace from 'Popery' and 'superstition'. The campaign failed, and the balance of population tilted even further away from the Protestants: about 3:1 at the beginning of the century, it was about 4:1 at the end.

Catholicism's failure in England to escape from its sixteenth-century demonisation was not inevitable; indeed, Catholicism was driven to accept a religious pluralism that anticipated much later ideals. In 1687 James II echoed Charles II's Declaration of Breda of 1660 in a declaration of indulgence: it had been his settled view, James announced, 'that conscience ought not to be constrained, nor people forced in matters of meer religion'. Many churchmen and Dissenters loudly denied his commitment to this principle, and the matter of sincerity became more pressing when the king reissued the declaration in 1688 and ordered the clergy to read it from their pulpits. Was Dissent no longer synonymous with disloyalty? Had James remained on the throne, a clear answer to that question might have been given, but his expulsion in 1688 meant that the situation remained ambiguous, different answers being offered from different points on the spectrum. Many (notably Protestant Dissenters) maintained after 1688 that Catholic Dissenters certainly were, as such, disloyal to the state; many churchmen preserved a lasting suspicion of Protestant Dissent, a fear spectacularly vindicated by the American rebellion of 1776; and into the early nineteenth century the idea that Britain enjoyed a 'Protestant Constitution' experienced a revival. The Revolution of 1688, in this respect, settled little: religious persecution declined in England (though not in New England, Scotland or Ireland), but religious exclusivism changed less. With the removal of the Stuart option in the 1740s, Irish Catholicism was a leaderless force until its politicisation by a brilliant organiser, Daniel O'Connell, in the 1820s. Catholicism's failure in the eighteenth century was dictated by politics; in Ireland at least, it was politics that finally reversed the verdict.

Challenges to the National Churches: Sectarianism

The second challenge to the national Church ideal was posed by the aftermath of civil war sectarianism, from the 1660s expressed in the new shape of separated denominations now termed Dissenters or Nonconformists. The largest of these were the Presbyterians, who generally accepted the idea of a national Church but rejected its governance by a separate order of bishops. Other sects rejected the idea of a national Church itself: the Congregationalists (also called Independents), who held the autonomy and equality of each congregation; the Baptists, who held the necessity of the baptism of conscious believers; and the Quakers, who dispensed with an ordained ministry in favour of the individual's 'inner light'. None of these were otherwordly, looking to the next life rather than to this, though some later became so; all were interpreted by churchmen as zealots and fanatics who had caused the civil war.

In 1660, some English clergy sympathetic to these sectarian positions chose to leave their livings; others were pushed, forced out by popular mass action in parish after parish. An exodus of about a fifth of its clergy is often held to have weakened the Church of England, though this has been debated. How many lay followers left with them? In 1676 Henry Compton, bishop of London, organised a religious census of England that revealed only about 5 per cent of the population to be Protestant Nonconformists. This was encouraging for churchmen; but sympathisers with Dissent, and occasional conformists, would have swelled this percentage. Nonconformity was more important than Compton's figures suggest. Scotland and Ireland were also more divided along denominational lines than England, and their divisions contributed to the new pattern of alignments within the British Isles. Where before 1660 the leading dynamic was a 'three kingdoms' one, after 1660 it increasingly became one of tension between denominations, reinforced in its effects by the different proportions of Catholics, Anglicans and Protestant Dissenters in Ireland, England, Scotland and the American colonies.

Nonconformists themselves differed in their composition and their aims. The English Presbyterians initially sought an accommodation with the establishment that would have allowed them to return to the fold of a national Church: this option was real, and the Presbyterians were lastingly weakened when it was frustrated in 1688–9. Dissenters who openly opposed the state Church ideal had more scope for action, but were drawn into a formulaic and ultimately futile litany of objections to certain English Church practices. Over time, English Nonconformity grew cool and declined in numbers.

English Dissenting sects lacked leadership except a London-based body, the Protestant Dissenting Deputies, launched in 1727, which took as its chief goal the repeal of the Test and Corporation Acts. Here it was unsuccessful; but this preoccupation merely locked Dissenters into a backward-looking legalistic confrontation with the Church, a quarrel in which they were the losers. Increasingly, Dissenting congregations tended to fragment as some ministers adopted Arian or Socinian theologies (demoting Christ from an equal partner in the Trinity to a subordinate figure, and, in the case of Socinianism, a purely human one); from the 1770s some separated from their brethren to worship openly as Unitarians. Only a few Anglicans joined them. It was to be the remaining Dissenters, revitalised in their Calvinism and Trinitarianism, who began to flourish in the new mood of evangelicalism that marked the decades from the 1790s on.

In Scotland, about a third of the clergy left the established Church after the Restoration. Following 1688, this exodus was reversed, for in that kingdom, unlike in England, William III imposed Presbyterianism as the principle of the established Church's government. It was this Church that now organised the persecution of Scots Episcopalians, linked as they were with Jacobitism. Again, persecution worked: although the numbers of Episcopalians and Presbyterians were probably equally balanced in 1688, the expulsion of 664 ministers from Scotland's 926 parishes between 1688 and 1716 meant that episcopalianism was driven into an exclusive association with Jacobitism and suffered the fate of that political option: legislation of 1746 virtually proscribed the Episcopalians, and it remained in force until 1792. Yet Scots Presbyterianism fell into schism again and again. The formation of the Secession Church (1733) and the Relief Church (1761) were only the start. The Secession itself split in 1747 into two groups, and each of these split again around 1800. From the 1790s, 'New Light' evangelicalism added to their expansionary zeal, so that by 1826 about 38 per cent of Scotland's population dissented from the Kirk.

These schisms were inevitably political: in 1733 Ebenezer Erskine, leading a secession group which claimed to be the true national Church, denounced the Act of Union for guaranteeing the continuance of the episcopal Church of England. Nevertheless, the Seceders of 1733 still subscribed to the ideal of a single state Church. The Relief Presbytery, formed in 1761, broke from this consensus to advocate disestablishment, but not until the early nineteenth century did most of the Seceders adopt that principle. From events like the Cambuslang revival of 1742, evangelical fervour was found at least as much within the Kirk as among the Seceders. Consequently, until the 1840s, Dissent was not nearly as disruptive in Scotland as it was in England, Ulster or the American colonies.

In England, the legal position of separated Dissent was deeply ambiguous after 1660. In response to this new challenge, some churchmen advocated toleration; others, comprehension within a Church whose terms of membership had been relaxed; others held that a degree of coercion was legitimate in order to encourage Dissenters to rejoin the Church as then constituted. In 1689 the measure nicknamed the 'Toleration Act' permitted freedom of worship to Trinitarian Protestant Dissenters only, on condition that certain terms were met. This was not the principled charter of religious liberty that Nonconformists had sought: the word 'toleration' appeared neither in the title of the Act nor in its text. Yet they soon hailed it as such a charter, and it acquired a political weight beyond its formal provisions. Ironically, Dissenters were the long-term losers in the system now established. The 'Toleration Act' provided a framework, not a full set of answers: the relations between Church and Dissent varied diocese by diocese and bishop by bishop. Yet, in general, the Dissenters found themselves marginalised by the working of 'the Toleration', since it conceded freedom of worship but continued to deny political power to those deemed to be threats to the state. By the time the Corporation Act (1661) and the Test Acts (1673, 1678) were passed local and national office was formally confined to churchmen. Although there was some non-implementation at local level, public life at national level was almost wholly restricted to genuine or nominal Anglicans until the 1830s.

The Dissenters' experience was generally of persecution before 1688, and sufferance thereafter. Historians have often been reluctant to admit the effectiveness of the established Church, and the contribution of the two policies can be debated; but the net result was that, in the century after 1660, the numbers of Protestant Dissenters in England approximately halved. Catholic numbers held steady where patronised by gentry families, but Protestant Dissent overwhelmingly lacked gentry support and suffered accordingly in a society in which elite backing counted for much. Dissenters were excluded from the universities and from the resources of scholarship; their isolated theologians tended to fall into private heterodoxy; and heterodoxy reduced the size of congregations.

If Dissent had major problems, monarchs remained unreliable allies of the Church of England. In England, High Churchmen (those who loudly defended the Church of England as a branch of the universal Catholic Church rather than as a Protestant denomination) were deeply alarmed by the accession in 1714 of the Elector of Hanover, a Lutheran: some saw him as little better than an Occasional Conformist, qualifying himself for office by a legalistic and insincere reception of Holy Communion. Yet in a legalistic age, this was enough: neither of the first two Georges was eager to imperil his hold on the throne by alienating the Church. Both conformed, and neither gave Protestant Dissent the encouragement for which it hoped.

Before 1760, English Dissent languished. Not so in colonial America, where the balance of denominations (as heavily weighted towards the Dissenters as in England it was towards the Church) produced an explosive situation, ignited when the sects put their seventeenth-century resistance theories into practice in 1776. Everywhere in the wider British polity, religion remained the best predictor of allegiance. In parts of the colonies, the backbone of the republican cause in the Revolution was often provided by the Scotch-Irish, emigrants from Ulster and the adjacent Scottish mainland who still nurtured the Covenanting commitments of the 1640s. In Ireland, it was the Protestant Dissenters again who were the keys to Ireland's attempts to break from London's control. Even in subservient Scotland, it was the evangelical Popular Party in the Kirk who in the 1770s sympathised with the American cause in opposition to the regime of the Moderates, who were in turn enthusiastic unionists in relation to England and eager participants in the patronage system of an imperial state machine. If the American Revolution had some of the character of a war of religion, the whole trajectory of Dissent in eighteenth-century Britain must be reconsidered: if it was a greater threat to the state, the Church's success in defeating it becomes much more important.

The English Nonconformist position was gradually revived after *c*. 1760 by two developments. The first was the rise within their ranks of various forms of theological heterodoxy, especially Arianism and Socinianism; these theological positions were adopted by a galaxy of talented figures including the philosophers Richard Price (1723–91) and Joseph Priestley (1733–1804), issuing in atheism with William Godwin (1756–1836) and James Mill (1773–1836). They finally made common cause with a convert to atheism from High Church Anglicanism, Jeremy Bentham (1748–1832). It was the heterodox Dissenting intelligentsia who framed the novel doctrine of universal manhood suffrage in the 1760s; even Bentham did not accept it until the 1810s. The Deist Major John Cartwright, though a churchman, included universal manhood suffrage, the secret ballot and annual parliaments in his pamphlet *Take Your Choice* (1776), doctrines not yet heard in colonial America but justifying the author in offering a similar rhetorically exaggerated choice between 'liberty' and 'a speedy subjection to arbitrary power' or 'slavery'.

These theological innovations placed a generation of Dissenters in the spotlight of politics, but did not swell their congregations. What increased numbers was the second development, one that pointed in the opposite direction: a revival of evangelical fervour, including Calvinism, from the 1770s, which gathered pace from the 1790s. Even so, it was not the 'pressure from without' of growing Protestant Dissent that forced a legislative dismantling of the confessional state in

1828–9, but the threat of civil war from Irish Catholicism (see below) as it impacted on Westminster politics. Religious change accelerated after *c.* 1790, but this does not mean that fundamental change of the sort later seen had always been immanent in British society since the Revolution of 1688, only waiting its opportunity to emerge.

Challenges to the National Churches: Internal Heterodoxy

The third challenge to the idea of a national Church was the most powerful: that of theological heterodoxy *within* the established Churches of Ireland, Scotland and England. In Ireland this trend was least fully developed and had least impact: the presence of a surrounding majority Catholicism gave little scope for the Church of Ireland to rest its self-image on anything other than a claim to the apostolic succession, the Fathers, the Councils and the creeds of the western Church. Irish churchmen were, in theory if not in liturgical practice, mostly High Churchmen. Heterodox Irishmen like John Toland (1670–1722) were in some peril, and often had to live abroad.

In Scotland the coercive and communal nature of parish church discipline after the restoration of Presbyterianism in 1689 left little room for theological heterodoxy to take root. The execution for heresy of an Edinburgh student, Thomas Aikenhead, in 1697 was an effective warning. Scots theological writing entered an arid age, and the talents of the most able were diverted instead into what became known from the 1960s as the 'Scottish Enlightenment'. Yet this movement had one remarkable characteristic: where similar 'Enlightenments' elsewhere in Europe were associated with anti-clericalism, religious scepticism and even atheism, the Scots literati normally tried to steer clear of religious speculations that might explode in their faces (a partial exception was David Hume, yet even he left his key work, *Dialogues Concerning Natural Religion*, to be published posthumously). They were content to soften the Calvinism of established Presbyterianism and generally did not seek head-on doctrinal confrontations. The established Scottish Church remained relatively united in doctrine, and was to fracture in the nineteenth century over the quite different matter of lay patronage, made non-negotiable by religious literalism. Heterodox

Scots, from David Hume in the 1740s to James Mill in the 1820s, often found it safer to live in England.

In England the scope for heterodoxy was greater. Pre-publication censorship ended in 1695, and opportunities for theological speculation steadily widened. Dissent's threat to the Church of England gradually subsided; the Church was increasingly relaxed and accommodating in tone; it was drawn from a population open to innovation in many areas of life. Curiosity, candour and free enquiry were the passports of many Anglican theologians to private theories that now went far beyond the agenda of the sixteenth-century reformers; indeed, the long eighteenth century may be seen as a Second Reformation. The initial targets of such later reformers were ecclesiastical, in the position of supremacy enjoyed by the re-established Church, and dynastic, as Charles II and James II came under increasing attack for their presumed or actual commitments. In the eighteenth century, and especially after the evaporation of the Jacobite threat in the 1740s, heterodox thinkers, sometimes heterodox Nonconformists but often churchmen, began to take further the implications of their beliefs.

It was from the 1760s that the heterodox generated the new idea of universal suffrage; revitalised natural law theory; explored a critique of their society's assumptions about the claims of ancient institutions or values, and of inherited or inherent rank or worth. With William Godwin in the 1790s this issued in a position now known as anarchism, a rejection of the legitimate role of the state. With others, including Jeremy Bentham, it led in the 1820s to the new ideology of radicalism, a novel combination of David Ricardo's economics, programmatic atheism and universal suffrage. Against successive generations of heterodox thinkers stood a long gallery of orthodox churchmen who sustained a quite different vision of the social order in terms of providential disposition, rank, order and prescription.

Modernity, Secularisation and the Enlightenment

The late seventeenth and early eighteenth centuries have recently come under the historical spotlight as some historians have tried to revive older ideas of secularisation and modernisation (now often questioned) by reasserting a picture of England as 'the first modern society', the home of 'modernity', the birthplace of 'the Enlightenment', an exemplary case of secularisation. Where fifty years ago these assumptions commanded widespread assent in academe, they now need careful scrutiny.

First, 'modernity'. Late seventeenth- and early eighteenth-century Britons often took sides in a literary debate between 'ancients' and 'moderns', but never understood the 'moderns' as being on the side of what we describe with the more recent term 'modernity'. This concept was formulated only in the late nineteenth century, when it meant something unknown in the seventeenth: a positivist, reductionist denial of Christianity and a faith in the natural and social sciences as the new matrices of human perfectibility in this world. Sir Isaac Newton, by contrast, was a churchman and a writer on religion, open to the concept of miracle. John Locke, in *Two Treatises of Government*, failed to depict a watershed between anachronistic and modern doctrines of politics, instead presenting the views of Sir Robert Filmer (1588–1653) as a very present threat. As late as 1769 the Huguenot and Anglican clergyman Louis Dutens, in *An Inquiry into the Origin of the Discoveries attributed to the Moderns*, argued that, in case after scientific case, the ancients had got there first. Just as the Church of England had long appealed to scripture, reason and tradition as its grounds of authority, so in various ways did secular writers; for any of them to make a special claim to reason to validate their positions was a rhetorical device, not a tenable historical analysis. That being so, for historians to draw up teams for their chosen period, some people being held to be for 'modernity', others against it, is one of the larger solecisms.

The nineteenth-century idea of 'modernity' is closely related to another concept, equally problematic. Some historians have celebrated the onset of those complex developments brought together (perhaps wrongly) by the label 'secularisation', but, inconsistently, have seen this phenomenon in many different periods. This ubiquity should arouse suspicion, since if secularisation is characteristic of one period it cannot be so of all. A case was once often made for the late seventeenth century as the crucial divide between an age of faith and an age of reason: worldly, pragmatic, licentious, the restored monarchy was hailed as an era whose secular values acquired an official sanction. The rise of the new science, symbolised by the Royal Society, and of latitudinarianism within the Church of England (the doctrine that no particular form of church organisation was divinely mandated), were depicted as essentially related. From the late seventeenth century a new theological position can be found, Deism, that was to flourish in the eighteenth, and was much later to generate another historians' category, 'the Enlightenment'.

The assumption that the new science of men like the chemist Robert Boyle (1627–91), the physicists Robert Hooke (1635–1703) and Sir Isaac Newton (1642–1727) and the astronomer Sir Edmund Halley (1656–1742) compromised religious faith is central to the scenario of secularisation. But that is not how these men saw it: most natural scientists in Britain (unlike many of their European contemporaries) entertained a fervent religious belief (if sometimes built around heterodox theologies; Newton was an Arian). They saw no contradiction between faith and reason: Newton used reason to show how his cosmos could only be sustained by the intervention at every moment of God, and used his astronomy to clarify the chronology of Old Testament events. The main challenge to religion came not from natural science but from the Deists, men who generally knew little of physics but read the Bible avidly to reveal what they saw as its contradictions or absurdities; they argued that God (often only an abstract idea in their thinking) related to Creation by invariable general laws that precluded 'special providences', miracles, and (by inference) an Atonement exercised in favour of some individuals but not of all.

Historians have sometimes used this scenario of secularisation to explain a change in the behaviour of the masses. It is argued that the conflicts of the seventeenth century discredited zealotry and eroded popular religious commitment. The ability of the Church courts to enforce moral behaviour was in decline; the Toleration Act was used not only by Dissenters but also by the lukewarm or sceptical to avoid hitherto mandatory church attendance. There is some truth to this; but, on the other hand, there is also much evidence of religious zeal and the conflicts it inspired, although denied and suppressed by the elite, as in 1776 in the American colonies or 1780 in London's Gordon riots. Religious zeal, or bigotry, was more entrenched in Scotland, Ireland and Wales, and even more vivid in New England. In England many of the moral functions of the Church courts were taken over, more efficiently, by JPs (who were Anglican gentry and increasingly, at the end of the eighteenth century, Anglican clergy). Much evidence for a powerful mainstream religiosity is now being uncovered, and the

Secularisation? Modernisation and secularisation have often been linked in historical explanation, but have they ignored the evidence for continuing religious allegiance by the great majority of people? This print shows Hackney Church, London, packed for a confirmation service in 1827, and the home of the High Church 'Hackney Phalanx'.

receptiveness of English-speaking populations to revivalism can be interpreted as a manifestation of this mainstream religiosity rather than a disproof of it: from Methodism through to early nineteenth-century evangelicalism, religion was the common coin of mass discourse.

The popular mind of the eighteenth century was shaped less by rationalism than by a growing evangelicalism. This was an international movement, spontaneously manifesting itself in Germany, the North American colonies, Scotland and England at the same times from the 1730s, its followers growing markedly in numbers and influence from the 1790s. An evangelical idiom spanned denominations, from High Church Anglicans like John Wesley in Oxford and London, to Congregationalists like Jonathan Edwards in Massachusetts, itinerant preachers like Howell Harris in Wales and Baptists like Robert Hall in Cambridge. It also spanned theologies, from Arminian beliefs that Christ died for all (again, Wesley) to Calvinist doctrine that He died only for the elect (George Whitefield). This movement ignored parish boundaries, and often denominational boundaries, to reach individuals with a message of both personal sinfulness and the possibility of atoning grace; the 'new birth' demanded of converts was often experienced, sometimes at mass open-air revival meetings like that at Cambuslang, near Glasgow, in 1742.

The most famous practitioner of this new style was John Wesley (1703–91). Why did he have such an impact? One interpretation sees him as essentially counter-cultural, speaking directly to the people, condemning the somnolence of the established Church and appealing to those unmoved by Nonconformity's routine condemnation of establishment. An alternative explanation sees him as a more typical churchman, expressing the strength of that tradition. He profited from his High Church background to flourish within an established Church that was already receptive to his literalistic interpretation of scripture and his Arminian confidence in grace offered to all. By contrast, where an Anglican religiosity was lacking, as in Scotland, Methodism did not take root. Wesley himself insisted that he was not a Dissenter, and only local hostility towards his followers led many of them from the 1760s to apply for licences under the Toleration Act to protect their preachers and places of worship.

Wesley was not alone within the Church of England: its evangelicals reached larger numbers and had more impact by deliberately targeting the social elite. This was the strategy of Selina, dowager countess of Huntingdon (1707–91), who used her wealth to sponsor her own 'connection'. Yet even she resorted to the Toleration Act to shield her followers in 1779, and they formally became a Dissenting Church in 1783 over the issue of unauthorised ordinations. John Wesley began to ordain his own ministers in 1784, although without acknowledging the implications of this act; Methodist independence became a reality after his death in 1791. George Whitefield's followers had tended to become Congregationalists after his death in 1770; in Wales, Howell Harris's followers left the Church in 1811. Their supporters believed themselves to have been expelled from the Church, but the rising tide of Anglican evangelicalism calls this explanation in question.

As yet, the mass movement was evangelicalism within Anglicanism. Wesley carried into his denomination a key principle of the Church of England, the resistance to 'enthusiasm', the pretence of private revelation and private exemption from the moral law ('anti-nomianism') that had caused revolution in the British Isles in the 1640s and did so again in North America in the 1770s. In their English social teaching, Anglicanism and Wesleyan Methodism were essentially in harmony; it has been urged that this partnership was important in the avoidance of revolution after 1789, and again in the turbulent years after 1815. Anglican evangelicals were also reformers, especially prominent in the anti-slavery movement, but their humanitarianism went with support of the government in all other respects: in the 1790s the 'Clapham sect' backed William Pitt, in the 1820s Lord Liverpool.

In Wales, evangelical revivalism stemmed very directly from a nearly ubiquitous Anglican Church and its labours for education, and popular literacy, in Welsh: this early Methodism was no rejection of the established Church, but a development of it. Only much later did Welsh-speaking Calvinistic Methodists and Baptists sweep the board. Wales, which in the seventeenth century had been a stronghold of royalism, became in the nineteenth heavily associated with the Liberal party and in the twentieth with Labour: this reorientation may have had its roots in the Principality's religious history. In Scotland the regime of the 'Moderates', associated with a softened Calvinism and the use of lay patronage to defend the political order, was revitalised during the French Revolution. It was challenged 'from below' less by democracy than by popular protests against the right of private patronage which allowed many landowners to nominate ministers rather than their parishes to elect them. This dispute became central when Thomas Chalmers, a leading Evangelical, became Moderator of the Church of Scotland in 1832, and massive conflict followed the 'Disruption' of 1843, the secession from the Kirk of a third of its ministers, opposed to lay patronage.

Britain's Thirteen Colonies saw a different situation again. If John Wesley stood for social order in England, in America his fellow Methodist George Whitefield, on successive preaching tours, acted as an important catalyst of a new consciousness, spanning denominations and linking very different colonies, that perceived a threat to religious liberty in metropolitan policies and gave a religious, revivalistic fervour to the drive to political mobilisation. In 1776 these colonies collectively experienced a 'new birth', to create a 'redeemer nation'. Historians who debated the question of whether Methodism saved Britain from revolution in the late eighteenth century overlooked the central test of their thesis, that of North America. There, its role in *promoting* revolution is clear.

Secularisation and modernisation run together in the idea of 'the Enlightenment', a term unknown in the eighteenth century, coined in the late nineteenth, popularised only in the late twentieth. From the

1960s the idea was developed as shorthand for values held to be antithetical to Nazism, enjoyed enormous vogue, and still carries heavy normative overtones. Confusingly, like 'class' and 'race', the word can be found in this period, but meant something different: not 'the Enlightenment', a *movement* with members, goals and values, but 'enlightenment', the *intellectual apprehension* of truth. In that sense the latitudinarian Whig Edmund Burke, on the reforming wing of English politics, objected against Richard Price that the seventeenth century 'appears to me to have been quite as much enlightened' as the eighteenth: he mocked the pretensions of 'this enlightened age', as some wished to call it. 'Enlightened' was a familiar adjective, often found in scripture, but not yet reified as 'the Enlightenment'. A vast range of people at all points on the political and social spectrum pursued 'enlightenment' without imagining themselves to be forwarding 'the Enlightenment'; to draw a line around the commitments of only a few of these people and call those goals 'the Enlightenment' is merely normative. It is especially normative to imply, by such a misuse of evidence, that a project of secularisation was at the heart of intellectual activity in this period. The British Isles demonstrated a variety of religious commitments; 'secularisation' is a poor explanation of that diversity. Many people pursued 'enlightenment' in its familiar form, spiritual truth; none invented the term 'the Enlightenment' to describe a social movement built on the premise that religion was an illusion.

Theology as a Model of the Social Order

Every social order is supported by a rationale; at this time it was still profoundly theological. Even so seemingly secular a work as William Blackstone's *Commentaries on the Laws of England* derived the specific content of English law from divine command: 'Upon these two foundations, the law of nature and the law of revelation, depend all human laws'; even the law of nature was 'dictated by God himself'. From these divine commands could be deduced the structure of the State and of the Church, two aspects, as many claimed, of a single body. In defining the position of the Church, the key elements were 'ecclesiology' (the theology that described the essential nature of a church) and 'ecclesiastical polity' (the branch of theology that described a church's proper organisation). Between them, they accounted for a vast printed output.

Throughout the 10,000 parishes of England and Wales, clergy taught obedience to 'the powers that be' as a Christian duty; theologians expounded the legal institutions entailed by such a doctrine. Judges on circuit were greeted with assize sermons that enforced a similar lesson, and from the bench the judges acted on the common law doctrine that Christianity was part of the laws of England. The Lords, the Commons and countless congregations were taught the same lesson on occasion of the state sermons of 30 January (the execution of Charles I), 29 May (the Restoration of Charles II) and 5 November (the Gunpowder Plot). Blasphemy was a common law offence, and was still punished by the civil courts after the Church courts shrank in their role.

In England and Wales, no clergy sat in the House of Commons, but two archbishops and twenty-six bishops sat in the House of Lords. Dissenters could vote in elections and sit in parliament; but although many voted, few stood for election. Of the 2,041 MPs who sat in the House of Commons in 1715–54, only fourteen were Dissenters. This hardly changed: of the 1,964 men in the House in 1754–90, only nineteen were Dissenters. Social leadership was overwhelmingly in the hands of churchmen. To be a member to the political and social elite it was almost essential to be a member of the Church. The elite had, moreover, a powerful set of defences designed to exclude those hostile to it. These defences were successful: the old elite survived, to be eclipsed in the twentieth century by the wealth and numbers of new groups, rather than being destroyed by them as happened in France after 1789.

Debate among historians continues as to the nature of this order. Some maintain that it was 'Erastian', i.e. that the Church was subordinated to the State. Few think it was 'theocratic', with the State dominated by the Church (although this could be argued in the case of Presbyterian Scotland and Congregational New England). A third and more persuasive alternative points to the wide acceptance of the doctrine worked out under Henry VIII in which Church and State were held to be aspects of a single body. This created an extremely durable state form in England, although its status was highly ambiguous, and largely ineffective, as a description of the composite polity created by England's relations with Scotland and Ireland.

Scotland had been a society fractured by religion from the sixteenth century onwards. There the conflict between Episcopalians (who advocated a 'top-down' theory of authority) and Presbyterians (who championed a 'bottom-up' principle) was decided only by outside intervention: Charles II established the former, William III the latter. This did not resolve the conflict: Scotland remained a divided society whose identity was weakened by having at its heart a quasi-theocracy that did not command sufficient support to sustain it, especially from the intelligentsia that developed from the mid-eighteenth century.

After 1688, the established Church in Scotland became and remained Presbyterian. It had no formal presence within the Edinburgh Parliament, and when this was abolished by the union of 1707 the Kirk acquired no formal share in the Anglo-Scots Parliament that met at Westminster. It did, however, exercise a much larger role in local government than did its English counterpart. Where in England Anglican clergy became JPs in larger numbers only after c. 1760, in Scotland the Kirk session was already the core institution of local government. In practical terms, the Scottish Church was strong; theoretically, it produced little to defend its established status, and the Union of 1707 was defended chiefly by the literati who are today identified as part of the Scottish Enlightenment.

Ireland was different again. William III avoided draconian action against Catholics there: he was too concerned about retaining the sympathy of his European Catholic allies in the struggle against France. It was under Queen Anne, when the Revolution was more secure, that most of the 'penal laws' against Irish Catholics were passed by the Dublin Parliament. Yet this code embodied more than mere persecution: it expressed the belief (the mirror image of the Catholic belief) that the opposite denomination could be made to wither away in the face of the progress of divine truth. Until the 1790s, there was much evidence that religious persecution worked in Ireland as everywhere else; it may be debated whether the return of Irish sectarian conflict in the early nineteenth century was the result of the unwisdom of the penal laws, or of their progressive abandonment to secure Irish support in the wars that followed 1776.

With colonial rebellion about to turn into a European war, Lord North's government backed a Catholic Relief Act for England in 1778. It recognised (what was already a fact) Catholic freedom of worship, but now put Catholics on the same footing as Protestants in the ownership and inheritance of land (provided they took an oath to renounce the Stuart claimant, styling himself Charles III, and the papal deposing power: 1745 did not seem as far off as it does to us). That same year, the Dublin Parliament also began the relaxation of the penal code with respect to Catholic landholding. Lord North's main concern was evidently recruiting to the armed forces. The Bill passed the Dublin Parliament only in the face of strong Ascendancy hostility that may have stimulated the growth of the Volunteer movement, an unofficial Protestant militia, and the parliamentary campaign that led to the attainment of Irish legislative independence in 1782. The same year two more Acts in the Dublin Parliament were passed, pushed through by the lord-lieutenant, that effectively extended to Ireland all the concessions in the English Relief Act of 1778. Only in Scotland did a bitter anti-Catholic outburst coerce the London government into abandoning plans for a similar Act.

Ireland's divisions were even greater than England's and Scotland's. First the Church of Ireland (the episcopal sister church of the Church of England), then Ulster Presbyterianism threatened to become the vehicle of a national consciousness. This phase ended with the rebellion triggered by Jacobin aspirations in 1798, for it turned into a war of religion and had the effect of lastingly preventing a united Ireland. It was Roman Catholicism that subsequently became the mould for Irish national identity, not Jacobin secularism.

Race: the Extent of Racialist Ideas in Britain

Ireland's direction after 1798 was not unusual, however, since religion still played a large part in shaping identities throughout the British Isles; and this role was important in explaining the lateness in Britain of the emergence of ideas of racial difference. 'Race' was a commonly used term in Britain in this period, but, like 'class', it signified something very different from its later meaning. 'Race' then meant chiefly 'descent', and could be synonymous with 'family' or with what we would today call 'nationality'. Subsequently, the term 'race' changed to denote certain characteristics allegedly set by inherent genetic disposition. In and before the eighteenth century, this usage was almost unknown.

Since the Church taught that humanity had originated in common parents, Adam and Eve, the word 'race' was normally found in the phrase 'the human race', which implied shared characteristics and was the opposite of nineteenth-century ideas of inherent, indelible group difference. This theory, technically called 'monogenesis', was loudly championed by English anthropologists, ethnologists and theologians, almost all of them churchmen. This was the dominant view within English academe until its opposite, 'polygenesis', arose in the mid-nineteenth century to claim that mankind originated in many, essentially different, stocks.

The intellectual dominance of the Church of England within England itself may therefore have had a major role in ensuring that by the twentieth century England, and perhaps Britain, was less receptive than many continental European societies to the siren strains of racialism. Whether Ireland and Scotland were somewhat more receptive to such doctrines is a question that historians have not been eager to ask, and no research yet addresses that point; it is, however, the case that few of the British thinkers to whom some modern historians point as examples of nineteenth-century racialists were English. Yet these differences were not yet apparent in the eighteenth century. The Scot James Boswell, encountering an African in the north of Scotland, commented only that 'A man is like a bottle, which you may fill with red wine or with white'. English speakers in the long eighteenth century were inclined to ascribe more importance to nurture than to nature, subscribed to ideas of the common origin of humanity, lacked scientific ideas of genetic difference, and were intolerant and aggressive on grounds of religion and culture instead.

3. Political and National Cultures

The political life of this period set up seemingly familiar landmarks, but each is the subject of intense historical debate: an adequate interpretation demands that we understand them as a whole rather than as discrete episodes. In 1660 the English republic failed, and Charles II was restored as a champion of the Church. In 1688 his Catholic brother, James II, was expelled by the invading troops of William of Orange, who became William III; by about 1714, this episode was hailed by the Whigs as 'the Glorious Revolution'. In 1714 a Whig coup installed the Elector of Hanover as George I; in 1776–83 thirteen of Britain's colonies dissented from the libertarian claims of this Hanoverian monarchy so strongly as to trigger a world war to secure independence. Far from collapsing in the face of this major defeat, the British state strengthened and even emerged triumphant after years of war (1793–1802, 1803–15) against revolutionary France. Despite this success, Britain's constitution was challenged and underwent a transformation in 1828–35 the extent of which is still disputed. Moreover, this fast-changing domestic political scene was played out within a European state system that was itself dynamic. Throughout, problems of interpretation are major ones.

The Parameters: Foreign Policy, 1660–1832

Since the 1980s, historians have generally moved beyond the preoccupation with English constitutional development that once saw it as the domestic achievement of the timelessly correct forms of limited monarchy and cabinet government; they now accept parallels and interactions, especially with continental Europe. English, then British, foreign policy in Europe was shaped in this period by four key elements: first, by England's small size vis-à-vis major continental states, this balance slowly changing through the progressive incorporation of Scotland, Ireland and Wales and as a result of population growth; second, by the ingrained Protestantism of England, Wales and Scotland; third, by successive struggles for national survival in the face of far more powerful enemies, chiefly, from 1689 to 1815, France; and fourth, by the long-running contest in Europe for naval supremacy. By comparison with these struggles to survive, it might be argued that any independent drive to overseas expansion was secondary.

In retrospect, the dramatic conflict with France that was to last well over a century was made to seem inevitable, but this was not obvious in 1660. In March 1657 even Cromwell's regime had concluded an alliance with Louis XIV to facilitate war against Spain in Flanders. From the 1670s, it was the Whigs who saw in Catholic France a pressing and immediate threat to England, but it is debatable how real this was: Louis XIV was not Hitler. Louis may have sought to secure more defensible borders, partly at the expense of the United Provinces, but may not have planned the takeover of western Europe and its forcible reconversion, goals with which paranoid anti-Catholics credited him. Not until the expulsion of James II did Louis intervene militarily against England, backing James with an army in Ireland. In this interpretation it was William of Orange more than Louis XIV who was responsible for a century of Anglo-French conflict. But the Whigs were not the consistent men of principle they claimed to be in retrospect. From the 1670s, it was not only Charles II who took French money; Louis bribed the Whig opposition also (including its heroes William, Lord Russell and Algernon Sidney) to prevent them leading England into war with France. How far the Whigs really did perceive a French threat is open to doubt.

In one respect France did come to pose a greater challenge than the United Provinces. So much rhetoric has surrounded the Royal Navy that it is important to remember that it was only one of the major navies of Europe, and seldom enjoyed a dominant position. France's rise as a sea power was, initially, unexpected. In 1660 the English navy was four times the size of the French. But the phenomenal naval building programme undertaken by Jean-Baptiste Colbert, Finance Minister from 1665 to 1683, then meant that France achieved superiority by 1670 and held it until *c.* 1700. It was to be a naval expansion as momentous in its implications as Tirpitz's creation of a major German battle fleet in the years before 1914; yet this was not as quickly grasped. In 1660 the United Provinces seemed England's major problem, and they responded to Colbert with a huge naval expansion of their own. The Commonwealth's commitment to naval power was therefore continued after the Restoration, and the second and third Dutch wars (1665–7, 1672–4) revealed a conscious plan to diminish England's main trading rival. This was not easy. England lacked the overseas trading bases that her rivals had collected, and was slow to make up lost ground. The East India Company did not aspire to the conquest of a continent. It was only from the 1740s that the English and French companies were drawn in to territorial expansion by the decline of the Moghuls: the Indian empire was not planned from London. James II was seriously interested in the reorganisation of England's North American possessions, but this was successfully resisted by colonial Dissenters. Some historians have depicted a sudden reorientation to a crusading Protestant imperialism after 1688, but this is doubtful. War with France in 1689 was not inevitable, and it meant that England's commitments became more continental, not less.

Once France was demonised as the national enemy, it posed a formidable challenge. France had three times England's population and far greater military resources, hardly yet counterbalanced by English (let alone Scots or Irish) wealth. Two main responses to this threat were possible: first, to ally with France and seek to restrain French expansion; second, to seek to assemble a coalition of European states willing to counter French power by war. Whigs claimed their interpretation of French intentions was proved by Louis' annexation of the Spanish Netherlands in 1667. With Spain ruled from 1665 to 1700 by the mentally retarded and childless Carlos II, the future of the Spanish empire would be in doubt on his long-anticipated death. Louis XIV may have long intended to engineer a union of the two powers, creating a powerful Catholic bloc: this threat was to become a reality with the accession to the Spanish throne of the Bourbon Philip V (ruled 1700–46); it was confirmed in the Bourbon Family Compact of 1761, creating a Franco-Spanish alliance that was to have disastrous consequences for Britain after 1776.

Both of these major responses to French power, alliance and confrontation were explored by successive ministries in London. The first option, pursued from the 1670s, was made unpopular by the

Counter Reformation Catholicism of Louis XIV's France and by England's militant Protestantism. The Anglo-French alliance effected by the secret Treaty of Dover (1670) was initially an agreement to wage war against the United Provinces; for this war, a French subsidy secured to the English crown independence from parliamentary finance. Sensationally, Charles secretly promised to declare his conversion to Catholicism 'as soon as the welfare of his kingdom will permit' in return for an increased subsidy and for six thousand French troops to aid in the reconversion of England. Charles never kept this promise, and it is doubtful that he ever intended to do so; he was nothing if not a politician. The second option, military confrontation, was pursued by William of Orange, who seized the English throne primarily to secure English backing in the struggle for survival being waged by the United Provinces against France. French support for the Stuart cause then dictated the same alignment in the Anglo-French war of Queen Anne's reign (1702–14).

Which of these two options was the more perilous may be debated. By 1688 the English navy had not caught up with the French; indeed, the peak of French supremacy at sea came in c. 1695 after a second great building programme that transcended Colbert's. This French navy was a formidable one in large ships, technological excellence and professional skill: the possibility in the 1690s of France's reversing the Revolution of 1688 was real. Had Louis XIV not ordered his fleet to fight at a disadvantage in 1692, leading to the defeat at La Hogue, its numerical superiority by 1693 or 1694 might well have tipped the scales, and made a restoration possible. As it was, Anglo-Dutch naval cooperation was only just sufficient to avert invasion until cooperation on land had a decisive effect in leading France to divert resources away from its navy to its army.

By 1714, the European balance of power had greatly changed. France had been drained of resources by war: its great navy was no more, cut to a quarter of the strength it possessed in 1695. The United Provinces, too, had suffered badly; although they had defended their territorial integrity, their predominance in European shipping was over. It was Britain's navy that emerged as the leader in Europe, not dominant in numbers but the largest and the most consistently resourced.

After 1714, however, the problem became France's steady revival. With a French Bourbon on the Spanish throne, which Anglo-Dutch efforts during the War of the Spanish Succession (1702–14) had failed to prevent, Spain now began to build a navy on Colbert's model. By 1740, France and Spain combined were little short of naval parity with Britain; Britain's naval dominance really only lasted from 1714 to c. 1740. The two stark alternatives in foreign policy therefore persisted. By the time a French alliance was again in place from 1716 to 1730, after the death of Louis XIV, religious animosities had cooled to the point where Sir Robert Walpole, Britain's Prime Minister in 1721–42, gained more from the low land tax that peace secured than he lost by association with a Catholic power. Even so, peace was fragile: during the War of the Polish Succession in 1731–5, Walpole kept the navy in readiness and used diplomatic pressure to deter France from invading the Austrian Netherlands; France, for the moment unwilling to resume war with Britain, complied. Nor was France the only possible enemy in war. British colonial conflicts with Spain, and Spain's intermittent interest in playing the Jacobite card, meant that Spain, with its revived fleet, now became a regular opponent. Such conflicts were tactically dramatic but strategically indecisive: the Royal Navy never succeeded in cutting off Spain's supply of gold and silver from the New World, or in seriously damaging Spain's position in Europe.

As long as France could be persuaded not to back the exiled Stuarts, France and Britain could be at peace. But global rivalry, especially in India and North America, was eventually resumed between Britain and both France and Spain; the Franco-British alliance was dead by 1731, having lasted barely fifteen years. Anglo-Spanish friction over trade, and conflicts between Spanish Florida and British settlers to the north, led to war with Spain in 1739. This eventually tempted Louis XV again to support a Stuart restoration as a way of destabilising the possessions of George II; the result was the French invasion attempt of 1744 and another Anglo-French war. This invasion ended in failure when a storm seriously damaged the French landing craft assembled at Dunkirk, and when Walpole's secret service uncovered the Jacobite plan for a domestic rising to coincide with a French landing. The failure of this serious prospect led Charles Edward Stuart into the quixotic and almost hopeless gamble of his rising in 1745. Landing on the west coast of Scotland with only a handful of men and private financial backing, he nevertheless scored a series of military victories against uninspired government forces and in December 1745 reached Derby, only 127 miles from London. The Hanoverian regime was seriously shaken, and after the duke of Cumberland's decisive victory at the Battle of

Culloden (April 1746) his forces embarked on a campaign of repression designed to crush the ability of the disaffected Highland clans ever to rise in arms again. This might be described as an act of genocide, perhaps an inappropriate term; yet even at the time, Cumberland acquired the nickname 'the Butcher'. Repression worked: Scotland never again rebelled.

Invasion in 1744 would have been sensational, but even the unresourced rising of 1745 served French interests well: the diversion of troops to suppress the rising helped to ensure the French army's victories in Flanders that tipped the military balance against Britain. Whether in India, North America or on continental European battlefields, France was the more successful power after 1714; the image of Britain as an effective, militaristic, expansionist, Protestant power, its triumphalism inspired by the newly composed 'Rule, Britannia!', is far from the reality of draws, reverses and insecurity. After the inconclusive war of 1739–48, France and Spain again pursued significant naval expansion: from 1746 to 1755 the Bourbon powers launched some 250,000 tons of naval shipping against Britain's 90,000, and by 1755 they had once more achieved parity. The Seven Years War began with significant naval reverses for Britain, and the French invasion attempt of 1759 was a genuine threat. This dire situation was suddenly and unexpectedly reversed by a string of British victories in that *annus mirabilis*, 1759, in which British astonishment reflected relief at having succeeded against the odds.

In January 1762 Britain declared war on Spain to pre-empt a Spanish attack. Efficient British expeditions now seized Manila, key to the Philippines, and Havana, key to the Caribbean. At the peace, Spain bought back Havana by the cession of the whole of Florida. Commentators urged that Britain return at least part of Canada, conquered four years earlier, to France as a way of ensuring the allegiance of the British colonists and of justifying a British garrison, but this was not done. The entire eastern seaboard of North America was now in British hands; France, to win support in a future war of revenge, ceded Louisiana to Spain. The failure of the Forty-five, and unprecedented military success in 1756–63, left the Hanoverian dynasty far more securely established and elevated it to be a symbol of national identity. But triumph in 1763 also isolated Britain in a Europe apprehensive of Britain's sudden accession to world power, and would deprive Britain of continental allies when war again broke out.

It has recently been argued by Bruce Lenman that in ceding these territories the French minister Choiseul laid a trap, isolating Britain internationally and setting the scene for future rebellion in North America; if so, Britain took the bait. Triumph in 1763 was short-lived. France and Spain embarked on naval building programmes, consciously aimed at worldwide theatres of war, to which Britain responded too late: by 1770 the balance of naval advantage had swung in favour of the Bourbon powers. From 1770 to 1785 all the major naval powers engaged in the greatest naval building programme seen in the age of sail. Colonial rebellion in 1776 was bad enough, but the war was made unwinnable by the entry on the side of the Thirteen Colonies first of France in 1778, and then of Spain in 1779; by Britain's preemptive declaration of war on the United Provinces in 1780; and by the signing the same year of the League of Armed Neutrality between Russia, Sweden and Denmark, intended to secure their trade with Britain's enemies. British dominance of the Channel was temporarily lost in 1779, and control of the American seaboard became intermittent: in 1781 the navy's failure to displace a superior French fleet led to the army's defeat at Yorktown and the independence of thirteen of the American colonies.

Military defeat in the American war of 1776–83 did not unseat George III, however: Britain's political system, like its financial one, was developing an ability to survive catastrophe that it had lacked during the recent and profoundly destabilising rebellion of 1745. Yet one key problem was not resolved. The naval advantage of the Bourbon powers was reduced, but not eliminated, by the mid-1780s; by 1790 France and Spain had opened up another distinct lead. Britain's survival in a future European war was no foregone conclusion.

The French Revolution accidentally reversed Britain's isolation of 1763. Initially it created an anti-French coalition of absolute princes with which Britain was reluctant to ally; but France's declaration of war on Britain of 1793, after identifying Britain as essentially akin to the princely states of continental Europe, created a host of potential allies and clients. Survival now depended as directly as ever on naval victory. Once more, France and her coerced allies, the United Provinces and Spain, launched more naval tonnage than Britain, but lost far more in ships captured or sunk. Successive naval victories steadily tilted the balance in Britain's favour. In c. 1795–6 France and her allies had an advantage in ships of the line over Britain of about 40 per cent; by 1800 this had returned to approximate parity; after Trafalgar, Britain enjoyed a superiority of about a third. Even so, France and the Netherlands engaged in large building programmes in 1804–8. Napoleon's ambitions at sea were real, and continued after Trafalgar; but his great battle fleet was not ready before his defeat on land in 1814.

The leading theme of British diplomacy up to 1815 was a series of attempts to hold together fragile coalitions to counterbalance the extraordinary dynamism of revolutionary France. In 1815 this strategy finally triumphed; but its victory left Europe dominated by the crowned heads and by a Catholicism increasingly centred on the papacy. This was not what Britain had entered the war to secure, and so into the late nineteenth century Britain tended to side with nationalism, seen as it still was as a liberal phenomenon, in wars of national liberation and unification in Greece (1821), Italy (1859–61) and Germany (1866–71).

The Constitutional Balance

England, Scotland and Ireland were monarchies, but how monarchy was to be understood was already a problem of long standing. One answer was the idea of 'mixed monarchy', already old in English and Scottish history (but not found in Ireland): the idea that the executive could be tamed by notionally dividing sovereignty between various social constituencies or institutions in the state. Historians debate whether this idea triumphed in the revolution of 1688, leading to the eighteenth-century idea of the 'mixed and balanced' constitution whereby authority was supposed to be divided between the sovereign, the Commons and the Lords, its components held in a mechanical system of opposing forces; or whether the idea of mixed monarchy failed in the late seventeenth century, and, by its failure, led to the stronger, more centralised states of the present day with their unified conceptions of sovereignty (notably the USA).

On the side of the second interpretation are the facts that one of the period's thinkers now most acclaimed, John Locke, ignored mixed monarchy theory altogether in *Two Treatises of Government* (1690), assuming instead a unified sovereign, 'the people', and that William III and succeeding monarchs similarly looked to the sixteenth-century notion that the legal sovereign was a unified trinity, 'the Crown in

The Revolution. This print, published only in 1790, shows William III being offered the crown together with a document intended to represent the Declaration of Rights; it implies that accepting the second was a condition of receiving the first. But is there any evidence that this occurred? If not, the picture, and others like it, may be evidence for the later Whig myth rather than for what happened in 1689.

Parliament', not a division of sovereignty between three independent players. But the mixed monarchy idea was open to use by those opposition groups who argued that political power was unbalanced; in their view the two rhetorics of 'checks and balances' and 'the Crown in Parliament' came to seem synonymous. Relations between crown and parliament developed significantly after 1689; but it is open to enquiry whether they developed primarily because of war rather than because of the Revolution. English history was already littered with attempts to restrain the executive, and the Test Acts (1673, 1678) had been deliberate restrictions of royal prerogative: they told the king whom he could not choose as a minister or military officer. But the only effective formal restrictions on the prerogative were for religious reasons, and this remained largely true.

For example, the Bill of Rights (1689), passed after the Revolution (formally an Act, not just a Bill) is often hailed as instituting a limited monarchy. In reality, the Act made its assertions in the name of 'the estates of the people of this realm', not 'the people'. The political compromises needed to ensure it a parliamentary majority meant that a list of new rights had to be dropped; the Act sought only to restate old rights. Even so, its provisions were often too vague to be legally enforceable (e.g. 'That election of members of Parliament ought to be free.' But what was 'free'? The succeeding century was marked by widespread corruption.) By contrast, the Act's really effective provision was that no monarch could henceforth be a Catholic.

If England, Ireland and Scotland were monarchies, they also possessed ancient representative institutions. In the period 1660–1832, they too continued to change, and their nature was equally a matter for debate. Just as the Westminster Parliament developed a system in which the king worked through a chief minister who could organise support, suppress dissent and deliver votes of taxation, so the London government came to manage the Dublin and Edinburgh Parliaments in the same way. English historians have tended to disparage the system of 'undertakers' in neighbouring parliaments, but it is debatable how far that system compromised Westminster's independence too. When this system of parliamentary management broke down, the results were the same: the incorporation of the Edinburgh and Dublin Parliaments into their Westminster neighbour (in 1707 and 1801), where management and manipulation had been raised to a higher power. The alternative was demonstrated in 1776, when the long-standing metropolitan failure to deal with colonial assemblies produced a new tradition of oligarchical representative institutions beyond metropolitan control.

A strong ministry, and parliamentary management, were responses to a common problem: instability. This was the major political issue in the British Isles in the seventeenth century, and many people reacted to it by preferring a strong monarchy. This came at the price of a strong executive branch in general: one which would have provided a more effective customs service, a larger and more intrusive excise, the abolition of local privileges and legal jurisdictions, larger and much more effective armed forces, the use of the army to suppress domestic rebellion or even riots. The Stuarts were made to take much of the blame; but the state continued to strengthen, whether the monarch was James II or William III. What changed in the early eighteenth century was the rise of a political rhetoric which ascribed a growing role and importance to parliament. Yet this happened in parallel with the development of techniques of political control which meant that parliament was increasingly subject to the executive. If the executive was more and more dependent on parliament to fund ever larger wars, it found ways of ensuring that parliament would comply. Over time, parliaments voted sums ever larger than their more wilful seventeenth-century predecessors. The executive therefore summoned them on a regular basis and kept them in being.

Whigs often claimed that the Revolution of 1688 created a wholly new polity, and some historians in succeeding centuries have echoed this rhetoric. It is legitimate to ask whether such transformations are common in human affairs, or whether, on the contrary, monarchs after 1688 had to cope with problems not dissimilar to those of their predecessors. It is questionable whether the Revolution made the state much less monarchical. Because the legal fiction was that James II had abdicated, no principles were established about deposing monarchs or calling them to account. William III had just as authoritarian a personality as James II. William, too, was a monarchist, and before 1688 had feared that James would provoke a civil war in England ending once more in a republic, so denying William the throne on James's anticipated death. Like James II, William had a religious mission and preferred centralised government to achieve it. Both were soldiers of God: William III, like James II, was an active military leader; the last sovereign to command in battle was George II, at Dettingen in 1743. Even afterwards, younger sons of the royal family continued to have military careers, and it remained a truth decorously expressed that the Hanoverian regime was ultimately secured by armed force.

What made most difference was not any legislation by the Convention Parliament of 1689 but the fact that the exile of James meant that the natural friends of monarchy, the Tories, were now cold or even hostile to William III. After 1697, they had their chance to restrict his power in what had angered them most. The Act of Settlement (1701) not only fixed the succession; it provided that in case a foreigner came to the throne, 'this nation be not obliged to engage in any war for the defence of any dominions or territories which do not belong to the crown of England without the consent of Parliament' (it became a dead letter); that no future monarch leave England, Scotland or Ireland without consent of parliament (it failed after the accession of the House of Hanover); that no foreigner be able to be a member of the Privy Council, or either House of Parliament, or hold any civil or military office, or receive any grant of lands; and that no salaried government officer sit in parliament following Anne's death (a provision repealed by the Whigs in 1706 in order to safeguard themselves under a Hanoverian successor).

Some people, therefore, continued to see the crown as a threat that needed to be limited; in the eighteenth century, many came to talk of a tripartite balance between crown, Lords and Commons. But how was this to be gauged? There had been no normal and identifiable balance in the seventeenth century or before that could have been used as a yardstick; nor was a balance then seen as the central feature of the constitution. The civil wars of the 1640s were not caused by any drive for supremacy on the part of the House of Commons, as was once thought. No such bid for power was present before the wars; none can be traced after 1660. The crown was still the central feature, and its powers were, if anything, enhanced: (1) in 1660 the king was recognised to have command of the militia, a point bitterly disputed before the war; (2) in 1664 the crown was effectively released from the obligation, imposed by the Triennial Act of 1641, to summon parliament at least every three years, with consequences evident in the 1680s; (3) in 1668 the terms of the judges' appointments were changed from 'quamdiu se bene gesserint' (during good behaviour) to 'durante bene placito' (during the king's pleasure). But these prerogative powers were not widely resisted; prerogative was a recognised part of government. If parliament was not trying to seize sovereignty, equally Charles II was not trying to effect a constitutional revolution, however much he may have admired Louis XIV. All government was absolute, as Sir Robert Filmer had argued in the 1640s: men well remembered that this was true of Cromwell's. Even during the Exclusion Crisis of 1679–81, a period of political strife during which the Whigs sought to disqualify James from the succession on the grounds of his Catholicism, the Whigs implicitly acknowledged that the crown could not be bound by conditions; an unacceptable monarch could only be replaced by an acceptable one.

Republicanism was not in origin about the institution of monarchy. Its origin was religious, a conviction that, since God alone was the supreme monarch, and Christ the head of the Church, the position claimed by worldly sovereigns was blasphemous. Republicanism was therefore a negation of monarchy rather than a thought-through programme for the structure of civil government, and this remained the case even in colonial America: the years 1763–76 saw a keenly contested and sophisticated debate in the American colonies on the nature and legitimacy of American grievances, but blueprints for a republican future were notable by their absence. Even Thomas Paine, in *Rights of Man* (1791–2), remarkably treated a republic as any government that was directed towards the public good. Republicanism had a poor record in Britain after 1660 chiefly because it was so lacking in intellectual content.

In the reigns of Charles II and James II, parliaments behaved more like their Tudor precursors than their Hanoverian successors. MPs were still men of their localities, and few displayed a wider vision. Information available to them on many detailed matters of national finance, trade and administration was scanty, and their position vis-à-vis the executive was weak. On foreign affairs they knew more; on constitutional law and religion they knew a great deal. What built up the role of parliament was neither any degree of informed, detailed involvement in the business of government nor any plan to secure such a larger role, but the unplanned and gradual emergence of two groups within parliament, 'Whig' and 'Tory', Whigs placing their anti-Catholicism before their allegiance to the monarch (and so, among Whig extremists, endorsing republicanism); Tories doing the opposite (and so, among Tory extremists, placing the crown above parliament). The impetus for their formation was electoral division, and none such occurred while the Cavalier Parliament sat without a general election, as it did in 1661–79. It was the dissolutions and general elections in the midst of the Exclusion Crisis, in 1679, 1680 and 1681, that changed all this.

Both Whigs and Tories then appealed to 'the people'. This term was commonly used in political rhetoric, but it usually meant the political elite, not everyone. Universal manhood suffrage was not on the agenda until the election for Westminster in 1780. Until then, politics might be populist, but was not (in our sense) democratic. In 1688 about 2.6 per cent of the English population voted in general elections; by 1716 about 4.6 per cent, roughly one in four adult males. Participation then steadily fell as turnouts declined, falling to about 2.6 per cent again by 1830, and the earlier peak was not regained until after the second Reform Act of 1867. The first Reform Act of 1832 was in some ways restrictive, explicitly excluding women from voting for the first time. Why was this? Some historians have written of 'exclusion' and the growth of 'oligarchy'; and something of this can be seen at work during particular periods. Others have pointed to low turnouts and a lack of widespread demand for popular involvement, with exceptions like the bitter party battles unleashed by 1688 and lasting at least until 1715 and the arrival of Walpole's political manipulation. 'Radical politics', the mobilisation of the poor, was not an ever-present possibility, codified in 'radicalism'. Popular engagement was episodic; radicalism was the proper name for a new political ideology, coined in the 1820s, which then meant a doctrine devised for the people, not by them. Popular politics was generally organised and elicited by the elite; it was not spontaneously generated 'from without' the world of Westminster and Whitehall.

The Dynastic Framework

The British Isles, like almost all of Europe, was composed of a series of polities that were assembled, and understood, in dynastic terms and in a dynastic age. Since Calvin's Case (1608), a test case used to define what we call 'citizenship' after the Union of Crowns in 1603, it was clear that national identity was defined in terms of personal allegiance to the natural person of the sovereign, not to an abstract 'state'; indeed, until the late eighteenth century, monarchical allegiance was the dominant way of defining and picturing national identity. This usage did not reveal some immature or subservient attitude. Rather, like the later doctrine of popular sovereignty, monarchical allegiance was a language that all could use in an attempt to secure their own ends. The nobility and gentry, bishops and clergy professing extravagant loyalty to Charles II retained much power in their own hands; more, indeed, than did the elites who rode the tiger of the Commonwealth in the 1650s.

Ideas of religious duty overwhelmingly reinforced this legal code and national symbolism. It was plausible in an age of text-centred Christian literalism that men should appeal to a doctrine of divine, indefeasible, hereditary right; most supporters of William III disagreed only with 'indefeasible', the claim that the succession could never be changed. Even then, most Whigs conceded the strong claims of hereditary right in seeking the next successor to Queen Anne by tracing a family tree and disqualifying only the Catholic claimants: when this bar ruled out fifty-seven individuals, the resulting heir, Georg Ludwig, Kurfürst von Braunschweig-Lüneburg, anglicised as

George I, still claimed an hereditary title. There was nothing 'modern' about the Hanoverians, nothing 'ancient' about the Stuarts: each was a dynasty in a dynastic age. It might be argued that the Stuarts were unsuccessful as a dynasty not because of personal failings, which they shared with all dynasties and all politicians, but because they had to deal with exceptional challenges to their rule in the form of Protestant Dissent, the resistance theories that went with it, and anti-Catholicism.

In 1689–92 the Whigs won the war in the British Isles, but not the argument: the debate about dynastic ideas went on being fought until the 1750s. The Revolution was a fact, but what did it mean? The challenge was to vindicate one's own interpretation of what had happened in 1688–9. This was not easy, and political allegiances were not black and white. Historians consequently dispute how many Stuart sympathisers there were. There is no simple answer to this question, for political commitment was a matter of degree, varied over time with the available options, and was often concealed; but it seems clear that Jacobitism was a more potent practical force in the early eighteenth-century British Isles than Marxism was to be in the early twentieth.

This threat had a geographical embodiment, initially nearby. Louis XIV gave James II the use of the former royal palace at Saint-Germain-en-Laye, near Paris; there the Stuart court numbered between 750 and 1,000 people, a substantial operation, generously funded by Louis. In 1713 the Treaty of Utrecht forced James III to leave France: he re-established himself at the Chateau of Bar-le-Duc in Lorraine. In 1716, after the failure of the first Jacobite rebellion (the Fifteen), he moved to Avignon, and in 1717 to Italy, eventually to Urbino; then to Rome in 1718, settling there from 1719. Even here, the British elite on the Grand Tour might pay a discreet visit to the Palazzo del Re.

The hard core of Stuart supporters were the Nonjurors. Samuel Johnson, in his great *Dictionary* of 1755, defined Nonjuror as 'One who conceiving James II unjustly deposed, refuses to swear allegiance to those who have succeeded him': he used the present tense for a commitment still persisting. Historians used to identify 'Nonjuror' with that tiny minority of clergy who declined the oath of allegiance in 1689 (and later the oath of abjuration, which specifically disavowed the title of James II or his son), were ejected from their livings, and thereafter worshipped in separated congregations, independently from the established Church. This usage was not wrong, but too limited: far more men were never in situations in which they faced demands to take the oaths, and the separated Nonjurors were probably only the tip of an iceberg whose size is impossible to determine. What is clearer is the insecurity and lack of zeal with which England and Scotland were taken into a major European war in the 1690s; Catholic Ireland was more openly hostile. In 1770 the Tory Samuel Johnson wrote of William III that 'half the nation' had denied him their allegiance. In 1776 the Whig Edmund Burke spoke of 'half of the kingdom' attached to 'their exiled Prince' in William's reign. Whatever the numbers, men on opposite sides in politics like Johnson and Burke could express the same apprehension at the scale of the problem.

Some people – Nonconformists and heterodox Anglicans – nevertheless tried to escape from the legal framework of monarchical legitimacy, chiefly for religious reasons. This had been one point at issue in the civil wars of the 1640s; but with the Restoration a monarchical understanding of society was reasserted. At the Revolution, this legal and political system was kept in being, and a commonwealth option rejected: even John Locke dedicated his *Two Treatises of Government* to William III. In a dynastic age, the only security from the claim of the Stuarts was another dynasty.

Yet William had no children: as a patriarchal deliverer his shelf life was short. At his death in 1702, the same was true of James II's daughter Anne, martyr to an illness that killed all her children in infancy. Everyone knew that on her death the Revolution would be refought. This indeed happened: 1714 saw a Whig coup when their candidate, the Elector of Hanover, was proclaimed, but this verdict was at once contested in the Jacobite rising of 1715. A precedent was set in 1660: restorations were possible. Recent work on the Fifteen has emphasised how plausible such a reversal was on this occasion.

The ideologies of two rival royal houses only made it more essential for the supporters of each to lay claim to dynastic propriety, and this competition for ownership of the dynastic idiom was intensified with the accession of the house of Hanover in 1714. Supporters of William III, George I and George II had to hail their monarchs, however implausibly, as bulwarks of liberty because lawfully entitled to the throne, and the same idiom was in full repair at the accession of the young, idealistic and as yet untarnished George III in 1760. The Jacobites replied in kind: James III (1688–1766) also claimed to respect the ancient constitution, and promised to rescue his country from an illegal regime. Some historians have argued that Jacobitism stood no chance because it was 'romantic' and therefore impractical; others have pointed out that Romanticism took root only in the early nineteenth century, and have reconstructed the very different world view that made dynastic allegiance a viable and powerful framework for public affairs. The exiled Stuarts were supported for somewhat different reasons in England, Scotland, Ireland and Wales; yet those reasons combined material advantage, libertarianism, national pride, religion and political ideology in durable combinations.

Where the exclusion of the Tory-Jacobite half of the nation from political office under George I and II had strengthened the monarchical idiom, both sides bidding for a monopoly of it, the removal from office in the 1760s of the old corps of parliamentary Whigs by George III's chief minister, Lord Bute (1713–92), had a different effect: with no other dynastic option to fall back on, and despite being eventually compelled to accept the patronage of the Hanoverian Prince of Wales (to reign as George IV in 1820–30), the Whig opposition gradually developed a far less dynastic attitude to politics.

Open republicans were still few in the British Isles before the French Revolution, and the American war had given little impetus to anti-monarchical thought at home. But 1789, and the execution of Louis XVI in 1793, became symbols of which the disaffected could make use. This was especially the case in Ireland and Scotland, where the ending of the Jacobite option had left large areas of local society politically decapitated, without a symbolic personal focus. In England the challenges of 1776 and 1789 led to a reassertion of the monarchy as a national symbol, but there were counter-currents, too: in treason trials the state came to be defined in more impersonal legal terms. Edmund Burke's defence of the whole social order in *Reflections on the Revolution in France* (1790) paradoxically meant that the spotlight moved away from the person of the king.

The last two decades before 1832 saw a reassertion of the role of the Church before that of the monarchy. What was most defended was increasingly pictured as 'the Protestant constitution': Catholic demands for 'emancipation' had the initial effect of strengthening the Protestant component of the state's self-image. Yet this measure narrowed the foundation of the state, for it applied most obviously to England. The most powerful challenge to it came from the threat of armed rebellion in Ireland, and Scotland too now began to slip away from the unionist commitments that the men of the Scottish Enlightenment had championed. After the reforms of 1828–35, especially the 1832 Reform Act, Robert Peel redefined the doctrine of the party of order and so, by implication, the nature of the state that it defended. Out went the old 'Toryism' focused on Church and king; in came the new 'Conservatism', a secular, pragmatic defence of property and power. Queen Victoria still headed a Europe-wide family, but for her British subjects dynasticism mattered little.

Centre and Periphery

The British Isles, and their overseas possessions in North America especially, were in a perpetual tension between definition as a federal or as a confederal polity, between centralisation or devolution; indeed, the same unresolved conflicts were inherited by the United States after independence in 1783. This is a recent way of putting it; at the time, many Europeans saw their polities in a seventeenth-century framework as either multiple kingdoms (a single sovereign ruling simultaneously over several kingdoms, the sovereign being the sole point of unity) or as composite monarchies (a unified polity created by a dominant core kingdom absorbing neighbouring kingdoms or principalities). It was the ancient distinction between the kingdoms of England, Scotland and Ireland that created the potential for tensions and conflicts, often over religion. This was especially true when England's growing power encouraged the country to see itself as a 'core' to which Wales, Scotland and Ireland were 'peripheries', and these problems now extended themselves across the Atlantic.

One tangible expression of this was commercial. The Union of Crowns in 1603 had not brought commercial integration: England's Navigation Acts, which from 1651 restricted the use of foreign shipping in English trade, initially applied against Ireland and Scotland just as much as against the United Provinces. Scotland's attempt to catch up economically in the 1690s took the form of a scheme for a trading company to Africa and the Indies, but in the face of London's hostility its outpost at Darien (near present-day Panama) withered and collapsed, involving a massive loss of the capital subscribed by an impoverished homeland. The independence of the 'peripheries' clearly had an economic price.

Cromwell's regime had embarked on the military conquest of the peripheries and their assimilation into a centrally directed godly commonwealth. Charles II, re-establishing the ancient autonomy of the thrones of England, Scotland and Ireland, necessarily looked in the opposite direction. James II, pursuing bureaucratic efficiencies, moved back towards centralisation in a way that offended the localities, and William III and his successors, whatever else they disavowed in James's policies, continued this trend towards centralised control. The first two Georges, aware of the fragility of their hold on power, found it prudent not to press the point of the regional loyalties that the Stuarts could exploit, and not to offend the sensitivities of Dissenters to rule from the centre. The end of the Stuart threat allowed a trend to central direction to reassert itself in the 1760s in the shape of metropolitan policies on colonial taxation, with – as 1776 demonstrated – significant consequences.

Yet centralisation was not necessarily an unwise or inappropriate option. Both James I and Charles I had pursued the integration of England and Scotland, notably the creation of a single national Church; the religiously-based resistance that this evoked may be evidence of the need for that strategy, or equally proof of its imprudence. It was the Westminster Parliament that refused an incorporating union after 1603 and later insisted that the Navigation Acts be applied to exclude Scots trade, even with England's colonies. Scotland gained little economically from the Union of Crowns in 1603, and this became yet clearer in the wars of the 1690s. London politicians rightly saw that Scotland threatened to break away from England after the Revolution of 1688: the Scots Parliament steadily gained control of its business and its composition in the 1690s, escaping from its old subordination to the crown. In that decade William's regime failed to find Scots grandees who could deliver local compliance, as was to happen in Dublin. The Edinburgh Parliament even refused to ratify the English Act of Settlement (1701). Its Act Anent Peace and War (1703) instead provided that foreign policy decisions made in London, after Anne's death, would need the consent of the Scots Parliament. The Act of Security (1704) asserted that the Scots Parliament would choose Anne's successor on her death (by implication, a Stuart, implying a French alliance), unless London conceded free trade. This was effectively a delayed declaration of independence, and made English intervention to secure Scots participation in the war inevitable. The English ministry's first response was the Alien Act (1705) which provided that if Scotland refused to accept a union it would be legally an alien nation.

This finally decided an old Scots dilemma, and commissioners began to negotiate. According to Sir John Clerk, one of the Scots who negotiated the terms, his fellow commissioners debated among themselves 'whether they should propose to the English a Federal union between the two nations, or an Incorporating union'. They recognised that 'The first was most favoured by the people of Scotland, but all the Scots Commissioners, to a Man, considered it rediculous and impracticable' since 'in all Federal unions there is behoved to be a supreme power lodged some where'; nor would the English Commissioners accept it. The terms agreed on were nevertheless anomalous: an incorporating union, creating a single government and armed forces, was to leave Scots law and Scots religion untouched. It was an illogical compromise, but it worked because the Scots Parliament was absorbed in and swamped by its Westminster cousin and because the Presbyterian coup of 1689 was preserved: just as, for the Frenchman Henri IV, Paris was worth a mass, so for the Dutchman Willem van Oranje Edinburgh was worth a General Assembly of the Kirk. But in the French-backed Jacobite invasion attempt that followed in 1708, James III promised to restore the Edinburgh Parliament: this remained a possibility, if the times should alter.

The union was unpopular in Scotland. Sir John Clerk confessed in his memoirs that of the Scottish people 'not even one per cent approved' of what the Edinburgh Parliament was doing in agreeing to that measure. The Scottish Commissioners had asked for the whole of the Edinburgh Parliament to be absorbed at Westminster; the English Commissioners offered only thirty-eight seats in the Westminster Commons (later raised to forty-five, but falling far short of the 159 constituencies of the Scottish Parliament) plus sixteen representative Scots peers in the Lords; they argued that representation should reflect property, not population or the size of existing institutions. Yet although these sixteen peers were 'elected' from the whole body of the Scottish nobility, control from London meant that they were largely official nominees: the Scots contingent at Westminster was henceforth usually subservient to the government of the day.

The union was unpopular in England, too. Scots dissatisfaction with its working led to a motion by a Scots peer in the Westminster Parliament in 1713 to repeal the treaty: it attracted much English support and failed by just four votes. When rebellion followed in 1715, the union was secured by military force. Only slowly did its economic benefits emerge. Under its terms, Scotland was brought within the ambit of England's Navigation Acts, evaded many of the duties under those Acts by widespread and flagrant smuggling, shouldered a disproportionately small share of the land tax and excise burdens, and retained its own Church and legal system. From the mid-1720s, Walpole built up a patronage machine in Scotland, run by the earl of Islay, later second duke of Argyll, to parallel that in Dublin; these political arts brought stability, of a sort, to the union of 1707. Scotland retained a large degree of self-government, but via an oligarchy. Nor was it invariably subservient: when Walpole's agent Argyll turned against him following the Porteous riots of 1736, Argyll's following at Westminster tilted the balance and helped ensure Walpole's fall in 1742. But control was re-established via the third duke of Argyll, who held Scotland for the London government from 1743 to 1761 and weathered the rebellion of 1745.

Union with Ireland, however, was resisted by the English throughout the eighteenth century: it came in 1801 only as a result of the Irish rebellion of 1798. Englishmen often looked on Ireland as a kingdom already subordinated: union was deemed unnecessary. In 1764 the American James Otis drew a distinction between the extensive liberties to which his fellow colonists were entitled and those of the Irish, since 'Ireland is a *conquered* country'. Ireland was seen as a trade rival, where Scotland was not. Ireland was also more populous than Scotland, and could not have been as easily assimilated at Westminster. An Irish unionist elite dedicated to moderating old religious passions and to promoting scientific, technological and social change therefore did not emerge, as it did in Scotland. Irish opinion oscillated during the eighteenth century, sometimes for a union, sometimes against. Union came in 1801 when both Irish and English elites agreed simultaneously.

Neither union was self-explanatory. Was 1707 an episode in state formation, part of a drive by England to assimilate surrounding cultures? Or was it a bid for security, an attempt to arrange political cooperation by concession to the peripheries where no easy military dominance was possible? In favour of the second interpretation was the London governments' preoccupation with dynastic instability after 1660, 1688 and 1714, and the resolute focus of William III and the first two Georges on continental European politics. None of these leaders had any record of 'state formation' in their native countries (the United Provinces was a ramshackle coalition, Braunschweig-Lüneburg a petty princedom among petty princedoms); the idea would have been above the head of Queen Anne.

Despite the Union, Scotland remained a remote and strange country until the reign of George III. From 1688, Scotland had a substantial disaffected intelligentsia, inward-looking and unreconciled. From the mid-eighteenth century, however, more and more professional careers in England and overseas opened up for the graduates of Scotland's efficient universities, and the disaffected intelligentsia gradually evaporated. This was not immediately obvious, but by the 1780s was undeniable: in 1763, one stagecoach a month left Edinburgh for London, which it reached in twelve to sixteen days; yet, twenty years later, sixty stagecoaches a month were making the same journey in four days. Even more than the professional middle orders, the Scots elite increasingly departed for England to pursue careers at court, in politics or the army. Consequently the Scots nobility was largely anglicised by 1760; short of a Stuart restoration, undoing the union was inconceivable. After the 1760s, Scots began to hold high office in England in substantial numbers, and began to fill more and more posts in the East India Company: by 1776, the empire had a distinctly Scottish look.

Something similar happened in Ireland, though to a lesser degree: far more of the Irish elite stayed at home, or joined the Jacobite diaspora on the continent. Yet whereas the Scots nobility and gentry had been in a time warp before 1707, reversing that stance dramatically after c. 1760, Irish patricians were already more cosmopolitan, the result of conquest, mobility and intermarriage over many centuries. Whatever the image of self-sufficiency devised by nineteenth-century Irish nationalism, the eighteenth-century Irish elite was assiduously part of an Anglo-Irish cultural world, as their magnificent houses still testify.

Both Scotland and Ireland came to be ruled from London in similar ways. Managers who could deliver local compliance (in Ireland nicknamed 'undertakers') were recruited from local elites. Colonial America differed in that such 'undertakers' tended not to emerge, and direct rule by royal governors, backed by inadequate patronage and weak military force, failed long before 1776. In subservient Scotland, by contrast, the system of 'undertakers' continued successfully into the

1790s with the ascendancy of Henry Dundas. In Ireland the presence of an English lord-lieutenant, appointed by London, meant a divided elite and encouraged the emergence of anti-unionist sentiment that secured its fullest expression during the American Revolution. This siding with Catholic opinion meant that a united unionist bloc was never born, and Ireland was prone to stresses which erupted in rebellion in 1798.

Centralisation did not go unchallenged. For the Thirteen Colonies, 1776 saw a rebellion against centralisation, a reaffirmation of the idea of creating a more libertarian polity by dividing up sovereignty. But no sooner had a confederal republic been born than much of its own political elite began to denounce it as dangerously weak, a trend that resulted in the establishment of a centralising, incorporating union with the American constitution of 1787. This in turn was only the precursor of a series of legal disputes in the American courts over states' rights that ended in civil war in the 1860s. In constitutions, no settlement is ever permanent; indeed, in the framing of constitutions, ten years is a long time.

National Identity

England, Wales, Scotland and Ireland were ancient societies: each in 1660 had long-standing, complex and continually developing ways of describing their identities that seldom strongly anticipated the new ideology, 'nationalism', that was to be coined in continental Europe after Napoleon. 'Nationalism' would later appeal to blood and soil, to nineteenth-century scientific ideas of racial difference, and to the allegedly separate and characteristic nature of folk culture, literature, art and music. Earlier ages had different attitudes to these things. Before the nineteenth century, as mentioned earlier, 'race' meant family lineage rather than indelible genetic identity, and related to family pride rather than to ideas of populist commonalities. Elite culture in any European society that possessed elites was saturated in the classics of Greece and Rome, and seldom regarded popular vernacular culture through the eyes of the Romantics as a guide to the unchanging inner essence of a 'people'. Before the nineteenth century, elites were far more cosmopolitan than they later became. But the societies of the British Isles were well aware of their special characteristics, and had other ways of picturing themselves that did not depend on 'nationalism'.

The English had a well-developed historiography that traced the deeds and achievements of Englishmen (and some women, notably Boudicca and Queen Elizabeth I) over many centuries. The cult of the English common law was already ancient, and was revitalised by texts like Sir Matthew Hale's *The History of the Common Law of England* (1713) and William Blackstone's *Commentaries on the Laws of England* (1765–9). But the biggest body of literature outlining a shared experience concerned the English Church. It was here especially that an image of a free, Protestant people was worked out and sustained, whether in bestsellers like John Foxe's *Book of Martyrs* (1559 and many later editions) or in heavyweight theological texts like Richard Hooker's *Of the Laws of Ecclesiastical Polity* (1593; first complete edition, 1662). Between them, these texts kept alive the interpretation long ago placed on English history by the Venerable Bede (d. 735) in his *Ecclesiastical History of the English People* that its unifying theme was providential destiny and survival in the face of overwhelming odds.

The identity of Wales, lacking universities and a major capital city, was far weaker. The Welsh in the seventeenth century, like the Welshman Judge George Jeffreys, often tried to be more loyal than the English loyalists. At the dawn of the eighteenth century, Wales was a stronghold of Stuart allegiance. The failure of this option, and the rise of the evangelical movement, provided Wales with a different idiom. A growing body of books printed in Welsh, especially works of devotion, laid the groundwork for revivalist Methodism, eventually outside the framework of English and Anglican culture. From royalism in the seventeenth century, Wales turned to liberalism in the nine-teenth and socialism in the twentieth. But neither liberalism nor socialism were to create a powerful national identity: even in the Romantic era, Welsh 'nationalism' was not a strong a political force.

Scotland in the seventeenth century was a society divided between Gaelic and English speakers, between Highlands and Lowlands, between clanship and market economy, between Presbyterian, Covenanter, Episcopalian and Catholic. Lasting rivalry meant that the victory of Presbyterianism in 1689 was hollow: the abolition of the Edinburgh Parliament by the Union of 1707 was a major symbolic loss, and Scots resentment long outlasted the Jacobite option. Unionism was always of more importance to the Scots literati than to the English, and what is now called the Scottish Enlightenment was oriented more to an English Whig myth about the centrality and probity of parliament, print and Protestantism than to supporting a tenable rival account of Scotland's past and identity. Appropriately, Hume chose to write a *History of England* (1754–62). Lacking a more intellectually defensible account of their homeland, many Scots imaginations were captured in the late eighteenth century by the fictions of 'Ossian', an invented Gaelic bard, and in the early nineteenth by the fake tartanry and biscuit-tin Jacobitism which succeeded Sir Walter Scott. It had few immediate political consequences. Engineering and empire later provided much more compelling images.

Ireland's identity was the most bitterly disputed among these four societies. Protestant Ulster necessarily subscribed to the earliest and most powerful version of the English Whig myth. Memories of the successful Protestant defence of Londonderry (1689) and of William III's victory at the Battle of the Boyne (1690) retain their potency in Ulster society even today. Yet this was a self-image that really owed most to the Covenanting tradition of south-west Scotland, and so offered only an uneasy basis for cooperation between Ireland and England: many Englishmen remained ambiguous about the Whig myth that some of the English had invented, and were uneasy about the literalistic implementation of that myth in Ireland to oppress the Catholic majority. If Scotland's identity was weakened by its union of 1707, Ireland's as yet had not benefited from the absence of a union. Indeed, the Irish Commons in 1703 petitioned for just such a union, although unsuccessfully. Irish patriotism, resisting English links, was a later development. Only from the 1770s did the Church of Ireland's adherents begin to construct a patriotism defined against England, but this belated flowering was first frustrated by Westminster, then swamped by the passions unleashed by the French Revolution. Meanwhile, the south of Ireland sustained an unmobilised identity, latently built around its Catholicism.

Éamonn Ó Ciardha has argued that this basic Irish loyalty to the exiled Stuarts was a much more potent force than the official adherence of the Ascendancy to the Hanoverians revealed. Jacobite allegiance was driven into a Gaelic culture that was extensive but cut off from Anglophone contemporaries and present-day historians alike; indeed, he argues, it prevented the emergence of a popular cult of loyalty to the wider polity (as the Scots came to celebrate their union by the 1760s) with major long-term consequences: a transition from Jacobite in the 1740s to Jacobin in the era of the French Revolution, the movement of the 1820s for Catholic Emancipation, and the eventual reversal of the settlement that followed 1688. This national conscious-ness was slow to arrive partly because Catholicism functioned in Ireland as a peasant church without significant gentry leadership: the political activation of Catholics was difficult, and when it happened was initially often conducted by Protestants like the revolutionary Wolfe Tone (1763–98). For a Catholic politician of genius, Ireland had to wait for Daniel O'Connell (1775–1847). Meanwhile, Williamite conquest in 1689–91 meant that the English in Ireland could now confidently depict themselves as Irish, look forward to the withering away of Catholicism, and use English constitutionalist arguments against England itself.

If English, Welsh, Irish and Scottish identities were ancient and deep-rooted, much debate has recently turned on when, why and how far a shared 'Britishness' emerged or was promoted after the Unions of 1707 and 1801. The thesis of the shallow roots of Britishness has seemed most persuasive to historians who use the term 'nationalism' as timelessly valid (so allowing a single answer to that question) and who find their postmodern preferences for claiming 'nationalism' to have been recently 'constructed' to be strengthened by the weakness of eighteenth-century 'Britishness'. Those who recognise the novelty of that new term 'nationalism' in the early nineteenth century have more reservations about the inclusiveness or acceptance of 'Britishness' in the eighteenth. Certainly, the term 'Britain' was used, though often for polemical purposes. Where Scots after 1707 made much of it, even rechristening their nation 'North Britain', the Irish elite, increasingly rejecting an image of themselves as colonists and affirming their Irishness, made fewer such bids for inclusion in a shared identity. The term 'British' was problematic for most Irish not least because it implied a common identity with Ulster Protestant Dissenters. Not until the 1830s did Daniel O'Connell offer the Whigs at Westminster the prospect that the Irish, if treated with justice, would 'become a kind of West Britons'; it has never been clear when exactly it became too late for such gestures. After 1714, however, the Irish Ascendancy less and less felt threatened by a Stuart restoration; even during the Fifteen and the Forty-five, the Catholics in Ireland were quiescent. As a result, Catholicism was strangely unimportant for national identities before O'Connell, whether by its affirmation or negation.

Protestantism has been proposed as the main foundation for a shared Britishness, but this is a simplistic generalisation. True, England, Scotland and part of Ireland predominantly described themselves as 'Protestant' and at times showed strong populist anti-Catholic sentiments, most notably at the time of London's Gordon riots (1780) but also when the 'Catholic question' was brought forward in Westminster politics after 1805. Yet despite its negations Protestantism was never able to create a strong shared identity, for it covered a range of mutually antagonistic positions from episcopal Anglicanism through Scots and Ulster Presbyterianism to Civil War sectarianism, and from High Churchmanship, which regarded Rome as a branch of the universal Church, to Low Churchmanship and Nonconformity, which had not all ceased to identify the pope with Antichrist.

Only when a foreign enemy was clearly Catholic, and perceived as posing a threat of the reconversion of the British Isles, did a sense of a common cause emerge. But this was not the case between 1660 and 1688, or after 1763; at times, Britain had Catholic allies, like Austria in the wars of Queen Anne's reign. In the American war, Britain faced a continental coalition including the undeniably Protestant United Provinces. After 1793, Britain was at war with atheist France in alliance with Christian states of many denominations. Protestantism was not enough; indeed, nothing was enough to unify the three kingdoms in a shared identity if 'identity' is conceived as an essence or principle. But this is a nineteenth-century assumption. Rather, 'identity' should be understood as a descriptive term, devised and deployed for practical political purposes, not the reflection of any 'underlying' reality. It seems more likely that 'British' was used during this period as a synonym for Englishness, Welshness, Scottishness and to a lesser extent Irishness without the meanings of those identities in popular discourse being essentially modified.

If so, we can see that the identities of the four component parts of the British Isles were not equally robust. Wales's identity was in long-term decline before the nineteenth century. Scotland was the loser from the Revolution of 1688, bound by force to an English Whig myth that condoned the extension of English influence and deprived of its Parliament by the Union of 1707. Protestant Ireland, which retained the Dublin Parliament until the Union of 1801, was similarly locked into an English Whig historical scenario, but one which was openly rejected by the Catholic majority of its population.

The commonly used name for this composite polity was 'England', a conventional usage, just as the citizens of the USA today refer to themselves as 'Americans' in disregard of the many other states on the American continent. Edmund Burke, whom everyone knew to be Irish-born, wrote of himself in c. 1790 as 'an Englishman'. The Scottish MP David Scott complained in the House of Commons about an Irish MP in 1805: 'we commonly, when speaking of British subjects, call them English, be they English, Scotch or Irish; he, therefore, I hope, will never be offended with the word English being applied in future to express any of his majesty's subjects, or suppose it can be meant as an allusion to any particular part of the united kingdom.' No other MP contested his claim. What changed this situation fundamentally was not the weakness of the English formula for describing a free, law-bound, patriotic people but the increasing participation of Irish and Scots in the military, overseas and imperial enterprise after c. 1776: the term 'British' now came into vogue, but mainly as a euphemism for the Irish, Scots and English when abroad.

With the exception of hated tax officials, England lacked powerful centralising institutions of government apart from the Church: law and religion rather than a bureaucracy had long functioned as the symbolic agencies of state building. Indeed, the term 'state' was not often used; the conventional term was 'kingdom'. Because England was usually seen as a personalised kingdom rather than an abstract and secular state, and because the notion of 'the community of the realm' had been strong since the Middle Ages, registering a sense of popular participation in the conduct of that kingdom, no clear antagonism developed in England between the ideas of 'the nation' and 'the state', as often happened in Europe, at least until the rise of radicalism after 1815. If so, it was not that 'the upper classes' appropriated 'patriotism' in a cynical manoeuvre to defend their ascendancy but rather that all groups, Whig and Tory, rich and poor, could more easily see themselves as patriotic participants in a national epic. In 1776–83 and 1793–1815 that epic took on tragic and sanguinary overtones that only bound its participants closer together. Although a strand of ruthless satire of monarchs continued throughout the century, George III emerged from his early unpopularity to win widespread respect and even affection among his subjects.

The identity that triumphed in the wars of 1793–1815 was largely England's. Wellington was born in Ireland, but pointed out that a man's being born in a stable did not make him a horse. Nelson was a loyal Norfolk man; Collingwood bore a famous Northumbrian name. England was repeatedly in the front line. It was English fleets that ruled the waves, whatever the Scot James Thompson had written in 1740 about 'Rule, Britannia!'. For this combination of xenophobia and military assertion the term used when overseas was 'British', but the English at home normally called themselves English, and local identities took priority in Wales, Ireland and Scotland also. The assembly of these societies into the union of 1801 were political more than cultural episodes.

War meant that English national identity was strengthened around the core of providential mission, a self-image Protestant and constitutionalist. So successful was this idea – attracting a wealth of images, iconography and celebration that reached a crescendo in 1814–15 – that the later doctrine of 'nationalism' never fully replaced it. By 'nationalism' we mean the racial-linguistic premises of national identity that took shape on the Continent in response to the advance of Jacobinism and the dictatorship of Napoleon. These new ideas had some points of similarity with the older premises of 'providential' identity, and later seemed to become synonymous with them; at the time there were fundamental differences.

Older ideas survived in England into the twentieth century, producing a society markedly less open to racialism than many other societies in Europe. This was less true of Scotland and Ireland, which in the nineteenth century were to develop forms of 'nationalism' (forms that never, however, persuaded all of the Scots and Irish). Scots and Irish identities in the eighteenth century were less triumphalist than England's, lacking the English sense of providential destiny, and their societies were less robustly successful; the scene was set for the rise of different ways of picturing collective identity in Scotland and Ireland in the idiom of Romantic nationalism. Yet in 1832 this could not be foreseen.

Imperial Connections:
the Significance of Empire

Empire has lately become a fashionable subject, often led by the preoccupations of American academe and fuelled by American postmodernism. This projection of US anti-imperialist sentiments onto

Britain has led to claims that eighteenth-century Britain was deeply shaped by its imperial experience; that British culture was profoundly 'imperialist'; that racialism was rampant in Britain, and British public opinion was oriented towards conquest at the expense of liberty. Yet this 'new imperial history' is at an early stage, and often rests on untested assumptions rather than on adequate research. It is challenged, for example, by Bernard Porter's study of British attitudes to empire in the nineteenth and twentieth centuries that attempts to quantify themes and preoccupations in popular culture. This research reveals a widespread British indifference towards, and ignorance of, all things imperial; it locates eager concern for empire primarily in those small social groups actively involved in its military or civil administration. Such a survey suggests that Britons' sense of superiority was based on cultural, as opposed to racial, assumptions; that strategic calculations revolved around defence against perceived foreign threats rather than 'militaristic' assertion; and that attitudes to the monarchy at home were not projected as imperialism abroad. If this is true of the nineteenth century, it is likely to be still more true of the eighteenth.

An exception to this general pattern of indifference was in attitudes towards colonies of settlement; but before 1776 these were generally called 'colonies' in the plural rather than 'empire' in the singular, and were unsystematically and miscellaneously understood in terms of discovery, lawful purchase, occupation or beneficial development rather than as the expropriation of and domination over native inhabitants; it is a view that continues to characterise the United States' attitude towards its own vast land empire in North America today. In the eighteenth century, apart from the east coast of North America, Britain's overseas possessions were scattered, small and heterogeneous, acquired for a bewildering variety of reasons. To analyse them historically, we need to question the demand to define them as an 'empire' sustained by 'imperialism'. Few Englishmen held such a theoretical vision.

The English, and to a lesser extent the Scots, sought trade and (though not as fervently as in the seventeenth century) security for their various religious denominations, not a great land empire integrated into the domestic polity. James II had pursued a clearer definition of colonial relations, but had no time to achieve it; the contested and ambiguous outcome of the Revolution of 1688 then meant that empire was left similarly undefined. The London government often found it prudent to adopt towards the colonies a stance summed up by the duke of Newcastle as 'salutary neglect'. This meant that the peripheries (Scotland, Ireland and the American colonies) could achieve leverage against England only by appealing to 'Revolution principles', the principles held to have been vindicated in 1688. Since people had often understood these differently, it was an argument that the metropolitan government could never decisively win.

Argument was possible partly because empire was not new, and antiquity had created complexity. England had had overseas possessions before: by the fifteenth century the English came to see large parts of France as 'their' territories more than they saw England as a subordinate kingdom still occupied by Normans as a result of the conquest of 1066. The final loss of these possessions after the Battle of Castillon (1453), the last battle of the Hundred Years War, turned England in on itself. Colonial expansion in the New World in the early seventeenth century looked set to reverse this insularity, but in the event was only ever the enthusiasm of relatively small numbers (more English and Scots emigrated to Ulster than to North America, and civil war in the 1640s made inhabitants of the islands look inwards once more). There was even a reverse migration of religious zealots from New England, eager to leap onto the bandwagon of reformation in the homeland. But in 1660 Charles II, and his brother James, returned with wider horizons. Both were fascinated by science, technology, maritime enterprise and trade; they were well aware that the customs revenue rather than the land tax was the backbone of royal finance. New York and Carolina both testify by their names to this new enthusiasm for overseas involvement. Although religious geopolitics played a part, and still influenced the decisions of individuals to emigrate, state policy became more and more focused on trade and naval power. Slowly, Britain realigned itself: in 1700–1701, about 85 per cent of Britain's trade by value was with continental Europe. By 1750–51, this had fallen slightly to 77 per cent, and thereafter fell dramatically: by 1772–3 it was 49 per cent, and by 1797–8 (although during major continental wars) 30 per cent. But after 1814, trade with Europe again grew as a proportion of total British trade: as these fluctuating trends demonstrate, there was no steadily growing orientation towards 'empire'.

Colonies were one thing; 'empire' was another. Some historians seek to depict 'an empire', and 'imperialism', from an early date. Others doubt that English, or British, policy had such a coherence of aim, and deny that the United Kingdom was established in 1707 to serve the purposes of overseas expansion. According to this view, the Union was an episode in the European war against France; the Scottish city that traded most with overseas territories, Glasgow, was the most hostile to the Union. England's and Britain's involvements overseas were diverse, and all such engagements depended on the unpredictable outcomes of military conflict. Britain's possessions were normally termed 'colonies', and there were few contemporary references to a 'British empire'. These territories were too diverse, too far-flung, acquired for too many different reasons, and too often looked on as counters to be traded in the great game of European power politics for a clear sense of 'an empire' to emerge. Nor were Britain's overseas possessions united by any systematic legal or political theory: the legal and constitutional relations between colonies and homeland were defined in imprecise and often contradictory ways, a problem that was demonstrated by the transatlantic controversies that followed 1763, and which paved the way for the breakdown of government in 1776.

The evolution of polities in America was still shaped chiefly by European dynastic contests. This was true of the dispute over the Spanish succession from 1700, for it entailed a decision over the future course of Spain's American possessions and triggered conflicts between English and French settlers there on just that issue. The War of the Spanish Succession was a world war, fought also in North America. It was at this point that French strategy became clear: to pen in the British settlements to the eastern seaboard by promoting a French colony in Louisiana, so ensuring control of the Mississippi; to secure a fortress at Detroit, commanding the Great Lakes and excluding the British from the north-west. French power would join the two, in alliance with Native American tribes.

British military involvements overseas did not therefore operate in some independent sphere, governed by calculations about 'empire'; they were, from an early date, peripheral extensions of European conflicts. This was true of Franco-British rivalries in North America from 1689 and in India from the 1740s; the Seven Years War began with a failed attempt to prevent such conflicts in the Ohio valley escalating into European conflict. At least until the 1750s, colonial conflicts were of secondary concern to London governments; from the 1760s it was North American colonists who demanded a redefinition of empire more than British imperialists who sought to impose it on them. Britain's concerns focused after 1714 on Hanover, and the continental entanglements that this brought; soon an added threat was identified by France's economic resurgence. French seaborne trade expanded from some 50 per cent of Britain's in the 1720s to over 80 per cent in the 1780s: British policy failed permanently to check this fundamental and adverse shift in the balance of power.

By 1763 the strategy on which Britain had set out in 1689, the attempt to reduce the power of France, seemed triumphantly vindicated. France had lost North America, was saddled with huge debts that it could hardly afford to service, and had suffered humiliating military defeats. But this only made Europe's superpower more determined to reverse that verdict, and from 1763 French policy was dedicated to doing just that at a time when Britain was reducing its involvement with Europe. That policy succeeded beyond Choiseul's dreams when, in 1783, the Treaty of Paris recognised American independence and granted the Thirteen Colonies their own extended territories. This had major implications for Britain's attitude towards her remaining overseas possessions, now finally, but belatedly, defined coherently as an 'empire'. It is debated how far the loss of the Thirteen Colonies redirected British attention to the East. Some have argued for a 'new imperialism' directed towards dark-skinned peoples; yet British commercial and colonial activity in India, China and the East Indies long predated 1783. Where the monopolies enjoyed by the Royal African Company and the Levant Company had been terminated in the 1750s, the East India Company (founded in 1600) retained its unique position, and continued to be the semi-official arm of the state in territorial acquisition as well as in trade; its charter was renewed, although reformed, in 1792. In economic terms, the 'first' British empire was still far more important than the 'second': after 1783, the area of fastest growth of trade was again North America, as prewar relations resumed. The East may have captured the imaginations of later anti-imperialists, but eighteenth-century merchants still looked to the bottom line: North America.

The American Revolution: an Episode
in British History

Historians have long been given to debating the question: why did Britain in the late eighteenth century not experience major revolution, as the assumptions of modernism led them to expect? Yet the problem was created by an arbitrary choice of categories. It could better be argued that Britain did experience major, transformative revolution; but it happened among fellow Britons in the North American colonies, and for reasons having nothing to do with class or industrialisation, those twin preoccupations of so many modern historians. Within the British Isles, the constitutional transformations of 1828–35 (discussed below) were similarly only distantly related to industrialisation and urbanisation, and their importance was for similar reasons long understated.

Seen in a transatlantic perspective, there was little that was new, and little that was specifically American, about the American Revolution: it was an episode that looked back more than it looked forward, and that took place within an English-speaking polity whose political language originated in the British Isles. The real puzzle about the American Revolution is that it happened in America. Just as Marx and Engels expected revolution to occur in industrial Germany rather than backward Russia, so revolution was, on the surface, far more likely in Britain (and especially England) than in the rural isolation of North America. Yet neither the American nor the French Revolutions were quite the modern episodes that they were later depicted as being, and neither displayed many ideas which students who are familiar with earlier centuries would recognise as novel or original. In the late eighteenth century it was England, not France or North America, that saw the birth of universal suffrage, anti-slavery and women's rights, and the British Isles into the 1840s still seemed to contemporaries to be on the edge of social upheaval: the American and French Revolutions, in the shape they took, were largely unexpected, and cannot simply be explained as self-evident conflicts between 'modern' and 'pre-modern'. Universal suffrage and a dynamic of conflict between rich and poor were themes absent from Thomas Paine's *Common Sense* (1776), the key pamphlet in catalysing the colonial decision to attempt independence, but a tract that came straight out of the mental world of English Deism in the early eighteenth century. Paine was out of date, and could only have an impact in a backward corner of the English-speaking world, where his tract, covertly heterodox, could have a catalytic effect on politicised but uninformed religious sectarianism that was worryingly reminiscent of the 1640s.

A better explanation of the American Revolution is a transatlantic one. Settlements of constitutional conflicts within the British Isles had often been attempts to cope with religious diversity and its consequences. At home, solutions were found, although sometimes by narrow margins, but frequently at the price of exporting them to North America. There they eventually recurred in an insoluble form, the American Revolution having many of the attributes of seventeenth-century wars of religion in Scotland, Ireland and England. In the British Isles, as we have seen, the Revolution of 1688 produced not settlement but lasting ambiguity and conflict; in 1776, again, both sides appealed to the 'rights of Englishmen'. British colonists had no monopoly on 'liberty'. Nor were they secular, like the official face of the republic that emerged in 1783.

The American Revolution. How secular were the causes of the American Revolution? Here four bishops dance around the Quebec Bill, which its opponents denounced as recognising 'Popery' in Canada, while the devil whispers suggestions to Lord North and Lord Bute plays the bagpipes. And how American were the Revolution's causes? This print appeared in *The New American Magazine*, 1 (October 1774), engraved by the American patriot Paul Revere; but he copied it from an English source, and Dissenting denunciations of 'arbitrary power' were already entrenched in England.

This is a controversial thesis only because the American Revolution has been swept up into the 'myth of origins' of the United States and is normally interpreted there for present-day purposes. Within these presentist adaptations, some common features emerge. The revolution is blamed on innovations in British policy alone, and George III or his ministers reproached for the inconsistency of their acts with 'fundamental law'; colonial society is defined as securely 'American' and transformingly 'modern' from its outset. These assumptions tell us more about the present day than about the 1770s. Innovations in metropolitan policy undoubtedly occurred in the 1760s (policy is always changing, like the constitution), but it is debatable whether they were adequate to explain the scale of what followed. They were more than matched by social and intellectual changes within North America that had created a volcano and now triggered its eruption. Similarly, the idea that colonial American society was 'modern' from its outset overlooks the fact that many of the features cited in support of this argument were found to a greater degree in England.

The common myth of 'the American Revolution' as a unified, consensual response to tyranny also ignores the fact that there was no 'America' before 1776 to make a revolution: a united nation was the result of the revolution, not its cause. In 1769 Burke wrote of twenty-six British colonies 'from Nova Scotia to St. Nevis': in 1776 half of them rebelled, half did not. Even within the Thirteen Colonies, some people campaigned for independence, some were loyalists and a body of opinion in the centre was initially undecided. Within the British Isles, too, opinion was divided, some like Edmund Burke agreeing with colonial grievances up to 1775, others like Samuel Johnson opposing for equally serious reasons. Like all great constitutional conflicts, this one took place in a legal grey area and greatly advanced the careers of lawyers. One such was that hard realist Jeremy Bentham. He later recalled his views in 1775:

> My opinions were at that time opposite to the American side. The turn they took was the result of the bad arguments by which I observed that side supported . . . The Declaration of Rights [Independence] presented itself to my conception from the first, as what it has always continued to be, a hodge-podge of confusion and absurdity, in which the thing to be proved is all along taken for granted . . . Absurdity, if I do not mis-recollect, went so far on that side as to pretend that, in point of fact, they had

all along been in a state of independence of the British Parliament, the contrary of which was proved so plainly by such a number of acts of parliament, which were produced.

Colonial lawyers and politicians found reasons to disagree, and this made the American Revolution to a pronounced degree an ideological conflict of a particular kind. The revolution was less a colonial war of liberation than a civil war among people who openly subscribed to similar ideals, but whose ideology had fallen into schism. Yet if the population of the Thirteen Colonies was made up of elements comparable to its British counterpart, the balance of its composition was wholly different: the Nonconformist denominations, minorities in the old world, hugely predominated in the Thirteen Colonies. Moreover, they had had the freedom to become more like themselves, to develop far further in an intolerant Congregationalist or Presbyterian direction, and to revitalise the seventeenth-century resistance theories that had been held in check at home by the Anglican ascendancy of the 1660s. As well as being a civil war, the American Revolution contained many of the elements of a war of religion.

Adopting an opposite interpretation, the 'Whig interpretation' of the revolution is still heard, and takes a variety of forms. Some authors have written of a 'radicalism' originating in the 1760s that flowered in the 1770s as a defence of liberty against heavy-handed metropolitan exactions, achieving timeless significance as an assertion of humanity's natural rights. This argument is vulnerable to the demonstration that 'radicalism' was a later ideology, born in England in the 1820s, and that its targets were absent in North America (no heavy tax burden was ever laid on American shoulders, or even threatened; universal suffrage was not at issue in 1776; no colonial economist like Ricardo had pointed a finger at American landowners; atheism was almost unknown in the colonies). Colonists, moreover, were pro-active from the 1760s, not merely reactive; women, slaves and Native Americans were so obviously excluded from the promise of natural rights language in the 1770s that this language itself becomes the historical phenomenon to be explained rather than the explanatory key that opens all locks.

The famous cry of the Revolution was 'no taxation without representation'. This was an ancient English idea, and therefore difficult for the metropolitan government to argue against. But it was almost always no more than a smokescreen: colonial Americans almost never sought their colonies' representation in the Westminster Parliament or more democratic colonial assemblies, and the idea was hardly ever seriously promoted on either side of the Atlantic. What part of the colonial elite sought, from an early date, was independence. Britain resisted, as England had long resisted the independence of Ireland and Scotland, and as America's northern states in the 1860s resisted by force the secession of the Confederacy. Resistance to dismemberment is not a puzzle; but rebellion is.

Some of the causes of the rebellion were practical and self-interested. Victory over the French brought territorial responsibilities. Partly in an attempt to minimise expensive conflict with Native Americans, partly to check the rapacity of settlers, the metropolitan government in 1763 drew a Proclamation Line around areas of existing white occupation in an attempt to regulate settlement beyond it. From then until 1773 a clear boundary was established stretching from New York to Florida, despite colonial attempts to cheat on land allocations. By the 1770s, this attempt to restrain the depredations of colonists upon the Native Americans was breaking down. Even so, it had involved stationing some 10,000 troops in America, mostly in the newly conquered colonies of Quebec and Florida, or in the back country to separate colonists and Indians. The army had lived amicably enough with the colonists, but the disaffected intelligentsia of the east coast now got up a heightened denunciation of 'standing' (i.e. regular) armies, held to be proof of a royal conspiracy to rivet the chains of slavery on the people.

What have been called the 'ostensible causes' of the revolution mostly concerned the legitimacy of taxation, and this problem became acute for the metropolitan government with the massive debt incurred in the Seven Years War. But it was not obvious that taxation would produce such a rhetorically exaggerated reaction. The founding myth of the revolution, as the Declaration of Independence put it, was that the colonies merely reacted against 'a design to reduce them under absolute despotism', namely George III's 'direct object' of 'the establishment of an absolute tyranny over these states'. The opposite was nearer the case: George III's ministers had reacted to illegality among the colonists (massive evasion of trade regulations, disregard of property rights, assertions of legislative autonomy) with a policy which combined an abstract theoretical assertion of sovereignty over the colonies with practical appeasement of local elites. From the Stamp Act in 1765 (which extended to the colonies a metropolitan tax on official documents) through the Townshend duties in 1767 (which lightly taxed certain commodities in order to free colonial judges and governors from local political control, and so allow them to enforce trade regulations) to the East India Company tea deal in 1773 (which would have halved its price and undercut the influential colonial merchants who smuggled tea), London attempted to find compromise formulae to raise modest sums in revenue but tended to back down when these provoked loud colonial resistance. Throughout, the real issue was expressed as one of constitutional principle, but this failed to disguise colonial self-interest and religious antipathy to English rule, perceived as a militantly Anglican regime: the colonies never groaned under a major tax burden, and were not going to be asked to do so. The army was never used (as it was to be in Ireland before 1798) to round up colonial leaders, break up meetings like the Continental Congress, or shut down printing presses. When troops finally arrived in Boston in 1768 they were at a loss how to act among a population that continued to enjoy the legal rights of Englishmen. No English bishop was ever going to pursue the descendants of those who had fled from Archbishop Laud; but many colonial Nonconformists feared, or said they feared, just that.

Meanwhile, the ministry had decided that the loyalty of newly conquered Quebec could only be secured by granting religious toleration and preserving French civil law. In this it was persuaded by Alexander Wedderburn, Solicitor General, who applied to Canada the formula successfully implemented in his native Scotland in 1707 (in 1777 Adam Smith continued to press Wedderburn to use the 1707 model to solve the American problem). The Quebec Act of 1774 was opposed at Westminster and received with outrage in the Thirteen Colonies, whose elites affected to be indignant at the concession to 'Popery' and claimed it as proof that the Whig George III and his Whig ministers were in league with the pope; they were perhaps more alarmed that the Act extended the boundaries of Quebec south and west, blocking the ambitions of many colonial land speculators including Patrick Henry and George Washington. Overnight, their investments in a speculative future settlement, to be called Vandalia, became valueless.

Just as threatening to many British colonists was the landmark ruling in *Somerset v. Stewart*, a case heard in London by Lord Mansfield in 1772, which made clear (as Blackstone had argued in his *Commentaries*) that

English common law did not recognise the status of slavery. In a transatlantic polity, it was only a matter of time before the same principle would have to be applied in North America also. Colonial slave-owners therefore joined colonial merchant smugglers, colonial Dissenters, colonial debtors and colonial land speculators as powerful groups with an interest in emancipation from British policy.

A growing mood of belligerence spread among colonists, who still included people long used to weapons and to murderous conflicts with Native Americans or slaves. Even so, the outbreak of fighting in 1775 was not bound to lead to the independence of the Thirteen Colonies. War in the early eighteenth century more often led to compromises. That this was not the outcome was not due to Congress, or to the patriot militia, but to the courts of Europe. Only the intervention on the rebel side of France and Spain created a strategic situation in which British victory and a compromised settlement were impossible. Even so, much more might have been achieved, but for Lord North's inadequacy as a war minister, for the lacklustre performance of the two senior British commanders, Admiral Howe and General Howe, and for Britain's failure to coordinate strategy with the colonial loyalists, who were in some areas numerous.

George Washington's regular troops were significant, but not decisive. A majority of the forces facing the British in the key battle at Yorktown (1781) were French regulars, whether of the army or the navy. Even here, France's intention was not altruistically to bring into being the new social experiment of an independent United States but to weaken both sides so that the French position on the American continent might be retrieved. That this did not happen after 1783 was by far the most significant outcome of the Revolution. It can be attributed not to the strength of the new republic but to the success of the Royal Navy in bottling up the French Revolution and in leading Napoleon to direct his attack ultimately against Russia. In 1783 Britain lost thirteen colonies, but not her navy; and in the next half century the navy was to matter more.

Why could disaffected colonists not be appeased? Both sides were led to war because of irreconcilably different world views that would not compromise on the constitutional questions of sovereignty and jurisdiction thought to be at issue. Yet neither colonies nor metropolis had seriously explored a federal solution: neither side wanted a compromise. The question is why not.

The British in Britain fought the American war out of a commitment to the indivisibility of sovereignty and the sanctity of allegiance;
from a calculation that colonial forces might disintegrate in the face of
regular troops; and in the belief that, as Wedderburn put it, the
colonies were 'to the trade and navigation of the kingdom essential'.
The last two were proved wrong: Britons from the Thirteen Colonies
were as militarily unskilled, but as brave and stubborn, as Britons from
the homeland; Britain's trade grew strongly after the colonies secured
independence. The first two, however, were remarkably vindicated,
and on both sides. The most important outcome of the American war
was not initially the independence of the Thirteen Colonies, which
only much later became significant in world terms, but (1) Britain's
political and ideological cohesion and practical success in the face of a
major coalition of European powers, and (2) the lasting political and
ideological cohesion of the new United States. Indeed, it was Britain
that boldly declared war on the United Provinces in December 1780 to
deprive the French and Spaniards of the Dutch carrying trade. The
American war was in this way a trial run for Britain's survival in the
more important conflicts that followed 1789. Out of the American
Revolution, the British polity emerged intact; although the kingdom of
Ireland threatened to break free, by 1800 this possibility was frustrated.
It was not the defeated party, Britain, that then collapsed in revolution,
but the chief victor, France. Britain, by contrast, emerged from the war
showing every sign of resilience and dynamism. But even the new
American republic emerged not as a confederal polity but, with the
constitution of 1787, as a unified one with a unitary conception of
sovereignty residing in 'we the people'.

The British in the colonies fought the home country out of a
conviction that their liberties were at peril from 'Popery' and 'arbitrary
power'; that the metropolis intended to load a heavy tax burden on
them; that they had a religious duty to resist; and that they had a
Providential destiny to spread (Protestant Nonconformist) civilisation
throughout the world (or, at least, North America). Military victory
seemed to prove the correctness of this analysis. In reality, since
metropolitan 'Popery' and 'arbitrary power' were mythical, the
problem had been wrongly diagnosed: the new republic therefore
inherited the unsolved legal and constitutional problems of its parent,
leading to decades of constitutional conflict and renewed civil war in
the 1860s. Its understandings of 'liberty' had to be adapted to the

militantly slave-owning, Indian-expropriating society that was born
less of idealism than of the bloody horrors of war and revolution. This
situation was disguised when the new nation constructed a sanitised
myth of origins, and when Britain distanced itself from the failures of
metropolitan policy by developing a 'Whig interpretation of history'
that blamed everything on George III and his ministers. What was
vindicated in the new republic were the self-interested motives of the
white elite: the release of many planters from debts contracted in
Britain; the freedom of merchants to trade outside the Navigation Acts;
the freedom greatly to extend black slavery; the freedom to disregard
treaties with Native Americans, to seize their lands with massive loss
of Native American life, and to make fortunes from the development
of an expropriated continent.

Despite these long-term sectoral advantages, in the medium term
the economic impact of revolution and war on the Thirteen Colonies
was severe: the destruction of property and trade, the huge states'
debts, the high taxes needed to service those debts for many years
afterwards and the rampant inflation that went with paper currency.
Much of the devastation was localised; but averaged across the
economy, one recent American estimate suggests that even after
some years of recovery US per capita income fell by a huge 46 per cent
between 1774 and 1790; recovery, moreover, was slow. Another
estimate places US wealth per capita 14 per cent lower in 1805 than in
1774. In Britain, the opposite was true. Although the national debt rose
from £127 million in 1775 to £232 million by 1783, manufacturing output
recovered quickly after the war. Exports were back at their 1772 level
by 1783, and 40 per cent higher by 1790. Trade boomed. Perhaps for the
first time, Britons began to sense that war was not always an
economic disaster.

The End of the Ancien Regime?

Britain survived the French Revolution only to experience its own
years of trauma after 1815 and an episode of upheaval, in 1828–35, which
saw an end to the legal hegemony of the Church of England,
fundamental parliamentary reform and a recasting of local government that, between them, amounted to a social revolution. How this
episode is to be analysed and explained is a major preoccupation of

historians, and debate continues. Much depends on what we take to be the starting point: what, after all, was Britain's state form in the first decades of the nineteenth century? Was it essentially open, democratic, dynamic? Or essentially closed, hierarchical, anachronistic? Are these alternatives wrongly framed? Are they even admissible as historical statements?

The starting point has traditionally been the history of parliamentary reform rather than the history of religious or local government reform. Before 1832 Britain possessed a system of representative government, but how was this to be understood? According to one revealing contemporary defence of that system, democracy in the sense it was later understood played only a minor part in it. As Charles Jenkinson, later Lord Liverpool, put it, speaking against Grey's motion in the Commons for parliamentary reform in 1793, 'We ought not then to begin first, by considering who ought to be the electors, and then who ought to be the elected; but we ought to begin by considering who ought to be the elected, and then constitute such persons electors as would be likely to produce the best elected.' The landed interest 'ought to have the preponderant weight' since it was 'the stamina of the country. In the second place, in a commercial country like this, the manufacturing and commercial interest ought to have a considerable weight, secondary to the landed interest'; plus, thirdly, 'professional people', who were 'absolutely necessary to the composition of the House of Commons'. These professional people 'made that House the representation of the people', exactly because they 'have collectively no *esprit de corps*' – they were not an 'interest' (still less, we might add, a class). And the professional people could only be returned 'by means of those boroughs which are called rotten boroughs'. Nor was representation intended to give effect to sectional self-interest: 'It was certainly a principle of the British constitution, that monarchy, aristocracy and democracy should serve as a control on each other; but it was likewise a principle that on ordinary occasions they should and must cooperate.' If so, it is open to debate how far the old order was destroyed by the positive advocacy of democracy, how far by the negative condemnation of the hereditary principle. But changes were certainly afoot.

In 1827 *Blackwood's Magazine* deplored a reversal in public discourse: John Bull, from boasting that the laws and constitution were 'the perfection of human wisdom', had been persuaded that they were 'so

erroneous and defective, that they inflict on him almost every
conceivable injury'. One target stood out: 'A war now rages against the
Aristocracy, the object of which is to degrade it from its place in
society, and to accomplish its virtual annihilation as a separate Estate
of the Realm.' Was this an exaggeration? Did the old order indeed have
a necessary, interlocking unity? Much here depends on definitions. In
the late eighteenth century Britain, like France, often pictured itself as
sophisticated and modern; British opinion was therefore often resistant
to the revolutionary allegation that Britain, too, represented an
instance of the outmoded aristocratic order that the new revolutionary
dawn was to dispel. To such Britons it was the French Revolution that
represented a step back to an age of barbarism, and many voices could
be found to echo Burke in this interpretation. France's declaration of
war in 1793 gave a practical but not an historical answer to the point at
issue: was British society anachronistic? To delve further into that
question we must review a number of areas.

First, the conceptual. A negative characterisation of British society
did indeed arise with the coinage of a key term, 'Old Corruption'.
It was an idea that enjoyed some currency after 1815; it claimed to
identify a world of status and hierarchy, and point to its alleged props:
privilege, patronage, places, pensions, sinecures. Against a world so
characterised stood, some claimed, a new set of values, sometimes
expressed in terms of natural rights and equality of opportunity,
sometimes in terms of Jeremy Bentham's new philosophy of
utilitarianism, sometimes in terms of that new political ideology,
radicalism, with its denigration of the landowner and the established
Church. Although the nexus of sinecures, pensions and contracts used
to support government was steadily scaled down from Pitt's ministry
of 1784 onwards, enough remained that radicals could ignore this
progressive abolition and paint what William Cobbett called 'The
Thing' in increasingly threatening hues. This concept, drawing a
variety of phenomena together and claiming that they constituted an
interlocking system, allowed people at the time to hail 1832 as a major
watershed, although it equally allowed others to complain that too
little had changed.

Second, the perception of general and widespread change in society
proceeding independently of the political events of 1828–35. In 1829 a
Yorkshire gentleman, A. H. Eyre, wrote:

For some time a *Revolution* has been commenced & is regularly *pro-gressing*, in our *feelings*, our *manners*, & our *principles political & religious*. We are no longer the same people that we were seventy years ago: there is no longer the same hospitality amongst acquaintance, nor the same warm attachment amongst connections, even the nearest; there are no *gradations* of rank in society, either in regard to *birth*, to *dress*, to *manners*, nor even to *acquirements*. A general appearance of equality pervades all classes without leaving any line of distinction between them. Even between the *rich* & the *poor* there is little apparent difference; all persons live alike however different may be their income; indeed the fluctuation of property is so rapid, that he who is poor to-day may by some fortunate speculation be rich tomorrow, & the great capitalist may be at once plunged into poverty.

It was already a cliché that people were not as they once were, and his remarks need to be interpreted; nevertheless, they were part of a wider body of comment on a shift from an aristocratic to a free-market society. Such transitions happen slowly: if correctly identified here, they must have begun long before 1832 and continued long afterwards. Yet such changes often have symbolic moments and determinative events that end the hegemony of one set of values and promote the extension of others. 1832 may have been one such moment.

Third, the impact of the major legislation of 1828–35. Some of the clearest and most testable evidence concerns the nature of the Reform Act of 1832, around which much historical controversy has raged. Yet the 1832 Act cannot be understood by reading its text alone; its impact must be judged against the circumstances that led to it. Here, the evidence does not support the idea that there was a pent-up demand for the franchise over the long eighteenth century that was triumphantly fulfilled with the passing of the Act: even in the 'first age of party', 1689–1714, this demand was not heard, while after the 1720s the numbers of people voting fell away substantially: many more men had the vote than cast it. Yet this need not imply a political quiescence from which 1832 was an awakening: in some boroughs with house-holder franchises, participation rates could be high, and borough seats were often in commercial and manufacturing centres like Leicester, Norwich and Nottingham, or ports like Bristol, Harwich, Newcastle upon Tyne and Liverpool. Much is often made of the 'unrepresented' state of growing manufacturing towns, yet their inhabitants normally voted in the counties within which the towns were located, and did so on the wide 40s. franchise that applied in the counties. One characteristic of the English representative system was that a sub-stantially plebeian electorate (and four-fifths of English MPs sat for boroughs) consistently returned patrician candidates. Of the one-sixth of MPs in 1790–1830 who were merchants or bankers, most sided with the ministry against parliamentary reform. So the absence of any long-term demand for 'democracy' may tell either in favour of or against the idea that the 1832 Act represented a fundamental change: 1832 may have initiated a new and democratic era, or this may have been brought about for other reasons entirely. On this reading, the significant increase after 1832 was not in the number entitled to vote, but in the proportion of seats contested; 1832 reinstated two-party politics and the alternation of parties in government (in abeyance since 1714) rather than initiating democracy.

It used to be conventional to treat parliamentary reform in 1832 as a response to an Industrial Revolution, but the plausibility of this scenario has also weakened in recent decades as the extent of economic change has been reassessed. Proposals for the reform of parliament long preceded industrialisation; the novel ideology of universal manhood suffrage was devised in the 1760s for reasons unconnected with economic change, and for half a century achieved no mass audience in growing cities or manufacturing districts. Parliamentary reform was a cry heard in London more than in Leeds, in Westminster more than in Wolverhampton. Not until 1816–17 did agitation for Reform become prominent in industrial areas, and it has not been established that it was the urban or the industrial nature of those areas that caused new political attitudes; rather, Reform was widely seen as a generalised remedy for an economic slump, and recovery in the 1820s silenced those demands until the next recession in 1829–30. The degree to which industrialisation had yet developed should not be exaggerated: in 1832 Britain possessed only 166 miles of railway, against the 20,266 miles of the mature system in 1913. If political change was not compelled by economic change, this may tell in favour of, or against, the idea that 1832 represented a watershed. Political change, if self-caused, might have been sudden rather than incremental; or it might alternatively have been largely irrelevant to the economy's long continuities.

Because of such uncertainties it is still debated how far an erosion in the position of the established order took place over time and was complete before 1832, or how far a hegemonic system retained its grip, despite some degree of numerical erosion, until a late and relatively sudden disintegration. If 'underlying' or 'long-term' change did not make a watershed inevitable, we can briefly sum up the other arguments for and against a fundamental transition.

The argument against a watershed points to the areas in which the 1832 Reform Act made little difference. The landed interest still filled the House of Commons, and the number of MPs who were merchants or manufacturers did not greatly rise. Numbers voting increased from 400,000, but only to about 600,000: there was no intention on the part of the ministry to initiate an age of democracy, and equally little recognition that the middle classes were now to be given political power, let alone the working classes. In the discussions of the Whig government on the contents of the 1832 Bill, the secret ballot was considered, but dropped: the intention was to preserve 'influence'. It was because voting was still open and subject to scrutiny that the qualification was reduced to the level of the £10 householder. Whigs continued to claim that 1832 was final. Even the firebrand Lord John Russell argued thus until 1848; Gladstone voted against reform in the 1850s, and backed it only from 1865. The really large extensions of the franchise waited for the Reform Acts of 1867 and 1884, and it was this later era that saw a marked further rise in the proportion of seats contested at general elections.

The argument in favour of major change looks at other aspects of the question. In one view the end of a social order came when its constitutional-libertarian tradition was brought to merge with resurgent Dissent, joined now by the programmatic atheism that an intelligentsia had propagated. By creating a uniform franchise, the 1832 Act has been argued to have played a large role in the formation of the notion of a singular 'middle class'. Reformers tried to define this middle class as those worthy of the franchise, as distinct from the mob; but class politics were antithetical to the old order.

The Act embodied major advantages for the landed classes in the short term, especially the rise in English county seats from 82 to 144, but may have ensured their eventual destruction. It had been passed amidst extra-parliamentary pressure: henceforth parliament would have to work in the shadow of a militant 'public opinion'. The Act was in some respects intended by its authors to be symbolic: the large number of small borough seats it abolished was a recognition of the validity of the critique of Old Corruption, and was pushed through despite the shock caused to the political classes. It was not final, as its defenders claimed, but led to further parliamentary Reform Acts in 1867, 1884 and 1918. Yet the extension of the franchise was not the key theme in 1832, and possibly not even in 1867; what mattered more were the mechanics of representation, not any principled affirmation of democracy in the sense of the direct representation of the individual.

By 1867, Walter Bagehot was arguing in *The English Constitution* that the state was already a republic in all but name, under a token monarchy. It was also a state significantly more secularised: the Church of England had been the great loser in 1832, vilified by radicals for siding with the old order (the bishops had voted against the first Reform Bill, in October 1831, by twenty-one to two). 'Old Corruption' was an idea that, thanks to that new group, the radicals, had centrally included the Church. A Unitarian, John Wade, had set out figures for the inequalities of clerical incomes in *The Black Book: or, corruption unmasked* (1820), reprinted as *The Extraordinary Black Book* (1832). From Jeremy Bentham to James Mill, some intellectuals from the middling orders had been hostile to the Church; from the 1800s populist reformers had taken up the cry, as was clear in the Captain Swing riots among landless agricultural labourers in England's south-east and the riots over the Reform Bill in several towns in 1830–32. Until 1914, English politics was heavily shaped by the Protestant Nonconformist assault on the surviving powers of the Church, one that largely succeeded in marginalising it.

Historians debate whether the changes of these years were part of an integrated programme, changes that share the label 'reform'. Those who deny this tend to conclude that the reforms themselves were not major changes; yet this may be a normative judgement. It seems likely that (except for small groups, like the followers of Jeremy Bentham) even the Whig parliamentary party did not come to office in 1830 with an organised agenda of legislative change. Most politicians reacted pragmatically to events. What was more in evidence, it may be suggested, was a law of unintended consequences, as each innovation changed the structure of the system and led on to further innovation.

A fourth, and final, consideration is the comparative dimension. The question of whether Britain was an ancien regime state might more helpfully be considered in a comparative framework, first between the British Isles and continental Europe, and second between England,

Ireland, Scotland and Wales; but little such analysis has yet been undertaken. It seems clear, however, that the internal dynamic within the British Isles did not cease in 1832. Rather, the balance of power tilted markedly, so that Wales, Ireland and Scotland carried far more weight in the century after 1832 than in the century before.

Such matters are hard to quantify, but one point of access is provided by the controversies of the age about the nature and position of the elite. Some historians have argued that Britain's social order should not be analysed as an ancien regime since, unlike in continental Europe, different social groups did not possess legal immunities. Peers, as well as people, paid taxes and were subject to the criminal law. There is much truth in that argument, seen from a present-day perspective; but it often appeared differently to people at the time. They were acutely aware that differences of status were expressed in terms of 'rank', and that rank was contested. In the countryside, where most people still lived, the idea of a social hierarchy was most palpable (indeed the crisis of 1828–35 was in part a clash between the values of country and town). In England there was one part of the legal code that was intended to, and did in fact, secure special privilege to landed gentlemen: the game laws, codified by the Act of 1671, supplemented and modified by legislation through the eighteenth century, but not fundamentally recast until 1831.

In such a mental world a recognition of privilege attached to rank was valued by some, as well as condemned by others. Defenders of the old order used a range of arguments: the positive contribution to society of country gentlemen residing on their estates; the need to keep this practical system in repair by not blurring the distinction between gentlemen and plebeians; the defence of a value system associated with the country against the values of townsmen; a siding with the economic plight of the rural labourer, ignored by the London government. The game laws thus came to symbolise the values of 'land' against the values of 'money'. The redefinition of game as private property rather than as elite privilege, and the collapse of the practice of duelling within a decade of the 1832 Act, is in this view evidence of British society's redefinition away from the assumptions of an old order.

Yet if comparisons with France before 1789 are revealing, comparisons within the British Isles make the pattern far less clear. The term 'Old Corruption' pointed to a particularly English formation, less characteristic of Scotland and Wales, and even less so of Ireland. Social

systems within the British Isles were diverse. In each of its component
parts some voices from the 1790s agreed with the Jacobin analysis,
developed critiques of Britain's leading institutions and practices, and
eventually found ways of pursuing their interests. Yet these varied
considerably between the polities: the intellectual critique of the old
order came from a number of sources. One large source was provided
by Scotland, whose intelligentsia had abandoned the fervent Unionism
of the mid-eighteenth century and from the 1790s proved receptive to
new ideas, especially political economy and Benthamite utilitarianism.
Englishmen educated at Scottish universities imbibed similar
doctrines. *The Edinburgh Review* (founded 1802) sold equally well in
England, and provided a rationale for the revived Whig party that
passed the 1832 Reform Act and the reforms that followed.

This was not a common model, however: where Scotland responded
to the problems of the world after 1815 with the mindset of *The
Edinburgh Review*, Ireland's response was the mindset represented in
O'Connell's Catholic Association. In Ireland, Catholic emancipation
was accompanied by raising the Irish county franchise from the
traditional English figure of 40s. (£2) to £10: the intention was to exclude

Radical reform, 1819. 'Radical reform', a synonym for universal suffrage, is here associated
with French Jacobinism, about to ravish Britannia, who defends 'Religion', armed with
'The laws' and assisted by 'Loyalty'. How effective was this characterisation in denigrating
or resisting a reforming impulse?

those who had supported the Catholic Association. But this formal barrier was to prove ineffective against the populist politics that O'Connell had created. In the nineteenth century, Scotland remained within the union, arguably at the price of the union's progressive penetration by Scots values; southern Ireland increasingly resisted both English and Scots world views, threatened to secede, and finally did so to embody a very different outlook that led to its neutrality between Britain and Nazi Germany in the Second World War. This was not the attitude that prevailed in Ireland before 1801.

The hegemony of a new social sector in England was immediately evident from the rejection by parliament in 1833 of the 'ten hours' movement (an attempt to limit the working day in factories) and the passage of the Poor Law Amendment Act in 1834. This ended the right of the poor to receive parish assistance in their homes and established instead a network of workhouses, far more than had previously existed, designed to be so much more miserable in order to promote industriousness as the lesser evil. This was not merely an English Whig innovation; it was inspired by practice elsewhere in the British Isles. Scotland had not developed a compulsory poor relief system, despite legislative efforts in the late sixteenth and early seventeenth centuries. By the eighteenth, Scotland in principle gave no relief to paupers who were classed as 'able bodied'; paupers who were aged or infirm depended on meagre charitable collections at church, allocated by the ministers and elders, and administered by the heritors (landowners). Now these quite different Scots assumptions were applied to England and Wales, and widely interpreted as ending an older set of customs and values.

On one side in the emerging debate on the 'condition of England question' were social campaigners, in alliance with Tory paternalists, who stressed the moral responsibility of landowners for the wellbeing of their localities; on the other were Liberal manufacturers, political economists and 'philosophic radicals', the followers of Benthamite utilitarianism, who thought that unconstrained choice maximised individual utility. Like most Benthamite schemes, the 1834 Poor Law was implemented only in part, with wide regional variations: work-houses were too expensive, and unemployment was too widespread, to allow such a tidy solution. Yet the point was one of principle. It might be argued that a new view of man as an independent, secular, rational calculator had gained the ascendant; and with the Municipal

Corporations Act (1835), which established a uniform ratepayer franchise and terminated local oligarchies, this view secured hegemony in local government in England and Wales. National politics continued for many decades to be dominated by the landed elite; but in the towns and cities, in which a growing section of the population spent their lives, a new social constituency was in charge, which came to seem to be self-evidently 'the middle class', defined now as enemies (not, as in the 1820s, as allies) of the working classes.

British society in the late eighteenth and early nineteenth centuries was steadily evolving, innovative, increasingly geographically and socially mobile, technologically minded; but it was all these things within the familiar structures of 'Church and State', and these were the primary targets of reformers. Some historians explain this survival in terms of ruthless and successful repression by the ruling orders. Others point to a considerable degree of social solidarity, and doubt the 'contradiction' between 'structure' and 'superstructure' that Marxist historians used to depict. Such weighty matters are still at issue when Britain's status as an ancien regime is debated.

4. Some Counter-Factuals

In a wider perspective nothing can be taken for granted, not even the course followed by population totals. It would be possible to envisage a situation in which England and Scotland had shared in Ireland's runaway population growth, with equally disastrous results. England and Scotland might then have dealt with such a population boom in the Irish manner, by a progressive sub-division of landholdings. This might have kept the custom-bound, corporatist local community in being for some decades more, but with such a response rampant population growth is likely to have immiserated the countryside more than enclosures did. Those who idealise the 'moral economy' assume that an old order could have survived, centred on smallholdings and customary use-rights for the poor; but this projection depends on the assumption that the 'customary society' would not have generated a population explosion. Since in Ireland and parts of the Scottish Highlands it did just that, this assumption is not secure. It may be that all the major options pointed forward to widespread distress; in England and Scotland that could have meant revolution, as it did in France after near-famine in 1788–9, rather than Ireland's politically quiescent response to the disaster of the 1840s.

That this outcome was avoided was chiefly due to the special case of England. England's pre-industrial and commercial economy was markedly successful even before the growth of manufacturing industry, and this success is generally taken for granted. Yet it would have been possible for England to have followed the pattern of that other notable commercial economy, the United Provinces, commercially dynamic in the seventeenth century yet stagnant in the eighteenth. A serious historical comparison of the two has yet to be undertaken, but it would greatly illuminate the English case.

Many of the differences between the United Provinces and England, then Britain, were political; and political counterfactuals are more easily framed. The collapse of the English Republic in 1660 was by no means inevitable; indeed, it might be argued that it was the result of a military coup by General Monck. Without the intervention of his army, England might have continued as a republic with a Presbyterian religious underpinning, again like the United Provinces. Yet against this possibility must be set the relative lack, within the British Isles, of regional bases of military power: English, Scots and Irish government therefore tended in the seventeenth century towards centrist rule. A powerful military regime in England implied England's military dominance of Scotland and Ireland, as Oliver Cromwell had clearly seen. Such a republican regime, centralised and militarised, would probably have led, in an age of religious ferment and denominational resistance theory, to far more religiously based armed conflicts than was the case after 1660. Edmund Burke looked back on the restored monarchy, even in the person of Charles II, as a crucial guarantor of political stability and internal peace, and in this he may have been right.

Internal stability was nevertheless not a secure possession, and stability gained in one decade might be lost in the next. So it proved with the fall of the Stuart monarchy in 1688, which led to six decades of external war, internal rebellion and religious schism. But the deposition of James II was by no means a foregone conclusion. William of Orange's naval expedition might have enjoyed the same logistical ill fortune that later dogged successive Jacobite invasion attempts (and, indeed, most combined operations in the age of sail). In that event James would have retained his authority, beyond challenge from internal enemies. A Catholic monarchy, continued after James II's death in 1701 by the son born to him in 1688 and dying only in 1766, would, in a still strongly Protestant polity, have been able to do little more than secure toleration for all religious groups: the Anglican hegemony of the long eighteenth century would have been unseated, and the religious pluralism that followed 1828–9 would have arrived decades earlier. Whether parliament would have emerged essentially weakened from this encounter is harder to gauge: the usual celebration of parliament's powers after 1688 and 1714 rests on a greatly exaggerated estimate of the ability of the Commons to control ministries. The reality was that ministries developed powerful means of controlling the Commons rather than vice versa. A continued Stuart monarchy might have made little difference to this. Although it would undoubtedly have been denounced by spokesmen for the strident anti-Catholicism still widespread within the British Isles, the experience of an avowedly Catholic regime might have meant that this ancient antipathy of Catholic and Protestant weakened two centuries before it did.

Even had William of Orange landed with a significant army in 1688, the result might have been a political compromise rather than James's expulsion. In that case, parliament's position would have been enhanced at the same time that a larger measure of religious toleration was secured. Even James II's expulsion in 1688 need not have been a final exclusion of the Stuarts: the wide unpopularity of the Williamite and Hanoverian regimes provided serious support for a Stuart restoration in all the component parts of the archipelago. This became practical politics only with military backing from overseas; yet this was often planned, and often possible. The French fleet might have covered a major landing in the 1690s or 1744 with every chance of linking with support in England. The last such invasion attempt was that of 1759, and only the astonishing series of victories of that year removed that possibility.

A Stuart restoration might have reduced or eliminated the bloodshed endemic in England's relations with Scotland and Ireland, but at the price of igniting armed conflict at an earlier date with the North American colonies, animated as they often were with an anti-Catholicism more extreme than anywhere else in the English-speaking world. An American Revolution in 1715 might have stood much less chance of success, with important long-term consequences. We now know that revolution did occur in 1776, and treat it as inevitable. The founding myth of the American republic, drawn from England's Whig political rhetoric of the Exclusion Crisis, presented the alternatives as 'liberty' or 'slavery', independence or permanent imperial subservience. But this was a false antithesis. It is difficult to see Britain's colonies in North America remaining within the empire for more than a few decades: many of the Thirteen Colonies were already developing towards de facto self-rule, and would have continued to do so. The real alternatives in the 1770s were between, first, a perilous bid for independence via world war and internal revolution, or, second, the expectation of independence a few decades later via commonplace political conflict and negotiation. If so, the path actually followed looks less attractive and less inevitable.

Much would have been different had the Thirteen Colonies followed Canada's peaceful route to negotiated independence. Within North America, the two major acts of genocide that marked the foundation of the United States would have been mitigated. The expropriation and murder of Native Americans by white settlers might have been under at least some degree of governmental restraint, since relations with the tribes were regulated in detail by the treaties into which the British government had entered with Native Americans in order to win their support against France in the Seven Years War; these commitments the new American republic disavowed. The phenomenon of black slavery, too, would have been checked, since Mansfield's landmark verdict in *Somerset v. Stewart* (1772) clearly established that English law did not recognise slavery, and the implications of this judgment for the colonies must soon have been confronted. The anti-slavery movement developed first in Britain, not America, and would have made greater headway at an earlier date without the American war. Even in an age of revolution, Britain was compelled by the opinion of its elite to act against the slave trade, first by the use of the Royal Navy to end the trade itself, then by buying out the slave-owners of the West Indies. The extent of slavery in North America was far less in 1776 than it became by the 1860s, and it was still a problem that could have been contained and solved by the metropolitan government. The possibility that North America's devastating and essentially related civil wars of 1776–83 and 1861–5 could both have been avoided by a managed evolution towards self-government is real.

Internationally, the absence of an American revolutionary war would have meant that France would not have collapsed in bankruptcy, as it did in 1788, leading to the recall of the Estates-General and revolution in 1789: the absence of revolution would have meant that France, and Europe generally, would have pursued a path of meliorist reform. Without the convulsions and losses of war in 1776–83, 1793–1802 and 1803–15, Britain's national debt would have fallen, capital would have been employed instead in manufacture, trade and agriculture, society would have been substantially more prosperous and the pressures for violent reform at home would have been mitigated.

All these affluent but mundane outcomes were blasted by war and revolution. In that setting, Britain's very survival within revolutionary Europe was not a foregone conclusion. Many historians claim that domestic insurrection was a real possibility in the 1790s, even in England. In Ireland, the potential for armed conflict was far greater, and greater again in the event of a French invasion. The failure of the French navy to deliver this outcome in the 1790s is highlighted by the scale of the Irish rebellion which materialised in 1798 even without significant French aid. In combination with mutinies in the fleet in 1797, a successful Irish rising would have destabilised the state and might easily have brought a version of the French Revolution to the British Isles, as happened so often elsewhere in Europe. Even if revolution had been avoided in the 1790s, all was not secure: the significance of the Battle of Trafalgar in 1805 was that it smashed a Franco-Spanish naval combination whose aim was to allow the landing in Britain of the vast army that Napoleon had massed at Boulogne. Had this army, the most effective in Europe, set foot on British soil, its success would have been highly likely.

Britain's course of development in the nineteenth century was set within limits established by her survival of war and the threat of revolution. This survival was a remarkable achievement. Historians have found a series of ways of describing it as inevitable: the Whig myth of English constitutional liberties; the model of successful capitalist exploitation; the strength of a fiscal-military state. All are open to major objections. At any point between 1660 and 1832, the future was wholly uncertain.

PART V

THE WORLD HEGEMON: THE LONG NINETEENTH CENTURY, 1832–1914

William D. Rubinstein

The Great Exhibition of 1851. Held in the Crystal Palace, an enormous building erected for that purpose in Kensington Park, London, the Great Exhibition was the first 'world's fair'. Attracting millions of visitors from Britain and overseas, it was symbolic of Victorian progress and peaceful development. What impact would such an unprecedented event have upon visitors? What realities did it conceal?

Introduction

In many respects, the nineteenth century belonged to Britain, just as the twentieth century was dominated in so many ways by the United States. For most of the period between 1800 and 1914, Britain was at the zenith of its power and influence, and, certainly prior to the last decades of the century, was universally seen as one of the world's superpowers, perhaps its greatest. It is a cliché that every period is a time of transition and change, but nowhere is this more true than in the nineteenth century, when Britain experienced seismic industrial upheaval, was transformed from a largely rural to a largely urban society, and formally became the head of a mighty empire. Yet, to a surprising extent, much about Britain did not change dramatically. In contrast to virtually all the other European nations its formal governmental structure was almost precisely the same in 1914 as it was a century earlier. The British Isles escaped revolution, invasion, internal turmoil and dictatorship, despite the transformations it experienced. Part V considers the major dimensions of British change and stability, and what these meant for its peoples' sense of identity, during the nineteenth century.

1. Material Cultures

The Demographic Background

Of all the changes Britain witnessed during the nineteenth century, possibly none was as dramatic, or easier to quantify, than the enormous growth in population and the increase in size of its cities. Britain recorded its first national census in 1801. Every ten years thereafter censuses have been held, and from them we have an accurate account of British population and change. (The first Irish census was not held until 1821; no British census was held in 1941, during the Second World War.) While no official figures exist prior to 1801, it is generally estimated that the population of England and Wales totalled about 3 million in 1600, rising to 5.5 million in 1700 and 6.5 million in 1750; Ireland's was approximately 2.7 million in 1700, 3.2 million in 1750 and 5 million in 1801; and Scotland's by 1755 was 1.3 million – in other words, the total population of what would become known as the United Kingdom probably totalled about 10.8 million in 1750. The extraordinary rate of growth of Britain's population during the nineteenth century can be seen from the following statistics.

Table 1. Population of the United Kingdom and its Components, 1801–1911 ('000)

	1801	1831	1851	1881	1901	1911
England	8,352	13,090	16,922	25,974	30,813	34,109
Wales	541	807	1,006	1,361	1,715	2,027
Scotland	1,608	2,364	2,889	3,736	4,272	4,751
Ireland	5,216	7,767	6,552	5,175	4,459	4,381
United Kingdom	15,501	24,028	27,369	34,885	41,259	45,268
% of Total in England	c. 54	54	62	71	75	75

During the half-century from 1750 to 1801, the population of Britain and Ireland probably increased by about 44 per cent. Over the course of the next century, however, it rose by nearly four times that amount, 166 per cent, a rate of increase without any parallel in history. The population of England more than tripled during the nineteenth century; by 1911, Britain was vastly more populous than it had been a century earlier. Britain's population explosion, moreover, occurred alongside massive and unprecedented emigration overseas, chiefly to North America and other areas of the white empire such as Australia. Without this unprecedented emigration, Britain's overall population growth would have been even greater.

While England, Scotland and Wales grew significantly during the nineteenth century, it is striking that, in complete contrast, the population of Ireland actually declined considerably. Ireland's population reached a peak of about 8.5 million in the mid-1840s, before being struck by the Great Famine of 1845-49, probably the greatest demographic catastrophe in any European country between the Thirty Years War of the seventeenth century and the First World War. In 1845, a fungus-borne potato blight substantially destroyed the single crop on which much of rural western Ireland depended for its sustenance. Starvation and disease, and an arguably inept British governmental response, meant that about 1.1 million people died in the famine, while more than two million Irishmen emigrated in the decade 1845-55 (more than a quarter of the total Irish population), creating great Irish Catholic diasporas in many cities in England and Scotland, and powerful communities in the United States, Australia and elsewhere. Although anti-English feeling was already deeply ingrained, the Irish Famine only exacerbated the lasting sense of hostility and grievance felt by nationalist-minded Irish Catholics towards the British government.

Elsewhere in Britain, however, there was uninterrupted population growth: an increase of 308 per cent in England, 195 per cent in Scotland, and 175 per cent in Wales between 1801 and 1911. What caused this enormous and unprecedented increase? While such a question cannot be answered precisely, many historians would attribute it to a lowering in the age of marriage after the mid-eighteenth century, as opportunities increased in the wake of economic growth. This enabled more children to be born into each family (illegitimacies represented only a small percentage of births). Particularly during the period 1800-70, large families were the norm, even among the middle classes. The reasons for this decline in the age of marriage are controversial, but might revolve around wider social and geographical changes in society such as a shift towards greater urbanisation. It would also appear that the incidences of virulent diseases declined compared with earlier centuries. Inoculation and, later, vaccination for smallpox (introduced by Edward Jenner in 1796) certainly saved many from this notorious killer, while the plague, the scourge of Europe's population down the ages, failed to appear in its old form in Europe after about 1727, possibly because the brown rat replaced the plague-ridden black rat. Nevertheless, one should not exaggerate how healthy Britain had become. In 1860, about 15 per cent of infants died before their first birthday, while death by such infectious diseases as tuberculosis, typhoid and scarlet fever were still commonplace.

In the last decades of the nineteenth century, the birth rate began to decline dramatically, a phenomenon first observed among the English middle classes from about 1870. It remained marginally higher in Scotland than in England and Wales, and higher in England and Wales than in Ireland after the 1840s, where the overall population continued to drop, and many young men and women emigrated. This decline in the birth rate was accompanied by an even sharper fall in the death rate, especially among children, meaning that it became more likely that some children would survive into adulthood even among smaller families. This process of smaller families becoming more common is known as the 'demographic transition', and was accelerated among middle-class (especially professional) families by the steep costs of educating sons at fee-paying schools and universities. By the close of the nineteenth century, late marriages became the rule, augmented in the twentieth century by contraception. By the 1930s, the British birth rate was less than half of what it had been in the mid-nineteenth century.

The other major factors in population change are emigration and immigration. The nineteenth century was the era, *par excellence*, of massive European migration overseas, especially to the United States and, in the British case, to areas of new settlement in the white empire such as Canada and Australia. Comprehensive statistics exist only from the mid-nineteenth century, but these are startling in their scale. In 1853, the first year when official statistics are available, 278,000 British people emigrated overseas, about 1 per cent of the population, of whom 191,000 went to the United States. Between 5 and 10 per cent of the British population emigrated overseas in most decades of the nineteenth century – extraordinary figures. While disproportionate numbers of these were probably impoverished Irishmen, emigrants came from all ranks on the social scale. Emigration overseas has often been seen as a 'safety valve' to relieve potential discontent at home, with tens of thousands of potential trouble-makers, even potential revolutionaries, leaving Britain each year. Many did well in their new homes and, paradoxically, often eventually became conservatives and empire super-patriots. The worldwide network of empire loyalty which Britain had built up by the time of the First World War was largely founded on just such successful émigrés. Immigration into Britain from Europe and elsewhere always existed, but, during the nineteenth century, was hardly noticed except in the last two decades of the century when about 150,000 eastern European Jews escaped poverty and oppression by migrating to Britain, chiefly to London's East End. Immigrant entrepreneurs, intellectuals and political refugees were, however, a notable part of the British scene; until 1905, Britain had *no* barriers of any kind to immigration, so anyone could come. By far the largest number of settlers in Great Britain, however, were impoverished Irish Catholics – who, of course, were British subjects, not foreigners.

Just as significant as the sheer growth in Britain's population was the enormous expansion in the size of Britain's cities, and the changes in the nature of British urban demography which occurred as a result of population growth and industrialisation. Down the ages, Britain contained a city which was vastly greater in size than any other, namely London, the capital. Many of the smaller cities and towns were, officially, the local administrative centres of Britain's counties, while a few of the largest – Bristol, Liverpool, Manchester – were commercial or industrial centres. At the beginning of the nineteenth century, the gap in size between London and Britain's other main cities was extraordinary: in 1801, the Greater London metropolitan area had a population of 1,117,000; remarkably, not a single other city in Britain had a population even a tenth this size, the six next largest being Edinburgh (83,000), Liverpool (82,000), Glasgow (77,000), Manchester (75,000), Birmingham (71,000) and Bristol (61,000). Only a handful of other cities had a population which exceeded 40,000. In Ireland there were no reliable population statistics before 1821. In that year, the population of Dublin was about 336,000, while that of Belfast was only about 35,000. By 1910, Dublin had about 395,000 inhabitants, while the population of industrial Belfast had risen dramatically, to about 380,000, up from only 200,000 in 1881.

By 1911, however, there were *forty* cities in addition to London with a population of 100,000 or more, including Glasgow (1,000,000), Birmingham (840,000), Liverpool (753,000) and Manchester (714,000). Britain now contained recognisable urban conurbations – distinctive groups of adjacent cities and their outlying areas – with South-East Lancashire (Greater Manchester) containing 2.3 million inhabitants, the West Midlands (Birmingham) 1.6 million, West Yorkshire (Leeds and Bradford) 1.6 million, and Merseyside (Liverpool) 1.2 million. These new urban areas dwarfed the old commercial and adminis-trative towns of Britain, whose population wholly failed to keep pace with the new areas of urban growth. For instance, Chester's population was 15,000 in 1801 but only 39,000 in 1911; King's Lynn numbered 10,000 inhabitants in 1801 but only 20,000 in 1911; Exeter grew from 17,000 to 59,000 in this period. Unless a town could attract new sources of industry or commerce, it often decayed. Some old towns such as Aberdeen, Derby, Norwich and Nottingham managed to find new industries, sometimes because a few local entrepreneurs fortuitously established new businesses there, developing the granite industry in Aberdeen and lace manufacture in Nottingham. Never-theless, without new forms of commerce and industry, numbers declined relatively, even absolutely. Counties bypassed by economic and population growth included Cornwall, most of northern Scotland and much of rural Wales and Ireland.

Within each of the old British counties, the growth of enormous new cities meant that the old structures of governance and the old ruling elites were swamped, even obliterated, by the new urban order. Lancashire's county town and capital, for instance, was Preston, which developed its own new industries and grew from 12,000 in 1801 to 117,000 in 1911. But its role as county administrative centre was largely irrelevant to the governance of the county's two huge cities, Liverpool and Manchester, and to the host of smaller, but still substantial, towns which grew with industrialisation, such as Blackburn, Bolton and Oldham. The traditional, pre-modern elite structure which had governed at the local level in Lancashire (as in all other counties), composed of aristocrats and the larger landowners, well-established merchants and lawyers, and some Anglican clergymen, was now largely eclipsed, in terms of wealth, economic power and ideologically driven political intent, by the new men of industrial and commercial Lancashire, often 'self-made' and uncouth, often Nonconformist in religion, often politically radical (at least initially), often regarding the traditional ruling elite – again, at least initially – as their enemies. Accommodating this new elite thrown up by industrial growth with the old elites became one of the major themes of nineteenth-century political life. The pattern found in Lancashire occurred throughout the new industrial areas of Britain. Birmingham in Warwickshire, for instance, became renowned as the great city where semi-socialist civic improvement and public works, led by the great radical (and, later, Tory) leader Joseph Chamberlain, went furthest.

Dwarfing every urban area in Britain – indeed, in the western world – was London, in every sense the capital of the nation and of the empire. Despite the fact that London was so large (perhaps because of it), it has been easy for contemporary commentators and later historians to overlook: Manchester, with its hundreds of billowing factory smokestacks, was somehow regarded as the norm and the standard from which other cities deviated. London's growth was indeed extraordinary: from 1.1 million in 1801, it grew to 2.7 million at the time of the Great Exhibition in 1851, and then to 4.8 million in 1881 and, remarkably, to 7.3 million in 1911, when it was almost certainly the largest city in the world. London's continuing expansion had been checked to a certain extent between 1831 and 1851 (when it grew in size from 1.9 million to 'only' 2.7 million, as newer industrial cities attracted the economically insecure and as London's own infrastructure floundered just before the development of suburban railways and trams, gaslight and running water), but then once again spurted enormously, nearly tripling over the next sixty years. London was virtually unique among the world's great cities in combining the formal role of national capital and administrative centre with a host of other functions of fundamental importance – the world's financial centre, in the 'square mile' of the City of London, a great shipping port, Britain's press and publishing centre, the focus of arts, entertainment and the intelligentsia, the centre of retailing, and the focus of all of High Society, the court, the aristocracy, and the wealthy. It was also the largest single manufacturing centre in Britain, producing a range of industrial and consumer goods, despite not being a factory town like Manchester or Leeds.

Since the Middle Ages, London had acted as a magnet for the footloose, and tens of thousands came to London from other parts of Britain each year to seek their fortunes. While some succeeded, the majority remained in the working classes. For women, the hazards of migrating to London were especially great, with prostitution a ubiquitous and shameful feature of life in the capital, probably more visible and unavoidable than anywhere else in Britain. London's eclectic combination of roles, and its vast size, place it in a different category from the rest of the world's great cities. Although New York was America's largest city, the capital was Washington, while in the late nineteenth century Chicago grew as something of a rival to New York. In many other countries – Russia, Canada, Australia – two rival large cities emerged. There were countries where a single capital metropolis paralleled London's multifaceted role, such as (most obviously) Paris in France, but none matched London's relative size in their respective populations. In 1911, for instance, London contained about 16 per cent of the entire population of the United Kingdom, while Paris was the home to only about 5 per cent of the French population. As a result, none of the great new cities of the north of England emerged to challenge London's dominance, which, if anything, increased in the course of the nineteenth century with its role as capital of the empire and world financial centre. (In 1911, it should be noted, Glasgow, with one million inhabitants, contained 21 per cent of Scotland's population, although its population was less than one-sixth of Greater London's. Edinburgh, with 401,000 people, held 8.4 per cent of Scotland's population. At the same time, Dublin and Belfast contained, respectively, 9.0 and 8.7 per cent of Ireland's population.)

The population of the entire western world grew enormously during the nineteenth century. This occurred, perhaps ironically, at a time when the British Isles never saw a revolution but emerged at the end of the century with arguably greater political and social stability than at its beginning. Could this have occurred without the 'safety valve' provided by the empire and massive emigration overseas? Was population growth in part the result of the fortuitous absence of old-style plagues and pestilence? Would it have occurred in the absence of an industrial revolution? Quite possibly; the population of Europe's backward areas, especially Russia, grew just as rapidly as Britain's, without the emergence of more than a skeletal urban working class in these regions. It is just possible, too, to imagine population decline, as in Ireland – if, for example, a cataclysmic plague visited Britain, or a period of sustained depression led to even more massive emigration overseas. Arguably, the long period of population growth throughout most of nineteenth-century Europe was merely fortuitous, the result of autonomous factors, and not the product of economic growth or industrialisation. These population changes helped to ensure the dominance of England within the United Kingdom. Nevertheless, as the rest of Part V demonstrates, population alone isn't everything, and in and of itself cannot explain the relations between the four parts of the United Kingdom. Ireland's population declined in absolute terms, yet the Irish contingent of MPs at the Westminster Parliament sometimes held the political balance of power between the major parties.

The Evolution of the British Economy

Parallel to the extraordinary changes in Britain's population during the nineteenth century was the growth and reorientation of its economy. Between 1801 and 1911 Britain's total gross national income grew from about £232 million to £1,643 million, a sevenfold increase, at a time when rates of inflation were either very low or non-existent. Economic growth thus outstripped population growth for the first time in British history. Historians from about the 1880s often began to depict the era after c. 1760 as that of an 'industrial revolution'. This was usually seen as centrally entailing the application of steam power and other forms of advanced motive power to manufacturing production, through the factory system, and to transport, via the railway and steam-powered shipping. While these things certainly occurred, one must not forget that the non-industrial component of the economy – finance, commerce, the professions, the service sector – grew at least as rapidly. Nor should one forget that agriculture and farming remained major components of the economy.

The 'industrial revolution' was also seen as fundamentally altering the class basis of British society, instituting the growth of a huge urban proletariat of workers in factories and mines, alongside a small class of wealthy industrialists. Again, while these changes certainly occurred, it is also the case that there was never a time when the classical industrial proletariat – workers in factories and mines – constituted more than about 40 per cent of the male workforce, while industrialists never comprised a majority of the wealthy or middle classes. Many recent historians question whether there was a 'take-off into sustained economic growth', to revisit the famous phrase of Walt Rostow, the American economic historian who believed that industrial revolutions, wherever they occur, are marked by spurts of much higher levels of economic growth, as measured by that country's national product. Instead, they argue that Britain's growth rate did not increase noticeably during the mid- to late eighteenth century, but was fairly steady throughout this period. Such an interpretation might help to explain the relative lack of political unrest in Britain, except in limited periods such as the aftermath of the Napoleonic Wars.

Historians have often debated why it was in Britain, rather than a rival nation such as France or the Netherlands, that these economic changes apparently occurred first. Put simply, Britain was well placed for early industrialisation. It was in many (but certainly not all) respects already a 'modern' society, with none of the feudalism, peasantry or serfdom that could be found throughout most of Europe until the nineteenth century (or sometimes even later). Instead, Britain was already what Thomas Carlyle later termed a 'cash-nexus'-based society, where reward was in the form of money wages, and enterprise for profit was broadly based. In the eighteenth century, Britain probably already had the highest per capita income of any European state, and was free of very sharp boundaries separating the traditional aristocracy from the rest of society. Many 'self-made' men became aristocrats. Private property was invariably protected by law, and could never be arbitrarily taken by the state. It has often been noted that England was the only part of Europe without any distinctive traditional peasant costume: bearing in mind social class differences, of course, everyone dressed alike. A high per capita income, a growing population and broadly similar tastes throughout society were major factors in creating strong internal demand for the goods which the British economy produced, especially for the cotton and woollen mass-produced goods emblematic of the first phase of industrialisation. This demand was augmented by increases in productivity and by Britain's fortunate position as a prime exporting nation.

Britain also controlled, or was dominant in, a large share of the world's foreign trade. Britain already had a large empire, centred in

India, Canada and the West Indies. It also exported to Europe, and ironically was significantly assisted after the rise of Napoleon when Britain successfully blockaded the French-dominated areas of the Continent, removing potential European rivals to Britain's export trade. After the American colonies gained their independence, strong economic ties between Britain and the United States resumed. When most of Latin America gained independence from Spain in the early nineteenth century, the Continent in many respects became an unofficial British economic colony. Above all, British world trading hegemony was crucially guaranteed by the dominance of the Royal Navy.

These potent factors were necessary, but not sufficient, preconditions for industrialisation. Arguably more important was Britain's propensity to engender both successful business entrepreneurs, especially in the newer manufacturing industries, as well as the new inventions which made industrialisation possible, which created the supply that matched home and foreign demand. Britain had always produced successful merchants and entrepreneurs; what was relatively new was their success in large-scale manufacturing industry as well as in trade and finance. Many of Britain's successful early industrialists were Protestant Nonconformists, whose 'Protestant ethic' of hard work and situation outside the Anglican-dominated elite structure probably drove this success. However, it should perhaps be noted that the two richest industrialists of the early nineteenth century, Richard Arkwright and Sir Robert Peel – the father of the Prime Minister – were Anglicans, and that there was certainly a very significant number of Anglican entrepreneurs. It is likely, in fact, that Anglican businessmen were just as successful as Nonconformist businessmen. Anglicans may have succeeded in different areas of the economy from their Nonconformist rivals – for example, overseas trade and brewing; likewise, it is quite possible that there were disproportionately more successful Nonconformist industrialists and manufacturers than Anglicans, especially in the new urban areas of the north of England, although, in the overall British wealth structure, comprising landowners, merchants and bankers, they were certainly outnumbered by Anglicans. The first wave of successful industrialists, especially in large-scale cotton and woollen manufacturing, achieved their success before steam power was used in factory production, their factories instead powered by water in remote rural areas.

When steam power became more widespread, from the 1820s on, a second wave of large-scale industrial production began, far greater than anything seen before. Most of this was done in city factories, where steam power could be used without the necessity of ample running water, and the classical factory towns of the Industrial Revolution, especially Manchester, grew enormously as a result. Factory production centred above all around the manufacture of cotton goods. Imports of raw cotton into England grew from 93 million pounds in 1815 to 554 million pounds in 1844, the decades when factory capitalism grew most dramatically. Steam power also generated a vast increase in its main source of energy, coal production (also required for domestic heating), while the manufacture of iron and engineering equipment likewise increased astronomically. This was the classical industrial revolution, an image recognisable to us all by belching smokestacks, small children employed as factory hands and hard-nosed factory owners alongside a proletarian army. By 1841 about 1.5 million people, nearly a quarter of the total employed labour force of 6.8 million, were employed in manufacturing in the United Kingdom, along with another 220,000 in mining. Their numbers continued to grow until after mid-century, reaching about 40 per cent of the workforce by 1861, but then remained fairly stagnant, as the service sector of the economy increased sharply.

The most enduring symbol of the new age was the railway, as emblematic of nineteenth-century Britain as the cathedrals and monasteries had become of the Middle Ages. Primitive railways, consisting of carts running on wooden tramways, had existed in mining areas since the sixteenth century; these were, of course, pulled by horses or human labourers. Although steam engines had existed since the 1760s, it wasn't until about 1803 that anyone combined the two, and it took until the mid-1820s for the railway revolution to begin, with the famous Stockton–Darlington railway. Britain's railway revolution and its railway 'mania' took another decade or more to erupt: in 1837 there were only 540 miles of railways in operation in the United Kingdom, and fewer than five million passengers carried. The slow development of Britain's railways suggests that, as some economic historians have argued, rapid and sudden transformations of the economy did not always occur in this period (see Part IV). The late 1830s and 1840s, however, witnessed the railway mania in full flood: by 1850 there were 6,084 miles of railways built, and sixty-seven million passengers. The rest of the nineteenth century saw the remainder of Britain's railway system fleshed out, reaching virtually every place of significance in the country, so that by 1911 there were over 20,000 miles of railways in operation, with 1.3 billion passengers carried. England always had more railway mileage, in terms of its size, than Scotland, Wales or Ireland. Nevertheless, by the early twentieth century much of the Scottish Highlands, Welsh hill country and Irish rural areas were connected to urban centres by rail.

As a system of transport, railways were vastly faster, more reliable and more efficient than anything known before, but they still had many deficiencies: accidents, often fatal, were frequent, and railways were extraordinarily labour-intensive, employing 373,000 people by 1911. By definition railways could not leave the track, and both persons and goods still had to be met and transported from the station to their final destination, which left ample room for widespread horse-drawn carriages, until the automobile age. Steam power was a mighty pollutant, and London's many mainline railway stations were deliberately situated at the edges of the central city, rather than at the hub. Perhaps uniquely in Europe, all Britain's railways were built, operated and owned by private capitalists and companies, rather than by the state, and the railway companies grew to become among the largest of nineteenth-century businesses. Some railway builders and managers became legendary, with Isambard Kingdom Brunel (1806–59), also a legendary shipbuilder, emerging as the very symbol of British industrial capitalism. The great edifices of Victorian engineering such as the famous railway stations, the viaducts and a structure like the Forth Bridge, were at the heart of industrialisation. The Forth Bridge, linking Midlothian with Fifeshire and opened in 1889 after taking over ten years to complete, impresses even today by its incredible size.

While industry and manufacturing were the most dramatic aspects of Britain's growing economy in the nineteenth century, they were not the only – or, arguably, the most – important sectors. Britain's service sector – commerce, finance, trade and the professions – was of central significance before the industrial revolution even began, although economic growth in the service sector is intrinsically more difficult to measure or quantify than in manufacturing or industry (a fact which calls into dispute the accuracy of Britain's statistics of economic growth). Britain had long been a world centre of trade, commerce and finance; during the nineteenth century its centrality in these spheres

The Forth Bridge. One of the greatest of all Victorian construction projects, the mighty
Forth Bridge linking Edinburgh with the north of Scotland opened in 1890. Its truly
staggering size, as seen in this photograph taken when under construction, must have
seemed like science fiction to observers at the time. What were contemporaries likely to
conclude from such projects about Britain's place in human evolution?

increased and consolidated. In particular, the role of the City of
London as the centre of the world's international finance reached its
apogee. The City – as the historical square mile centring around
Threadneedle Street, which contains London's financial district,
analogous to Wall Street in New York, is known – financed much of
the world's economic growth and development through merchant
banks owned by renowned families such as the Rothschilds and
Barings. It also contained the Stock Exchange, Lloyd's of London
insurance, the headquarters of the great clearing banks and insurance
companies, and many company headquarters. The City established a
reputation for probity, and for the ability to finance large-scale
government loans, which made it the world's financial capital until this
mantle passed to New York after the First World War.

Much in the world's international economic life was governed by
the Gold Standard, whereby the value of any currency was fixed
against gold bullion, and redeemable in gold. Each country's central

bank set its exchange rate, which had to be maintained by the use of its gold reserve. (The Gold Standard appeared to work harmoniously until the First World War destroyed the world's existing currency system.) London, too, was a great centre of commerce as well as finance, containing innumerable retail shops, wholesalers, warehouses, import-export houses and the great docks of the Thames. Other major British cities, such as Liverpool and Bristol, were primarily oriented around commerce and trade rather than manufacturing. While employment in manufacturing reached 40 per cent of the total workforce in 1861, and then hardly grew, the service sector increased during the late nineteenth century from about 21 per cent of the workforce in 1861 to about 30 per cent in 1901. Edinburgh and Dublin flourished as governmental centres and as homes of the local professional elite, as did parts of London on a vastly greater scale. The service sector also included an ever-larger segment of professionals and semi-professionals. While the older professions – traditionally law, medicine, the Anglican clergy, and perhaps military officers, always regarded as occupations for gentlemen – increased substantially during the nineteenth century, they were joined by newer professions such as accountancy and engineering, as well as the so-called 'sub-professions' – schoolteachers in the state sector, nurses, librarians – with an increasing female presence. Nursing, in particular, emerged as arguably *par excellence* the woman's sub-profession, a nurturing, life-saving occupation whose icon was Florence Nightingale, but one in which its largely female workforce was expected to work like slaves, in highly unpleasant ways, for a pittance, almost always ultimately directed by male doctors.

While industry, commerce and the professions comprised the bulk of the nineteenth-century workforce, it is important to remember that agriculture was still extremely important to the British economy. In 1811, about 35 per cent of families in England, Wales and Scotland (to use the somewhat peculiar categories of the census) were engaged in agriculture. There was a continuous decline in agriculture as a component of the employed workforce throughout the century, to 27 per cent in 1861, 19 per cent in 1881 and 11 per cent in 1911, but these still comprised substantial numbers of persons. In 1851 nearly 1.8 million males were employed in agriculture and farming, more than any other occupational category. Britain's overall national income still included a large, albeit declining, agricultural and farming sector, which accounted for 33 per cent of the national income of England, Wales and Scotland in 1801, 20 per cent in 1851 and 6 per cent even in the early twentieth century. Many parts of Britain still remained visibly rural and pre-industrial down to the First World War, with farmers and agricultural labourers, to say nothing of the country house life of the aristocracy and gentry, being familiar props of English novels, poems and other literary depictions throughout the nineteenth century. Indeed, given the relatively efficient and progressive nature of much of British agriculture (outside southern Ireland and other Celtic areas), Britain's landowners and farmers grew ever wealthier at least until the late Victorian agricultural depression, which began around 1880 when the large-scale importation of foreign foodstuffs undermined Britain's farming sector. The Highlands of Scotland, the Welsh-speaking areas of Wales, and most of Ireland retained a larger rural sector than did most of England, although rural areas predominated in parts of England such as Cornwall and East Anglia until the twentieth century.

British agriculture had been based, throughout modern history, on the so-called 'triple division of land tenure'. Land was usually owned by a wealthy aristocrat, and was worked by a tenant farmer who sold what produce he grew, paid a rental income to the landowners, and in turn employed agricultural labourers. (There were also smaller owner-occupiers of land, especially in the north of England, Scotland and Wales.) This type of landownership made efficiencies of scale and investment in the land and new equipment and methods of production possible, and gave many of those landowners a vested interest in increasing the profitability of the land. British agriculture was, as a rule, more profitable and advanced than anywhere else in Europe, where small peasant holdings were the rule. Only when British agriculture was itself challenged by the gigantic farms and their output of the United States, Canada and Australia, in the latter part of the nineteenth century, did it come under serious challenge.

During the eighteenth and nineteenth centuries, enclosure continued. Landowners secured Acts of Parliament to 'enclose' fields previously owned in common, taking them over as private property in exchange for fencing them and providing agricultural improvements. The alleged loss of rights by the rural poor, whose access to these fields often provided a significant component of their incomes, became a matter of great controversy, then and since. Proponents of enclosure argued that it greatly increased both agricultural productivity and demand for labour. It should also be noted that different parts of Britain had relatively dissimilar farming patterns, with some areas specialising in cattle and sheep farming, others in growing crops. In general, regions of cattle and sheep production were harder hit by foreign competition after 1880, when the large-scale importing of foods from America and Australia began, than were others. Ireland, with its reliance on the single crop of potatoes, paid a heavy penalty for its lack of diversification.

By the dawn of the twentieth century, there was a pervasive sense that all was not well with Britain's economy. In particular, there was a sense that Britain was being overtaken by Germany and the United States as the world's economic superpower – Germany appeared to be far ahead of Britain in harnessing what is often now termed the 'second industrial revolution' based on electricity, chemicals and novel technologies, while America's assembly lines of mass production dwarfed anything elsewhere. Unemployment in Britain is thought to have risen, while rates of economic growth appeared to stagnate. Net national income per head in the United Kingdom, at 1900 prices, had increased from £18 in 1855 to £38 in 1890, but thereafter hardly grew at all, totalling £44 per head in 1913. Identifying and ameliorating Britain's apparent decline became an obsession at the time, as it was to become again from the 1950s until the 1990s. Yet although there were areas in which Britain was undeniably being overtaken by its major rivals, important sectors of the economy remained profitable and successful in the years leading up to 1914. These included the old staple industries – cotton, coal, shipbuilding – and the service sector, which was growing strongly.

The reason why Britain failed to maintain its old lead across the board has been vigorously debated. Many argue that it would have been inherently almost impossible to maintain its old lead once such powerful international competition emerged. Others have pointed to the 'cult of the amateur' in Britain, with the sons and grandsons of the dynamic founders of a firm being educated at a public school and university and joining the landed gentry. Some have also singled out the alleged sharp division between the City of London and British industry, with British banks declining to invest in new industries, or the propensity to invest overseas rather than in Britain itself. A number of economic historians, however, have questioned the notion of a real British decline by 1914, viewing the growth of the service sector as itself evidence of a dynamic and modernising economy. What is undeniable is that the economic changes brought about by the First World War deleteriously affected, after 1918, Britain's staple industries – coal, cotton, shipbuilding, iron – leading to high unemployment in these areas during 1919–39, concentrated especially in those regions of Britain, such as South Wales, the North East and Clydeside, where they had been strongest.

Modes of Identity: Social Class

Social class is not easy to define precisely, and, as a concept, is made more difficult by the fact that while one might situate an individual within an ascribed social class, he or she might perceive their own class in quite a different way. By time-honoured usage, it is common to divide British society into three main social classes, the upper, middle and working classes, with many sub-divisions within each. While, broadly, it may be reasonable to draw this division, we must be wary of oversimplification – British society as a whole evolved and changed during the nineteenth century in ways which transformed its apparently straightforward class structure into something else entirely.

During the nineteenth century (as before and after), Britain contained a titled aristocracy composed of peers, baronets (hereditary knights) and knights. Down the ages, Britain's aristocracy differed markedly from its continental equivalents. It was very small, comprising fewer than about 550 men at the end of the nineteenth century; only the eldest son of a peer inherited the title, younger sons and daughters being commoners; the eldest son normally inherited all the family's land and most of their wealth. Most peers sat in the House of Lords, and their number increased over the course of the century: in 1833, 366 peers were entitled to sit there, which rose to 551 in 1900, and 616 in 1910 (overall, the British peerage numbered about 600 in 1833 and 750 in 1900). Several hundred Scottish and Irish peers did not have an automatic right to sit in the Lords, and neither did female peers in their own right or peers who were minors. Above all, Britain's aristocracy was not exempted from any tax and enjoyed no legal privileges (apart from trial by their 'peers' in the House of Lords, if accused of a crime). Baronetcies (about 1,000 in number in 1900) were also inherited by the eldest son, while knighthoods (also numbering about 1,000) ceased with their holder's death. Many aristocrats were very rich, owning vast amounts of land. The very greatest aristocrats, such as the Dukes of Westminster, Bedford, Devonshire and Northumberland, and the Earls of Derby, were among the richest men in Europe. On average, about ten new peerages were created every year. After about 1870 (but not before) many new creations were great industrialists or business-men who, generally, had bought landed estates, thus integrating a component of the new wealth with the old.

The upper classes also certainly included very rich businessmen, who also increased rapidly in number during the nineteenth century. Gauging just how rapidly is, of course, difficult, but the number of estates left for probate of £100,000 or more (about £6 million in today's money) rose from about 25 per year early in the nineteenth century to about 250 per year by 1900, a tenfold increase, although the value of money was virtually unchanged. The very wealthiest businessmen of the century, such as the banker Lord Overstone (d. 1883), the ware-houseman James Morrison (d. 1857) or the railway builder Thomas Brassey (d. 1870), were nearly as rich as any landed aristocrat. Many bought landed estates, and the West End of London and other upper-class areas swelled with their numbers. More – perhaps 60 per cent – appear to have earned their fortunes in London and other commercial centres than in the industrial north of England. It is difficult to provide more than an estimate, but if one defines the 'wealthy' as those earning £5,000 or more per year (that is, an annual income of 5 per cent of a fortune of £100,000 or more), then certainly only a fraction of 1 per cent of the adult male population could be considered 'wealthy'. Even if all their relatives be included as 'wealthy', certainly no more than 1 per cent of the population could be so classified. The wealthy lived primarily in the West End of London, in Mayfair, Belgravia and Kensington, in similarly exclusive districts in other large cities such as Victoria Park in Manchester, and in large country houses throughout the country.

Defining the middle class (or classes) has always been notoriously difficult, the nineteenth century providing no exception. Should the category 'middle class' be delineated by occupations (businessmen and professionals), incomes (with, say, anyone with an income between about £150 and £5,000 being included), lifestyles (living in large houses with several servants but not mansions), or in some other way? To most Victorians, the 'middle class' consisted of businessmen and professionals below the very rich; following this criteria, about 15–20 per cent of the population could be said to be middle class in some sense. The middle classes probably comprised a larger share of the population in London and the smaller towns of the south of England than in the newer industrial areas. The proportion of middle-class citizens employed in public administration and the professions rose rapidly during the nineteenth century, increasing by nearly 350 per cent between 1841 (there is no earlier data) and 1911 compared with just 154 per cent among the employed male population. Most middle-class men were businessmen or superior shopkeepers, with a minority in the professions. Most university-educated men emerged from the professional middle classes and themselves became professionals. It has always been particularly difficult to distinguish the lower middle classes of small shopkeepers, minor officials and schoolteachers from the solid middle classes. Even more problematic is how to categorise farmers and rural owner-occupiers. Including all these categories on their widest definition probably raised the overall middle-class share to around 30–35 per cent of the adult male population.

The nineteenth century also saw the rise of the elite fee-paying public schools as institutions where the upper and middle classes could, in a sense, merge intergenerationally, although one must be careful not to exaggerate this. Most aristocrats and the super-rich sent their sons to the most exclusive public schools, Eton and Harrow, although these also contained many sons of barristers, Anglican vicars and middle-ranking businessmen. Most of the new or reformed public schools which appeared during the nineteenth century – Rugby, Cheltenham, Marlborough, Wellington or Mill Hill, to name but a few – were basically schools for the sons of upper middle-class parents, not the sons of the aristocracy. Oxford and Cambridge universities also provided venues where the sons of genuine blue bloods, the nouveau riche and the very fortunate or talented nobodies could meet and interact, to a certain extent as equals, and form lifelong networks of friendship and employment. In many ways, by the interwar period (1918–39) in Britain, education at a public school and Oxbridge had replaced landownership or even titled status as the chief determinant of high social status. To say that someone was an 'old Etonian' or an 'old Balliol man' (a leading college at Oxford) was enough to identify and define his social status: whether his father was a duke, a millionaire or merely an ordinary solicitor or business proprietor became less and less relevant. To most observers, it seems that the great class barrier, often almost insurmountable, increasingly lay between the upper and middle classes on the one hand and the working class on the other. This barrier was *probably* greater than in the eighteenth century, with higher start-up costs for successful entrepreneurs and more obvious markers of upper middle-class status, such as education at a public school, although accurate research on this matter is very difficult.

Most people belonged to the working classes, those employed for wages in factories or mines, or in a variety of menial occupations such as carrying and hauling, on railways or as domestic servants. There was also a very large class of agricultural labourers, probably the most poorly paid sector of the workforce. It is common to divide the working class into three segments: the higher skilled working class – about 14 per cent of the employed population in Great Britain (England, Wales and Scotland) in the 1860s; the lower skilled working class – about 26 per cent of the population; and the unskilled working class and agricultural labourers – about 25 per cent of the population. (However, this percentage was much higher in Ireland.) The higher skilled working class comprised mainly artisans who required some training, senior male factory operatives, locomotive engine drivers, even the best paid among coal miners. Many of these groups were protected to a certain extent by trades union organisations; in Britain these originated among the skilled artisanal male working classes, and often had an important role as insurance providers and even as lodge-style fraternal orders. Incomes among the skilled working classes could reach £100 per year or even more among such groups as locomotive engine drivers and skilled printers, although £75 per annum was probably the average. Many in the skilled working class could aspire to a standard of living not far below the lower part of the middle class with little beside their occupations to distinguish them. The lower skilled working class comprised most factory operatives and miners, senior shop assistants and what has become known as the 'uniformed working class' – soldiers and sailors, policemen, postmen, firemen and railway station personnel, among others – who were often surprisingly poorly paid. The normal rate of pay for an ordinary London policeman was about £1 per week, for which he was expected to risk his life virtually every day. The unskilled working class comprised the miscellaneous residuum, ranging from carters to stablehands to casual dock workers, stevedores and merchant sailors, down to the demi-monde of semi-criminality carving out a catch-penny income as best they could.

The leitmotif of most of the nineteenth-century British working class was its insecurity: there was, of course, no welfare state, and no government safety net in the twentieth-century sense to protect anyone (from whatever class background) from unemployment, old age, sickness or accident. The famous New Poor Law of 1834 mandated that there would be no 'outdoor relief' provided by the government – that is, any kind of government welfare or insurance payments to the poor or needy. Instead, virtually the *only* form of state-provided welfare was to be the workhouse, of which hundreds dotted the country. Anyone could enter a workhouse, where he or she would receive a parsimonious meal and a bed of sorts. It was a requirement that one remained overnight, and the sexes were separated. By the notorious 'principle of less eligibility', conditions in workhouses had, by law, to be worse than anything likely to be encountered outside. The aims of the workhouse were to compel the poor to save for bad times and old age, and to keep the cost to taxpayers as low as possible. Little in the way of a state-provided welfare net of any kind existed in Britain, even skeletally, until 1908, while the modern welfare state is largely a product of the 1940s. The assumption regarding the relief of poverty in Victorian Britain was that any excessive generosity to the poor would simply deter honest work, lead to drunkenness and dissolution, and remove the disincentive to early marriage.

In the main, however, unemployment was not caused by deliberate malingering, but by wider economic conditions, which differed from industry to industry and from place to place. Unemployment in factory areas of the north was highly cyclical, and largely dependent on economic patterns of boom and bust: in boom times, when all the factories in Manchester, Bolton, Bradford or Paisley had full order books, everyone worked and, indeed, labour was scarce; during a periodical recession, many were unemployed. On the other hand, among the poor in London, in other port and commercial cities, and in agricultural areas, there was chronic unemployment caused by the fact that the ever-swelling population almost always exceeded the amount of work available. In neither case were the presuppositions of the New Poor Law, that there would be idleness without its severe deterrence, valid. Some parts of the working classes which enjoyed tenure, such as policemen and postmen, were to a certain extent protected from either cyclical unemployment or chronic underemployment, but they were very much the exception. The structure for the relief of poverty in nineteenth-century Britain, such as it was, also largely failed the sick, accident victims, and, above all, the elderly and most women.

One of the best-known twentieth-century historical debates about the British working classes is whether their standard of living rose or fell: the 'optimists' (as they are known) believe that it rose, at least in the long run; the 'pessimists' that it certainly did not rise during the first half of the nineteenth century, while the sheer awfulness of Britain's slum districts, especially in factory towns, or the hellishness of the life of a coal miner, simply cannot be quantified. It is likely that the 'pessimists' are correct for the situation in Britain before 1850. The main variables in this debate are the increase in population compared with the rate of economic growth and the pace at which the economic benefits of industrialisation reached the working classes. Given the unprecedentedly rapid rate of population growth in the first half of the nineteenth century, it seems reasonable to conclude that the relatively slow and steady pace of economic growth failed to provide perceptible economic benefits to many in the working class. After 1850, however, it equally seems very likely that per capita incomes and living standards rose for everyone, the product of what the historian Harold Perkin described as 'a viable class society' which emerged in mid- and late Victorian Britain.

The objective facts of social class must be considered in conjunction with the subjective facts: to what class did people feel they belonged and how did this matter? A number of well-known episodes of nineteenth-century British politics were indeed fought out in class terms, for instance the movement for the Reform Bill of 1832 and for the repeal of the Corn Laws in the mid-1840s, which were widely perceived as benefiting the middle classes. Given the vast size of the nineteenth-century British working classes, and the chronic poverty they suffered, it might seem as if class bitterness, even class war, would be endemic to British society. Although the notion of the industrial working class in the sense we recognise is often dated to the years just after the Napoleonic Wars, specifically to the period around 1820 or so, it is striking that the concept of an active, oppositionist working class never really emerged in nineteenth-century Britain, at least until the 1890s and arguably not even then. That social class appears to have been so *unimportant* in nineteenth-century British politics is evidence, perhaps, that its significance was exaggerated by later observers and historians, especially Marxist historians who believed that class conflict 'should' have been present during Britain's industrialisation and urbanisation. But Britain (like the United States, which, it is often argued, is 'exceptional' in never having produced a class-based politics) might well have been different.

While major socialist parties and strong socialist movements took shape throughout the European continent after about 1870, these had no parallel in nineteenth-century Britain: the Labour party was first formed only in 1900, and then clearly as a small tail to the Liberal party. One might adduce several reasons for this, including the multiplicity of other salient loyalties, especially religious allegiances, which united persons of different social classes; the long tradition of left-liberal reforms being led and enacted by the upper classes; the willingness of both the Conservative and Liberal parties to accommodate the trades unions and some working-class demands; the genuinely widespread traditions of working-class self-help; and the 'safety valve' of large-scale emigration. While Britain thus contained the oldest and possibly the largest industrial working class in Europe, it was, paradoxically, also one of the least demonstrative and least radical. Trades unions remained relatively small until the late nineteenth century, with the Trades Union Congress (the TUC), the representative body of the British trades union movement, not formed until 1868. While Karl Marx and Frederick Engels lived most of their adult lives in Britain, ironically they had less impact there than in most other European countries. The British experience probably shows that the rise of a self-conscious, oppositionist and politically significant trades union and working-class organisation was not inevitable in an advanced industrial society. (Similarly, the United States never developed a socialist movement of any importance.) The European pattern, of the growth of large and highly significant socialist movements such as in Germany and France, did not occur in the same form in nineteenth-century Britain.

By 1914 there is some evidence that this was changing, with the Labour party increasingly influential, especially at the local level, in England, Wales and Scotland, and the government keen to bring the trades unions into the circle of governance through active negotiations with them to satisfy their demands. Labour militancy – which had erupted during the late nineteenth century in such acts as the great

London dockers' strike of 1889 – definitely increased, especially around 1910–11 when a wave of crippling strikes hit Britain. Yet Britain remained different from Europe, and, had it not been for the First World War, the Labour party might not have emerged as the dominant left-of-centre party in British politics. Similarly, the unions might not have become as powerful as they did after 1914.

These class differences were by no means uniform throughout the United Kingdom. In Scotland, although deference to aristocratic clan or regional leaders still existed and probably exceeded anything in England, assertive working-class consciousness, especially in Glasgow and Clydeside, was also strong. In Wales the influence of the gentry and aristocracy was much weaker than in many parts of England, and in industrial South Wales was virtually non-existent. In Ireland the religious conflict arguably overshadowed everything, and the role and influence of the largely Anglican landed aristocracy declined markedly

The Stately Home. This is Eaton Hall in Cheshire, the home of the Duke of Westminster. In its vast palatial size it was typical of the country houses of the very richest aristocrats and landowners, as well as those purchased by some nouveau-riche businessmen. The Duke of Westminster (whose surname was Grosvenor) was probably Britain's wealthiest man. His affluence derived from owning the ground rents of much of Mayfair and Belgravia, two of the richest parts of London. He also owned landed estates, especially in Cheshire. Yet the first Duke of Westminster was a Whig and then a Liberal, that is, on the moderate left of the British political spectrum. What does this suggest about the ways in which many aristocrats viewed their role in British society?

in the later nineteenth century in the south. In Ulster, Protestant loyalties were dominant in a largely urban, industrial society. In England itself, aristocratic and 'Society' figures and influence remained strongest in London, the south and rural England. They were far less strong in northern and industrial England, although in places like Liverpool the divide between Protestantism and Catholicism largely determined politics after mid-century. A charismatic political leader could make a major difference to loyalties throughout society from top to bottom. In Birmingham, Joseph Chamberlain carried most of the local population with him in his journey from the political left to the right, including most of the local working class.

Modes of Identity: Gender

Gender is arguably the most basic of all modes of identity and self-identification. While this has been a constant throughout all human history, in some periods gender has arguably been more of a constant than in others. Many would argue that Victorian Britain marked the zenith of ascribed gender differences and gender roles in modern history. Men and women, according to this viewpoint, were confined almost comprehensively to 'separate spheres', male domination, with the rarest exception, being the norm. Like most historical generalisations, such a view is partially true; it should be noted, however, that we know far less about the attitudes of women in Scotland, Wales and Ireland than in England, especially among women of the upper and middle classes in England.

Britain was a western, liberal state, and such institutions as arranged and child marriage, the virtual imprisonment of widows, and, *a fortiori*, such enormities as female infanticide, female circumcision, polygamy, suttee and the range of anti-female habits routinely practised in the non-European world were unknown or illegal, and regarded with universal horror when reported in Britain. Yet there were undeniably areas of public and private life from which women in Britain were systematically excluded, by law, custom or institutional bias. *Legally*, in nineteenth-century Britain women were debarred from voting or holding public office (except at the local level, where women rate-payers were increasingly given the right to vote and hold office), serving on juries or entering most professions such as the law, although medicine was open to women by the end of the century. Most hereditary titles of nobility passed to the eldest male heir. Until 1882, the property of married women became, upon their marriage, the legal property of their husband, although trusts were regularly established by the rich to get around this. After 1857 (and, indeed, until the 1920s), the grounds for divorce were different for husband and wife, a husband having to prove only adultery by his wife to be granted a divorce, while a wife had to prove not merely adultery, but some other heinous activity such as cruelty, incest or bestiality, the assumption apparently being that many normal men would routinely commit adultery, and wives should simply grin and bear it unless the husband was truly a swine as well. Virtually all private educational institutions automatically refused admission to women, although by the end of the nineteenth century there were women's private schools, and women's colleges at Oxford and Cambridge, with women admitted to many other universities.

While this list of *legal* disabilities suffered by women in nineteenth-century Britain is significant, it is also probably exhaustive: legally, women in Britain could do anything else, such as own, inherit and leave property, live where they wished, sue or give evidence in court, or emigrate. Some degree of de facto equality also existed in public spaces: men and women, for instance, sat together in churches, performances and meetings and on public transport. Women could, and frequently did, write books and comment on public affairs. They could organise societies and associations and often, but not always, join learned and serious bodies. A queen sat on the British throne from 1837 until 1901, an era we know as the Victorian age.

Of course, spelling out the legal and de facto rights of women offers no realistic description of their actual status. In fact, women's roles were automatically constrained and diminished in ways which men's never were. Women were at almost all times restricted by the pervasive notion of 'separate spheres', which dictated that women belonged in the home, as mothers and home-makers. While virtually all able-bodied adult males were in the labour force, only a minority of women were. (This situation might well have differed from that in pre-industrial Britain, when 'domestic' industries were often carried out in the home, allowing more home-makers to work.) In 1841, while 76 per cent of males over the age of ten living in Great Britain (England, Wales and Scotland) were listed in the census as having an occupation, only 25 per cent of females of the same age were so listed. Seventy years later, in 1911, this had barely changed: 84 per cent of males listed an occupation compared with 32 per cent of women. Although these figures can be disputed – many women, listed as having no occupation, actually were involved in the businesses of their husbands or fathers – in fact *most* adult women spent the majority of their adult lives without gainful employment, and were dependent upon a male breadwinner for their incomes. The female occupational structure was also very different from its male equivalent. By far the largest single occupation among employed women during the nineteenth century was domestic service, with nearly a million female employees in 1841 and over two million in 1911. Textiles and clothing were the next largest occupational categories, with over half a million female employees in 1841 and 1.7 million in 1911. Many components of the factory production of textiles and clothing were female preserves, and wages were relatively high.

As the nineteenth century progressed, a female service and professional sector grew, based especially in the 'sub-professions' of teaching and nursing. A female clerical sector began rapidly increasing in size in the late nineteenth century (although not before), especially with the widespread use of typewriters in the 1890s. At the very top, a tiny handful of women became successful in business life, or even rich in their own right, such as Harriet Mellon (*c.* 1772–1837), an actress who became the wife of Thomas Coutts (d. 1822), the great banker, inheriting his fortune and becoming the chief director of Coutts' Bank and, eventually, duchess of St Albans, or, at the end of the century, Helen Carte (née Black, 1852–1913), a talented Scotswoman who became the secretary and business manager of Richard D'Oyly Carte (d. 1901), the chief producer of Gilbert and Sullivan operas, whom she later married. Before her marriage, however, she was paid a salary of £1,000 per annum plus 10 per cent of Carte's profits as his business manager, and was probably the highest paid woman in England. Among other things, Helen Carte oversaw the rebuilding of the famous Savoy Hotel in London, and left over £100,000 at her death. While there were a number of other such examples of highly successful businesswomen, even in the 1890s they were, of course, exceptionally rare. Inevitably, the mid- and late nineteenth century saw a range of female 'firsts', as a microscopic number of highly qualified women were able to break through into the professions: the first woman architect in 1898, the first woman administrative civil servant in 1874

(Mrs Nassau Senior, the sister of the novelist Thomas Hughes, who was appointed a Poor Law Inspector), the first woman dentist in 1895, the first woman doctor, Elizabeth Garrett Anderson, in 1865. Despite these breakthroughs, only after the First World War could British women enter such professions as the law.

One of the main obstacles to women's employment was the almost complete absence of a career structure in any female occupation (again, with teaching and nursing the exceptions). Invariably, the high peaks of every profession were dominated by men, while unskilled or semi-skilled women could expect to rise no higher than the factory floor. Below this was the street. As Henry Snell, an early Labour politician put it,

> What of the women who had no male relatives, the young women with children to support, and the lonely working girls? How were they to live? . . . [E]verybody knew the dangers to which they were exposed. The statesmen knew of them, the economists and the Church knew, but there was no evidence that their complacent philosophy of life was seriously disturbed.
>
> (Lord Henry Snell, *Men, Movements, and Myself*, London, 1936, p. 88.)

There is no accurate way of knowing the extent of prostitution in nineteenth-century Britain other than that it was a ubiquitous part of life, especially urban life. Prostitution in London's West End, especially in the Haymarket and surrounding streets, was so flagrant and unavoidable that it was commented upon by most foreign visitors. In 1888, when 'Jack the Ripper' brutally murdered five prostitutes in London's East End, the Metropolitan Police were asked how many others were potentially at risk. It reported that 1,200 prostitutes and sixty-two brothels were known to the police in the single district of Whitechapel. Estimates of the total number of streetwalkers in mid-Victorian London ranged from 40,000 to 120,000, although Henry Mayhew pointed out, in 1861, in an oft-quoted remark, that the census had no occupational category for prostitutes, and so, officially, the number of women who made ends meet in this way was zero.

Mayhew was here noting the Victorian 'double standard' at its most egregious: few ever discussed the subject of prostitution, except in the context of venereal disease, or asked why so many women were driven beyond the fringes of respectable society to earn a living. As a general rule, prostitution was accepted as an unfortunate fact of life with which it was pointless for the state to interfere. Above the level of the streetwalker, many women certainly lived as the mistresses of rich men. St John's Wood, north of the West End, with its many blocks of flats, is often said to have been developed in part for wealthy City men to keep a second household; it was also conveniently near Lord's Cricket Ground, allowing pleasure to be combined with pleasure. The fact that divorce was both legally difficult and socially stigmatised arguably meant that second households of this type were (de facto) widely tolerated. Only occasionally did the press intrude into the private lives of leading politicians, unlike the situation in our time. There is some evidence that prostitution declined, at least in its visibility, in the Edwardian era, presumably as more opportunities in the sub-professions and service sector opened for young women.

Because the life of unprotected and single women was often so precarious, it was probably the case that a higher percentage of women married in the nineteenth century than before or since. About 85 per cent of women in Victorian Britain eventually married, and conventional marriage was regarded as the normal and only really acceptable fate for most women, followed of course by motherhood. While many working-class women did work after their marriage, for the most part married women seeking fulfilment beyond the home had to be content with voluntary work for charities and church groups. There was, therefore, an almost total reliance on the husband as head of the household and breadwinner. A fortunate marriage could bring lifelong security and affluence, while marriage to a ne'er-do-well or an alcoholic, or to a man simply unlucky in business or professional life, represented ever-looming disaster, as did the possibility, always real, that the husband would die young.

Given the central importance of marriage and its ubiquity, the historian naturally wants to know more about its inner nature: how many marriages were happy? A comprehensive answer to this is beyond our knowledge, since so little reliable evidence exists, and a range of conclusions is possible. It seems clear that a great many marriages were extremely happy, with the husband and wife as true companions in life, the wife sharing the husband's intimate concerns. Historians have pointed out that many of the surviving letters of British Cabinet ministers to their wives show an extraordinary level of intimacy, and there were many men who preferred the company of women, for instance Benjamin Disraeli. On the other hand, the image of the heavy, often brutal, even sadistic Victorian husband and father was a powerful one, and the nature of the institution of marriage in Victorian Britain gave ample scope for domestic male oppression. It is likely that unhappy marriages increased as one went down the social scale, where a lack of income, outside interests and communications skills greatly enhanced the potential for marital warfare, as did alcohol and domestic claustrophobia. Probably many men were only too happy to leave their wives in charge of the home, and to get out as often as possible to the world of social clubs, political societies and, above all, fraternal orders such as the Freemasons, which at the time were all-male domains; for the working-class male, there was the pub, the social club and, increasingly, weekend sporting fixtures, especially football – far more options than the Church and charitable groups with which women were expected to be content. The Primrose League, a Tory fundraising organisation founded in 1883, was possibly the first mass political movement actively to include women, and the Conservatives, then and later, probably mobilised women to a greater extent than did the Liberals or the nascent Labour parties, whose political culture was (at the time) arguably more male-dominated and male-centred.

Concrete political gains for British women in the nineteenth century were few, with the Married Women's Property Act of 1882 probably the most important. This gave married women the right to retain their incomes and property upon marriage. Such measures as the Divorce Act of 1857 and the Matrimonial Causes Act of 1878, which allowed a wife beaten by her husband to apply for a separation order, were among the few other measures which directly affected women's rights. The key was granting women the franchise, but there was no movement here until 1894, when women received the vote in local elections on the same terms as men, enfranchising mainly well-off widows and unmarried women. Intellectually, the case for women's rights had been made by writers such as Mary Godwin and John Stuart Mill, but the suffragette movement was still in relative infancy. Motions in parliament to enfranchise women had attracted a measure of support, but never enough to see it enacted, and the main female suffrage movement, the Women's Social and Political Union, was founded only in 1903. Indeed, a component of social Darwinist theory as it emerged in the late nineteenth century saw what is now termed the 'separate spheres' of men and women as a product of natural selection, while many women, including very clever ones, actually remained opposed to women's suffrage or their direct participation in public life. The seriousness of the political, military and economic issues facing the British empire in the late Victorian era also weighed against extending the vote to women, with their alleged lack of practical experience or realism, and their supposed naïve idealism. The enfranchisement of women, when it finally came in 1918, would by no means have been a certainty without the First World War.

Men are the other half of the gender equation, a fact often overlooked. The relative absence of career opportunities for women, and the crucial importance of marriage and the family, weighed heavily on the life and career choices of adult men, adding to the sense of individual responsibility that was so important as a determinant of worthiness in Victorian life. Not all men embraced this responsibility: there was, for instance, the little-explored world of the bachelor, exemplified in such institutions as Oxbridge colleges (whose Fellows had to be unmarried until late in the century) and the posh London club, many of whose members were lifelong bachelors. There was also a homosexual underground, which allegedly and notoriously existed in

Suffragettism. This lady is campaigning very demurely for female suffrage on Kingsway in central London in August 1913, at the height of the political struggle for giving women the vote in parliamentary elections. She is advertising the monthly magazine *The Suffragette*, edited by Christobel Pankhurst. Many of the tactics employed by the suffragettes were far more militant. You might want to think about how novel these tactics were, and whether they were successful in securing women the vote.

the public schools, universities and Guards' regiments, but was always illegal and regarded with near-universal repulsion except in some artistic circles. Probably the most famous nineteenth-century British homosexual, Oscar Wilde (1854–1900), was almost universally condemned and ostracised after his jailing in 1895. As in many other spheres of life, social class played a major role in tolerance for male homosexuality, with public school and university men allowed a much greater degree of latitude by the police than their social inferiors, unless they engaged in grossly scandalous activities in public. The evidence suggests that attitudes towards anything resembling homosexuality probably hardened during the nineteenth century. For instance, it seems that (heterosexual) male friends often walked arm-in-arm in public until the closing years of the century, when this appeared to have ended due to its implications of improper intimacy. On the other hand, there was far less prejudice against lesbianism, which was never illegal, and women were (and are) always allowed to kiss and hold hands with other women in a way which few men would tolerate with other men. In the real world, however, there were certainly so many variations and permutations in individual behaviour and lifestyles that historians could probably find many exceptions to any stereotype of what nineteenth-century Britain, especially Victorian Britain, was supposedly like.

2. Religion, Nationalism and Identity

Modes of Identity: Religion

Religion was arguably the most fundamental mode of individual self-identity in nineteenth-century Britain; quite possibly its importance actually grew compared with the previous century, although this was disguised both by the intellectual assault on faith and religion associated with Charles Darwin and by the consistent steps towards religious equality which took place during the nineteenth century. Certainly we look at Victorian Britain as a religious society, with evangelical Christianity at the heart of our image of it.

The continuing centrality of religion was supported by a host of intellectual, social and legal forces. Virtually everyone in nineteenth-century Britain *believed* in religion: death often came suddenly, especially to infants and children. A family with eight children could routinely expect to lose two or three in infancy or childhood. Religion, with its central promise of eternal life, was an ever-present source of solace. (In many ways, the decline of organised religion in Britain followed upon the limitation, except in rare tragedies, of death to the elderly.) Organised religion, especially the Church of England, continued throughout this period to enjoy a virtual monopoly in the conducting of the *rites de passage* (baptisms, marriages, funerals). In 1844, for instance, 91 per cent of marriages in England and Wales took place in an Anglican church, while only 7 per cent took place in non-Anglican places of worship (the remaining 2 per cent were most probably civil marriage registrations). Even as late as 1911, 61 per cent of marriages were conducted in an Anglican church, compared with just 18 per cent in some other place of worship, and 21 per cent in civil ceremonies. The Anglican clergy probably constituted the largest single profession in England, outnumbering lawyers and doctors. In 1871 there were 21,000 Anglican clergymen; in 1911, over 25,000. Until the 1870s, more than half of *all* graduates of Oxford and Cambridge universities became Anglican clergymen. The two Anglican arch-bishops and twenty-four bishops sat in the House of Lords, and the senior hierarchy of the Anglican Church still exerted enormous influence at the local level, normally being regarded as among the most powerful and prestigious of local notables, whose views on a wide variety of subjects were sought and respected.

The surprising growth of the Anglican clergy was paralleled among the main Nonconformist denominations, with, for instance, the number of Wesleyan Methodist ministers more than doubling between 1831 and 1901. There were 4,270 ministers of all strands of Methodism in 1910, as well as 3,195 Baptist ministers and 4,908 Catholic priests in Great Britain (excluding Ireland). In Ireland in 1911 there were nearly 4,000 Roman Catholic priests, along with 1,575 Anglican clergymen, 667 Presbyterians and 244 Methodists. As Catholics comprised 74 per cent of the Irish population, it will be seen that Protestant clergymen were far more numerous in comparison to the size of the Protestant minority (26 per cent) of the population, contradicting the frequently heard Protestant claims of a 'priest-ridden' mass of Catholic peasants. Religious worship offered one of the few public spaces in which women were not merely allowed to participate but encouraged to do so. Women almost certainly constituted the majority of worshippers at most church services, and were increasingly the backbone of the ancillary structure of volunteers and minor employees on whom all churches relied, as Sunday School teachers, voluntary assistants, local committee members, home visitors and the like. Many women took readily to these supplementary roles, despite the total monopoly which males continued to enjoy in the power structure of all Churches except for a few, such as the Salvation Army (founded in 1878), which existed on the fringes of Nonconformist religious life.

Intellectual life in nineteenth-century Britain continued to revolve around religious questions. Probably most books and pamphlets published in Victorian Britain were religious in nature, and were printed in vast numbers. In the 1860s, for instance, the Religious Tract Society printed thirty-three million books and pamphlets *each year*. A major religious controversy, such as the quasi-Catholic challenge presented by the Oxford Movement to the Church of England, had the power to divide the entire literate nation. The most important intellectual debate of the nineteenth century, that sparked by the publication of Charles Darwin's *Origin of Species* in 1859, became central to Victorian intellectual life *because* it was seen primarily as an attack on orthodox Christian religion. In part because of Darwin and the apparent conflict between science and religion, the 'Victorian crisis of faith', as it has been termed, affected many young, well-educated middle-class citizens of late Victorian Britain: those raised on strict literalistic belief in the Bible read Darwin and the works of freethinkers and agnostics, and experienced internal crises of doubt which persisted throughout their lives.

At least as importantly, from the Reformation through the nine-teenth century religion in Britain was an aspect of national identity: the Church of *England* was the national Church of the English people, the religious component of being English in the same way as were English citizenship and speaking the English language. So, too, the Church of Scotland was the national Church of the Scottish people. In a real sense, those who failed to conform to the national churches of the English and Scottish peoples, Protestant and Reformed, were seen as disloyal to their national identities, in particular Roman Catholics, whose religion went hand in hand with allegiance, explicit or implicit, to the papacy and to Britain's traditional enemies France and Spain. Arguably, it was primarily for this reason that religion, now seen as chiefly if not wholly a private matter, was so bitterly contested during the three or four centuries after the Reformation.

The religious history of nineteenth-century Britain consists to a significant extent of the gradual disassociation of specific religious affiliations from any concept of national loyalty or identity, Ireland being the obvious exception. This occurred both because non-established religions were given full citizenship rights, and because the notion of citizenship became increasingly redefined such that religion became irrelevant to the concept of loyal citizenship, a change strongly reflected in the undeniable growth of a mass democratic polity in which all adults eventually participated. In particular, nineteenth-century England saw the gradual incorporation of the large Protestant Nonconformist sects within the 'Pale of the Constitution', while the Church of Ireland, the minority Anglican Church in Ireland, was disestablished in 1869. Nevertheless, there were limits to the changes which occurred: the Church of England and the Church of Scotland were still established Churches in 1914, just as they had been in 1800. In many respects, indeed, the Anglican Church was stronger in 1900 than a century earlier. Only in the case of Ireland did this process of the removal of religion from the concept of national loyalty and identity fail to diminish religious dispute: there, the religious basis of communal loyalty became central and paramount, ironically as the religious disabilities of the Roman Catholic majority were gradually removed, leading to a situation of virtual religious civil war by 1914. Catholicism in the south and Protestantism in Ulster provided the framework for Irish politics, which was seldom a secular phenomenon as on the European continent. The religious histories of Scotland, Wales and Ireland are intimately bound up with their national identities and will be considered separately from the dominant system of organised religion in England: the Anglican Church.

The Anglican Church

In 1800, and for several decades thereafter, the Church of England continued to hold a monopoly position as the Church of the English political nation, since only Anglicans – those prepared to testify their assent to the Thirty-Nine Articles of the Anglican creed – could hold any political office in England and Wales. The Test and Corporation Acts, which enforced this monopoly, had long become a dead letter in the case of most Protestant Dissenters, especially at the local government level, but the overwhelming majority of members of parliament were Anglicans. The Anglican Church oversaw the coronation of the monarch, the coronation being in large measure a religious ceremonial attesting to the monarch's role as head of the Anglican Church. The Anglican Church also had a role in areas seemingly far-removed from religious worship. For instance, until 1858 it enjoyed a legal monopoly on the probating of wills in England and Wales, through a system of Anglican Ecclesiastical Courts. England's only two universities, Oxford and Cambridge, were exclusively Anglican institutions until 1871.

In the course of the nineteenth century, however, this major component of the Anglican Church's privileged position was modified or removed entirely. Protestant Dissenters (in 1828), Roman Catholics (in 1829), Jews (in 1858) and avowed agnostics (in 1885) were allowed to take their seats in the House of Commons. After the sweeping local government reforms of 1835, probably a majority of elected local councillors and mayors in England's large cities were Protestant

Dissenters. Although some forms of legal discrimination remained in place against Roman Catholics, by the late nineteenth century only a handful of public offices existed which were not open to men of any religion.

Despite its initially privileged position, all was not well within the Anglican Church. Although their range and scope may be exaggerated, well-known abuses such as pluralism (one cleric holding two or more parochial appointments) and a vast differential between the princely incomes of most bishops and the near-poverty of many ordinary clergymen certainly existed. Areas of rapid population growth, such as the northern industrial towns, lacked churches or vicars, with the cumbersome structure of the Church of England, and its need to receive parliamentary approval for any changes in its framework, making reform extremely difficult. The arguably unfortunate condition of the Anglican Church in the eighteenth and early nineteenth centuries resulted in the rapid growth of Protestant Dissent in regions where Anglicanism was weak – remote rural areas such as Cornwall and East Anglia, the new urban centres of the north, London and Wales – which brought a more immediate, vivid and personal form of worship. By the middle of the century it was clear that many English citizens' personal allegiances lay elsewhere – in March 1851, at the time of the famous Religious Census, it was found that 10.4 million persons attended a religious service in England and Wales, of a total population of 17.9 million. Of these, while 4.9 million attended an Anglican service, 5.1 million attended a Dissenting service (and 365,000 a Roman Catholic service).

The Church of England was also wracked by bitter internal disputes which were nationally known. During the eighteenth century, the evangelical movement, aimed at religious regeneration through sincere repentance and conversion, earnestness and austerity, became extremely influential. Its best-known leader, John Wesley, was originally an Anglican clergyman, but found the structure and hierarchy of the Church of England too rigid and, from about the 1770s, organised his followers outside of Anglicanism (these followers later fragmented into many separate Wesleyan sects). Wesley always denied that he was forming a separate Church, but sometime between about 1790 and 1810 Wesleyanism generally became recognised as a denomination independent of the Church of England. Many Evangelicals remained within the Church, prominent in such groups as the Clapham Sect, formed around 1790 under the leadership of the Rev. John Venn. Influential in such reforms as the campaign for the abolition of slavery, evangelicals like Hannah More were tireless writers of religious tracts. Evangelicalism is, in particular, often seen as one of the most important forces behind the abolition of slavery throughout the British empire in 1834. Evangelicals and Quakers were among the progenitors of the Slave Trade Abolition Act of 1806, and were central in mobilising public opinion against the horrors of slavery. Parliament abolished slavery with compensation to their owners (almost all in the West Indies), a radical and profound humanitarian act to which religion was central. In the United States, slavery remained institutionalised in the Southern states until it was ended by a civil war in which 600,000 soldiers died.

From the 1830s, another influential movement arose from the opposite end of Anglican theology, the Oxford Movement (also known as the Tractarians or Puseyites, after one of its leaders, Edward Bouverie Pusey, 1800–82). The Oxford Movement claimed that, despite the Reformation, the Church of England remained a 'Catholic' Church whose authority derived from its unbroken linkages with the Apostles and the original bishops of the Christian Church. The main intellectual leader of the Oxford Movement, John Henry Newman (1801–90), is regarded as one of the greatest theologians of modern times. The Oxford Movement seemed to many to want to pull the Anglican Church away from Protestantism and towards Roman Catholicism, an outcome feared by its critics. Newman's conversion to Catholicism in 1845 deeply shocked many, and was an event of national importance. Broadly speaking, the evangelical and Oxford movements were associated with what became known as 'Low Church' and 'High Church' Anglicanism (although 'High Church' Anglicanism predated it and in some respects was separate from it) which persisted throughout the century and, indeed, persist to the present.

Despite the internal challenges it faced, in 1914 the Anglican Church appeared to be in a (perhaps surprisingly) satisfactory state. Although non-Anglican churches had been granted equal status, Anglicanism unquestionably remained the religion of the great majority among the English upper- and middle-class Establishment, and had found a new role as a major religious force throughout the white empire and through its successful missionary activity in the Third World, especially black Africa and Oceania. By the beginning of the twentieth century, the Anglican Church had recovered some of the ground it had lost to Nonconformity. It had halted the worst abuses routinely committed a century earlier, and appeared to have discovered a new vigour and even a new popularity.

Across England as a whole, however, the nineteenth century in many ways belonged to the Nonconformist churches. It is common to divide Protestant Nonconformity into 'Old Dissent' – sects such as Congregationalism, Baptism and Quakerism, founded in the seventeenth century – and 'New Dissent', chiefly Methodism, and a variety of newer, often strange Churches founded in the nineteenth century such as Mormonism. Both 'Old' and 'New' dissent grew during the nineteenth century, although it is very difficult to give anything more than a general estimate of numbers. The Religious Census of 1851 found that, in England and Wales, 1.2 million people had attended Independent or Congregationalist services that Sunday, 930,000 Baptist services, and no fewer than 2,484,000 any Methodist service, with smaller but not insignificant numbers attending services led by the Unitarians (50,000), Quakers (23,000), Plymouth Brethren (18,000) and Moravians (11,000). These figures may well be exaggerated – they count morning, afternoon and evening services separately, and devout individuals might well have attended more than one service – and group together denominations with a range of distinctive, often rival sub-sects (for instance, nine varieties of Methodism were detailed in the Census). Nevertheless, they give something of the sense of how widespread and important Nonconformity had become. Nonconformity, especially Methodism, arguably became the dominant religion in Britain's industrial areas. It usually – although not always – went hand in hand with political Liberalism, and with the package of ideals – free trade, opposition to aristocratic 'privileges', 'self-help', temperance – which were bound up with mid-Victorian Liberalism, just as Anglicanism was seen as connected with Toryism.

By the late nineteenth century, however, many viewed Nonconformity as past its best, or at least as not likely to make further significant gains. Sunday School enrolments, a potent indicator of the health of a religion, after a long period of steady growth appear to have peaked around 1900, before beginning a notable and then a catastrophic decline after the First World War. About 55 per cent of school-age children attended Sunday School (of any denomination) in 1900. This percentage never rose in the period to 1914, although it is also true that it did not markedly decline until the early 1930s. (In 2000, about 4 per cent of school-age children attended a Sunday School of any Christian denomination.) Evangelical Nonconformity, what many commonly see as the essence of 'Victorianism', probably reached a peak in the 1840s before being overtaken by increasing signs of proto-secularism. By granting legal religious equality to Nonconformity, parliament removed much of the sense of grievance which lay behind Dissent, the shared sense of historical persecution which helped to bind Dissenters together. By 1900, there was little to 'dissent' from, although Nonconformist grievances could still explode in nationally significant ways, as they did at the time of the 1906 general election over education and other matters.

As Dissenters climbed the economic ladder and sent their sons to public schools and universities, many inevitably became Anglicans and moved to the right both politically and socially. Probably the best-known Nonconformist in politics in the later nineteenth century, Joseph Chamberlain (1836–1914), illustrates this common progress. A Unitarian and originally a fiery radical leader of the Liberal party's left wing, Chamberlain broke with the Liberals and, within a decade, had become the country's best-known Tory imperialist, the main architect of the Boer War. Chamberlain's two sons, Sir Austen (1863–1937) and Neville (1869–1940), were both educated at Rugby, a leading public school; both were Anglicans and both became leaders of the Conservative party. To be sure, the pre-1914 decline of Nonconformity should not be exaggerated. The greatest victory of the Liberal party in 1906 owed much to Nonconformist discontent, especially over the Education Act of 1902, and the 1906–10 parliament was said to have been the first since Cromwell's time with a Nonconformist majority. But this proved to be Dissent's last political triumph.

Roman Catholicism in England also grew during the nineteenth century. English Catholicism was composed of pre-Reformation recusant families, numerous in Lancashire and Sussex and often well connected, to which were added significant numbers of converts and very large numbers of Irish and some European Catholic migrants. The Roman Catholic Church re-established an official hierarchy in England in 1850, amidst great controversy. Considerable anti-Catholicism still remained in England, even in 1914, at both the elite and mass levels, fanned in places like Liverpool by the Orange Order and extreme Protestant activists and societies. In contrast, the small

Jewish community in England, which grew from about 25,000 in 1800 to 200,000 a century later, is noteworthy for attracting little or no hostility. In contrast to much of the Continent, Jews did not 'control' the economy and were not strongly associated with radical or modernist movements; on the contrary, they were often admired by Protestant philo-semites. As a result, Britain escaped the anti-semitism of tsarist Russia or Dreyfusard France, with hostility to Jews emerging only in the wake of large-scale immigration to London's East End after 1881, and then only fitfully. It is often said that the career of the century's best-known Jewish politician, Benjamin Disraeli (1804–81), who became leader of Britain's *right*-wing party, would have been impossible anywhere else.

Modes of Identity: Nationality

The nineteenth century was a time of intense national loyalties in Britain, but whether or not Britain as a whole possessed a significant or cohesive ideology of nationalism is open to question. Britain never had to achieve independence. It felt no sense of national 'relative deprivation' – to use a well-known sociological term – and, throughout the period 1800–1914, was always a successful and satiated nation which never felt a need for national revenge or aggrandisement (though Britain's minority nations, Scotland, Wales and Ireland, might well have failed to share in this sense of national satisfaction). In general, the success enjoyed by the United Kingdom as a whole was enough to dampen strong nationalistic movements aimed at achieving national independence in the minority nations, with the exception of Catholic Ireland. The nationalisms which emerged in Ireland in the later nineteenth century were not paralleled elsewhere in Britain in the nineteenth century, although they might be seen as being precursors to the Scottish and Welsh nationalisms which emerged later. There were other ways, too, in which Britain was anomalous. Virtually alone among European states, Britain had no conscription and relied entirely upon a voluntary military and naval force. Until the First World War, passports were not legally required to leave Britain, and, as noted, Britain had no effective immigration barriers of any kind until 1905. Britain had no annual national holiday like the Fourth of July in the United States, with its tradition of tub-thumping patriotic speeches, the nearest equivalent, perhaps, being Guy Fawkes Day, which (as early as 1661) was transformed from a rather sinister anti-Catholic commemoration to a noisy celebration.

British patriotism was notable for almost never being officially compelled. Nevertheless, it was real and deep, and could occasionally erupt unexpectedly. Lord Nelson's state funeral in London early in 1806 possibly saw the highest percentage of the city's population as spectators to a state occasion of any event in history. Coronations, royal weddings and the two jubilees of Queen Victoria, in 1887 and 1897, also saw vast outpourings of apparently genuine public enthusiasm and support, while Mafeking Night, following the relief of the Boer-besieged British outpost in Bechuanaland in May 1900, became notorious for the totally unexpected saturnalia which accompanied London's spontaneous public celebrations. There were radical gatherings which were attended by tens of thousands, for instance the great Chartist meetings at Kennington Common in April 1848 (the first topical event in Britain to be photographed), but these were dwarfed in number and possibly enthusiasm by ceremonies of patriotic feeling. In 1914, whatever was the case in Ireland, Great Britain enthusiastically went to war as a united nation, political differences being put aside.

What, precisely, *British* patriotism celebrated was also never really made clear. If there was a central British narrative commonly depicted and probably consensually agreed upon, it was, overwhelmingly, an *English* narrative consisting of the familiar triumphalist verities of English history, essentially a Whig narrative of perpetual improvement, which was evidence of the favour of Divine Providence. In recent decades, historians have often depicted British history in terms of the co-existence, peaceful or otherwise, of the four 'nations' which comprised the United Kingdom, but it should not be forgotten that, in popular terms, the United Kingdom was predominantly English. It is therefore not surprising that the ruling historical narrative was primarily English. Paradoxically, however, it is difficult to identify a specifically *English* nationalism during the nineteenth century, in contrast to the situation in Scotland, Wales and, most emphatically, Ireland. England was widely seen as being hallmarked by a number of readily identifiable alleged national qualities – justice tempered by mercy, fair play, gentleness, 'stiff upper lip', eccentricity and marked individuality – which distinguished the English from foreigners, and which was underpinned by the enduring English myth of continuous improvement and success. It is probably fair to say that most of these alleged English qualities became widely accepted as actual hallmarks of the English only in the nineteenth century, and generally in its second half. For instance, few in the late eighteenth century would have conceived the English as particularly gentle, or, perhaps, as especially 'eccentric'. Like all national stereotypes, they are, of course, half-truths – which means (as is sometimes now forgotten) that they are half true as well as half false.

There were alternative historical narratives of 'Englishness', but these did not necessarily dissent from the mainstream account as much as one might suppose. The best known radical narrative emphasised the 'free-born Englishman' who had been corrupted by (it was often said) the 'Norman yoke' (in other words, the traditional landed aristocracy) and grasping London politicians. As enunciated by such populist publicists as William Cobbett, it also attacked 'Old Corruption' (venal office holding and lavish official incomes paid to the aristocracy and their minions), London, the finance capital, and looked to champions of Protestant liberty such as John Milton and John Bunyan as heroes. This radical populist tradition was certainly still alive among radical Liberals of the Boer War period. Just how radical the 'free-born Englishman' narrative actually was might be disputed: its populism could have a very nasty edge and was often anything but benign. It is doubtful, too, whether a *more* radical narrative about 'Englishness' existed. There were other widely held historical myths about English history, but these were often rather odd and are now virtually forgotten. For instance, there was belief in some quarters in the movement which became known as the British Israelites there was belief that the British were – literally – one of the Lost Tribes of Israel, who had migrated in ancient times from Palestine to the British Isles. Made popular in such works as the Rev. John Wilson's *Our Israelitish Origins* (1840), this notion struck a chord in extreme Protestant circles, by setting out and emphasising a view of British 'Chosenness' similar to that found in Judaism (and similar, too, to other notions of 'Chosenness' so popular in the United States, for instance, the religious doctrines of the Mormon Church, which claims that Jesus lived and preached in America in ancient times). The great vogue for Freemasonry and other secret fraternal orders in late Victorian Britain plainly drew on similar sensibilities and roots.

Nevertheless, alternative visions of 'Englishness' never challenged the common one. Indeed, the notion of an English national 'grand narrative' was seldom explicitly articulated in detail, because it was never seriously challenged. Those who might have been engaged in constructing an alternative vision of English history normally found other modes of presenting a challenge to the deficiencies of the Establishment. After 1835 (when local government was reformed) urban civic governance, for instance, often came into the hands of Nonconformist business and civic leaders whose challenge to the Establishment took the form of developing cities which were to be models of progressive improvement and reform, and which were also to challenge *laissez-faire* by the active use of state powers and money for social improvement. The best known example of this was probably in Birmingham where, from the 1860s, Joseph Chamberlain and his allies attempted to create a model city. The foundation of new civic universities in Manchester (1851), Newcastle (1852), Birmingham (1900), Liverpool (1903) and elsewhere were important hallmarks of this movement.

There are many ways in which Scotland, Wales and even Ireland became less *sui generis* and more fully integrated into a United Kingdom in the period 1832–1914. The Welsh, Scots Gaelic and Irish Gaelic languages steadily declined in terms of the number of their speakers, and monolinguistic speakers of these languages were increasingly confined to remoter rural areas. This process occurred even in Wales, where the old Celtic vernacular survived the longest. In 1800, virtually everyone in Wales spoke Welsh as his or her vernacular; by 1900, two-thirds of the population were bilingual in Welsh and English while, especially in the industrial south, the majority of the population was almost purely English-speaking. For instance, Aneurin Bevan (1897–1960), probably the greatest Welsh Labour politician of the twentieth century, could not speak any Welsh, although he grew up in a coal-mining town in the Rhondda. The tiny number of speakers of Cornish, Manx and Norn (a Norse dialect spoken in parts of the Shetlands and Orkneys) declined to zero, or nearly to zero, by the early twentieth century.

By 1900, probably all significant political and even cultural discussion and debate took place in English, and attempts by nationalists and romantics to revive the pre-English vernaculars almost always came to little or nothing. Even in southern Ireland, where a Gaelic

League was founded in 1893 to revivify Ireland's ancient language, and where Gaelic was made an official national language when the Irish Free State achieved independence in 1922, today only 2 per cent of the Irish population speaks Gaelic on a regular basis. All of the others, including the entire Irish political leadership, spoke and speaks English, the language of their alleged oppressors and conquerors, and all attempts to reverse the dominance of English have failed. With minor exceptions, *all* significant writing and literature in the British Isles during the period 1832–1914 was in English, even among Irish writers with a nationalistic edge such as Yeats, Synge or Joyce. There were minor exceptions, especially among some Welsh authors, but in effect British literary culture was monolinguistically English. Moreover, *spoken* English came increasingly to recognise the upper and upper middle-class speech forms of respectable London, Oxford and Cambridge – the so-called 'Queen's (or King's) English' – as the norm of correct speech, and all other accents and dialects as below standard, mimicked on stage and in cartoons as humorous or ignorant. These depictions applied to regional accents in Scotland, Wales, Ireland and northern and rural England, as well as to working-class accents, above all, perhaps, to the cockney accent of London's East End. The explicit or unconscious acceptance of the 'Queen's English' as the norm from which all other accents departed was arguably an important force in creating and maintaining a status hierarchy centred in middle-class London. Acquisition of proper speech, too, became an important marker of social respectability.

The English language became the near-universal vernacular of the British Isles (except in central and northern Wales and parts of the Scottish Highlands) in part because of profound technological changes, and changes in transport and communications, which did not and could not occur before the nineteenth century. Although it is a schoolchild's cliché that Britain after *c.* 1825 was in the 'railway age', one must remember that *all* of British history before the nineteenth century took place in times of pre-modern, and invariably slower, transport and communications, and that this had fundamental consequences for the unity of Britain. By 1880 or so at the latest, probably any town, even the remotest in Great Britain, could be reached from London in less than a day, and any town in Ireland, even the remotest, in two days, whereas a journey from London to the Scottish Highlands even in Samuel Johnson's time took weeks. By the

1880s, a trip by rail from London to Edinburgh on a fast steam train took about eight or nine hours, a time which would have seemed unimaginably rapid in the eighteenth century, and was vastly more comfortable than on stagecoach or other means of pre-railway travel. Communications, thanks to the telegraph, were even more rapid. News in London reached any major provincial city almost instantaneously, and was reported in local newspapers on the same day. This astonishing increase in the speed and ease of transport worked both ways: tens of thousands of those living in provincial Britain, even among the working classes, travelled to London. The first world's fair, for example, the Great Exhibition of 1851, lured several million to London on the new railway network, often for the first time.

There were other major institutional changes and circumstances which also worked to unify the British Isles. The nineteenth century was the first century in a thousand years in which no attempt was made to change the ruling dynasty by force of arms. Even in the eighteenth century, and despite its largely peaceful constitutional changes, two serious attempts were made, in 1715 and 1745, to restore the Stuart dynasty by armed invasion. The death of the last Jacobite pretender, Henry Benedict Stuart, Cardinal York, in 1807 (known to his Jacobite supporters as King Henry IX, and generally called 'Cardinal York' because he was the duke of York in the Jacobite peerage), closed the dynastic question. At his death, Cardinal York left the Jacobite Crown Jewels to King George III. By the Napoleonic Wars, if not before, the very notion of an armed invasion to place a different king on the English throne was surely absurd to the great majority of people. In so far as the question of the British head of state was ever raised again, it occurred in the context of proposals by some extreme Liberals or socialists to replace the monarchy with a republic. These surfaced, in particular, in the decade or so after the death of Prince Albert, the Prince Consort, in 1861, during which Queen Victoria withdrew almost entirely from public life.

But any republican sentiment then completely disappeared in the last three decades of the queen's life, when she re-emerged as a genuinely popular figure linking all parts of Britain and the empire. Her Jubilee celebrations in 1887 and 1897 were occasions for triumphant and heartfelt national rejoicing. It should be remembered that, with the exception of France after 1870–71 and the United States, all of the world's major nations at this time were monarchies, and would

continue to be until the European cataclysms at the end of the First
World War. In the twentieth century, King George V was forced
to change his surname from the German Saxe-Coburg-Gotha to
Windsor, and republican sentiment could only have re-emerged
during the First World War had Britain lost. But popular anti-
monarchial sentiment did not become a significant force in twentieth-
century Britain, even with the rise of the Labour party, with the
possible exception of a brief period around the time of Prince Charles's
divorce from Princess Diana in the early 1990s. Queen Victoria (and her
successors) maintained a Scottish residence at Balmoral from 1848, and
made infrequent but highly popular trips to most important provincial
towns in Britain – but much less frequently to Ireland, visiting it only
four times during her reign of sixty-three years, in itself a likely cause
of Irish dissatisfaction with the British government. In 1911 George V
visited remote India, one year after he came to the throne and three
years before the outbreak of the First World War.

Most of the aristocrats and members of the landed gentry in the four
countries certainly moved closer to a unified traditional upper class in
the period 1832–1914 than earlier, although the process was already well
underway before then. This occurred in a variety of ways and for
several reasons. Most wealthy, senior aristocrats from (in particular)
Scotland, Wales and (probably to a lesser extent) Ireland were educated increasingly at a leading English public school and at Oxbridge,
just as were their English counterparts. For instance, Archibald
Primrose, the fifth earl of Rosebery (1847–1929), Liberal Prime Minister
in 1894–5, was educated at Eton and Oxford, married a Rothschild
heiress and spent most of his adult life in London and the Home
Counties. Similarly, his contemporary Henry Petty-Fitzmaurice, fifth
marquess of Lansdowne (1845–1927), Foreign Minister and one of the
largest landowners in Ireland (who declined the title of duke of Kerry),
was also educated at Eton and Oxford, where he was heavily
influenced by Benjamin Jowett, the famous Master of Balliol College.
Aristocrats, wealthy gentry and the rich and titled came together every
year in London for the 'Season', a period of several months in which
levées, soirées, and coming-out dances for debutantes were held in the
great London town houses, sometimes presided over by royalty.
While the aristocracy had, of course, been centred in London for many
centuries, the ease of travel and universal acceptance of the norms of
High Society made such gatherings more popular and central, down to

the First World War, than before. Intermarriage between aristocrats and near-aristocrats of all four countries (and, internationally, with the overseas wealthy, especially the so-called 'Dollar Princesses', mega-rich American heiresses) almost certainly became more common. For instance, in 1908 Winston Churchill, then a rising Liberal MP and the grandson of the duke of Marlborough, married Clementine Ogilvie Hozier, the daughter of Sir Henry Hozier, a wealthy ground-rent landlord in Glasgow. Traditional Welsh and Irish aristocrats and gentry were also increasingly drawn into this pattern, as were some Irish landowners. But, once again, Ireland was an exception because much of its landed elite were Roman Catholics, at the time a virtually insuperable bar to intermarriage with Protestants, although they often married into the English 'Catholic Cousinhood' of aristocratic recusant families or recent converts.

In some respects, this cross-border merging of the elites also occurred among the business and professional middle classes, although in different ways and less categorically. The growth of the public schools, many of which were founded or re-established during the nineteenth century, and which became the most popular form of secondary education among the upper middle classes, greatly facili-tated this. With a common and virtually ubiquitous programme of education among all of the many dozen public schools in existence by 1914, based in the Greek and Latin classics, games and 'muscular Christianity', they instilled a common outlook among most of their graduates, whatever their geographical origins. So, too, did Oxford and Cambridge universities, although these educated a smaller portion of the middle classes after the foundation of London University and the provincial 'redbricks' which became increasingly popular in the second half of the century.

But perhaps the greatest source of unity among the upper and upper middle classes was their increasing fear of socialism and radical Liberalism, with their agendas of paying for social reform by taxing the well-off. In particular after the Liberal Unionist split of 1886, when many moderate Liberals left the party led by Gladstone, *most* (but not all) of the well-off belonged, increasingly as a matter of course, to the Conservative party (known at the time as the Unionists). Increasingly, the Tories united wealthy businessmen fearing trades union power, higher taxes or outright socialism, landowners fearing land national-isation in the wake of confiscatory reforms to landholding in Ireland

and proposals for a 'single tax' on land throughout Britain. These two groups came together with Irish Protestants who feared a Catholic-dominated Home Rule Parliament in Ireland to form a unified upper-class movement of resistance. While some Nonconformist businessmen and many middle-class intellectuals remained loyal to Liberalism, this marked trend to a *class*-based British politics after about 1880 was a common feature in most parts of the United Kingdom. The rise of the (in theory) explicitly class-based Labour party in the twentieth century, and the regrouping of anti-socialist forces in the Conservative party, in itself probably acted as a major deterrent to a nationality-based British politics, especially after the Irish question was seemingly settled in 1922, the same year that the Labour party first became the official opposition.

On the other side, however, there was a range of movements and ideas that could have resulted in the 'four nations' that comprised the British Isles moving further apart, and in nationality politics becoming more important and divisive in the period 1832–1914. The Romantic movement, with its emphasis on folk and national traditions and national historical narratives, was arguably of central cultural importance throughout virtually the whole of this period, as exemplified, for instance, by the popularity of Sir Walter Scott's historical novels set in medieval and early-modern Scotland. The Romantic movement might well have given rise to a politics of national assertion, such as explicitly developed in Catholic Ireland. During this period, too, the direction of British national life was firmly rooted in the central government in Westminster and in the civil service in Whitehall. Ireland was largely governed from Dublin Castle, but with the Chief Secretary for Ireland, always a member of the Cabinet, and the Lord-Lieutenant of Ireland, also an appointed member of the government and almost always a British aristocrat, constituting, in effect, the governors of Ireland. Scotland was even more centrally governed from London: the first Secretary for Scotland was appointed only in August 1885. Before that date, Scotland had no specific representative in the British government of the day, although the Lord Advocate (a Scottish legal official) acted through the Home Office as the 'manager' of Scottish affairs in parliament. Wales had no specific government minister responsible for its affairs until the first Minister for Welsh Affairs was appointed in 1951, and no separate Cabinet minister until 1964. Prior to the First World War, the only specifically Welsh administrative office of any kind was a Welsh Department of the Board of Education, established in 1907. It would be easy to understand if Scotland and Wales, as well as Catholic Ireland, had each developed a powerful feeling of what sociologists term 'relative deprivation', the sense that they are treated invidiously and gratuitously worse than others.

Yet, except in the case of Catholic Ireland, such resistance did not occur in our period, at least not with the urgency and significance that Scottish and Welsh nationalisms emerged in the latter part of the twentieth century. Explaining why a historical event or phenomenon has not occurred is always more difficult than explaining why it has (which can itself be hard enough!) but one might point to a number of important reasons why no such powerful nationalisms arose. Within Scotland, Wales and Ireland there were serious internal divisions that prevented the emergence of any consensus on such goals as increased internal self-rule. A movement for Welsh Home Rule briefly appeared in the 1880s, for instance, paralleling the major movement for Home Rule in Ireland. While this movement had some following in Welsh-speaking Wales, it had none in English-speaking South Wales, where many inhabitants were actually recent immigrants from elsewhere in Britain (or abroad), and which was economically dependent upon its links with England. Welsh self-assertion at this time concentrated instead on achieving the disestablishment of the Anglican Church in Wales, a goal which was finally realised in 1920. Scotland was similarly divided into a more 'Gaelic' Highlands and an English-speaking Lowlands, with Edinburgh, its capital, being more conservative and more closely linked with other parts of Britain than Glasgow, its largest city. There were, as well, other reasons why Scotland baulked at anything like Home Rule, above all that it was doing well out of its existing arrangement. Only in Ireland, with its Catholic peasant masses, did a genuinely popular and ultimately successful Home Rule movement arise at this time, one which was bitterly opposed by the Protestants of Ulster and elsewhere.

Similarly, the later nineteenth century and the earlier twentieth century saw the zenith of the empire and of imperial loyalty. It also seemed to most observers that the twentieth century would certainly be the century of world-empires rather than of small nations, which would inevitably be absorbed into larger units or face decline. For a small component of the United Kingdom actively to seek to go its own way – which many feared would be the ultimate aim of 'Home Rule' – seemed to many Scotsmen, Welshmen and even Irishmen totally contrary to the spirit of the times. So long as the British empire remained an existing world superpower, pressures for independence or semi-independence from any component of the United Kingdom were almost certain to be muted. The exception, as always, was Catholic Ireland. But even here it should be remembered that the stated aim of the Home Rule party in Ireland was not full independence from the United Kingdom but a local parliament in Dublin with powers over purely local matters. Under all of the three Home Rule Bills considered by parliament (in 1886, 1893 and 1913), such powers as foreign policy, war and income taxation were entirely reserved to the Westminster Parliament, and Ireland was to remain a part of the United Kingdom. Only after the Dublin Easter Uprising of 1916 and the rise of Sinn Féin was actual independence for Ireland a mainstream goal, an aim abetted by the Wilsonian settlement of Europe in 1918–19, which favoured independence for small national groups.

As well, in the period 1832–1914 England itself and the United Kingdom seemed to many to represent progressive values, in contrast to the 'backwardness' associated with, in particular, Britain's Celtic areas. Welsh speakers were often despised by other Welshmen as quaint peasants who spoke a primitive language, with the English language seen as a ticket to modernity and the United Kingdom itself at the forefront of progress. Similar views were held by many Scotsmen about Scots Highlanders, and by virtually everyone else about the majority of the Irish Catholic peasantry, viewed as a priest-governed mass of sometimes humorous but generally feckless, illiterate, alcoholic semi-barbarians, who stood in stark contrast to the industrious Protestants of the north.

Finally, an important reason for the failure of strong nationalist movements to emerge is that each needed allies in other parts of the United Kingdom, and these did not eventuate, again with the exception of the Irish, both north and south. Instead, disproportionate numbers of Scotsmen and Welshmen became members or allies of the Liberal party, joining with the larger group of English Liberals to elect Gladstone, Campbell-Bannerman and Asquith as prime ministers. Many of these English Liberals were themselves Protestant Non-conformists, and thus political and social 'outsiders' to the Anglican-centred Establishment. Most of the time after 1832, and certainly after the 1867 Reform Act, it was normal for many more Liberals than Tories to be elected in Wales and Scotland. In 1868, for instance, 22 Liberals and eight Tories were elected in Wales, 52 Liberals and eight Tories in Scotland, compared with 243 Liberals and 220 Tories in England. At the last general election before the First World War, in December 1910, Wales elected 26 Liberals, 5 Labourites (closely allied with the Liberals) and only 3 Tories. In Scotland the totals were, respectively, 58, 3 and 9. In the United Kingdom as a whole, the Liberals and Tories each elected 272 MPs, with 42 Labourites and 84 Irish Nationalists keeping Asquith and the Liberal party in office. Throughout this period, as will be clear, England often elected a Tory majority, whatever the case in the 'Celtic fringe'. In 1895, for instance, the Tories and their Liberal Unionist allies elected 293 MPs in England, compared with 112 Liberals, Ireland, as always, was a separate case, with the Irish Nationalist party normally winning virtually all of the seats in southern Ireland, the Ulster Unionists most of the seats in the north. The Irish Nationalists were almost always allied with the Liberals, although never incorporated into any Liberal government, while the Ulster Unionists were an active part of the Conservative and Unionist party, as it was known after 1886. The Celtic areas thus depended politically at all times on the goodwill of England with its much larger population, while in general forming an important component of the Liberal party, its Liberal MPs serving in Liberal Cabinets. This situation, of simultaneous dependence and active participation, almost certainly worked to diminish political nationalism in Scotland and Wales.

These two countervailing trends, towards separateness and towards unity, occurred against a backdrop of English predominance in the United Kingdom, always constituting a clear majority of its population.

National Identities: Scotland

England, being dominant, had no need to specify what constituted 'Englishness' or an English national identity. The need to define their national identities was greater, however, in the other parts of the United Kingdom, Scotland, Wales and Ireland. Yet each of these polities was quite separate, with obviously distinctive histories and cultures. Scotland, with 1.7 million inhabitants in 1801 and 4.5 million a

century later, and religiously relatively unified, might, as noted, have
been expected to have evolved a serious and continuing tradition of
overt opposition to English rule, perhaps as extreme as in Catholic
Ireland. Scotland had, of course, been a separate country with its own
Parliament until 1707. Unlike Wales, it had its own distinctive established religion, aristocracy and legal system. Unlike Ireland, its
established religion was that of the majority while its traditional
aristocracy was not necessarily hated by the majority. During the late
eighteenth and early nineteenth century it had experienced what in
recent years has become known as the Scottish Enlightenment, more
renowned throughout Europe than its English equivalent, and it
possessed four old and distinguished universities, compared with just
two for the whole of England (and none at all in Wales) before the
1820s. The image of Scotland was arguably reinvented during the
eighteenth and early nineteenth centuries to emphasise the age-old
historical legitimacy of the Highlands as authentically Scottish,
famously depicted in works of art and literature, above all in Sir Walter
Scott's novels. Despite its internal differences, the materials were
seemingly all there for a vigorous, perhaps subversive, assertion of
Scottish autonomy, even of Scottish independence. Yet this did not
occur. Why not?

The most important reason is that Scotland and the Scots did very
well out of their membership of the United Kingdom. The industrial
revolution made Glasgow into one of the world's greatest manufacturing and industrial centres, and sparked the economic development
of its surrounding areas and of its other Scottish cities such as Dundee,
which became the world centre of jute manufacturing. Scotland itself
was at the core of a worldwide web of overseas Scottish entrepreneurship. It is, indeed, almost no exaggeration to view the nineteenth
century as the time when Scottish entrepreneurship conquered the
world. Scottish firms such as Jardine Matheson predominated in Hong
Kong and the Far East. Australia was virtually a Scottish (and Scots-
Irish) continent in terms of the extraordinary number of successful
Scottish pastoralists and merchants, as were New Zealand and the
English-speaking parts of Canada. Scottish merchants were a
significant component among the leading British entrepreneurs in
Britain's 'unofficial empire' in Latin America, as were many of the
leading British merchants in Russia and eastern Europe. (This trend
had begun earlier: the father of Immanuel Kant, the great German

philosopher, was a Scottish merchant named Cant who had settled in Germany.) Even in the United States, probably the most famous rags-to-riches millionaire tycoon was Andrew Carnegie, who began as an operative in a Scottish factory.

Scottish entrepreneurship and its spread around the world went hand in hand with other Scottish-led activities overseas at this time, such as missionary work on behalf of the Protestant Churches. Dr David Livingstone (1813–73), the celebrated explorer and missionary who was 'found' by Henry Stanley in 1871, was a poor Glasgow boy who educated himself at Scottish colleges before being sent to Africa by the London Missionary Society; there were hundreds of Dr Livingstones around the world at the time and later. Scotsmen (and, perhaps in particular, the Scots-Irish from Ulster) also certainly formed a disproportionate share of the officers and men of the British Army, the East India Company and its successors, and even the Royal Navy. Without the worldwide empire presided over and governed from London, it would have been very difficult for this worldwide saga of success to have occurred.

It is often said as well that although the Scots had no means of governing themselves, through their role in the British government they governed the empire. Such a view might be an exaggeration in the earlier part of the nineteenth century but not in the late Victorian or Edwardian periods. The only Scotsman who became Prime Minister in the early and mid-nineteenth century was Lord Aberdeen (1852–55), although every Cabinet necessarily had its share of Scots. William E. Gladstone (1809–98), four times Prime Minister between 1868 and 1894, and arguably the greatest British political leader of the century, was a Scot by descent, the scion of a typical Scottish merchant who made a fortune in the West Indies and Liverpool and then joined the landed gentry. After Gladstone, however, came the deluge: his successor, Lord Rosebery, was known as the 'King of Midlothian' (owing to his extensive and valuable landed holdings near Edinburgh), and his successor as Liberal Prime Minister, Sir Henry Campbell-Bannerman, was another successful émigré Scottish merchant, this time to Manchester. Toryism, too, became a Scottish lake, with Arthur Balfour – although a Cecil on his mother's side, by paternity the son of a great Scottish untitled landowner – succeeded as Tory leader by yet another émigré Scot of a very different type indeed, the Canadian-born Andrew Bonar Law, son of a Free Church of Scotland minister. Even the early

Labour party imitated the bourgeois parties in one respect at least, that its two most important early leaders, Keir Hardie and Ramsay MacDonald, were Scotsmen.

What constituted Scottish national identity was also contested among the Scots themselves. Religiously, Scotland was officially Presbyterian, with an established Church, the Church of Scotland, based upon a hierarchical system, in which authority theoretically went from the bottom up rather than from the top down, with congregations electing ministers (Presbyters) and representative elders in the alleged manner of the early Christian Church. These in turn elected various more senior bodies, culminating in the General Assembly of the Church of Scotland, headed by a moderator elected for a year or two, although the sovereign was the official Head of the Church. Presbyterian doctrine is Calvinistic, and is often seen as grim and unforgiving, while the Church of Scotland has always been concerned to create a 'godly community' of well-behaved and devout believers. Since the Reformation, the Church of Scotland has certainly functioned as the Scottish national Church, much more fully an aspect of Scottish national identity than the Anglican Church in England, with the annual meetings of the General Assembly of the Church of Scotland often being seen as a kind of substitute, after 1707, for a Scottish Parliament. Yet religious dissent always existed in Scotland, usually stemming from sources which were even more extremely Protestant and Calvinistic than the official Church. During the eighteenth century, an evangelical Secession Church, which from 1847 was known as the United Presbyterian Church, was formed, generally from among extreme Protestants, mainly in Glasgow and Edinburgh.

A much more serious and traumatic fissure in the Church of Scotland, however, appeared in the 1830s and 1840s, leading in 1843 to what became known as the Free Church of Scotland. Ostensibly the disputes that led to the formulation of a breakaway Church included the non-recognition by the official Church of ministers appointed to newer parishes in urban areas, and the widespread use within the Church of Scotland of lay patronage, where (as in the Church of England), a lay patron, normally a wealthy landowner, had the power to appoint ministers to churches of which he was the patron, a custom regarded by many as contrary to Presbyterian practice. The movement towards forming a new Church was led by the Rev. Thomas Chalmers (1780–1847), a professor at Edinburgh University, and a tireless champion of this cause. Led by Chalmers, in May 1843, at the annual General Assembly of the Church of Scotland in Edinburgh, there occurred the famous 'Great Disruption', when about 40 per cent of both the clergy and laity of the Church of Scotland broke away from the old Church, dramatically symbolised by a mass walk-out from the General Assembly's meeting.

The Free Church of Scotland, as the breakaway movement was known, was strongly Protestant and Calvinistic, and drew its support from, in particular, nouveau riche Scottish businessmen, often living embodiments of the 'Protestant ethic' and from remote areas in the north of Scotland. Within a few years it had not only attracted a mass following, equal to the established Church, but a remarkable network of new churches, schools and institutions – of the third of the 2.9 million Scottish population that attended a religious service in 1851, 37 per cent attended a mainstream Church of Scotland service, and 31 per cent attended a Free Church of Scotland service (with 17 per cent attending United Presbyterian Church services, 10 per cent other Protestant services and 5 per cent Roman Catholic services). The intensity and spirit of the new Church continued until the 1870s, when it was widely noted that rigorous Calvinism began to decline among all three Presbyterian Churches. In 1900 the United Presbyterian and Free Church merged, with most of its members joining the established Church of Scotland in 1929. It is significant that Scottish 'nonconformity' almost always arose among believers who kept the name and structure of the old established Church, insisting on a purer and more uncompromising form of Calvinism. Although English Nonconformist sects such as the Baptists did exist in Scotland, and there was a growing Roman Catholic presence (deeply resented by many Scottish Protestants), the nature of 'Dissent' in Scotland differed from that in England, where many sects, from the Quakers to the Primitive Methodists, were entirely outside the structure of the Anglican Church and made no attempt to retain any remnant of its worship or dogma. One reason for this, arguably, was the self-consciously Scottish nature of the large breakaway movements: Scottish religious identity was almost consensually formulated through Scottish Presbyterianism.

That this was so might well have enhanced moves towards Scottish autonomy or even independence, but in the event this did not occur. Apart from Scotland's continuing success within the United Kingdom, the still very influential Scottish aristocracy and other components of its elite were probably drawing closer to their English counterparts. The notorious Highland Clearances, which began under the first duke of Sutherland, the great Scottish magnate, in 1807–21, were motivated in part by the desire to introduce the highly efficient English 'triple division of land tenure' and large-scale sheep breeding into the Highlands, in place of farming by the impoverished crofters, small owner-occupiers or tenants. Sutherland, the largest landowner in Scotland, was also the marquess of Stafford and a great English landowner. Thousands of crofters were cleared from the Highlands, many emigrating to Canada, leaving a lasting residue of bitterness. By the late nineteenth century, most Scottish aristocrats had probably been educated at a great English public school and university, although many also spent some time at a Scottish university. By the twentieth century, Scotland's aristocrats were janus-faced: linked ever more strongly to their English peers, but also still enjoying considerable local power and prestige at home.

Scottish 'nationalism' during the nineteenth century was extremely limited in its demands, centring around the desire for the appointment of a Secretary of State for Scotland in the Cabinet. This demand, first voiced in the 1850s, was crowned with success in 1885, with the appointment of the Tory duke of Richmond as the first Scottish Secretary. Vociferous Irish Nationalist demands for a Home Rule Irish parliament had their parallels in Scotland, and the idea of 'Home Rule All Round' had many supporters in Scotland and elsewhere. But Irish Nationalist demands and extremism triggered a Protestant Unionist backlash, which had important echoes throughout Protestant Scotland. Whereas in 1885 Scotland had elected fifty-eight Liberal and eight Conservative MPs to parliament, a year later, following the breakup of the Gladstonian Liberal party over Home Rule, the number of Unionist (Conservative and Liberal Unionist) MPs rose to twenty-seven. In 1900, for one of the only times at a normal two-party general election, Scotland elected a majority of Unionist MPs. In the twentieth century, with the long-term bifurcation of British politics along class lines and the rise of Labour, the middle and upper classes largely unified under the Conservatives. Until the 1990s, both the Labour and Conservatives opposed increased Scottish autonomy. The Scottish National Party, formed in 1928, did not elect an MP until 1945 and did not become a major force until the 1970s. Their rise occurred half a century after Scotland began its long-term decline as a major industrial centre.

National Identities: Wales

The situation in Wales presented some parallels with Scotland, but also many differences. Since the Middle Ages Wales had been not an independent state, but rather a kind of appendage of England. It had never (since that time) had a Parliament or legal system of its own, or separate aristocracy. Cardiff, which became acknowledged as the capital of Wales, was on the Principality's south-east coast, and had a population of only about two thousand in 1801, compared with Edinburgh's 83,000. Wales's largest city in 1801 was Swansea, also on the south coast; it had a population of only about 10,000 and was smaller than Colchester or Shrewsbury. Most Welsh people lived in remote, often almost inaccessible rural areas, and spoke Welsh. A far higher percentage of the population of Wales – about one-half in 1851 – spoke Welsh as their vernacular tongue than did the Irish or Scots who spoke Irish or Scottish Gaelic. Wales was considered remote, exotic, even uncivilised, by many Englishmen; Anglican parishes in Wales were considered the least desirable in the country and were generally

Lloyd Family Butchers, Aberystwyth. This picture, taken in 1911, is of a typical family-run retail shop, similar to thousands of others at the time. The lines of unrefrigerated carcasses in the outdoors will probably seem utterly unhealthy to many today.

among the lowest paid. There was little or nothing in Wales to compare with the Scottish Enlightenment, and it had no real university of its own until 1871.

In the eighteenth and early nineteenth centuries one very significant change came over the Welsh people: most ceased to be Anglican and became adherents of one or another variety of Protestant Non-conformity, such that by 1880 'Wales' and 'Nonconformist' were virtually interchangeable terms. By the early twentieth century, when Welsh Nonconformity was at its peak, only about 25 per cent of the people of Wales and Monmouthshire were Anglicans, compared with 23 per cent who were Congregationalists, 25 per cent who were Calvinistic Methodists, 18 per cent Baptists, 6 per cent Wesleyans and 3 per cent other religions, chiefly Roman Catholics. Although the four main Nonconformist sects had broadly similar doctrines, they had somewhat different clientele and histories and were, in many ways, rivals. They also had in common the ironical fact that all were English imports, while the Anglican Church regularly claimed to be the authentically Welsh ancient Church of the Principality, the successor to the early Christian Celtic Churches, and that its translation of the Bible into Welsh probably saved the language from extinction. (Calvinistic Methodism was officially founded at Bala in 1811 by the Rev. Thomas Charles (1765–1814), a Welsh Anglican vicar, but drew its doctrinal origins from English and Scottish sources.) By the early nineteenth century, the Welsh religious situation thus differed in many ways from the Scottish in that three-quarters of the Welsh people made no pretence to belonging to the established Church of the country in any sense, but viewed it, rather unhistorically, as a 'foreign' imposition. Nineteenth-century Welsh Nonconformity also developed a religiosity that, to many, embodied the essence of 'Welshness', emphasising rousing hymns in the 'Land of Song', and greatly prizing the minister capable of delivering spirited and gripping sermons (hwyl). In the absence of an entrenched local gentry or professional class, Nonconformist ministers often comprised a major part of the local leadership elite. Most Nonconformist sects in Wales were also associated with radical politics, first Liberal and then Labour, and their ministers normally emerged from working-class backgrounds, in marked contrast to the Anglican clergy.

Nevertheless, for much of the nineteenth century, Welsh Non-conformity was arguably not a disguised form of *political* nationalism:

at least it had no nationalistic political agenda. Welsh politics in the nineteenth century before about 1868 was dominated, perhaps surprisingly, by its anglicised gentry, often Tory or Whig-Liberal, who were regularly returned to parliament with little opposition. Historians have argued that the backwardness of 'Welsh Wales', and its lack of either a leadership elite of its own or a single charismatic leader akin to Daniel O'Connell in Ireland, were major factors in this, as was the relatively limited extent of the franchise in Wales before 1867, given that the right to vote was based largely on property ownership. A major turning point in Welsh politics came at the 1868 general election, the first held after the 1867 Reform Act, when a clear majority of Liberals were elected for the first time since 1832, twenty-two compared with the Tories' eight. By the end of the nineteenth century, Toryism in Wales was reduced to a fringe remnant in border and very middle-class areas, even in years of Tory triumph. Moreover, the social character of most Welsh MPs changed considerably, going 'downmarket' in a way unusual in the nineteenth century. One winner in 1868 was the Rev. Henry Richard, a Congregationalist minister, who became leader of the Welsh MPs.

The mid- and especially the late nineteenth century also saw the very rapid industrialisation of South Wales, symbolised by its coal mines, the very emblem of *laissez-faire* industrial capitalism at its grimmest and nastiest. Other forms of heavy industry and commerce developed rapidly in and around Cardiff, which increased in size from only 18,000 in 1851 to 182,000 in 1911, and Swansea, which grew in the same years from 31,000 to 144,000. Sharing in the bounty provided by the mantle of the British empire at this time almost certainly acted to dampen serious separatist aspirations, as did the growth (for the first time) of a class of native Welsh industrial tycoons, who were eventually ennobled with titles such as Lords Merthyr, Swansea and Glantawe. Culturally, too, this was a time of the favouring of English over Welsh, epitomised by the famous 'Blue Books' controversy of 1847, when the authors of a government commission on education in Wales criticised the continuing use of the Welsh language as a significant factor in hindering the 'moral and religious progress' of the 'poorer classes' and in keeping Wales generally backward. While their conclusions scandalised the Welsh-speaking community, it was consistent with a long-term decline in the use of Welsh, especially in the south. Welsh 'nationalism' generally focused on improvements in

Welsh education, some land reform, and, especially, on a move towards the disestablishment of the minority Anglican Church in Wales. A very typical Welsh historical myth and narrative also developed at this time, focusing on the (alleged) ancient Druids, the medieval kings of independent Wales, and the figure of Owain Glyn Dwr (c. 1354–1416), the medieval warrior king. Welsh disestablishment was almost achieved in 1895, and was finally enacted in 1919 when there was a Welsh Prime Minister, although a Tory parliamentary majority.

During the late nineteenth century, because of rapid industrial-isation the Welsh population evolved from largely rural and agricultural to largely industrial and urban (or situated in mining villages). As in Scotland, the rapid and comprehensive growth, first of Welsh radical Liberalism, and then of Welsh Labour, probably acted to reduce the somewhat contradictory pressures towards Welsh nationalism or even independence. By 1914 Wales was still firmly a part of the United Kingdom, although always on the left of politics and usually somewhat wary of imperialism and of Anglican gentry England. Its national mood was summarised in the career of the most famous and important Welsh politician of the age, David Lloyd George (1863–1945). Although Lloyd George was an almost perfect representative of Wales's national political culture, his life and career also illustrated the often contradictory nature of Wales and its place at this time: he was born in Manchester; grew up in the rural north of Wales and had little to do with the industrial south; he magically transformed himself in 1914–18 from a 'Little Englander' and the 'scourge of the dukes' to the great champion of the empire, and died an earl. As in Scotland, overt Welsh nationalism came late to Wales, with Plaid Cymru, the Welsh nationalist party, founded only in 1925 and electorally unsuccessful until it elected its first MP in 1966.

National Identities: Ireland

Ireland came to dominate British politics to such an extent that British political history between about 1845 and 1922 might, with little exaggeration, be said to consist of Ireland plus footnotes. If anything, the Irish question became more central to British political life after the 1870s than before, leading to the breakup of the Gladstonian Liberal party in 1886, to a near-civil war situation in Britain in 1910–14, to the downfall of Lloyd George in 1922 and to the decades of Tory ascendancy which followed. Presumed dead, the Irish issue sprang back to life in the late 1960s in a form deadlier than before.

The Irish question is so complex and proved so insoluble because it entailed several related but differing and very serious issues which, although linked in the minds of most Irish people, were not necessarily causally connected. Addressing one – no mean task in itself – would not necessarily resolve any of the others. Religion and ethnicity, the nation's economic structure and performance, modes of domestic governance and the nexus between the Westminster government and Ireland and its various communities were the principal elements in what was known as the 'Irish question', as was the fact that Ireland, of course, is a separate geographical entity. To some extent, therefore, Ireland could not be governed from London, and some form of local autonomy (at the very least) seemed inevitable. From 1297 until 1801 Ireland – the whole island – had its own Parliament with limited powers under the British crown, with an administration headed by a lord-lieutenant appointed by the British government. In 1800 the Irish Parliament, whose powers had been increased in 1782, consisted, like the Westminster Parliament, of two houses, an Irish House of Lords comprising 20 Anglican bishops and (at the time) 228 Irish peers, and an Irish House of Commons of 300 members. As in Britain, voting at elections was heavily restricted to a tiny number of electors, with Irish peers and other landowners de facto controlling nearly all elections. From 1727 only Protestants could vote, although the vote was restored to Catholics who met the requisite property qualifications in 1793. No Roman Catholic, however, could sit in the Irish Parliament, which was restricted to members of the Church of Ireland.

In the late eighteenth century, as a result of the French Revolution, a number of potentially serious revolutionary bodies were formed, such as Wolfe Tone's Society of United Irishmen, which developed links with revolutionary France, and a revolt among Munster peasants actually occurred in 1798. As a result, William Pitt's government in 1801 took the drastic step of securing the consent of both parliaments to a union. Pitt envisaged this as part of a strategy including Catholic emancipation (which King George III refused to allow and which was not enacted until 1829) and an enlarged market for Irish goods. From 1801 until 1922, 100 (150 from 1832) Irish MPs sat in the Westminster House of Commons, with Ireland governed both indirectly from

London and directly by the Irish Viceroy and his staff at Dublin Castle, while 28 Irish peers (out of a total of 228) elected from their own number sat in the House of Lords. Ireland thus had no national legislature, although each county and borough provided local government. Increased agricultural prices during the Napoleonic Wars kept Ireland relatively quiescent, but after Waterloo agitation began again to secure 'Catholic emancipation' – the right of Irish Roman Catholics to be elected to the Westminster Parliament and hold the full range of civic offices – and, if possible, the restoration of the Dublin Parliament. This agitation was led by Daniel O'Connell (1775–1847), an Irish Catholic barrister who became known as the 'Liberator'. O'Connell's Catholic Association, formed in 1823, skilfully exploited the fear of rural unrest to gain, with remarkable speed, the granting of 'Catholic emancipation' by parliament in 1829. O'Connell is seen by historians not merely as one of the great figures in modern Irish political history, but one of the first leaders of a rural proletariat to emerge in Europe, who used mass public meetings to great advantage. O'Connell's political triumph in 1829 might have been expected to go very far towards resolving the Irish question, and O'Connell, a moderate property owner, did not further exploit the political power he and his Irish Catholic bloc held at the Westminster Parliament.

'Catholic emancipation' did not resolve the 'Irish question', but was only one step on a troubled road which lasted for nearly another century. This was largely because of the underlying religious demography and power structure of the country. In 1821 about 80 per cent of Ireland's population of seven million were Roman Catholics. About 10 per cent were adherents of the Church of Ireland, the Protestant episcopal church on the island, and about 10 per cent were Presbyterians or other Protestant Nonconformists. Catholics existed in great numbers throughout the island, except in the north-east corner, the Province of Ulster. Church of Ireland membership was also widely spread, but was especially concentrated in and around Dublin, where it comprised most of the Anglo-Irish Establishment, its governmental, military and mercantile leadership. Many (but not all) significant landowners were churchmen, many of whom spent part of the year in other parts of Britain, where they often owned estates. Ulster was the home of the Scots-Irish Protestants, who had come over from Scotland in the seventeenth century and whose national ethos and historical narrative revolved around a triumphalist anti-Catholicism. Despite being the religion of only 10 per cent of the Irish population, the Church of Ireland was the established Church, and was closely inter-twined with Ireland's governing classes. It was headed by no fewer than four archbishops, compared with only two (Canterbury and York) for the whole of England. Protestant Nonconformists like the Ulster Presbyterians did not form a true part of the Anglo-Irish Establishment, although, as Protestants, they faced fewer obstacles and barriers than did the Catholics. Today, when we are used to the Northern Irish conflict being depicted in terms of Irish Catholics v. Ulster Scots-Irish Presbyterians, it is important to realise that a third religious element, the Irish churchmen, existed at the time and were, in fact, the ruling elite.

Irish Catholics thus felt a deep sense of grievance which was aug-mented by economic reality. Catholic landowning Ireland consisted chiefly of small sub-lessees and very small farmers, eking out a living in a manner reminiscent of a continental peasant society. Beneath even this, the mass of rural Irish Catholics were not farmers at all, but an impoverished rural proletariat of agricultural labourers, comprising an estimated 59 per cent of the rural population in 1841. Industrial growth largely bypassed – and would continue to bypass – Catholic Ireland, in contrast to Ulster, which became a major industrial centre after about 1850, the population of Belfast growing from 103,000 in 1851 to 387,000 in 1911.

Nevertheless, Ireland remained reasonably quiescent and rather off politics' centre stage from 1832 until the Great Famine of 1845–9, one of the greatest demographic catastrophes in modern history. The popu-lation of the west of Ireland declined precipitously, County Galway diminishing from 440,000 in 1841 to 322,000 a decade later, County Tipperary from 436,000 to 332,000 in the same period. These areas continued to decline through emigration after the famine, with Galway, for instance, dropping to 271,000 in 1861 and to only 182,000 in 1911. Relief of the famine by Britain's Whig government under Lord John Russell was uninspired and half-hearted, although it must be said that, with the transport and communications available at the time, it would have been difficult to get food from overseas to the stricken area in time to save many, while other areas of the United Kingdom, not dependent upon a one-crop economy, avoided famine. Observers reported scenes of starvation and utter misery strongly resembling the horrors which greeted the liberators of Belsen and Dachau a century later and, indeed, it was not long before Irish nationalist writers such as John Michel charged the British government with a deliberate act of genocide in its minimal response.

The famine had a number of lasting effects of considerable importance. It altered the class structure in much of rural Ireland, eliminating a large portion of the agricultural labourer class, increasing, through mergers and purchases, the size and viability of farms, and also, in the long run, increasing the power of the landlords. The famine enormously increased the number of expatriate Irishmen, especially in the United States, who felt a bitter hatred towards England. In 1858, expatriate Irishmen in America founded the Fenian Society, known officially as the Irish Republican Brotherhood, which advocated and paid for armed insurrection in Ireland and terrorism in England (and Canada, a symbol of British imperialism), and which came close to assassinating Queen Victoria. Its methods, of random bombings and murders, foreshadowed the policies of the IRA and more recent terrorists. In Ireland itself, the famine became a central historical myth, fundamental evidence of English wickedness and racism. The famine also probably acted to enhance the power of the Catholic clergy, relatively more numerous post-famine, who now adopted a more vigorous and visible role as leaders of the Irish rural masses, whereas previously they had been largely quiescent.

Nevertheless – although it may seem perverse to view such tragic events in this light – the famine actually had several beneficial effects in the medium term, reducing the size of the impoverished class of agricultural labourers and making Irish agriculture more profitable along English lines. It is possible that, Fenianism notwithstanding, Ireland might have remained quiet and relatively unnoticed. Probably the first dent in this veneer of quiescence came with the election of Gladstone's Liberal government in 1868 with a large majority. Gladstone, a strange combination of Evangelical and High Church Anglican, whose religiosity strongly influenced his actions according to rules which only he and the Deity understood, decided, out of the blue, that his central mission was to 'pacify Ireland'. His religious outlook and perception of the centrality of the religious question for Irish politics led him to make the centrepiece of his Irish policies the disestablishment of the Anglican Church in Ireland. For Gladstone, such a move would contribute greatly to the pacification of Ireland's Catholic majority, as well as its Presbyterian minority, who were also outside the established Church. It would also solidify Nonconformist support in Britain for his agenda, since the eventual disestablishment of the Church of England was high on the long-term programme of radical Nonconformity. Although Gladstone's Irish Church policies were opposed, they did not meet the same vigorous disapproval with which a previous attempt, in 1833, at reform of the Church of Ireland was opposed (when the number of its archbishops was cut from four to two and eight Irish bishoprics were abolished). This measure of 1833, the Irish Church Temporalities Act, led directly to the Oxford Movement and was regarded by strong Anglicans as sacrilege. In 1868, the main questions were how generous financial terms should be given to the Church of Ireland, and whether there should be 'concurrent endowment' for all Ireland's denominations instead, a move favoured by some Catholics. Disestablishment of the Church of Ireland became law in 1869, making Ireland one of the few places in Europe without an established Church. Gladstone also passed an Irish Land Act in 1870 which made the eviction of tenants more difficult.

Gladstone and many others thought that a healthier, happier Ireland would emerge, but this was not to be. While Irish unrest initially subsided, within ten or twelve years it re-emerged in a new, more extreme form. The English agricultural depression, which began around 1879 largely as a result of foreign competition, and a catastrophic downturn that struck the United States at the same time, which reduced the still large number of Irish emigrants, produced considerable unrest again in Ireland. By about 1880, dissent had centred around demands for Irish Home Rule, i.e. the restoration of an Irish Parliament for the whole island with considerable powers. This renewed radicalisation coincided with the ascendancy of Ireland's greatest political leader between O'Connell and the 1916–22 civil war, Charles Stewart Parnell (1846–91). Parnell, an upper-class Anglo-Irish Protestant, became leader of the Irish parliamentary party around 1878, and from then made the achievement of Irish Home Rule his goal. In 1885, Gladstone, once again Prime Minister, announced his conversion to Home Rule, and proceeded to introduce such a measure into parliament in 1886. It would have created a unicameral Irish Parliament consisting of two 'orders', one representing the old Irish aristocracy and the upper classes, the other the mass of the people, with limited powers to legislate on Irish affairs. The Westminster Parliament was to retain many powers, including exclusive control over foreign policy and defence, and Irish

MPs would continue to sit in the Westminster Parliament. The Home Rule Bill was accompanied by another Land Purchase Act, designed to buy out many absentee landlords.

Gladstone's Home Rule Bill set off an enormous storm of hostility and opposition without any parallel since the repeal of the Corn Laws in the mid-1840s. Opposition came from several sources. The first and most important was the Presbyterian community in Ulster, the Orangemen, who feared inevitable rule by the Catholic majority. Their fierce anti-Catholicism was augmented by a belief in the progressive nature of Protestant society in Northern Ireland, in contrast to the Catholic south. Orangemen pointed out the enormous progress made by Belfast as an industrial powerhouse under Protestant domination, strongly linked to Protestant Glasgow and the industries of the Clyde. Belfast's largest business, Harland & Wolff, was the largest shipbuilders in the world, and many other major industries were located there, although the most famous ship ever built by Harland & Wolff did little to enhance its reputation: RMS *Titanic*. In contrast, Catholic southern Ireland, priest-ridden and backward, had hardly any industries at all: Dublin's largest business was Guinness Breweries, and even the Guinness family was Protestant.

This notion of the inevitable superiority of Protestant to Catholic Europe was, in 1905, given apparent scholarly credence when the famous German sociologist Max Weber published his renowned work *The Protestant Ethic and the Spirit of Capitalism*, which introduced the notion of the 'Protestant work ethic'. Protestant fears were that an impoverished Irish Catholic majority, led by Catholic priests with an ideology from the Dark Ages, would inevitably destroy the achievement of the Protestant minority through deliberate taxation and perhaps overt persecution. The Ulster Protestants wanted either a continuation of the existing state of affairs or, at the very least, the exclusion of Ulster from the Home Rule Bill's provisions. They, and their supporters, also argued that Gladstone's appeasement of those who hated Britain at the expense of those loyal to it was immoral, and would not work: Irish nationalists would inevitably be back ten years later with some proposal still more extreme.

The Ulster Protestant community was strongly backed by many English Tories, who saw in them a winning cause. 'Ulster will fight, Ulster will be right' was Lord Randolph Churchill's famous phrase. Over the next thirty years Protestant Ulster evolved into a community whose *raison d'être*, almost to a man and woman, revolved around fierce opposition to Catholic-dominated Home Rule, underpinned by a spirit of militant national resistance. While the other minority nations within Britain looked back to a romantic, legendary past, reviving the Druids and the medieval Irish kings, Ulster saw its history as beginning with the Protestant conquest of Northern Ireland in the seventeenth century and celebrated the suppression of the Catholics. Alone among the historical narratives and myths of Britain's minority nations, Ulster celebrated victory rather than mourning defeat and conquest; it did not look to a lost golden age before foreign oppression began. Gladstone and the Home Rulers certainly underestimated the strength of Ulster's determination to resist a Catholic majority, arguing that these inhabitants' civil rights would be protected, while a Home Rule parliament would bring the communities together by forcing them to take part in the mundane process of local government administration, necessarily entailing compromise.

Apart from the Ulster Protestants and the Tories, several other major sources of opposition to Home Rule quickly emerged, most seriously from within the Liberal party itself. Both the party's Whig, moderate right wing and, rather surprisingly, a major portion of its left wing led by Joseph Chamberlain, were bitterly opposed to Home Rule, Chamberlain and others arguing that it would weaken the British empire. Many strong Protestants in England and Scotland also turned against Home Rule. As a result, in June 1886, Gladstone's Home Rule Bill was defeated by 341 to 311, when 94 Liberals voted against it. Many formed a new political party, the Liberal Unionists, which, by the mid-1890s, had effectively joined the Conservatives. A further attempt by the minority Liberal government of 1892–5 to enact Home Rule also failed. A Home Rule Bill, excluding Ulster for six years, finally passed in 1914 but was put into cold storage by the First World War. After the war and the Dublin Uprising of Easter 1916, it proved impossible to reach any agreement short of Irish independence and the total exclusion of Ulster. In the period, too, an Irish nationalist historical myth and narrative based around the ancient and medieval independent kingdoms of Ireland, took shape, aiming at total independence, if necessary by force. Although confined to the fringes until the First World War, its strength was enhanced by the failure to enact Home Rule and by the lack of inspiring political leadership in Catholic Ireland after Parnell's career was destroyed in a divorce scandal in 1891, followed by his early death. It should perhaps be noted that the appeal of extreme Irish nationalism grew dramatically during the First World War, with the 1916 uprising, and in the wake of the settlement imposed upon Europe by American President Woodrow Wilson in 1918–19, which viewed language and nationality as the major basis for revised national boundaries and national independence.

The successful enactment of Irish Home Rule is one of the great might-have-beens of British history. Conceivably, a successful Home Rule parliament, concentrating solely on down-to-earth local issues and respecting the rights of all, might have satisfied and disarmed Ulster while damping down extreme Catholic Irish nationalism. A united Ireland might have supported the First World War, and a significant number of southern Irish MPs would have remained in the Westminster Parliament, probably enhancing the electoral success of the British left in the twentieth century. On the other hand, the nationalistic forces of both Catholic Ireland and Ulster were probably too strong to make compromise possible, while Gladstone's pro-gramme was – as Chamberlain noted – profoundly antipathetic to the spirit of the times, with its perception of great empires as a prerequisite for great power status in the twentieth century.

Although somewhat removed from the central discussion of this section, it is worth noting that the nineteenth century saw the emergence and growth of many colonies settled by British émigrés, in Canada, Australia, New Zealand and parts of South Africa. While these might have developed strong separatist tendencies, especially as many settlers constituted Britain's dispossessed, in fact without exception they developed strong feelings of loyalty to Britain, seen nostalgically as the 'Mother Country', with all loyally fighting on Britain's side in the war of 1914–18 and, indeed, in the war of 1939–45. Britain's white colonies developed as British outposts overseas, the majority rejoicing in British law, government and civilisation. Only where large communities of Irish Catholics resided in the white empire was this sense of loyalty contested.

Perhaps the most important lesson to be drawn from this discussion of local nationalisms within the United Kingdom is that, Catholic Ireland alone excepted, a sense of Britishness and British triumphalism became ubiquitous everywhere, with Scottish, Welsh, Ulster and even moderate southern Irish opinion loyal to Britain and the empire. Nothing succeeds like success, and the unquestioned success of Britain in every sphere until, at the earliest, the end of the nineteenth century, proved sufficiently strong to dampen down centrifugal opinion, helped by the 'safety valve' of migration to the white empire and elsewhere. The doctrine of evolution helped, too, with large empires and continental nation-states (such as the United States) seemingly, by the end of the century, preordained to domination in the twentieth century. So, too, did Protestantism (outside of southern Ireland, of course), seen as a progressive religion generally in accord with scientific progress and democracy, as opposed to the backwardness of Catholicism and non-Christian religions. The nineteenth century was a time of the integration of the disparate parts of the United Kingdom into something like one whole, southern Ireland always being the exception.

3. Political Cultures

Queen Victoria, who reigned from 1837 until 1901, was the sovereign during most of the nineteenth century, and lent her name to that age. This schemata continues to be a fruitful way of viewing Britain's nineteenth-century political history, and will be used here to describe the broad political trends of the nineteenth century.

In terms of its legal and constitutional forms, Britain changed less markedly between 1800 and 1914 than virtually any European nation. One might contrast this situation with that in France, which, in the course of the nineteenth century, transformed itself from a republic to an empire headed by an emperor, to a monarchy with broad monarchical powers, to a constitutional monarchy, a republic, another empire with an emperor, and finally to a republic again, having experienced three revolutions and numerous attempted *coups d'état* along the way. By way of comparison, Britain had almost precisely the same formal institutions of government in 1914 as in 1801. Indeed, it is difficult to think of *any* formal change in the institutions of national governance which occurred in nineteenth-century Britain after the Act of Union with Ireland in 1801. Moreover, there was also a fair degree of genuine continuity in many of the informal institutions of British government: in 1800 Britain's actual executive consisted of a Cabinet headed by a prime minister, just as in 1914, while, by 1820, everyone knew that there was a Tory, right-of-centre party (although it was not called the Conservative party until the 1830s) and a liberal or radical party, then generally known as the Whigs. In 1914 these two parties still existed, broadly and with many permutations the descendants of the two earlier parties, now known officially as the Unionists and the Liberals.

There was also something of a continuum among the families which produced a disproportionate number of the ministers in successive governments, mainly drawn from Britain's traditional landed aristocracy, although occasionally from families outside the aristocracy. For instance, Frederick John Robinson (1782–1859), who entered parliament in 1806, served as President of the Board of Trade and Chancellor of the Exchequer in the 1820s, was created Viscount Goderich in 1827 and briefly served as Britain's Prime Minister in 1827–8. In 1833 he became earl of Ripon. Many decades later his son, the second earl (and first marquess) of Ripon (1827–1909), served as Colonial Secretary in the Liberal government of 1892–5 and even continued to hold Cabinet office as Lord Privy Seal from 1905 to 1908 in Sir Henry Campbell-Bannerman's Liberal government. The foremost political leader of the late Victorian period, Robert Gascoyne-Cecil, third marquess of Salisbury (1830–1903), was a direct descendant of Lord Burghley, Queen Elizabeth I's great minister, and some other leading politicians of this era, such as Lord Rosebery, the eighth duke of Devonshire, Lord Randolph Churchill and Arthur J. Balfour, could also trace their lineage back for many centuries.

To be sure, however, such evidence of continuity, impressive as it is, conceals far more than it reveals. The British political nation changed drastically and in many respects fundamentally, probably far more than it had in the eighteenth century. During the nineteenth century Britain evolved from what for want of a better phrase might be termed a popular oligarchy to a broadly based mass democracy in which most adult males had the vote and the nature of general elections and political leadership was, in many respects, recognisably similar to today.

While this process was continuous across the decades it has been common for historians to divide Britain's nineteenth-century political history into three different eras of approximately equal length, marked by different characteristics. The first, from the start of the century until the passage of the Great Reform Act of 1832, and which clearly forms a component of the 'long eighteenth century' (c. 1660–1832), as it has come to be termed, was the last phase of what is sometimes called Britain's ancien regime (see Part IV), and was characterised by an aristocratic oligarchy but also, perhaps, by a consensual Tory rule which drew in much of the mercantile and professional middle classes. This period occurred during the reigns of King George III (1760–1820) and his son George IV (1820–30), who had previously held the legal powers of the sovereign as Prince Regent during his father's madness, in the years generally known as the Regency (1811–20). George IV was succeeded by his brother William IV (1830–37). The second period, lasting roughly from 1832 until the passage of the Second Reform Act of 1867 (or, perhaps, until Disraeli's famous Crystal Palace speech of 1872), is often termed 'the Age of Reform', and was marked by the ascendancy of *laissez-faire*, free trade, a series of key governmental reforms in the interests of modernised, liberal government, a fluctuating series of party alliances and governments, and a view of Britain's worldwide empire as secondary to the country's other international interests. The third period, roughly from 1867 (or 1872) until the outbreak of the First World War, is sometimes termed that of 'Imperialism and Social Reform', and was marked by the growth of a genuine mass political nation and modern parties, a mass press of growing importance, increasing awareness of poverty and inequality at home, with the enunciation of increasingly influential collectivist theories aimed at ameliorating poverty, and the centrality of the British empire as crucially important to Britain's continuing great power status, even to its continuous existence.

That profound changes occurred in Britain's governance during the century can also be illustrated by considering many of the major political leaders in 1900. Such figures of central importance as Joseph Chamberlain – arguably Britain's most important political leader at the opening of the twentieth century – a Unitarian screw manufacturer, Sir Henry Campbell-Bannerman (1836–1908), a Scottish-born Manchester cotton manufacturer, H. H. Asquith (1852–1928), a barrister who was the son of a small Congregationalist woollen merchant in the West Riding, or, still more, John Burns (1858–1943), in 1906 the first working man to hold Cabinet office, could simply not have risen to the top of British politics a century before or perhaps fifty years before. These men and others of similar background, born with no connections to the traditional aristocracy or governing circles, were able to rise only because of the profound political and social changes which had come over British society during the nineteenth century. It can be argued that what is known as the Edwardian period (technically, 1901–10, the years of the reign of King Edward VII, Queen Victoria's son, but generally used for the years between 1901 and the outbreak of the First World War in 1914) saw social class conflict enter British politics in a major way, with the 'New Liberalism' that emerged after 1905 aiming at providing benefits to the working classes which were to be paid for by taxing the well-off. At this time, however, both the Liberal party and the opposition Unionists increasingly looked to collectivist measures of social improvement.

Although the three-phase schema used here is a fruitful one, there are also other ways of viewing the 'long nineteenth century'. Some historians see a broad continuity in British political culture from the eighteenth century until perhaps the mid-1880s, when a polity which for decades had revolved around a limited electorate, with parliament always dominated by landed aristocrats in the Lords and their close relatives or associates in the Commons, was ruptured. From about the time of the Third Reform Act of 1884, in this view, the bases of British political life changed, with a genuine mass electorate and mass-based political parties replacing the former system. The old aristocracy, while it still existed and was certainly not negligible, became progressively less important than middle-class political leaders, and even a few working-class ones, who were able to organise mass constituencies around adversarial programmes, assisted by the mass popular press which arose for the first time in the 1890s and by mass political associations. British politics, according to this view, became dominated by rival collectivist visions, with the Liberal party increasingly looking to progressive taxation and the Unionist (i.e. the Conservative) party to a high tariff wall to raise revenue and exclude foreign imports, as the means of paying for a greatly enlarged state apparatus. This is also a fruitful way of viewing the 'long nineteenth century', and should be kept in mind.

The Political Nation, 1800–32

While parliament was dominated in the first of these three periods by the landed aristocracy and its close relatives, a significant number of self-made businessmen, wealthy professionals and East and West India 'nabobs' and merchants managed to get elected to the House of Commons. This was because the very small electorates in many borough seats were open to influence – or something like overt bribery – from any source, and wealthy businessmen regularly took advantage of this situation. Because of the continuing presence of businessmen in the pre-1832 House of Commons their number was not markedly lower after the 1832 Act, which supposedly gave political power to the middle classes. (There were about 179 businessmen in the House of Commons elected in 1830; 186 in 1831; and about 215 in 1832, in the first reformed parliament.) That businessmen figure so prominently in the pre-reformed parliament is evidence of what might be termed the consensual nature of the Tory government which dominated British political life between the 1780s and 1830. The *raison d'être* of pre-1832 Toryism was to augment Britain's national interests by increasing Britain's worldwide commercial greatness as well as by defending its traditional social structure and institutions, the landed interest and a traditional 'Church and King' vision of British patriotism.

Despite the unrest of the pre-1832 years, particularly the very troubled years of mass strikes and civil unrest between about 1815 and 1820, there was no British revolution and no really serious threat of one. That there 'should' have been a powerful revolutionary move- ment in industrialising Britain has long been a presupposition of radical and Marxist historians; indeed, on even a superficial view it is some- what surprising that no serious revolutionary effort occurred on British soil. One might suggest a number of reasons for this, bearing in mind that few events in history which 'should' have occurred and did not were actually preordained. The aims of Britain's radicals at this time were primarily political in nature, chiefly targeted at the reform of parliament and other institutions, rather than socio-economic, as they lacked any concept of proto-socialist collectivism. Economic theory at the time revolved around removing state barriers and restrictions and establishing *laissez-faire*. Although its origins were found earlier, a collectivist economic vision of society would not fully emerge until the time of Marx and Engels, a generation later. Popular disturbances which were straightforwardly economic in nature – by food rioters or machine breakers – were often spontaneous and almost always localised to a few communities. The French Revolution, with the bloodbath of the 'Reign of Terror' and dictatorial rule by Bonaparte, deeply affected moderate opinion in Britain, alienating many who might have been sympathetic to reform. The British government was relentless and very effective in nipping much serious popular protest in the bud, employing a network of spies, the apparatus of local and national government, and severe punishments in a successful effort to suppress insurrectionary movements.

No genuinely charismatic national radical leader emerged who might have given such a movement a central focus. There was also a religious dimension to the failure of the working classes to rise up. Many historians, beginning with the great early twentieth-century French historian of England Elie Halévy, have credited the growing Methodist movement with preventing an English revolution during these years. Wesleyanism was extremely hostile to radical political action outside those channels which were legally permissible, and gave consistent advice to its followers to obey legitimate authority. So, too, did other forms of evangelicalism, including the growing evangelical movement within the Church of England, disseminated in countless tracts by influential writers such as Hannah More. With the possible exception of a few fringe religious leaders, the whole body of organised religion in Britain, now of growing importance and popularity, was set against radical, insurrectionary change, and especially against anything which threatened to usher in the equivalent of the French Revolution.

The Reform Act of 1832, the crowning achievement of the Whig government of 1830–34 headed by Lord Grey, was, of course, one of the most important pieces of legislation in British history. Briefly, it abolished nearly ninety 'rotten boroughs' – tiny seats with virtually no inhabitants – and added 125 new seats in their place, generally in populous new areas of urban growth, but also in rural counties where (as was noted) the Whig landowners were strong and influential. Secondly, it rationalised the basis of the electorate, extending the vote, on the basis of the ownership or rental of houses or landed property, to much of the middle classes. In many respects, the Great Reform Act, as it is known, signalled a revolutionary change, although its limitations should be kept in mind. The electorate increased in size by an estimated 49 per cent, although 80 per cent of adult men (and all women) still lacked the vote. Large cities such as Bradford, Leeds and Sheffield received separate parliamentary representation for the first time (although its qualified inhabitants had previously voted in local county seats), but nothing had happened to the majority of parliamentary seats and, indeed, the influence of the great landowners remained the same or even grew. Most certainly, democracy as we now understand it was not introduced into Britain in 1832. Separate Acts covered Scotland and Wales. Scotland gained eight parliamentary seats, and its electorate vastly increased, from only 4,579 in 1831 to 64,447 (one adult male in eight) in 1833. Ireland gained five seats, although its electorate increased by only 16,192 (from 75,960 to 92,152) between 1831 and 1833, or one adult male in thirty, largely because so few Irishmen met the new property qualification.

Perhaps the most important effects of the 1832 Reform Act were ancillary, creating the conditions and environment for a raft of other reform measures. For instance, in 1833–5 the Church of Ireland was reformed, the New Poor Law, which restricted welfare largely to the workhouse, was enacted, local government was rationalised and a wider electoral system was introduced at the local level. Taxes on newspapers were greatly reduced and, in 1840, the first postage stamp was introduced. The spirit of 'the Age of Reform' seemed to be predominantly liberal and utilitarian. Traditionally, it has been seen as benefiting the middle classes through a variety of measures aimed at reducing 'Old Corruption' (perquisites for aristocrats and their minions) and enhancing *laissez-faire* capitalism. On the other hand it is important to realise that the landed aristocracy and gentry certainly did not suffer as a result of the actual changes introduced by 'the Age of Reform', and were probably just as politically important in the early 1860s as thirty years earlier. British liberalism in this period built on the foundations of Whig liberalism – religious freedom, freedom of the press, limits on the authority of the executive – to denote an attitude towards the role of government which wished to limit its authority to what was absolutely necessary, giving the maximum degree of liberty to the individual in most spheres, including the economic. A recognisable ideology of conservatism, based upon the veneration of traditional institutions and a mistrust of liberal and radical theorists and extremists, also grew up.

The Political Nation, 1832–67

The new political order left the Whig party (increasingly known as the Liberal party) in control of parliament. The party's new name, generally used from about the 1850s, implied a commitment of its members to the reformist values of political, intellectual and religious liberty, and to *laissez-faire* and free trade in economics, and also looked back to the landmarks in the establishment of 'British liberty' such as Magna Carta and the 'Glorious Revolution' of 1688. At the 1832 general election, the first fought after the Reform Act, the Whig-Liberals gained 479 seats, the Tories only 179. Dominated by Whig aristocrats, it enacted the string of reform measures noted above, including the rationalisation of local government and the enactment of the New Poor Law. Yet Lord Grey and his successor as Whig Prime Minister, Lord Melbourne (in office 1835–41), soon came under a renewed challenge from the Tories, and in 1841 they were ousted by the Conservative party (as it was now called, although they were – and are – also known as the Tories), now led by Sir Robert Peel. Peel (1788–1850) was one of the great figures of nineteenth-century British politics. The son of a millionaire cotton manufacturer, but educated at Harrow and Oxford, he was a reforming Home Secretary in the 1820s, and had very briefly headed a minority Tory government in 1834–5. In 1834 Peel delivered what is known as the 'Tamworth Manifesto', in which he pledged future Conservative governments fully to accept the Reform Act and, indeed, to introduce 'careful' measures of reform aimed at 'the correction of proved abuses'. Peel thus began a long tradition wherein the Conservative party almost always accepted reform measures introduced by radical governments; the post-1832 Tory party would not aim at turning the clock back, and – unlike continental European right-wing movements – would accept increasing democracy and careful measures of reform.

Peel's formula proved very popular with moderate Liberals, who remained wary of extremist tendencies in their party. On the other hand, this stance threatened to alienate many on the right wing of the Conservative party, especially landowners, who often believed that they had been weakened by Reform, and who also feared the removal of tariff protection entailed in the mid-1840s by the repeal of the Corn Laws. While no one doubted Peel's competence, he was also seen as unusually supercilious and lacking in the common touch. Peel became Prime Minister in 1841 at a time of renewed economic difficulties: the decade is often known as the 'hungry forties'. While economic growth, especially the 'railway mania' of the decade, certainly existed, the rapid rise in Britain's population, especially in the urban slums, arguably engendered a considerable increase in poverty, while shortly afterwards Ireland experienced its catastrophic famine. In the late 1830s a new radical mass movement arose, known as 'Chartism' because of its Charter, advocating universal male suffrage and annual elections. Strikes and radical violence increased, and a repetition of the situation of mass unrest of the 1815–20 period seemed probable.

While forcefully repressing violent unrest, Peel believed that some

The great Chartist meeting at Kennington Common, in south London, held in 1848, the year of revolution throughout Europe. Chartism was a radical movement to establish democracy in Britain by enacting the 'People's Charter'. This remarkable photograph, taken by police while the meeting was being held, is regarded as the earliest photograph to be taken of an historical event as it actually occurred. It was unknown until it was rediscovered in 1977. What does it reveal about the fears of the authorities concerning the likelihood of a violent uprising?

very basic measure of reform, aimed at improving the living standards of the working classes, was necessary. In 1845 he became convinced, through a consideration of pro-*laissez-faire* economic arguments, that the best hope for raising living standards lay in the repeal of the Corn Laws. ('Corn' in England is the term given to what would elsewhere be known as wheat, the basic component of bread, at the time the main foodstuff of the working classes.) In order to protect British land-owners and farmers, a tariff had long existed on the importation of corn from overseas. This kept the profits of the agricultural sector high, but also artificially increased the price of bread. Peel, a convinced free trader (as advocates of the removal of tariffs were known), was won over to the view that Repeal (as repeal of the Corn Laws was known) would have profoundly beneficial effects for working-class standards of living. According to its proponents, by reducing the cost of bread it would also enable factory owners and manufacturers to cut wages, at least marginally, to lower the cost of their products and to compete

more successfully in international trade. Peel thus foresaw a com-
monality of interests between the middle classes, especially in
manufacturing, and the urban working classes. The drive for Repeal
was also aided by an efficient and powerful free trade lobby, headed by
Richard Cobden (1810–65) and John Bright (1811–89), two manufacturers whose names became synonymous with Victorian free trade
liberalism. Unfortunately for Peel, most Tory backbench MPs were
landowners who were opposed to Repeal. Early in 1846, after a lengthy
national debate, the Corn Laws were repealed. Peel managed to obtain
the votes of 113 Conservative MPs, but 242 of his party voted against
him and he fell from power in June 1846.

Within a few years, this split in the Conservative party became
permanent: Peel and the 'Peelites' (those Tory parliamentarians who
followed him) increasingly sided with the Whig-Liberal opposition,
with most eventually joining them on a permanent basis. The fight
over Repeal also helped bring to pre-eminence the two most famous
politicians of the next generation. One of Peel's most talented deputies,
who loyally followed him, was William Ewart Gladstone (1809–98).
Originally a right-wing Tory, enormously gifted, from a mercantile
family background somewhat similar to Peel's and a product of
Eton and Oxford, Gladstone moved steadily to the political left,
becoming, by the late 1860s, the renowned leader of Victorian
liberalism. The Peelites included most of the younger men of talent in
the Conservative party, creating a vacuum of leadership and ability.
Into this void stepped the man who was unquestionably the most
implausible British political leader of the nineteenth century, Benjamin
Disraeli, eventually Gladstone's great rival. Disraeli, a London Jew
who became an Anglican as a teenager, was a celebrated novelist, but
unconnected by birth, marriage, education or lifestyle with the party of
landowners he eventually led. Disraeli had initially attempted to enter
parliament as a radical – like Gladstone he started out on the 'wrong'
side of political life – but became one of the greatest intellectual and
political figures of nineteenth-century British Conservatism. He was at
this time a backbencher, but became one of the leaders of the
Conservative party in the House of Commons a few years after Peel's
resignation. The residuum of the Tories in parliament was officially
headed, from 1846 until 1868, by their leader in the House of Lords, the
fourteenth earl of Derby (1799–1868), who was known from 1834 to 1851
as Lord Stanley.

The next twenty-two years in British political life saw the Whigs, increasingly with the assistance of the former Peelite Conservatives, dominate British political life under a series of aristocratic Prime Ministers. Lord John Russell was Prime Minister in 1846–52 and again in 1865–6. He introduced the Reform Act into the House of Commons and was a consistent supporter of Whig liberalism, the introduction and furtherance of liberal measures of reform by the Whig aristocracy and its supporters. His successor of 1852–5 was George Hamilton-Gordon, fourth earl of Aberdeen, a former Tory and then leader of the Peelites in the House of Lords. His government, in which William E. Gladstone served as Chancellor of the Exchequer, signalled the movement of many Peelites into the Whig-Liberal camp. Britain's longest serving Prime Minister during this period was Henry John Temple, third viscount Palmerston: a colourful, outspoken, moderate Whig who had first held government office in 1807, he was known for his rousing (some would say bombastic) assertions of British patriotism. As Foreign Minister in 1850, Palmerston had staunchly defended gunboat diplomacy against Greece when the house in Athens of a British citizen of Portuguese-Jewish background, 'Don Pacifico' (David Pacifico), had been pillaged by a mob, concluding, 'As the Roman, in days of old . . . could say "Civis Romanus sum" [I am a citizen of Rome], so also a British subject, in whatever land he may be, shall feel confident that the watchful eye and strong arm of England will protect him against injustice and wrong.' Palmerston's stirring words became immensely popular with middle-class Britain, even those normally very lukewarm about the use of military force. As Prime Minister for nearly ten years, Palmerston did oversee the use of military force on several occasions. His government was responsible for the suppression of the Indian Mutiny in 1857–8, and for the Second Opium War of 1856–60, but remained pointedly neutral during the American civil war of 1861–5, despite considerable pressure to recognise the South's independence.

The one major war of this period was fought not by Palmerston but by his predecessor, Lord Aberdeen. In 1854, in an effort to keep the Ottoman empire (Turkey) neutral and out of Russian hands, Britain and France declared war on Russia, sending a large contingent of men to southern Russia in what became known as the Crimean War, which lasted until 1856. This strange and destructive affair, which was 'won' by Britain and France in the sense that the peace treaty at the war's end guaranteed Turkish neutrality, is famous for a number of rather unenviable reasons. The incompetence and generally poor military leadership of the British troops led to the celebrated Charge of the Light Brigade at Balaclava in the Crimea in November 1855. Britain's heavy casualties brought lasting fame to the renowned nurse sent to Constantinople to attend to wounded British soldiers hospitalised there, Florence Nightingale (1820–1910), 'the lady with the lamp'. Journalism took a quantitative leap forward with the reporting of The Times' correspondent in Crimea, William Howard Russell, whose brutally frank reports of appalling conditions, telegraphed back to England in a few hours, created a sensation. The conflict also engendered probably the first anti-war movement in the modern sense, led by John Bright, the free trader and Quaker. The war did, however, arguably check Russian expansionism into the Ottoman areas for several generations, although the Aberdeen government's handling of it proved so unpopular that he fell from office. He was replaced by Lord Palmerston, who had not held office under Aberdeen.

This era also saw three minority Tory 'Protectionist' governments briefly holding office for three short periods, composed of the anti-free trade core of the Conservative party. The Protectionists (those in favour of a tariff) first held office in 1852 under Lord Derby; this government is famous as the first in which Disraeli served as a minister, as Chancellor of the Exchequer, and, despite its name, for not re-enacting a tariff. The minority Tories were in power again in 1858–9, and finally in 1866–8. In February 1868, after Derby's retirement, Disraeli became Prime Minister for the first time. The third minority Tory government enacted the Second Reform Act in 1867.

Governance and related public discourse during the 1832–67 period is seen by many historians as the zenith of national debate and careful discussion by informed members of the intelligentsia and politicians who acted in the national interest rather than in their party's interests. Famed writers such as Macaulay and Bulwer-Lytton actually held Cabinet posts; Disraeli, the leader of the Tories, was one of the greatest novelists of his age, while Gladstone, leader of the Liberals, wrote many books on topics ranging from Homer to theology; John Stuart Mill, the great philosopher, sat in parliament from 1865 till 1868. This period also marked the peak of intellectual journals of informed debate such as The Fortnightly Review and The Westminster Review. Most, if not all, of the great debates and movements of opinion of the time were carried forward by well-informed, often brilliant, intellectual amateurs, rather than by university academics. Strikingly, the proponents of the theory of evolution – Charles Darwin, Thomas Huxley and Herbert Spencer – had little or nothing to do with the established universities during their careers (although Huxley held professorships for several years at two London medical schools). Many attributed these circumstances to the political conditions which existed between the 1832 and 1867 Reform Acts, when only a minority of propertied men held the vote, before the political process was corrupted by a mass press and well-organised party machines, and while the existence of the Peelites meant that no government was necessarily safe for a full parliamentary term.

The years from about 1850 until 1867 are also sometimes known as the 'age of equipoise', the height of Britain's mid-Victorian stability and prosperity. Britain avoided the revolutions which erupted throughout Europe in 1848, cleverly and decisively crushing any violent unrest from the Chartists or other radicals. The mood of stability was symbolised by London's famous Great Exhibition of 1851, at which the fruits of British and foreign industry were displayed. In part a brainchild of Prince Albert (1819–61), Queen Victoria's German-born husband, it has been seen as ushering in two decades of prosperity and rising living standards, and was emblematic of how industrialisation, the growth of the railways and other modern developments had now improved working-class living standards and introduced peace and prosperity.

In political terms, this mood of stability was to change in 1867. It was widely recognised in public commentary at this time that a much larger percentage of adult males would, sooner or later, have to be given the vote, and that the great cities were still under-represented at the expense of small towns and rural areas. The death of Palmerston in 1865 also seemed to presage the end of a long parliamentary truce. It was Disraeli and the Tories, in their third minority government, who brought in the Second Reform Act. Disraeli firmly believed that the lower middle classes of smaller shopkeepers and tradesmen, and the superior working classes, likely to be given the vote in any future reform, were probably more pro-Tory than their social superiors. The possibility of reform also attracted the fierce opposition of a group of conservative Whig politicians and intellectuals, headed by Robert Lowe, formerly the minister responsible for education, which became known as the 'Cave of Adullam', men who (in Carlyle's phrase) thought that enfranchising a component of the working classes would constitute 'shooting Niagara' – going over the waterfalls in a barrel. Nevertheless, Disraeli and the Tories proceeded to enfranchise virtually all male householders and lodgers in boroughs, took fifty-two seats away from very small boroughs and gave new or increased representation to large and middle-sized towns. The size of the electorate was increased by 88 per cent, although about two-thirds of adult males in England, Wales and Scotland, and five-sixths in Ireland, were still not entitled to vote. If, however, Disraeli expected immediate political gains from his move, he was doomed to disappointment. In the general election held in 1868, just after the passage of the Second Reform Act, the Liberals scored strong gains in Scotland, Wales and Ireland (although not in England) and found themselves with a majority of 106. William E. Gladstone now took office as Prime Minister for the first time.

The Political Nation, 1867–1900

There is agreement among many historians that the last third of the nineteenth century was the period when a recognisably modern political culture came into existence in Britain, with the 1880s often seen as a decisive turning point. This evolution came about in large measure as a result of both the Second and, perhaps more importantly, the Third Reform Act, in 1884, which created a largely class-based electoral geography. By the early twentieth century this had become well established: middle-class seats were largely Tory, working-class seats largely Liberal (or, in some areas, Labour). There were occasional variations in this pattern due to regional peculiarities or personal factors (for instance, the personal ascendancy of Joseph Chamberlain in Birmingham) but the overall picture is well documented. The fact that the electorate became so large necessitated the establishment of mass political machines and organisations, and elevated the leaders of the major parties to something more than first among equals. This apparent modernisation of politics was also augmented by such factors as the growth of a mass newspaper press, and of such institutions as the trades unions and of special-interest lobbying groups.

Gladstone's government of 1868–74 is usually seen as the greatest of the four ministries he headed. Although his Cabinet did not differ too markedly from previous Whig-Liberal governments, it was the first to have a significant representation from middle-class businessmen and professionals, including Protestant Nonconformists, which reflected the heightened importance of the middle classes among all Liberal MPs. Gladstone also had an agenda of reform, which included the disestablishment of the Church of Ireland, discussed above, along with Irish land reform, and the reform of the elementary education system of England and Wales. The Education Act of 1870 created Boards of Education and required all children to be educated to the age of thirteen. It also outlawed religiously sectarian education in state schools. In a separate act, Oxford and Cambridge universities were opened to non-Anglicans. (This Act did not affect universities in Scotland, which were always non-denominational, or Ireland's university, Trinity College, Dublin, which Catholics could attend despite being discouraged from so doing by the Catholic hierarchy.) The army and the law courts were reformed and, by the Ballot Act of 1872, voting by secret ballot became the rule at all elections. Previously voting was conducted publicly, with the voter openly stating the candidate for whom he voted. This was held to be more honest and honourable than secret voting, though critics felt that this procedure could be used by employers or landlords to penalise those who voted the 'wrong' way. Yet although it was seen at the time as a major step forward, in practice the Ballot Act made little actual difference to voting patterns, and after this enthusiastic spate of legislation political commentators and politicians began to wonder if reformist mid-Victorian liberalism had run its course. The 'radical programme' of the 1880s, as it was termed, centred around such less grandiose matters as the possible disestablishment of the Church of England and temperance reform, both strongly favoured by Nonconformists, but neither capturing the progressive imagination in the same way that the legislation of the 1870s had. These were more decisive than other reform measures and attracted much less support, even within the Liberal party. This subdued mood persisted for perhaps another quarter of a century – only with the growth of the so-called 'New Liberalism' at the end of the century, with its quasi-collectivist presaging of the welfare state, did the Liberal party again develop a potentially nationally popular agenda.

The sense that liberalism had had its day worked to the advantage of the Conservative party. At the general election of 1874 Disraeli and his party won a large majority. The English middle classes, perhaps frightened by Gladstone's Irish policies, now gave a significant majority of their votes to the Tories, with the City of London (which elected four MPs) now moving decisively into the Tory camp. Almost as many English borough seats went to the Tories as to the Liberals, justifying Disraeli's faith in the conservative instincts of much of the lower middle class and superior working-class voters enfranchised in 1867.

Disraeli's government lasted for six years and is known for a raft of social legislation which is often said to have introduced what in the twentieth century became known as 'One Nation Toryism' into the centre of Conservative party policy, where it remained for a century. He sought to develop a social policy agenda which was seemingly to the left of the Liberals, for whom *laissez-faire* liberalism remained in the ascendancy. Disraeli (and his Home Secretary R. A. Cross, who was responsible for much of this legislation) gave greater legal recognition to the trades unions, made slum clearance possible through an Artisans' Dwelling Act, and improved public health, river pollution and safety aboard British ships through enacting the famous 'Plimsoll Line' on merchant vessels. The government did not, however, go beyond this, failing, for instance, to introduce any form of national insurance as Bismarck's right-wing government did in Germany. In foreign policy, Disraeli's government achieved a triumph at the Congress of Berlin, which again guaranteed Turkish independence and secured Cyprus for the British empire. Prior to the Congress, Britain came close to war with Russia over events in the decaying Turkish empire in the Balkans, and a pro-war mood gripped much of England, symbolised by the famous music-hall song which began 'We don't want to fight/But by jingo if we do . . .'. 'Jingoism', outspoken xenophobia, entered the language of political abuse. That the mid-Victorian mood of little-Englandism had changed was also symbolised by the enactment of the Royal Titles Act of 1876, which gave Queen Victoria the title of Empress of India (but no additional or revised powers), thus declaring her to be at the head of an officially recognised empire. The British monarch was officially to remain Emperor (or Empress) of India until independence was granted to the sub-continent in 1947.

Disraeli signalled his fundamental changes in policy in a number of well-known speeches in London and Manchester in 1872 at which he expounded the need for 'social . . . improvement' and the virtues of the British empire, even foreshadowing the establishment of a 'representative council' for the whole empire in London. 'Imperialism and Social Reform' had increasingly become the watchwords of both parties by the end of the century.

Yet Disraeli's popularity plummeted in the last two years of his great government. He was old and ill and his government apparently ran out of steam in domestic legislation. Worse, a severe depression, affecting both industry and agriculture, began in 1878–9, which undermined his government's popularity. Gladstone took advantage of Disraeli's predicament, guiding the spotlight back upon himself through the so-called Midlothian Campaign, a series of popular speeches and mass meetings in and around Edinburgh in 1879–80, where he was campaigning for the forthcoming general election. Gladstone put international morality and religion at the centre of his campaign, denouncing the so-called 'Bulgarian Atrocities' carried out by the Turks against the Christians of the Balkans, and thus attacking Disraeli's defence of Turkey at the Congress of Berlin. The campaign, which was centred in Scotland because it was organised by Lord Rosebery, Gladstone's successor as Prime Minister in 1894 and a major figure in Midlothian, is often seen as the first modern election drive, at which the leader of a party seeks national attention for himself and his views. (It might be worth noting that, by tradition, peers cannot become directly engaged in an election campaign; this tradition debarred both Disraeli, now an earl, and his successor Lord Salisbury, from responding in kind.) The Midlothian Campaign succeeded brilliantly: Gladstone and the Liberals found themselves back in power after the 1880 general election, where they remained until 1885. Gladstone's second government, it has often been noted, had fewer achievements than his first, and was increasingly dominated by the Irish issue.

The late 1870s and early 1880s also saw the beginnings of a collectivist movement, fanned by the success of Henry George's famous book *Progress and Poverty* (1879), which advocated a single tax on land, and by the formation of both the Fabian Society and the Social Democratic Federation (SDF) in 1884. The Fabian Society, founded by intellectuals such as Sidney Webb and George Bernard Shaw, advocated the gradual but inevitable growth of collectivist measures in the interests of an efficient and rational society. The SDF, founded by

H. M. Hyndman, organised working-class rallies and demonstrations involving tens of thousands of protestors. Although some mainstream Liberals such as Joseph Chamberlain were now advocating moderate redistribution, these movements as yet had little major impact on British politics, and nor did the death in London in 1883 of Karl Marx, who wrote *Das Kapital* (published in three volumes from 1867, the last appearing twelve years after Marx's death) in the British Museum.

Despite these harbingers of collectivism, Gladstone's second government was still centrally concerned with completing the nineteenth-century British reform agenda. In 1884 it passed the Third Reform Act, which gave the vote to agricultural labourers and most other adult males to whom the two previous reform acts had not applied, and further redistributed seats in parliament to urban areas on the basis of population. The 1884 Reform Act greatly increased the size of the electorate, which, it is estimated, grew in England and Wales from 2.6 to 4.4 million, and gave much more real political influence to the poorer classes than before. That Britain now had something like a mass democracy was increasingly recognised by the two major parties. They began the organisation of mass parties in the modern sense, with annual party conferences, an infrastructure of party agents responsible to each party's central office and the enrolment and mass canvassing of voters. Although these had existed skeletally before, seen, for example, in Gladstone's Midlothian Campaign, from the mid-1880s it became an absolute prerequisite for electoral victory to arouse enthusiasm among one's potential supporters across the nation. Each party developed a network of newspapers, both national and local, normally supportive of it, which, as newspaper circulation grew, made the great 'press lords' who owned these newspapers increasingly influential. Both parties also used armies of volunteer workers – increasingly, women, especially among the Tories – and rewarded wealthy donors with peerages and knighthoods. Both parties became recognisably identified with ideologically based agendas and drew their support from different types of constituencies, the Tories from the middle classes and (most but not all) rural areas, the Liberals from the working classes, many Nonconformists, and the Celtic areas. In many respects, the Third Reform Act marked a major departure from the assumptions of informed government by qualified voters underpinning the period after 1832, although it was generally seen at the time as following naturally and inevitably from the two previous Reform Acts. It did not

attract as much heated controversy as did the 1832 and 1867 Reform
Acts. After the 1867 Act, one adult male in three in England and
Scotland, and one adult male in six in Ireland, had the right to vote.
After the 1884 Reform Act, two-thirds of adult males in England, three-
fifths of those in Scotland and half of those in Ireland, had the vote.
While all adult males were given the vote in 1918, real democracy
would not come to Britain until 1928.

The mid-1880s were increasingly dominated by Gladstone's
proposal for Irish Home Rule, described above. Following the 1885
general election, but before he had adopted Home Rule as a policy,
Gladstone was defeated on a vote of no confidence after the Irish MPs
voted with the Tories, and the Conservatives formed a minority
government headed by their new leader Lord Salisbury, a skilful, very
intelligent and cynical politician whose main forte was his mastery of
foreign policy. Salisbury had succeeded to the leadership on Disraeli's
death in 1881. In domestic policy he was almost equally adept, and
gradually emerged as the dominant political leader of the last fifteen
years of the century. A general election in late 1885 produced a Liberal
win, although with the Tories and Irish just able to bring down the
government if they combined. Gladstone now formed his third
government, which lasted for six months in 1886. It was then that he
attempted to introduce Irish Home Rule, with the disastrous results
discussed above. After Gladstone was defeated in the House of
Commons, another general election was held in July 1886 which
resulted in the Tories winning 316 seats, the Liberals only 190, the
Liberal Unionists 79, and the Irish Nationalists 85.

Salisbury now formed his second administration, which lasted until
1892. Although it could be defeated if the opposition parties combined,
the Liberal Unionists – former Liberals, headed by Joseph Chamberlain
and Lord Hartington, who were opposed to Home Rule – never
rejoined Gladstone's party, but increasingly became open allies of the
Conservatives. The two groups, the Tories and Liberal Unionists, were
usually referred to in the press as the 'Unionists', i.e. those favouring
the continued union of Britain and Ireland. The Liberal Unionists also
brought with them most of the Whig and Liberal landed aristocracy
and gentry, and much of the upper middle classes, especially in
London, such that by 1900 the Unionists were the normal party of
Britain's Establishment, which the Conservative party had not
previously been. Salisbury's government lasted until 1892, and was

marked by policies of moderate reform, including a reform of local government in London and the counties. This was the period of Queen Victoria's Golden Jubilee in 1887, marked by spontaneous outpourings of patriotic fervour, and by an unusual number of scandals and sensations played for all they were worth by the mass press – the divorce scandals of Sir Charles Dilke, a leading radical politician, in 1885, and Charles Stewart Parnell (cited in a divorce case in 1891), the spectacular resignation of Lord Randolph Churchill, the Chancellor of the Exchequer, at the end of 1886, the death of General Charles 'Chinese' Gordon at the hands of the Mahdi (a Muslim religious and political leader) in the Sudan in 1885 and the suppression of the Mahdi's forces by Horatio (later Lord) Kitchener, and the horrifying 'Jack the Ripper' murders in 1888, regarded as the first serial killings. Many thought that 'Victorianism' had ended well before the end of her reign.

There were two more general elections in the nineteenth century, in 1892 and 1895. In 1892 Gladstone briefly returned at the head of a minority Liberal government for the fourth and final time. He again attempted to pass an Irish Home Rule Bill, which was defeated in the House of Lords. In March 1894 Gladstone finally retired and was succeeded, for fifteen months, by Lord Rosebery, a brilliant, wealthy 'golden boy' who had become Foreign Secretary at the age of just thirty-eight. Already unsympathetic to most of his colleagues, he resigned amidst much bitterness. Rosebery, a pro-imperialist moderate, never held office again, but was long regarded as a potential 'Prime Minister in Waiting'. In the general election which followed, the Unionists scored a sweeping victory. Lord Salisbury formed his third administration, making his nephew Arthur Balfour (1848–1930) First Lord of the Treasury (head of the government in the House of Commons) and bringing several Liberal Unionists leaders into the Cabinet, most notably the duke of Devonshire (formerly Lord Hartington) as Lord President of the Council and Joseph Chamberlain as Colonial Secretary. Although seemingly a middle-ranking post, the Colonial Secretaryship became, under Chamberlain, arguably the focal point of the government, and was used by him to expand the British empire, especially in South Africa. There, a long-running and controversial feud with the Boers in their independent republics, fanned by the discovery of gold and diamonds, led, in 1899, to the outbreak of the Boer War (or Second South African War). It continued until May 1902, when Britain, after many travails, annexed the Boer republics. The last

five years of the century arguably marked the zenith of the British
empire and of patriotic imperialism, as evidenced by the Queen's
Diamond Jubilee celebrations in 1897, whose lavishness outdid the
festivities for her Golden Jubilee a decade earlier. Although the death
of Queen Victoria in January 1901, and the succession of her eldest son
Edward VII, is generally seen as marking the end of an era, in fact
policies, ideologies, expectations and political conflicts continued as
before.

The Edwardian Era, 1901–14

In the wake of the patriotic enthusiasm aroused by the Boer War,
Salisbury's Unionists scored another sweeping electoral victory in the
autumn of 1900, winning a general election with 402 seats to only 184
for the Liberals and 82 for the Irish Nationalists. At this stage, the
Tories appeared impregnable, while the Liberals, wracked by bitter
internal divisions and without a recognised leader, appeared doomed
to indefinite opposition. (Lord Rosebery was, formally, leader of the
Liberal party until early 1896 when he resigned in favour of his bitter
rival Sir William V. Harcourt, who was replaced by Sir Henry
Campbell-Bannerman in 1898. Campbell-Bannerman, who was sixty-
four in 1900, was widely seen as a stop-gap leader until a younger, more
commanding head arose.) In July 1902 Lord Salisbury retired as Prime
Minister. Probably the dominant political leader of his time, he was
replaced, without opposition, by Arthur Balfour, a brilliant and
wealthy Cambridge-educated politician and philosopher (his works on
philosophy are still highly regarded), who took office in circumstances
possibly more favourable than virtually any recent Prime Minister
entering office for the first time: on 31 May 1902, a few months earlier,
the Boer War had ended with a British victory over the Boer republics.
Yet within just a couple of years the situation of the Unionist party had
disintegrated beyond recognition.

There were several causes for this remarkable and sudden decline.
In May 1903 Joseph Chamberlain, the Colonial Secretary and architect
of the Boer War, made one of the most important speeches of the age,
in which he announced his conversion to 'Imperial Preference', the
erection of a tariff wall around the whole British empire, to exclude
cheap foreign goods, and to finance measures of social reform by

'making the foreigner pay' rather than through increasing direct taxation on the well-off. Although both Germany and the United States had prospered exceedingly behind high tariff walls, so great was the force of the doctrine of free trade in Britain – it was often compared to a religion – that Chamberlain's proposals amounted to a fundamental break with the basic economic policies of Britain as they had existed during the previous sixty years. At this time, Chamberlain occupied a position in British politics arguably without parallel in the post-1832 world. Although he was widely regarded as the most powerful man in the Cabinet, and was probably the best known politician in Britain, he held only a middle-ranking office as Colonial Secretary. Chamberlain's speech was made without seeking Balfour's approval; there has been no parallel in modern British politics to a middle-ranking Cabinet minister positing such a fundamental change of British policy without securing the approval of the Prime Minister and Cabinet.

Chamberlain's speech set off a tidal wave of controversy and debate. He resigned from the Cabinet in October 1903 and quickly organised a group of enthusiastic supporters – for whom tariff reform and imperial unity became core beliefs – as well as a Tariff Reform League to further his cause. But he also aroused bitter hostility, leading to the resignation of several of his senior Cabinet colleagues who favoured free trade. Furthermore, Chamberlain's proposals served to unite the Liberal party, who, virtually to a man, remained strong opponents of tariffs. Balfour, the Prime Minister, attempted to meet Chamberlain's difficult challenge by prevarication. In October 1903 he appointed Chamberlain's elder son, Austen Chamberlain, as Chancellor of the Exchequer, but also appointed a strong free trader, Victor Cavendish, as his deputy. Balfour, a moderate but not fanatical supporter of tariff reform, was faced with a very difficult task, and his handling of his government during the last two years of his premiership is generally viewed as inept. As noted, tariff reform immediately unified the Liberal party, which, in conjunction with pro-free trade elements, organised a campaign to fight Chamberlain's proposals. Central to their opposition was the contention that tariff reform would mean a tax on bread and other basic foods, which would fall most heavily on the working classes. The 'tax on bread' claim would prove fatal to tariff reform whenever it became central to the Tories' electoral proposals, as it did in 1905 and again in 1923.

There were other important factors that served further to

undermine the Unionists' position. In 1901 there occurred the famous legal case *Taff Vale Railway Co. v. Amalgamated Society of Railway Servants*. The *Taff Vale* decision, as it became known, made it legal for a company to sue a trades union for damages and losses incurred during a strike, reversing the immunity unions had enjoyed since the 1870s and inflicting a potentially crippling blow to the trades union movement. Reversing the *Taff Vale* decision became a major aim of the union movement, which the Liberal party could use to their advantage. Another major cause of Tory unpopularity was the Education Act of 1902, which had given enlarged powers to local authorities to provide secondary education. However, this brought the voluntary (i.e. religious-based) schools under the authority of local governments, using ratepayers' money, for the first time, to pay their teachers. This greatly alienated Nonconformists, who launched a great campaign against the payment of rates (local taxes) to pay for what were normally Anglican schools. Nonconformist and Evangelical Anglican opinion was also aroused by the growth of High Church, quasi-Catholic practice within the Church of England. In 1904–5 there also occurred a significant religious revivalist movement within the Nonconformist churches, especially in Wales. Many Nonconformists now bitterly opposed to the Tory government turned their support to a revived Liberal party.

Nevertheless, Balfour viewed the Liberal party as hopelessly divided, in particular between the so-called 'Liberal Imperialist' champions of empire, whose parliamentary leaders included the future Prime Minister Herbert H. Asquith, Sir Edward Grey and the so-called 'little Englanders', who were more radical and generally uneasy with 'jingoist' policies. Their supporters included the leader of the Liberal party, Sir Henry Campbell-Bannerman, and a radical solicitor from Wales, David Lloyd George, both of whom had been opponents of the Boer War. In December 1905, faced with increased unrest within his own party, and acting under the assumption that the Liberals would be unable to form a viable minority government, Balfour resigned, although he still enjoyed a working majority in parliament.

Sir Henry Campbell-Bannerman now became Prime Minister, and with surprisingly little difficulty formed a Liberal government which was both stable and able. Asquith became Chancellor of the Exchequer, Grey Foreign Secretary, and Lloyd George President of the Board of Trade. This famous government included many men who would make a lasting mark on British political life, among them the thirty-one-year-old Winston Churchill (1874–1965), who was appointed Under-Secretary for the Colonies. The son of Lord Randolph Churchill, Winston had entered politics as a Conservative but had become disenchanted with a range of Unionist policies, especially tariff reform, and, in 1904, joined the Liberal party. Campbell-Bannerman called a general election, held early in 1906, which resulted in a great victory for the Liberal party, entirely reversing the former political dominance of the Unionists. The Liberals won 400 seats compared with only 157 Unionists. In addition, 30 Labour MPs were elected as well as 22 so-called 'Lib-Lab', members officially counted with the Liberals. This phalanx of more than 50 Labour MPs was widely regarded as the most important – and, to many, unnerving – result of the election. To the anti-Tory majority in parliament were added 83 Irish Nationalist MPs, making an impregnable left-of-centre majority unknown since the 1832 election. While the British electoral system greatly exaggerated the actual scale of defeat suffered by the Unionists, who secured 44 per cent of the total vote, 1906 certainly marked a major climacteric in British political history. In 1906, the Unionists won 122 seats in England, none in Wales, 10 in Scotland and 16 in Ireland. In contrast, the Liberals won 306 seats in England, 33 in Wales, and 58 in Scotland. Labour won 27 seats in England, 1 in Wales, 2 in Scotland. Eighty-two of Ireland's 101 seats were again won by the Irish Nationalists.

While Campbell-Bannerman was Prime Minister, the Liberal government was largely Gladstonian and fiscally orthodox in its policies, and actually cut overall government expenditure. It reversed the *Taff Vale* decision, and, in 1908, introduced the first old-age pensions (of up to 5s. – 25p – per week, perhaps £15 today, paid to those aged seventy or over), but otherwise did not differ very markedly from previous Liberal governments, and certainly did not engender radical changes. Modernisation of the army, brought about by War Minister Richard Haldane, was one of the few measures for which it is remembered. In April 1908 Campbell-Bannerman died, and was replaced as Prime Minister by H. H. Asquith. Asquith's appointment as Prime Minister (he served until December 1916) ushered in a period of vigorous and radical measures for which the Edwardian Liberal government became famous. In particular, we associate these measures with David Lloyd George, who became Chancellor of the

Exchequer, serving in the post until May 1915, and with the appointment of other reforming ministers, including Winston Churchill, who entered the Cabinet this time as President of the Board of Trade.

The Asquith government proceeded to adopt a number of quasi-collectivist measures associated with the 'New Liberalism', which were to be paid for by increased direct taxation of the well-off, and which were accompanied by left-wing rhetoric previously unknown. Probably the most important was the National Insurance Act of 1911, which provided unemployment insurance to manual workers in heavy industry. The trades unions were given increased rights, and were brought visibly into the affairs of governance, being frequently consulted by the government. Lloyd George, in particular, launched extravagant rhetorical attacks on the House of Lords and the aristocracy which were seen as keen to block the majority of radical measures, most notably in a speech in Limehouse, east London, in July 1909 which was couched virtually in terms of class warfare. Aware of the growing likelihood of war in Europe, the government also greatly increased spending on the Royal Navy, which was widely seen as Britain's shield against a German attack. To finance both welfare and naval spending, in 1909 Lloyd George proposed a greatly increased Budget, known as the 'People's Budget', which was to be paid for by seven new taxes, most of which were to fall on the rich and upper middle classes, especially landowners. The People's Budget also set the stage for a showdown with the House of Lords, which in November 1909 threw out it out.

The Liberals now called a general election, held in January 1910, which produced an indecisive result, the Liberals electing 275 MPs compared with 273 Tories, 40 Labour and 82 Irish Nationalists. While the Liberals still enjoyed a working majority, it was dependent upon the votes of the Irish MPs, whose long-standing demands for Home Rule it had ignored between 1905 and 1910. In May 1910, Edward VII died, and his son George V (reigned 1910–36) came to the throne. A strict martinet very different in personality from his *bon vivant* father, he nevertheless proved to be an excellent and very popular king, and was universally respected during his reign. After 1918, as one of the few surviving European monarchs of a major nation, he became a great symbol of continuity and unity throughout the British empire.

In order to pass the People's Budget and other legislation the Lords was likely to block, Asquith had to secure a promise from the new king to create hundreds of new peers who would give the Liberals a majority in the upper house. He would secure this promise only if another general election were held first. The Liberals then called an election for December 1910, which resulted in a virtually identical result to the one held in January of that year: 272 Tories, 272 Liberals, 42 Labour, 84 Irish Nationalists. In August 1911, after a terrible struggle, the government passed the Parliament Bill, which took away the right of the House of Lords to reject money bills (such as the People's Budget) and limited the power of the Lords to delay passage of any other Bill passed by the House of Commons to two years. This second proviso was enacted in order to deny the Lords the power to veto any new Irish Home Rule Bill, making the implementation of such a measure almost inevitable. The government did not, however, alter the composition of the Lords or further reform the upper house, as many radicals demanded. As Prime Minister, Asquith created sixty-one new peers, many wealthy Liberal businessmen, finding, like all prime ministers, the patronage powers of creating honours and titles irresistibly useful. The composition of the Lords was, in fact, not altered in a serious way until 1999, when most (not all) hereditary peers lost their seats.

The three years before the outbreak of the war focused politically on the Irish question, which once again took centre stage in British political life. Dependent upon the votes of the Irish Nationalist MPs for its political survival, the Asquith government was forced to attempt to enact an Irish Home Rule Bill. But once again this provoked the adamant hostility of the Ulster Protestants, who opposed Irish Home Rule and, at the very least, wished Ulster to be excluded from any Home Rule Act, something which the Liberals consistently refused. Even more than in the past the Ulster Protestants were supported by a reinvigorated Unionist/Tory party. After losing three general elections, Balfour had been forced to resign as leader in November 1911 (although he would continue to hold senior Cabinet positions until 1929); his replacement, a compromise choice, was a wholly unexpected one: Andrew Bonar Law (1858–1923), a competent, dour Canadian-born Scottish businessman with strong links to Ulster. Bonar Law served as Prime Minister for seven months in 1922–3, and is often referred to as the 'unknown Prime Minister', but he is widely regarded by historians as an unusually accomplished political leader who revivified the Unionist party, ably served as Lloyd George's deputy from 1915 to 1921, and as leader never lost an election. Bonar Law was emblematic of the fact that the centre of gravity in the Conservative party had passed from the landed aristocracy – with which Bonar Law had no connection – to the business and professional middle classes, who now dominated the party. Indeed, only a handful of landed aristocrats remained in senior leadership positions in the Conservative party, such as George Nathaniel Curzon, Lord (later Marquess) Curzon of Kedleston (1859–1925), the former Viceroy of India renowned for his superciliousness. Instead, the leadership of the Conservative party under Bonar Law largely consisted of men drawn from the middle classes (although often educated at a major public school and Oxbridge), such as F. E. Smith (1872–1930; later earl of Birkenhead), a brilliant, buccaneering barrister, and Sir Edward Carson (1854–1935), another celebrated barrister who was the leader of the Ulster Protestants.

Whatever their social backgrounds, nearly all Tories felt a deep sense of frustration at being excluded from power for so long. This discontent took several forms. Many Tories believed that the House of Lords had a duty to defeat the Liberals' radical legislation, and actively fought to save its power. After 1910, others gave all-out support to the Ulster Unionists, with some appearing to countenance arguably unconstitutional behaviour in defence of Ulster. Many Tories looked at Edwardian Ulster as a model for future conservatism – the nation in arms, but united for patriotic rather than seditious ends. Bonar Law, the new Unionists' leader, famously said in July 1912: 'I can imagine no lengths of resistance to which Ulster will go in which I shall not be ready to support them and in which they will not be supported by the overwhelming majority of the British people.'

The last few years of peace were thus dominated politically by the Irish question, with the Liberal government's Home Rule Act, passed in May 1914 after the Lords had vetoed the Bill for two years, due to come into force later in the year. Although Ulster was promised exemption for six years from being subject to an all-Irish Parliament, both sides were aiming for what appeared to be an inevitable armed conflict ahead. In March 1914, many army officers of Ulster Protestant background stationed at Curragh in Ireland signed a letter stating that they would resign rather than engage in the coercion of Ulster – this was the so-called 'Curragh Mutiny', perhaps the only occasion in modern times when the British Army appeared to 'mutiny' against parliament. Although a compromise solution to the Irish conundrum might well have been found, the mood in some important parts of British society on the eve of the outbreak of the war was deeply troubled. A spirit of discontent also enveloped many key parts of the Labour movement. In 1912, thirty-four million working days had been lost through strikes, the highest total in British history up to that point, including a bitter miners' dispute involving one million workers. The atmosphere in the mining areas of South Wales was particularly ugly, with an undercurrent of violence which was actually compared in some newspapers to the mood in Russia in 1905 just before the first Russian revolution.

The struggle for women's suffrage had also sparked major and highly visible divisions. The Women's Social and Political Union, founded in 1903 in part by Emmeline Pankhurst (1859–1928) and her daughters Christabel (1880–1961) and Sylvia (1882–1960), spearheaded a campaign of militancy which included attacks on property, picture slashing, hunger strikes and the famous suicide under the king's horse at the Derby. The Liberal government of these years stubbornly refused to grant women the vote in parliamentary elections. Without the First World War and its political and social consequences, it is (probably) unlikely that most women would have received the parliamentary vote in 1918, as they actually did. The multifaceted forces of unrest in Edwardian England have caused some historians to ask whether there was a *Strange Death of Liberal England*, as George Dangerfield put it in a famous book published in 1935.

More broadly, historians have also asked whether the 'New Liberalism', emphasising the deliberate use of extended state powers to ameliorate social evils, was really radically different from anything in the past, and, in particular, whether it would have been strong enough to prevent what actually took place after 1918, the rise of the Labour party, now independent of the Liberal party, as the normal left-of-centre party in British politics, with the Liberals shrinking to near-disappearance. The replacement of the Liberal party by Labour has given rise to an extended debate among historians over whether it was in some sense inevitable, whether it was in the process of occurring before 1914, and whether the war itself, or other factors, was responsible for what occurred. Many historians believe that the next general election, scheduled for 1915 (but postponed until December 1918 because of the war), was likely to produce a Unionist majority, with

Bonar Law becoming Prime Minister. In opposition, the Liberals could conceivably have disintegrated and given way to an irresistible Labour tide.

But in the summer of 1914, a *deus ex machina* changed literally everything. In far-off Sarajevo, the assassination of an Austrian archduke by Bosnian nationalists set off a chain reaction of war declarations and mobilisation around the Continent. On 4 August 1914 Britain declared war on Germany and, eight days later, on Austria-Hungary. In August came the retreat from Mons by the British regular army and, in October, the first Battle of Ypres, with its extraordinary casualty figures, the first of many full-scale slaughters to come. While some far-sighted observers such as Lord Kitchener expected a long war, what ensued was very different from what they had imagined. The Royal Navy effectively blockaded Germany's ports, but – contrary to what had been widely expected – played only a limited role in the fighting, which was carried out by land armies, largely in France, of incredible size and subject to nightmarish levels of casualties. Quite conceivably, had Britain's leaders known what was to come, the country would have remained neutral, even at the cost of giving Germany a probable victory and hegemony on the Continent. But Germany's plans to defeat France necessarily entailed the invasion and occupation of Belgium, and it was the invasion of 'little Belgium', accomplished with much brutality, that brought a virtually united nation into the war, including those radical and Nonconformist elements which had opposed the Boer War. Having entered the war, Britain was doomed to see it out, with the inevitability of a Greek tragedy, until its conclusion. So, too, was most of Europe, engendering a series of conflicts and near-conflicts which, it might be argued, continued until Stalin's death in 1953, or perhaps until the collapse of the Soviet Union in 1991.

Looking Outward: the World and the Empire

England had been a significant European power for several centuries before 1800; Britain emerged from the Napoleonic Wars as arguably the most powerful nation in the world, certainly the strongest naval power, and already the possessor of a worldwide empire. While Britain's foreign policy priorities remained broadly consistent, its imperial policies – those affecting the British empire – changed considerably over the century, with imperial expansion matched by a growing awareness of the empire as the dominant element in Britain's great power status, and by the growth of movements of self-government within the white empire. While many were, at best, lukewarm about the British empire in 1850, by 1900 it seemed to most observers to be central to Britain's survival as a great power.

Throughout the nineteenth century Britain's foreign policy continued fairly consistently, four overriding elements repeatedly determining its diplomatic and military actions. The first was the central desire to preserve the balance of power in Europe by preventing any one European nation from becoming the dominant hegemon. This was a policy of long standing: for centuries, Britain had fought Spain, France and Napoleon for this very reason. With the eclipse of French military power after Waterloo, the necessity of preventing one hegemon from arising in Europe went into abeyance for many decades, although Britain's actions in the Crimean War were directed against Russia becoming too powerful. With the rise of a unified Germany to world-power status after 1871, its ruling elite adopting a stance which often seemed belligerent and expansionist, Britain gradually discarded the philosophy of 'splendid isolation' which defined its attitude to overt military alliances, and entered, early in the twentieth century, into agreements, just short of binding alliances, with France and Russia. Growing hostility to Germany was triggered in part by that country's stubborn drive to build a large-scale ocean-going navy to rival Britain's, despite the fact that Germany possessed only a handful of far-flung colonies. In the late nineteenth century, although some influential men in Britain, such as Joseph Chamberlain, initially favoured an alliance between Britain and Germany, Germany's seemingly ominous threat to British sea power, and its growing sword-waving in Europe, made this impossible. By 1914, it was apparent to virtually all British observers that Germany represented Britain's greatest foreign threat, a powerful state which threatened to upset the balance of power in Europe and which represented a potential challenge to the British empire. While few expected a great war to break out when it did, in the summer of 1914, many saw a conflict between Germany and its allies and those states ranged against Germany, including Britain, as inevitable.

The second theme of nineteenth-century British foreign policy was somewhat less consistent than the first. After Waterloo, Britain was seen as the liberal European superpower, in contrast to the 'reactionary' Holy Alliance (as it was known) among the European monarchies, especially France under the restored Bourbons, Austria under Metternich and tsarist Russia. Most influential Englishmen instinctively supported Greek independence from the Ottoman empire in the 1820s, a cause to which many liberals and romantics devoted themselves, and also supported Latin American independence from Spain at the same time, the British Foreign Secretary George Canning famously claiming that he had 'called the new world into existence, to redress the balance of the old'. Britain generally opposed repression by oppressive regimes: it actively supported the suppression of the slave trade after it abolished slavery, and, in its colonies, put down barbaric practices such as suttee in India. In some respects these policies anticipated the more aggressive posture of the United States after the First World War in 'making the world safe for democracy', although it must be emphasised that Britain's elites were very uneasy in entering into potentially dangerous foreign policy entanglements for abstract ideological reasons.

It must also be emphasised that Britain's perceived self-interest usually took precedence over moral outrage. Occasionally, too, morality and self-interest split the British Establishment. In the 1870s the Conservatives under Disraeli were anti-Russian, fearing Russian expansionism into the Ottoman empire, and therefore pro-Turk, wishing to prop up the declining Ottoman empire, while the Liberals under Gladstone were visibly anti-Turk, viewing Turkey as the oppressor of Christians in the Balkans during the so-called 'Bulgarian Atrocities'. Nevertheless, Britain's instinctive, if low-key, liberalism brought it closer, at least haltingly, to the United States, its daughter nation, when America assumed superpower status during and after the First World War, leading to the consistently potent alliance between the two which shaped twentieth-century world politics, despite America's (long) tradition of isolationism.

The third and fourth pillars of British foreign policy were its insistence on maintaining both freedom of the seas and its worldwide empire, especially India, the 'jewel in the crown' of imperial rule, and all routes that led to it. Throughout the nineteenth century, the Royal Navy effectively enforced freedom of navigation in the world's oceans, a policy which, of course, directly benefited Britain as the pre-eminent trading nation. The Royal Navy was regarded as a virtually sacred institution, such that, as noted above, any attempt by an unfriendly power such as Germany to build up a rival ocean-going navy was regarded as unequivocally threatening. The centrality of maintaining the empire as one of the fundamental props of British foreign policy never vanished, even during the period between roughly 1840 and 1870 when the empire was somewhat passé in liberal circles. After 1870, however, it re-emerged as one of the major factors in Britain's continuing dominance as a great power.

In 1800, Britain already had an extensive worldwide empire, controlling most of the coastal areas of south India and Bengal, much of the Caribbean, Canada and Australia, among other places. Victories and treaties during and just after the Napoleonic Wars gave it a further range of territories in India, and elsewhere, ranging from Malta to British Guiana to Sierra Leone to South Africa. India was already regarded as the most important British colony, taking over this role from the West Indies, which rapidly declined in importance. The white colonies – Canada and Australia (consisting of separate colonial areas), New Zealand (annexed in 1840) and the South African states – were seen as places where Britain's excess population could usefully settle (or be settled). Britain's colonies were, however, very much of secondary importance until the latter half of the century. In 1857 the suppression of the great mutiny in India and the consequent replacement of the East India Company (the legal administrative government in British India) by direct rule from London (with a Secretary of State for India sitting in the Cabinet), prepared the way for the empire to become more central to Britain's political concerns. Many new areas were annexed, including most of the black African colonies; on the other hand, increasing measures of internal self-government were given to the white colonies, with Canada, for instance, being given the status of a Dominion in 1867. In 1876, as noted, Queen Victoria was proclaimed Empress of India. By the end of the century, the empire had become fundamental to the political world view of most British politicians, especially to Tories and the 'Liberal imperialist' majority of the party. Joseph Chamberlain's 1903 proposal for a tariff wall around the whole empire seemed to many to be the way of the future, a proposal made at the end of a brutal war in South Africa in which Britain emerged victorious only after a fierce struggle against the Boer republics.

Historians, however, have viewed the empire in different ways. For some, its most striking feature was its economic *unprofitability* and its lack of popular appeal except on patriotic occasions. Others have, in contrast, seen it as a central prop of 'gentlemanly capitalism', the commercial-financial capitalism of the City of London which dominated the British economy down to 1914 (and beyond). Many Liberal imperialists of the late Victorian and Edwardian periods were happy for Britain to control the white, English-speaking colonies such as Canada and Australia, but were unhappy with the necessarily dictatorial and elitist control exercised over India and Africa, while many Nonconformists and others saw in the empire what Rudyard Kipling termed 'the white man's burden', the necessity and opportunity of converting the natives to Christianity or educating them in western ways and values. Few, however, failed to be both moved and comforted by seeing all the areas coloured red (indicating British possession) on the map of the world: indeed, an empire 'on which the sun never set'.

Most well-informed observers expected the twentieth century to be a time when only immense world-empires and highly populated, technologically advanced states would survive as great powers, if they survived at all. To remain powerful, it was argued, Britain must build on its global empire as the only way to remain in the same league as Germany, the United States and perhaps Russia (unless it disintegrated). Without an empire, and considerable internal reforms aimed at producing 'national efficiency', Britain was doomed to decline. Few could foresee the forces which were to shape Britain during the next century, such as Keynesianism, the rise of Labour and the welfare state. Nevertheless, to an extent this critique of British decline was valid, although, again, few could foresee that two murderous world wars would be the result of the great power rivalries they acknowledged, or that the outcomes they feared would in a sense be realised, even though Britain emerged victorious.

4. Some Counter-Factuals

It is easy to imagine several alternative political histories for Britain in this period. The most obvious, perhaps, is a refusal by the House of Lords to endorse parliamentary reform in 1831–2, leading to a revolution which would have swept away much more of the British 'old regime' than the 1832 Act did. Many contemporary observers, such as Macaulay, expected a revolution if the Reform Act was not passed by parliament, one perhaps involving insurrection repressed by violence. France experienced a revolution in 1830 which overthrew the Bourbon monarchy, and it is possible that something similar might have occurred in Britain. Such a revolt might have established a British republic, although this is probably less likely than the enactment of much wider modes of democratic government, perhaps including manhood suffrage and the disestablishment of the Anglican Church. Whether the British Establishment would have lost control of the situation so comprehensively as to have allowed a sweeping revolution to have occurred is, however, arguable: Whigs as well as Tories were united in opposing anything like what we would term democracy. It is also possible that a working-class uprising might have occurred, although it is safe to say that the whole of established society would have opposed it, and any concomitant violence would certainly have been ruthlessly suppressed. Any purported revolution in the United Kingdom in 1831–2 might also have seen the establishment of an independent Ireland and of greater self-rule in Scotland.

An even more intriguing possibility is that the Whig-dominated 'Age of Reform' might not have occurred at all, in which case Britain would have continued indefinitely as a Tory-led, unreformed, neo-mercantilist state where 'Church and King' Anglicanism also continued to predominate. Such a possibility is not as fanciful as it might seem: support for parliamentary reform, which hardly existed in the early 1820s, grew suddenly and dramatically just before 1832, when Britain experienced industrial and commercial growth in a regulated economy with tariff protection. Even in 1839, John Stuart Mill, in a perceptive article in *The London and Westminster Review,* acknowledged the sheer strength of the forces *opposed* to free trade liberalism which, he claimed, included almost the whole of the landed classes, the older professions, the Church of England and a range of trades such as 'the shipping interest, the timber interest, the West Indies interest' where foreign competition was still prohibited.

The modernisation process did indeed occur in societies which did not experience the liberalism associated with Britain's 'Age of Reform', most strikingly in Germany between 1848 and 1918, whose so-called 'special path' to modernity combined particularly rapid industrialisation (behind high tariff walls) with the continued ascendancy of pre-modern elites, and the military in pursuit of largely nationalistic ends: economic growth based on self-sufficiency rather than free trade; a more narrow elite based on continuing Anglican and landowning domination without modification by liberal values. Nevertheless, such a possibility was far less likely in Britain than in Germany. Britain's powerful Whig aristocracy was pervaded by liberalism in a way which had no parallel in Germany; the fact that Britain had already experienced both industrialisation and urbanisation had itself created both an urban-industrial elite and an industrial working class generally permeated by radical and liberal values. Germany had no parallel to Britain's large Nonconformist religious minority or to Scots Presbyterianism; Britain seemingly had no parallel to the Prussian tradition of militarism or to the German habit of obedience, although it can certainly be argued that Britain's military traditions, as well as that of 'Church and King' Toryism, offered more in the way of similarities than Whig and liberal historians might credit. Britain was already a unified nation-state (albeit composed of three separate kingdoms), while German unity was defined and imposed in 1864–71 by Bismarck, the Hohenzollern monarchy and the Prussian Junkers, along with their own historical values.

Just as for the earlier part of the nineteenth century, it is possible to imagine and consider a number of alternative scenarios in the political history of later nineteenth-century Britain. Perhaps the most plausible is the electoral triumph, in the 1880s, of a radical Liberal government with a large majority which would have enacted the radical programme of advanced liberalism, a programme which would potentially have included the abolition or thorough reform of the House of Lords, universal manhood suffrage, the disestablishment of the Church of England, 'land reform' giving farmers the right to buy out the estates of the great landowners and abolishing the 'strict settlement' of land, measures giving local governments much wider powers to enact 'municipal socialism' and a scaling back of British involvement in the empire. At its most extreme, ending the monarchy and establishing a British republic might conceivably have been considered, although Queen Victoria's return to carrying out public duties in the 1870s after an extended period of mourning following the death of Prince Albert in 1861 probably ruled this out as a realistic possibility. By the 1880s, a major portion of the Liberal party, especially that part associated with Joseph Chamberlain, was amenable to these measures. Such a programme would have encountered fierce resistance, with, for instance, the House of Lords being viewed by both conservatives and moderates as a bulwark against socialism, while the Church of England would certainly never have agreed to give up its legal establishment. Had such a programme been enacted, however, Britain would probably have looked much more like the United States of America, a republic with no established Church and wide measures of local autonomy rather than central rule.

This radical programme is also notable for what it did not contain: it did not propose to enact 'socialism' in the sense this is commonly understood, with public ownership, at a national level, of key industries, and high rates of taxation on the rich. Increased direct taxation of the rich (but at much lower rates than anything known since 1914) did become part of the agenda of the left at a slightly later date, with the Harcourt Death Duties of 1894 (higher levels of taxation on wealthy estates passing at death, enacted by Chancellor of the Exchequer Sir William Harcourt) and higher rates of income tax enacted by the Asquith government from 1909 to 1914, but were not a part of the mainstream radical agenda before then. At that time many, perhaps most, influential radicals were wealthy businessmen, especially northern manufacturers, who defiantly opposed 'confiscatory' levels of taxation. Socialism in the twentieth-century sense was hardly known in Britain at all at this time; the Fabian Society (a society of middle-class intellectual socialists) was not founded until 1884. Until much later, the trades unions had no socialist agenda, and national-

isation did not really become a debatable issue in the mainstream until
the rise of the Labour party in 1918–22. Had the radical programme of
the 1880s been enacted, however, it might have set the stage and
provided the conditions for a socialist programme earlier and more
extreme than actually occurred in twentieth-century British politics. It
might also have opened the door for aspects of the radical agenda
which are mainly forgotten today, such as the temperance movement
which, at its most extreme, wanted to outlaw all alcoholic beverages
(as was actually done in the United States between 1919 and 1933).

In fact, however, the radical programme was not enacted. The
Liberal party was still controlled by relative moderates until the Liberal
Unionist split of 1886. Gladstone, liberalism's leader, was concerned
with other things, especially Ireland; he was a deeply religious Anglican
and something of a partisan of the Whig aristocracy who was unlikely
to enact such a sweeping programme. The man who was most likely
to enact it, Joseph Chamberlain, paradoxically left the Liberal party in
1886 and, by the mid-1890s, was a key member of the Tory Cabinet. By
1900 the radical programme itself looked distinctly old-fashioned, with
the extreme left now in favour of measures of collectivism to enact
social reform and a strong Liberal imperialist wing within the Liberal
party that championed the empire. Politically, the Liberals were never
in a position to enact their programme between 1884 and 1906, when
new issues came to dominate the political scene. Ireland and Irish
Home Rule moved to the centre of British political life, and many
wealthy industrialists and businessmen had moved into the Unionist
(i.e. Conservative) party.

At the centre of British political life in this period was Ireland, and it
is also worth considering what might have happened had Ireland been
successfully 'pacified' – as Gladstone put it – by a Home Rule Bill
enacted in 1886. A successful solution to the Irish question would
necessarily have required the Catholic south and Protestant Ulster to
cooperate harmoniously over the range of areas in local government
delegated to Ireland under Gladstone's proposals. This possibility is not
far-fetched, and it is likely that a Home Rule Ireland would have seen
growing links and cooperation between politicians of both religions in
such mundane realms as railways, harbours, civic improvements,
public health and so on. Successful cooperation would obviously have
diminished mutual hostility and increased mutual respect. One might
assume, too, that it would have weakened the forces of extreme

nationalism in southern Ireland later responsible for the creation of the Irish Republic. On the other hand, such a rosy scenario may well be far too optimistic. Even within the areas of legislation reserved for an Irish Home Rule Parliament, there was ample room for mutual conflict in such areas as education (with its continuing sectarian dimensions) and, more importantly, the overall division of an Irish budget among the communities. A 'normal' Irish political system, based largely on class, might have emerged, although it is difficult to imagine the rural-based poor of the south and the Protestant urban proletariat of Ulster ever realistically coming together. More broadly, the prospect of southern Irish nationalists being genuinely satisfied with this situation as a permanent settlement seems even less plausible. They would surely, almost inevitably, demand wider measures of self-government. The 1916 Easter uprising might well have occurred despite Gladstone's best efforts.

Because the war began so suddenly in 1914 and resulted in a fundamental break in European history, it is seemingly easier to reflect on what might have occurred for the 1900–14 period than for the earlier decades surveyed here in Part V. In reality, it is perhaps more difficult to arrive at plausible alternative scenarios for this period than before. Had the war not broken out, it seems very likely that some kind of violent civil war would have been fought in Ireland later in 1914 once Irish Home Rule finally became law. This conflict would have been led by Ulster's Protestants, who enjoyed almost unanimous support in their own community and among Tories in other parts of Britain, and who were armed and desperate. Had conflict erupted in Ireland in 1914–15, its consequences are simply too unclear for an obviously plausible scenario to be posited; it would have depended on the reaction of the Catholic south, of the Liberal government and of the British Army. It is likely that extreme nationalists in the south would have been greatly strengthened by an armed uprising in Ulster, leading, perhaps, to a similar division of Ireland to that which actually occurred in 1922. Much would have depended on the government in power in Westminster. A general election was due to be held in 1915. Most historians believe that the Unionists under Bonar Law would have won such an election. The party had consistently been winning by-elections, while most of southern Ireland's MPs would have been excluded from the Westminster Parliament under the Home Rule Act due to take effect. Bonar Law was a remarkably able party leader who easily took the Tories to a predominant position at both the 1918 and 1922 general elections, the only ones he contested as party leader. Had the Tories been in power from 1915, it seems certain that more would have been done to mollify Ulster, probably leading to a backlash in the south.

The Tories lost power in 1905. They did not return to government for ten years, until they joined the Asquith-led wartime coalition in 1915. While they were the largest single party in parliament following the 1918 general election, the Conservatives did not form another government in their own right until October 1922, seventeen years after the last exclusive Conservative government resigned in December 1905. Had the Tories been in power in the years 1905–15, would events have been much different? On one level, probably not: Britain entered the First World War in August 1914 under a Liberal government, one which spent millions on building an advanced navy equipped with Dreadnought battleships and which reformed the army. If the Tories had been in power during this period, probably much the same course of events would have occurred. After the First World War, some critics blamed the Liberal government for not making crystal-clear beforehand to Germany that Britain would have immediately declared war if Germany launched an aggressive attack on Belgium or any other country, a warning which, it was claimed, might have deterred German aggression. While it is possible that German militarism might have been deterred by outspoken British firmness, it is probably more likely that it would have made no difference: Britain's army was too small in 1914 to have had any real effect on the actions of Germany's high command. For British military (as opposed to naval) power to have successfully deterred Germany's sweep through Belgium on the way to encircling Paris, the British Army would have had to have been vastly larger, a standing army of hundreds of thousands backed by an even larger, well-trained reserve force, on continental lines.

For Britain to have had such a force in place in 1914 would have required a fundamental change not merely in British military thinking (which *always* viewed the Royal Navy as primary) but in the essence of British liberalism itself, for it would certainly have required the introduction of universal male conscription, with men obliged to perform reserve training for several months a year until they were perhaps fifty. Some voices in the Unionist party indeed wanted such a development, along with other right-wing collectivist measures, especially the enactment of Chamberlain's tariff reform proposals to unify the British empire. Such a view was by no means dominant in the Unionist party during the period 1905–15, and would almost certainly have been electorally disastrous. Nevertheless, it is just possible that a thorough-going right-wing programme, including conscription, would, if enacted, have made Germany's leaders regard the launching of a war against France in 1914 as too costly to contemplate, leading to an armed truce which might have continued indefinitely.

Such a right-wing programme would also almost certainly have been harsher against trades union and labour militancy than was the Liberal government of 1905–14 which, thanks largely to Lloyd George's influence, did its best to accommodate labour demands and to end strikes and workplace militancy on a negotiated basis. Especially in the coalfields and docks, Britain would probably have seen more labour unrest than actually occurred, had such a right-wing programme been in place. On the other hand, a central claim made by the advocates of tariff reform is that a tariff would have produced lower levels of unemployment than did free trade: if these claims proved accurate, one assumes that labour unrest would have subsided. Over Ireland, it goes without saying that a Unionist government would have been unsympathetic to Home Rule. Presumably, therefore, militant Protestant Unionism in Ulster would not have arisen in the same form as it actually did in 1900–14, although extreme Catholic Irish nationalism was likely to have been stronger and more visible. Whether the course of Irish history as we know it, comprising the 1916 Easter uprising, the Irish civil war of 1918–22, and the emergence of the Irish Free State, would have been radically different, is much more arguable, for its essence was the rise to centrality of just such an extreme Catholic Irish nationalism, sweeping away the relative moderation of Home Rule.

The most widely discussed counter-factual question in recent British political history, however, concerns the long-term fate of the Liberal party, specifically whether Labour would inevitably have replaced it as the predominant party of the left, as happened after 1918–22. Labour was indeed making many gains at the expense of the Liberals (and Tories) at the local level in the period 1900–14, and a class-based politics was clearly emerging, at least in many heavily industrialised areas. Yet there are reasons for supposing that Labour would not have replaced the Liberals if war had not broken out. The war itself was the principal cause of the political realignment which followed, engendering the wartime split between Asquith and Lloyd George, the 'coupon' election of 1918 which marginalised Asquith's followers, and the decision of Labour's leaders in 1918, especially Arthur Henderson, to form a genuinely separate party with a radical and socialist constitution. The war also sparked massive social and economic changes which worked to the Liberals' disadvantage and to Labour's advantage, such as the decline of Nonconformity and a considerable growth in trades union membership. The Representation of the People Act 1918 gave the vote to all adult males (including perhaps 40 per cent of the adult male population still without a vote) and to women over thirty, measures which benefited both Labour and the Tories, but not the Liberals. The war moved all of European politics to the left, at least temporarily, with Bolshevism in power in Russia. Presumably, in the absence of a war, none of this – and certainly not the range of events which together worked to Labour's advantage – would have occurred, although most women would inevitably have been given the vote. It is quite possible, even likely, that the Liberal party would have remained the normal left-of-centre party in Britain indefinitely (with, for instance, Winston Churchill quite possibly becoming Liberal Prime Minister around 1930, rather than Tory Prime Minister in 1940!), probably and ironically espousing a position not much different from that of Tony Blair and 'New Labour' at the end of the twentieth century.

Had there been no First World War, too, Europe's empires and traditional societies would presumably have remained intact. The lives of up to ten million soldiers killed in the war would have been spared, and neither Communism nor fascism would, presumably, have come to power anywhere. Lenin, Stalin, Mussolini and Hitler would be unknown to history. It is at seminal junctures such as that of the 1914–18 war that 'counter-factual' history is both most rewarding to the imagination and most likely to be inaccurate, since the whole of contemporary history from August 1914 until today would have been utterly different and essentially incalculable. For example, three men who served as front-line soldiers in the First World War (Attlee, Eden and Macmillan) eventually became Prime Ministers of Britain. But how many among the 720,000 British dead in the war would otherwise have lived to become Prime Minister, giving us a list of prime ministerial names very different from that which we know? Or was the First World War inevitable in some form? Europe, consisting of two armed camps, needed only a spark to ignite, and if this had not been provided in Sarajevo in 1914 it might well have been somewhere else in 1915 or 1916, with similarly cataclysmic results. Or, in such a conflict, would Germany have managed to win quickly – as she was not able to do in August 1914 – and become Europe's hegemon for generations? We can posit a series of seemingly credible possibilities, but hind-sighted plausibility leaves no room for accident, happenstance or the simply unknowable. By definition the plausible, or a range of plausi-bilities, leaves no room for the unexpected.

That the British economy generally performed well throughout the nineteenth century was due in large part to its successful multiplicity of functions, which to a certain extent were fortuitous developments. Had any of these been thwarted, it is possible that Britain's economy would have been very different and much less productive. For instance, it is entirely possible that France under Napoleon or his successors might have emerged as the leader of the industrial revolu-tion, or that London's role as the world's greatest financial centre might have been taken instead by Amsterdam, Paris or Hamburg. Britain's economic ascendancy was also based in its links with the empire, the so-called 'unofficial Empire' in Latin America and the Far East, and the United States, which in turn rested on Britain's control of the seas. None of this was preordained, but was largely the result of fortunate circumstances.

Could Britain have developed otherwise between about 1830 and 1914? There are grounds for answering that question in the negative. The forces which challenged the growth of constitutional democracy were, arguably, never strong enough to have prevented what occurred, while the economic forces of industrialisation and commerce were already in place by the early nineteenth century. There were, of course, points at which history might have turned but did not, although these probably always reflected contingencies rather than more basic trends. As has been noted, it was *possible* that, for instance, a genuinely revolutionary situation might have arisen in 1830–32 had not the Reform Act been passed: certainly many Liberals such as Macaulay feared that a violent revolution was possible had the Lords not given way and enacted Reform. Here larger considerations weighed against such a dramatic outcome: the 'safety valve' of empire and foreign emigration were already in place, as was the moderating force of Methodism, while the British Cabinet in 1830–32 was in the hands of Whig liberals, not ultra-conservative Tories. Similarly, it is possible that the long tragedy of Ireland might have been avoided had the pre-1801 Irish Parliament remained in place, or, many decades later, that Ireland's centrally divisive role in late Victorian and Edwardian politics might have been avoided had Gladstone succeeded in enacting Home Rule in 1886. By 1914–18, it is possible that Catholic Ireland, its reasonable demands satisfied, might have produced a majority patriotic to the United Kingdom, while Protestant Ulster might have learned to coexist and cooperate with the Catholic south. It is arguable that the forces of extreme nationalism in the south, Sinn Féin and the IRA, would have remained tiny fringe groups or never existed at all. Against this, however, it must be said that no attempt to appease Catholic Ireland had ever diminished the forces of Irish nationalism in the long term, and it is unrealistic to imagine that a successful Home Rule Act would have been any different.

It is also worth asking what Britain would have been like in the twentieth century had there been no First World War. Its class system, institutional structure and pre-1914 party politics would have remained intact for many decades, and the British empire would have lasted longer than it did and, indeed, might well still exist. It is unlikely, although not impossible, that Labour would have replaced the Liberal party as the major left-of-centre party, although it seems certain that the trades unions would have played a major role in British politics. It is perhaps rather difficult realistically to see a pacific 1914–18 as having led to a British future radically or fundamentally different from what actually ensued. Although Britain plainly changed in many ways as a result of the First World War, it emerged in the interwar years arguably less altered than any European society: Britain's government and institutions were virtually identical in 1935 to what they had been in 1910. To be sure, there was some change: southern Ireland was independent (although nominally still a British dominion); women had the vote; Labour had replaced the Liberals. But, in terms of formal and institutional change, that was it. Whereas throughout central and eastern Europe all the old landmarks were gone and society had altered fundamentally, Britain came through the Great War with surprisingly little changed and its major institutions still standing – sadder, certainly; not necessarily wiser; but victorious and intact.

The years since the Great War of 1914–18 saw, at least for the period until about 1980, a great increase in the power, roles and economic resources of the central government, far beyond what would have been imaginable to most observers in our period. It saw the equally unimaginable reality of the end of the British empire and a second catastrophic world war, as well, especially after the 1960s, of sweeping social changes, such that the assumptions of British politics and society of the period 1832–1914 would arguably seem infinitely remote.

PART VI

TWENTIETH-CENTURY BRITAIN: A SUCCESS STORY?

Robert Skidelsky

Introduction

'What is a prosperous nation? Is it one in which the greatest number enjoys material and moral wellbeing? Or is it one which covers itself with military glory? There is no criterion which I could apply to determine which of us is right and which of us is wrong.'

Vilfredo Pareto

What follows is not a full-blown narrative history of Britain in the twentieth century. It is an essay in interpretation. It is an exploration of what happened to Britain, and in Britain, over roughly the last hundred years. How much changed and how much stayed the same? And how might an historian judge these islands' experience as a whole? This final Part is an attempt to answer the question: how successful was Britain in the twentieth century?

Broadly speaking, there are four issues which I believe any historian of twentieth-century Britain needs to address. The first is the decline of Britain's world power, at the centre of which was 'the decline and fall of the British Empire'. This is familiar ground, and requires no further elaboration at this point. The second, more complex, theme is 'the rise of the people', the grand narrative of the century's political, economic and social history. In a word, 'the people' became more active in shaping the history of the British state, and while this was generally true in all developed countries, the way in which this came about in Britain is particularly fascinating. The third theme concerns the effects of the people's rise on morals and taste. 'The decline of authority' is the best way of thinking about this. As description it is, I think, relatively uncontroversial, but the consequences of this decline are certainly contentious. The final theme is 'the preservation of liberty'. This provides the strongest element of continuity in the story, and is perhaps the least controversial measure of British success in the twentieth century.

Apart from the first two chapters, which provide a century-long overview, it did not feel appropriate to dispense with a chronological treatment, because the four topics are so laterally interlinked. For example, the end of empire, the spread of affluence, the loosening of morals and the commercialisation of culture came together to transform British society in the middle years of the century, and one would lose the sense of context by isolating them from each other. I have followed convention in one further respect, by treating the two world wars, especially the second, as the central transforming experiences. To justify this, I simply ask the reader to imagine what would have happened to Britain, or in Britain, had these wars not taken place, or had Britain stayed out of them, or lost them.

Germany started two European wars in the twentieth century; it was Britain's response which transformed them into 'world wars'. From Britain's standpoint the crucial question to ask, in language more recently made familiar, was whether they were wars of choice or wars of necessity. The defence of Britain's going to war in 1914 is that the Germans were proto-fascists who, had they won, would have subjected Europe, and sooner or later Britain, to the jackboot. More generally the war takes its place in the western grand narrative of the struggle between democracy and dictatorship, which opens in 1914, takes in the Second World War and the Cold War and carries on today in the 'War on Terror'. Democracy has so far emerged triumphant.

Looked at coolly, this is simply the international version of the Whig theory of history, which has its roots in the Protestant–Catholic wars of the sixteenth to eighteenth centuries. Such an interpretation of twentieth-century history is particularly congenial to the Americans, who like to see themselves as the shining city on the hill, but also to the British, who, like a tiring relay runner, were able to hand on the torch of freedom to the Americans before their final collapse. Yet its weaknesses are those of all Whig history. It reads backwards into the past subsequent events; it is teleological, assuming that history has a finite goal; it is crudely Anglocentric, assuming that progress towards this goal is exclusive to Anglo-American civilisation; it is static, assuming that the protagonists in the struggle have fixed character-istics; and it is heedless of costs, most notably the cost of millions of lives. In the matter under discussion it has to ignore the extent to which the First World War turned the allegedly proto-fascist characteristics of Germany in 1914 into full-blown ones in 1939; and the extent to which the world as a whole was made irrevocably poorer by the collapse of European civilisation.

As a consequence, I have treated the two world wars as part of the story of the 'decline and fall' of British, and European, liberal civilisation – the cutting off of its civilisational possibilities, and a retardation of the growth of material prosperity. Although in the causal chain, the First World War is primary, in the sense that the Second World War was the sequel, in terms of its transforming power the Second World War was more important. High bourgeois civilisation was shaken but not destroyed by the First World War, whereas after 1945 it was replaced altogether by something which might be called 'democracy'.

It is, of course, a tenable proposition that the two world wars, by transferring violence abroad, prevented violent internal convulsions in British society, including a break-up of the British state itself. From this point of view, the positive effect of the wars was to promote social equality, deepen democracy and widen the bounds of citizenship. I believe, on the contrary, that the 'collectivist' model of society created by the wars was a dangerous distraction, which led to economic regression and political illiberalism. I have therefore rejected this popular interpretation of the two world wars – that, while immensely destructive, they nevertheless facilitated the 'rise of the people' – but I have aimed to allow the reader to make up his or her own mind.

It is partly in this context that I address the theme of Britain's relative economic decline. It has been much chewed over by economists and economic historians; attempts to reverse it absorbed a huge amount of intellectual and political energy from the 1950s to the 1980s. I have been influenced by interpretations offered by the historians Correlli Barnett and Nick Crafts. In essence, these are that the success of the wartime model (especially in the Second World War), vindicated as it was by victory, diverted British governments from tackling the 'supply-side' problems of the British economy, particularly the dysfunctional nature of Britain's system of labour relations, and the lack of technical training for the workforce.

This standpoint influences my treatment of Thatcherism. Most people agree that the 1970s was an exceptionally bad ten years – the worst peacetime decade in twentieth-century British history. The centre collapsed, Britain became 'ungovernable', and the territorial integrity of the United Kingdom was threatened. But the way the story is told is bound to reflect the biases of the teller. For me, Thatcherism, for all its failings, represented an authentic *English* road to economic revival and political governability. Less drastic cures might have worked, especially if undertaken earlier. But Thatcherism was not a complete solution to the problems either of Britain or of capitalism in general, as the current global recession make clear.

By the beginning of the twenty-first century, culture had become 'democratised' throughout the developed world. But the British form of cultural democratisation was heavily influenced by the association of culture with class. This bred a populist culture to which the term 'dumbing down' has been applied.

The twentieth century British story can be largely told in terms of class – not only has Britain remained a class society throughout this period, but class consciousness, for better or worse, is constitutive of British civilisation, resisting every attempt at its dissolution. Nevertheless, the role of class did not stay the same throughout the century. For much of it class was the basis of political allegiance, even though the two main political parties had a cross-class appeal. In the last quarter of the century it became less important for politics – class consciousness remained, but shifted from politics to culture. Class position became less a matter of income than of taste, and of the social prestige attached to different types of education, occupations and lifestyles, all of them capable of arousing strong feelings of superiority and inferiority, condescension and resentment.

It is in this sense that class has had a pervasive influence on culture. The twentieth is the first century in which religion was not a dominant force in shaping the law, social attitudes and behaviour. The collapse of religion was not just a collapse of belief, but the collapse of identities shaped by religion. The weakening of hierarchy and deference, the search for new forms of authority, the commercialisation of culture, and the increasingly contractual view of rights and obligations are part of the vast social transformation of Britain in the twentieth century. What has survived is a particularly British vein of moralism, yet one which has been detached from its previous institutional expressions in family duties, sexual and moral codes, good behaviour, politeness and self-restraint.

The phrase 'democratisation of culture' is partly misleading. As in all periods of history, culture has been shaped by the elites. The elites do not have a free hand; limits to cultural change are set by the customs and traditions of the people. Popular opinion does exist. But it is incoherent. Every survey of public opinion shows that people want many contradictory things. So elites have always had enormous scope to shape attitudes and beliefs. It has been the traditional task of political parties to aggregate broad swathes of opinion into political pro-grammes on which to seek the support of voters in competitive elections. As long as the elites are competitive, it can just about be claimed that 'the people' decide on the broad direction of political development. However, the struggle for votes has made oligopolistic competition the norm in politics, and the struggle for revenue has made this even truer in culture. Only the big players survive, and this has inevitably restricted political and cultural choice.

In the second half of the twentieth century money became the main arbiter of culture. On the one side, it has concentrated cultural propaganda on the capture of the lowest common denominator; on the other it has made it the sport of advertisers and oligarchs. To argue that this is the 'choice of the people' is naïve. Popular culture is just as constructed as elite culture used to be. What the people 'want' is never clear; what they get is what the elites encourage or allow them to get. 'Giving people what they want' is as much an act of management as giving them what is 'good for them'. Marxists are therefore right to regard contemporary mass culture as a manipulated culture (but wrong to think there is an alternative to manipulation).

The British state has proved to be a hardy plant. David Marquand has identified 'Whig imperialism' as its central political tendency – the tradition of undogmatic accommodation to the forces of change, which, for most of the century, saw off the 'democratic collectivism' of the Left and the 'Tory nationalism' of the Right. The Thatcherite revival of the 1980s marked the start of its disintegration; the historically oblivious Tony Blair carried its decay a stage further, and today the future of the British state, and of 'Britishness' itself, are problematic.

However, for much of the twentieth century this remarkable political construction preserved the liberties which the British had come to expect as their birthright. The formula of fictional monarchy was one of the most successful legitimating devices ever invented – not that anyone ever set out to invent it. The monarchy was the buckle which bound the four kingdoms together, and it still binds to Britain the three kingdoms overseas – Australia, New Zealand and Canada. Its survival, almost unchanged, throughout the century shows that Britain was not just an artificial amalgam of nations created by foreign enemies which was bound to unravel as soon as the continental threat subsided. There was a powerful reservoir of allegiance and loyalty to Britain, and not just to England, Scotland, Wales and Ireland. The exception was southern Ireland, which was unique in having a national church – Anglicanism – to which the majority of its people did not belong. But Ireland was not just the first to break away from Britain in the twentieth century, it was the last. Elsewhere the British state fulfilled important services for the 'nations' of Britain by compressing regional differences and ensuring a non-violent pluralism.

The persistence of this inherited framework, together with the modest revival of Britain's world position at the end of the century, still makes Britain one of the most stable and civilised countries in the world, as well as the destination of choice for political and economic migrants. The argument that the protection of Britain's own liberties required preserving the liberties of Europe is the main and, to my mind, the only justification for Britain's participation in the two world wars. Whether it was sufficient justification the reader must judge for himself.

1. Material Cultures

Britain grew immensely richer in the twentieth century. Population growth slowed down while productivity went up, allowing a four and a half times increase in real income per head. Contemporary British civilisation was built on a base of massively increased purchasing power. This was mainly spent on buying consumption goods and services, which in the course of the century increased hugely in quantity and variety. The fact that the British people are so much 'better off' today than they were in 1900 does not mean that they are happier or better. They just have more money to spend.

Population

The most striking facts about Britain's population in the twentieth century are the slowdown in its rate of increase, its ageing and the change in its composition. The population of the UK, excluding southern Ireland, grew by just over 50 per cent between 1900 and 2000 – from thirty-eight million to sixty million.

The birth rate began falling in the late nineteenth century, from 5.5 children per woman in 1871 to 1.8 today. This decline in fertility was caused by three factors: the fall in infant mortality (infant deaths per 1,000 births fell from 110 in 1910–11 to 5.4 in 2001, reducing parents' incentives to have large families), the spread of modern birth control methods (most notably with the contraceptive pill of the 1960s), and the increased participation of women in the labour market. Today, men work less, women work more (outside the home). Since the 1960s they have been marrying later or not at all, and postponing births or remaining childless. Marriage was sacrificed to career; children to income.

Britain's population aged steadily as the century progressed. About 5 per cent of the population was sixty-five or over in 1900, a proportion relatively unchanged for centuries. This increased to 11 per cent in 1951, to 16 per cent in 1995 and is expected to reach 23 per cent by 2031. In 1901 the average expectancy of life at birth was forty-seven; today it is seventy-eight, with women living on average five years longer than men, and Scots living five years less than both. The incidence of the leading causes of premature old-age death – coronary heart disease, strokes, cancer and respiratory diseases – declined in the second half of the century as a result of medical improvements and healthier lifestyles: in 1949, 81 per cent of men and 39 per cent of women over fifteen smoked; only 25 per cent of the population do so today. The fall in the 'population support ratio' – roughly the ratio of the economically active to the economically inactive – from 12 to 1 in 1900 to 4 to 1 today has increased 'grey power' in politics, which coincides with the increasing difficulty in financing pension provision.

The British population is not just older, but healthier and better educated than before. The National Health Service (introduced in 1948) was a milestone in the transformation of health care, and the school leaving age was raised in stages from eleven to sixteen, and is set to go up to eighteen when affordable. The number of students in full-time university education has risen from 20,000 in 1900 to over a million today. Longer exposure to education has been an important factor in raising productivity.

Aggregate figures mask significant regional, ethnic and class variations, however: over the century Scotland, Ireland and Wales lost population while England, and especially southern England, gained it. This reflected the industrial decline of these 'peripheries' and the pull of England, which would in due course stimulate Scottish and Welsh nationalism. In 1900, 46 per cent of the UK population lived in the north (including Scotland) and 54 per cent in the south; by 2000 the figures were 38 per cent in the north and 62 per cent in the south. Also, most foreign immigrants settled in the south – in 2001, 45 per cent of the non-white population in the UK lived in the London region.

Migration has affected both the size and the composition of the population. The nineteenth-century pattern of net emigration continued until the 1930s, when net outflows were replaced by net inflows. In the middle years of the century inflows and outflows more or less balanced: Britain lost whites, gained coloureds. From the 1990s onwards net immigration trebled, from under 100,000 per year to a peak of over 300,000 in 2006. As a result, net immigration, and the higher fertility of immigrants, became the main driver of British population growth. Britain started the century colonising the empire; it ended with the empire colonising Britain.

Prior to the 1950s, immigration had been mainly 'white' (Irish and Jewish), and it became so again in 2004 when Britain gave unrestricted entry to labour from the enlarged EU. Before 1914, the Irish settled in England and Scotland in large numbers, sucked into big cities by the demand for cheap factory labour. Irish immigration briefly revived in the 1940s and 1950s but soon dried up and its place was taken by coloured immigration. Of the 60.2 million inhabitants of Britain in the 2001 census, 92 per cent were classified as 'white', and 8 per cent as Asian, Black and 'other ethnic'. This is close to the average for western Europe. The largest non-white group today is by origin Indian (2 per cent of the total population but 25 per cent of the ethnic minority population), the second largest is Pakistani. New Commonwealth immigration transformed major cities into racially mixed populations that would have been unimaginable in 1900.

Supporters of immigration point out that not only is it good for immigrants, but it has helped economic growth by restraining wage

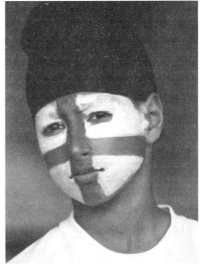

Left: A young boy with a sticker saying 'Stop this multicultural madness' plastered on his forehead makes a Hitler salute at a British Movement rally in Notting Hill, London, *c.*1980. *Right*: A young England fan watches the action during the 4th One Day International between India and England, Bangalore, November 2008. What defines Britishness today? Can the British constitution survive the strain of accommodating such divergent visions?

inflation and provided Britain with a variety of cultural, economic and culinary services beyond the wit of the native population. Anti-immigrant feeling has been driven by fear of job losses, but also by racial prejudice. Many object to Britain being turned into a 'multicultural' society. Earlier panics have recently been reignited by terrorist attacks and the fear of 'Islamisation'.

The Economy

The most important thing to say about the experience of the British economy in the twentieth century is that it closely resembled that of other developed economies. National income, as already noted, expanded faster than population; the structure of the economy shifted from industry to services; the state's role in the economy grew; taxes went up to pay for it.

Britain's real income per head increased from about $8,000 in 1913 to $36,000 in 2008 (measured in 2008 dollars), an average growth of 1.9 per cent a year. The twentieth century was an inflationary one, though the extent of inflation is exaggerated, partly because it took place in short bursts. Price increases over the century averaged only 0.4 per cent per year: hardly catastrophic. The price of services has risen much more than the price of goods. The servant problem much complained about by the middle class after the Second World War was largely the result of wages having risen faster than prices. Unemployment averaged 5 per cent a year between 1910 and 2000, but there were severe fluctuations in the course of the century: from 7 to 15 per cent between the wars, but between just 1 and 3 per cent in the 1960s and 1970s. At 5.6 per cent, average unemployment in the last decade of the twentieth century was very close to that of the first decade, and indeed to that of forty years before the outbreak of the First World War. These figures suggest a 'normal' British unemployment rate of about 5 per cent, which was widely assumed, even by Keynes, to be equivalent to full employment in British conditions.

Once again, however, there were important regional variations. Real wages in the peripheral nations rose more slowly than in England, where they rose faster in the south than in the north. Unemployment, too, was higher in the peripheries. For much of the twentieth century the northern and western parts of the UK stagnated, the southern and south-eastern parts boomed. This was in contrast to the nineteenth century, and the pattern persisted despite regional policies.

Over a hundred-year period what emerges is the long-run *stability* of Britain's economic performance. Whatever the policies adopted for its improvement, the trend rate of growth of the British economy could not be dislodged from between 2 and 3 per cent a year – higher than in the nineteenth century, as one would expect from a more fully industrialised economy, but lower than its main competitors.

It was not, of course, an unchanging economy. In 1911 56 per cent of the workforce was employed in agriculture and industry and 44 per cent in services, but by 2001 the equivalent proportions were 22 per cent and 78 per cent. Britain started the period with a smaller share of agricultural employment (12 per cent in 1911) and a smaller share of agriculture in GDP (3 per cent) than any other industrial nation, and this may have restricted its growth potential in the twentieth century.

The British economy was restructured in three stages. Before the First World War it was 'fabric and mineral-intensive'. The staple industries were iron and steel, textiles, coal mining and shipbuilding. Employment and production in all these sectors declined between the wars, as British costs rose relative to those of competitors. Most inter-war unemployment was concentrated in them, and their locations: Lancashire, South Wales, the north-east coast and the Clyde. The service sector also began to change: domestic service fell, a new professional class rose – school teachers, nurses, accountants. Employment in government also expanded.

From the 1930s a new economy grew up, based on houses and housing appliances, cars, chemicals, metals, cheap consumer goods and retail distribution. It was built on green-field sites in the south-east and midlands. It was this new economy, based on mass production and mass consumption, which laid the basis of the new British civilisation. The share of industry in both employment and GDP declined very little from the 1930s to the 1970s. But by the 1970s many of the manufacturing firms created in the 1930s had become 'lame ducks' and could only be kept going by government support. This was due largely to poor industrial relations and erratic investment. When Thatcher ended protection and subsidies in the early 1980s, Britain's manu-facturing base went into steep decline: between 1973 and 1990 industrial employment fell from 42 to 28 per cent of total employment, most of it after 1979. The decline and fall of the British car industry – which had

developed the iconic and world-beating small car, the Mini, in the 1960s
– is emblematic of industrial decline.

What industry lost in investment and resources to the accom-
paniment of massive unemployment went into a 'post-industrial'
economy based on services – retail, real estate, financial and business,
health and social work, educational, transport and leisure. Mines and
industrial plants closed; shopping malls and offices rose in their place;
under Blair the creative, financial and retail services dominated the
private sector; health, education and welfare services the public sector.
Marketing replaced production. 'Public relations' became an increasingly frequent response to the question, 'Where do you work?'

In the nineteenth century, Britain was the world's leading trading
nation. In 1913, 30 per cent of British GDP was traded, and Britain still
accounted for 25 per cent of world trade, owned 43 per cent of the total
stock of overseas assets, and was investing £200 million a year abroad.
By the end of the twentieth century Britain's foreign trade was still just
under 30 per cent of GDP and London remained the world's busiest
financial capital. Britain's *relative* position, however, had declined. Its
share of world trade was now only 7 per cent, and the City of London,
which in the past had channelled British savings abroad, had
metamorphosed into a financial entrepôt, importing and re-exporting
world savings.

The fate of the trades union movement mirrored the changing
structure of the economy. For most of the twentieth century the trades
unions bestrode the land like a colossus, making Labour governments,
unmaking Tory ones, and in the end making both unworkable. At their
peak, half of all workers were members of one or other union. Trades
unions were made by industrial society and the law and were unmade
by de-industrialisation and changes in the law: the huge shrinkage of
the extractive and manufacturing economy cut the ground from under
their feet, and Margaret Thatcher's trades union laws removed their
legal foundation, the Trades Disputes Act of 1906, which freed them
from collective liability for strike action. Strengthened enormously by
the two world wars, the Trades Union Congress came close to
becoming an estate of the realm in the 1960s and 1970s, running, or
ruining, the economy with the government and employers, even
signing up to 'incomes policies'. However, two factors stopped British
corporatism in its tracks. First, trades unions, having grown out of the
craft unions of the nineteenth century, remained too fragmented,

outside wartime, to act cohesively even within individual plants, much less nationally. Secondly, they were too suspicious of governments of either persuasion to give up 'free collective bargaining' for wages and conditions. Today they survive mainly in the public service and public utility sectors, with their names all changed through amalgamations and disappearances, like those of famous British regiments of bygone years.

Urbanisation

The most striking feature of twentieth-century urbanisation was the colonisation of the countryside by the town. Towns expanded outwards, not upwards. The growing middle classes wanted houses and gardens, not flats; and the working class were entitled to no less. The English, when given the chance, instinctively gravitated to that mixture of town and country known as suburbia. Cities, especially London, spilled over into conurbations and commuter belts. Today, over much of England, 'rural' signifies simply lower densities than in towns. The countryside became an endangered habitat which, like its wildlife, had to be protected by special legislation from the encroachment of human predators.

Outward expansion went hand in hand with the gradual depopulation of inner cities. London's population fell from a peak of 8.3 million in 1951 to just over 7 million in 2001. Post-1945 dispersal brought about urban decay as the middle classes fled, old factory jobs disappeared and inner-city populations were relocated in council estates which sprung up in the late 1940s and 1950s. In the 1960s local councils replaced decaying inner-city terraced houses with concrete tower blocks. Brutal in architecture, bereft of amenities, often alien to their residents, they replaced one form of urban decay by another, as the single-class new housing estates became vandalised slums and centres of urban crime. Governments countered with a spate of regeneration policies, which mostly failed to regenerate.

Urban areas had to accommodate the rising demand for household units as families grew smaller. The average size of households fell from 4.6 in 1901 to 2.4 by the century's end: the outcome of declining fertility, the virtual extinction of residential domestic servants and lodgers, and the increase in single-person households of the young and the old.

Although the population was not growing by much, there was always an excess of families over housing units.

In 1914 only an estimated 10 per cent of the population owned their own homes; by the end of the twentieth century Britain had become a 'property-owning democracy', with 70 per cent of the population (or the banks and building societies from whom they had borrowed) owning houses, and most of the rest renting from private or 'social' landlords. (The pattern in Scotland, Wales and Northern Ireland is little different.) For the first time since the Industrial Revolution the majority owned an asset other than their labour-power.

Technologies

Twentieth-century British lives were transformed by inventions. By creating what became known as a 'democracy of consumerism' these inventions are a central element in the story of the 'rise of the people', and one of its most important sub-sets, the emergence of a teenage culture.

From being a society where few people moved much, or often, from their jobs and homes, twentieth-century Britain became a nation on the move. Motor cars and lorries gradually crowded out railways as means of moving people and goods, and rising real incomes produced a predictable explosion in car ownership – in 1913 there were 34,000 cars; today there are twenty-five million. Cars created the supermarket and destroyed the neighbourhood shop. The railways could not compete, and so in the mid-1960s the railway network was cut by a quarter. Today it is half what it was at the beginning of the twentieth century. An exception to this decline was the city 'metro', a Victorian innovation. The government responded to growing car ownership by building more roads, but, from the motorist's standpoint, never enough. The number of trunk roads (including two thousand miles of motorway, started in 1958) has doubled in the last sixty years, but road space remains scarcer in the UK than elsewhere in Europe – eleven miles per thousand cars as opposed to the European average of fifteen.

The considerable gain in mobility carried large external costs, however: congestion and pollution got worse, and the crime rate increased. Not only did the car offer a new object of theft and vandalism, but it spawned a rash of new motoring regulations, and, with them, motoring offences. Already by 1938 these accounted for 60 per cent of all convictions. For the first time the middle class found themselves on the wrong side of the law.

It was the aeroplane which put 'abroad' within reach of the average British family. Mass air travel was made possible by a huge fall in the cost of air transport and the development of the package holiday in the 1950s. The number of passengers recorded at Britain's airports has risen from two million in 1950 to 150 million today. Britons flock to the French and Spanish rivieras while thousands of football fans travel round European stadia.

'Going to the pictures' was the dominant form of entertainment in the forty years between the rise of radio in the 1920s and television in the 1960s. Picture palaces, sometimes of neo-gothic splendour, were built in every city. Hollywood dominated the production and distribution of films, as it still does, contributing mightily to the Americanisation of British culture. The much smaller British film industry had a golden age in the 1940s and 1950s but, despite enjoying a common language, it lacked the mass audience size to compete with Hollywood without heavy subsidy.

The telephone became the twentieth century's favourite means of communicating, and an estimated twenty billion telephone calls are now made every year. In 1965, the first commercial telecommunications satellite was launched, and the first cordless telephone went on sale two years later. Today the British Isles are more interconnected than ever before: there are seventy-four million mobile telephone connections in Britain, and eleven million UK homes and small businesses now have broadband internet connections via their telephone lines, the highest percentage in Europe. The internet revolution led to some surprising and counterintuitive trends: sixteen-to twenty-four-year-olds now spend seven hours less time per week watching television than do their elders.

The British Broadcasting Corporation was started in 1922. The BBC's radio monopoly lasted over a half-century, broken only with the legalisation of commercial radio in 1973. Although today there are nearly seven hundred radio broadcast stations, radio's heyday was in the 1940s, with millions tuning in to the three BBC programmes on offer. Television, which extended the 'wireless' concept to images, replaced the radio as the main source of non-print information and home entertainment. The BBC Television Service was launched in

1932, and five years later, in June 1937, the Wimbledon Tennis Championships were first broadcast. Like radio, television started as 'serious', with the majority of programmes focusing on drama, politics and sport. The decisive change came with the birth of commercial television, with revenues from advertising, in 1954. This started the race to the bottom, as television programmes had to compete for audience ratings, which they did by becoming as commercial as possible. By the end of the century, 97 per cent of British households had a TV licence, and radio survived largely as a service for the car commuter, the housewife and the insomniac.

Television took its toll on the print media. Well into the twentieth century newspapers were the main source of news, political debate and literary and artistic discussion. The peak of newspaper circulation was reached in 1951 with a total of almost seventeen million daily, and twenty-seven million Sunday newspapers sold. Thereafter a decline set in as television took over their main news functions. The result was shrinking circulation (with dailies down to twelve million, Sundays to 13.5 million in 2000), increasing reliance on advertising revenue, consolidation of national titles and contraction of the local press. Broadsheets were transformed into bulky magazines with features, commentary, supplements and less and less news or reportage, while the tabloids filled up with gossip about celebrities from the world of royalty, pop music, football and television. The challenge posed to print media by television was compounded towards the end of the century by the pressures of catering to a new generation who, instead of buying newspapers, choose to get their news and gossip online, for free, from a much wider variety of outlets.

The Role of the State

The role of the state grew enormously in the twentieth century as it stepped in to compensate for the economic inequality between both classes and regions. Indeed, scholars have argued that it was its role in 'compressing' both sets of inequalities which ensured the survival of the 'unitary' state in the twentieth century; and that the diminution of this role since Thatcher weakened its legitimacy and made Scottish nationalism a political force.

In 1910 the government owned only the post office and a few ordinance factories, employed 2 per cent of the population and spent 12 per cent of the national income. At its peak in 1976, it owned 20 per cent of the economy, employed 25 per cent of the workforce and spent or transferred 47 per cent of the national income. By the century's end, government spending was down to 39 per cent of GDP, though it has since gone up again. In 1910, 3 per cent of GDP went on defence (the British empire was cheap to run), 3 per cent to repay the National Debt and 4 per cent on social spending. Today defence spending – without an empire – is still around 3 per cent, but social expenditure – on education, health, social services and social security – has climbed steadily to roughly 50 per cent of government expenditure – equivalent to 20 per cent of GDP – with the biggest increase being in the cost of old-age pensions. Spending on the tax-financed National Health Service increased twenty times from 1948 to 2008, although the population grew by only 20 per cent in that period.

Taxes therefore rose steeply in the twentieth century. They began to increase at the start of our period to finance rearmament (Dreadnoughts), old-age pensions and national insurance. Income tax was 5p in the £ in 1909 and people on incomes below £100 – that is, the working class – were exempt, paying only indirect taxes, mainly on drink. In his People's Budget of 1909, Lloyd George introduced a 'super-tax' of 13 per cent on incomes over £5,000 a year – the birth of the graduated income tax. During the First World War, the basic rate of income tax rose sevenfold to 35p and super-tax to 70p. In the interwar years the basic rate ranged between 20p and 25p, with a top rate of 60p. In his 1941 Budget, Kingsley Wood raised the basic rate to 50p with a top marginal rate of 97.5p. He also lowered the threshold, creating over three million new taxpayers who paid by compulsory deduction from wages at source. In 1939 fewer than four million paid income tax; in 1979 nearly twenty-six million did.

This was a revolution in the relationship between workers and the state: in return for their taxes the government looked after the people. But from the Thatcher period onwards there was a noticeable decline in the burden and 'progressivity' of direct taxes, with revenue losses partly offset by increases in indirect taxes like VAT. Top rates on unearned and earned income fell from 98 and 83 per cent respectively to 40 per cent in 1988–9 (put back up to 50 per cent in 2009), with the basic rate cut from 33 per cent to 25 per cent; there were also big reductions in corporation tax and death duties. Income tax (standard and top-rate) was lower in 1989 than in 1938, but many more people paid it.

The welfare state rose with the warfare state. The Second World War had greatest impact in this respect. The trend, however, might well have been upwards in any case: spending increases in the 1960s and 1970s were driven by 'the explosion in entitlements', which resulted in millions of new benefit claimants as income support was claimed by those who fell below a defined poverty line, independently of their work status. Thatcher's cuts allowed for a slight downward trend in the late 1980s and 1990s, but this was reversed under New Labour. Today, public spending as a share of GDP is once again above 40 per cent; in the current slump both spending and taxes are certain to rise again.

All indicators of living standards went up in the twentieth century but this was accompanied by changes in the distribution of wealth and incomes. Incomes grew more equal over the first decades, and between 1938 and 1949, followed by more hesitant redistribution in the postwar period. From the 1980s there was a sharp reversal, with the returns to labour falling relative to the returns to capital, and redistributionary policies partly reversed. The heroic age of the 'redistributionary state' is now evidently over. Even in its heyday it failed to eradicate a large residue of poverty, which was 'rediscovered' in the 1960s, when researchers found that 3.8 per cent of the population was living below the minimum National Assistance scale. Pensioner poverty was particularly acute. However, since poverty is now defined in relative, not absolute, terms, there is no stable yardstick against which changes in poverty can be measured.

2. Culture and Society

The End of Victorianism

This chapter is about what happened to Britain's immaterial culture in the twentieth century – its morals and what are known collectively as 'the arts'. This is a subject on which few would presume to pronounce with confidence. Two broadly contrasting views predominate, the first being part of the narrative of progress, the second of the narrative of decline. The debate between the two is not so much over the facts as over the interpretation of those facts, with changes which are seen as liberating by the first school being viewed as ruinous by the second. A classic example concerns the freeing of women from domesticity. This can be regarded either as enlarging human freedom or as destroying the institution of marriage. The answer that it is both, and that therefore sensible societies recognise the need for trade-offs, is too easy, since it depends on a definition of freedom – as absence of constraint – which is philosophically incomplete.

What is undeniable is that British moral and cultural habits were subject to two massive forces for change – secularisation and relativism. The decline of religion changed both the moral code and aesthetic culture. Moral purpose in the arts remained strong in the first half of the century, but gradually faded with the evaporation of a religious view of life. Detached from any purpose outside themselves the arts inevitably became self-contained: 'art for art's sake'.

By relativism we mean the collapse of agreed standards of good and bad in both morals and the arts. Large swathes of moral and aesthetic life became matters of personal preference. Artistic achievement was divorced from skill and came to inhere in the self-expression of the artist, particularly his perceived 'originality'. The inevitable tendency of both secularisation and relativism was towards 'anything goes'.

Many would see commercialism as the decisive influence on twentieth-century British culture: the elevation of the market into the position of arbiter of all values, immaterial as well as material. It seems more plausible to see commercialism as stepping in to fill the void left by the forces of secularisation and relativism. If qualities intrinsic to certain behaviours or attitudes are no longer recognised, the market – the predominant locus of personal choice in a secular society – is bound to become the main arbiter of value. However, the process is not all one way. Commercialism also tends to obliterate the older moralities which would have acted to restrain it. It does this by imposing the logic of gainfulness on an ever-widening range of activities.

What we now think of as popular culture was shaped by films, popular newspapers, television and advertisment. The content and style of the mass media in turn helped shape moral attitudes and behaviour: television and tabloids have largely replaced the pulpit and literature as agents of moral commentary and instruction. This capture of culture by commerce, accelerating from the 1960s onwards,

The Tube Train, c. 1934, colour linocut by Cyril E. Power. Modernism could be an ambiguous aesthetic. The dizzily rhythmic patterns convey something of the machine age's fascination with speed. But the excitement is offset by the blank faces of serried commuters. Modernity also meant alienation.

was made possible by the disappearance of ways of life which had sustained the traditional class cultures. In the new 'weightless' economy of post-Thatcherite Britain, culture became a branch of the tourist industry, morality a department of the caring services.

The three pillars of Victorian culture were religion, social deference and a strong sense of 'Britishness'. The Church regulated morals, the aristocracy and the upper middle class regulated manners, and 'Britishness' provided a national myth which bound together the classes as well as the nations of the British Isles. The Victorian ideal of the 'Christian gentleman' neatly combined Christian, social and 'British' values. By the end of the twentieth century, morals had become secularised, taste was a matter of opinion, 'gentleman' had become a condescending obituary description of an obsolescent species, and the national project – forged over centuries of warfare and imperial exertion – was gone. For the older generation, Britain had become unrecognisable and deeply distressing; for the young it was bursting with new and strange vitalities.

The Decline of Religion

Decline in religion meant not just decline of belief in God, but the decline of religion as a source of moral thinking and cultural inspiration. Nineteenth-century Britain was a religious society with secular bridgeheads; twentieth-century Britain was a secular society with religious residues. In the twentieth century there was a gradual fall in all measures of religiousness – denominational membership, worship, Sunday School attendance, baptism, church marriage – until the 1960s, then a collapse.

The falls were most striking in inner cities and council estates, less in the countryside, suburbs and small towns; more in England than in Scotland, Ireland and Wales; more among the unskilled working class than among the middle class, less among women than among men. Catholicism bucked the trend but only because its congregations were swelled by working-class Irish immigrants. Late in the twentieth century there were signs of a religious revival – new Pentecostal religions appeared in the wake of immigration from the Caribbean and Africa, Islam established its presence through immigration from the Indian sub-continent, and evangelical Christianity spread among the young, signifying the arrival of American-style fundamentalism with its rejection of doctrinal and moral compromise. Whether these trends will be strong enough to reverse secularisation is doubtful. At present only 20 per cent of the population can be described as institutionally religious.

What brought about the the decline of religion? The standard explanation is sociological: urbanisation increased people's distance from nature, and therefore from God; with increased material abundance Christianity could no longer rely on poverty and misery in this world to enhance the attraction of the next.

But sociological explanations of religion's decline cannot explain the loss of belief itself. Religious beliefs are not merely socially useful habits which fall away when they are no longer required. To some degree the decline of religion was elite-driven, with the conversion of an influential fraction of the intellectual class to atheism. Whereas the Victorians had promoted Christianity as a civilising force, at home and abroad, progressive twentieth-century thinkers like Bertrand Russell, H. G. Wells and George Bernard Shaw attacked religion as mere superstitition, and the churches as the main obstacle to the rational treatment of social-moral questions such as birth control, divorce, homosexuality and the role of women. Twentieth-century analytic philosophy was aggressively atheist, with religious belief denounced as a species of 'non-sense'. Thus the repudiation of religion was part of the intellectual demand for the reconstruction of society on 'rational' lines. The demand for the scientific treatment of morals was satisfied in the 1950s and 1960s with its raft of permissive legislation removing 'moral' censorship of films, plays and books, legalising abortion and adult homosexuality, and providing divorce on demand. In the second half of the twentieth century, state education was secularised with the abolition of collective acts of Christian worship. As a result the door to the rich cultural heritage of Protestant Christianity – the Bible, prayer book and Wesleyan hymnary – became closed to most schoolchildren. By the 1990s, 27 per cent of the population called themselves atheists, a threefold increase since the 1960s.

Of course, a great deal of Christian ethics survived in secular form. It could hardly be otherwise; Britain was no longer a Christian country, but it was a christianised one. Yet the authority of religion had gone. The Christian frame of reference simply dissolved, to be replaced by secular creeds and material demands.

The Decline of Social Deference

At the start of the century social deference bound together the political, religious and aesthetic cultures of Britain. Culture was hierarchical. A vertical scale was implicit in the terminology used; high culture was at the top and low culture at the bottom. Like accent, culture was a mark of distinction. It was about having good taste, in books, painting, music, furniture, clothes. It involved knowing about the classics and not knowing about science. It was connected to wealth and leisure and fine houses. At the same time aristocratic culture was a shared culture because it arose naturally from the life of the countryside, with its big houses and estates. It was the replacement of this vertical society of ranks by the horizontal society of classes which ruptured the cultural transmission belt. Neither middle nor working class could plausibly be said to embody a national culture.

Early in the century the left was hopeful that working-class culture, suitably purified by socialist thought, contained the kernel of a superior national culture – one which was inherently democratic, not hierarchical. Writers like D. H. Lawrence, Arnold Wesker, Raymond Williams and Richard Hoggart took the values of 'solidarity' and 'neighbourliness' , expressed through working class practices and institutions, to be emblematic of this superior culture. Uncontaminated by wealth, the workers were seen, in a tradition going back to primitive Christianity, as repositories of original virtue, the main resource for moral renewal. A workers' state would extend this virtue to the whole society. But the working class never saw itself as the ruling class. Trades union leaders saw their role as being to fight the bosses not to be the bosses. The defeat of the socialist project in 1951 with the return of the Conservatives to power for thirteen years, followed by the erosion of traditional working-class jobs, closed off the socialist dream of a national culture based on working-class values. The last stand of the miners against the logic of the market ended in their total defeat in 1985. By the time Tony Blair won for Labour in 1997, a working-class project no longer made sense. Scotland, Northern Ireland, Wales and northern England have a more working-class 'feel' to them than the Midlands and southern England, but this is a working class largely shorn of its former occupations, and heavily penetrated by commercial culture.

The idea of a superior national culture based on middle-class values proved only slightly less delusory. The middle class saw itself as the 'general' class: recruited from all classes, it would transcend both class interests and class *cultures*. It saw itself as the new hegemonic class, superior in virtue to the aristocracy and in culture to the working class. Middle-class thinkers looked forward to the convergence of both top and bottom on middle-class values. In practice, the middle class was able to wrest the commanding heights of politics and administration from the aristocracy; its reforms helped make the working class better educated and more prosperous. But it failed to establish its own cultural hegemony. An important index of this is the failure of the late Victorian 'intellectual aristocracy', lauded by Noel Annan, to reproduce itself. There were no heirs to Bertrand Russell and Keynes; to Bernard Shaw, H. G. Wells, or T. S. Eliot, the intellectual and literary giants of the first half of the twentieth century.

Most explanations of the failure of the middle class to provide the cultural leadership expected of them revolve round the connection between culture and class. Left-wing thinkers like Perry Anderson and Tom Nairn argue that Britain did not experience a middle-class revolution like the French Revolution. This meant that it failed to develop a distinctive *bourgeois* culture as an alternative to aristocratic and working-class culture. Middle-class intellectuals saw themselves not as a republican vanguard, but as heirs to the aristocratic Establishment. Their spiritual home was not the civic centres of nineteenth-century Britain, but Oxford and Cambridge. By the time Thatcher's bourgeois revolution arrived in the 1980s, it was too late for a middle-class culture to take root, except in the narrow sphere of economics, and even here it was the City and finance which triumphed over the provinces and industry. Because it attempted to mimic the aristocracy, the English middle class developed a social snobbism inimical to the generalisation of its cultural values. This made it easy for the media to stir up populist feeling against 'elites'.

The abolition of the free grammar schools in the 1960s and 1970s stands out as a milestone in the failure to sustain a culture based on middle-class values. The grammar schools, being the main conduit of higher-order cultural values to the working class, offered Britain its best opportunity to build a high-quality culture detached from class. The opportunity was lost because the grammar schools' meritocratic ideal fell foul of both middle-class exclusiveness and working-class egalitarianism. The virtual disappearance of the grammar schools accentuated the cultural divide between the high brow and the low brow. As prosperity spread, the working class became middle class in income, but not in taste. And the middle class itself experienced a cultural degradation. It used to aspire upwards towards the aristocracy, now it aspired downwards to avoid being thought elitist.

However, the main reason for the cultural failure of the middle class was that its habits of thought were essentially critical, not constructive. It sought liberation from conventional morality and cultural restraint, but had nothing constructive to put in their place. Keynes understood this. As a young man he believed that individuals were sufficiently evolved to be safely released from the 'outward restraints of convention and traditional standards' to pursue their own 'pure motives and reliable intuitions of the good'. This was the standard progressive view. As he grew older – and grew up – he realised he had been wrong. He admitted to having had a 'disastrously mistaken' view of human nature; he and his friends had ignored the 'insane and irrational springs of wickedness in most men' and the dependence of civilisation on 'rules and conventions skilfully put across and guilefully preserved'. He began to wonder whether morality was possible without religion. Yet the generation of the 1960s simply reproduced the naivety which Keynes abandoned, with the consequences of which we are stuck.

The cultural watershed of the 1960s saw the coming of age of two distinctive middle-class doctrines: utilitarianism and expressive individualism. Utilitarianism, derided by Nietzsche as a philosophy for traders, clearly had deep roots in British thought, and was an expression of the practical genius of the British people. However, its influence on legislation concerned with conduct had been limited by strong residues of Victorian morality. In the mid-twentieth century these disappeared. The new doctrine was that law should be subjected to the single test of 'utility'. The state was justified in restraining the actions of individuals only to prevent harm to third parties: the moral feelings of the community, or religious teaching, furnished no criteria for criminalising behaviour or setting a tariff of legal penalties. Four notable applications of utilitarianism to law, all dating from the 1950s and 1960s, were the legalisation of both suicide and homosexual acts between consenting adults; the establishment of divorce by consent; and the abolition of capital punishment. The test of utility did not point only to liberation from existing law. In the name of preventing harm to third parties, utilitarian doctrine has brought a range of hitherto 'free' activities like drug-taking, smoking, drinking and fox-hunting within the ambit of restrictive law. The strength and weakness of utilitarianism as the basis of legislation is well illustrated by its attitude to families. The state has become increasingly intrusive in regulating relations between adults and children to protect minors from abuse or harm of various kinds; but indifferent to the social value of marriage as a nurturing institution for children.

Utilitarianism contested the ground of middle-class thought with the doctrine of expressive individualism. Derived from the romantic view of the self, expressive individualism claimed that the expression of one's personality was necessary for true authenticity. If self-expression is good, it is wrong to repress any parts of it for the sake of hollow social convention.

This view of the self had three large consequences. First, as art was reduced to self-expression, judgements of higher and lower disappeared, because every artistic happening became a self-contained event or experience. Second, it enabled consumption to be sold by advertisers as a primary means of self-expression, removing the moral restraint on greed. Third, it reduced the political to the personal. This started with the slogan 'the personal is the political'. Politics became the expression of gender and race, as well as youth and identity. Political issues became intertwined with lifestyle issues. The gap between the public and private sphere narrowed. Key events in the onset of identity politics were the Campaign for Nuclear Disarmament and the student occupations of university buildings of the 1960s. Although such events were said to herald a more intense political commitment, the more profound effect of identity politics was to trivialise politics. People became more interested in the personalities and private lives of their leaders than in their policies; the personal foibles of the royals became more interesting than their function.

The distinction between utilitarianism and expressive individualism is more apparent than real. Utilitarianism can accommodate expressive individualism on the assumption – made by Mill, and the early Keynes, but not by Bentham – that individuals are the best judges of their own interests. So to maximise liberty (within the harm constraint) is to maximise general happiness. This, in a nutshell, is the argument of Mill's hugely influential treatise *On Liberty*, and the principle behind the social reforms of the 1960s. But outside the 'constraint', all moral and aesthetic judgements are a matter of personal preference. There is nothing *intrinsically* right or wrong, good or bad.

The Decline of Britishness

Historians have familiarised us with the notion that the 'British nation' was a myth, born of the long struggle between Protestant England and Catholic Europe, a myth which was associated with the expansion of the English crown throughout the British Isles and also overseas. In extreme form this thesis has it that the three 'nations' of Ireland, Scotland and Wales were colonies of England, and 'Britishness' was a colonial myth invented to disguise the reality of their subordination. One implication of this perspective is that Britain has long been a culturally diverse society – in 1989 Professor Hugh Kearney identified eight cultures – held together by a national project. Once this project dissolved there might be little to hold Britain together culturally, and even politically.

As long as 'Great' Britain was a leading world and imperial power the smaller nations could take pride in their partnership with England. As long as there was no European Union, 'Britain' offered the only alternative to small-nation isolation. With empire gone, the European Union offering wider links, and Britain no longer a unique success story, union no longer seemed to offer the same advantages. The bulwarks against fragmentation were Protestantism, empire and welfare state. The end of empire, together with mass coloured immigration, dissolved the glue of 'Britishness' and from the late 1960s the submerged national cultures started to assert themselves in Northern Ireland, Scotland and Wales. Process replaced project.

From this perspective, the end of empire is a particularly significant event in the dissolution of traditional 'British' culture. Victorian moral standards were closely linked to the maintenance of Britain's position as a world power. Empire required an imperial ruling class, born into and bred for the job of ruling, and the production (and reproduction) of such a class was the chief aim of the Victorian public school. The code of the officer and gentleman, with its high sense of duty and its repression of personal feeling, was the morality of ruling. Although few Britons worked in or visited the empire, elite values serving the vocation of imperial rule had a disproportionate influence on the moral life of the nation. With the liquidation of empire in the aftermath of the Second World War this moral code lost its hold on the ruling class. Just as the elites had upheld traditional morals, so their repudiation of these spread down the social scale.

The kind of culture which developed in the second half of the twentieth century was connected with the end of empire in four ways. Popular culture replaced imperial mission as an expression of national identity; the 'soft power' of football and pop music compensated for the waning of Britain's 'hard power'; British culture became Americanised as the USA replaced Britain as the centre of the English-speaking world; and cultural transformation was brought about by mass immigration from the 'New Commonwealth', most obviously in music, food, fashion and drugs.

The collapse of the British mission was not unresisted. Among the conspicuous losers from twentieth-century social change were the 'patriotic' groups who upheld some earlier version of 'what it means to be British'. These ranged from the aristocratic diehards who resisted the end of empire, to the coal miners with their patriotic socialism, to the football fans of Thatcherism, whose drunkenness and violence were a pathetic attempt to display the qualities which had supposedly made Britain great. Other losers included the white Rhodesian settlers, the Northern Irish Protestants, and the dockers and Smithfield meat porters who marched in support of Enoch Powell to resist coloured immigration. They were deemed obsolete and retrograde. What they shared was a reminiscence, however distorted, of Britishness.

The Fruits of Social Change: Morality

Has the ending of Victorianism borne out the expectations of cultural optimists or pessimists? What happens to human beings when social control is loosened?

Moral optimists point to advances like the occupational liberation of women, rising educational attainment, tolerance of homosexuals and ethnic minorities, while pessimists focus on the breakdown of the family, the rise in crime and the increase in teenage sexual activity, alcoholism and drug abuse. Cultural optimists point to the many and various outbursts of cultural vitality, while pessimists concentrate on the spread of low taste and mediocrity. Optimists often view the distempers of the times as teething troubles on the advance to a superior civilisation; while pessimists take them as portending the dissolution of society.

The advance of women – to equal status in jobs, to fulfilment in sexual life, to control over their own bodies – has been unambiguously welcomed by the optimists. But the mirror image of these advances was the collapse of the traditional family structure, the main indicators of which were fewer marriages, more divorces and more children born out of wedlock. The marriage rate increased rapidly in mid-century, but then fell dramatically from 404,700 a year in 1971 to 283,000 in 1995. Marriage is now preceded and often replaced entirely by cohabitation. There was a startling increase in the number of divorces from 812 a year in England and Wales in 1901–5 to 159,964 a year in 1991–5, having jumped after the Marriage Act of 1969, which introduced the principle of no-fault divorce. Pre-marital sex became more popular than ever: by 1974–5, 42 per cent of single girls aged sixteen to nineteen were no longer virgins (although only 17 per cent in Scotland). Today, the figure is well over 60 per cent. In the past, extra-marital conceptions usually led to marriage; today, they mostly end up as abortions or illegitimate births. The percentage of children born out of wedlock remained around 5 per cent from the reign of Elizabeth I to the beginning of Elizabeth II's reign when it began to rise sharply, but by 2001 almost 40 per cent of births were illegitimate. Eighty-eight per cent of children born to teenage mothers today are born outside marriage. The trend is the same across the British Isles.

The support of Britons for the institution of marriage is stronger than their behaviour would indicate: 70 per cent believe that it is better for parents to be married, and 57 per cent are even happy for governments to encourage marriage as the 'normal' state. This is markedly different from the supposedly non-judgemental public discourse on the subject, which claims that marriage is only one of a number of family options. This suggests that some part of moral behaviour is conditioned by the law, and would be different if the law were different. Since changes in the law are almost always elite-driven, the elites cannot escape responsibility for changing the moral behaviour, if not outlook, of the people.

The rise in crime has been cited as another result of weakening social control, but the perception that we have become a much more criminalised society is largely a reflection of disappointment of the

hope that better education and economic prosperity would bring
down the crime rate (as well as the result of media-fuelled moral
panic). In Edwardian Britain it was widely believed that crime would
yield to material and moral progress. In fact, the number of crimes
recorded by the police per 1,000 population over the age of 10 rose from
3 in 1900 to 86, in 1997, 29 times higher. This partly reflects more
opportunities for criminal behaviour – we have already noted the huge
increases in the number of motor cars, and hence of car-related
offences. However, there was no century-long consistent increase in
the crime rate. After doubling during the years of depression, 1927–37,
and doubling again during the Second World War, recorded offences
actually fell between 1951 and 1955. But the five-year period 1955–60 saw
the largest percentage increase ever recorded: a rise of 69.8 per cent in
total offences. The rate continued to increase until 1992, when the
number of recorded crimes began to fall. Violent crime remained a
small proportion of total crime throughout the twentieth century,
even though it has more than doubled as a percentage in the last four
decades of the century from 2.4 to 5.6 per cent of the total. Contrary to
popular perception, the number of sex offences, while growing in
absolute terms, decreased as a proportion of total crime. The homicide
rate (which includes murder, manslaughter and infanticide) is not
much higher today than it was in 1900, but this masks the fact that the
rate halved in the first fifty years of the century before doubling in the
second. Prison numbers tell a similar story: the total prison population
fell from 18,000 in 1907 to around 10,000 in the interwar years, but from
1945 it began to grow sharply. By 2008, it had reached 80,000, with
existing prisons overflowing.

Contrary to popular opinion, drunkenness and consumption of
alcohol per head decreased slightly in the twentieth century. But drug
use has increased, partly because more drugs have become available.
The main trends are: big increases in use in the 1970s and 1980s,
comparative stability in the 1990s. In the UK (as in the US) there was an
escalation of cannabis use in the 1970s and 1980s, followed by a drop,
followed by a slow increase over the 1990s. 'Recreational drugs' are
widely available, despite the law. Ecstasy became the most popular
teenage party prop in the 1990s; cocaine has become the drug of choice
for metropolitan party-goers in early middle age.

Although there are problems with all the data, the trends seem clear
enough. Between the late 1950s and the 1970s, there was an increase in

practically all socially dysfunctional behaviour. By comparison with the century's first fifty years, Britain became a violent and unruly country, and Geoffrey Gorer's picture of 'football crowds . . . as orderly as church meetings', and Orwell's vision of 'a gentle-mannered, undemonstrative, law-abiding' people faded into memory. In a conversation in 1961 with John Osborne, Lady Violet Bonham Carter noted that great poverty in her youth had coexisted with 'far higher moral standards among the very poorest . . . Why had savagery taken the place of high spirits? We both agreed that real civilization had gone down since material prosperity had risen.'

The older generation has never accepted the emancipation of the young from parental control, and the greatest concern of adults is with teenage behaviour. One survey of opinion notes that 'as many as 84 per cent now agree that young people have too much freedom and need more discipline. Similarly, when you ask the British what educational issues concern them most, pupil behaviour and discipline comes out far ahead of attainment, exams, class sizes or anything else' – that is, far ahead of what legislators think important.

The blood-curdling tabloid picture of end-of-century young people as no-good layabouts, violent, criminal, sex-crazed, drunken and drug-addicted, a terror to little old ladies and a burden on the welfare state, is mainly piffle. What the tabloid picture does reflect is the behaviour of a minority of young people. Even more, it creates the reality it claims to depict, and thus stokes up the 'social pessimism' which sells papers. Nevertheless, there has been some increase in what most people would call bad behaviour, and this is, in the broadest sense, a consequence of the triumph of permissiveness. The great fault of 'Our Age', wrote Noel Annan, was that 'they could never say no'.

The Fruits of Social Change: Taste

The picture of British society presented by media, especially TV, is often deeply depressing, but this is partly due to the relentless pressure to fill in time, which gives a cumulative impression of triviality. Large chunks of TV time – chat shoes, soap operas and 'reality' TV – are devoted to the problems and relationships of ordinary and untalented people, thus exposing a previously hidden banality to the public gaze. Largely gone is the 'improving' urge which inspired early radio and TV.

In the course of the twentieth century Britain changed from being a working-class nation with a small middle class and a much smaller aristocracy into a largely lower middle-class nation with a proletarian flavour chiefly featured in a flat sub-middle-class accent, a national obsession with sport, especially football, and a dumbed-down commercialised sentimental culture. Three cultural signposts on the road to the twenty-first century are worth special attention.

Bloomsburies and Fabians

Bloomsbury is both the label attached to a group of Edwardian friends of the 'lower upper middle class' who made their homes in that part of London, and a generic name for the dominant cultural movement of the first third of the twentieth century. It tells us a great deal about efforts to create a high culture fit for a secular age, and about why they failed, ultimately, to resist the rising tide of consumerism. The Bloomsbury Group were the first iconoclasts of the twentieth century. Their attacks on Victorian morals, Victorian taste and the British empire set in motion the intellectual dismantling of the Victorian moral and social order. In rejecting the symbols of Victorian authority they taught a generation to doubt authority as such. From Bloomsbury, wrote Noel Annan, 'came our distaste for the Establishment'. Yet they failed to lay the ground for a mass culture of high quality. Bloomsbury culture remained coterie culture.

A paper read by the Cambridge undergraduate Desmond McCarthy to the Apostles – a secret 'conversation' society – in December 1900, can serve as Bloomsbury's manifesto for the twentieth century. The key difference from their predecessors, McCarthy says, was that his generation took 'everything more *personally*' than they did. This was due to 'all institutions, the family, the state, laws of honour, etc which have a claim on the individual . . . having failed to produce convincing proofs of their authority'. 'Shaken belief in rules of thumb and the usual aims in life' have made for much 'greater interest taken in personal relations'. The new generation had much more 'trust in their immediate judgment'. The full consequences of this change in consciousness took a century to roll out, and were retarded by two world wars, which reinstated the claims of duty.

McCarthy's generation was greatly influenced by G. E. Moore's

Principia Ethica, published at Cambridge in 1902, which developed an intuitionist theory of ethics. We perceive, or 'intuit', what is good, Moore claimed, just as we know what is green, and what is best are personal relations and aesthetic values. The Bloomsbury artist and art critic Roger Fry tried to use Moore's intuitionist method to develop a purely 'internal' way of judging a work of art. This was expounded in his doctrine of 'significant form'. He wrote: 'The aesthetic emotion is an emotion about form. In certain people, purely formal relations of certain kinds arouse peculiarly profound emotions.' Just as Moore's moral intuitionism was an attempt to protect society from bad morals, so Fry's aesthetic intuitionism was an attempt to protect it from bad art. Philosophically, intuitionist ethics and aesthetics were little more than stepping stones on the road to 'emotivism' or value relativism. But they are important in the history of the revolt against Victorian values.

Edwardian Bloomsbury championed not just Post-Impressionism but openness about sex. The Bloomsbury 'moment' in 1904, when Lytton Strachey, pointing an elongated finger to a stain on Vanessa Bell's dress, enquired 'Semen?' challenges Philip Larkin's conceit that 'Sexual intercourse began/In nineteen sixty-three'. But the turning inward demanded by McCarthy was possible only to an intellectual and artistic elite possessed of some private income. Bohemia was traditional, Bloomsbury was new. But Bloomsbury was not hedonistic. Liberation from Victorian convention was not identical to permissiveness. Its ideal was beauty, contemplation and personal relations, not consumption.

Bloomsbury was closely associated with the cultural movement known as Modernism. In sociological terms, modernism can be interpreted as an attempt to protect culture from bad taste. But its cultural exclusiveness had the effect of surrendering popular culture to commerce. It rejected narrative and plot in the novel, story-telling in painting, metre and rhyme in poetry, tonality in music and decoration in architecture: the very things that made the arts part of a 'shared' culture. Before 1914 Bloomsbury writers and painters aggressively challenged conventional opinions in both morals and art. In the interwar wars, the 'high-brows' scorned the 'middle-brows' and the 'middle-brows' scorned the 'low-brows'. T. S. Eliot epitomised this attitude when he asserted that 'Poetry in our civilization, as it exists at present, must be difficult.' Or as Roger Fry put it: 'In proportion as art

becomes purer, the number of people to whom it appeals gets less.'
Through modernism high culture became elite culture, inspiring a
wave of populist ridicule.

The Fabians, another fraction of the dissident Edwardian intelligentsia, were more clearly Victorian in outlook, mainly because they
were about twenty years older. They hated Bloomsbury because of its
lack of concern with public causes and what Beatrice Webb called its
'anarchic ways in sexual questions'. Sidney Webb deplored any undue
stress on self-expression. 'We have no right,' he said, 'to live our own
lives. What shall it profit a man to save his own soul, even if thereby one
jot less good is done to the world?' The Fabians were collectivists, who
saw themselves as the 'scientific' managers of a socialist state, a role
which has often appealed to intellectuals of modest birth and wealth.

Both were in the business of elevation: Bloomsbury wanted to raise
the general culture of the middle class; the Fabians to elevate the
material and, through that, the cultural condition of the working class.
But from a longer perspective, one can see that they espoused partly
complementary, partly contrasting, but equally high-minded alternatives to the Christianised ethics and social structure of Victorian
Britain. They attacked Victorianism, but at the same time sought to
construct a high cultural ideal from the wreck of religious and social
authority. They were more successful in their undermining than in
their constructive efforts.

Mid-Century Watersheds: the Generation War

The 1950s and 1960s bisect the culture of the century into two halves.
Traditional culture came under simultaneous assault from so many
different directions that it is difficult to make a coherent narrative of
the changes. Its anti-Establishment mood and atmosphere of sexual
liberation link it to Bloomsbury. But the new movements of literary
realism and kitchen-sink drama deliberately attacked Bloomsbury's
esotericism and modernism: they represent the coming of age of the
first (and last) grammar school generation of lower middle-class
writers. A third element was the eruption of teenage spending power,
and a specific teenage culture based on pop music and clothes. Yet a
fourth element was the student revolts of the late 1960s, which were
simultaneously protests against atomic weapons and marked the

emergence of politics as self-expression. If anything united these disparate movements it was a sense of generation: the young felt they were in revolt against their parents and grandparents. These seismic cultural shifts reflected both the discredit of Britain's great power pretensions following the collapse of the Suez expedition in 1956, and the onset of mass affluence and with it the enlargement of consumer choice. To stress the continuity of cultural habits across mid-century as writers like Dominic Sandbrook have done seems somewhat beside the point. Most of life changes slowly; it is the transforming effect of minority movements that historians rightly notice.

The early 1950s were the last years of the 'classic' collectivised urban working-class culture, with extended family networks going back to the late nineteenth century. The contrast is with the more isolated and individualistic working class of the new postwar council-housing estate, motor-car manufacturing culture of Dagenham studied by Ferdynand Zweig in his *The Worker in the Affluent Society* (1961). The 'shiny barbarism' of affluence began to replace the authentic working-class culture of brass bands and working-men's clubs. Evenings were increasingly spent in front of the television instead of down at the pub, and the working class replaced its authentic culture with the nostalgic simulacra of television shows like *Coronation Street*, first broadcast in 1960.

The first explosion of protest at Macmillan's 'you never had it so good' society was the 'anger' of the Angry Young Men – John Osborne, Colin Wilson, Kingsley Amis, Alan Sillitoe, John Braine, a rag-tag group of writers and playwrights with no coherent agenda, of working-class or lower middle-class provincial background – against upper middle-class metropolitan elites. However, Jimmy Porter's gloomy assertion, in John Osborne's 1956 *Look Back in Anger*, that 'there aren't any good brave causes left' was not shared by everyone. While working-class youths were politically apathetic, their middle-class counterparts took up moral causes in time-honoured fashion: the Campaign for Nuclear Disarmament, formed in 1958 to protest against nuclear weapons, and the student 'rebellions' of the later 1960s triggered off by the Vietnam War. If Britain protested, the world was bound to take notice! It became increasingly difficult to separate politics from culture, as political demands became the direct expression of cultural, sexual and racial identity.

Affluence brought youth culture, and youth culture became mass culture. Macmillan's premiership (1957–63) was the golden age of the working-class teenager: freed from the incubus of school at fifteen, he could, unskilled and without family responsibilities, step straight into a steady job with wages that rivalled those of adults. Before the 1950s the cash of teenagers was only enough to buy cigarettes and sweets; now, with money in their pockets, the whole world of consumption was at their feet.

They were avid consumers of novelty and ephemerality. The Teddy boys of the 1950s, aping the Edwardian style, were the first in a long line of teenage fads and movements. This provoked another round of fear-baiting over the Americanisation of British culture. In the immediate postwar years, popular music remained conservative. Big bands supported trained voices like Vera Lynn and Dickie Valentine. But in December 1954, Bill Haley and the Comets gave British teenagers their first taste of rock 'n' roll, the musical style that would come to dominate all others in the second half of the twentieth century. Their second single, 'Rock Around the Clock' reached number one in November 1955. Rock 'n' roll – a white man's black music – gave teenagers what they wanted: a visceral, informal, accessible and sexually charged soundtrack, music that, in the words of Tony Bicat, 'anyone with a fiver for a guitar and a minimal amount of intelligence could have a go at'. Elvis Presley soon became the main rock 'n' roll reference, along with his numerous British impersonators like Billy Fury and Cliff Richard.

The Beatles were the most famous beneficiaries of this cultural upheaval; their music started to hit the shops in 1962–3 at the height of the teenage consumer boom. Their sheer novelty and cheeky-chappy working-class charm offered a wholesome contrast to a corrupt Establishment mired in scandal. Their success abroad was hailed as a contribution to the nation's shaky balance of payments, and they were the first of many cultural substitutes for Britain's waning 'hard power'. The prestige of Beatlemania was not lost on the Labour Prime Minster Harold Wilson, who awarded them OBEs in 1965.

But the teenager also became a metaphor for a society in flux. The emergence of the teenager symbolised the decline of traditional authority, the instability of the family, and the breakup of settled communities. With the coming of rock 'n' roll the image of 'bad' teenagers supplanted that of the 'good' children of the early 1950s, and has dominated the tabloids (and therefore public perceptions) ever since. This image proved to be highly exploitable for the teenage market.

The 1960s was an unstable decade from which some reaction back to 'normality' was inevitable. Yet the pendulum did not swing back mechanically. Moral and aesthetic culture had shifted into a new gear, in which deviant behaviours such as homosexuality and pre- and extra-marital sex, previously tolerated as signs of human frailty, became rights, backed by legislation. Affluence turned consumption into a 'right'. As Joe Lampton, hero of John Braine's *Room at the Top* (1957), explained: 'I wanted an Aston Martin, I wanted a three guinea linen suit, I wanted a girl with a Riviera suntan – these were my rights.' The right to consume towered over all others, linking Macmillan's children to Thatcher's children.

Celebrity Culture

Despite a few notable outbreaks of cultural vigour – in the early years of the last century, in the 1950s and 1960s, and in the postmodernist architecture and post-colonial literature of the 1980s and 1990s – there has been a gradual drift downwards. It is not that there is not much 'good' culture around, but the centre of gravity has shifted. The dominant tone in the media is the production and celebration of low taste, as much in the world of books as in that of television. The book trade, once a prestigious world based in London's Bloomsbury and prone to allegations of snobbish elitism, has become in many ways a branch of the television industry. Most bestsellers originate as ideas for television programmes, and, apart from a small strand of prize-winning, quality books, the titles which sell the most are to do with hobbies ('special interests'), lifestyle revelations (celebrity or 'misery' memoirs) or are overwhelmingly mass-market fiction, packaged for supermarkets and no less ephemeral than most other consumption goods, to be read and thrown away on holidays. In high culture, biography has become the main literary art form, reflecting the public's hunger for sexual revelation. In the arts, as in politics, traditional British reticence has vanished without a trace: stiff pricks have replaced stiff upper lips.

The journalist and former Conservative politician George Walden makes a powerful argument that 'dumbing down' was manufactured by the elite out of guilt and greed. His argument is not that elites have disappeared, but that the big money is to be made from exploiting bad taste. This cannot be the whole story. Walden assumes that the elites know what is good but will the bad. This leaves out the degradation of elite taste – their loss of any sense of what it is which makes a work of art good or bad, interesting or disgusting. It is not the people's demand which inflates the prices and reputations of Tracy Emin, Damien Hirst and Chris Offili but the demand of a handful of collectors like Charles Saachi and Nicholas Serota. The 'rebranding' of Britain as Cool Britannia, low on power but high on ecstasy, is simply a marketing gimmick, 'spiritual larceny' as the art critic Roger Kimball describes it. Such productions reflect the diseased condition of the elites far more than that of the masses.

There remain, of course, pockets of excellence and achievement in all the arts – a total collapse of culture would require a total collapse of economic life. High value continues to be attached to professionalism, with a demand for increasingly high standards of performance. This is because, in many areas of skill, standards can be measured. That is why education is expected to be 'skills based'. Football, the most pervasive expression of popular culture, demands a high level of professionalism.

Authority has survived in some cultural forms. Science enjoys a unique prestige in contemporary civilisation. Cinema and theatre have partly resisted the celebration of mediocrity, because they are art forms which demand technical prowess. Actors are more often than not still required to convey the vision and language of a director or playwright, not merely to express themselves. It is the very lack of technical proficiency required by the performers of pop music which has made it the most ephemeral of today's cultural products: thrust into the limelight by the music money-men, most groups are here today and gone tomorrow, their members enjoying brief moments of genuine fame before entering celebrity purgatory, where they remain famous only for once having been famous. The few survivors like Oasis and Coldplay remain commercially durable only because middle-aged men in a state of arrested cultural development continue to buy their records.

The celebrity culture has passed most trained professionals by; when professionals become celebrities it is usually less for their on-field than off-field exploits. Most celebrities are famous only for being famous. Many of them are models or TV presenters, which does not require any special talent. Celebrity actors are not necessarily or even typically the best ones, celebrity rock stars are often mediocre musicians. And now there is the phenomenon of celebrities who have no professional talents at all, like the late Jade Goody of *Big Brother* fame. The whole point of celebrities is that they are *not* special in any way, professional or otherwise – a celebrity is averageness on a pedestal. Princess Diana is the supreme example of this, her death in 1997 producing an astonishing outbreak of mass sentimentality and counterfeit emotion.

Celebrities are expected by politicians to be 'role models' for supposedly rudderless youth. However, their attraction for the public stems more from their private lives than public performances. We want to know what they are really like in private, how they struggle with their demons of drink and drugs, how they fight their battles against cancer. 'Full disclosure' memoirs and biographies fuel the public's desire to get between the sheets. The tabloids are eager to make of irregular private lives the stuff of spurious moral fables. All true celebrities have feet of clay, so that the populace can see in them a reflection not only of their dreams but of their own banality.

Anyone who was young in the 1950s and 1960s is bound to be ambivalent about the fruits of progress. Conservatives have attacked these decades as a mere outburst of egotism and licence, but they were more than that, at least in self-perception. There was hope – naïve in retrospect, but sincere at the time – that the unleashing of erotic energy would create a new form of community based not on power or money but on love (a version of the old Christian fellowship, only with sex and drugs added) and unlock creative powers repressed by convention and class. This was absurd, of course, but it is better to be a deluded romantic when young than cynical from the start, like the subsequent generations so often seem to be.

3. Political and National Cultures

The Constitution

The British state survived mighty political blows in the twentieth century. This survival testifies to the robustness as well as the flexibility of its 'ancient constitution'. It has outlasted the loss of world power, economic decline, Britain's troubled, often violent, engagement with Europe, the separation of southern Ireland, the growth of Scottish and Welsh nationalism, the 'rise of the people' and, last but not least, frequently indifferent political performance. The survival of the British state is *the* grand narrative of Britain's twentieth-century political history. Irish and Scottish nationalism are secondary threads. Reformers railed against its unfitness for the tasks of the modern world, but they ignored its success in perpetuating itself, and with it the liberties it has fostered, and which were protected by its survival. Its system of adversarial politics was an unrivalled mechanism for channelling conflict into Westminster and thus robbing it of its revolutionary sting. Never was it so evidently an advantage than in the interwar years.

By the end of the century there was a feeling that the 'ancient constitution' had run its course. It was paternalist, increasingly centralist, and based on manners and conventions that were disappearing. It was not suited to an era of identity, regional and multicultural politics, and it discouraged active citizenship. Reformists wanted it to be replaced with a written constitution that provided for a proper federal structure and a real separation of powers.

The British constitution was not a contract between the state and its citizens, but an accumulation of laws and behaviours – as J. M. Roberts wrote, 'the institutional core of the story which runs from Anglo-Saxon times to our own is the story of a state structure built round the English monarchy and its effective successor, the Crown in Parliament'. The House of Commons replaced the closet and preceded the ballot. This has given the British state its 'ancient' character.

Over the century, the Prime Minister became much more important. Britain today is still commonly described as having Cabinet government, but except in periods of crisis Cabinet government has become prime ministerial government. This change was foreshadowed by Lloyd George with his 'garden suburb', advanced by Harold Wilson with his 'kitchen cabinet' and consummated by Tony Blair with his 'sofa cabinet'. The institutional foundation of prime ministerial power lies in the fact that the Prime Minister is the party's (not monarch's) choice, and the source of all preferment. The key relationships have become those between the Prime Minister and his sources of power: his court, his party, the media and, through the media, the people.

The growth of state functions has shifted the locus of policy-making from the minister and his civil servants to powerful outside organisations, who negotiate with Whitehall before parliament rubber-stamps the results. In the heyday of the nationalised industries the key relationship was between government and the trades unions; today it is between government and the social service providers and lobbyists. Of all the great independent institutions of state, the most surprising survival is the Treasury, as aloof and powerful at the end of the century as it was at its start.

Parliament still has two houses, Commons and Lords. The House of Commons has hardly changed, though great parliamentary occasions are rarer, and it now has standing and select committees to scrutinise the actions of the executive. The House of Lords remains outwardly the same, but some new wine has been poured into this very old bottle. The Parliament Act of 1911 restricted its power to veto Bills passed by the Commons to two years; this was reduced to one year in 1949. The Life Peerages Act of 1958 created a new class of 'life peers' – peers whose titles expire with them. In 1999, 660 hereditary peers were culled from the Lords, with ninety-three remaining temporarily. Apart from them, the House of Lords now consists entirely of life peers, law lords and bishops. Lords, lunatics and prisoners are still voteless.

The basic trend in local government was towards its emasculation. Progressives hoped that local government would be the laboratory of democracy, performing social experiments on a small scale. This hope was not realised: despite the increasingly frequent reshuffling of its tiers, local government decayed. No twentieth-century civic government could compare with Joseph Chamberlain's rule in nineteenth-century

Birmingham; and the tradition of business philanthropy so successfully practised by the Rowntrees and Cadburys also died out. The reason is clear: local taxes declined from almost one-third of total government revenue in 1900 to less than 3.5 per cent in the 1990s, because central government took over the financing of the main local authority services in order to secure economies of scale and uniformity of provision. With devolution to Scotland and Wales, an elected Mayor of London (since 1998) and the promise of further elected mayors, there has since been a mild reversal in the centralising trend.

The structure of British politics has been hugely shaped by the voting system. The electorate to which parliament is responsible has been enlarged by several extensions of the franchise: to women in 1918 and 1928 and to eighteen-year-olds in 1969. The traditional voting system – known as 'first past the post', whereby the winning candidate must gain more votes than any rival in that constituency, as opposed to a majority of the votes cast – remains intact for national and local elections. (Proportional representation has been introduced for European, Welsh and Scottish elections.) It might have been tailor-made to ensure the executive its ability to act royally, by guaranteeing it, in normal times, a parliamentary majority.

As with culture, much of what happened in twentieth-century British politics can be explained by the replacement of a hierarchical view by a class view. At the core of the aristocracy was a patrician landowning class which stretched across the 'four nations', but was linked, often by family connection, to the army, the Anglican Church, the ancient universities and the higher reaches of the professions and civil service. This was the old governing class, to which the mass of the people 'deferred'. Why? Partly it was because the longevity of the families concerned linked them directly to British history; partly because they embodied widely shared facets of the 'national character'; partly because their position and training seemed to fit them uniquely for the task of ruling. It was especially important that the ruling class was not a closed elite: real, but limited access to merit softened resentment from below, and, via education, particularly the public school system, promoted a downward transmission of upper-class values.

The politics of hierarchy were replaced by those of class. As in the nineteenth century, Britain exhibited a tripartite structure – upper, middle and working – but the classes were much more sharply separated by class consciousness: the Conservatives represented the upper and middle class, Labour the working class. This is not what the parties said, of course – the Tories wrapped themselves in Church, flag, rural values and 'One Nation' rhetoric, which was effective enough to win a substantial minority of working-class votes (one could say that women and drink sustained them in the twentieth century). Labour, which also claimed to stand for the national interest, took a smaller but still substantial section of middle-class votes. This overlap was crucial in tilting both parties towards the centre. Wherever religion helped bond together nation or group, however, politics continued to be divided on religious rather than class lines. Since 1921, Northern Ireland has been politically divided along sectarian lines, and this was also true of some parts of Britain, notably Merseyside and Clydeside, where the Protestant working class voted Conservative, and the Irish Catholic workers Labour. From Thatcher onwards, however, class politics receded, though social class has not.

The peak of the two-party duopoly was in 1951, when Conservative and Labour each received nearly 50 per cent of the vote. Since then the percentages voting for both parties, and indeed turnouts at general elections themselves, have declined. Breakaways from the main parties flourished briefly, then disappeared, killed off by their inability to establish positions in parliament commensurate with the votes cast for them. The most successful of the small parties were those with regional concentration. The Unionist parties of Northern Ireland have returned an average of twelve seats between them since 1974, when they broke from the Conservatives. Minor parties have occasionally played a pivotal part: for example, Scottish Nationalists and Ulster Unionists toppled the minority Labour government in 1979. The Communist party never got more than two seats in parliament (in 1945), and finally expired in 1991. Its strength lay in the Labour movement, infiltrating small cadres of militants into key positions in local Labour parties and trades unions. 'Red Robbo', Derek Robinson, a radical folk hero, almost brought the car industry to a standstill in 1970s. The century's end brought a proliferation of small parties – Greens, British National Party, United Kingdom Independence Party – none of which have gained parliamentary seats, but which have varying influence within larger parties.

Although today the parties remain outwardly recognisable, they have been robbed of their deliberative force. The main traditional

indicators of political interest – membership of political parties, identification with political tendencies, attendance at political meetings,
voting – have been in steep decline. Since the 1970s, the parties have
lost two-thirds of their members. Political oratory is a shadow of its
former glory, replaced by comforting sound bites and evasive
interviews on television and radio. Rhetoric was always a key part of
persuasion, but as the century wore on the politics of gesture and 'spin'
increasingly replaced those of choice. Issues and interests, the bread
and butter of the old politics, have lost their force, and political parties
no longer 'educate' democracy – that task is left to the media and think
tanks. Thatcher dismantled the local base of the Conservative party;
Blair dismantled the trades union base of the Labour party. As a result,
British political parties have become top-down electoral machines,
rather than bottom-up shapers of political opinion. They no longer
exist to mobilise support for policies, but to mobilise votes behind
leaders competitive in their lust for power. In the nineteenth century
democracy arose as a check on oligarchy. Today it may well be giving
way to a new form of moneyed oligarchy. But perhaps it has always
been thus: the 'ancient constitution' was inherently oligarchic, and it
has remained so.

The First World War

The First World War features in the master narratives of both the
'decline and fall of British power' and the 'rise of the people'. Despite
the horrific slaughter it brought about, left-leaning historians have seen
it as an engine of progress: it made the state responsible for the welfare
of the people, and pointed to state planning as an alternative to
capitalism. But equally plausible is an opposite hypothesis, that victory
was a poisoned chalice, deluding and exhausting at the same time.

Once war momentum had built up on the Continent, following the
assassination of Archduke Franz Ferdinand, heir to the Austro-
Hungarian throne, in Sarajevo on 28 June 1914, Britain on its own could
not have stopped a European war. What it could do was to prevent
Germany and its allies from winning it quickly, or winning at all.
Britain's role in preventing Germany establishing a Prussianised
European Union, at a cost of four years' bloody fighting, was a decisive
event in its own and European history.

There was a radical non-interventionist tradition in British foreign policy, strongly represented in Asquith's Liberal Cabinet of 1908. This was challenged by Gladstone's 'moral interventionism' on behalf of small nations. The radicals needed a moral excuse to go to war, which Germany provided by invading 'neutral' Belgium on their expected way to Paris. The German blunder of invading Belgium, dictated by the logic of the Schlieffen plan, provided Asquith's Cabinet with the necessary reconciliation of morality with realpolitik. In particular it swung the Chancellor of the Exchequer, the Welshman David Lloyd George, an outsize product of a small country, behind the war.

Having entered the war, how should Britain fight it? The Foreign Secretary, Sir Edward Grey, hid from parliament the fact that Britain was bound by a secret treaty with France to fight a continental war. This was a break from the British tradition of fighting European wars with subsidies to its allies and naval power, with its armies intervening only in peripheral theatres and at decisive moments. It reflected the fact that Britain was no longer arbiter of Europe. For Britain, the First World War was a war both of subsidies and of large armies, continuously engaged for four years on the western front. As a result it suffered prodigious losses of both manpower and treasure.

Lloyd George's War Machine

Lloyd George was Britain's man of the war. His reputation as a dynamic man of action was sealed by his success at the newly created Ministry of Munitions to which he had been transferred from the Exchequer in May 1915. The Ministry's record stood out from the dreadful military reverses of the war's first year, for a much greater mobilisation was needed to fight the war the generals demanded. As A. J. P. Taylor describes it, 'By the autumn of 1916 liberalism was played out. The only logical alternatives were to abandon liberalism or abandon the war.' Lloyd George's success in producing shells made him Asquith's obvious successor. A palace coup accomplished the deed, and Lloyd George became Prime Minister on 7 December 1916 with the Conservative leader Bonar Law as Chancellor of the Exchequer. His new government was supported by nearly all the Conservatives, the Irish Nationalists and the Labour party, but about half the Liberals went into opposition under Asquith. This split the

Liberal party and ensured that Labour became the main alternative to the Tories in the postwar two-party system.

The war brought an unprecedented expansion of government intervention in the economy. The Munitions of War Act of May 1915 brought the munitions industry under government control. The trades unions agreed to 'dilution' (allowing unskilled workers to do the jobs of skilled craftsmen), and compulsory arbitration in return for government promises to restrict wartime profiteering and uphold the principle of free collective bargaining. Intervention spread with the Military Service Act of 27 January 1916, which imposed military conscription on all bachelors between eighteen and forty-one; this was extended to all men between these ages in July 1916. Military conscription ended the system of voluntary enlistment and the free market in labour which depleted vital industries haphazardly, and thus pointed to industrial conscription. Failure on the Somme in the summer of 1916 led, by stages, to food rationing and coal, manpower and shipping control. New war ministries – of Labour, Shipping, Food,

British troops 'go over the top' during the battle of the Somme, France, 1916. On the opening day of the battle 21,000 British troops were killed and 40,000 wounded, the greatest loss of life on a single day in British military history. A gain of 7 miles between July and November 1916 cost the British 420,000 casualties all told. Why did they go like 'sheep to the slaughter'?

Health and National Service among them – and over a hundred new boards, were set up to direct the flow of resources to priority sectors, most of them run by businessmen and temporary civil servants. Prices, wages, rents and profits were brought under government control, and subsidies for food-growing started in 1917, with four million acres brought back under plough.

War hugely expanded the government's financial resources. At first the government covered its war spending by heavy short-term borrowing, the accepted device for a short war. This proved inflationary, with purchasing power spilling back into the private economy. The squeeze on private consumption started with Liberal Chancellor of the Exchequer Reginald McKenna's first Budget of September 1915, which, in addition to a steep increase in taxes, imposed the 'McKenna Duties' on luxury imports, ending seventy years of free trade. By 1918 an excess-profits tax of 80 per cent was providing the Exchequer with nearly half its revenue. There were also four war loans which raised more than £2 billion. Of the government's domestic war expenditure, 32 per cent was raised by taxation, and the rest borrowed – worse than Pitt had achieved in the 1790s, but better than the other belligerents. This left the government's domestic debt at the end of the war at just over £6 billion, or 300 per cent of national income. Seventeen million Britons held some form of government debt, mostly in post office savings certificates. The millions of bondholders created by the war made up the deflationary coalition of the 1920s.

Wartime propaganda was an essential part of Lloyd George's war machine, foreshadowing the whole machinery of 'spinning' which became a normal part of twentieth-century government's relationship with the people – and the truth. Lord Northcliffe, owner of *The Times* and the *Daily Mail*, was put in charge of propaganda aimed at enemy cities; Lord Beaverbrook, who acquired the *Daily Express* in 1916 together with his peerage, was made Minister of Information by Lloyd George in February 1918, both press lords neatly combining two disinformation roles in one. Lloyd George cynically remarked to the *Manchester Guardian*'s C. P. Scott in December 1917: 'If the people really knew, the war would be stopped tomorrow. But of course they don't . . .'

War planning's biggest failure was its inability to impose political control over the military. The First World War was a war run by civilians for generals. Military demands were never considered in relation to political strategy but as determining it. The purpose of planning was to supply the armies with what the generals wanted, rather than to sustain the economy, society and Britain's postwar position. The result was a labour surplus in the armed forces and shortages everywhere else. This put a massive strain on the government's partnership with labour.

There was a limit to how far the TUC would, or could, contribute to military and industrial enlistment without losing control to the radical shop stewards' movement, particularly powerful in the engineering and shipbuilding industries. Most of the strikes in the war were about cost-of-living questions. The government rarely used its strike-breaking powers, preferring to settle on the men's terms. Bonar Law remarked prophetically in January 1918: 'Once the workpeople got the notion that they were dealing with the Treasury, and not with the employers, there could be no end to their demands, and future strikes would be against the government.' Finally, there was no central planning body to impose priorities. The war industry ministries simply grabbed the scarce resources, especially labour, for themselves, at premium prices. Despite Lloyd George's efforts, the machine created for winning the war was palpably defective, which drastically diminished its attraction as an instrument of peace.

The Costs of the War

By 1918 Britain had mobilised more than six million troops, over a quarter of its male population. Some 723,000 British soldiers were killed – almost 10 per cent of the workforce – and more than twice that number wounded. This was not just a quantitative but a qualitative loss. For the aristocracy and officers, the ratio of those killed to those who fought was one to four, twice as high as for ordinary ranks. The disproportionate toll the voluntary recruiting system took of the aristocracy, middle classes and skilled workers led to a loss of energy and talent. Quite simply, Britain failed to preserve its human capital.

External war spending had to be covered by selling gold and foreign assets and borrowing from the United States. By the end of the war, Britain had sold £1.25 billion, or a quarter of its foreign assets. It had borrowed £2 billion from America (the whole of its prewar national income), £842 million in 'Liberty Loans' owed to the US Treasury.

Britain had paid not only for its own external spending but for much of its allies'. Furthermore, though these allies quickly reneged on their debts to Britain, Britain spent the next ten years paying off its debt to the United States. It also failed to renew its capital stock – real income per capita in 1926 was lower than it had been in 1913. Had the First World War not happened, or had Britain stayed neutral, it would have been a much richer country in the 1920s and 1930s than it was.

Although the British empire had acquired new limbs – former German colonies in Africa, parts of the Ottoman empire in Mesopotamia, Transjordan and Palestine, formally held under mandate from the League of Nations – the war weakened Britain internationally. True enough, Britain emerged stronger than its defeated enemies. But Europe itself was weakened relative to the rest of the world. It lost its place as a centre of world civilisation and economy, and Britain went down with it. Ideologically Europe was hit by the twin assaults of Wilsonian national self-determination and Bolshevism. The one challenged imperial rule; the other liberal capitalism, both of which had defined pre-war European civilisation. The war also disrupted the global trading and financial system on which Britain relied for its living: Britain never enjoyed full employment between 1920 and 1940, and a weakening economic base supported undiminished global commitments.

After 1918, there could be no doubt that the United States was the most powerful nation in the world. Henceforth, the British empire existed by permission of the United States. The rise of both the United States and the Soviet Union to superpower status was delayed, in the first case by self-imposed isolationism and in the second by the domestic convulsions accompanying the Bolshevik Revolution. This left Britain the sole world power, *faute de mieux*, and nurtured the illusion that the medium-sized European states with their huge external appendages continued to be arbiters of their own fate and the world's.

The Benefits of the War

The reason why some historians have seen the war as an agent of advancement is that it fits their model of political and social progress. It advanced democracy and strengthened organised Labour. Women over thirty got the vote for the first time as a 'reward for war service' (in 1928 women of twenty-one got the vote also, equalising the genders) and millions of extra men were also enfranchised. This almost trebled the electorate, from 7.7 million in 1910 to 21.4 million in 1918. The Labour party replaced the war-shattered Liberal party as the main political opposition to the Conservatives. The trades union movement doubled in numbers – from four million to eight million – in prestige, and in power. During the war it had bargained with the government almost as a sovereign power; in 1920 the TUC set up a General Council as a 'general staff' for organised labour.

The war left, in Kenneth Morgan's words, 'a mighty leviathan of government'. If the government could produce munitions, why not houses? Lloyd George promised homes, farms, schools and hospitals for heroes. The Haldane Committee was set up in 1918 to rationalise the machinery of government, and the Bryce Report of the same year recommended a partly-elected House of Lords. But the 'British revolution' obstinately failed to materialise. There were some achievements after 1918: the start of state-financed municipal housing, the extension of unemployment insurance to almost all workers. But most of the reconstruction projects were wish lists. None of them had been properly costed; it soon turned out that they were 'unaffordable'. One by one they were abandoned. There was, also, a reaction against the methods of war for their inefficiency, extravagance and curtailment of freedom. Soon after the war ended, the popular press started an 'anti-waste' campaign which called for the curtailment of inflated war spending. The loudest call, from both employers and unions, was for 'back to normalcy', despite the fact that 'normalcy' now included a much-strengthened labour movement. Reconstruction and Reform expressed a fleeting mood, not a philosophical choice.

After the war the British rediscovered the pleasures of mental inertia. The war confirmed them in what Tom Nairn called their 'sense of underlying insular identity and common fate'. Prewar social reformers who had called for the state to organise 'national efficiency' rediscovered the virtues of individualism, private property and muddling through. The war gave amateurism a boost: had not make-do, after all, won out against Prussian preparations? With amateurism went sportsmanship. 'The British soldier is fighting for fair play,' declared Lloyd George vacuously. Sport – especially football – could bring social peace. For workers on strike to play football with the police was considered to be typically, and helpfully, 'British'. The war produced a generation of defeated politicians who clung to the frail lifeboat of decency.

The political hopes of the left were not fulfilled. Labour emerged from the war with a new constitution, pledging itself, alarmingly, to the 'common ownership of the means of production'. There was also a new provision for individual membership, which opened up the party to middle-class radicals. But Labour had no clear aims. More importantly, by giving birth to the bogey of socialism its advance consolidated the hegemony of the Conservatives.

There was a modest advance in social equality. The landed aristocracy lost most of its remaining political clout, partly because, with fixed rents and falling agricultural prices after the war, a quarter of landed estates were sold off and divided up into 'villas'. It had become unthinkable to have a prime minister in the Lords – as the magnificent Marquess Curzon, Foreign Secretary and ex-Viceroy of India, discovered in 1923. After the war, England was more middle class than aristocratic, although it was a middle class permeated by Arcadian longing. Women gained a new political status but their employment was not maintained after the war, with the postwar depression sending them back to domesticity, whether as housewives or domestic servants.

The war's effect on morals was more equivocal. Historians like Arthur Marwick and Samuel Hynes have argued that it loosened traditional morals. Sexual behaviour and artistic expression became freer. Yet the interwar years were conservative decades, despite Bloomsbury and the Bright Young Things. The king and queen and Mr and Mrs Baldwin symbolised the domestic virtues; Joynson Hicks (in the mid-1920s) provided moral stiffening at the Home Office; King Edward VIII had to sacrifice his throne in 1936 to marry a divorced woman. There was a modest increase in the number of divorces as a result of changes in legislation. The prewar literary and artistic avant-garde remained the post-war avant-garde.

What the war did do was to destroy the heroic military ideal. The pity of war and the suffering of the individual became paramount; the defectiveness of the leaders taken for granted. The old men of 1914 had betrayed the young by sending them to the front for no good cause. There they were betrayed by stupid generals – 'the fierce and bald, and short of breath' and those bloodthirsty padres who perverted sacrifice to God into killing for country.

The literary reaction to the war from such enduring voices as Sassoon, Brooke, Rosenberg and Owen launched the pacifist mood, which had such an influence in the 1930s. It also explains the wary, sceptical and mocking mood of those who fought in the Second World War: 'the dominant feeling in 1939 among the young', according to Noel Annan, 'was that although the bloody old men had got us into this mess we had to fight – only this time with no bloody heroics'.

In summary, whereas the First World War was a tremendous shock, its main result was not to shock the British out of old habits, but to reinforce them. Pulling back from the excesses of the war occupied most of the energies of the political class, leaving it bereft of new ideas. Nevertheless, it did change the momentum of political economy. It ended the liberal era of British-managed globalisation. The postwar world was more nationalistic. One clear sign was the end of mass emigration. When the British economy slumped in the nineteenth century it exported people; in the interwar years their successors joined the dole queues. The war also made the British economy less flexible. In the interwar years consolidation was the order of the day, on both sides of industry. This inevitably gave rise to the notion of a negotiated rather than competitive industrial system, and with it the notion of a negotiated rather than hierarchical social order. The middle way of the Baldwin–MacDonald era of the 1920s and 1930s was thus markedly less confident than the 'liberal imperialism' of the Asquith years.

The Decline and Fall of Lloyd George

Lloyd George looked set to dominate postwar politics. The 'man who had won the war' won an overwhelming electoral victory on 14 December 1918 as head of a coalition of Conservatives and Lloyd George Liberals, promising 'to make Britain a fit country for heroes to live in' – as well as to hang the Kaiser and make Germany pay the whole cost of the war. Yet just four years later he was chased from power, never to return. The straightforward explanation for this debacle is the collapse of the coalition and resumption of party politics, snuffing out Lloyd George's hope of forming a permanent centre party under his leadership.

The coalition failed because it was saddled with commitments which overstretched Britain's reduced means, as well as having a leader who carried hugely exaggerated expectations of what he could accomplish in peace. The retreat from illusion would have been painful under any circumstances, but it coincided with the sharpest economic contraction since the Industrial Revolution. There was a similar retreat from victory in foreign policy. The Versailles Treaty, signed on 7 June 1919, failed to produce a pacific world in which imperial dominion could be quietly enjoyed. This was because the war failed to solve the German problem. Lloyd George spent the first six months of his peacetime premiership negotiating the peace treaty with Germany, and much of the rest of it trying to undo its consequences.

The most important act of British scaling-down was the jettisoning of the policy of naval supremacy. The Americans were determined to end the anomaly by which the Monroe Doctrine depended in part on British control of the Atlantic. They told the British that unless they accepted naval parity with the United States they were prepared to outbuild the British navy. Before 1914, Britain had taken up the German naval challenge; now it gave way to the United States. It realised that in America it faced a more powerful, but also less hostile, rival. The Washington Naval Agreement of 1921 fixed the relative strength of the American, British and Japanese navies at 5:5:3. As a result, wrote the historian Max Beloff, 'a permanent shift in world power was consummated without a shot being fired'. As a condition of the agreement, the United States insisted that Britain give up its alliance with Japan. This proved to be fatal for the future of the British empire in Asia, since in the Far East America would be the challenger, not the underwriter.

Lloyd George must take credit for 'solving' the Irish question. More than the Easter uprising of 1916, brutally suppressed, it was the British attempt to introduce conscription in 1918 which killed prewar Home Rule, uniting Catholic Ireland behind Sinn Féin, the political wing of the Irish Republican Army. Michael Collins, the IRA's commander, worked out the blueprint for a new kind of 'asymmetric' warfare, whose aim was not to win military victory but to render a continuation of repressive policy politically and psychologically impossible for the occupying power. Collins's tactics worked brilliantly against the shell-shocked British forces. Lloyd George's use of the Black and Tans and Auxiliary police, who became notorious for the use of reprisals, failed to quell the insurgency, while infuriating American opinion. While claiming to have 'murder by the throat', he opened unofficial negotiations with Arthur Griffith, acting president of Sinn Féin, and in July 1921 a truce was declared. Four months later a treaty was signed which made Catholic Ireland a self-governing dominion under the crown, like Canada, Australia, New Zealand and South Africa. Protestant Ulster accepted 'home rule' as second-best to direct rule from London. In 1937, the Prime Minister Eamon De Valéra would send the king's governor-general packing. In 1949, Ireland formally became a republic, outside the Commonwealth. Lloyd George took Ireland off the radar screen of British politics till the 'troubles' in Northern Ireland started in the 1960s.

Indian nationalism learned from Ireland's successes – and failures. What Ireland showed was that the British had no stomach for repression of the 'Prussian' kind. In response to rioting in the Punjab, on 23 April 1919 General Dyer ordered his troops to fire on an unarmed crowd of thousands assembled illegally in a square in the middle of the Sikh holy city of Amritsar, killing 379 and wounding hundreds of others. Dyer's action restored order – Mahatma Gandhi, the leader of passive Indian resistance to British rule, called off the Punjab campaign – but radicalised the National Congress party, hitherto a constitutional pressure group. For the next twenty years the British alternated between locking up Gandhi, Nehru and other nationalist leaders, and trying to win them for a programme of constitutional progress to modified Dominion status at an undefined future date.

The most pressing political issue dominating the Coalition, however, was Lloyd George's future. Was he the problem or the solution? As long as the Conservatives felt they needed him, he had some hope of constructing a new Centre Party to resist Labour. As the Coalition's fortunes declined so did Lloyd George's attraction for the Tories. He tried to safeguard his position by accumulating a personal fund made up from selling peerages and other honours for use for any party which would have him. His reputation never recovered from the stench of the honours scandal.

In 1922 Lloyd George hoped for foreign policy triumphs to 'restore his star to its zenith'. But his plans for pacifying Europe relied on American money or security guarantees which were unavailable: an unwelcome reminder of Britain's shrunken power. In the end it was his adventurism which brought him down. When British and Turkish troops found themselves facing each other at Chanak, on the Asiatic shore of the supposedly demilitarised Dardanelles, Lloyd George called on the empire to support Britain in a war against Turkey. But the French deserted him, and this time so did the Conservatives. Their leader Bonar Law published a letter in *The Times*, on 7 October, which said that Britain could not be the 'policeman of the world'. A meeting of Conservative MPs at the Carlton Club on the morning of 19 October unhitched the Conservative party from the Lloyd George chariot. Lloyd George resigned at four o'clock and the king sent for Bonar Law.

The breakup of the Coalition in 1922 poured domestic politics into the two-party mould which has lasted, with some aberrations, to this day. As Keynes put it in 1926, the future task of liberalism would be to supply the Conservative party with Cabinets, and the Labour party with ideas.

From Dynamic Centre to Soft Centre

The age of Lloyd George was succeeded by the age of Baldwin and MacDonald. Hyperactivity gave way to an inactivity more in keeping with Britain's postwar fatigue. In 1923 MacDonald, Labour's new leader, claimed that 'there are only two parties in politics today . . . the capitalist party and the Labour and Socialist party'. This set up the rhetorical debate which was to dominate British politics for most of the century. The reality was less dramatic. The socialist advance MacDonald envisaged was of the imperceptible variety. This enabled him to form a close political partnership with the Conservative leader Baldwin, even before they got together in the same government in 1931. Together the two leaders dominated interwar British politics. Each was Prime Minister for seven years, Baldwin in 1923, 1924–9 and 1935–7, MacDonald in 1924 and 1929–35. MacDonald reined in the left and Baldwin reined in the right. Their partnership was fortified by their common loathing of Lloyd George.

The challenge facing any Conservative party in an era of independent working-class politics was how to offset the huge working-class preponderance of voters. The middle class was still very small: in 1938, only 14 per cent of the population were salary earners and 6 per cent self-employed. Baldwin understood that the only path to electoral success was to refuse to fight the class war. He also understood that the working class was not synonymous with the trades unions and Labour party. Women were not unionised; Protestant workers voted

Conservative in regions of high Irish Catholic immigration; a section of the working class had a vested interest in capitalist success as a result of their savings. He was the first practitioner of what came to be known as consensus politics: government from the moderate centre. Baldwin was a master at expressing non-political, 'soft' Christian, family and patriotic ideas in moving words; he evoked a gentlemanly ideal of 'Englishness'. His ruminating oratory gave him a moral authority unique in interwar politics. The Baldwin style brought electoral but not political hegemony. The Conservatives deferred to working-class sensibilities more than the workers deferred to upper-class leadership. They won a large proportion of the working-class vote by not frightening them. The price paid was the party's inability to carry out its preferred policies, or indeed any coherent policy. Accommodation was the order of the day. This constantly threatened breakaway movements to the right.

In foreign policy, Baldwin displayed a similar inactivity, his refusal to fight the class war being matched by a refusal to prepare for any other. An astringent critic, John Strachey, saw him as 'a perfect statesman for an empire in decline; he realises instinctively that almost anything anyone does will only make matters worse'. One of his favourite ruminating spots was Aix-les-Bains, where he spent lengthy annual holidays. Holiday time was the time he liked best.

Labour faced a similar dilemma. Like the socialist Fabians, MacDonald believed in the 'inevitability of gradualness' – 'Socialism,' he once wrote, 'comes as the dawn.' This meant one did not have to do too much to bring it about. MacDonald's opposition to the war made him a hero of the left to which he never belonged. Once he became leader of the Labour party in 1922, he was determined that Labour should prove itself 'fit to govern' in its own right, and not as a junior partner of the Liberals. This meant doing nothing that would frighten the middle class. He also enlarged Labour's appeal to the radical intelligentsia, chiefly the anti-war Liberals, the notorious vagueness of his oratory helping in both respects, before it finally descended into incoherence. (His unique ability, Churchill noted, was to 'compress the largest number of words into the smallest amount of thought'.) He was eager to encourage upper-class recruits: his first Cabinet was stuffed with Liberal as well as Tory grandees. When he formed his first government in 1924, the rich locked up their silver: a few fled abroad, never to return. After a few months of MacDonald they breathed more easily. He made Labour respectable. This was his service to social democracy.

The Baldwin–MacDonald duumvirate helped keep Britain free from the violent social and political convulsions which wrecked democracy over much of Europe between the wars. This was a notable achievement, which we can appreciate better today than could the impatient radicals like Keynes, Mosley and Orwell who lived through it. The cost, though, was stagnation, complacency and loss of energy. These men, and the society they reflected, recoiled from the blood-letting of the First World War. They craved 'peace in our time', but the times were out of joint.

Stagnation in the 1920s

Foreign policy did not make too many demands of Britain in the 1920s. Lloyd George had failed to pacify Europe, but the French army, American money and the passage of time brought about some healing. The 'Ten Year Rule' adopted in 1919 assumed that that there would be no great war for a decade and that Britain would not need an expeditionary force in that time; the 'rule' further allowed defence expenditure to be slashed from £604 million in 1919 to £111 million in 1922, and it was cut even further in the mid-1920s by Churchill at the Treasury. In 1923 Britain finally settled its war debt with the United States, and the following year the Dawes Plan fixed the total amount and annual schedules of German reparations at levels which the Germans said they accepted. The Locarno treaty of 1925 completed the work of Versailles, with Britain, France, Germany and Italy guaranteeing the Franco-German frontier. These steps led to the return of American private capital to Europe and the first tentative moves to European unification. There were hints, in China and the Middle East, that Britain's grasp was weakening. But generally the 1920s was a silver age for British power: like Baldwin, it did not have to work all that hard.

The war had shown the worth of empire, but failed to produce an imperial policy – the prewar effort to unite it economically had failed, as had the wartime effort to unite it politically. The empire lacked a doctrinal basis. In place of imperial doctrine there was imperial sentiment. Its hold on the popular imagination grew, its symbols and rituals serving as a unifying myth and a comforting evocation of greatness. Imperial decorations like CBE, OBE and MBE entered the honours' lists under George V in 1917. 'Empire Day' was started on 24 May 1902, the date of Queen Victoria's birthday, but only became an official holiday in 1916, when commemoration for the imperial dead started to mingle with imperial festivity.

Nor was there yet any need to think about Europe. In 1930, the Foreign Office responded to the Briand Plan for European unification with the discouraging message that it could not 'help to create any political or economic group which could in any way be regarded as hostile to the American . . . continent, or which would weaken our political co-operation with the other members of the British Commonwealth' – words which reappeared throughout the century.

The flaw in Britain's world position, even in the relatively benign decade of the 1920s, was the malfunctioning of its economy, hitherto the bedrock of its international role; and this was to contribute to the collapse of the world economy in 1929–30. Unemployment averaged 10 per cent between 1923 and 1929, double from before the war. Governments of both parties simply stood aside. Economic policy was left to the Treasury and the Bank of England, who put their faith in sound money, balanced budgets and international trade.

The problem was not just that Britain's old trades – cotton, coal, ship-building and metals – were losing world market share, and Britain was losing its share of that. It was that Britain was also failing to win a leading share in the export of *new* products. In 1924 the volume of exports was only 72 per cent of prewar, with imports at their prewar level.

It now seems clearer than it did at the time that between 1919 and 1922 the British economy suffered from two major 'shocks'. The first was a 'supply' shock – a once and for all increase in British unit labour costs. Second was a 'demand' shock: the savage deflation of prices to prepare for the return to the gold standard at the prewar parity. These shocks left the real wage, the purchasing power of the money wage, higher at the end of the depression in 1922 than it had been in the boom of 1920. Britain's export performance would have been significantly better, and its unemployment less, had Keynes's policy of low interest rates and a 'managed' exchange rate been adopted.

Instead, the commitment to refixing the pound to gold at its prewar parity of $4.86 to the pound entailed deflating the economy by raising interest rates. The restoration was accomplished by Churchill at the Exchequer on 28 April 1925. Churchill soon judged his decision to put sterling back on the gold standard as the worst mistake of his life. A paternalist at heart, he would have preferred 'Finance less proud and Industry more content'. But financial discipline, argued his Treasury advisers, was the only way of restoring 'reality' to wage bargaining. Keynes was scathing: 'The policy [of restoring the prewar parity]', he wrote, 'can only attain its end by intensifying unemployment without limit, until the workers are ready to accept the necessary reduction of money wages under the pressure of "hard facts".'

Keynes's prediction that the Bank of England would shrink from applying in full rigour the measures that its policy entailed was soon borne out. The return to gold led to the first and only general strike in British history, with coal at its heart. The Miners' Federation refused to accept wage reductions. On 5 May 1926, the General Council of the TUC called a general strike in support of the miners. Terrified by the thought that this might be a revolutionary act, it called it off a week later. The miners were starved back on the owners' terms in the autumn. Though devoid of revolutionary intent, the general strike was enough to deter employers from any concerted attack on wage levels. So heavy unemployment remained, especially in the export sector, with the overvalued pound maintained by high interest rates and short-term borrowing from abroad.

Mass unemployment was, in fact, the condition of the Baldwin–MacDonald consensus. For one thing it tamed the unions. The twentieth-century pattern is clear: the unions slept when prices were falling, and became alertly wakeful when they were rising. Given the industrial militancy which accompanied inflation, it is not altogether surprising that policy-makers chose deflation. What made heavy unemployment tolerable was the relatively generous amounts, and conditions for the receipt of, unemployment benefit, and the ability of employers, especially in the cotton trade, to manipulate the 'dole' to keep their employees working 'half time'. Industrial stagnation was the price of industrial peace.

Politicians and the Slump

In the 1930s external shocks destroyed the hope that Britain might enjoy its diminished estate in peace. Two portents foretold a much more troubled world: the great depression of 1929–33 and the

appointment of Hitler as German Chancellor. These, and especially
the last, confronted the pacific duo of Baldwin and MacDonald with
problems which threatened to overwhelm them.

MacDonald formed his second minority Labour government,
dependent on Liberal support, in 1929 just before the great depression
hit. The slump raised unemployment to over 20 per cent between 1931
and 1933. It was still nearly 12 per cent when war broke out in 1939.
Britain escaped relatively lightly from the depression, partly because its
economy was already quite depressed. Between 1929 and 1932
industrial output fell by 12 per cent, compared with 41 per cent in
Germany. MacDonald's image of the world helplessly engulfed in an
'economic blizzard' appealed to a nation wearied of political stunts. In
a blizzard a government, like a household, was supposed to batten
down the hatches and wait for the storm to pass. Economic battening-
down took the form of governments reducing their spending as their
income from taxes fell. Why this would do anything to promote
recovery was not very well explained.

In MacDonald's government, the dynamic spirit was represented by
the thirty-two-year-old Chancellor of the Duchy of Lancaster, Sir
Oswald Mosley, a convert to socialism from the Tory backwoods.
When his proposals for fighting the depression with big public
spending were rejected, he resigned in May 1930, making a resignation
speech so masterful that only his later fall from grace prevents it from
being remembered as one of parliament's great oratorical occasions. A
few months later he started the 'New Party' in which his associate John
Strachey soon detected 'the cloven hoof of Fascism'.

With unemployment rising, it proved impossible to balance the
budget on the basis of existing revenue. In 1931 the Conservatives and
Liberals told MacDonald that £56 million of economy cuts was
insufficient. Instead of resigning, MacDonald, on 25 August 1931,
accepted King George V's invitation to form a 'National Government'
with the Conservatives to 'save the pound'. He was followed into the
new government by four members of his Cabinet but supported by
only thirteen of his party, the rest, led by Arthur Henderson, going into
opposition.

The pound, however, refused to be saved. Following a 'mutiny' of
naval ratings at Invergordon which seemed to portend the end of the
empire, the flight from sterling accelerated, and on 21 September 1931
the gold standard was suspended, never to be restored. Urged on by

the Conservatives, MacDonald appealed to the country for a 'Doctor's Mandate' just five weeks later. The result was the greatest landslide in British electoral history, the government winning 554 seats to Labour's 52. Of the 554 MPs, 473 were Conservatives. MacDonald had been worth three million votes to them, and a further four years as Prime Minister was his reward.

The economic engine started stuttering back into life as soon as Britain left the gold standard. The pound sank, stimulating exports; interest rates fell to 2 per cent, producing a private-housing boom with its associated level of high demand for consumer durables, and the growth of building societies to finance home buying; the war debt was refinanced at lower cost; help was provided for the older industries to shed their surplus capacity; the introduction of Protection and a favourable shift in the terms of trade left more purchasing power to be spent on home-produced goods. The essence of the 'business conservatism' of the 1930s was that it raised profits relative to wages, through devaluation, Protection, cheap money, restriction of capital exports and encouragement of cartels and collusive behaviour. This stimulated business to invest: extra investment provided extra employment.

This mixture of policy and events enabled the national government to preside over a substantial market-based recovery which helped the growth of a mass-consumption economy. The big political beneficiary of the recovery was the Conservative party. Baldwin replaced MacDonald as Prime Minister in June 1935, a general election in October 1935 confirming what was now a purely Conservative regime with another massive, though reduced, majority. Neville Chamberlain replaced Baldwin in May 1937. Little has been written about the domestic policies of the national governments, because there was little to write about. It was a period of legislative lull. Budgets were regularly balanced without the aid of Keynesian stimulants; there were no significant innovations in social policy. A miserly £8 million was allocated between 1934 and 1938 to the 'special areas' of heavy unemployment. Baldwin handled the abdication of King Edward VIII with consummate tact and skill. The national government fulfilled its economic purpose simply by being there.

Why did the slump of the 1930s fail to shake Britain's social and political order? The Webbs argued that MacDonald had succumbed to the 'aristocratic embrace'. The more general thesis of the left, reproduced in dozens of publications down to the 1980s, after which such discussions appeared redundant, was that the British working class had been betrayed, as it would continue to be, by a leadership wedded to parliamentarism, compromise and respectability. But the premise is false: there was very little evidence of working-class radicalism. Trades unions were reactionary, not revolutionary. More interesting is the failure in the interwar years to develop a middle-class radicalism in opposition to the restored forces of Treasury orthodoxy and City finance. John Maynard Keynes and Sir Oswald Mosley were almost alone. It was in this respect that the collapse of the historic Liberal party was a great misfortune. The replacement Labour party was debarred by its socialist commitment from having new ideas about how to make the capitalist system work better. As a Labour party manifesto of 1934 put it: 'There is no halfway house between a society based on private ownership . . . and a society [based on] public ownership.' The halfway house was, in fact, the work of two Liberals, Keynes and Beveridge, but it took another world war for it to be built.

The device of a national government was a superb political ploy, neutering both right and left, in the classic style of Whig statecraft. MacDonald and Baldwin could now do, yoked together, what they had done separately in the 1920s, which was to crowd out extremism. However, the main reason for lack of political ferment is that the interwar years were not nearly as bad as folklore made them out to be. Historians have long since demolished the Orwellian orthodoxy of a Britain of dole queues, means tests and hunger marches. Persistently high unemployment was confined to the 'special areas'. These included Scotland, whose disproportionate industrial decline led to the foundation of the Scottish Nationalist party in 1928. Elsewhere it was balanced by the spread of modest prosperity. Between 1932 and 1937, real GDP rose by 23 per cent, or 4 per cent a year – a faster rate of growth than anywhere outside Scandinavia. Business confidence was boosted by the size of the Conservative majorities; Conservatives majorities were boosted by the prosperity spreading in the south and Midlands through ribbons of new housing to new factories built on green-field sites. Suburban, neo-Elizabethan Britain was born, serviced by new retail outlets, and linked to factories and offices by branch railways lines and motor cars. Fifteen million Britons could now enjoy a week's annual holiday by the sea in Butlins' camps or Blackpool. 'By 1939', wrote the Canadian historian Susan Pedersen, 'the British as a whole were drinking and brawling less, and reading, smoking, and gambling more.' Britain remained highly divided by class, but there was enough easement of working-class conditions to blunt an overt class-war appeal.

MacDonald and Baldwin were also successful in lowering the political temperature in, and on, India. Throughout the interwar years the Indian Raj was slowly slipping from Britain's grasp, but there was no policy available except to postpone the rate of slippage. The MacDonald–Baldwin strategy for keeping India in the empire was to involve the Indian political class in its government. This would avoid the mistakes over Ireland. The problem, as with Ireland, was the Tory party, the diehard wing of which now found an improbable leader in Winston Churchill, scornful of any 'appeasement' of the 'half-naked fakir' Mahatma Gandhi. Baldwin adroitly managed to confine Churchill's following of MPs to fewer than one hundred. Both sides were deluding themselves: the moderates in their belief that India could be peacefully groomed for Dominion status, Churchill in believing it could be held by force without 'frightfulness'. Churchill failed to derail the Government of India Act of 1935 which created an All-Indian Federation of British-ruled provinces and princely states. What he derailed was his own career.

The Indian context is important for understanding Britain's slowness in 'facing up' to the dictators. Almost single-handedly Churchill kept India at the centre of Tory politics during the first two years of Hitler's dictatorship, with most of Baldwin's waning energy devoted to preventing a split in the Tory ranks. 'Appeasement' was Churchill's dirty word for policy to Gandhi, not to Hitler. It was not until August 1935 that Churchill himself started to mend his political fences by pointing to dangers 'larger and nearer than Indian dangers'. By then he was completely discredited with the Baldwin loyalists, who assumed that his new campaign for rearmament was simply a further step in a career devoted largely to self-promotion.

Chamberlain's Decade

Had events – that is, Hitler – been kinder to him, Neville Chamberlain, Chancellor of the Exchequer from 1932 to 1937, and Prime Minister from 1937 to 1940, would have gone down as one of the greatest British statesmen, the 1930s as one of Britain's most successful decades, the

Chamberlain dynasty, father and two sons, as the most remarkable British political family of the century.

With the negotiation of the imperial preference system at Ottawa in 1932, Chamberlain accomplished his father's dream of uniting the empire through trade. The 'sterling area' which emerged at the time of sterling's devaluation in 1931 was the financial counterpart of these preferential trade arrangements. About twenty countries, not all of them in the empire, devalued their currencies in line with sterling, and some agreed to hold their foreign exchange reserves in sterling in return for privileged access to the British capital market.

Imperial economics pointed to isolation from the continent of Europe. The diplomatic framework for this had been the Locarno treaty of 1925, negotiated by Austen Chamberlain, Neville's elder brother and Baldwin's Foreign Secretary. This apparently achieved what had eluded British diplomacy before 1914 – the security of western Europe against German attack. (It did not cover frontiers in eastern Europe.) Yet, despite Locarno, twenty years after the Treaty of Versailles Britain found itself once more at war with Germany. Why was this? Many historians question the wisdom of Britain going to war in 1914; hardly any doubt that the war which started in 1939 was a 'good war'.

The consensus is somewhat mysterious, given the fact that Hitler's Germany seemingly posed less of an obvious threat to Britain than had the Kaiser's. British policy-makers believed rightly that Hitler's long-term goals were to the east, and even here they were reasonably acquiescent, Baldwin remarking in 1936 that if there was 'any fighting in Europe to be done' he would like to see 'the Bolshies and the Nazis doing it'. So why did Britain go to war to stop Hitler from recovering Danzig, a German city in Poland which the Versailles treaty had detached from Germany against the will of its inhabitants, and which most people in Britain, if they thought of it at all, agreed he could have for the (decent) asking?

There was an almost unanimous consensus for peace before 1939. Churchill, leader of the anti-appeasers, was an isolated figure until after the Munich Agreement of 1938. Churchill took his stand on the balance of power: any German expansion beyond its Versailles treaty limits was *ipso facto* a threat to Britain, which must be resisted by big armaments and encircling alliances. This would have made sense when Hitler was weak, but it hardly did so after 1936, when Hitler had rearmed and the USA and the Soviet Union could not be brought into the 'balance'. So Churchill's 'realism' was in fact pie in the sky, except in its call for a much earlier British rearmament.

Accommodation with Hitler was the object of Neville Chamberlain's appeasement policy. But Britain's leaders lacked the ruthlessness (and public support) to pursue it to its bitter end. Leaders cannot for long run a foreign policy that conflicts with the moral instincts of their people. Like most foreigners Hitler mistook the British character, assuming that because Britain was so successful as an empire builder its moral vocabulary was simply a cloak for self-interest. Self-interest, he thought, would bring it to see the advantages of a deal with Germany. But he missed a crucial dimension. Ever since Protestant England had first taken up the cudgels against Catholic Europe, the British had defined their self-interest in moral, even religious, terms. Once Chamberlain's appeasement policy started to seem to the British people a shameful betrayal of their values it was doomed.

The real indictment of British foreign policy in the 1930s is not that it tried to appease Germany when Germany was strong but that it failed to keep it weak. For this failure Baldwin and MacDonald had an obvious excuse: the pacifist state of public opinion. To the retrospective horror of the trenches was added the threat of destruction from the air. By appealing to the principle of national self-determination, Hitler was also able to exploit the widespread feeling that Germany had been unjustly treated at Versailles. The Labour party's hostility to rearmament was an important constraint, mainly because of the need for trades union cooperation. However, with a majority of 470 in the Commons, the government's political timidity was at least partly self-generated.

This political constraint was reinforced by the financial constraint. Germany's rapid rearmament was based on Hitler's full employment policy, which hugely improved Germany's 'guns versus butter' trade-off. Britain missed the chance to do the same thing. A full-employment policy would have changed the political context of rearmament by providing the unemployed with jobs in the derelict areas. Instead, Britain's recovery from depression, market-led and largely confined to the south-east and the Midlands, was slower and less complete than Germany's. Failure to add full employment policy to his recipe for resisting Hitler was a major gap in Churchill's polemics. But Churchill never understood economics.

The best chance of 'nailing down' Hitler was between 1933 and 1936. In principle British policy was to bind Germany and Japan to arms limitation agreements. Hitler played skilfully on this by offering a succession of plausible arms pacts. Japan also seemed receptive to a new naval agreement. These propositions ran into resistance from France in Europe and the United States in Asia, and the opportunity was missed. The only arms pact concluded was the bilateral Anglo-German naval agreement of 1935, which limited the German navy to 35 per cent of Britain's. This assured Britain its much needed naval supremacy in the North Sea. But Japan remained unappeased in the Pacific.

In 1935–6 British foreign policy unravelled in the face of increasing assertiveness by Italy and Germany. Willing neither to resist nor to conciliate the dictators, Britain and France acquiesced in a series of bold coups which weakened their prestige and prepared the ground for further assaults. This dismal sequence started in October 1935 when Mussolini invaded Abyssinia; Hitler, noting the infirmity of the western response to Italian aggression, sent German troops into the demilitarised Rhineland on 7 March 1936, claiming that the Franco-Soviet pact had abrogated the assumptions of Locarno. France and Britain did nothing. The last chance for a costlessly firm stand came with the outbreak of the Spanish civil war in July 1936. When Italy and Germany started supplying arms to the rebel General Franco, and Russia to the republican government, Britain devised a policy of 'non-intervention' to localise the conflict. Britain's failure to enforce this policy by a naval blockade reinforced the lesson of Abyssinia and the Rhineland: gambles could safely be taken by the brigand powers in face of extreme war fear by the democracies.

This phase of drift was terminated when Neville Chamberlain succeeded Baldwin as Prime Minister in May 1937. He was determined to take over control of foreign policy from the palsied grip of the Foreign Office. His last act as Chancellor had been to authorise, at long last, a massive British rearmament drive (£1.5 billion over five years, £400 million of which was to be borrowed). This was heavily concentrated on defence of Britain and its trade routes, Chamberlain believing that Britain lacked the resources to create 'a million men Army' for continental warfare. Indeed, the British army of 154,000 (plus 50,000 troops in India) was smaller than it had been in 1914. Chamberlain intended to settle all outstanding issues with Hitler and

Mussolini on a businesslike basis. 'I believe the double policy of rearmament and better relations with Germany and Italy will carry us safely through the danger period, if only the Foreign Office will play up', he wrote on becoming PM. This was the start of appeasement as a systematic policy. In his earlier imperial policy, and now in his search for agreement with Germany, Neville Chamberlain had taken up the mantle of his father. Britain would allow the Reich to expand to include ethnic Germans beyond its borders provided, as Chamberlain's emissary Halifax told Hitler in November 1937, this could be done peacefully and through 'reasonable agreements with Germany reasonably reached'.

The flaw in this strategy of peaceful German expansion was the lack of any mechanism for accomplishing it if some of the victim countries chose to resist having their Germanic limbs chopped off. The incorporation of Austria into the Reich on 12 March 1938 caused no problem because Austria was ethnically German. It was different when appeasement meant the dismemberment of democratic, multi-national Czechoslovakia. The Munich Agreement of 30 September 1938 was brought about by two acts of bullying: Britain's pressuring of the Czech government to cede the ethnically German Sudetenland to Germany, and Hitler's intimidation of Chamberlain to concede to the German demand for immediate military occupation of the ceded area. Chamberlain returned from Munich waving a piece of paper signed by Hitler, which, he claimed, promised 'peace with honour, peace in our time'. 'How horrible, fantastic, incredible,' he broadcast just before Munich, 'that we should be digging trenches and trying on gas masks here because of a quarrel in a far-away country between people of whom we know nothing.'

The Munich settlement was very popular – Chamberlain was cheered from the balcony of Buckingham Palace – though more out of a sense of relief than of pride. Thereafter appeasement was under-mined by Hitler himself. Surprised and emboldened by the ease with which he had secured a British capitulation, he convinced himself that he could, if necessary, discount further British interference with his plans. The unleashing of Kristallnacht against the German Jews on 7 November 1938 showed how indifferent he had become to world opinion. The disintegration of the Czech state in March 1939 was a natural consequence of the Munich Agreement; nevertheless, the German occupation of Prague on 15 March 1939 was sufficiently triumphal to turn public opinion decisively against further unilateral concessions to Germany. Yet Britain's guarantees to Poland and Romania, which almost immediately followed, were the panicky responses to rumours of an imminent German invasion of one or other of these countries, circulated by the Romanian ambassador, Tilea, which turned out to have no foundation. It was the first commitment Britain had ever made to the unstable territorial status quo in eastern Europe.

Chamberlain still hoped that the transfer of Danzig to Germany could be negotiated between Germany and Poland. (The League of Nations' interest in the matter had long become academic.) But Britain's guarantee of Poland's frontiers, as well as the Poles' unfounded belief in the strength of their armed forces, deprived the Polish Foreign Minister, Beck, of any incentive to parley. Hitler looked on Britain to put pressure on the Poles as they had on the Czechs, but this time the British would not say 'Boo to Beck'. Hitler decided to settle the Polish question by force, freeing himself from the threat of a two-front war by the Ribbentrop–Molotov pact with Russia of 23 August. This thieves' contract divided Poland between them. When German troops crossed the Polish frontier on 31 August, Britain and France, in fulfilment of their guarantee, declared war on Germany on 3 September. Britain declared war on behalf of the non-white empire. Australia and New Zealand felt honour-bound by the British declaration. Canada and South Africa declared war separately, South Africa after a change of government. The Irish Free State stayed neutral.

The Anglo-French declaration of war had no effect on Poland's fortunes. German troops entered Warsaw on 27 September; the next day Germany and Russia settled their zones of occupation. Although Chamberlain immediately brought Churchill back into his old post as First Lord of the Admiralty, the first eight months of hostilities have been rightly called the 'phoney war'. Britain and France were in no position to stop Germany conquering Poland, and had no offensive plans of their own. Hitler's path to the Ukraine was blocked by the pact with Russia, and, in view of Britain's refusal to make peace, he saw no alternative but to force both France and Britain out of the war. On 10 May 1940, the Third Reich sprang its military might on Belgium, Holland and France. The same day, Chamberlain, his appeasement policy in ruins, resigned as Prime Minister, and Winston Churchill became Prime Minister at the head of a coalition with the Labour and

Liberal parties. France soon fell to the German 'blitzkrieg'; Britain's expeditionary force was extracted, with much difficulty and minus its equipment, from the French port of Dunkirk. The new war leader offered his people 'blood, toil, tears and sweat'.

The Finest Hour and Churchill's War Machine

Bolingbroke said of Marlborough: 'He was so great a man that I have forgot his vices.' There is a strong temptation to write similarly of Marlborough's great descendant Winston Spencer Churchill. Yet Marlborough won an empire, Churchill lost one. Both were heroes, but their heroic acts had different consequences. Churchill is the most ambiguous figure in the 'decline and fall' story. Rhetorically, he was an unashamed imperialist. The empire was in his blood; his early years were spent on its frontiers. Yet he achieved totemic status as the conduit by which imperial, aristocratic Britain passed into the post-imperial, social democratic age. Did he understand what he was doing? Or did he care? By the 1930s he needed, as he put it, a war to 'win the Derby'; he also needed several gigantic strokes of luck to win the war.

Unlike the First World War, the Second falls neatly into two halves. In the first half Britain was losing, in the second it was winning. The change in fortunes was due mainly to Hitler's hubristic blunders. Britain started the war with only one significant ally, France, and France was knocked out in June 1940. Hitler added two more: by invading Russia on 22 June 1941 and gratuitously declaring war on the United States on 7 December 1941. Neither power would have come in on its own volition – or at least in time to avert a British defeat. This fact vindicates Chamberlain's strategy, not Churchill's.

Britain's 'finest hour' was the RAF's defeat of the Luftwaffe in the 'battle of Britain' in August–September 1940, which put paid to Hitler's immediate plan to invade Britain. As Churchill famously put it 'never in the field of human conflict was so much owed by so many to so few'. The 'battle of Britain' was succeeded by the 'battle of the Atlantic', Hitler's attempt to force Britain out of the war by cutting off its supplies from America. The naval war was hard fought. The British navy commanded the waves, German submarines the depths. For much of 1941 and 1942 tonnage sunk exceeded tonnage replaced. It was only American help short of war which enabled Britain to hold on in 1941. The 'battle of the Atlantic' was not finally won until mid-1943, with the breaking of the German naval codes. Meanwhile, the British had lost their East Asian empire to Japan. On 15 February 1942, Singapore surrendered, together with 100,000 British and imperial troops. Churchill called it 'the greatest disaster to British arms which our history records'.

The rapid collapse of France forced Britain to fight the 'peripheral' war which the 'easterners' had unsuccessfully demanded in 1915, and which was the only one it could now fight on its own. For two years Britain's Eighth Army fought the German Afrika Corps across the deserts of Egypt and Libya, in an almost self-contained war. This only joined up with the main war in 1943 once Anglo-American forces started to fight their way up the spine of Italy.

After the end of 1941, there were still defeats to come, but victory was no longer in doubt. Three events in November–December 1942 mark the turning point: the Anglo-American invasion of North Africa, Montgomery's victory over Rommel at El Alamein in Egypt, and, most important of all, the surrender of a huge German army at Stalingrad. The rest was essentially mopping up, though the Germans and Japanese, being martial nations, fought hard and resourcefully against increasingly unfavourable odds. British armies under Montgomery took part with the Americans in the liberation of France in 1944 and the push into Germany in 1945. Britain played a minor part in the American defeat of Japan in the Pacific. Its other key contributions were off-stage, breaking the German secret codes (it was the British who invented 'Colossus', the first computer) and contributing to the development of the atomic bomb which hastened the end of the war in the Pacific. By contrast the Anglo-American aerial bombardment of German cities, which killed 600,000 German civilians, strengthened, rather than weakened, German morale. With Germany's surrender on 7 May 1945, Britain, still led by Churchill, emerged as one of the 'Big Three' victors, with the ordering of the world in their hands.

Compared with the Russians and the Germans, or indeed with their own casualties between 1914 and 1918, the British had a 'light' war. The home population suffered more, starting with the blitz in September 1940 and ending with the 'doodlebugs' of 1944–5. Altogether, 60,000 were killed through aerial bombardment. Physical destruction of property was estimated at £1.45 billion. But manpower losses, at 300,000 killed (plus 35,000 in the merchant navy), were less than half those in the First World War.

Churchill was a more dominating war leader than Lloyd George, chiefly because he had more political support, and because there was less fighting to do, which reduced the role of the military. The Second World War was also better run than the First. The planning instruments, which had taken four years of experiment to discover in the earlier conflict, were almost immediately ready for use in this one. Churchill headed a Defence Committee which ran the military side of the war. He chose the strategy, the generals implemented it. Sir John Anderson headed a Lord President's Committee which organised the home front. This second super-committee became the hub of the domestic planning effort, charged with allocating resources – manpower, raw materials, transport – in line with national priorities.

War finance was also better handled. This time the government imposed swingeing taxes early on. Kingsley Wood's Budget of 7 April 1941 raised the standard rate of income tax to 50 per cent, the top marginal rate to 97.5 per cent, and brought in 3.25 million new working-class taxpayers. More importantly for the future, it was the first use of the government's Budget to try to 'balance the accounts of the nation' rather than just the accounts of the government, in line with the new macro-economics of Keynes. A further innovation of 1943 was the Pay as You Earn scheme of compulsory wage deductions at source, needed for the new mass base of income tax payers. In addition to taxation, the war was partly financed by 'cheap money': the government's maximum borrowing rate was 3 per cent, and most of its war debt was borrowed at negative real interest rates. The government covered 54 per cent of its domestic spending by taxation in the years 1940–45 as opposed to 32 per cent between 1914 and 1918 and the price level in 1945 was only 30 per cent higher than in 1939, as compared to a doubling of prices in the 1914–18 war, almost the whole of the rise having occurred before the 1941 Budget.

The problem of external finance was solved differently. This was because this time the United States gifted rather than lent about half Britain's external cost through the 'Lend-Lease' programmes started in March 1941, and because, unlike in the first war, Britain drew heavily on its empire for loans. The decisive contribution of these two sources of external financing to Britain's ability to wage war can be seen in the figures. Of Britain's cumulative external deficit of approaching £10 billion over the six years of war, £4.5 billion was covered by Lend-Lease from the USA, £500 million by 'Mutual Aid' from Canada, a further £1.2

billion by the sale of foreign assets – roughly a quarter of its overseas investments – and £3.4 billion from the sterling area.

Unlike in the First World War, Labour was fully integrated into the war effort from the moment Churchill took over, with Labour's Ernest Bevin, Minister of Labour, the second man in the government. Between 1940 and 1941 a 'social contract' was forged whereby the trades unions were induced to accept income tax for the workers and wage restraint in return for government commitment to stable prices, subsidisation of necessities and a 'fair' distribution of sacrifice, largely through rationing and punitive taxation on the rich, with an Excess Profits Tax of 100 per cent. This 'social contract' approach to economic and social policy set the framework for postwar politics.

State and people came much closer together than in the First World War. Bombing to some extent abolished the distinction between the home front and the fighting forces, and the spread of discomfort was regarded almost as a benefit, not least because it was fairly distributed, from Buckingham Palace downwards. The high level of wartime consensus meant that voluntarism worked better in the second than in the first conflict, both in industrial relations and civil society. The government took the usual powers – to forbid strikes, suppress any subversive publications, to lock up anyone suspected of sympathising with the enemy. However, it made little use of these powers, since opposition to the war was confined to small political fringes. The war exemplified a spirit of national unity which retained a permanent hold on the imagination, not just of the left. The war was doubly blessed, by victory and by war socialism.

Consequences of the War

However successful in its own terms, war finance mortgaged Britain's postwar future. On the domestic side, it left a dreadful legacy of high taxation which survived into the 1980s. War expenditure took 56 per cent of national income; capital depreciation 14 per cent of non-war plant. On the external side, Britain entered the war as an independent great power; it emerged from it a client of the United States, shorn of a large chunk of its net overseas assets. The 'sterling balances' enabled Britain to maintain sterling as a major postwar reserve currency, to the benefit of the City of London, but at the cost of continuous sterling crises. Less profligate in manpower than its predecessor, the Second World War was more profligate in material.

In theory, the Second World War vindicated Churchill's historical thesis. The removal of the German, Japanese and Italian challenges to the British position should have made it easier for Britain to continue as a great power. Battered though it was, its economy was in much better shape than those of its defeated rivals, and European states like France. The British empire was intact, with the defeats in the Far East reversed. In practice, Britain's 'finest hour' was the prelude to its exit as a power of the first rank. Its economy, burdened by imperial nostalgia and dysfunctional labour relations, went into a long period of relative decline; this in turn denuded it of the resources to maintain its imperial position. Most important of all, Britain was not the real 'victor' in the war. It had 'hung on' against Germany; but Germany and Japan had been defeated by the United States and the Soviet Union. These were the new dominant powers.

The Second World War is still an indispensable point of reference for the notion of 'Britishness'. For years rulers and ruled lived in the shadow of the 'finest hour': 'When the bombs rained indiscriminately on Coventry and Clydesbank we knew we were one nation.' There was a sense of profound pride – victory had vindicated British institutions and the British view of themselves as a uniquely 'good' nation. By its exertions Britain had preserved its own freedom, and restored freedom to Europe. At the same time, the fruits of victory were undoubtedly disappointing. Postwar Britain looked like a defeated nation – grey, shabby, neglected, pitted with bomb craters. It should have been doing better. This feeling grew over time, as empire faded away and the defeated nations started to overtake Britain in all kinds of ways. The truth is that Britain's victory was pyrrhic. If war is, as Alan Milward has argued, an 'investment decision by the state', it is hard to see where the returns lay. Britain had lost, like the other countries of Europe, but was handicapped by the illusion it had won, and that there were fruits of victory to enjoy.

Labour in Power, 1945–1951

It was in this triumphant but stricken state that Labour's first majority government, elected in July 1945, set out both to build a British version of socialism and to maintain Britain's position as a world power. The wherewithal for both would come from a mixture of high taxation and an 'export drive'. Unlike after the First World War, the wartime spirit spilled over into peace. Probably the two most important reasons were a revulsion against the 1930s and the egalitarian 'social contract' of the war itself, which induced the middle class, if only temporarily, to accept a readjustment of its lifestyle. The war also legitimised Labour as a governing party. As a result, the war forged the 'postwar settlement' which lasted till the 1970s. The Baldwin–MacDonald middle way acquired substance in full employment, 'democratic planning', a 'mixed economy' of private and public sectors and a welfare state which embraced all in a universal citizenship.

The settlement did not amount to a consensus. Friedrich Hayek's *The Road to Serfdom* (1945), a searing attack on central planning which had six print runs in sixteen months, marked the start of the individualist fight-back. The Conservatives never accepted public ownership, the core Labour policy, and were lukewarm about the welfare state. The huge Labour majority of 1945 concealed the fact that the Conservatives retained 41 per cent of the popular vote: they lost because their share of the working-class vote fell.

The foundation of the postwar settlement was full employment. The 1944 Employment White Paper committed governments to 'maintain a high and stable level of employment'. The 1944 pledge soon evolved into a target rate of unemployment of between 2 and 3 per cent, and this rate was, in fact, achieved, even overachieved, for almost thirty years, abolishing the dreaded business cycle.

The welfare state was built on this foundation. Its intellectual basis was laid in the Beveridge Report of 1942. William Beveridge was the archetype of the Superior Person who knows best. Accepted by the Coalition government, his report proposed a comprehensive scheme of universal compulsory national insurance to cover the main contingencies of industrial life – unemployment, disability and retirement. This would replace the patchwork quilt of voluntary and compulsory insurance and charity which, badly sewn and full of holes, made up Britain's existing social security arrangements. The Beveridge approach was a compromise between individualism and collectivism: the insurance contribution would make benefit an earned entitlement, not state charity. To balance his insurance fund Beveridge assumed not just full employment, but a tax-financed National Health Service and family allowance system, both set up. By

1950, 46 per cent of government spending was devoted to the social budget.

Less popular, and less durable, was the nationalisation programme, though this was closest to the socialist heart. The nationalisation of the Bank of England in 1946 was symbolic. But between 1945 and 1951 Attlee's government took into public ownership the coal, gas, railway, road haulage and iron and steel industries, responsible for producing about 10 per cent of GDP, and which would receive 20 per cent of total investment. This was the core socialist programme of seizing the 'commanding heights' of the British economy. The dispossessed owners received generous compensation.

Nationalisation took the form, invented by Herbert Morrison when he created the London Passenger Authority in 1931, of setting up quasi-autonomous 'public corporations' which were supposed to be run by the old managers on business principles, but with social objectives – a contradiction which was never resolved in principle, and only resolved in practice by continuous subsidies. Labour ministers held the naïve belief that nationalisation would cause workers to work more enthusiastically and for less pay. The disappointments attendant on these hopes led to downgrading of public ownership in the socialist agenda of the 1950s.

In all the reformist flurry, there was no demand for institutional renovation. Wartime victory had vindicated British democracy. The successful state was there to be used, not to be reconstructed; the conventional character of British political and social arrangements was affirmed. The social revolution for which Labour stood was to be a top-down exercise in planning.

Full employment introduced a new problem: inflation. The Employment White Paper of 1944 urged the need for 'pay restraint' in return for full employment. However, this restraint tended to break down as conditions of peace returned. There was, then, a need to repress excessive wage growth by 'pay policy'. Evoking the wartime spirit, the Chancellor of the Exchequer, Sir Stafford Cripps, got the union leadership to agree to a 'wage freeze' in 1948. This lasted for three years; attempts to reproduce this success dominated industrial relations in the 1960s and 1970s. But the union commitment to 'free collective bargaining' precluded anything more than ad hoc bargains with governments deemed to be pro-Labour. Failure to define a legal role for trades unions in a peacetime private enterprise system proved to be the Achilles heel of postwar industrial relations.

Wartime success misled in two other ways. The Labour government had no incentive to tackle the underlying British problem of low productivity. With most European industries knocked out, imperial markets still captive and collusive agreements covering 60 per cent of manufacturing output, British businessmen at first had an easy time. So technological backwardness was not addressed. Secondly, the egalitarian system of incentives which united the nation for war proved unsuitable for a successful peacetime private enterprise economy. This was especially true of the tax system. The Beveridge universalist approach was very expensive, since a high proportion of benefits went to the non-poor. Had flows to the middle class been eliminated, direct taxes could have remained at the 1938 level without unbalancing the budget. However, the taboo against means-testing was then absolute. Helped by a continuation of food subsidies, working-class consumption in 1949 was estimated to be 22 per cent higher than in 1938, while that of the middle and wealthy classes was 18 and 42 per cent lower respectively. The combination of full employment and reduced post-tax incomes brought about the final demise of that fixture of middle-class life, domestic service.

Though Britain was exhausted, Labour leaders were just as determined as their Conservative predecessors to maintain the world position won by British arms. As Lord Franks put it, world leadership 'is part of the habit and furniture of our minds'. After the war, Churchill had insisted, in his famous metaphor of the 'three circles', that Britain would remain the head of the Commonwealth, the closest ally of the United States and the leading power in non-Communist Europe, the three tripods supporting each other. This remained the charter myth of British foreign policy till the 1970s, and even then it did not entirely vanish.

When the war ended, Britain had millions of men under arms controlling large parts of Europe, the Middle East, the Mediterranean and most of south-east Asia. But it was world power on American credit. In 1945 Keynes told the Labour government that the alternative to an American loan was 'to retire for the time being as a Great Power'. Despite the loan of $3.75 billion he negotiated in 1945 to bridge the huge peacetime balance of payments gap, retirement proved permanent. Over the years Britain's power ebbed away, the victim of a succession of economy cuts.

As Paul Kennedy tells it, the British empire 'receded spasmodically from one defensive line to another' until it finally disappeared.

The proximate cause of most retreats was a 'sterling crisis'. The first came in 1947, when Britain made the pound convertible on current account, in fulfilment of the terms of the American loan. Convertibility had to be suspended a month later, as holders of sterling rushed to convert their pounds into dollars. Four billion dollars of reserves, or more than the amount of the loan, were lost in 1947. With the help of a 30 per cent devaluation of the pound against the dollar in September 1949 (from $4.03 to $2.80 dollars), Britain's current account was turned round. But balance of payments crises continued to plague Britain till the 1970s.

The first sterling crisis precipitated Britain's withdrawal from Greece and surrender of the Palestine mandate. On 15 August 1947, it left India precipitately, causing hundreds of thousands of deaths as Hindus and Muslims started massacring each other. India and Pakistan became self-governing dominions within the British empire, but in 1949 the former chose to become a republic. By allowing republican India to stay in the Commonwealth, acknowledging only the British monarch as commonwealth head, the Attlee government took the decision to turn a club of whites into a creaking bridge between the white and coloured parts of the world. A year later Britain was gone from Burma and Ceylon.

The loss of India made the strategic aim of 'protecting the routes to India' redundant. However, a new mission was discovered. With Germany out of the way, the Foreign Office and military chiefs reinvented, as if by reflex, the great nineteenth-century game of checking Russian expansion, now in the guise of Soviet imperialism. The Foreign Secretary Ernest Bevin, who had spent his life fighting home-grown communists in the Transport and General Workers' Union, was an enthusiastic convert. 'Give me a million tons of coal,' he told a meeting of miners, 'and I will give you a foreign policy.' In 1947 the Labour Cabinet made the decision to build a British atomic bomb; peacetime conscription was introduced, for the first time. Bevin played a leading role setting up the North Atlantic Treaty Organization (NATO) in 1949, which committed Britain to a permanent garrison in central Europe. Britain's military expenditure ranged from 5 to 12 per cent of GDP for most of the Cold War years, much higher than that of the European members of NATO. However, economic weakness made British resistance to Soviet encroachments a pale shadow of the great game of the past.

The loss of Britain's East Asian empire prompted Whitehall, for the first time, to take an interest in Africa, which would be the new jewel in the crown. It encouraged postwar emigration, the white population of Southern Rhodesia increasing from 80,000 in 1945 to over 200,000 a decade later, and allocated money for 'colonial development'. The imperial preference system and the sterling area were also maintained, partly because they seemed to offer a relief from too great a dependence on America.

The strain of running a dual policy of a welfare state at home and world power abroad took its toll on the Labour government. Its decision to give the United States military support in resisting Communist North Korea's invasion of South Korea in June 1950 created a terminal crisis when it imposed prescription charges to help pay for rearmament, losing in the process Aneurin Bevan, architect of the welfare state. The Conservatives under the now-aged Churchill returned to power in October 1951.

Labour's first experience of majority government raises a question mark. Why was its attempt to build a New Jerusalem followed by thirteen years of Conservative rule? Usual explanations centre on exhaustion, splits, deaths, crises and bad luck. And there is a great deal in them. But the suspicion remains that what Labour was trying to achieve – the goals of the gentlemen in Whitehall who 'knew best' – was not exactly what the British people wanted. They wanted full employment and the welfare state, but they also wanted to relax after twelve extremely unrelaxing years saving the world from Hitler and building socialism. Churchill made 'easement' at home and abroad the main goal of his new administration. He aimed to 'give the working man what he had never had before – leisure. A four-day week and then three days of fun.'

The Empire's Last Stand: Conservative Britain, 1951–64

The Attlee government of 1945–51 was the furthest socialism was to reach in British life. This was not apparent at the time. The electoral struggle in the 1950s was very close, with Labour winning more votes than the Conservatives in 1951, and Labour might have done better still had the party not torn itself to pieces. The Conservatives only half believed that the future lay with them, so they were in an accommodating mood. 'Butskellism' was the word used to describe acceptance by the new Conservative Chancellor, 'Rab' Butler, of his predecessor Gaitskell's full employment policy.

The practical aim of Conservative policy during this period was to remove the taint of the 1930s. The Conservative governments of 1951–64 accepted full employment and the welfare state. There was no denationalisation except for the iron and steel industry, the most controversial of Labour's nationalisation measures. In these crucial respects, the postwar settlement was maintained. However, Conservative policy was not a mere replica of Labour's. Public spending was restrained to make possible tax cuts. There was modest deregulation – notably of the housing rental and retail markets – and a switch in emphasis from public to private housing. The positive Tory social vision was summed up in the phrase 'a property-owning democracy', and, as Health Minister, Harold Macmillan took pride in building 300,000 houses a year as against only 200,000 by his predecessor, Aneurin Bevan.

While the taint of the 1930s may have been forgotten, however, Conservative Britain was ruptured by the Suez crisis of 1956, which bifurcates the Conservative years. After this catastrophe it was never glad, confident morning again, though Macmillan retrieved a first-class political disaster with astonishing skill.

With the overthrow of the royal dynasty in 1952, Egypt had been converted from a restive British client into a spearhead of Arab nationalism under its charismatic leader Gamal Abdul Nasser. In 1954, with British resources overstretched by the conflicting demands of rearmament (to fight the Korean War) and Macmillan's domestic house building programme, Britain decided to abandon its almost besieged military base at the Suez Canal. On 26 July 1956, as soon as the last British soldiers left their Canal base, Nasser nationalised the Suez Canal Company, a joint Anglo-French consortium charged by an international treaty dating from 1881 with maintaining free navigation through the Canal. He did so partly to secure revenue to pay for his pet project the Aswan Dam, from which America had abruptly withdrawn funding. Claiming that free passage was endangered, France and Britain agreed to reverse the act of nationalisation, by force if

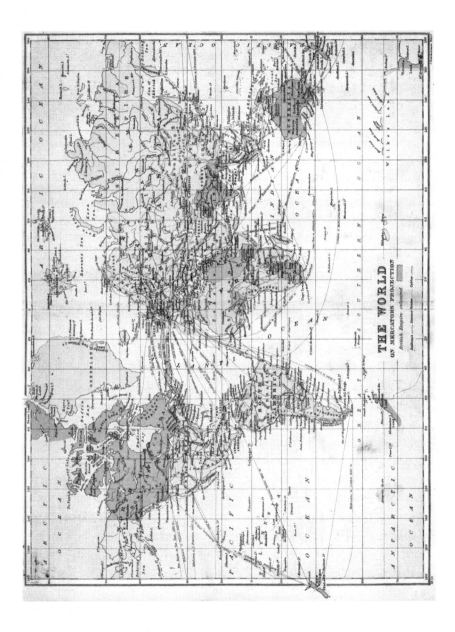

A Mercators Projection map of the World in 1900. The territories of the British Empire, here a darker shade, were originally highlighted in pink. The map shows the Empire's strength – its vast extent – and weakness, its dispersal across five continents. Its loss was the price Britain paid for the preservation of liberty. Was it worth it?

necessary. There was also, for the British, the matter of character. Nasser reminded Anthony Eden, Winston Churchill's neurotic successor, of Hitler. He was a dictator, and you cannot have a man like that, Eden said, 'with his finger on our windpipe'. Both nations resolved to act unilaterally – in defiance of the United Nations and, more importantly, the United States.

An Anglo-French expeditionary force of Second World War dimensions landed at Port Said on 5 November and advanced down the canal, meeting with little resistance. Then America said 'Boo', and the British caved in, bullying the French into agreeing to stop the operation. The majority of the public supported Suez; the big disappointment was with its failure. A young miner summed up a popular reaction: 'We should have gone right in there, but we can't do it any more. Not even against the bloody wogs.' Suez is important for another reason. It stands out in the history of imperial retreat as the only effort by the two leading colonial powers to defend their positions by pooling their policy and resources. Britain, in effect, undertook to underwrite French rule in Algeria, and France to underwrite the British client system in the Middle East. It offers a glimpse of that alternative *European* future foreclosed by the Second World War. But it came too late in the day; and its defeat turned retreat into rout.

Suez destroyed the last pretension of Britain and France to be great powers, even jointly. Power was now in the hands of men who were no longer willing to take the risks associated with its use. For Britain, its failure led directly to the collapse of its position in the Middle East, and indirectly to the dismantling of its African empire and its application to join the European Economic Community. In domestic affairs, the 'end of empire' brought about a cultural and social upheaval. Suez destroyed the prestige of the old governing class, especially with the young.

Scuttlemac

Macmillan's reward for being 'first in, first out' was to replace the ailing Eden as Prime Minister on 10 January 1957. With his faux Edwardian style, Macmillan was the great conjurer of twentieth-century British politics, masterly in restoring the illusion of greatness while complet-ing the scuttle from empire.

Macmillan's immediate priority was to restore damaged relations with the United States. To this aim he brought one of his sweeping historical analogies: Britain would play Greece to America's Rome. In this he succeeded: once Britain's pretensions to independence were squashed, the United States was happy to accept it as a 'junior partner' in the 'war against communism'. By 1958 the economy had recovered from its mid-decade stop, and with the help of a give-away Budget, Macmillan led the Conservatives to their third successive electoral victory in 1959 with an increased majority.

Tory hegemony was confirmed, and Britain's pride restored, but Macmillan realised that all was not well. Britain's undynamic economy was not sharing in Europe's economic miracle, and its relative economic decline would damage Britain's influence with Washington. People were beginning to ask a rather awkward question: why was Britain growing slower than continental countries like Germany and France? Following his election victory in 1959 Macmillan decided on a major change of course: withdrawal from empire, joining the European Economic Community and 'planning for growth'. These formed the core of his strategy for restoring Britain as a great, though no longer imperial, power.

In a famous speech to the South African Parliament in Cape Town in January 1960 Macmillan signalled the end of British rule in Africa by referring to the 'winds of change' that were blowing through that continent. Like France under de Gaulle, Britain had decided that it was not worth trying to hold on to its African colonies by force. Having abandoned conscription in 1958, it in any case no longer had the manpower to do so in the face of increasing nationalist unrest, notably by the Mau Mau in Kenya.

Britain and France were not chased out of Africa: there was no longer any pressing reason for them to stay, and better opportunities for earning money and projecting power were opening up in Europe. In a crash programme the African colonies were 'prepared' for independence. By 1968 – tiny Swaziland being the last – all seventeen had gone. The process of withdrawal took the form of suppressing 'violent' nationalist agitation, but conceding to the substance of nationalist demands. Thus, imprisoned or exiled leaders were, after a short interval, placed at the head of their newly independent countries. Brief incarceration by the British became the main qualification for post-colonial leadership. Nearly all the ex-African colonies changed their name; most became one-party dictatorships under their first leaders. Most joined the Commonwealth, adding black faces to the queen's dinner table.

Scuttle was the order of the day elsewhere: Malta (1954), Cyprus (1960), Guyana (1966), most of the tiny island colonies of the West Indies in the 1970s and 1980s. In 1967, following yet another sterling crisis, Britain announced that it would withdraw all its military forces 'east of Suez' by 1970, except for a small garrison in Hong Kong. Hong Kong was handed back to China in 1997. So the empire of conquest passed into history. Today it survives only in the honours list, the dames, knights and companions, annually created, of an empire which no longer exists.

One element only of the Macmillan wind-up programme failed to go according to plan. When the Central African Federation broke up in 1964, Northern Rhodesia and Nyasaland became independent as Zambia and Malawi. Britain refused to grant Southern Rhodesia equivalent independence unless it scrapped its settler-dominated constitution. Ian Smith, the leader of the white Rhodesian Front, declared independence unilaterally in November 1965, in defiance of the British crown, but with some support in Britain itself. The settlers were, after all, a part of Britain; 'Smithy' himself had been a fighter pilot in the Battle of Britain. Their problem was that they were frozen by their situation into a Britain which was ceasing to exist. The incoming Labour government was dissuaded from military intervention for fear, as at Curragh in 1914, that the army would not carry out orders if called on to shoot their 'kith and kin'. Pleading logistical obstacles to using military force, Labour's new Prime Minister Harold Wilson imposed sanctions, which he promised would 'work in weeks rather than months'. Initially supported by white South Africa, and buttressed by the Portuguese who still ruled Angola and Mozambique, 200,000 British settlers hung on till 1979 in face of international obloquy and mounting guerrilla activity, an inconvenient reminder of obsolete loyalties. Independence for what was now relabelled Zimbabwe came in 1980 on a one-man-one-vote basis, which handed power to the black leader Robert Mugabe. Over the next twenty-eight years, Mugabe reduced a once thriving British colony to a state of Africanised destitution, but few in Britain any longer cared.

Loss of empire deprived the British of an important part of their national identity. Empire abroad had reinforced union and hierarchy at

home. Britons could not even retire from the imperial enterprise with
the satisfaction of a job well done, since history books soon started
filling them with guilt at their shameful exploitation of the subject
peoples. Not only was Britain in rapid descent from the pinnacle of
world power, it was slipping down the moral league table as well.
Virtually ignored were two of the greatest blessings of imperial rule:
peace and capital for development.

Britain turned to Europe by a process of elimination. The
Commonwealth was too insubstantial as a prop for British power, and
Macmillan realised that the continuation of a 'special relationship' with
the United States depended on Britain having influence in Europe. This
meant joining the newly established European Economic Community.
British policy had, almost by reflex, tried to sabotage the drive for
European unity, which reminded it of earlier attempts to unite the
Continent by force. The Foreign Office had a nightmare of 'an empire
on our doorstep'. Britain's failure to prevent the signing of the Treaty
of Rome in 1957 and the start of the six-member European Economic
Community the following year led to the British decision to try to
sabotage this 'empire' from the inside.

Economics complemented high politics. Britain faced the prospect
of being shut out from the world's most dynamic market, with whom
it did nearly 40 per cent of its trade. Joining the 'common market'
would provide exactly that scale of operation and spur of competition
needed to revive Britain's sluggish economy.

'Leadership in Europe' thus became the new role canvassed to
replace leadership of the Commonwealth. But it turned out that
Britain needed Europe more than Europe needed Britain. The French
leader de Gaulle would not forgive Britain for its 'betrayal' at Suez, and
for many previous slights. Claiming that Britain would be an American
Trojan Horse inside the community, de Gaulle vetoed the British
application for entry. With de Gaulle's veto, a central plank of
Macmillan's strategy for reviving British power had collapsed. There
remained 'planning for growth', which, under Macmillan's intelligent,
indolent and corrupt Chancellor, Reginald Maudling, turned into a
'dash for growth' to try to ensure the Conservatives a fourth electoral
victory. The dash produced an inflationary boom, but it was not
enough to save a Tory government now discredited by sex scandals
and an atmosphere of sleaze. Thirteen years of Conservative government ended in a shambles.

Thirteen Wasted Years?

This was Labour's election slogan in 1964. In fact, the Tories delivered thirteen years of uninterrupted full employment. In 1964 GDP was 40 per cent higher than in 1951, the average standard of living had gone up by 30 per cent and the Tories were well on the way to fulfilling Butler's promise to double living standards in a generation. British society in the early 1950s looked like it had in the 1930s and 1940s, down to fashions in clothes, models of cars, household furniture and architecture. This was because there was not so much to buy and identity was still defined by collective, not individual, taste. After the mid-1950s this started to change. Affluence was starting to transform society. There was a huge growth in the number of private cars, television sets and other consumer durables. Attitudes to personal debt were transformed through 'hire purchase' (buying goods on the 'never-never') and, in 1966, by the introduction of the first credit card, Barclaycard. By 1964 the five-day week, plus two weeks' paid holiday, had become standard: seven million went to Blackpool, five million went abroad, for holidays. Fashions in clothes and popular music were revolutionised by the arrival of 'teenagers' and with them teenage taste and youth 'problems'. By 1965 Andrew Shonfield could talk about the birth of a new economic order that converted capitalism from cataclysmic failure 'into the great engine of prosperity'.

Following Labour's third electoral defeat in a row in 1959, Labour's Barbara Castle had had to concede that 'our ethical reach was beyond the mental grasp of the average person'. Hugh Gaitskell, Attlee's successor as leader, tried to lower the reach, but failed to rid Labour of its commitment to public ownership. Labour's two main intellectual protagonists were Anthony Crosland, who argued in *The Future of Socialism* (1956) that nationalisation was largely irrelevant, and Richard Crossman who predicted 'with mathematical certainty' that the publicly owned economies of eastern Europe would grow faster than privately owned ones. Harold Wilson, Gaitskell's successor as Labour leader, thought such theological disputation sterile. The trouble with the Conservatives, he proclaimed, was that they were too archaic, hidebound and amateur to run a modern, science-based economy. Labour would harness socialism to science. This line appealed to the expanding white-collar and professional sectors. 'Scientific planning' also sounded socialist. Wilson narrowly won the general election of

October 1964 from Macmillan's successor, Sir Alec Douglas Home, who imprudently confessed to economic illiteracy, and established a more solid majority in 1966. But Labour came into office poorly equipped to deal with Britain's continuing economic problems, which revolved round the still imperial role of sterling and the unresolved issue of labour relations.

The 'British Disease' Debate

What eroded the postwar settlement was the relatively slow growth of the British economy: 2.2 per cent per capita for the decade of the 1950s as against 3.5 per cent for France and 6.3 per cent for Germany. To cure the disease of slow growth became the avowed object of British governments, and would be achieved by 'indicative planning'. Planning for growth damaged the delicate balance between capitalism and socialism, individualism and collectivism, which sustained the postwar settlement. Far from curing the economic disease, it made Britain harder to govern.

Earlier in the century the context of economic debate was Britain's future as a world power. In the 1950s attention finally switched to the welfare of the inhabitants of Britain itself. Since the developed world as a whole was getting richer, relative economic decline meant that the British people were getting relatively poorer. For Labour, Britain's slow rate of growth posed a special problem: the slower the growth rate, the less revenue the government would have to improve public services. 'Raising the rate of growth' was the only way of advancing socialism without killing off capitalism.

In the 1950s, a new panel of expert diagnosticians appeared, as well as a new sense of urgency, even desperation. The diagnosticians identified three main 'constraints' on faster growth: the balance of payments, Britain's archaic political economy and its anti-commercial culture. At full employment the British economy imported more than it exported, causing 'balance of payments crises', whose resolution required growth-destroying bouts of deflation. This was the famous 'stop-go' cycle. Various cures were proposed for this, the chief one being devaluation. At the centre of the archaic political economy was the dominant position of the City and the overpowerful trades unions. But no one had much idea of how to reform either. The incoming

Labour government set its hopes on 'voluntary' cooperation in wage restraint, of the kind Stafford Cripps had achieved in the 1940s. The cultural critique, which goes back to the American economist Thorstein Veblen, claimed that the British elites had chosen not to be competitive in order to enjoy a more civilised way of life. In the late 1950s, the term 'Establishment' came into use to denote the narrow network of personal and family relationships which ran the country. Anthony Sampson's *The Anatomy of Britain* (1962) concluded that Britain and its people were carrying on a 'pattern of relationships' which had 'robbed them of their dynamic'.

From today's vantage point, the discussion has an old-fashioned ring to it in three respects. The first lay in the assumption that a 'desired' rate of economic growth could be brought about by deliberate government policy. Secondly, national wellbeing was still identified with the prosperity of 'smokestack' industry – few grasped that higher living standards might be achieved by producing something other than coal, steel, ships and textiles: satire, for example, at which the British excelled. Finally, the discussion was overwrought. Britain might have been losing ground, but not nearly as disastrously as the agonising suggested. The old 'patrician hegemony' was not serving the economy or society that badly.

Later post-Thatcherite analysis puts the discussion in a different framework. Entrepreneurial failure is not denied, but it is attributed less to deep sociological causes than to the adverse incentive structure facing British management, characterised by very high marginal income tax rates (still over 80 per cent till the Thatcher years) and lack of competition throughout most of the economy.

The main legacy of the discussion was an intellectual consensus on the need to fit the British state and society for what Wilson called the 'white heat of the technological revolution'. Wilson claimed that Labour was the answer to the British disease.

Wilson's Growthmanship

The 1964 election result showed that Labour was electable, not that it could govern. The incoming premier, Harold Wilson, had been a brilliant leader of the opposition, and this created high expectations for his premiership. He embodied the rise of grammar school Britain. He talked an executive language but proved to be an incompetent executive, with no sense of strategy, addicted to gimmicks and increasingly to paranoia. The government machine was a shambles throughout his premiership.

A new planning ministry, the Department of Economic Affairs, headed by the ebullient if frequently drunken George Brown, was supposed to develop a creative rivalry with the Treasury and gear up economic growth with detailed national and sectoral targets – the start of the target culture. Tony Benn headed a new Ministry of Technology to promote research and development.

Labour's economic plan was excellent – on paper. Expansionary fiscal and monetary policy would be run in tandem with 'indicative' planning to produce a 'sustainable' rate of growth. A higher rate of growth would allow a controlled growth of wages and expanding social services, validating free collective bargaining and modest redistributionary policies. However, the government failed to develop a balance of payments strategy consistent with its growth targets. Wilson's chief advisers, notably Nicholas Kaldor, urged a devaluation of the pound as soon as he took office. But Wilson refused to saddle Labour with another devaluation; a strong pound was a sign that Britain was still a great power. This negative decision meant that defence of sterling once more took priority over growth. It gave the Treasury and Bank of England a whiphand over the DEA, making the latter's function increasingly redundant.

Wilson compounded his error by refusing to impose a sufficient measure of deflation to defend the sterling–dollar exchange rate. This left sterling vulnerable to any passing shock. There were two sterling crises, in 1964 and 1966, before a third one forced the government to devalue the pound against the dollar by 14 per cent on 17 November 1967, Wilson going on television to deny that devaluation meant a devaluation of 'the pound in your pocket'. In rejecting a devaluation in 1966, Wilson had imposed £500 million of economies, a six-month wages freeze and two years of 'severe' pay restraint. This antagonised the unions: planning was supposed to make incomes grow, not stop. Wilson hoped that micro-investment in 'growth' industries could offset the major act of deflation. In 1966 Labour set up an Industrial Reorganization Corporation to subsidise business mergers, then considered to promote efficiency. Its fruits were the new giant companies like the General Electric Company, Ransom, Hoffman and Pollard,

International Computers Ltd and British Leyland. In British Leyland, the merged motor-car industry, the efficient car manufacturers were rapidly dragged down by internal chaos. Like Macmillan before him, Wilson turned to the EEC as a substitute for Britain's vanishing world role, to be met once more by de Gaulle's veto.

Many commentators cited as Wilson's main mistake his failure to devalue the pound quickly enough – Wilson, the cocky grammar school boy, had succumbed after all to the mystique of the City and imperial nostalgia. This aborted growthmanship from the start. Stop-go had not been overcome: in fact, the stops were longer and growth slower than under the Tories. A deeper explanation is that the whole planning project was misconceived. Peter Sinclair finds the most depressing feature not the specific mistakes of policy, but the government's 'extravagant claims of omnicompetence'. Planning was undertaken in an industrial relations system notably unsuited for the task. The trades unions failed to deliver the pay restraint which the Wilson government needed to achieve its growth targets. The number of working days lost through strikes rose steadily under Labour to peak at six million in 1969 – much below peak prewar periods but higher than under the Tories. Britain's problem was not long-drawn-out official stoppages, but lightning 'unofficial' strikes' – groups of workers downing tools on impulse and at the slightest provocation. This reflected the shift in power from union officials to shop stewards elected by the workforce in a factory or plant, partly to overcome craft-based fragmentation. Wilson realised that something had to be done to curb wildcat strikes, but his attempt in 1969 to impose a 'cooling off' period was overruled in the Cabinet and he had to be content with the TUC's 'solemn and binding undertaking' (Solomon Binding as it was irreverently known) to do its best to curb them.

Social Reform

A key object of Labour's social reforms was to plug the gaps in the Beveridgean welfare system. The managers of the post-1945 welfare state did not expect welfare expenditures to expand exponentially. The Beveridge system offered a single route – temporary interruption of earnings – to the benefit system. The expectation was that full employment and rising incomes would limit claims for social protection.

However, the anti-poverty goal implicit in Beveridge was a much wider ambition than just to provide a replacement income for contingencies. Logically it applied to those at work as well as those whose earnings were interrupted, and also to those who had no earnings. In addition, poverty was redefined in relative terms: from being a concept related to subsistence it became one related to average income. So poverty elimination became, *ipso facto*, a project for minimising income inequalities. Under Wilson insurance benefits were made more generous, especially for pensioners; family allowances (child benefits) increased; and earnings-related benefits and redundancy payments were introduced in an effort to shake skilled workers out of declining industries. Means-tested National Assistance, renamed Supplementary Benefits to rob it of its stigma, was extended in 1966 to the poor outside the labour market. The new claimants included widows, invalids and single mothers. Means-tested rent and rate rebates produced one million extra claimants within a year. This 'entitlements explosion' brought a far larger population into the benefits system than the residuum of 'cripples . . . and physical and moral defectives' for whom Beveridge had intended it. Between 1960 and 1970 the population relying on benefits crept up from under one million to three million and the cost of social services as a percentage of GDP climbed from 10 to 15 per cent.

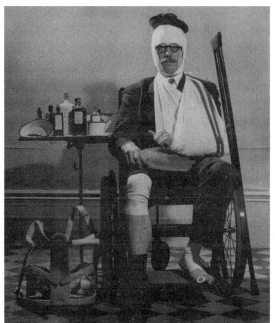

Demonstration of what a subject could get under Britain's original National Health Service programme, 1 April 1951. The NHS left Britons free to spend straight away what they had once saved to cover medical costs. It gave Britons the 'right' to free bandages and free medicines. It also gave birth to the world of entitlement and dependency culture.

Increased social spending under Labour did not produce increased quality in the public services. This was particularly true of housing, Bevan wanted municipal housing to create pleasant, socially mixed neighbourhoods, but by the 1960s council estates had become high-rise monstrosities, increasingly dumping grounds for problem families whose children wrecked the new comprehensive schools being set up to rescue them from 'underachievement'. Modernism in architecture never recovered from the massive, badly constructed tenements and urban regeneration schemes of the 1960s, which paved the way for Prince Charles's attacks on 'monstrous carbuncles' in 1984.

The Wilson government tried to tackle what was seen as Britain's straggling educational system. New business schools, universities and training programmes rolled off the socialist conveyor belt. The Open University, set up in 1969 to provide long-distance university education for adults, was especially close to Wilson's heart. However, the main instrument Labour relied on to raise national educational standards was the comprehensive school. Comprehensive schools were supposed to overcome the class divide in education by abolishing the so-called tripartite system of grammar, technical and secondary modern schools – in practice a bipartite system of grammar schools and secondary modern schools – established by the Butler Act of 1944. The *coup de grâce* to this system was delivered by the Education Secretary, Tony Crosland. His Circular 10/65, together with subsequent directives, ordered local authorities to go comprehensive, with financial penalties for non-compliance. Crosland famously said: 'If it's the last thing I do, I'm going to destroy every fucking grammar school in England and Wales and in Northern Ireland.' (Scotland had its own separate system.)

The comprehensive revolution offers a textbook case of the law of unintended consequences. The 'skills gap' it was designed to remedy got worse, not better: social expectations may have been raised, but academic expectations declined. The destruction of the grammar schools undercut Labour's own meritocratic ideal, by kicking away the ladder by which bright working-class children, including many of Labour's own leaders and middle-class supporters, had risen into the professions. Labour unintentionally strengthened the class character of elitism. In a corrupt bargain with the Tories, the independent sector was left untouched, Tory politicians being content to sacrifice the grammar schools to safeguard the entry of their own children into the private sector. The grammar schools had been a mechanism for creating a meritocracy, and their dissolution strengthened the link between elite and class, destroying the legitimacy of elitism.

Cultural Watershed

Both political parties were committed to improving the condition of the people. But what constituted 'improvement' depended partly on what one expected of the people. Two contrasting views of the working class were held by the elites. The financial journalist Nicholas Davenport, who served on the football commission which Wilson set up, believed that the working man 'still lived for the three F's – fun, football, and fucking . . . Like any other [he] could become bloody-minded and revolutionary when conditions went against him . . . but fundamentally he was a hedonist, with his eye on a good time without too much hard work.' Davenport's view was shared by Harold Macmillan and was reflected not just in his expansionary economic policies, but in specific acts of Tory legislation: the establishment of a commercial television station (ITV) to compete with the BBC in 1954, the liberalisation of gambling laws and the relaxation of licensing hours for pubs.

Labour's approach was collective and egalitarian: collective effort leading to collective reward in the form of improved public services paid for by taxation. Personal consumption was to be repressed to make room for public consumption. This reflected the Reithian programme of elevating the moral condition of the working class. It was the old conflict between Cavalier and Roundhead, pub and chapel, played out under conditions of growing affluence.

Cutting across this classic right-left divide was a strong strain of radical middle-class individualism, with a home in both parties, which saw improvement in terms of self-expression and release from restraint. The Tory 'Rab' Butler and Labour's Roy Jenkins were the two great liberalising Home Secretaries of the middle years of the century, laying the legal foundations of what Jenkins called the 'civilised' and others have called the 'permissive' society'.

The Ungovernable Seventies

The 1970s were the lowest point of British government in the twentieth century. At no time since before the First World War was there such a feeling that Britain had become ungovernable, and that a change of system – not just a change of government – was required. Punk rock music was an authentic cultural response to the sense of desolation which the failures of the 1970s engendered. The change came about, not through the violent breakup of British society, but through the victory of the Conservative party in 1979 under Margaret Thatcher, which would inaugurate eighteen years of what came to be known as Thatcherism.

Britain was clearly unlucky in the 1970s. First, it was hit by the quadrupling of oil prices in 1973–4. This misfortune it shared with the oil-importing countries, all of which were plunged into an inflationary recession: prices went up, living standards went down. Particular to Britain was the bad luck of having, in effect, minority governments between 1974 and 1979. Personality and political circumstances are both important, but they are not sufficient explanations of what went wrong. The truth is that the consensual approach to governing had run its course. The consensus had collapsed because it was never really a consensus, simply habits of behaviour created by the war and by pragmatism. Its lack of an institutional basis was most obvious in industrial relations. Faced with national emergencies, neither capitalists nor workers would give up their freedom of action; eventually the capitalists won because they got a government strong enough to crush the unions. But the crises of the 1970s also showed up in imperfect arrangements for governing the restive peripheries of the United Kingdom, differentially hit by the decline of British industry. On paper, Edward Heath, Conservative Prime Minister from 1970 to 1974, was a 'strong' leader. But he was rigid, overbearing and politically inept, with a weak and untried team. He took office and pledged to reverse Wilson's economic policies. Instead, he reversed his own policies, in a spectacular series of U-turns.

Heath promised 'tight money'. But when British unemployment reached the 'magic' figure of one million in January 1972, the economy was massively reflated in the 'Barber boom'. Inflation doubled in two years, while unemployment fell only by a third. Heath had promised not to bail out 'lame ducks', yet ailing companies like Rolls-Royce were not only rescued, but nationalised, and the Industry Act of 1972 created new interventionist powers to subsidise industrial projects. Heath promised to abandon 'incomes policies': instead he made them statutory in September 1972. All this was before the OPEC price hike of the following year ratcheted up stagflation. Under Sir Keith Joseph, Secretary of State for Social Services 1970–74, wrote Nicholas Timmins, the 'scope of social security saw almost unremitting expansion'.

None of this brought any relief from rising inflation and growing industrial disorder, as the unions, led by the miners, fought all attempts to control pay. It was under Heath that unions started to use methods of intimidation against employers and other workers in flagrant breach of the (weak) laws that his government had enacted to restrain them. Heath was brought down in February 1974 when he asked the electorate to decide 'Who Governs Britain?' at the precise moment when it was perfectly clear it was not he. Rejecting any policy reminiscent of Heath became the obsession of Margaret Thatcher, his successor as Conservative leader.

Heath's one positive achievement was finally to negotiate Britain's entry into the EEC. Following de Gaulle's resignation in 1969, Britain was admitted in 1972, on somewhat humiliating terms. It was forced to accept the Common Agricultural Policy, and had to jettison the remaining scaled-down imperial preferences, finally ending Joe Chamberlain's dream of imperial economics. The sterling area was also scrapped. Achieving EEC entry was the last victory of the Whig elite which had governed Britain since the war.

When Wilson took office for the second time in February 1974, without an overall majority, inflation, already raging under Heath, was being fed by the explosion of oil and commodity prices. The programme on which Labour fought the February 1974 election reflected the left's assessment that British capitalism was in terminal decline and that the British economy could not prosper unless it was comprehensively socialised. So the Labour party espoused a programme which would have led to the decapitation of the private sector and what its manifesto of 1973 called a 'fundamental and irreversible shift in the balance of power and wealth in favour of the working people'. Wilson, like his predecessor, found himself saddled with policies he did not believe in. He did his own U-turns, spending his first year and a half in office reversing or emasculating his party's manifesto commitments (helped in this by his wafer-thin majority and by the device of a referendum on Europe). He could not, however, prevent the further expansion of trades union privileges (notably the right to insist on a pre-entry 'closed shop') as the price of his much-trumpeted 'social contract'. Britain in the 1970s was governed by men who stood still in the middle while their party activists bolted in opposite directions.

Wilson let the economic situation deteriorate to the point when expenditure cuts and another pay policy could be imposed by external events. By mid-1975 the annual inflation rate was running at 26.5 per cent, the current account deficit was 1.48 per cent of GDP, public spending reached 58.4 per cent of GDP, the budget deficit stood at 7.3 per cent of GDP and business profitability was at an all-time low. It took the sterling crisis of 1976 and humiliating recourse to the IMF for a loan to bring runaway public spending under control. The combination of public spending cuts and pay policy brought down the annual rate of inflation from over 20 per cent to 8 per cent over two years. But when the government announced a 5 per cent wages 'norm' for 1978, the public sector unions responded with a series of strikes that paralysed the nation and the pay policy collapsed in the 'winter of discontent'. By 1979 inflation was back up to 13 per cent and unemployment was 5 per cent. Growth over the whole Labour period was 1.4 per cent a year, the lowest five years in the postwar period. This was the immediate background to the victory of the Conservative party in the 1979 election.

The renewed debate about Britain's economic prospects which opened up in the mid-1970s was more desperate than in the late 1950s. Then it had been about the causes of relatively slow growth; now it was about the style of government itself. Economic and political failure, it was claimed, had created a 'crisis of governability'. As a consequence, the state had become 'overloaded' with tasks: its reach had come to exceed its grasp: by the mid-1970s the government controlled the flow of more than 50 per cent of the gross national product, contributed more than 40 per cent of all new investment, employed 27 per cent of the working population, paid about one-third of all wages and salaries and owned nearly half the national fixed assets. It also influenced the private sector through price controls and industrial development certificates. Heath had offered employers and unions a chance to 'share fully with the government the benefits and obligations involved in running the economy'. Labour's left-leaning, but vaguer, 'social contract' had the same goal: economic policy would be agreed over 'beer and sandwiches' with Jack Jones and other union leaders at No. 10 Downing Street. But British economy and society were never suited to tripartism: the industrial structure was too fragmented, the people too individualistic.

The left and right agreed that the postwar settlement had disintegrated, but naturally disagreed on what to do about it. Marxist thinkers discerned a 'crisis of legitimacy'. The left, led by Tony Benn, promoted an Alternative Economic Strategy, which amounted to a command economy, withdrawal from the EEC and import controls. This was socialism's last hurrah: the more significant intellectual break was to the right. 'Free markets', long trumpeted by the Institute of Economic Affairs set up in 1955, was the right's answer to ungovernability. Now it captured the intellectual high ground in the Tory party.

The seminal texts of the Conservative intellectual rethink were the speeches and writings of the New Right's leading politician-intellectual Sir Keith Joseph, who, repenting of his extravagances as Social Security Secretary, announced his conversion to the true faith of Conservatism. Joseph identified the full employment commitment as the fundamental error. It forced government to take the pay policy route which led to ungovernability. Joseph made the point, soon to be commonplace, that it was taking more and more inflation to achieve a given reduction in unemployment, so that over successive cycles both inflation and unemployment tended to rise together. But trying to dampen down inflation by restricting pay was 'like trying to stop water coming out of a leaky hose without turning the tap off'. Reflecting the new 'monetarism' of the American economist Milton Friedman, Joseph declared that inflation was a monetary phenomenon caused by the government printing too much money. Government's task was to control money, not pay. If money was controlled, excessive pay awards would lead not to higher prices, but higher unemployment.

On 22 July 1976 the Bank of England publicly announced the adoption of money-supply targets, though it had already started using them. In 1975, public expenditure started to be 'cash limited', and for the first time since the war was cut during a major recession, Tony Crosland telling the local authorities that the 'party is over'. In October 1976 Wilson's embattled successor, James Callaghan, announced to a startled Labour party conference that governments could no longer 'spend their way' back to full employment. Although the intellectual elements of Thatcherism were falling into place, few believed that any government would have the will to implement the policies suggested by them. *The Times'* columnist Peter Jay reckoned that to eliminate inflation would require unemployment in the 'low millions' for a decade or more. He concluded that this was politically unfeasible. 'Governments depending on consent,' he wrote, 'cannot suspend the full employment commitment.'

The British Question

Until the 1970s, the breakup of Britain seemed inconceivable. But economic failure made the unitary state less attractive. The postwar settlement had also presumed an imperial United Kingdom with a stable social structure and a homogeneous 'British' population. The 'end of empire' raised the issue of British national identity. The gentlemen in Whitehall were finding their plans for a smooth British transition to a post-imperial role in Europe being derailed by a series of 'peasant revolts'.

In the late 1960s the demons of Irish history re-emerged. The existence of Northern Ireland was a permanent source of grievance to Republican Ireland; the way it was governed, to the Catholics inside its

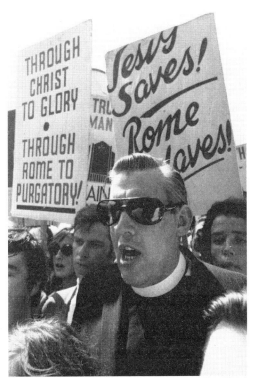

Ian Paisley, the militant Protestant leader of the DUP, sings during a demonstration in 1970 outside Canterbury Cathedral against the first Roman Catholic Mass to be held there for 400 years. Should we see Ian Paisley as a symbol of a lost kind of Britishness? Or is he merely a hang-over from a pre-secular age?

borders. Reunification was never a realistic possibility. With the Republic having a per capita income only a fraction of the North's, there was no chance of the Protestants accepting 'rule from Dublin'. At the same time, the settlement of 1922 had left a large Catholic minority in Ulster. Although officially there was no discrimination, in practice there was a Protestant ascendancy maintained through a set of interlocking political, economic and security institutions which had no parallel elsewhere in the UK. London politicians turned a blind eye to the situation as long as Northern Ireland stayed off in-trays. When middle-class Catholics took to the streets in 1968 – the year of failed revolutions all over Europe – to demand, in essence, the dismantling of the Protestant state, Whitehall reacted in the approved style of colonial retreat. It forced concessions on the Unionist governments of Terence O'Neill and James Chichester-Clark. These destroyed the authority of Ulster Unionism with the Protestant working class, without appeasing the Republicans. Both sides prepared for the 'armed struggle'. The IRA 'Provisionals' started up in 1969, and Protestants re-formed the Ulster Defence Volunteers. Violence escalated, and the British Army appeared on the streets of Londonderry in 1969. IRA violence spread to the British mainland, bomb explosions became regular in London and elsewhere, and there were several political assassinations, including that of the last Indian viceroy, Lord Mountbatten.

Since the Protestants refused their exit lines, Whitehall was stuck with the six provinces and their archaic enmities – the moth-eaten Protestant parades celebrating the Battle of the Boyne and other glorious victories over the Catholics, the decaying shipyards and factories of Belfast, once strongholds of a Protestant 'labour aristocracy', the run-down housing estates of Ballymurphy. The Protestant sub-state had lost its connection with those forces pushing British society towards a secular, history-free future, but it clung to the Union Jack with pathetic, unrequited loyalty.

Edward Heath had to bear the brunt of the Irish troubles. More and more British troops were poured in; the pace of reform was quickened. Far from enlarging the 'constitutional' centre, the reform measures shifted power to the extremists. Faced with the surge of sectarian violence, Heath reacted by reintroducing internment in August 1971, a disastrous move which swelled the ranks of the IRA. In January 1972 soldiers of the Parachute Regiment killed fourteen Catholics in Londonderry ('Bloody Sunday'). As recruitment to the paramilitaries on both sides soared, Heath removed control of security from the subordinate government at Stormont. This move, in February 1972, precipitated the resignation of the last Unionist government headed by Brian Faulkner, and Heath replaced 'home rule' by direct rule. Five hundred were killed that year as the two sides' murder gangs let rip. But Heath – or more particularly his jovial Secretary of State for Ireland, William Whitelaw – blundered on. The British would restore devolved government if Faulkner accepted a 'power sharing' executive with the Catholic parties, and a 'Council of Ireland'. Faulkner's acceptance of the latter, in the so-called Sunningdale Agreement of May 1974, precipitated a general strike of Protestant workers, organised by the Ulster Workers' Committee.

Within a few days, the strike paralysed the Northern Irish state. Harold Wilson, back at No. 10 Downing Street, was impotent to break it. As in Southern Rhodesia, the key to the situation was the attitude of the army and police. Not only was there considerable sympathy for the strikers in the lower ranks of both, but the army declared itself unable to keep the local power supply going. By 27 May, Faulkner's civil servants told him that the loss of power would destroy the sewage system, opening Belfast to flooding, typhoid and dysentery. The next day he resigned; the British government responded by suspending the power-sharing assembly and promising fresh elections. The same day the strike was called off. The Protestant workers' revolt of 1974 is the only example of a successful general strike in British history, not least because the Catholic workers, who also wanted the power-sharing executive to fail, did not oppose it. The British learned their lesson and embarked on the long process of scaled-down, but more precise, counter-terrorist measures, covert operations and secret negotiations which would eventually bring about an end to the violence in the Good Friday Agreement of 1998.

The Irish Protestants were mainly Scottish in origin, and the Ulster Protestant revolt against Westminster stimulated latent Scottish nationalism. The Scots had exported engineers, doctors and scientists to the empire. As the British empire retreated, the Scots, deprived of their share of imperial glory, started to portray themselves as victims of imperialism. A disproportionate economic decline, and an autonomous legal, religious and educational system heightened their sense of separateness. The discovery of North Sea Oil in 1969 and Britain's entry into the EEC seemed to offer rich pickings to 'An

Independent Scotland in Europe'. By the late 1960s, the Scottish
National Party was showing signs of political life. Labour, which
regarded Scotland as its political fiefdom, had no interest in Scottish
'devolution', but was forced to rethink its position when large Scottish
Nationalist gains in the 1974 general elections left a weak Labour
government dependent on Scottish Nationalist support. (In the two
general elections of that year the SNP won 22 per cent and 30 per cent
of the votes, and seven and eleven parliamentary seats, on a platform
of independence from Britain, and separate membership of the EEC.)
The Labour government passed a measure of devolution in 1978, but
this failed to reach the 40 per cent hurdle required, in a referendum, for
its passage into law.

A third challenge to the British sense of identity came from large-
scale coloured immigration. The first boatloads of Jamaicans arrived in
the late 1940s, and their numbers were soon swelled by immigrants
from the Indian sub-continent. In 1951 the coloured population was
about 80,000. In 1961 it reached 500,000; by 1971 it was 1.5 million, or 3
per cent of the total population, and highly concentrated in decaying
inner-city areas. Race riots broke out in Notting Hill, London, and
Nottingham in 1958. Warned by Cyril Osborne, the MP for Louth, that
it was 'time to speak up for the white man', the Conservatives introduced a restrictive, though 'colour blind', regime of work vouchers in
1962, which, however, contained a loophole allowing the entry of
spouses and children of immigrant workers. The winding up of
Britain's African empire brought another wave of immigrants, as Asian
British passport holders in Kenya and Uganda started to flee racial
discrimination in these newly independent African states. In a clear
break with the 'colour blind' approach, Wilson's government passed
an Act in 1968 denying them right of settlement while retaining free
entry for non-British subjects of British origin. At the same time, it
passed two Acts, in 1965 and 1968, modelled on US race relations
legislation, outlawing racial abuse and discrimination in employment
and housing, with a Race Relations Board to enforce its provisions.

Popular resentment at mass coloured immigration found an
unlikely champion in an austere classical scholar turned politician,
Enoch Powell. Powell was a dominating force in British politics from
1967 to 1975. He was the strangest popular tribune to emerge in
postwar Britain, in his mixture of extreme romanticism and extreme
rationality. On 20 April 1968, he made a speech in the Midland Hotel,

Birmingham, that made him a popular hero. Powell proposed to cut the flow of immigrants immediately to 'negligible proportions' and to provide grants for voluntary repatriation. Unless this were done, Britain, by the century's end, would have between five and seven million coloured people. (Powell was prescient about this.) This would inevitably produce large-scale racial violence (Powell was wrong here, but was speaking against the background of the American race riots of the 1960s). He foresaw 'the river Tiber foaming with much blood'.

Powell's populist handling of the most sensitive topic of domestic policy was condemned by the political elites. For Harold Wilson he was the 'evil guru from Wolverhampton', and Heath dismissed him from his Shadow Cabinet. Popular reaction, however, was different. Powell received 100,000 letters of support; 74 per cent of a Gallup Poll sample agreed with what he said; dockers and meat porters in London and factory workers in Birmingham marched in his support.

In the short run, the party leaderships successfully kept immigration 'out of politics'. In the longer run, immigration damaged the political nation by opening up, in Andrew Roberts' words, 'a profound gap . . . between the opinions of the governors and the governed'. It explains a lot of the sourness of the politics of the 1970s. It snapped social deference in the Tory party, facilitating its capture by middle and lower middle-class leaders closer to the outlook of their constituents. Powell attracted working-class voters away from Labour in 1970, and the Powell effect still worked for Thatcher in 1979.

Powell's importance was that he explicitly raised the question of Britain's post-imperial identity. How far would the unravelling of empire have to go? These questions have never since left the stage. For Heath, Britain's destiny was to be part of Europe. It would discover a new vocation as a member of the European Economic Community. But Europe offered no real equivalent role for Britain. By usurping some of the functions of the established nation-states, the EEC pointed not to a Europe of states but to a Europe of nationalities, which threatened the unity of the United Kingdom. For Powell, Britain's post-imperial identity was constituted by its island institutions, developed over centuries, which required a high degree of cultural homogeneity. But Powell too suffered from the illusion that the United Kingdom could be preserved as a unitary state. His call for island unity flew in the face of advanced centrifugal forces in both Northern Ireland and Scotland. In the short run, Powell was defeated by Heath. In the long run, he paved the way for Margaret Thatcher's more carefully circumscribed brand of free markets and populist nationalism.

Mrs Thatcher's Perestroika

The Thatcher governments from 1979 to 1990 demolished the ruined postwar settlement. Of its three pillars – the full employment commitment, the mixed economy and the welfare state – only the third remained standing. Margaret Thatcher achieved three things: she found a successful way of governing the country; she restored national pride and she brought to an end Britain's relative economic decline. These successes only became obvious later. At the time her revolution encountered almost universal scepticism, and indeed opposition, from the thinking classes; it also divided the country. It only continued because she was determined it should, and the voters elected four Conservative governments in a row, the last under John Major. That is why the Thatcher years turned out to be a watershed. It was only with the global financial meltdown of 2008 that her revolution, in turn, started to unravel.

Thatcher's vision, like Powell's, was insular. She was a nationalist who drew on a tradition of Protestantism and free markets. The historical moment she continually evoked was 1940, when Britain stood alone against a Hitler-dominated Europe. She seized on a favourable historical opportunity. Her predecessors had got rid of the empire, and therefore there was no imperial overhang. She had no time for the insubstantial Commonwealth, and not much more for the EEC, giving the impression that she viewed Brussels as the capital of a new Carolingian empire. Over the few remaining imperial problems – Southern Rhodesia, South Africa and Hong Kong – Thatcher bowed to the inevitable, though not always with good grace; she even nudged along the 'peace process' in Northern Ireland, despite an IRA assassination attempt in Brighton in 1984 which almost destroyed the Prime Minister and her Cabinet. In practice, rejection of a European vocation left Britain with its 'special relationship' with the United States, whose military dimension was now fortified by the ideological love fest between Thatcher and US President Ronald Reagan.

Margaret Thatcher was the most passionate and embattled of twentieth-century prime ministers. She transformed British lives, but failed to capture their hearts. She was intensely ideological, unashamedly partisan. 'Is he one of us?' she would ask of someone brought to her attention. But she was also practical. She knew when to give way. The clue to her success in government was that she was visionary in aim, cautious in method. The key to her success with voters was the distinctive style of her 'statecraft' – setting objectives, leading from the front, holding her position. She often gave the impression of running against her own Cabinet. She was not one for U-turns. All of this marked a radical change in style from the accommodating Tory leadership stretching from Baldwin to Macmillan. At the same time, she was able to play a long game. The Thatcherite ministry was a never-ending campaign, punctuated by set battles, with the miners, teachers, health workers, local authorities, sometimes broken off, but always resumed. Roy Jenkins attributed her success to the fact that she was 'almost totally impervious to how much she offends other people'.

Thatcher enjoyed three strokes of luck. First, North Sea oil started to come on stream at the end of the 1970s. At its peak it contributed 8 per cent to tax revenues. This 'gave a healthy kick start', wrote Nigel Lawson, 'to the very rapid reduction in the Budget deficit in the course of the 1980s'. It also caused a rise in the exchange rate which increased unemployment and became an unintended part of the anti-inflationary cure. From the mid-1980s she benefited from another windfall, the shift in the terms of trade in Britain's favour. Thatcher was lucky for the same reason that Gorbachev was unlucky.

The second stroke of luck was the Falklands War. In 1981 the Argentinean dictator General Galtieri seized the Falkland Islands, a tiny windswept British colony off the coast of Latin America, inhabited by three thousand hardy British settlers. Britain still had the third largest navy in the world, and Thatcher had no hesitation in despatching a formidable armada to the southern Atlantic, where British forces, in extremely adverse conditions, and with some help from Presidents Ronald Reagan of the USA and Auguste Pinochet of Chile, recaptured the islands. The Falklands were a throwback: the curtain had already fallen on empire. But the British victory in the Falklands was a defining moment in Thatcher's relationship with the British people. It restored British pride, and gave her a psychological mandate to govern: it was popular with the miners who would soon be fighting her pit closures. Equally important, it established her authority in her own party.

Finally, Thatcher was massively helped by the decline and disarray on the left. In the early 1980s the Labour party reached a point of crisis which many thought might be terminal. In 1974 its share of the popular vote dropped below 40 per cent for the first time since 1945; in 1983, at 27.6 per cent, it reached its lowest point since 1918. Affluence and de-industrialisation had shrunk its traditional working-class base; its growing ideological extremism alienated the 'progressive' middle class. By the 1970s its heartland had become the non-competitive, non-market sector of the economy, with the lower reaches of the academic estate – the 'polytechnocracy' – serving it as a 'socialist intelligentsia'. Thatcher saw that she no longer had a cohesive working class to confront. She could win pitched battles in the new war between capital and labour.

Thatcherism in Theory and Practice

Thatcher is the only Prime Minister who has given her name to an 'ism'. This is not because she was an intellectual, but because she had a set of instincts and values around which ideologies could coalesce and strategies develop. Thatcherism was a theory of macro-management based on stable prices and sound finance; a theory of micro-policy based on market deregulation and improved incentives for enterprise; and a theory of social policy based on individual responsibility and a wide distribution of private assets.

Inflation was to be conquered by gradually reducing money supply growth over four years by pre-announced amounts; a concurrent reduction in the budget deficit would enable the monetary targets to be achieved at lower interest rates. The government expected that the announcement of the monetary targets would lower the inflationary expectations of wage bargainers, enabling prices to come down with only a moderate increase in unemployment. It did not work this way: the monetary targets were consistently overshot, but inflation fell sharply and ahead of plan, from 17.8 per cent in 1980 to 4.6 per cent in 1983.

What brought inflation down was not monetarism but a government-created depression. A 17 per cent interest rate drove up the exchange rate, already strengthened by North Sea oil; super-imposed on this was Sir Geoffrey Howe's savage deflationary Budget in March 1981, which took £4 billion out of the economy when unemployment was already rising. The Howe Budget had a crucial effect, not on expectations about inflation, but on expectations about government policy. Its message was clear: Keynesianism would not be reactivated whatever the unemployment cost. This was heavy: between 1979 and 1982, unemployment rose to 10 per cent, as bad as in the 1920s, and went on creeping up until it hit three million in 1986. Three hundred and sixty-four economists anathematised the government's policy in a letter to *The Times* on 30 March 1981. The fact that recovery from the depression started a few weeks later has passed into Thatcherite legend. Between 1982 and 1987 the British economy grew by 4 per cent a year, the same as in the 1930s.

By 1984, the new Chancellor of the Exchequer, Nigel Lawson, was publicly ready to stand Keynesianism on its head. In his Mais lecture of 1984 he enunciated the new wisdom: 'The conquest of inflation should be the objective of macroeconomic policy. And the creation of conditions conducive to growth and employment should be the objective of micreconomic policy.'

Concomitantly with its inflation-busting programme, the government vigorously set about creating an 'enterprise economy'. The showpieces of this effort were deregulation, trades union reform, privatisation, reducing the size of the state and reforming the welfare state.

Deregulation of the financial sector came first, with the removal of capital controls in 1981, followed in 1986 by 'Big Bang', the freeing of banks to compete with building societies in the mortgage market. These measures strengthened the primacy of the City in the British economy, and over the years restored its global pre-eminence.

The trades unions were in Thatcher's sights from the start. A raft of labour legislation cumulatively reduced the scope of the unions' legal immunities to vanishing point; heavy unemployment and de-industrialisation, precipitated by the soaring pound, helped her legislation take root. Her anti-union offensive was massively helped by the hubris of Arthur Scargill, leader of the National Union of Mineworkers, who led the NUM into a carefully prepared trap; the failed year-long coal strike of 1984–5 resulted in the destruction of the mining industry and the ending of the 'coal factor' in Britain's industrial relations. Except for the year of that battle, the number of days lost through strike action fell steadily in the 1980s and 1990s to their lowest level in the twentieth century: from 957,000 in 1980 to 48,000 in 1992 and 30,000 in 1998. Union density – the proportion of the workforce unionised – fell from 55 per cent in 1979 to 31 per cent by 1993, its lowest since the 1930s. Individual contracts replaced collective contracts over large sectors of the economy. In political economy terms, all this meant a decisive break from the old project, inspired by the war economy, of achieving centralised wage bargaining within the framework of an incomes policy. The unions no longer mattered.

Privatisation started in Thatcher's first term, but accelerated in the second. It turned out to be her most striking policy innovation, taken up and copied all over the world, finally in the ex-Communist countries. Fiercely resisted by the nationalised industries and their unions, it proved very popular; millions of their employees, as well as the general public, bought shares in the new private companies. This created as many shareholders as trades unionists. By 1992 two-thirds of the formerly state-owned industries in the UK had been transferred to the private sector, consisting of forty-six major businesses, employing 900,000 people. With the sale of British Coal and British Rail in the 1990s, the commercial public sector virtually disappeared. The privatisation programme, 'selling off the family silver' as the aged Macmillan called it, had a double fiscal benefit: it reduced budget deficits (and therefore public spending) and raised £32.5 billion of revenue, allowing tax cuts.

The Tories were committed to a smaller state – one that taxed less, and spent less. The most important step in tax reform was Nigel Lawson's 1988 Budget which both reduced direct taxes and simplified the tax system. Six previous bands of income tax running from 27 per cent to 60 per cent were replaced with two rates of 25 per cent and 40 per cent, covering both earned and investment income. The rates of capital gains tax and inheritance tax were aligned with income tax; corporation tax came down in stages from 53 to 35 per cent. By 1987 a deficit of 5 per cent of GDP in 1979–80 had become a surplus of 0.75 per cent and 3 per cent a year later.

Thatcher's policy for building a 'popular' capitalism centred on the old Tory dream of a 'property-owning democracy'. Its keynote was selling council houses to their tenants. Under the 'right to buy' policy, 1.7 million tenants bought their own properties between 1979 and 1992 at heavily subsidised prices, nearly all for the first time. The proportion of home owners has almost doubled from 40 per cent in the 1960s to almost 80 per cent today, higher than anywhere else in Europe. Fifty per cent of pensioners became house owners. The sales raised £24 billion. Industrial privatisation plus selling off council houses was the greatest dispossession of public property since the dissolution of the monasteries.

These were the main lines of the Thatcher reform project. In October 1990, the Iron Lady was sacked by the Tory party, following her failure to win a sufficient majority to secure re-election as party leader against Michael Heseltine – the first incumbent Prime Minister ever to be deposed by his or her party. Her fall was a product of both hubris and inattention. Like all long-serving Prime Ministers, she had accumulated too much disaffection on the back benches of her own party. There were also palpable policy failures: by the late 1980s inflation again seemed out of control, and the disaster of the poll tax was dragging down the government's popularity. But moderates were also antagonised by Thatcher's increasingly strident tone over Europe.

Britain's role in the EU under Thatcher was not entirely obstructive. Britain largely shaped the Single European Act of 1986, which aimed to complete the 'single market'. It was to the political pretensions of the European Union that Thatcher objected. Her speech in Bruges in 1988 opened a rift in the Tory party which would not only destroy her government, but also that of her successor, John Major. In her reading of British history the special British contribution to Europe had been 'to prevent Europe from falling under the domination of a single power'. That power was now being exercised from Brussels, and Britain was bound to resist it if it was to remain true to itself. This was Thatcher speaking with the voice of Elizabeth I. It was not the voice that her Deputy Prime Minister, and erstwhile Foreign Secretary, Geoffrey Howe, wanted to hear, and two weeks after his resignation from government in October 1990 Thatcher was gone.

Benefits, Omissions and Costs of Thatcherism

When Thatcher came to power Sir Douglas Wass, Permanent Secretary of the Treasury, told her that the Treasury's task was to 'manage decline'. Thatcher not only managed, but ended, decline by making the British economy more competitive. In external policy Britain broke decisively with Protectionism, rediscovering its free trade tradition. Its domestic policies were designed to fit Britain for life in a free trade world. In Professor Crafts' view the reforms pursued by the Conservatives after

1979 improved the incentives facing firms and workers. This implies that 'growth performance has been better than would have been expected under a continuation of the policies of the 1970s'.

The Thatcher solution to the 'crisis of governability' has proved durable in three crucial respects. First, the macroeconomic framework of Lawson's Mais lecture 1984 is now orthodox. It is accepted that government's responsibility – at least in normal times – is to control inflation, not to determine the level of employment. Margaret Thatcher's second decisive achievement was the destruction of classical socialism. None of the privatised industries have been renationalised and there have been no further nationalisations. Thirdly, British trades unionism remained, in Robert Taylor's words, a 'pruned back plant' whose strength has been confined to the public sector. The main plot of twentieth-century British industrial relations disappeared.

The Thatcherite legacy has also been apparent in foreign policy. Thatcher mapped out a distinctively British path to economic revival which resonated with the general nationalist thrust of her policies. The Macmillan–Heath idea that Europe was, in some sense, an answer to the British disease disappeared, being replaced with the glorification of the 'special relationship' with the United States.

Although Thatcherism created a new settlement, it resembled its predecessor in not being a complete settlement. First, Thatcherite policies put the unitary state under unprecedented strain. She wanted to strengthen central government, not weaken it. She wanted to use it to implement her policies, just as Attlee and Heath had done. Thatcher was also a British nationalist who wanted to preserve the British nation state identity from being absorbed in a European 'superstate'. So she had no interest in the staples of constitutional reform aimed at limiting the power of central government: checks and balances, voting reform, dispersal of power to localities and nationalities. However, her ruthless use of power to carry out highly divisive policies put constitutional reform back on the map for the first time since 1909 when the Lords threw out Lloyd George's Budget.

Second, the question of the future of the welfare state remained unsettled. Thatcher herself favoured a 'safety net' concept of welfare, with a limitation of entitlements to those in genuine need. However, reform of the welfare state along these lines proved impossible. In fact, there was continuing pressure to increase, not reduce, public spending on welfare, since the very policies used to create an 'enterprise culture' had produced an even larger dependency culture by increasing unemployment, which in turn automatically increased relative poverty. By 1985 the population at least partly dependent on cash benefits had risen to five million: it was to creep up to almost six million ten years later. By the 1980s it had become common to talk about the growth of an 'underclass', a stagnant pool of poverty, entirely dependent on benefits, which was impervious to the general improvement in economic conditions. The 'internal markets' on which the Thatcher governments and their successors relied to improve 'variety' and 'choice' in the NHS and state education were monuments of complexity and over-regulation, with scant improvements in efficiency.

The greatest question mark over Thatcherism's legacy concerned its social and moral values. Thatcherism was avowedly a revivalist doctrine, not a complete social philosophy. 'There is no such thing as society,' she notoriously proclaimed in 1987; 'there are individual men and women. And there are families.' People must help themselves and each other, and only rely on the government as a last resort. But it was a one-sided distillation of British experience. The thrusting and often brutal individualism which made Britain so successful has always been softened by a protective collectivism, embedded in the social structure itself, and only fitfully imposed by the state. In emphasising market efficiency, Thatcherism embraced the economism of Victorianism without its paternalism. It weakened all those intermediate associations which stood between the state and the market, producing a flattened landscape.

'Moral' Thatcherism failed to offer convincing social underpinnings for the 'British values' which Thatcher upheld. The truth was that those Methodist virtues, shared with much of Old Labour, which provided Thatcher with a moral context for economic liberalism, had already been eroded to a large degree, and the intensified pursuit of material wealth which she encouraged eroded them still further. Gratification of wants – maximal and instant, natural or artificially stimulated – does not accord with the ethics of saints, soldiers and scholars.

The unavoidable question is: could the benefits of renewed entrepreneurial vigour have been achieved at less cost? Between 1979 and 1981 there was a rapid decline in British output – 5 per cent of GDP, 15 per cent of manufactured output – and a doubling of unemployment to over 10 per cent. Two million jobs went from manufacturing. The economy started growing rapidly after 1982, but there was no complete recovery. The boom of 1983–7 led to another collapse, with another million jobs lost in manufacturing in 1990–92. The pattern of recovery and collapse was strikingly similar to that of the 1930s. Between 1979 and 1993, unemployment fluctuated between 6 and 12 per cent, a record at least as bad as that of the interwar years which gave birth to Keynesian economics. The social price was equally heavy. In creating a society in which limitations are brutally exposed, Thatcherism tore apart the easy-going traditional fabric of British society. Industrial deserts were created, from which phoenixes were left to rise. There was a legacy of inner-city problems. Abandoned warehouses were commandeered for 'raves' – drug-fuelled dystopian reminiscences of 1968. Eighteen years after Margaret Thatcher left office, the pendulum has started to swing back to government interventionism, as the world economic downturn reveals the flakiness of the financially driven British economy she created.

The Major Interlude, 1991–7, and Resurgent Labour

John Major's decency, even diffidence, helped win Tories a fourth term in April 1992 in the depth of the recession, disproving the theory that elections are won and lost according to the state of the economy. Despite this promising start, the Major years of 1992–7 saw the unravelling of Conservativism under weak leadership. The mishandling of sterling's exodus from the European Exchange Rate mechanism on 16 September 1992 ('Black Wednesday') cost the government its reputation for economic competence, which not even Kenneth Clarke's successful custodianship of the Treasury could retrieve. Historically, the two most important achievements of the Major government were to negotiate the 'opt out' of sterling from the euro in the Maastricht Treaty of February 1992 and to set Northern Ireland on the path to peace.

Europe exposed irreconcilable differences between left and right within the Tory party. Euro-sceptics and hardcore Thatcherites – helped by unhelpful interventions from the Lady herself – held the party hostage and prevented it from re-engaging with the political centre. Major failed to reconcile the warring factions under his leadership. This enabled a resurgent Labour party, now called New Labour, under a bold and dynamic young leader, Tony Blair, to capture the initiative. Blair was careful to wound but not kill Major, and allowed the Tory party to kill itself. In this way he became what the electorate had wanted from Major, namely 'Thatcher with a human face'. Everyone expected Labour to win in 1997, though not by such a large margin. With an identically big victory in 2001, followed by a smaller one in 2005, Labour seemed poised to take command of the twenty-first century just as the Conservatives did of the twentieth.

Labour had had a torrid time in the 1980s. The left wing's capture of the party had produced the first breakaway since 1931 when Oswald Mosley formed the New Party. The Social Democratic Party (SDP) was started on 26 March 1981, under the leadership of the 'Gang of Four' – Roy Jenkins, formerly deputy leader of the Labour party, who had just retired as President of the European Commission, and three Labour ex-minister MPs, David Owen, William Rogers and Shirley Williams. Eventually thirty MPs joined. Together with eleven Liberal MPs they formed an 'Alliance', initially under Jenkins' leadership. The Alliance narrowly failed to overtake Labour in the popular vote in 1983, with Labour getting 27.6 per cent to the Alliance's 25.6. Overtaking Labour would have given the Alliance a tremendous psychological boost. Nevertheless, the Alliance left a powerful legacy. Roy Jenkins' 'break to the centre' foreshadowed the much enlarged Liberal Democratic party of the 1990s and David Owen's 'social market economy' pointed the way to Tony Blair and New Labour.

The electoral challenge of the Alliance as well as its drubbing by Thatcher in 1983 shocked the Labour party into sobriety. Neil Kinnock, who succeeded Michael Foot, Callaghan's successor, as Party leader, rapidly moved the party to the right. There were still huge obstacles to recovery in the shape of the miners' Arthur Scargill and Ken Livingstone, the leader of London's GLC, whose attempt to build 'socialism in one city' helped to ensure the continuance of Thatcherism at Westminster. Nevertheless, Kinnock's leadership brought about a revival: he stood up to the Trotskyist Militant Tendency and dished Labour's unpopular policies. He also took marketing seriously by appointing Peter Mandelson in 1986 as Labour's first marketing director.

Efforts to make Labour electable were helped by seismic changes in world politics. The collapse of the Soviet Union and the advance of globalisation enabled Labour to discard the most electorally crippling elements of its old baggage: public ownership, 'tax and spend' and the promotion of trades union privilege. Soviet collapse also removed the right's most potent message: that the left was weak on communism and so on national defence. Without communism, the left was free to rediscover patriotism.

When Blair was elected leader of the Labour party in 1994, following the death of Kinnock's successor John Smith, his political life had hardly begun. He gave the impression of having wandered into politics. He was a portent of a new kind of political man, for whom politics was a temporary job opening up lucrative financial opportunities, rather than a life-time vocation. He never had to jettison his socialist faith, because he never had one. This made it easier for him to understand that socialism was a busted flush, and that the Labour party had to rebrand itself as the heir of the reformist liberalism of Edwardian England. If Labour could offer Thatcherism, plus competent economic management, plus the social entitlements which Thatcherism threatened, it had a potentially winning formula. Just as Thatcher had appealed to the working class, Blair targeted his appeal to a middle class rendered insecure by negative equity, corporate downsizing, crumbling public services and rising crime. He understood the power of symbols – in 1995, he jettisoned Clause IV of the Labour party constitution, which had promised 'common ownership of the means of production, distribution and exchange'. His chief colleague and lieutenant Gordon Brown followed this by jettisoning egalitarianism in favour of the vaguer promise of inclusion. The party no longer needed to speak with forked tongues.

Labour in Power

The driving force of New Labour was the Blair–Brown axis. Under their 1994 'deal', forged when Brown agreed not to stand against Blair for leadership of the party, Gordon Brown would run economic and social policy, leaving Blair the world stage and any domestic initiatives that did not cost money. Their political philosophies were not identical. Blair was a social liberal, Brown a social democrat. Their political personalities were also strikingly different: Blair was the rhetorician, Brown the thinker; Blair was eloquent and expansive, Brown dour and adamantine. Their outlooks and qualities proved surprisingly complementary, and, despite many sour moments, they formed the most successful duumvirate in postwar British politics.

Gordon Brown, Chancellor of the Exchequer from 1997 to 2007, believed that politicised monetary and fiscal policy had led to cycles of 'boom and bust'. His first decisions as Chancellor were to give the Bank of England an inflation target and control over interest rates, to bind himself to explicit fiscal rules and to stick to his Tory predecessor's spending plans for two years. This signalled pre-commitment to financial stability, in full conformity with neo-liberal rigour, but not Conservative practice. Equally, Brown accepted the Thatcher doctrine that competition is the best spur to innovation and efficiency, simply adding to Tory labour market policy enlarged schemes of training for 'employability'.

Brown faced the familiar problem of a Labour Chancellor: how to increase the share of social spending in GDP with taxes low enough to maintain business confidence. His solution to the problem was drastically to scale down Labour's social ambitions. 'Inclusion' signified a much more modest goal for social policy than equality. Brown characteristically claimed that 'inclusion' would improve economic efficiency. 'What is right on ethical grounds is good for the economy too,' he insisted. The use of the language of inclusion rather than equality allowed Labour to target money on those most in need without alienating the better-off. This meant greater use of means-testing than Old Labour would have countenanced. In social policy abandonment of universalism was New Labour's biggest break with Old Labour.

The centrepiece of social policy in Labour's second term was a vast expansion in spending on the National Health Service. From 2002 to 2007 spending went up by over 7 per cent a year, rising from 2.6 per cent of GDP in the Major years to 7.4 per cent by 2008. Payments to hospitals would be determined by their success in meeting the targets set. The National Health Service is the last relic of undiluted socialism in Britain, and encounters all the problems which brought the Soviet central planning system crashing down – most of the extra cash went into the salaries of doctors and nurses and expensive capital projects, with little left over for improving 'outcomes' for patients. Despite all the efforts of efficiency experts, the reforms failed. The Treasury had advocated moving to a system of compulsory insurance, like in France, as early as 1952, but New Labour was no more willing than previous governments to risk the slaughter of Britain's favourite sacred cow.

Despite his stress on 'prudence', Brown was forced into endless juggling to reconcile fiscal probity with social commitments. He called all borrowing which did not meet his 'golden rule' criteria 'investment', recalibrated the timing of the 'cycles' over which current spending and taxation were supposed to balance, and imposed a variety of what the Tories called 'stealth' taxes while respecting the Tory limits on income tax. The juggling was helped by a benign environment which for years brought in larger than expected revenues. But these expedients ran out and the government entered the 2008 recession with a projected deficit of £60 billion, or 5 per cent of GDP in the fifth year of a boom when there should have been a surplus. This left fiscal policy partly disabled in dealing with the deepening economic crisis.

Blair's main domestic priority was education; he had only a modest interest in constitutional matters. But New Labour, bereft of its socialist project, revived the 'new' Liberal agenda of constitutional reform. A Scottish Parliament, with limited tax raising, and more extensive social, powers finally came into being in 1999, together with a Welsh Assembly with more restricted powers, both were housed in grandiose buildings and provided an enlarged platform for self-important politicians.

With the signing of the power-sharing agreement on 26 March 2007, the Blair government was able to bring to an end the forty-year conflict in Northern Ireland, though at the time of writing the deal has not yet been implemented. Economics and secularisation have combined to bring the two halves of Ireland closer together. Catholic Ireland, which De Valéra had tried to keep as a Catholic peasant backwater, uncontaminated by modern influences, exploded into the 'Celtic tiger', while Northern Ireland went into industrial decline. Demographic change – both Britain and Ireland receiving large influxes of European and Asian immigrants – weakened the relevance of Protestant–Catholic conflicts going back to the seventeenth century. There will be no 'united' Ireland as Sinn Féin wanted, and the IRA fought for, at least not for the foreseeable future. But the boundaries between North and South, and between the rest of Britain and Ireland, are bound to become increasingly blurred as the British state loses its unique claim to the allegiance of the British 'nations'.

Blair's premiership will always carry the taint of the invasion of Iraq in 2003. That at the dawn of the new century the British elite was once more willing to take up the 'white man's burden', this time as a very junior partner of the United States, is an ironic conclusion to a century of imperial retreat.

Into the Future

Between the two opposed views that history can teach us nothing and that the future is simply a reflection of the past lies the sensible middle position that history, like any other way of experiencing the past, can give us 'vague' knowledge of what lies ahead. Looking back from the vantage point of 2009, two things have become clearer: first, Britain's determination to carve out a future separate from that of the continent of Europe; second, the recently revealed fragility of its reborn Thatcherite economy, which makes economic independence distinctly less inviting. The tension between these two pulls will surely form a major plot in the history of the next century.

By 2007 it could be claimed that Thatcher's reversal of Keynesian and socialist priorities had proved itself. Between 1993 and 2007 price inflation averaged 3 per cent, about the same as during the 'golden age' of the 1950s and 1960s. At the same time, unemployment fell steadily from 9 to 4 per cent, confirming a decline in the 'natural rate' of unemployment – the rate necessary to keep prices stable. By 2007 the number of people in work stood at almost 30 million, or 75 per cent of the workforce, the highest in the G7 countries, with four million new jobs since 1986, half of them added after 1997, and with women gaining two-thirds of them. Between 1993 and 2007, GDP growth averaged 2.8 per cent a year, no better than the postwar average, but the longest period of stable growth in Britain's history. Since 1997, more than half a million children have been raised above the poverty line.

However, the very factors which brought Britain success in the globalised market economy went into reverse as the economic tsunami hit in 2008. The post-Thatcherite British economy had been built on services. Of a workforce of 29 million in 2006, 8 million worked in financial and business services, 8 million in the public sector, 7 million in distribution, hotels and restaurants: 79 per cent of the total. Manufacturing was down to 3.3 million or 11 per cent, much of it in construction. It is an exaggeration to say that the British economy has become a colony of the City of London, but a major financial collapse has been especially disturbing to a country so dependent for its living on producing and exporting financial, business and insurance services. Thatcherite and post-Thatcherite indifference to the distribution of income also proved to be a weakness. The combination of stagnant post-tax incomes and the relentless pressure to consume produced an economy built on debt. Britain's households save less than they have ever done. In place of savings there has been a hectic accumulation of debt-financed assets, especially houses and flats. Rising house prices were supposed to provide all the security of traditional savings, while enabling increasing borrowing for consumption. The fall in house prices has undermined the British way of life championed by Thatcher.

What all this adds up to is that the Anglo-American model of economic life, inaugurated by Thatcher and embraced by New Labour, has started to crumble. Keynesianism and socialism, which were pronounced dead and buried, are coming back to life. The balance between the private and public ownership, between freedom and regulation is starting to shift again. The battle between right and left is resumed.

One consequence of this shift is sure to be a questioning of Britain's positioning vis-à-vis Europe and the United States. From being one of the powerhouses of the global economy, Britain has been shown up to be one of its weakest links. In face of the global recession, the advantages of globalisation itself seem less certain, with the more efficient allocation of resources which it brings about being offset by its instability and (especially for the wealthy nations) job losses. If, as seems likely, there is a move back to Protectionism, the future of a medium-sized economy outside the main emerging protective systems will seem increasingly insecure. This development, as well as the meagre rewards it derives from the 'special relationship' with the United States, will push Britain towards, rather than away from, Europe.

The so-called 'West Lothian question' still bedevils the devolution project. For how long, asked Tim Dalyell in the House of Commons in 1977, will English MPs tolerate Scottish MPs at Westminster legislating on purely English business, when they themselves cannot legislate on equivalent Scottish matters? The answer to the West Lothian question is a federal Britain, or what used to be called 'devolution all round', with an English Parliament set up to deal with the range of issues within the competence of the Scottish Parliament. But no one is yet ready for this.

Equally fraught is the future relationship between the nations and religions within England itself. On present projections the non-Christian population of England is expected to be about 20 per cent of the total by 2050. Much of this will be actively religious, i.e. Muslim. This leads to a fascinating question: will the trend towards secularisation continue or will there be a religious revival? Will the religious groups, both Christian and Muslim, cooperate in an attempt to roll back the permissive legislation of the last century, or will they start fighting each other? Will the twenty-first century usher in a new wave of religious conflicts as Europeans rediscover in Christianity a source of civilisational identity? One thing is clear: in accepting mass immigration from outside Europe, the European nations, Britain included, opened themselves up to a whole host of unintended consequences, which amount to irreversible changes in the character of their societies. The only questions are what these will be, and whether they will come about peacefully or violently.

4. Some Counter-Factuals

It was Anglo-German rivalry which destroyed British power and ruined Europe's liberal civilisation. What would have happened had Britain handled its relations with Germany differently and avoided the wars of 1914–18 and of 1939–45? Let us consider both the foreign policy and domestic consequences for Britain of not being involved in war in the two periods. Each case is different.

Take first an Anglo-German alliance or accommodation. This was mooted both before 1914 and in the 1930s, so it was not beyond the bounds of the possible. It would not necessarily have avoided continental wars, but they would have been smaller-scale, and would not have involved Britain. In either case, Germany would most probably have established a qualified domination over the continent of Europe through quick victories. The cost to European civilisation would have been high, though much higher in the 1930s than before 1914. Britain's abstention from war in 1914 would most probably have led to the establishment of a Prussianised European Union. This would have been insufferable, but not barbaric.

Had Britain in the 1930s reached the kind of agreement with Hitler that Hitler wanted, most of eastern Europe and the Ukraine at least would probably have fallen under German sway. At some point, Hitler's empire might well have imploded through genocidal excess, with incalculable consequences.

An alternative war avoidance policy would have been effective resistance to German expansionism along balance-of-power lines. The core of this would have been an Anglo-French military alliance, backed up by British forces stationed on the Continent. The most probable result of this before 1914 would have been no war at all, since there would have been no hope of the Germans 'breaking out'.

In the 1930s there were two possibilities. Between 1933 and 1936

Britain and France could simply have prevented Germany rearming. Hitler would probably have fallen from power as his foreign policy crumbled. By the later 1930s, when Germany had rearmed, the chances of containing Hitler were much smaller, since neither the Soviet Union nor the United States were part of the European balance. The object of an Anglo-French alliance would then rationally have been to turn Hitler away from the west, giving him a 'free hand' in the east. How such a scenario would have played out is very unclear. Though Europe would have become an armed camp, war in the west would probably have been avoided for several years more, and may never have happened.

What would have been the domestic consequences of a British acquiescence in German expansion or a successful resistance to it short of war? Again the pre-1914 and pre-1939 cases must be distinguished.

In his classic book *The Strange Death of Liberal England* (1935), George Dangerfield argued that 'liberal' England was dead or dying before 1914. This has been interpreted wrongly to mean that the Liberal party was dead. The Liberal party was certainly not dead. It was the war which split it and made Labour dominant on the left. Dangerfield's other hypothesis is that, but for the war, there would have been a civil war in Ireland spilling over into England and Scotland. More likely, but for the war Home Rule would have gone through in 1914 with the six counties of Ulster temporarily, and eventually permanently, excluded. With Home Rule in place, a growing net flow of revenue from the British Exchequer to Ireland would have made it much harder for Ireland subsequently to break free. *Pace* Dangerfield, it was the war, not the pre-war troubles, which killed Home Rule for Catholic Ireland.

In her novella *Alfred and Emily* (2008) Doris Lessing imagines what would have happened to her parents' lives but for the First World War. 'The war-free England that gives Alfred his harmonious, productive life has conserved its Edwardian / Georgian self with remarkable purity. Its dominant culture is bucolic; sport, practical and neighbourly charity, and a cheerfully carnal uxoriousness are its outstanding features. Prosperity has continued, though poverty, mostly urban, does exist, and is fought by individual dedication and private resource-fulness. (The People's Budget of 1909 clearly had no real consequence.) In the wider world, we learn that Austria-Hungary and Turkey imploded in the earlier 1920s, affecting little in English life except metropolitan fashion. But men . . . do come to feel a lack in their lives which they think only wars can fill. Alfred's sons, though not Alfred himself, will hear the call to battle.' (Paul Binding's review, *TLS*, 30 May 2008). This is a possible, and by no means implausible, future.

The consequences to British domestic politics of war avoidance in the 1930s would have depended on how it came about. Preventing German rearmament, with Hitler's removal from power as the most likely consequence, would have empowered all the democratic forces in Europe, including those in Britain. Acquiescence in a Nazi rampage through eastern Europe and Russia would have tilted the European ideological balance towards fascism. Whether Hitler's empire eventually imploded or simply subsided, the political complexion of Britain would have been different – authoritarian and nationalistic. At the very least, fascism would have become more powerful.

There is another possibility, much fancied by fiction writers, which is that Britain went to war with Germany but lost. This applies only to the second war, since there was no realistic possibility of Germany defeating Britain in 1914. In 1940–41, though, Britain did face a real possibility of defeat. Again, it would have depended on how it happened. Had Britain lost the 'battle of Britain' or the 'battle of the Atlantic' and opened peace overtures before all its resources for continuing the fight had been exhausted, it might have preserved something of its empire and domestic institutions which, in a perverse way, Hitler rather admired. Lloyd George was often canvassed in 1940 as a possible leader for a compromise peace. Had Britain been invaded and occupied, the best that could have been hoped for was a Vichy status in Hitler's European empire.

A similarly tantalising question is, what if Britain and France had succeeded at Suez in 1956? The following sequence assumes that Britain resists American pressure to bring the Suez invasion to a premature halt. Britain and France restore ownership of the Canal to the Suez Canal Company, and re-establish the Canal base, this time with a joint Anglo-French garrison. The pound is de-linked from the dollar and floats downwards, giving a boost to British exports. The United States is severely miffed, but there is nothing it can do.

Following the successful invasion, Britain and France sign a wide-ranging agreement to coordinate their foreign and defence policies, and build a joint nuclear deterrent. Nasser is toppled in an internal coup. Arab nationalism is aborted, and a post-imperial system of indirect rule takes shape, based on Anglo-French military bases in

North Africa and the Middle East. There are no further Arab–Israeli wars.

The European Economic Community is set up under Anglo-French leadership. It incorporates Britain's and France's African colonies and the Middle East in a giant preference system which also includes Britain's 'white' dominions. Britain and France join together to form a political union. This 'European Union' is built outwards to include Germany and the main European countries. The dynamics of the Cold War are changed. Europe becomes a Third Force. Germany is reunited on condition of neutrality.

It is obvious that if any of these counter-factuals had come to pass, the moral conditions of the world would have been very different. Whether they would have been better or worse is a matter of judgement. But in narrow national terms, Britain would not have had to 'sacrifice' over a million killed and three million injured in two world wars, its world position would have been better preserved and it would (almost certainly) have been richer than it is today.

Afterword

Paradoxically, readers often look to history for a guide to the future. In this implicit task of prediction, historical writing has had very limited success: the only securely established historical law is that *the unexpected always happens*. This limitation was once thought to disqualify history from the status of a science, but from the late twentieth century it became increasingly clear that the 'social sciences', mostly devised in the nineteenth century, shared a similar limitation: human experience is as fluid and inscrutable for economists and psychoanalysts as for historians. However much some historians sought to claim authority, Clio will not be usurped. History offers the reassurance of hindsight, not the peril of foresight.

All histories are therefore overtaken by events. All histories embody, more than their authors can fully appreciate, the perspectives and priorities of the moment of their composition. But this intellectual equipment is both helpful and limited: the economic, political and intellectual dynamics of life are of such complexity that (like Europe's weather) outcomes cannot be reliably predicted for more than a few days in advance. Long cycles are clearly evident in nature (for example, the advance and retreat of glaciers in successive ice ages), but the lifespans of individuals are too short for them to place themselves reliably against long-term trends. The long continuities of human history discussed in this book are never experienced as statistical averages or as functional processes, but as conscious participation in a shared history that the inhabitants of a society regard as their own.

One problem is that humanity's goalposts are regularly moved. The history of these islands shows a succession of agendas: no sooner has some approximate agreement been reached on old issues than a new and unexpected set of problems arise. This may be especially the case at the moment of publication, when the conflicts born in the era of modernism are (at least in the British Isles) often reduced to formalities, and the alternation of political parties in power results in only modest shifts of national expenditure.

At this moment, however, we may be witnessing the possible emergence of a different set of problems caused by (among many possible candidates) religious conflicts, epidemic disease, major climate change, economic collapse, mass migration, political integration into a trans-national polity or the independence of component parts of the Union. All these have the potential to change the future history of these islands profoundly, yet, despite appearances, none of them is exactly new. All of them have clear parallels in the history of these islands, yet these parallels are never sufficiently exact to yield simple lessons for the future. History is always repeating itself, but never in quite the same way. Like all forms of organised knowledge, the historical perspective is essential exactly because the process of discovery continues.

Guide to Further Reading

This Guide does not claim to be a comprehensive bibliography: the materials for the history of the British Isles are so immense that any fair listing would itself need many volumes. The intention here is to engage the interest of readers and to whet their appetites for further explorations. To that end, each contributor has provided a short list of books that, in the contributor's view, the reader will find stimulating. Partly they are writings of the time; partly classic works of history; partly the books of the present day. They are starting points, not a canon of classics or a party list of correct interpretations. Indeed, the authors of this volume do not necessarily endorse all the modern works of scholarship that they include; but they are works that the reader will wish to know about.

Part I. The Romans to the Norman Conquest, 500 BC–AD 1066
The best modern introductions are the relevant volumes of the *Short Oxford History of the British Isles*, which all have good bibliographies: Thomas Charles-Edwards (ed.), *After Rome* (Oxford, 2003) and Wendy Davies (ed.), *From the Vikings to the Normans* (Oxford, 2003). Peter Salway (ed.), *The Roman Era: The British Isles: 55 BC–AD 410* (Oxford, 2002) has chapters on all aspects of Roman Britain by leading experts with good bibliographies. Sheppard Frere, *Britannia: A History of Roman Britain* (3rd edn, London, 1987) is a standard survey with strong archaeological emphasis. Other recent works have introduced a welcome element of contentious debate into study of the end of Roman Britain: Neil Faulkner, *The Decline and Fall of Roman Britain* (Stroud, 2000) is a good example.

A well-illustrated survey is James Campbell (ed.), *The Anglo-Saxons* (Oxford, 1982, also available in paperback, London, 1991); it provides more of a narrative than the other works mentioned. David Hill, *An*

Atlas of Anglo-Saxon England (Oxford, 1981) is important both as a work of reference and as a stimulus to thought. An attractive element in the study of Anglo-Saxon history is that the student can read a much higher proportion of the sources than is possible for other periods. Dorothy Whitelock (ed.), *English Historical Documents, c. 500–1042* (2nd edn, London, 1979) provides a wide range of translations. Everyone should read Bede's *Ecclesiastical History* and *Beowulf*. A good translation of the former is that by Judith McClure and Roger Collins (Oxford, 1994); Seamus Heaney's translation of the latter (London, 1999) is arresting. A very important internet source is the *Prosopography of Anglo-Saxon England* (PASE) http://www.kcl.ac.uk/cch/pase which provides biographies of all Anglo-Saxons known before the time of Domesday Book.

For Wales, Wendy Davies, *Wales in the Early Middle Ages* (Leicester, 1982) is a spirited introduction and although Rees R. Davies, *Conquest, Coexistence and Change: Wales 1063–1415* (Oxford, 1987) begins very near the end of our period it forms in some ways a most valuable introduction to it. Also fascinating is D. Simon Evans' translation *A Medieval Prince of Wales: The Life of Gruffudd ap Cynan* (Felinfach, 1990). The best brief introductions to early Ireland are Gearoid Mac Niocaill, *Ireland before the Vikings* (Dublin, 1972) and Donncha Ó Cróinín, *Ireland before the Normans* (Dublin, 1972). A fuller, more modern and excellent textbook is Dáibhi Ó Cróinín, *Early Medieval Ireland, 400–1200* (London, 1995). Thomas Charles-Edwards, *Early Christian Ireland* (Cambridge, 2000) is a major and magisterial account. For sources see Kathleen Hughes, *Early Christian Ireland: Introduction to the Sources* (London, 1972). A lively and provocative introduction to the early history of Scotland is Alfred P. Smyth, *Warlords and Holy Men* (London, 1984). Archibald Duncan, *Scotland: The Making of the Kingdom* (Edinburgh, 1975) is much fuller, and a good work of reference. Finally, W. B. Morgan's *Agriculture in the Third World* (London, 1977) offers valuable comparable insights.

Part II. Conquests, Catastrophe and Recovery, 1066–c. 1485

Contemporary works well worth reading include *The Canterbury Tales*, the masterpiece by Geoffrey Chaucer, one of the makers of our language, a revealing and often entertaining commentary on late fourteenth-century English society. The first great work of Scottish literature is John Barbour's *The Bruce*, the rousing tale of a fight for freedom (edited and translated into modern English by A. A. M. Duncan (Edinburgh, 1997). The ethos of an honour-centred society is vividly recaptured in P. Ford (ed.), *The Mabinogi and Other Medieval Welsh Tales* (Berkeley, 1977).

For the greater part of this period, the most distinguished literature produced in these islands was in French and Latin, part of a culture that was international rather than insular. French can be sampled in collections such as *The Birth of Romance*, translated by Judith Weiss (Everyman, 1992), and in reworkings of Celtic tales such *The Lais of Marie de France* (Penguin Classics, 1986). There are some accessible translations from the Latin, e.g. Gerald of Wales, *The Journey through Wales/The Description of Wales* (Penguin Classics), innovative works by an Anglo-Welsh author torn by his own ambiguous loyalties. Jocelin of Brakelond's *Chronicle of the Abbey of Bury St Edmunds*, translated by Diana Greenway and Jane Sayers (Oxford World Classics, 1989) offers insights into the daily reality of monastic life.

Both in volume and variety of type so much more evidence survives from England than from Ireland and the rest of Britain that there are some aspects of these centuries for which it is hard to go beyond England. Two cases in point are M. T. Clanchy's seminal study of literacy, *From Memory to Written Record: England 1066–1377* (Oxford, 1979, 2nd edn, 1993) and P. J. P. Goldberg, *Medieval England: A Social History 1250–1550* (London, 2004). Robert Bartlett's volume in *The New Oxford History of England* series, *England under the Norman and Angevin Kings 1075–1225* (Oxford, 2000), is uncompromisingly – and fascinatingly – concerned with what was going on in people's heads. Two other volumes in the same series, despite the choice of unfamiliar terminal dates, are masterly treatments of largely familiar themes: Michael Prestwich, *Plantagenet England 1225–1360* (Oxford, 2005) and Gerald Harriss, *Shaping the Nation 1360–1461* (Oxford, 2005). Excellent one-volume guides to the other parts of Britain are R. R. Davies, *Age of Conquest. Wales 1063–1415* (Oxford, 1987) and A. A. M. Duncan, *Scotland: The Making of the Kingdom* (Edinburgh, 1975). Seán Duffy's *Ireland in the Middle Ages* (Dublin, 1997) provides a succinct introduction to the subject.

A feature of the historical writing of recent decades has been the more systematic adoption of a comparative approach to the histories of Britain and Ireland. No one did more to encourage this movement than R. R. Davies, whose *The First English Empire: Power and Identities in the British Isles 1093–1343* (Oxford, 2000) is the most recent of his contributions to the field. Other stimulating studies along similar lines are Robin Frame, *The Political Development of the British Isles 1100–1400* (Oxford, 1990) and David Carpenter, *The Struggle for Mastery: Britain 1066–1284* (Penguin History of Britain, 2003). Richard Britnell's pioneering *Britain and Ireland 1050–1530: Economy and Society* (Oxford, 2004) does much the same for economic history. A useful guide to recent historiography on Britain and Ireland is S. H. Rigby (ed.), *A Companion to Britain in the Later Middle Ages* (Oxford, 2003).

Part III. Reformations, Unions and Civil Wars, 1485–1660

Among the wealth of printed sources for this period is the clarion call of John Knox's *History of the Reformation in Scotland* (1566); there is a good Anglicised edition by W. Croft Dickinson (two vols, Edinburgh, 1950). He was a master of prose. So was that prolific author James VI and I; his major political writings, crucial to the understanding of his kingship, are in *King James VI and I: Political Writings*, ed. J. P. Somerville (Cambridge, 1994). Anyone should read Milton and Marvell; and what a source for the crisis of the mid-seventeenth century in England: John Milton, *Poetical Works*, ed. D. Bush (Harmondsworth, 1966) and Andrew Marvell, *The Complete Poems*, ed. E. S. Donno (Harmondsworth, 1972). And for stunning insight into one man's faith in this troubled period, John Bunyan, *The Pilgrim's Progress* (Harmondsworth, 2008) and *Grace Abounding* (Oxford, 2004). Scotland's crisis is recorded in the agonised *Diary of Archibald Johnston of Wariston, 1632–1639* (Scottish History Society, Edinburgh, 1911).

The classic secondary work for the seventeenth century remains S. R. Gardiner, *History of England, 1603–1642* (ten vols, London, 1883–4), still well worth reading for its astonishing range of scholarship even if his approach has been challenged; there is no equivalent for the sixteenth century. General modern introductions are found in Patrick Collinson (ed.), *The Sixteenth Century* and Jenny Wormald (ed.), *The Seventeenth Century* in *The Short Oxford History of the British Isles* series (Oxford, 2002 and 2008).

The Reformation has produced such an impressive number of books that it is hard to narrow down the citations. Felicity Heal, *Reformation in Britain and Ireland* (Oxford, 2003) is a unique and successful attempt to cover the British Isles. Eamon Duffy, *The Stripping of the Altars: Traditional Religion in England 1400–1580* (New

Haven, 2003) is justly famous for its compelling discussion of the vigour of the pre-Reformation Church. Of the many works of Christopher Haigh, who demolished the idea that England became Protestant in the reign of Henry VIII, *English Reformations: Religion, Politics and Society under the Tudors* (Oxford, 1993) is an excellent starting point. The master of the understanding of English Puritanism is Patrick Collinson; *Godly People: Essays on English Protestantism and Puritanism* (London, 1984) shows why. Diarmaid MacCulloch, *The Later Reformation in England, 1547–1603* (Basingstoke, 1990) is a short book, long on fascinating insights. With her cultural and social analysis, Margo Todd, *The Culture of Protestantism in Early Modern Scotland* (New Haven, 2002), opens up a new approach to the Scottish Reformation. A notable collection of essays is Elizabethanne Boran and Crawford Gribben (eds), *Enforcing Reformation in Ireland and Scotland 1550–1700* (Aldershot, 2006).

Of the many books on 'the British Problem', Brendan Bradshaw and John Morrill (eds), *The British Problem, c. 1534–1707: State Formation in the Atlantic Archipelago* (Basingstoke, 1996), Brendan Bradshaw and Peter Roberts (eds), *British Consciousness and Identity: The making of Britain, 1533–1707* (Cambridge, 1998) and Glen Burgess (ed.), *The New British History: Founding a Modern State, 1603–1715* (London, 1999) are notable examples of this genre, all containing essays on the four parts of the British Isles, with bibliographical reference to other such books and more specific studies; so readers should not stop there. Conrad Russell is a name to conjure with on this subject; his *The Causes of the English Civil War* (Oxford, 1990) is in fact a wide-ranging 'British' study, from 1559 to 1642. Finally, in an age of much confusion, there was one thoroughly enjoyable innovation: the public theatre. A thoroughly enjoyable book about it is Andrew Gurr, *Playgoing in Shakespearean London* (Cambridge, 3rd edn, 2004).

Part IV. Restoration to Reform, 1660–1832

Compelling contemporary writings abound. *The Diary of Samuel Pepys*, which covers 1660–69 (the complete text is edited by Robert Latham and William Matthews, eleven vols, London, 1991; there are abridgements), shows that individualism did not begin with the Romantic era. John Locke's *Two Treatises of Government* (1690; the classic edition is edited by Peter Laslett, Cambridge, 1988) was once taken as a blueprint for a modern, contractarian society, but is increasingly seen as a call for

armed resistance to the Stuarts in the Exclusion Crisis of 1679–81, a
rebellion that Locke, remarkably, expected would leave society
otherwise intact. Daniel Defoe's *The Life and Strange Surprizing
Adventures of Robinson Crusoe of York, Mariner* (1719; ed. J. Donald
Crowley, Oxford, 1998) is a pilgrim's progress in the tradition of
Bunyan, still often mistaken for a rationale for capitalist accumulation.
Adam Smith's *An Inquiry into the Nature and Causes of the Wealth of
Nations* (1776; eds R. H. Campbell and A. S. Skinner, two vols, Oxford,
1979; the same excellent edition, in paperback, Indianapolis, 1981)
pursues national aggrandisement and is not the apologia for
individualist acquisitiveness that its later reputation depicts. Edward
Gibbon's *The Decline and Fall of the Roman Empire* (six vols, 1776–88; ed.
David Womersley, three vols, London, 1994) is still Britain's most
famous historical monograph, and James Boswell's *The Life of Samuel
Johnson, LL.D.* (1791; in a single-volume edition, ed. R. W. Chapman,
Oxford, 1998) is still the greatest biography in the language. Edmund
Burke's *Reflections on the Revolution in France* (1790; ed. J. C. D. Clark,
2001) summed up the tensions of the old world and looked forward to
the totalitarianism and genocide of the new.

Among classic works of scholarship, the pioneering book on social
structure was Peter Laslett's inspirational *The World We Have Lost*
(London, 1965; 3rd edn, 2000), and the great prophet of labour history
was E. P. Thompson, especially in his classic *The Making of the English
Working Class* (London, 1963; Harmondsworth, 1968). Among more
recent works, Martin Daunton's *Progress and Poverty: An Economic and
Social History of Britain 1700–1850* (Oxford, 1995) ranges widely. J. C. D.
Clark's *English Society 1660–1832: Religion, Ideology and Politics during the
Ancien Regime* (2nd edn, Cambridge, 2000) offers an overview of
religion and politics. The world of science is marvellously recaptured
in R. S. Westfall's *Never At Rest: A Biography of Isaac Newton* (Cambridge,
1980). Roy Porter's infectious enthusiasm is irresistible in
Enlightenment: Britain and the Creation of the Modern World (London,
2000), and naval history is made compelling by N. A. M. Rodger's *The
Command of the Ocean: A Naval History of Britain 1649–1815* (London,
2004). Henry D. Rack's *Reasonable Enthusiast: John Wesley and the Rise of
Methodism* (3rd edn, London, 2002) is wide-ranging and fascinating. For
Ireland, see, for example, Thomas Bartlett, *The Rise and Fall of the Irish
Nation: The Catholic Question 1690–1830* (Dublin, 1992) and Toby
Barnard, *A New Anatomy of Ireland: The Irish Protestants, 1649–1770* (New

Haven, 2003). For Wales, start with Geraint H. Jenkins, *The Foundations of Modern Wales: Wales 1642–1780* (Oxford, 1987). T. C. Smout's *A History of the Scottish People, 1560–1830* (see Part III) is a classic; it should be read with Alexander Broadie, *The Scottish Enlightenment: The Historical Age of the Scottish Nation* (Edinburgh, 2001) and Susan Manning (ed.), *The Edinburgh History of Scottish Literature*, vol. II, *Enlightenment, Britain and Empire (1707–1918)* (Edinburgh, 2007).

Part V. The World Hegemon: The Long Nineteenth Century, 1832–1914

No list from this deeply researched period can do anything more than present a microscopic selection from among dozens of valuable works. Contemporary works should, of course, be read. Lord Macaulay's *Essays and Speeches*, written from the 1820s until his death in 1859, are still delightful and often very funny, arguably the best introduction to the assumptions of optimistic early Victorian liberalism. They are available in many editions. Frederick Engels's *The Condition of the Working Class in England in 1844* (originally published in German in 1845; no English translation appeared until 1887), while obviously tendentious and wholly negative, presents a contrast to Macaulay's optimism about the effects of political and economic change. Many famous Victorian novelists and authors, including Dickens, Disraeli, Trollope, Hardy and Shaw, commented on social class and social conditions of their time, but the reader should never forget that they are works of the imagination. Many general histories of all or part of the period 1832–1914 exist. Perhaps the closest approximations to 'official' histories are the three relevant volumes of *The New Oxford History of England*: Boyd Hilton, *A Mad, Bad, and Dangerous People? England 1783–1846* (Oxford, 2006); K. Theodore Hoppen, *The Mid-Victorian Generation, 1846–1886* (Oxford, 1998), and G. R. Searle, *A New England? Peace and War, 1886–1918* (Oxford, 2004). These works survey the field, and have lengthy bibliographies, but – reflecting the growth of historical research in this area during the past forty years – are rather discursive, and less tightly organised than the relevant volumes in the old *Oxford History of England*, which they do not wholly displace. Despite their titles, all of these works discuss Scotland, Wales, Ireland and the empire.

Many post-1945, but now relatively older, works of history are still valuable. These include Harold Perkin's ambitious attempt to explain the main dimensions of modern English social history in *Origins of Modern English Society, 1780–1980* (London, 1969) and *The Rise of Professional Society: England since 1880* (London, 1989), and E. J. Hobsbawm's survey of economic and social history, *Industry and Empire: An Economic History of Britain since 1750* (originally London, 1968; revised edn, 1999). Asa Briggs's *Victorian Cities* (London, 1963) remains valuable. Bernard Semmel's *Imperialism and Social Reform: English Social Imperialist Thought 1895–1914* (Cambridge, Mass., 1960) is still a highly important work on the British right and left just before the First World War.

British politics is perhaps most approachable through well-written biographies of the major political leaders. Some of the best known are noted here, although in the case of older biographies listed here, more recent and sophisticated accounts are available. Classical political biographies include Lord David Cecil, *Melbourne* (two vols, London, 1939 and 1954); Robert Blake, *Disraeli* (London, 1966); Sir Philip Magnus, *Gladstone* (London, 1954; revised edn, 1963); Andrew Roberts, *Salisbury: Victorian Titan* (London, 1999); and Roy Jenkins, *Asquith* (London, 1964).

On the Victorian landed aristocracy, F. M. L. Thompson, *English Landed Society in the Nineteenth Century* (London, 1963), is still the classic work. A recent excellent introduction to the mysteries of the Irish situation is Alvin Jackson, *Ireland, 1798–1998* (Oxford, 1999). Women's history has been a major recent growth area. Jane Lewis, *Women in England 1870–1950: Sexual Division and Social Change* (Hemel Hempstead, 1984) introduces the contemporary debate. Religion, though central, is easy for secular historians to neglect. Kenneth Hylton-Smith, *The Churches in England: From Elizabeth I to Elizabeth II: Vol. III, 1833–1998* (London, 1998) gives a good recent overview of all Christian denominations in the period.

Part VI. Twentieth Century Britain: A Success Story?

Contemporary writings are so numerous that the student is in danger of being overwhelmed by numbers, but some works still hold classic status. George Dangerfield's *The Strange Death of Liberal England* (first published 1935; 2nd edn, London, 1997) argued that 'liberal' England expired before the First World War. A classic account of ordinary soldiers' experiences (and their language) in that war is Frederic Manning, *Her Privates We* (first published in a limited edition in 1929 as

The Middle Parts of Fortune, this edition is London, 1999, with an introduction by William Boyd). Lord Beaverbrook's *Men and Power 1914–16* (London, 1928) is the first volume of his classic trilogy dealing with the rise and fall of Lloyd George. J. M. Keynes himself described his *Essays in Persuasion* (London, 1930) as 'the croakings of a Cassandra'. The same might be said of Winston Churchill's *The Gathering Storm* (London, 1948) the first volume of his six-volume history of the Second World War. Noel Annan's *Our Age: Portrait of a Generation* (London, 1990) is a scintillating account by one of its great survivors.

Classic works of scholarship include Keith Feiling's *The Life of Neville Chamberlain* (London, 1946), the first attempt to do justice to the much pilloried author of appeasement. Francis Williams, *A Pattern of Rulers* (London, 1965) has lively sketches of the leading politicians of the interwar period. A. J. P. Taylor, *English History 1914–1945* (Oxford, 1965) is the most sparkling statement of war-induced optimism, with its concluding epiphany: 'Few now sang "Land of Hope and Glory". Few even sang "England Arise". England had risen all the same.' C. L. Mowat, *Britain between the Wars 1918–1940* (first published 1955, new edn London, 1968) lacks Taylor's sparkle but is too useful a workhorse to be put out to grass. A. J. P. Taylor's *Origins of the Second World War* (London, 1961) is a superb example of the strengths and weaknesses of his 'green fingers' approach to history writing.

Vernon Bogdanor and Robert Skidelsky (eds), *The Age of Affluence 1951–1964* (London, 1970) is still indispensable for its survey of the 'thirteen wasted years'. Readers fortunate enough to obtain a copy which has not fallen to pieces will see that its pages, which started to yellow soon after the book was published, look as if they have come out of the age of austerity. Corelli Barnett's *The Collapse of British Power* (London, 1972) is the first of four volumes in which he tries to explain it. Edmund Dell, *A Strange and Eventful History: Democratic Socialism in Britain* (London, 1999) applies the Dangerfield touch to the Labour party, without its literary distinction, but with much more inside knowledge; it is especially good on the Harold Wilson/James Callaghan years.

Robert Skidelsky's *John Maynard Keynes: Economist, Philosopher, Statesman* (London, 2003) is the single-volume abridgment of his three-volume biography. The best insider's view of Thatcherism is Nigel Lawson's intellectually superior *The View from No. 11: Memoirs of a Tory Radical* (London, 1992). The failure of British policy towards Europe has been expertly analysed by Hugo Young in *The Blessed Plot: Britain and Europe from Churchill to Blair* (London, 1999). Ross McKibbin's *Classes and Cultures: England 1918–1951* (London, 1998) argues that 'class', however imperfect as a unit of analysis, is still the best way of understanding British politics and society in the first half of the century. David Marquand's superbly written and argued *Britain since 1918: The Strange Career of British Democracy* (London 2008), another Dangerfield inspiration, reminds us that that there was 'no single, authoritative narrative of Britain's long march towards democracy'.

Counter-Factuals

All historians use counter-factual analysis: the familiar claim that '*A* caused *B*' is also the counter-factual claim that 'without *A*, *B* would not have occurred'. Nevertheless, history can often look importantly different when its hidden counter-factual assumptions are made explicit. Readers new to the theoretical and practical implications of this approach should begin with two texts: Niall Ferguson (ed.), *Virtual History: Alternatives and Counterfactuals* (London, 1997), especially the editor's Introduction, and Philip E. Tetlock, Richard Ned Lebow and Geoffrey Parker (eds), *Unmaking the West: 'What-if' Scenarios that Rewrite World History* (Ann Arbor, MI, 2006).

Index

The British Isles in the early 21st century

Most traditional counties in England were defined by the 12th century (in Wales after 1282); following successive minor modifications many were abolished by local government reform in 1974. Regional government was anticipated by the rule of Oliver Cromwell's Major Generals; in its modern form it was introduced in 1994 at the instigation of the European Union following the Maastricht Treaty. These regions are also constituency boundaries for the European Parliament.

Numbered Northern Ireland Unitary Authorities

1 Derry
2 Limavady
3 Coleraine
4 Ballymoney
5 Moyle
6 Ballymena
7 Larne
8 Carrickfergus
9 Newtownabbey
10 Antrim
11 Ards
12 North Down
13 Castlereagh
14 Belfast
15 Lisburn
16 Banbridge
17 Craigavon
18 Dungannon
19 Omagh
20 Strabane
21 Magherafelt

Numbered Scottish Unitary Authorities

1 Aberdeen City
2 Dundee City
3 Clackmannanshire
4 Falkirk
5 North Lanarkshire
6 Glasgow City
7 East Dunbartonshire
8 West Dunbartonshire
9 Inverclyde
10 Renfrewshire
11 East Renfrewshire
12 West Lothian
13 City of Edinburgh
14 Midlothian
15 East Lothian

Numbered English Unitary Authorities

1 Tyne & Wear
2 Hartlepool
3 Darlington
4 Stockton-on-Tees
5 Middlesbrough
6 Redcar & Cleveland
7 City of Kingston-upon-Hull
8 North East Lincolnshire
9 North Lincolnshire
10 Blackburn with Darwen
11 Merseyside
12 Halton
13 Warrington
14 Greater Manchester
15 Stoke-on-Trent
16 Derby
17 Nottingham
18 Peterborough
19 Rutland
20 Leicester
21 West Midlands
22 Telford & Wrekin
23 Milton Keynes
24 Luton
25 Southend-on-Sea
26 Thurrock
27 Medway
28 Greater London
29 Slough
30 Bracknell Forest
31 Windsor & Maidenhead
32 Wokingham

Scottish border
(Established 1237)

Republic of Ireland border
(Established 1948)

Atlantic Ocean

North Sea

SHETLAND ISLANDS

ORKNEY ISLANDS

OUTER HEBRIDES

Eilean Siar

Highland

Inverness

Aberdeenshire

Aberdeen

Moray

Angus

Dundee

Perth & Kinross

Perth

Fife

Scotland

SCOTLAND

Stirling

Glasgow

Edinburgh

Scottish borders

Clyde

East Ayrshire

South Lanarkshire

South Ayrshire

Northumberland

Tyne

Northern Ireland

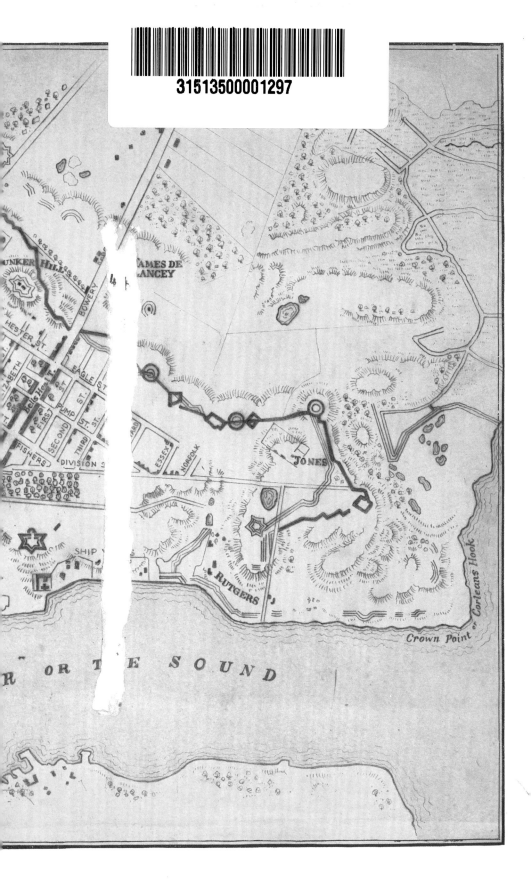

UNKER HILL

AMES DE
LANCEY

BOWERY

HESTER ST.

EAGLE ST.

ELIZABETH

PUMP ST.

FIRST

SECOND

THIRD

FISHERS

DIVISION S

ESSEX

NORFOLK

JONES

SHIP Y

RUTGERS

Corleans Hook

Crown Point

R OR TE SOUND